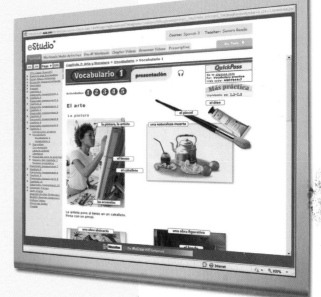

3 Glencoe Spanish

¡Así se dice!

Experience
ONLINE LEARNING
at its best!

eStudio®
powered by Quia

Conrad J. Schmitt

McGraw Hill **Glencoe**

Information on featured companies, organizations, and their products and services is included for educational purposes only and does not present or imply endorsement of the ¡Así se dice! program. Permission to use all business logos has been granted by the businesses represented in this text.

The **McGraw·Hill** Companies

 Glencoe

Send all inquiries to:
Glencoe/McGraw-Hill
8787 Orion Place
Columbus, OH 43240-4027

ISBN: 978-0-07-660425-8
MHID: 0-07-660425-X

Printed in the United States of America.

4 5 6 7 8   RJE   15 14 13

About the Author

Conrad J. Schmitt

Conrad J. Schmitt received his B.A. degree magna cum laude from Montclair State University, Upper Montclair, New Jersey. He received his M.A. from Middlebury College, Middlebury, Vermont, and did additional graduate work at New York University. He also studied at the Far Eastern Institute at Seton Hall University, Newark, New Jersey.

Mr. Schmitt has taught Spanish and French at all academic levels—from elementary school to graduate courses. He served as Coordinator of Foreign Languages for the Hackensack, New Jersey, public schools. He also taught courses in Foreign Language Education as a visiting professor at the Graduate School of Education at Rutgers University, New Brunswick, New Jersey.

Mr. Schmitt has authored or co-authored more than one hundred books, all published by The McGraw-Hill Companies. He was also editor-in-chief of foreign languages, ESL, and bilingual education for The McGraw-Hill Companies.

Mr. Schmitt has traveled extensively throughout Spain and all of Latin America. He has addressed teacher groups in all fifty states and has given seminars in many countries including Japan, the People's Republic of China, Taiwan, Egypt, Germany, Spain, Portugal, Mexico, Panama, Colombia, Brazil, Jamaica, and Haiti.

Contributing Writers

Louise M. Belnay
    Teacher of World Languages
    Adams County School District 50
    Westminster, Colorado

Reina Martínez
    Coordinator/Teacher of World Languages
    North Rockland Central School District
    Thiells, New York

Contenido

Student Handbook

Repaso

Capítulo 1 Cocina hispana

Objetivos

You will:
- talk about foods and food preparation
- talk about a Hispanic recipe

You will use:
- the subjunctive
- formal commands
- negative informal commands

Capítulo 2 ¡Cuídate bien!

Objetivos

You will:
- identify more parts of the body
- talk about exercise
- talk about having a little accident and a trip to the emergency room
- discuss physical fitness

You will use:
- the subjunctive with impersonal expressions
- **ojalá, quizás, tal vez**
- the subjunctive of stem-changing verbs
- the comparison of like things

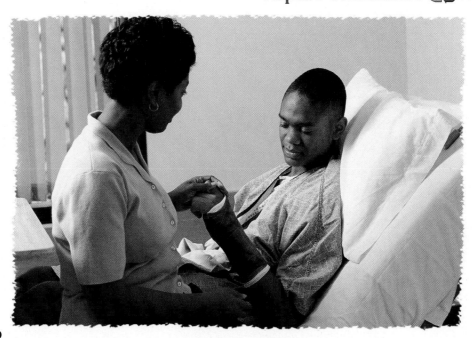

Capítulo 3 Pasajes de la vida

Objetivos

You will:
- talk about passages of life: weddings, baptisms, birthdays, and funerals
- read a poem by the Peruvian writer Abraham Valdelomar

You will use:
- the subjunctive to express wishes
- the subjunctive to express emotions
- possessive pronouns

Capítulo 4 Quehaceres

Objetivos

You will:
- talk about errands
- discuss preparing for a trip through Andalusia
- read a short story from Argentina

You will use:
- the subjunctive with expressions of doubt
- the subjunctive with adverbial clauses
- the pluperfect, conditional perfect, and future perfect tenses

Capítulo 5 ¿Buenos o malos modales?

Objetivos

You will:
- discuss manners
- compare manners in Spanish-speaking countries to manners in the United States
- read a famous episode from *El conde Lucanor* by Don Juan Manuel

You will use:
- the imperfect subjunctive
- the subjunctive vs. the infinitive
- suffixes

Capítulo 6 Viajes

Objetivos

You will:
- discuss several modes of travel
- talk about a trip to Bolivia
- read a short story by the Spanish author Emilia Pardo Bazán

You will use:
- the subjunctive with conjunctions of time
- the subjunctive to express suggestions and advice
- irregular nouns

Capítulo 7 Arte y literatura

Objetivos

You will:
- discuss fine art and literature
- talk about a mural by the Mexican artist Diego Rivera
- read a sonnet by the Spaniard Federico García Lorca
- read a poem by the Cuban poet Nicolás Guillén

You will use:
- the present perfect and pluperfect subjunctive
- **si** clauses
- adverbs ending in **-mente**

Capítulo 8 Latinos en Estados Unidos

Objetivos

You will:
- talk about the history of Spanish speakers in the United States
- read a poem by the Puerto Rican poet Julia de Burgos

You will use:
- the subjunctive with **aunque**
- the subjunctive with **-quiera**
- definite and indefinite articles (special uses)
- apocopated adjectives

Capítulo 9 Historia de la comida latina

Objetivos

You will:
- identify more foods
- describe food preparation
- discuss the history of foods from Europe and the Americas
- read a poem by the famous Chilean poet Pablo Neruda

You will use:
- the passive voice
- relative pronouns
- expressions of time with **hace** and **hacía**

Capítulo 10 Carreras

Objetivos

You will:
- talk about professions and occupations
- have a job interview
- discuss the importance of learning a second language
- read a short story by the famous Colombian writer Gabriel García Márquez

You will use:
- **por** and **para**
- the subjunctive in relative clauses

CONTENIDO

Student Resources

Guide to Symbols

Throughout ¡**Así se dice!** you will see these symbols, or icons. They will tell you how to best use the particular part of the chapter or activity they accompany. Following is a key to help you understand these symbols.

 Audio link This icon indicates material in the chapter that is recorded on compact disk.

 Recycling This icon indicates sections that review previously introduced material.

 Paired activity This icon indicates activities that you can practice orally with a partner.

 Group activity This icon indicates activities that you can practice together in groups.

 Critical thinking This icon indicates activities that require critical thinking.

 InfoGap This icon refers to additional paired activities at the end of the book.

 ¡Bravo! This icon indicates the end of new material in each chapter. All remaining material is recombination and review.

Why Learn Spanish?

¡Viva el español!

Spanish is currently the fourth-most-spoken language in the world. Studying Spanish will help you explore other cultures, communicate with Spanish speakers, and increase your career possibilities.

It's fascinating!

Culture Hispanic culture is full of diverse expressions of music, art, and literature. From dancing the tango or salsa to admiring a modern painting by Salvador Dalí, your studies will introduce you to an array of what the culture has to offer. You'll learn about the various customs, traditions, and values in Latin America and Spain. From food and family to school and sports, you'll learn all about life in the Hispanic world.

▲ **Dancers of the tango on the streets of Argentina**

It's all around us!

Communication The United States is home to more than fifty million Hispanics or Latinos. Whether on the radio, in your community or school, or in your own home, the Spanish language is probably part of your life in some way. Understanding Spanish allows you to sing along with Latin music on the radio or chat with Spanish speakers in your school, community, or family. No matter who you are, Spanish can enrich your life in some way.

If you plan to travel outside the United States, remember that Spanish is the official language of twenty-one countries. Experiencing another country is more fun and meaningful when you can understand restaurant menus, read newspapers, follow street signs, watch TV, and better yet converse with the locals.

◀ **Singer Shakira performs.**

▲ **A Spanish-speaking dentist**

It's a lifelong skill!

Career Do you know what career you plan to pursue? Medicine, business, social work, teaching? What will you do if you have a Spanish-speaking patient, client, or student? Speak Spanish, of course! Whatever your career, you will be able to reach more people if you are able to converse in Spanish. After all, it's spoken by more than 16 percent of the U.S. population. You will also be open to many more career opportunities if you know Spanish. Businesses, government agencies, and educational institutions are always looking for people with the ability to speak and read more than one language.

It's an adventure!

Challenge When you study a language, you not only learn about the language and its speakers but also about yourself. Studying a language requires that you challenge yourself and more fully develop your skills. When you know about the customs and values of another culture, you are better able to reflect upon your own. Language is a means of self-discovery. Enjoy!

▼ **Fans of Enrique Iglesias**

Reading in a New Language

Following are skills and strategies that can help you understand what you read in a language you have just begun to learn. *Reading and Succeeding* will help you build skills and strategies that will make it easier to understand what you are reading in your exciting new language.

The strategies you use frequently depend on the purpose of your reading. You do not read a textbook or standardized testing questions the same way you read a novel or a magazine article. You read a textbook for information. You read a novel or magazine article for fun.

In the early stages of second-language learning, your vocabulary is, of course, very limited in comparison to the vast number of words you already know in English. The material presented to you to read in the early stages must accommodate this reality. Your limited knowledge of the language does not have to deter you from enjoying what you are reading. Most of what you read, however, will come from your textbook, since original novels and magazine articles are not written for people who have limited exposure to the language.

As you develop your reading ability in Spanish, you will encounter basically two types of readings.

Intensive Readings

These readings are short. They are very controlled, using only language you have already learned. You should find these readings easy and enjoyable. If you find them difficult, it means you have not sufficiently learned the material presented in the chapter of the textbook. The vast majority of these informative readings will introduce you to the fascinating cultures of the Spanish-speaking world.

A very important aspect of reading in Spanish is to give you things to "talk about" in the language. The more you read, speak, and use the language, the more proficient you will become. Whenever you finish reading one of the intensive reading selections, you should be able to talk about it; that is, you should be able to retell it in your own words.

Extensive Readings

Since it is unrealistic to assume that you will never encounter new words as you branch out and read material in Spanish, you will also be presented with extensive readings. The goal of these extensive readings is to help you develop the tools and skills you need in order to read at some future date an original novel or magazine article. They do indeed contain some words and structures that are unfamiliar to you. In this *Reading and Succeeding* section, you will learn to develop many skills that will enable you to read such material with relative ease.

Use *Reading and Succeeding* to help you:

- adjust the way you read to fit the type of material you are reading
- identify new words and build your vocabulary
- use specific reading strategies to better understand what you read
- improve your ability to speak by developing strategies that enable you to retell orally what you have read
- use critical thinking strategies to think more deeply about what you read

Identifying New Words and Building Vocabulary

What do you do when you come across a word you do not know as you read? Do you skip the word and keep reading? You might if you are reading for fun. If it hinders your ability to understand, however, you might miss something important. When you come to a word you don't know, try the following strategies to figure out what the word means.

Reading Aloud

In the early stages of learning a second language, a good strategy is to sit by yourself and read the selection aloud. This can help you understand the reading because you once again hear words that you have already practiced orally in class. Hearing them as you read them can help reinforce meaning.

Identifying Cognates

As you read you will come across many cognates. Cognates are words that look alike in both English and Spanish. Not only do they look alike

but they mean the same thing. Recognizing cognates is a great reading strategy. Examples of cognates are:

cómico	nacionalidad	entra
popular	secundaria	clase
cubano	matemática	prepara
video	blusa	televisión

Identifying Roots and Base Words

The main part of a word is called its root. From a root, many new words can be formed. When you see a new word, identify its root. It can help you pronounce the word and figure out its meaning.

For example, if you know the word **importante,** there is no problem determining the meaning of **importancia.** The verb **importar** becomes a bit more problematic, but with some intelligent guessing you can get its meaning. You know it has something to do with importance so it means *it is important,* and by extension it can even carry the meaning *it matters.*

Identifying Prefixes

A prefix is a word part added to the beginning of a root or base word. Spanish as well as English has prefixes. Prefixes can change, or even reverse, the meaning of a word. For example, the prefixes **in-, im-,** and **des-** mean *not.*

estable/inestable **posible/imposible**
honesto/deshonesto

Using Syntax

Like all languages, Spanish has rules for the way words are arranged in sentences. The way a sentence is organized is called its syntax. Spanish syntax, however, is a bit more flexible than English. In a simple English sentence someone or something (its subject) does something (the predicate or verb) to or with another person or thing (the object). This word order can vary in Spanish and does not always follow the subject/verb/object order.

Because Spanish and English syntax vary, you should think in Spanish and not try to translate what you are reading into English. Reading in Spanish will then have a natural flow and follow exactly the way you learned it. Trying to translate it into English confuses the matter and serves no purpose.

Example

English always states: *John speaks to me.*
Spanish can state: *John to me speaks. or*
To me speaks John.

The latter leaves the subject to the end of the sentence and emphasizes that it is John who speaks to me.

Using Context Clues

This is a very important reading strategy in a second language. You can often figure out the meaning of an unfamiliar word by looking at it in context (the words and sentences that surround it). Let's look at the example below.

Example

The glump ate it all up and flew away.

You have no idea what a *glump* is. Right? But from the rest of the sentence you can figure out that it's a bird. Why? Because it flew away and you know that birds fly. In this way you guessed at the meaning of an unknown word using context. Although you know it is a bird, you cannot determine the specific meaning such as a robin, a wren, or a sparrow. In many cases it does not matter because that degree of specificity is not necessary for comprehension.

Let's look at another example:
The glump ate it all up and phlumped.

In this case you do not know the meaning of two key words in the same sentence—*glump* and *phlumped.* This makes it impossible to guess the meaning and this is what can happen when you try to read something in a second language that is beyond your proficiency level. This makes reading a frustrating experience. For this reason all the readings in your textbook control the language to keep it within your reach. Remember, if you have studied the vocabulary in your book, this will not happen.

Understanding What You Read

Try using some of the following strategies before, during, and after reading to understand and remember what you read.

Previewing

When you preview a piece of writing, you are looking for a general idea of what to expect from it. Before you read, try the following.
- Look at the title and any illustrations that are included.
- Read the headings, subheadings, and anything in bold letters.
- Skim over the passage to see how it is organized. Is it divided into many parts? Is it a long poem or short story?
- Look at the graphics—pictures, maps, or diagrams.
- Set a purpose for your reading. Are you reading to learn something new? Are you reading to find specific information?

Using What You Know

Believe it or not, you already know quite a bit about what you are going to read. Your own knowledge and personal experience can help you create meaning in what you read. There is, however, a big difference in reading the information in your Spanish textbook. You already have some knowledge about what you are reading from a United States oriented base. What you will be reading about takes place in a Spanish-speaking environment and thus you will be adding an exciting new dimension to what you already know. Comparing and contrasting are important critical skills to put to use when reading material about a culture other than your own. This skill will be discussed later.

Visualizing

Creating pictures in your mind about what you are reading—called visualizing—will help you understand and remember what you read. With the assistance of the many accompanying photos, try to visualize the people, streets, cities, homes, etc., you are reading about.

Identifying Sequence

When you discover the logical order of events or ideas, you are identifying sequence. Look for clues and signal words that will help you find how information is organized. Some signal words are **primero, al principio, antes, después, luego, entonces, más tarde, por fin, finalmente.**

Determining the Main Idea

When you look for the main idea of a selection, you look for the most important idea. The examples, reasons, and details that further explain the main idea are called supporting details.

Reviewing

When you review in school, you go over what you learned the day before so that the information is clear in your mind. Reviewing when you read does the same thing. Take time now and then to pause and review what you have read. Think about the main ideas and organize them for yourself so you can recall them later. Filling in study aids such as graphic organizers can help you review.

Monitoring Your Comprehension

As you read, check your understanding by summarizing. Pause from time to time and state the main ideas of what you have just read. Answer the questions: **¿Quién?** *(Who?)* **¿Qué?** *(What?)* **¿Dónde?** *(Where?)* **¿Cuándo?** *(When?)* **¿Cómo?** *(How?)* **¿Por qué?** *(Why?)*. Summarizing tests your comprehension because you state key points in your own words. Remember something you read earlier: reading in Spanish empowers your ability to speak by developing strategies that enable you to retell orally what you have read.

Thinking About Your Reading

Sometimes it is important to think more deeply about what you read so you can get the most out of what the author says. These critical thinking skills will help you go beyond what the words say and understand the meaning of your reading.

Compare and Contrast

To compare and contrast shows the similarities and differences among people, things, and ideas. Your reading experience in Spanish will show you many things that are similar and many others that are different depending upon the culture groups and social mores.

As you go over these culturally oriented readings, try to visualize what you are reading. Then think about the information. Think about what you know about the topic and then determine if the information you are reading is similar, somewhat different, or very different from what you know.

Continue to think about it. In this case you may have to think about it in English. Determine if you find the similarities or the differences interesting. Would you like to experience what you are reading about? Analyzing the information in this way will most certainly help you remember what you have read.

- Signal words and phrases that indicate similarity are **similar, semejante, parecido, igual.**
- Signal words and phrases that indicate differences are **diferente, distinto, al contrario, contrariamente, sin embargo.**

Cause and Effect

Just about everything that happens in life is the cause or the effect of some other event or action. Writers use cause-and-effect structure to explore the reasons for something happening and to examine the results of previous events. This structure helps answer the question that everybody is always asking: Why? Cause-and-effect structure is about explaining things.

- Signal words and phrases are **así, porque, por consiguiente, resulta que.**

Using Reference Materials

In the early stages of second-language learning, you will not be able to use certain types of reference materials that are helpful to you in English. For example, you could not look up a word in a Spanish dictionary as you would not be able to understand many of the words used in the definition.

You can, however, make use of the glossary that appears at the end of your textbook. A glossary includes only words that are included in the textbook. Rather than give you a Spanish definition, the glossary gives you the English equivalent of the word. If you have to use the glossary very frequently, it indicates to you that you have not studied the vocabulary sufficiently in each chapter. A strategy to use before beginning a reading selection in any given chapter is to quickly skim the vocabulary in the **Vocabulario 1** and **Vocabulario 2** sections of the chapter.

Expand your view of the Spanish-speaking world.

¡Así se dice! will show you the many places where you will be able to use your Spanish.

Cultural and geographic information is at your fingertips with **GeoVistas**, your virtual field trip to the Spanish-speaking countries.

Start your journey into language and culture.

Opening photo provides a cultural backdrop for the chapter.

Aquí y Allí introduces you to the chapter theme and invites you to make connections between your culture and the cultures of Spanish-speaking countries.

Objectives let you know what you will be able to do by the end of the chapter.

Access your eBook with QuickPass at glencoe.com.

Get acquainted with the chapter theme.

Explore each chapter's theme with vivid cultural photos and informative captions.

Introducción al tema
Viajes

Cada día hay miles de personas que están viajando. Hay muchos motivos para hacer un viaje—vacaciones, negocios, visitas familiares, etc. Como vas a observar en este capítulo, hay más de una manera de viajar y de vez en cuando es necesario cambiar de planes al último momento.

El Salvador TACA, una línea aérea centroamericana, como todas las líneas aéreas, tiene etiquetas que los pasajeros pueden poner en su equipaje. La etiqueta es muy importante porque tiene la dirección del pasajero. Nunca se sabe si una maleta se va a perder o extraviar.

República Dominicana Este señor tiene que hacer un viaje importante y no importa que tenga una pierna quebrada. Una agente de la línea aérea le puede ayudar en el aeropuerto.

Puerto Rico El maletero en el aeropuerto Luis Muñoz Marín en San Juan ayuda a los pasajeros con su equipaje.

Argentina Es un tren de cercanías en Buenos Aires. El tren no está completo. Sin embargo hay unos pasajeros de pie.

Guatemala Estas dos jóvenes están de vacaciones en Guatemala. Acaban de visitar las famosas ruinas en Tikal y ahora están llegando al aeropuerto de Santa Elena.

Panamá El tren está en la estación de ferrocarril en la Ciudad de Panamá. Es el tren que corre a lo largo de las orillas del Canal de Panamá.

España ¿Es una cafetería en un parque tropical? No. Está en la sala de espera de la estación de ferrocarril Atocha en Madrid.

166

167

See how the theme relates to different countries in the Spanish-speaking world.

Talk about the chapter theme with your new vocabulary.

Learn colloquial phrases to make conversation easy.

Vocabulary is introduced and practiced in two manageable sections.

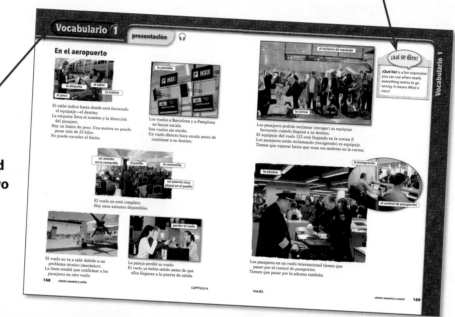

Recorded presentation ensures proper pronunciation.

Watch video clips to experience the diversity of the Spanish-speaking world while reinforcing the language you have learned and improving your listening and viewing skills.

Photos and illustrations aid comprehension and vocabulary acquisition.

New words are used in a meaningful context.

Practice and master new vocabulary.

Graphic organizers make practice clear and easy.

Use QuickPass to easily access additional vocabulary practice at glencoe.com.

Practice and master your new vocabulary with your Workbook and StudentWorks™ Plus.

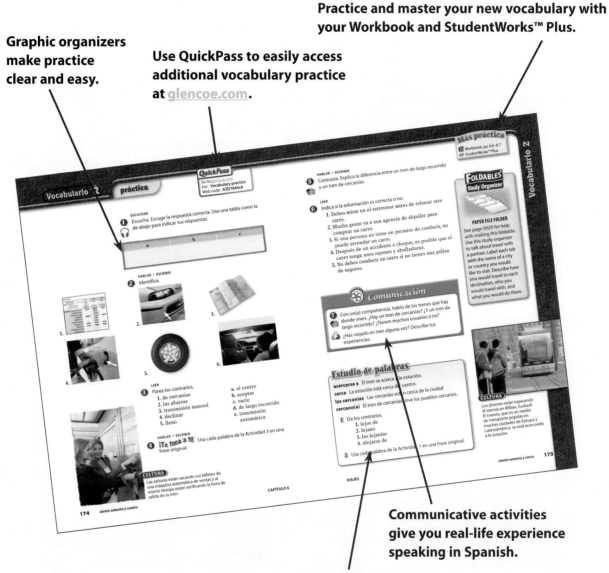

Communicative activities give you real-life experience speaking in Spanish.

Estudio de palabras helps you understand, form, and use words from a common root.

Learn grammar within the context of the chapter theme.

Expansión enables you to tell and retell a story, using your new words.

Use QuickPass to access additional grammar practice at glencoe.com.

Reinforce pronunciation and aural comprehension with audio activities.

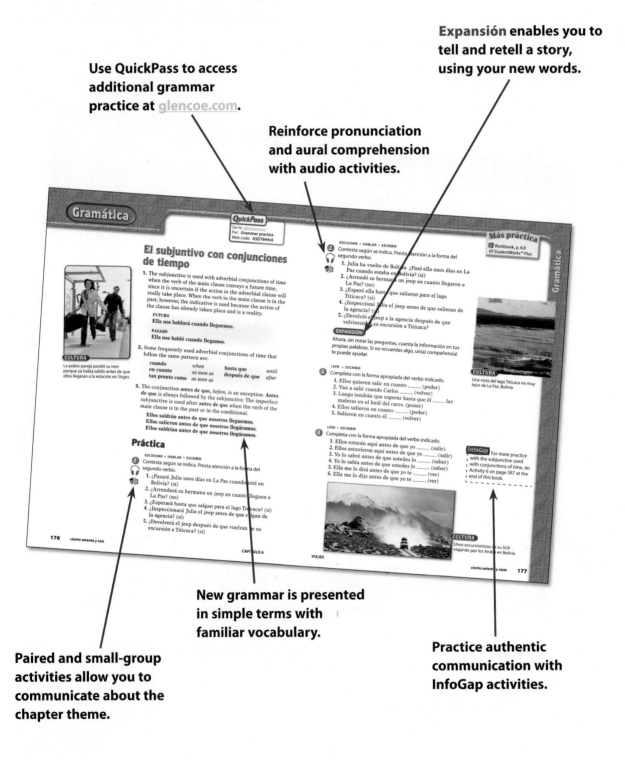

New grammar is presented in simple terms with familiar vocabulary.

Paired and small-group activities allow you to communicate about the chapter theme.

Practice authentic communication with InfoGap activities.

Build on what you already know.

Use your new vocabulary as you practice the new grammar points.

Have fun using your Spanish to figure out the meaning of Spanish proverbs.

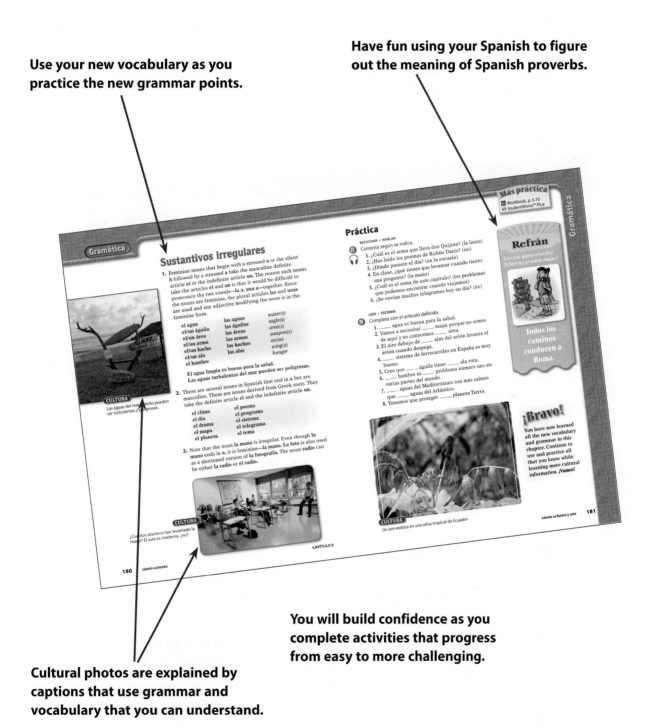

Cultural photos are explained by captions that use grammar and vocabulary that you can understand.

You will build confidence as you complete activities that progress from easy to more challenging.

Engage classmates in real conversation.

Use QuickPass to access the Conversation online at glencoe.com.

You will have a sense of accomplishment when you are able to comprehend the conversation.

Look for this symbol to find additional information to help you meet the National Standards for Foreign Language Learning.

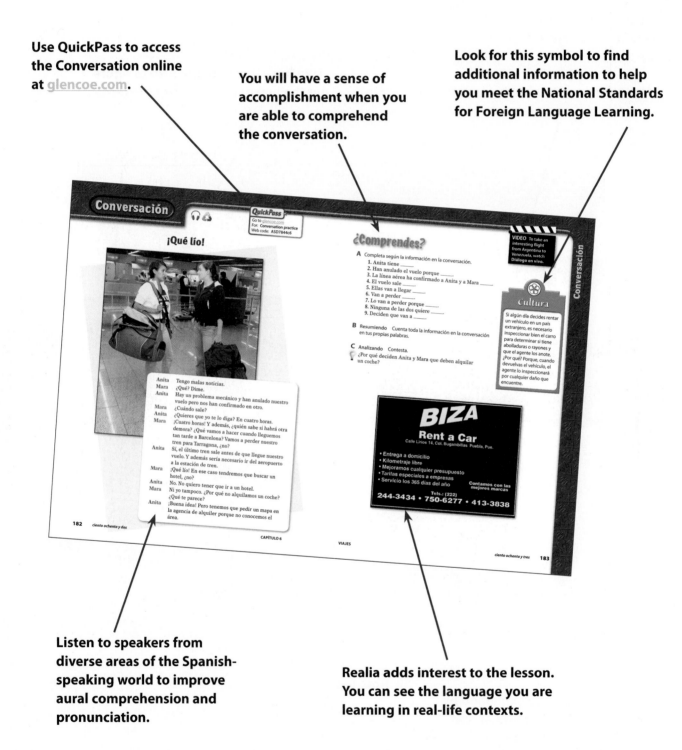

Listen to speakers from diverse areas of the Spanish-speaking world to improve aural comprehension and pronunciation.

Realia adds interest to the lesson. You can see the language you are learning in real-life contexts.

Heighten your cultural awareness.

Lectura cultural uses learned language to reinforce the chapter theme and to expand your understanding of the Spanish-speaking world.

Recorded reading online and on CD provides options for addressing various skills and learning styles.

Questions follow the reading to check comprehension.

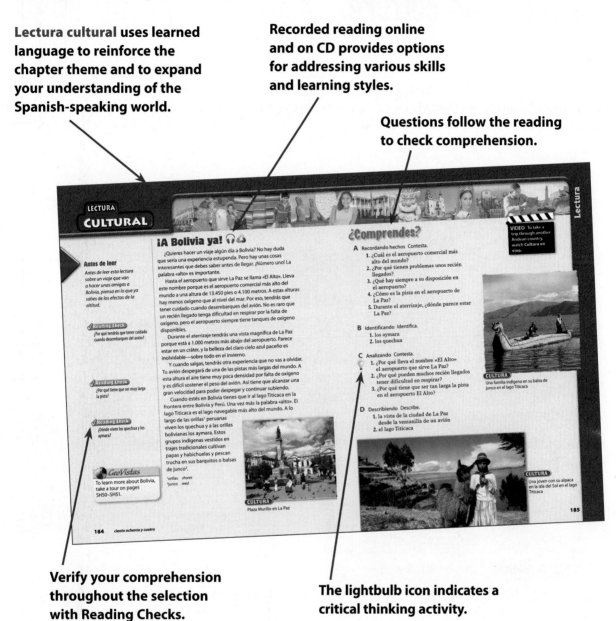

Verify your comprehension throughout the selection with Reading Checks.

The lightbulb icon indicates a critical thinking activity.

Enhance your appreciation of Hispanic literature and culture.

Literatura gives you another opportunity to apply your reading skills in Spanish and to further acquaint you with authentic prose and poetry of the Spanish-speaking world.

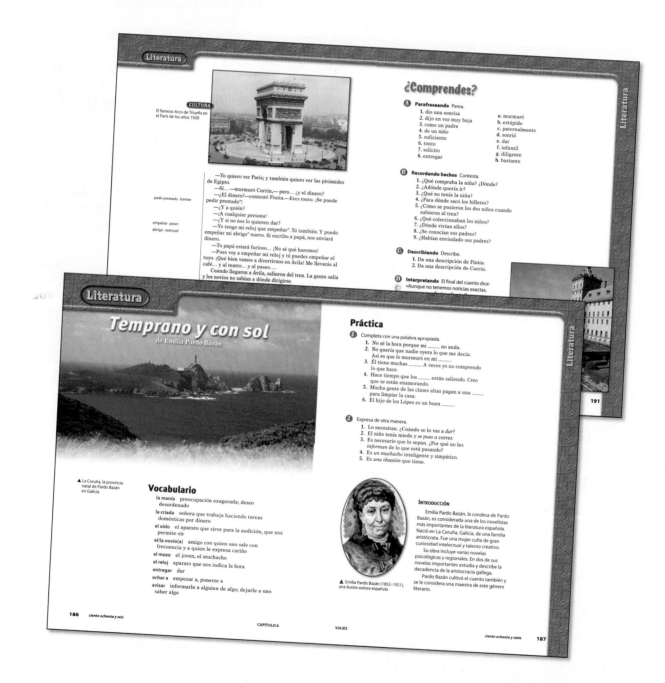

Literatura

CULTURA
El famoso Arco de Triunfo en el París de los años 1920

pedir prestado *borrow*

empeñar *pawn*
abrigo *overcoat*

—Yo quiero ver París; y también quiero ver las pirámides de Egipto.
—Sí... —murmuró Currín,— pero... ¿y el dinero?
—¿El dinero?—contestó Finita.—Eres tonto. ¡Se puede pedir prestado°!
—¿Y a quién?
—¡A cualquier persona!
—¿Y si no nos lo quieren dar?
—Yo tengo mi reloj que empeñar°. Tú también. Y puedo empeñar mi abrigo° nuevo. Si escribo a papá, nos enviará dinero.
—Tu papá estará furioso... ¡No sé qué haremos!
—Pues voy a empeñar mi reloj y tú puedes empeñar el tuyo. ¡Qué bien vamos a divertirnos en Ávila! Me llevarás al café... y al teatro... y al paseo....
Cuando llegaron a Ávila, salieron del tren. La gente salía y los novios no sabían a dónde dirigirse.

¿Comprendes?

A Parafraseando Parea.
1. dio una sonrisa
2. dijo en voz muy baja
3. como un padre
4. de un niño
5. suficiente
6. tonto
7. solícito
8. entregar

a. murmuró
b. estúpido
c. paternalmente
d. sonrió
e. dar
f. infantil
g. diligente
h. bastante

B Recordando hechos Contesta.
1. ¿Qué compraba la niña? ¿Dónde?
2. ¿Adónde quería ir?
3. ¿Qué no tenía la niña?
4. ¿Para dónde sacó los billetes?
5. ¿Cómo se pusieron los dos niños cuando subieron al tren?
6. ¿Qué coleccionaban los niños?
7. ¿Dónde vivían ellos?
8. ¿Se conocían sus padres?
9. ¿Habían envidiado sus padres?

C Describiendo Describe.
1. Da una descripción de Finita.
2. Da una descripción de Currín.

D Interpretando El final del cuento dice: «Aunque no tenemos noticias exactas,

191

Literatura

Temprano y con sol
de Emilia Pardo Bazán

▲ La Coruña, la provincia natal de Pardo Bazán en Galicia

Vocabulario

la manía preocupación exagerada; deseo desordenado
la criada señora que trabaja haciendo tareas domésticas por dinero
el oído el aparato que sirve para la audición, que nos permite oír
el/la novio(a) amigo con quien uno sale con frecuencia y a quien le expresa cariño
el mozo el joven, el muchacho
el reloj aparato que nos indica la hora
entregar dar
echar a empezar a, ponerse a
avisar informarle a alguien de algo; dejarle a uno saber algo

Práctica

❶ Completa con una palabra apropiada.
1. No sé la hora porque mi _____ no anda.
2. No quería que nadie oyera lo que me decía. Así es que lo murmuró en mi _____.
3. Él tiene muchas _____. A veces yo no comprendo lo que hace.
4. Hace tiempo que los _____ están saliendo. Creo que se están enamorando.
5. Mucha gente de las clases altas pagan a una _____ para limpiar la casa.
6. El hijo de los López es un buen _____.

❷ Expresa de otra manera.
1. Lo necesitan. ¿Cuándo se lo vas a *dar*?
2. El niño tenía miedo y *se puso a* correr.
3. Es necesario que lo sepan. ¿Por qué no les *informan de* lo que está pasando?
4. Es *un muchacho* inteligente y simpático.
5. Es *una obsesión* que tiene.

INTRODUCCIÓN

Emilia Pardo Bazán, la condesa de Pardo Bazán, es considerada una de los novelistas más importantes de la literatura española. Nació en La Coruña, Galicia, de una familia aristócrata. Fue una mujer culta de gran curiosidad intelectual y talento creativo.
Su obra incluye varias novelas psicológicas y regionales. En dos de sus novelas importantes estudia y describe la decadencia de la aristocracia gallega.
Pardo Bazán cultivó el cuento también y se le considera una maestra de este género literario.

▲ Emilia Pardo Bazán (1852–1921), una ilustre autora española

Show what you know.

Review what you have learned and prepare for your chapter test.

Reference notes direct you to the correct pages for review.

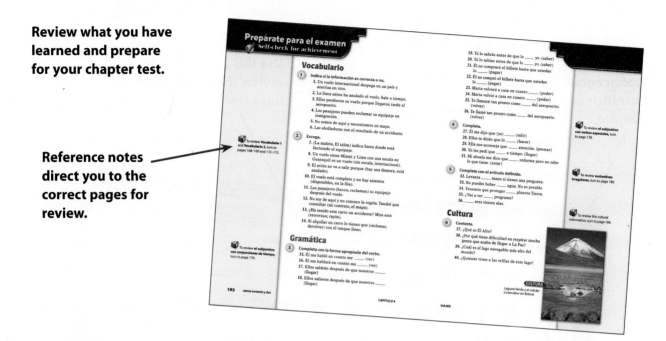

Apply what you have learned.

Use your new skills to communicate orally in meaningful, open-ended activities.

Practice what you have learned while improving your written Spanish.

Writing Strategy gives you the tools you need to develop better writing skills.

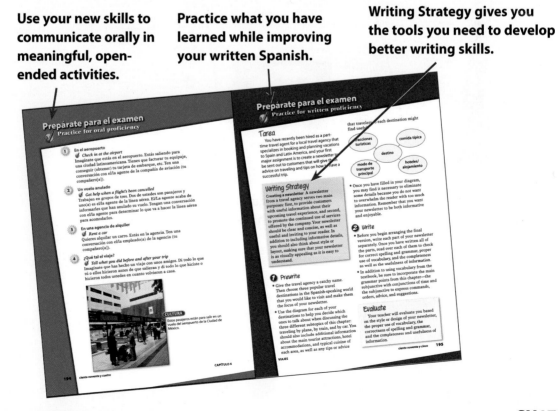

Review grammar and vocabulary at a glance.

Succinct grammar notes help you efficiently review chapter material.

Use this vocabulary list to review the vocabulary you have learned in this chapter.

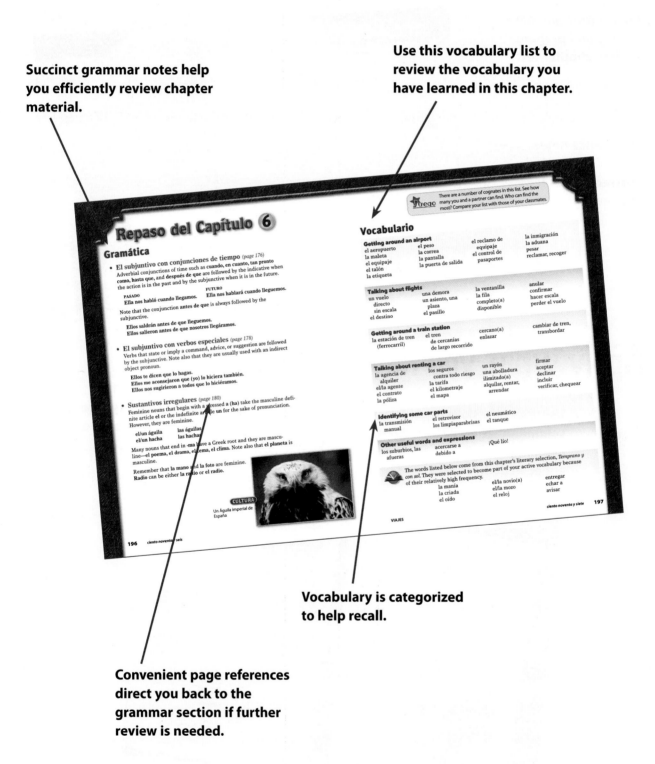

There are a number of cognates in this list. See how many you and a partner can find. Who can find the most? Compare your list with those of your classmates.

Repaso del Capítulo 6

Gramática

- **El subjuntivo con conjunciones de tiempo** *(page 176)*
  Adverbial conjunctions of time such as **cuando, en cuanto, tan pronto como, hasta que,** and **después de que** are followed by the indicative when the action is in the past and by the subjunctive when it is in the future.

  PASADO   FUTURO
  Ella nos habló cuando llegamos.   Ella nos hablará cuando lleguemos.

  Note that the conjunction **antes de que** is always followed by the subjunctive.

  Ellos saldrán antes de que lleguemos.
  Ellos salieron antes de que nosotros llegáramos.

- **El subjuntivo con verbos especiales** *(page 178)*
  Verbs that state or imply a command, advice, or suggestion are followed by the subjunctive. Note also that they are usually used with an indirect object pronoun.

  Ellos te dicen que lo hagas.
  Ellos me aconsejaron que (yo) lo hiciera también.
  Ellos nos sugirieron a todos que lo hiciéramos.

- **Sustantivos irregulares** *(page 180)*
  Feminine nouns that begin with a stressed **a (ha)** take the masculine definite article **el** or the indefinite article **un** for the sake of pronunciation. However, they are feminine.

  el/un águila   las águilas
  el/un hacha   las hachas

  Many nouns that end in **-ma** have a Greek root and they are masculine—**el poema, el drama, el tema, el clima**. Note also that **el planeta** is masculine.

  Remember that **la mano** and **la foto** are feminine. **Radio** can be either **la radio** or **el radio**.

CULTURA
Un Águila imperial de España

Vocabulario

Getting around an airport
el aeropuerto / el peso / el reclamo de equipaje / la inmigración
la maleta / la correa / el control de pasaportes / la aduana
el equipaje / la pantalla / pesar
el talón / la puerta de salida / reclamar, recoger
la etiqueta

Talking about flights
un vuelo / una demora / la ventanilla / anular
directo / un asiento, una plaza / la fila / confirmar
sin escala / el pasillo / completo(a) / hacer escala
el destino / disponible / perder el vuelo

Getting around a train station
la estación de tren (ferrocarril) / el tren / cercano(a) / cambiar de tren, transbordar
de cercanías / enlazar
de largo recorrido

Talking about renting a car
la agencia de alquiler / los seguros / un rayón / firmar
el/la agente / contra todo riesgo / una abolladura / aceptar
el contrato / la tarifa / ilimitado(a) / declinar
la póliza / el kilometraje / alquilar, rentar, arrendar / incluir
el mapa / verificar, chequear

Identifying some car parts
la transmisión manual / el retrovisor / el neumático
los limpiaparabrisas / el tanque

Other useful words and expressions
los suburbios, las afueras / acercarse a / ¡Qué lío!
debido a

The words listed below come from this chapter's literary selection, *Temprano y con sol.* They were selected to become part of your active vocabulary because of their relatively high frequency.
la manía / el/la novio(a) / entregar
la criada / el/la mozo / echar a
el oído / el reloj / avisar

VIAJES

196 ciento noventa y seis

ciento noventa y siete 197

Vocabulary is categorized to help recall.

Convenient page references direct you back to the grammar section if further review is needed.

Practice what you have learned so far in Spanish.

A wide variety of activities allow you to practice what you have learned so far in Spanish class.

The Cumulative Review always begins with an audio activity to give you more listening practice.

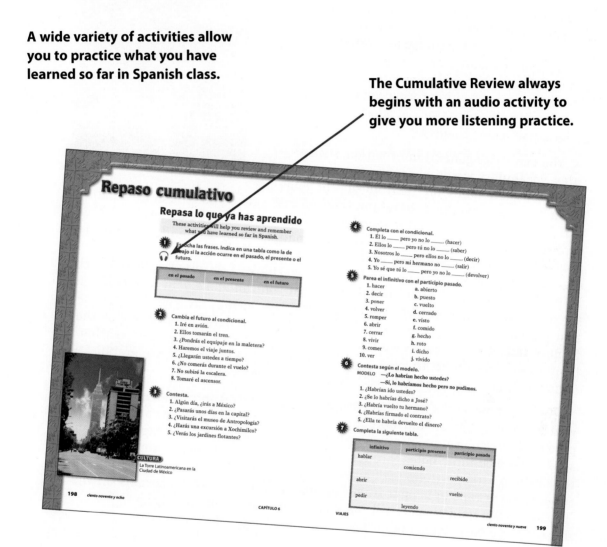

Dear Student,

Foldables are interactive study organizers that you can make yourself. They are a wonderful resource to help you organize and retain information. Foldables have many purposes. You can use them to remember vocabulary words or to organize more in-depth information on any given topic, such as keeping track of what you know about a particular country.

You can write general information, such as titles, vocabulary words, concepts, questions, main ideas, and dates, on the front tabs of your Foldables. You view this general information every time you look at a Foldable. This helps you focus on and remember key points without the distraction of additional text. You can write specific information—supporting ideas, thoughts, answers to questions, research information, empirical data, class notes, observations, and definitions—under the tabs. Think of different ways in which Foldables can be used. Soon you will find that you can make your own Foldables for study guides and projects. Foldables with flaps or tabs create study guides that you can use to check what you know about the general information on the front of tabs. Use Foldables without tabs for projects that require information to be presented for others to view quickly. The more you make and use graphic organizers, the faster you will become able to produce them.

To store your Foldables, turn one-gallon freezer bags into student portfolios which can be collected and stored in the classroom. You can also carry your portfolios in your notebooks if you place strips of two-inch clear tape along one side and punch three holes through the taped edge. Write your name along the top of the plastic portfolio with a permanent marker and cover the writing with two-inch clear tape to keep it from wearing off. Cut the bottom corners off the bag so it won't hold air and will stack and store easily. The following figures illustrate the basic folds that are referred to throughout this book.

Good luck!

Dinah Zike

Dinah Zike
www.dinah.com

Category Book

Los números Use this *category book* organizer to review dates and numbers.

Step 1 **Fold** a sheet of paper (8½" x 11") in half like a *hot dog*.

Step 2 On one side, **cut** every third line. This usually results in ten tabs. Do this with three sheets of paper to make three books.

Step 3 **Write** one Arabic number on the outside of each of the tabs. On the inside write out the respective number. As you review more numbers, use *category books* to categorize numbers in this way.

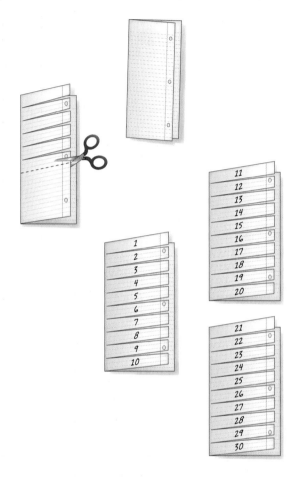

Other Suggestions for a *Category Book* Foldable

You may wish to use *category book* foldables to practice forming adverbs. On the front of each tab, write an adjective. Then your partner will rewrite the adjectives as adverbs on the inside of the tabs.

A *category book* foldable may also be used to practice conjugating Spanish verbs in various tenses. On the top tab, write the infinitive form of a verb.

On the following tabs, write the subject pronouns: **yo, tú, él, ella, Ud., nosotros(as), ellos, ellas, Uds.** Then open each tab and write the corresponding form of the verb in the tense you wish to practice.

Forward-Backward Book

Las estaciones Use this *forward-backward book* to compare and contrast two seasons of your choice.

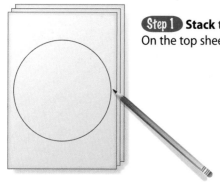

Step 1 Stack three sheets of paper. On the top sheet, trace a large circle.

Step 2 With the papers still stacked, **cut out** the circles.

Step 3 Staple the paper circles together along the left-hand side to create a circular booklet.

Step 4 Write the name of a season on the cover. On the page that opens to the right list the months of the year in that particular season. On the following page draw a picture to illustrate the season.

front

inside

El invierno

Step 5 Turn the book upside down and write the name of a season on the cover. On the page that opens to the right list the months of the year in that particular season. On the following page draw a picture to illustrate the season.

back

inside

El verano

Other Suggestions for a *Forward-Backward Book* Foldable

You may wish to use a *forward-backward book* foldable to organize vocabulary pertaining to television and the press. On the front cover, write **La televisión**. Inside, illustrate and name your favorite television programs. Close your book and flip it over. On the back cover, write **La prensa**. Inside, illustrate and write about a news event and different types of press. Discuss your books with a partner.

It may be helpful to use a *forward-backward book* foldable to organize the food groups. You could use the name of a food group in Spanish (meat, vegetable, fruit, etc.) as the title. On the inside, list as many foods in this food group as you can on the right-hand page and illustrate these foods on the opposite page. Give the same information for a second food group by reversing the book.

Pocket Book

La geografía Use this *pocket book* organizer in your ongoing study of all the countries in the Spanish-speaking world.

Step 1 **Fold** a sheet of paper (8½" x 11") in half like a *hamburger*.

Step 2 **Open** the folded paper and fold one of the long sides up two inches to form a pocket. Refold the *hamburger* fold so that the newly formed pockets are on the inside.

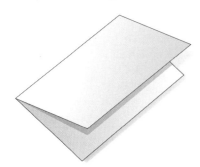

Step 3 **Glue** the outer edges of the two-inch fold with a small amount of glue.

Step 4 **Make a multipaged booklet** by gluing six pockets side-by-side. Glue a cover around the multipaged *pocket book*.

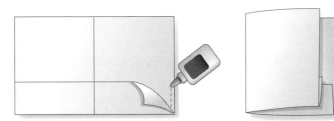

Step 5 **Label** five pockets with the following geographical areas: **Europa, la América del Norte, la América del Sur, la América Central,** and **Islas del Caribe.** Use index cards inside the pockets to record information each time you learn something new about a specific country. Be sure to include the name of the country (in Spanish, of course) and its capital.

Other Suggestions for a *Pocket Book* Foldable

A *pocket book* foldable may be used to organize information about several subjects. For example, to organize information about airplane and train travel, label pockets with topics such as *taking a flight, taking a train,* and *renting a car* in Spanish. You can also organize information related to the passages of life. Make one *pocket book* for each passage of life that you study. Make cards for all the words and phrases you know that go with each topic.

If you wish to organize what you are learning about important people, works of art, festivals, and other cultural information in countries that speak Spanish, a *pocket book* foldable may be helpful. You can make a card for each person, work of art, or event that you study, and you can add cards and even add categories as you continue to learn about cultures that speak Spanish.

Tab Book

Preguntas Use this *tab book* to practice asking
and answering questions.

Step 1 **Fold** a sheet of paper (8½" x 11") like a *hot dog* but fold it so that one side is
one inch longer than the other.

Step 2 On the shorter side only, **cut** five equal tabs. On the front of each tab, **write** a
question word you have learned. For example, you may wish to write the following.

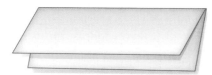

Step 3 On the bottom edge, **write** any sentence you would like.

Step 4 Under each tab, **write** the word from your sentence that answers the
question on the front of the tab.

Other Suggestions for a *Tab Book* Foldable

You may also use a *tab book* foldable to
practice verb conjugations. You would need
to make six tabs instead of five. Write a verb
and a tense on the bottom edge and write the
pronouns on the front of each tab. Under each
tab, write the corresponding verb form.

You may wish to use a *tab book* foldable
to practice new vocabulary words. Leave extra
space on the bottom edge. Choose five or six
vocabulary words and write each one on a tab.

You may also use a *tab book* to practice
the subjunctive. On the top of each tab, write
an expression that requires the subjunctive,
for example **Es imposible que...** . Then open
each tab and write a sentence using that
expression with the subjunctive.

Single Picture Frame

Dibujar y escribir Use this *single picture frame* to help you illustrate the stories you write.

Step 1 **Fold** a sheet of paper (8½" x 11") in half like a *hamburger*.

Step 2 **Open** the *hamburger* and gently roll one side of the *hamburger* toward the valley. Try not to crease the roll.

Step 3 **Cut** a rectangle out of the middle of the rolled side of paper, leaving a ½" border and forming a frame.

Step 4 **Fold** another sheet of paper (8½" x 11") in half like a *hamburger*.

Step 5 **Apply** glue to the picture frame and place it inside the *hamburger* fold.

Variation:
- Place a picture behind the frame and glue the edges of the frame to the other side of the *hamburger* fold. This locks the picture in place.
- Cut out only three sides of the rolled rectangle. This forms a window with a cover that opens and closes.

Other Suggestions for a *Single Picture Frame* Foldable

You may wish to discuss a meal—ingredients and preparation—using a *single picture frame* foldable. Work in small groups. One student will draw a picture of a meal or find one from a magazine. The next person will identify as many ingredients as he or she can.

Other members of the group can add any that were left out. The next person will explain how a certain item was prepared. Continue until everyone has contributed information. Then begin again with another person drawing another meal.

Minibook

Mi autobiografía Use this *minibook* organizer to write and illustrate your autobiography. Before you begin to write, think about the many things concerning yourself that you have the ability to write about in Spanish. On the left pages, draw the events of your life in chronological order. On the right, write about your drawings.

Step 1 **Fold** a sheet of paper (8½" x 11") in half like a *hot dog*.

Step 2 **Fold** it in half again like a *hamburger*.

Step 3 Then **fold** in half again, forming eight sections.

Step 4 **Open** the fold and **cut** the eight sections apart.

Step 5 **Place** all eight sections in a stack and fold in half like a *hamburger*.

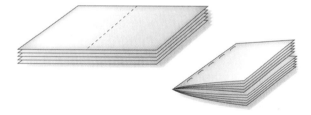

Step 6 **Staple** along the center fold line. **Glue** the front and back sheets into a construction paper cover.

Other Suggestions for a *Minibook* Foldable

Work in pairs to practice new verbs and verb forms using a *minibook* foldable. Illustrate different verbs on the left pages. If it is not clear what pronoun is required, you should write the pronoun under the drawing, for instance to differentiate between *we* and *they*. Then trade *minibooks* and write sentences to go with each picture on the right pages, using the new verb and the pronoun illustrated or indicated.

A *minibook* foldable can be used to talk about errands. On each page, illustrate a person on an errand. Under the illustration, write a sentence describing what the person is doing.

Paper File Folder

Las emociones Use this *paper file folder* organizer to keep track of happenings or events that cause you to feel a certain way.

Step 1 **Fold** four sheets of paper (8½" x 11") in half like a *hamburger*. Leave one side one inch longer than the other side.

Step 2 On each sheet, **fold** the one-inch tab over the short side, forming an envelope-like fold.

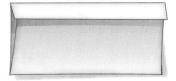

Step 3 **Place** the four sheets side-by-side, then move each fold so that the tabs are exposed.

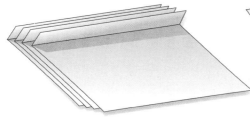

Step 4 Moving left to right, **cut** staggered tabs in each fold, 2⅛" wide. Fold the tabs upward.

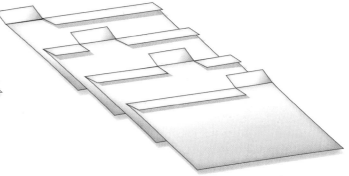

Step 5 **Glue** the ends of the folders together. On each tab, write an emotion you sometimes feel. Pay attention to when it is that you feel happy, sad, nervous, etc. Describe the situation in Spanish and file it in the correct pocket.

Other Suggestions for a *Paper File Folder* Foldable

You may use a *paper file folder* organizer to keep track of verbs and verb forms. You should make a folder for each type of regular verb and for each type of irregular verb. Write the conjugations for some important verbs in each category and file them in the *paper file folder* organizer. Add new tenses to the existing cards and new verbs as you learn them.

A *paper file folder* organizer can be useful for keeping notes on the cultural information that you will learn. You may wish to make categories for different types of cultural information and add index cards to them as you learn new facts and concepts about the target cultures.

Envelope Fold

Un viaje especial Use this *envelope fold* to make a hidden picture or to write secret clues about a city in the Spanish-speaking world you would like to visit.

Step 1 **Fold** a sheet of paper into a *taco* to form a square. Cut off the leftover piece.

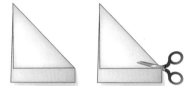

Step 2 **Open** the folded *taco* and refold it the opposite way, forming another *taco* and an X-fold pattern.

Step 3 **Open** the *taco fold* and fold the corners toward the center point of the X, forming a small square.

Step 4 **Trace** this square onto another sheet of paper. Cut and glue it to the inside of the envelope. Pictures can be drawn under the tabs.

Step 5 Use this foldable to **draw** a picture of the city you would like to visit. Or if you prefer, **write** clues about the city and have your classmates raise one tab at a time until they can guess what city the picture represents. Number the tabs in the order in which they are to be opened.

Other Suggestions for an *Envelope Fold* Foldable

An *envelope fold* can be useful for practicing vocabulary related to airports, trains, Hispanic cooking, passages of life, or careers. To talk about careers and professions, describe on each tab a task that is part of a particular career or profession. Your partner will use these clues to guess the profession.

You may want to use an *envelope fold* to review a selection you have read. Depict a scene from the selection on the paper covered by the tabs. Number the tabs in the order they are to be opened and have a partner open the tabs one at a time to guess what scene is illustrated. The partner should then write a description of the scenes.

Large Sentence Strips

El presente y el pasado Use these *large sentence strips* to help you compare and contrast activities in the past and in the present.

Step 1 Take two sheets of paper (8½" x 11") and **fold** into *hamburgers*. Cut along the fold lines, making four half sheets. (Use as many half sheets as necessary for additional pages in your book.)

Step 2 **Fold** each half sheet in half like a *hot dog*.

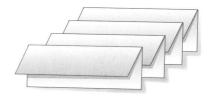

Step 3 Place the folds side-by-side and **staple** them together on the left side.

Step 4 About one inch from the stapled edge, **cut** the front page of each folded section up to the top. These cuts form flaps that can be raised and lowered.

Step 5 To make a half-cover, use a sheet of construction paper one inch longer than the book. **Glue** the back of the last sheet to the construction paper strip, leaving one inch on the left side to fold over and cover the original staples. Staple this half-cover in place.

Step 6 With a friend, **write** sentences on the front of the flap, either in the present tense or in the past tense. Then switch your books of sentence strips and write the opposite tense inside under the flaps.

Other Suggestions for a *Large Sentence Strips* Foldable

You may work in pairs to use *large sentence strips* to practice using direct and/or indirect object pronouns. On the front of each flap, write full sentences that have direct or indirect objects or both. Then trade sentence strips. You and your partner will each write sentences under the flaps replacing the direct or indirect objects with object pronouns.

You may wish to use *large sentence strips* to practice using the subjunctive. On the front of each strip, write a sentence that uses the present subjunctive after verbs

such as **querer, insistir, esperar,** and **dudar.** Then on the back of each strip, your partner will rewrite the sentence in the past, using the imperfect of verbs like **querer, insistir, esperar,** and **dudar** with the imperfect subjunctive. When you are finished, reverse roles. Make sure you check each other's work.

Project Board With Tabs

Diversiones favoritas Use this *project board with tabs* to display a visual about your favorite movie or event. Be sure to make it as attractive as possible to help convince others to see it.

Step 1 **Draw** a large illustration, a series of small illustrations, or write on the front of a sheet of paper.

Step 2 **Pinch** and slightly fold the sheet of paper at the point where a tab is desired on the illustrated piece of paper. Cut into the paper on the fold. Cut straight in, then cut up to form an L. When the paper is unfolded, it will form a tab with the illustration on the front.

Step 3 After all tabs have been cut, **glue** this front sheet onto a second sheet of paper. Place glue around all four edges and in the middle, away from tabs.

Step 4 **Write** or draw under the tabs. If the project is made as a bulletin board using butcher paper, tape or glue smaller sheets of paper under the tabs.

Think of favorite scenes from a movie or cultural event that you enjoyed and draw them on the front of the tabs. Underneath the tabs write a description of the scene or tell why you liked it. It might be fun to not put a title on the project board and just hang it up and let classmates guess the name of the movie or event you are describing.

Other Suggestions for a *Project Board With Tabs* Foldable

You may wish to use a *project board with tabs* to practice your formal commands. Think of the food words you know in Spanish and use them to create a recipe of your own. Draw a small picture of each ingredient in the order you will use it in your recipe. Next, lift each tab and write instructions about how to prepare each ingredient for your recipe using formal commands. For a more complex recipe, combine two or more *project boards with tabs*.

You may also use a *project board with tabs* to illustrate a party, museum, sport, or concert. Draw one aspect of it on the outside of the tab and write a description of your drawing under the tab.

You may work in pairs to practice the comparative and superlative. Each of you will make a *project board with tabs*. On the outside of each tab, draw a different comparison or superlative. Then trade with your partner and under each tab write a sentence describing the other's illustrations.

You may also wish to use a *project board with tabs* to practice the use of object pronouns. Draw a series of scenes involving two or more people on the outside of the tabs. Write sentences using object pronouns describing the people's conversations.

▼ México

Spanish is the language of almost 400 million people around the world. Spanish had its origin in Spain. It is sometimes fondly called the "language of Cervantes," the author of the famous novel and character, *Don Quijote*. The Spanish **conquistadores** and **exploradores** brought their language to the Americas in the fifteenth and sixteenth centuries. Spanish is the official language of almost all the countries of Central and South America. It is the official language of Mexico and several of the larger islands in the Caribbean. Spanish is also the heritage language of more than fifty million people in the United States.

Perú ▶

▲ Puerto Rico

▲ España

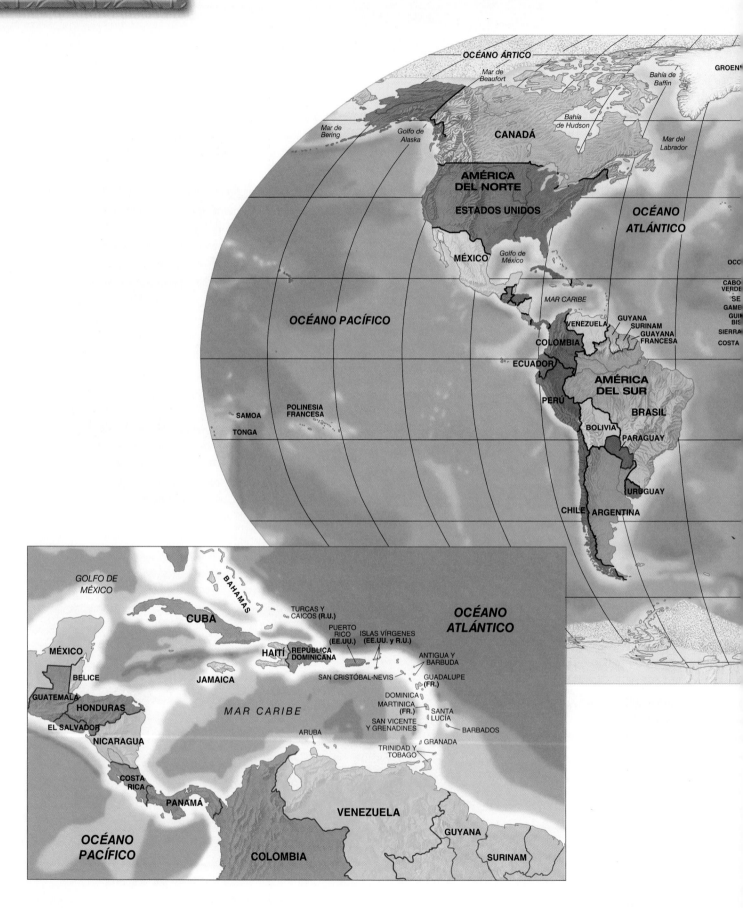

OCÉANO ÁRTICO

GROEN

Mar de Beaufort

Bahía de Baffin

Mar de Bering

Golfo de Alaska

CANADÁ

Bahía de Hudson

Mar del Labrador

AMÉRICA DEL NORTE

ESTADOS UNIDOS

OCÉANO ATLÁNTICO

MÉXICO

Golfo de México

OCÉANO PACÍFICO

MAR CARIBE

OCC

CABO VERDE

'SE

GAME

GUIN

BIS

VENEZUELA

GUYANA

SURINAM

GUAYANA FRANCESA

SIERRA

COSTA

COLOMBIA

ECUADOR

AMÉRICA DEL SUR

PERÚ

BRASIL

SAMOA

POLINESIA FRANCESA

BOLIVIA

PARAGUAY

TONGA

URUGUAY

CHILE

ARGENTINA

GOLFO DE MÉXICO

BAHAMAS

TURCAS Y CAICOS (R.U.)

OCÉANO ATLÁNTICO

CUBA

PUERTO RICO (EE.UU.)

ISLAS VÍRGENES (EE.UU. y R.U.)

MÉXICO

HAITÍ

REPÚBLICA DOMINICANA

ANTIGUA Y BARBUDA

BELICE

JAMAICA

SAN CRISTÓBAL-NEVIS

GUADALUPE (FR.)

GUATEMALA

DOMINICA

HONDURAS

MAR CARIBE

MARTINICA (FR.)

SANTA LUCÍA

EL SALVADOR

SAN VICENTE Y GRENADINES

BARBADOS

NICARAGUA

ARUBA

GRANADA

TRINIDAD Y TOBAGO

COSTA RICA

PANAMÁ

VENEZUELA

OCÉANO PACÍFICO

GUYANA

COLOMBIA

SURINAM

España

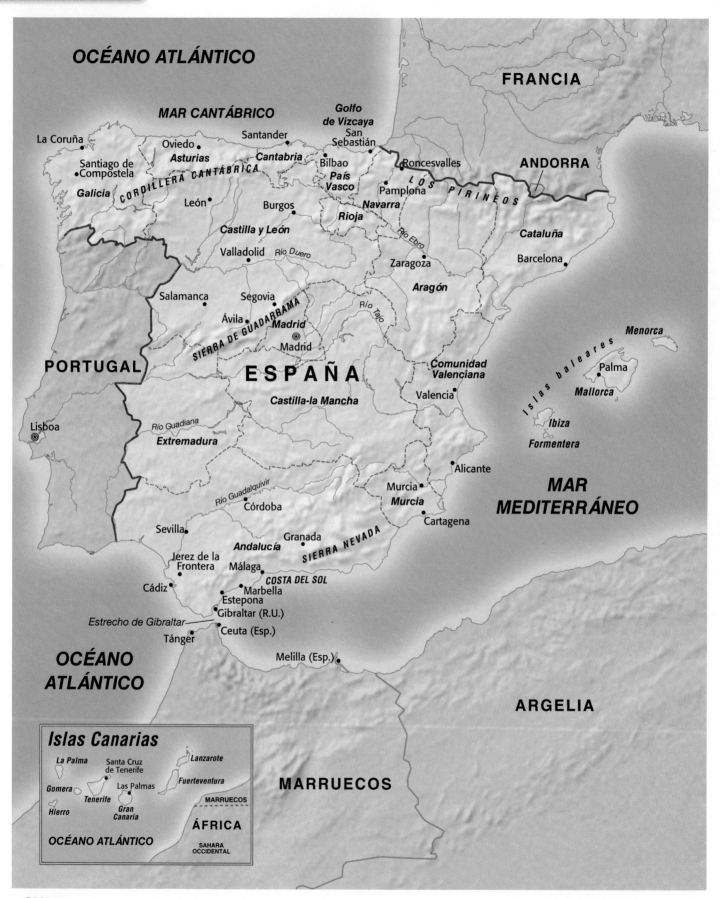

OCÉANO ATLÁNTICO

FRANCIA

MAR CANTÁBRICO

Golfo de Vizcaya

ANDORRA

La Coruña

Santiago de Compostela

Oviedo

Asturias

Santander

San Sebastián

Roncesvalles

LOS PIRINEOS

Cantabria

Bilbao

País Vasco

Pamplona

Galicia

CORDILLERA CANTÁBRICA

León

Burgos

Navarra

Rioja

Río Ebro

Cataluña

Castilla y León

Valladolid

Río Duero

Zaragoza

Barcelona

Aragón

Salamanca

Segovia

Río Tajo

Ávila

SIERRA DE GUADARRAMA

Madrid

Madrid

PORTUGAL

ESPAÑA

Comunidad Valenciana

Menorca

Islas baleares

Palma

Castilla-la Mancha

Valencia

Mallorca

Lisboa

Río Guadiana

Ibiza

Extremadura

Formentera

Alicante

MAR MEDITERRÁNEO

Río Guadalquivir

Murcia

Córdoba

Murcia

Sevilla

Cartagena

Granada

Andalucía

SIERRA NEVADA

Jerez de la Frontera

Málaga

COSTA DEL SOL

Cádiz

Marbella

Estepona

Gibraltar (R.U.)

Estrecho de Gibraltar

Ceuta (Esp.)

Tánger

OCÉANO ATLÁNTICO

Melilla (Esp.)

ARGELIA

Islas Canarias

La Palma

Santa Cruz de Tenerife

Lanzarote

Gomera

Las Palmas

Fuerteventura

MARRUECOS

Tenerife

Hierro

Gran Canaria

ÁFRICA

OCÉANO ATLÁNTICO

SAHARA OCCIDENTAL

MARRUECOS

MAR CARIBE

OCÉANO ATLÁNTICO

Barranquilla
Maracaibo
Caracas
Cartagena
Lago de Maracaibo
Río Orinoco
Medellín
VENEZUELA
GUYANA
Santafé de Bogotá
SURINAM
GUAYANA FRANCESA
Río Magdalena
COLOMBIA
Cali
Ecuador
Otavalo
Quito
ECUADOR
Río Amazonas
Islas Galápagos (Ecuador)
Guayaquil
Cuenca
PERÚ
BRASIL
El Callao
Lima
Cuzco
CORDILLERA
Lago Titicaca
BOLIVIA
Brasília
La Paz
Cochabamba
Santa Cruz
Sucre
Trópico de Capricornio
PARAGUAY
DE
CHILE
Asunción
Río Paraná
LOS
Vicuña
Córdoba
Valparaíso
Rosario
URUGUAY
ANDES
Santiago
Buenos Aires
Montevideo
ARGENTINA
La Plata
Río de la Plata
Mar del Plata
OCÉANO PACÍFICO
PATAGONIA
OCÉANO ATLÁNTICO
Puerto Montt
Estrecho de Magallanes
Islas Malvinas (R.U.)
Tierra del Fuego
Punta Arenas
Cabo de Hornos

México, la América Central y el Caribe

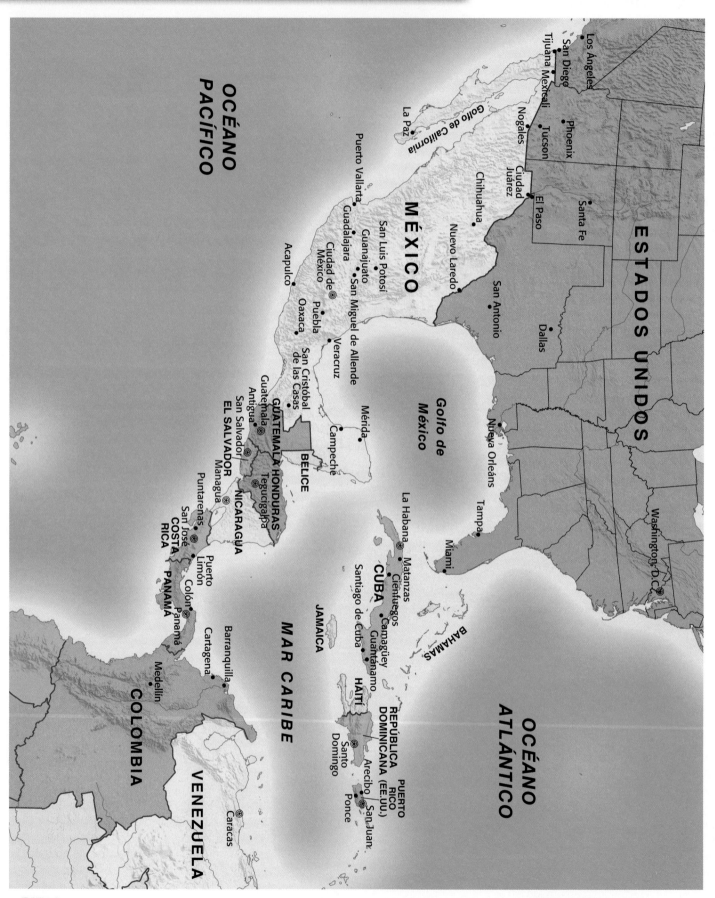

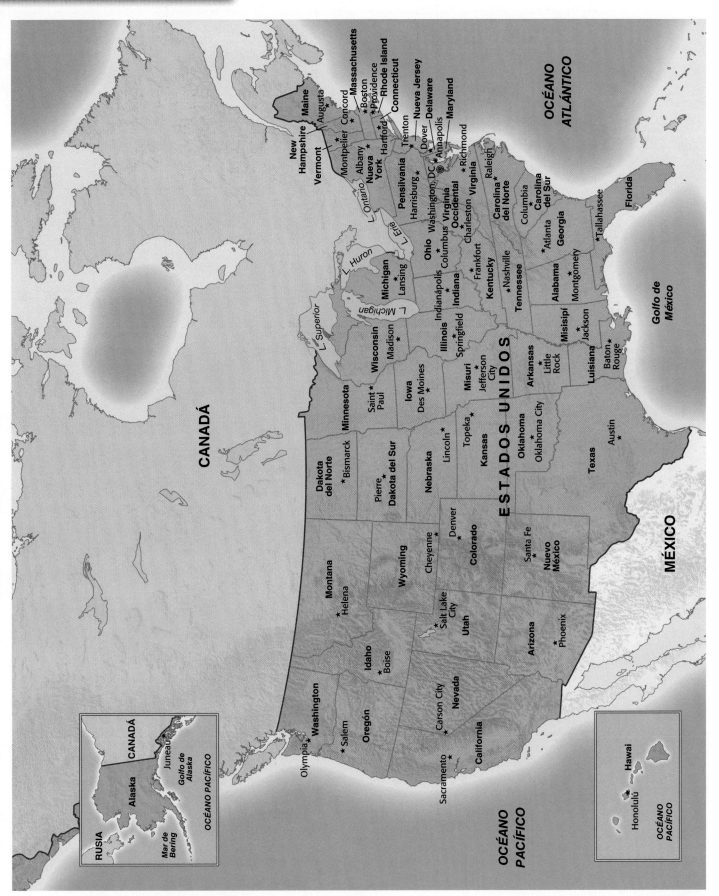

GeoVistas

◀ Un excursionista mira
la majestuosa vista del Fitz Roy y
del Cerro Torre en el Parque Nacional de
los Glaciares en la Patagonia, Argentina.

Explorando el mundo hispanohablante

GeoVista

Geografía España y Portugal en el sudoeste de Europa forman la Península Ibérica, nombre que viene de los iberos, sus primeros habitantes. Como es una península, tiene agua a los tres lados. Y España es el segundo país más montañoso de Europa después de Suiza.

Clima España tiene una variedad de climas. Hay mucha lluvia en el nordeste donde todo es de color verde. En el centro donde todo es de color oro-amarillo, hace mucho frío en invierno y mucho calor en verano. El sur es una región de poca lluvia y mucho calor (aunque los picos de la Sierra Nevada están cubiertos de nieve).

Picos de Europa, Asturias ▲

Playa de Nerja ▲

Gente El español es una mezcla de las muchas razas que han habitado la península. En Galicia, la gente tiene el pelo rubio o rojo con ojos azules o verdes—influencias de los celtas. En el sur hay gente morena con el pelo negro y ojos castaños—influencias de los árabes.

Alcázar de Segovia ▼

▲ Fallas de Valencia

Ferias España es famosa por sus ferias. En Valencia se celebran las Fallas en el mes de marzo. Los valencianos hacen fallas o sea figuras cómicas. Las exhiben por toda la ciudad y a la medianoche del 19 de marzo se queman, iluminando toda la ciudad.

El AVE—El tren de alta velocidad española en Zaragoza ▼

Museo Guggenheim en Bilbao ▼

Hoy España se ha modernizado mucho en los últimos cincuenta años. Tiene uno de los trenes y aeropuertos más modernos del mundo. Las ciudades de Madrid y Barcelona figuran entre las más sofisticadas de Europa. Y el nuevo museo Guggenheim en la ciudad industrial de Bilbao se considera una joya artística y arquitectónica.

Políticamente España se divide en diecisiete comunidades autónomas.

GeoVista

▲ Mar de Cortés en Baja California

Clima Templado, cálido, lluvioso, seco, húmedo son todos adjetivos que describen el clima de las diferentes regiones de México. Se dice que en México se encuentran todos los climas del globo terrestre.

Alfombras de flores para una fiesta en Patambán ▶

Geografía México, que forma parte de Norteamérica, es un país vasto, cuatro veces mayor que España y Francia. Es un país de una gran variedad geográfica con grandes mesetas, desiertos, montañas, sierras volcánicas y unos 8.000 kilómetros de costa en el este y el oeste del país.

Gente En cuanto a la composición étnica de México un gran porcentaje de sus habitantes son de origen indígena y europeo. El idioma oficial es el español y además se hablan sesenta y seis lenguas autóctonas. La influencia indígena se ve en los majestuosos monumentos históricos de las civilizaciones maya, tolteca, olmeca y azteca entre otras.

▼ Antes de una boda en Coyoacán

▼ Vista de Toluca

Ferias México, el país de los mariachis, es un país de música y fiestas. Cada ciudad y pueblo tiene sus ferias locales, muchas de ellas de índole religiosa. Dos fiestas populares por todo el país son el Día de los Muertos que les rinde honor a los parientes difuntos y la fiesta en honor de la Virgen de Guadalupe, la santa patrona de todo México que se celebra el 12 de diciembre.

▲ Castillo o pirámide de Kukulkán en Chichén Itzá

▲ Comida mexicana

▼ Fábrica de cemento en Monterrey

Hoy El México de hoy se divide en treinta y un estados y el Distrito Federal—término que se refiere a la capital, la Ciudad de México, una de las ciudades más grandes del mundo. México es un país de contrastes con ciudades industriales como Monterrey y Tampico y remotos pueblos indígenas en Chiapas y Oaxaca.

▲ Una joven indígena de Guatemala

Gente Hay una gran diversidad de gente en Centroamérica. La población de la mayoría de los países es de origen indígena y europeo. Los muchos grupos indígenas que habitan Centroamérica no comparten todas las mismas costumbres ni tradiciones. Costa Rica es el país que más europeos tiene; muchos son del norte de España. En la costa oriental de Costa Rica hay gente de ascendencia africana. Panamá es el país de mayor influencia africana.

Estela maya en Copán, Honduras ▼

Geografía Centroamérica es un istmo que fusiona Norte y Sudamérica. Tiene una gran variedad de geografía con montañas que corren del norte al sur en el centro del istmo, selvas tropicales de una vegetación densa a lo largo de la costa del Caribe y en la costa del Pacífico playas de arena volcánica negra.

Cataratas del río Azul en Costa Rica ▼

La isla de Ometepe y el volcán de la Concepción, Nicaragua ▼

▲ **Avenida Balboa en la Ciudad de Panamá**

Clima Los centroamericanos dividen su año en dos estaciones—el invierno, la estación calurosa y lluviosa, y el verano—la estación caliente y seca. El invierno es por lo general de mayo a noviembre. Muchas de las ciudades más importantes de Centroamérica como Tegucigalpa y San José son conocidas como ciudades de «primavera eterna».

▼ **Barcos haciendo la travesía del canal de Panamá**

Hoy Al hablar de Centroamérica es imposible generalizar. La situación económica y política es diferente en cada país y cada país tiene su propia atracción—pueblos coloniales e indígenas en Guatemala; lagos y volcanes en Nicaragua; parques nacionales de interés ecológico en Costa Rica; empresas bancarias y nuevos rascacielos en Panamá. Cada país tiene algo suyo.

▲ Callecita típica del Viejo San Juan de Puerto Rico

▲ Vista del Condado en San Juan

◄ Estatua de Cristóbal Colón en Santo Domingo

Geografía Las islas llamadas las Grandes Antillas se encuentran en el mar Caribe al este de Estados Unidos. Tres de ellas son hispanohablantes y la más cercana de Estados Unidos es Cuba a solo 90 kilómetros de Cayo Cabo. La Española se divide en dos naciones—la República Dominicana de habla española y Haití de habla criolla. Más al este está Puerto Rico, un estado asociado de Estados Unidos. Las tres islas son montañosas y en Puerto Rico, por ejemplo, en un pico del centro del país se puede ver el Atlántico mirando hacia el norte y el Caribe hacia el sur.

▲ Escena montañosa de Puerto Rico

Clima Las tres islas tienen un clima tropical. Hace calor durante todo el año con la sola excepción de algunas bajas de temperaturas en las montañas sobre todo de noche. Suele llover más de junio a septiembre. Como son regiones tropicales cultivan una gran variedad de productos agrícolas tropicales como el azúcar, el coco, la banana y muchas otras frutas tropicales.

▲ Castillo del Morro a la entrada del puerto de La Habana

Gente En las tres islas se ve mucha influencia africana. Aunque hay africanos y europeos un gran porcentaje de la población tiene en sus venas sangre africana y europea. Hay poquísima influencia indígena porque la población indígena fue diezmada poco después de la llegada de los conquistadores. Murieron del trabajo forzado y de muchas enfermedades traídas por los europeos. Cada isla se conoce por sus sonidos y ritmos del tambor, la guajira y las marimbas. La gente es conocida por su viva personalidad «de sal y pimienta».

Estatua de José Martí, el gran poeta y héroe cubano ▼

Una de las muchas playas de la República Dominicana ▶

GEOVISTA

▲ Vista panorámica de Bogotá

Geografía Colombia y Venezuela en el norte del continente de Sudamérica tienen en común una variedad de características geográficas. Cada país tiene una costa larga; Colombia es el único país sudamericano con costa en el Pacífico y en el Caribe. Tienen también sierras andinas, grandes extensiones de llanos y sabanas y selvas tropicales en la cuenca del río Amazonas y sus tributarios.

Ciclistas en la Candelaria—el casco antiguo de Bogotá donde se prohíbe el tráfico vehicular los domingos. ▼

◀ **Medellín, ciudad colombiana famosa por sus flores**

Clima Como ambos países están cerca del ecuador, son cálidos y no hay mucha variación de temperatura durante todo el año—con una excepción. La temperatura cambiará según la altitud. Puede hacer mucho calor al nivel del mar mientras hace mucho frío en las montañas. Hay dos estaciones—el verano o la estación seca y el invierno o la estación lluviosa. Las estaciones varían según la región y están cambiando debido a la influencia de «El Niño».

Hoy Más del 90 por ciento de los 46 millones de colombianos viven en la parte occidental del país que incluye la región andina y las dos costas. De los 26 millones de venezolanos, la mayoría vive en Caracas y en las ciudades de la costa.

Venezuela es un gran productor de petróleo y también de oro y diamantes. Colombia es famosa por la calidad de sus esmeraldas y café y Medellín, la segunda ciudad del país, se conoce como la «capital mundial de orquídeas». La tierra de los dos países es rica en una variedad de minerales.

▲ Pozos petroleros en el lago de Maracaibo, Venezuela

▲ Esmeralda preciosa de Colombia

Gente En cada país entre el 70 y el 75 por ciento de la población es una mezcla de indígenas, europeos y africanos. Se ve mayor influencia africana en las regiones litorales que en las montañas. Si lees un libro de turismo, leerás que los venezolanos y colombianos son gente simpática, cortés y abierta y no les molesta nada entablar una conversación con extranjeros.

▲ Turistas en una excursión en una canoa en la cuenca del Orinoco en Venezuela

Salto Ángel en Venezuela, dieciséis veces más alto que los saltos de Niágara ▼

GeoVista

Geografía Aunque no son los únicos países con majestuosos picos andinos, son Ecuador, Perú y Bolivia los países que se consideran la región andina. Los Andes corren del norte al sur. Ecuador y Perú tienen tres zonas geográficas—la costa en el oeste, la sierra o cordillera en el centro y la selva tropical en el este. Bolivia es el único país de la región que no tiene costa. Se divide en dos cordilleras separadas por un altiplano ventoso. Como sus vecinos, Perú y Ecuador, tiene selvas tropicales en el este.

Universitarios en Pichincha, Ecuador ▲

Paseo a orillas del río Guayas en Guayaquil, Ecuador ▼

Flamencos en la laguna Hedionda en Bolivia ▼

Clima Al mirar el mapa verás que el ecuador cruza el país de Ecuador y no queda muy lejos de Perú. Sin embargo en la costa de Ecuador y Perú no hace mucho calor y no llueve mucho. Una corriente fría llamada la corriente Humboldt pasa por la costa bajando la temperatura y la precipitación. En la sierra hay un clima más templado. La temperatura suele variar de unos 40 a 70 grados aunque unos picos andinos se ven cubiertos de nieve durante todo el año. En las selvas del este el clima es tropical y hace mucho calor.

◀ **Músicos tocando la zampoña en Cuzco**

Gente En cada uno de los países andinos un 50 por ciento de la población total vive en la sierra. Ecuador, Perú y Bolivia son los países de mayor población indígena pura o una mezcla de indígenas y europeos.

▲ **Plaza de Armas en Lima**

Hoy Los tres países son productores de petróleo pero no en cantidad tan grande como en Venezuela. Bolivia produce gas natural y estaño; Perú, hierro y fosfatos. Aunque La Paz es la capital de Bolivia y Quito es la capital de Ecuador, Sucre en Bolivia y Guayaquil en Ecuador son centros de gran importancia comercial y financiero.

◀ **Paceños admirando la vista de su capital, La Paz.**

Geografía La geografía de Chile, Argentina, Uruguay y Paraguay, los países del Cono sur, varía mucho. Chile, un país largo y estrecho, es conocido por sus picos andinos y el Atacama—el desierto más seco del mundo. Argentina es un país de llanuras y pampas donde pace el mejor ganado del mundo. Argentina y Chile comparten la Patagonia que se extiende desde el estrecho de Magallanes hasta la famosa región de los lagos. Uruguay, el país más pequeño de Sudamérica, es también una tierra de llanos conocidos por sus estancias grandes. Paraguay, como su vecino andino—Bolivia— no tiene costa. En el este, Paraguay tiene un bosque tropical y en el oeste el Chaco, una zona árida.

Avenida Nueve de Julio en Buenos Aires, Argentina ▼

▲ **Pescadores en Puerto Montt, Chile**

Clima La mayor parte del Cono sur goza de un clima templado con cuatro estaciones. Pero la Patagonia tiene un clima frío, lluvioso y ventoso durante casi todo el año. La tierra y el clima de una gran parte de Argentina, Chile y Uruguay son propicios para la agricultura. En el Chaco, la región seca de Paraguay, se explota mucha madera.

Pingüinos en Patagonia ▼

Vista del Fitz Roy al amanecer en el Parque Nacional de los Glaciares en la Patagonia argentina ▼

▲ **Vista de Punta del Este, Uruguay**

Gente De todas las regiones de Latinoamérica la que tiene la menor influencia indígena es el Cono sur con la excepción de Paraguay. Igual que a Estados Unidos emigraron muchos europeos a Argentina, Chile y Uruguay. Hay mucha gente de ascendencia española, italiana, británica, alemana y en menor grado del este de Europa. En Paraguay, siguen viviendo muchos guaraníes, los indígenas de la región. Paraguay tiene dos idiomas oficiales—el español y el guaraní, y la moneda del país se llama el guaraní.

Gauchos en las pampas argentinas ▼

▲ **Valle de la Luna en el desierto de Atacama en Chile**

GeoVista

Gente Es posible que Estados Unidos sea el país de población más heterogénea del mundo. Hay indígenas americanos, gente que ha emigrado de todas partes de Europa, grandes grupos de asiáticos y mucha gente de ascendencia africana cuyos antepasados llegaron en gran parte como gente esclavizada. Actualmente hay más de cincuenta millones de latinos de todas partes de España y Latinoamérica. El grupo latino mayoritario son los mexicanoamericanos y sigue llegando gente sobre todo de la República Dominicana, Centroamérica, Ecuador y Perú, entre otros. En algunos lugares de Estados Unidos se oye más español, o por lo menos tanto español como inglés.

Misión San José en San Antonio, Texas ▶

Washington Heights en el norte de Manhattan ▼

▼ Librería en Miami, Florida

Desfile en la calle 18 en Chicago para celebrar el día de la Independencia de México ▶

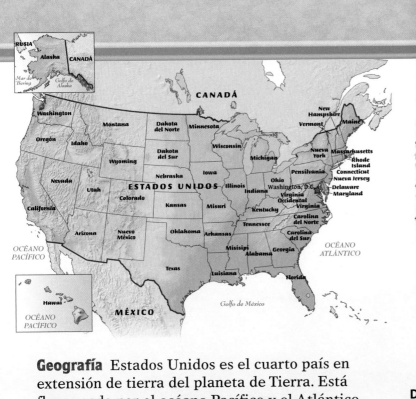

▲ Puesto de comida colombiana durante un festival culinario en Manhattan

Geografía Estados Unidos es el cuarto país en extensión de tierra del planeta de Tierra. Está flanqueado por el océano Pacífico y el Atlántico. Siendo tan grande es un país de gran variedad geográfica—un tercio está ocupado por grandes bosques, al este hay tierras bajas y llanas interrumpidas por los Apalaches, una cordillera que corre desde el Golfo de México hasta la península de Labrador. En el oeste hay una sucesión de montañas y altiplanicies de las cuales destacan las Montañas Rocosas. La región central, llamada el Medio Oeste, es una vasta llanura fértil.

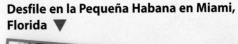

Desfile en la Pequeña Habana en Miami, Florida ▼

Basílica de la Misión de Alcalá en San Diego, California ▼

◀ Alumnos delante de la escuela San Lorenzo en el Parque José Martí en Cienfuegos, Cuba

En casa y en clase

Objetivos

In this chapter you will review:

- vocabulary associated with home and school

- the present tense of regular verbs

- the verbs **ir, dar, estar**

- verbs with an irregular **yo** form in the present tense

QuickPass

Go to glencoe.com
For: **Online book**
Web code: **ASD7844rc**

QuickPass

Go to glencoe.com
For: **Vocabulary practice**
Web code: **ASD7844rc**

Vocabulario 🎧

la cocina

la comida

La familia prepara la comida.

el comedor

José pone la mesa.
La familia come en el comedor.

la sala

Después de la comida la familia va a la sala.
En la sala algunos ven la televisión.
Y papá lee una revista.

En la escuela los alumnos aprenden
   mucho.
El profesor enseña.
Una alumna levanta la mano.
Hace una pregunta.
El profesor contesta la pregunta.

Las hermanas salen de casa.
Van a la escuela.
Van a la escuela a pie.

la computadora

Elena está en su cuarto (de dormir).
Recibe unos correos electrónicos.
Envía correos también.

Repaso A

Práctica

LEER

1 Indica en una tabla como la de abajo donde se hace todo.

	en casa	en clase	en casa y en clase
1. Ellos preparan la comida.			
2. Ellos hacen muchas preguntas.			
3. Él enseña.			
4. Usan la computadora.			
5. Reciben y envían correos electrónicos.			
6. Habla en su móvil.			
7. Él lee el periódico después de la comida.			
8. Comen en el comedor.			
9. Ven la televisión en la sala.			
10. Toman apuntes y aprenden mucho.			

HABLAR • ESCRIBIR

2 Contesta.

1. ¿Dónde prepara la familia la comida?
2. ¿Dónde comen ellos?
3. ¿Adónde van después de la comida?
4. ¿Qué hacen en la sala?
5. ¿A qué hora salen los hermanos para la escuela?
6. ¿Cómo van a la escuela? ¿En el bus escolar, en carro o a pie?
7. ¿Quiénes enseñan en la escuela?
8. ¿Quiénes estudian y aprenden mucho?

3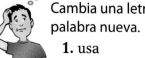

Cambia una letra en cada palabra para formar una palabra nueva.

1. usa
2. todo
3. casa
4. ve
5. son

Más práctica

Workbook, pp. R.3–R.5
StudentWorks™ Plus

Repaso

LEER • ESCRIBIR

4 Identifica.

1. las tres comidas
2. algunos vegetales
3. algunas frutas
4. algunas carnes
5. lo que lleva una ensalada
6. tu comida favorita
7. lo que pones en la mesa antes de comer
8. a tus parientes
9. la ropa que llevas
10. los cursos que tomas

LEER • HABLAR

5 Parea.

1. dar
2. tomar
3. prestar
4. leer
5. escribir
6. vivir
7. salir
8. conocer
9. asistir

   a. atención
   b. en la calle Bolívar
   c. una fiesta
   d. una composición
   e. notas (apuntes) en clase
   f. a muchos amigos
   g. una novela
   h. por la mañana
   i. a clase

¡Ojo!

Ya sabes que las palabras afines son palabras que se parecen en dos o más idiomas y tienen el mismo significado. Ejemplos son **importante, atleta.** Hay también lo que llamamos «amigos falsos». Son palabras que se parecen en dos idiomas pero no tienen el mismo significado. Ejemplos son **pariente** (relative) y **asistir** (to attend).

CULTURA

Estos jóvenes de ascendencia maya estudian en una escuela secundaria en el estado de Chiapas, México.

QuickPass

Go to glencoe.com
For: **Conversation practice**
Web code: **ASD7844rc**

Conversación 🎧

La escuela Abraham Lincoln

Antonio	¡Oye, Roberto! ¿A qué escuela asistes ahora?
Roberto	Asisto a la escuela Abraham Lincoln.
Antonio	¿Llevan los alumnos uniforme a la escuela?
Roberto	¡Uniforme! De ninguna manera. No estamos en Latinoamérica.
Antonio	¿Cómo vas a la escuela? ¿Tomas el bus?
Roberto	No, voy a pie. Salgo de casa muy temprano por la mañana.
Antonio	¿Cuántos cursos tomas este semestre?
Roberto	Cinco. Y algunos son bastante difíciles.

¿Comprendes?

A Contesta según la información en la conversación.

1. ¿A qué escuela asiste Roberto?
2. ¿Asisten Roberto y Antonio a la misma escuela?
3. ¿Sabe Antonio mucho sobre la escuela de Roberto?
4. ¿Cómo va Roberto a la escuela?
5. ¿Cuándo sale de casa?
6. ¿Cuántos cursos toma este semestre?
7. ¿Cómo son algunos de sus cursos?

B **Analizando** Contesta.

¿Asiste Roberto a una escuela norteamericana o latinoamericana? Defiende tu respuesta.

Gramática
Presente de los verbos regulares e irregulares

1. Review the forms of regular **-ar, -er,** and **-ir** verbs in the present tense.

	hablar	comer	vivir
yo	hablo	como	vivo
tú	hablas	comes	vives
Ud., él, ella	habla	come	vive
nosotros(as)	hablamos	comemos	vivimos
vosotros(as)	*habláis*	*coméis*	*vivís*
Uds., ellos, ellas	hablan	comen	viven

2. Most irregular verbs are irregular in the **yo** form only. Note that the verbs **ir, dar,** and **estar** are like an **-ar** verb in all forms except **yo.**

	ir	dar	estar
yo	voy	doy	estoy
tú	vas	das	estás
Ud., él, ella	va	da	está
nosotros(as)	vamos	damos	estamos
vosotros(as)	*vais*	*dais*	*estáis*
Uds., ellos, ellas	van	dan	están

3. The following verbs have an irregular **yo** form. All other forms are those of a regular **-er** or **-ir** verb.

hacer	→	hago	saber	→	sé
poner	→	pongo	conocer	→	conozco
traer	→	traigo	producir	→	produzco
salir	→	salgo	conducir	→	conduzco

4. Review the forms of the important irregular verb **ser.**

ser			
yo	soy	nosotros(as)	somos
tú	eres	*vosotros(as)*	*sois*
Ud., él, ella	es	Uds., ellos, ellas	son

Los padres de estos niños venden mantas en el mercado en Sololá, Guatemala. Los niños ayudan de vez en cuando pero ahora les ha captado el interés el móvil.

Cultura

Casi todos los aparatos tecnológicos se ven y se usan hasta en zonas muy remotas.

Práctica

ESCUCHAR • HABLAR

① Personaliza. Da respuestas personales.

    1. ¿Cuántas lenguas hablas?

    2. ¿A qué escuela asistes?

    3. ¿Cómo vas a la escuela?

    4. ¿Cuántos cursos tomas este semestre?

    5. ¿Cómo son tus cursos?

    6. ¿Quién es tu profesor(a) de español?

    7. ¿Haces muchas preguntas en clase?

    8. ¿Aprendes mucho en la escuela?

    9. ¿Llevas tus materiales escolares en una mochila?

    10. ¿Conoces a muchos alumnos en tu escuela?

LEER • ESCRIBIR

② Completa.

    1. Yo voy y él _____ también.

    2. Yo lo sé y ellos lo _____ también.

    3. Yo lo pongo aquí y tú lo _____ allí.

    4. Yo leo mucho y ustedes _____ mucho también.

    5. Yo vivo en California y ellos _____ en Texas.

    6. Yo conozco a mucha gente y tú _____ a mucha gente también.

    7. Yo conduzco un carro viejo y ella _____ un carro nuevo.

    8. Yo hago mucho trabajo y ellos _____ mucho trabajo también.

    9. Yo soy alumno(a) y ellas _____ alumnas también.

Más práctica

📖 Workbook, pp. R.6–R.7
💿 StudentWorks™ Plus

Repaso

HABLAR • ESCRIBIR

 3 Contesta.

1. ¿Dónde viven ustedes?
2. ¿A qué escuela asisten ustedes?
3. ¿Cómo van a la escuela?
4. ¿Qué hacen ustedes en la clase de español?
5. ¿A qué hora salen ustedes de la escuela?

LEER • ESCRIBIR

4 Forma frases con los siguientes verbos.

mirar   ver   vivir

comprar   leer   ir

escribir

conocer   poner   ser   estar

✤ Comunicación

 5 Con un(a) compañero(a) de clase discute todas las cosas que haces en casa. Luego tu compañero(a) te va a decir lo que él o ella hace. Comparen sus actividades.

 6 Trabaja con un(a) compañero(a). Describe tu día típico en la escuela. Luego tu compañero(a) va a hacer lo mismo. Comparen sus actividades.

CULTURA

Estas muchachas van a una escuela en Buenos Aires, Argentina. ¿Lo pasan bien después de las clases?

Holanda juega contra España durante la Copa Davis en Palma de Mallorca, España.

Deportes y rutinas

Objetivos

In this chapter you will review:

- vocabulary related to sports and daily routine

- the present tense of stem-changing verbs

- the present tense of reflexive verbs

QuickPass

Go to glencoe.com
For: **Online book**
Web code: **ASD7844rc**

QuickPass

Go to glencoe.com
For: **Vocabulary practice**
Web code: **ASD7844rc**

Vocabulario 🎧

Hola. Me llamo Felipe. Y tú, ¿cómo te llamas? Soy jugador de fútbol. ¿Juegas fútbol también?

Los jugadores se acuestan temprano.
Mañana juegan (tienen) un partido
(juego) importante.

el tanto

el balón

Es el campo de fútbol.
Empieza el segundo tiempo.
Los dos equipos vuelven al campo.

La muchacha se despierta temprano.
Va al cuarto de baño.
Se lava la cara.

el guante

Es un equipo de béisbol.
El jugador (beisbolista) corre
de una base a otra.

la cancha de tenis

la red

Las tenistas juegan individuales.
La pelota tiene que pasar por encima de la red.
Una jugadora devuelve la pelota.

el cesto,
la canasta

la cancha de básquetbol

El balón entra en el cesto.
Cuando el muchacho encesta, marca
un tanto.

Nota

The contexts in which
campo and **cancha** are used
here is the most common.
However, their use can vary.
Most countries, for example,
use **un campo de fútbol,**
but you will sometimes hear
la cancha de fútbol.

Práctica

LEER

1 Categoriza indicando el deporte.

	el béisbol	el baloncesto	el fútbol	el tenis
1. El lanzador lanza la pelota al bateador.				
2. Driblan con el balón.				
3. Hay once jugadores en el equipo.				
4. Hay que tirar el balón con los pies, las piernas, las espaldas o la cabeza.				
5. La jugadora atrapa la pelota con un guante.				
6. Es posible jugar dobles o individuales.				
7. Corren de una base a otra.				
8. La pelota pasa por encima de una red.				
9. El portero guarda la portería y bloquea el balón.				
10. Cada vez que un jugador encesta marca un tanto.				

ESCUCHAR • HABLAR • ESCRIBIR

2 Personaliza. Da respuestas personales.

1. ¿Tiene tu escuela un equipo de fútbol?
2. ¿Siempre quiere ganar el equipo?
3. ¿Gana siempre o pierde a veces?
4. ¿Juegan tus amigos fútbol?
5. ¿Cómo se llama el capitán del equipo?

Más práctica

Workbook, pp. R.10–R.11
StudentWorks™ Plus

Repaso

LEER • ESCRIBIR

3 Escoge la respuesta.

en la cocina	a las once	enseguida	Pepe
para desayunar	a las seis y media	cepillarse los dientes	en el cuarto de baño

1. ¿Cómo se llama el joven?
2. ¿A qué hora se despierta?
3. ¿Cuándo se levanta?
4. ¿Dónde se lava la cara y los dientes?
5. ¿Por qué se sienta a la mesa?
6. ¿Qué tiene que hacer antes de acostarse?
7. ¿A qué hora se acuesta?

No, no. No quiero levantarme. Tengo sueño y quiero dormir más.

ESCRIBIR

4 Identifica las partes del cuerpo en español.

LEER • ESCRIBIR

5 Forma frases con las palabras.

la pasta dentífrica   el jabón   el champú

el peine   el cepillo para los dientes

Comunicación

6 Trabaja con un(a) compañero(a). Piensa en un(a) atleta que consideras héroe. Describe a la persona. Tu compañero(a) tratará de adivinar de quién hablas. Túrnense.

CULTURA

Los jóvenes juegan fútbol delante de la iglesia de la Sagrada Familia en Barcelona, España.

QuickPass

Go to glencoe.com
For: **Conversation practice**
Web code: **ASD7844rc**

Conversación

Un partido

¿Comprendes?

A Contesta.

1. ¿Cuándo va a acostarse Daniel esta noche?
2. ¿Por qué quiere dormir bien?
3. ¿Contra qué equipo juega?
4. ¿Pierden ellos mucho?
5. ¿Qué tienen?

B **Resumiendo** Relata toda la información en la conversación en tus propias palabras.

QuickPass

Go to glencoe.com
For: **Grammar practice**
Web code: **ASD7844rc**

Repaso

Gramática
Presente de los verbos de cambio radical

1. Many Spanish verbs have a stem change in the present tense. Review the forms of verbs that change their stem from **e** to **ie.**

	empezar	querer	preferir
yo	empiezo	quiero	prefiero
tú	empiezas	quieres	prefieres
Ud., él, ella	empieza	quiere	prefiere
nosotros(as)	empezamos	queremos	preferimos
vosotros(as)	*empezáis*	*queréis*	*preferís*
Uds., ellos, ellas	empiezan	quieren	prefieren

2. Review the forms of verbs that change their stem from **o** to **ue.**

	volver	poder	dormir
yo	vuelvo	puedo	duermo
tú	vuelves	puedes	duermes
Ud., él, ella	vuelve	puede	duerme
nosotros(as)	volvemos	podemos	dormimos
vosotros(as)	*volvéis*	*podéis*	*dormís*
Uds., ellos, ellas	vuelven	pueden	duermen

3. Remember that the verb **jugar** changes the **u** to **ue.**

juego   juegas   juega   jugamos   *jugáis*   juegan

4. Note that in all cases the only forms that do not have the stem change are **nosotros** and **vosotros.**

Práctica

HABLAR

1 Contesta.

1. ¿Quieren ustedes ganar el partido?
2. ¿Pueden ustedes ganarlo?
3. ¿Juegan ustedes bien?
4. ¿Pierden ustedes a veces?
5. Tú y tus amigos, ¿prefieren ustedes participar en el partido o ser espectadores?

HABLAR • ESCRIBIR

2 Forma frases.

1. el segundo tiempo / empezar
2. los jugadores / volver al campo de fútbol
3. cada equipo / querer ganar
4. los dos equipos / no poder ganar
5. un equipo / perder
6. los Osos / perder

LEER • ESCRIBIR

3 Completa.

Yo __1__ (jugar) mucho (al) fútbol y Diana __2__ (jugar) mucho también, pero ahora ella no __3__ (poder).

—Diana, ¿por qué no __4__ (poder) jugar ahora?

—No __5__ (poder) porque __6__ (querer) ir a casa.

Sí, Diana __7__ (querer) ir a casa porque ella __8__ (tener) un amigo que __9__ (volver) hoy de Puerto Rico y ella __10__ (querer) estar en casa. Pero mañana todos nosotros __11__ (ir) a jugar. Y el amigo puertorriqueño de Diana __12__ (poder) jugar también. Su amigo __13__ (jugar) muy bien.

CULTURA

Los amigos juegan fútbol en la Ciudad de México.

Diana tiene un amigo que vuelve hoy de Puerto Rico y todos van a jugar fútbol. ¿Quieres también?

Comunicación

4. ¿Cuál es tu deporte favorito? Descríbelo. Explica por qué lo consideras tu deporte favorito.

5. Habla con un(a) compañero(a) de clase sobre todos los equipos deportivos que hay en tu escuela. Decidan cuáles son sus equipos favoritos y cuáles consideran los mejores. ¿Por qué?

Verbos reflexivos

1. A reflexive construction is one in which the subject both performs and receives the action of the verb. A reflexive verb in Spanish is accompanied by a pronoun called a reflexive pronoun. Review the forms of some reflexive verbs. Note too that some reflexive verbs also have a stem change.

	lavarse	levantarse	acostarse (o → ue)
yo	me lavo	me levanto	me acuesto
tú	te lavas	te levantas	te acuestas
Ud., él, ella	se lava	se levanta	se acuesta
nosotros(as)	nos lavamos	nos levantamos	nos acostamos
vosotros(as)	os laváis	os levantáis	os acostáis
Uds., ellos, ellas	se lavan	se levantan	se acuestan

2. In sentences where one person performs the action and another person or thing receives the action, a verb is not reflexive. It is only reflexive when the same person performs and receives the action of the verb. Review the following.

Federico lava el carro.   Federico se lava.
Patricia mira a su amigo.   Patricia se mira en el espejo.

3. When you refer to parts of the body or articles of clothing with a reflexive verb, you use the definite article rather than the possessive adjective.

Él se lava las manos.
Me pongo la camisa.
Ellas se lavan la cara.

La muchacha tiene frío por la mañana y se pone la bata mientras toma su desayuno. ▶

R19

Práctica

ESCUCHAR • HABLAR

6 Personaliza. Da respuestas personales.

1. ¿Cómo te llamas?
2. ¿A qué hora te despiertas?
3. Cuando te despiertas, ¿te levantas enseguida o pasas un rato más en la cama?
4. ¿Te sientas a la mesa para tomar el desayuno?
5. ¿Cuándo te lavas los dientes, antes o después de tomar el desayuno?
6. Cuando hace frío, ¿te pones un suéter antes de salir de casa?
7. ¿A qué hora te acuestas?
8. Cuando te acuestas, ¿te duermes enseguida o pasas tiempo dando vueltas en la cama?

LEER • ESCRIBIR

7 Completa según las fotos.

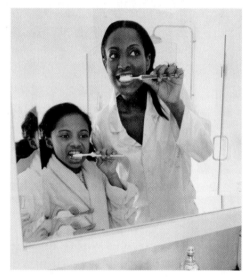

1. Yo _____.
   Él _____.
   Tú _____.
   Usted _____.

2. Nosotras _____.
   Ellas _____.
   Ustedes _____.
   Ella y yo _____.

Más práctica

📘 Workbook, pp. R.12–R.14
🌐 StudentWorks™ Plus

Repaso

8 Completa con un pronombre reflexivo cuando necesario.

1. ¿A qué hora ____ levantas?
2. Ana ____ pone su traje de baño en la mochila.
3. Ellos ____ divierten mucho en la fiesta.
4. Julia ____ cepilla al perro.
5. Nosotros ____ acostamos temprano.

Comunidades

¿Hay muchos gimnasios privados donde vives? ¿Son tú y tus amigos socios de tal gimnasio o usan mayormente el gimnasio de su escuela?

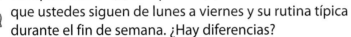

Comunicación

9 Describe un día típico para los miembros de tu familia.

10 Compara con un(a) compañero(a) de clase la rutina que ustedes siguen de lunes a viernes y su rutina típica durante el fin de semana. ¿Hay diferencias?

CULTURA

Un joven anda en bici en un parque de Santiago de Chile.

Un snowboarder en una estación de esquí cerca de Santiago de Chile

REPASO
C
Vacaciones

Objetivos

In this chapter you will review:

- vocabulary related to summer and winter activities and vacations
- vocabulary related to traveling by plane and by train
- the preterite of regular verbs
- the preterite of irregular verbs

QuickPass

Go to glencoe.com
For: **Online book**
Web code: **ASD7844rc**

R23

QuickPass

Go to glencoe.com
For: **Vocabulary practice**
Web code: **ASD7844rc**

Vocabulario 🎧

el aeropuerto

el billete, el boleto

la tarjeta de embarque

las maletas

el equipaje

José y sus amigos hicieron un viaje.
Fueron a Puerto Rico.
Fueron en avión.

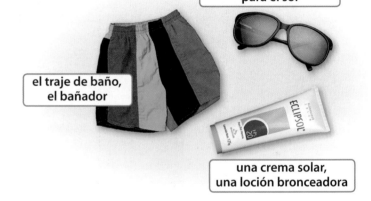

las gafas (los anteojos) para el sol

el traje de baño, el bañador

una crema solar, una loción bronceadora

la playa

la piscina, la alberca

La familia pasó un mes en la playa.
Todos tomaron el sol y nadaron.

los esquís acuáticos (náuticos)

la arena

Maricarmen esquió en el agua.
Ella alquiló (rentó) los esquís acuáticos.

la estación de tren (ferrocarril)

la boletería, la ventanilla

Elena y un grupo de amigos estuvieron en Perú.
Decidieron visitar Machu Picchu.
Tomaron el tren de Cuzco a Machu Picchu.

la pista

el telesilla

Los esquiadores subieron
la montaña en el telesilla.

el pico de la montaña

Penitentes

Anita bajó una pista avanzada.
Ella esquía bien.
Es muy aficionada al esquí.

Práctica

HABLAR

1 Categoriza. Pon cada palabra o expresión en el lugar apropiado.

	la playa	una estación de esquí	un camping	más de uno
1. las botas				
2. el bañador				
3. los esquís acuáticos				
4. los bastones				
5. la carpa, la tienda de campaña				
6. la pista				
7. el telesilla				
8. la plancha de vela				

ESCUCHAR • HABLAR • ESCRIBIR

2 Contesta.

1. ¿Qué tiempo hace en el verano donde vives?

2. ¿Qué tiempo hace en el invierno?

3. ¿Cuál de las dos estaciones prefieres? ¿Por qué?

CULTURA

Hay muchas actividades de verano y de invierno en La Angostura, Argentina.

Más práctica

▢ Workbook, pp. R.16–R.17
⬤ StudentWorks™ Plus

Repaso

LEER

3 ¿Sí o no?

1. Es necesario tener una tarjeta de embarque antes de poder embarcar (abordar) un avión.
2. En el aeropuerto los pasajeros esperan en el andén.
3. En la estación de ferrocarril se venden los boletos en una boletería (ventanilla) o en un distribuidor automático.
4. Antes de ir a la puerta de salida en el aeropuerto es necesario pasar por el control de seguridad.
5. Abordo de un avión es posible dejar el equipaje de mano en los pasillos del avión.
6. El revisor revisa los boletos en el tren.
7. Los aviones despegan de una vía.
8. Por lo general, los aeropuertos están en el centro de la ciudad y las estaciones de ferrocarril están en las afueras.

EXPANSIÓN

Corrige las frases falsas.

✿ Comunicación

4 Describe el dibujo. Di todo lo que puedes. Trabaja con un(a) compañero(a) si quieres.

QuickPass

Go to glencoe.com
For: Conversation practice
Web code: ASD7844rc

Conversación 🎧

La plancha de vela

¡HOLA, ANITA! ¿CUÁNDO LLEGASTE AQUÍ AL BALNEARIO SOL Y LUZ?

AYER.

TANTO GUSTO EN VERTE. ¿CÓMO VINISTE?

VINE EN TREN PORQUE MI PADRE NO ME PERMITIÓ TENER EL CARRO. ¿Y TÚ? ¿CUÁNDO LLEGASTE?

ELENA Y YO LLEGAMOS EL MIÉRCOLES. AYER YO HICE LA PLANCHA DE VELA. ¡QUÉ EXPERIENCIA!

¿TE CAÍSTE?

¿ME HABLAS EN SERIO? ¿POR QUÉ NO ME PREGUNTASTE CUÁNTAS VECES?

PUES, JOSÉ ME DIJO QUE TÚ SUPERAS EN TODOS LOS DEPORTES.

PUES, NÚMERO UNO: ÉL EXAGERA. Y NÚMERO DOS: FUE LA PRIMERA VEZ QUE INTENTÉ HACER LA PLANCHA DE VELA.

CULTURA

Los jóvenes hicieron la plancha de vela en el lago Nahuel Huapi en Argentina y no se cayeron.

¿Comprendes?

A Completa según la información en la conversación.

1. Anita llegó al balneario _____.
2. Ella vino _____.
3. Vino en _____ porque su padre _____.
4. Su amiga Sandra llegó al balneario _____.
5. Ayer ella hizo _____.
6. Ella se cayó _____.
7. Lo que dijo José fue _____.
8. Ayer fue la primera vez que Sandra _____.

QuickPass

Go to glencoe.com
For: **Grammar practice**
Web code: **ASD7844rc**

Gramática
Pretérito de los verbos regulares

1. Review the forms of the preterite tense of regular verbs.

	mirar	**comer**	**subir**
yo	miré	comí	subí
tú	miraste	comiste	subiste
Ud., él, ella	miró	comió	subió
nosotros(as)	miramos	comimos	subimos
vosotros(as)	*mirasteis*	*comisteis*	*subisteis*
Uds., ellos, ellas	miraron	comieron	subieron

2. Review the following spelling changes.

jugué → jugó   empecé → empezó   busqué → buscó
leí → leyó   caí → cayó

3. Note that in the preterite the verb **dar** is conjugated like an **-er** or **-ir** verb.

di   diste   dio   dimos   *disteis*   dieron

4. Remember that you use the preterite to express an action or event that started and ended at a specific time in the past.

Llegué ayer.
Lo estudiamos el año pasado.
Ellos me invitaron el viernes pasado.
Él salió hace un año.
Ella vendió su carro ayer y enseguida compró otro.

CULTURA

Este pavo real dio un gran *show* en un jardín en Cotacachi, Ecuador.

Práctica

HABLAR • ESCRIBIR

1 Contesta.

1. ¿A qué hora saliste anoche?
2. ¿Te acompañaron unos amigos?
3. ¿Comieron ustedes en un restaurante mexicano?
4. ¿Vieron ustedes un filme en el cine o alquilaron un DVD?
5. ¿Quién volvió a casa a pie?
6. ¿Quién o quiénes tomaron el autobús?
7. ¿A qué hora volviste a casa?
8. Al volver a casa, ¿te acostaste enseguida?

LEER • ESCRIBIR

2 Cambia al pretérito.

1. Esquío en las montañas.
2. Mi amigo Carlos compra los tickets para el telesilla.
3. Tomamos el telesilla para subir la montaña.
4. Yo pierdo mi casco.
5. Elena y Carlos bajan una pista avanzada.
6. Daniel baja una pista más fácil.

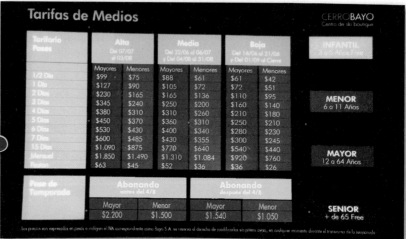

CULTURA

Las tarifas para usar las pistas en la estación de esquí Cerrobayo en Argentina

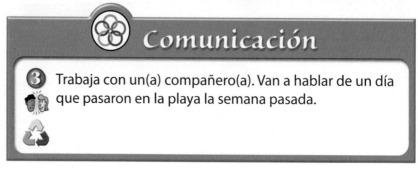

Comunicación

3 Trabaja con un(a) compañero(a). Van a hablar de un día que pasaron en la playa la semana pasada.

Más práctica

📘 Workbook, pp. R.18–R.20
💿 StudentWorks™ Plus

Repaso

Pretérito de los verbos irregulares

1. Many verbs have an irregular root in the preterite. Review
the following.

hacer	→	hic-	poner	→	pus-
querer	→	quis-	poder	→	pud-
venir	→	vin-	saber	→	sup-

tener	→	tuv-
andar	→	anduv-
estar	→	estuv-

	hacer	poner	tener
yo	hice	puse	tuve
tú	hiciste	pusiste	tuviste
Ud., él, ella	hizo	puso	tuvo
nosotros(as)	hicimos	pusimos	tuvimos
vosotros(as)	*hicisteis*	*pusisteis*	*tuvisteis*
Uds., ellos, ellas	hicieron	pusieron	tuvieron

2. Note the ending **-eron,** not **-ieron,** for verbs with a **j** or **y.**

decir	→	dijeron	leer	→	leyeron
traer	→	trajeron	construir	→	construyeron
conducir	→	condujeron			

decir		
yo dije	nosotros(as)	dijimos
tú dijiste	*vosotros(as)*	*dijisteis*
Ud., él, ella dijo	Uds., ellos, ellas	dijeron

3. Review the forms of **ser** and **ir.** Remember that
they are the same in the preterite.

ir, ser		
yo fui	nosotros(as)	fuimos
tú fuiste	*vosotros(as)*	*fuisteis*
Ud., él, ella fue	Uds., ellos, ellas	fueron

Una muchacha patinó en línea
y otra anduvo a bicicleta en el
Parque Palermo en Buenos Aires,
Argentina.

CULTURA

Práctica

HABLAR

4 Contesta.

1. ¿Hiciste un viaje una vez?
2. ¿Cuándo hiciste el viaje?
3. ¿Adónde fuiste?
4. ¿Fuiste solo(a) o estuviste acompañado(a) de unos amigos o parientes?
5. ¿Fueron ustedes en carro?
6. ¿Quién condujo?
7. ¿Pusieron ustedes sus maletas en la maletera del carro?
8. En la autopista, ¿tuvieron que pagar un peaje?

CULTURA

Los jóvenes fueron a admirar la vista bonita en El Cruce en el distrito de los lagos en Argentina.

LEER • ESCRIBIR

5 Completa la tabla.

	querer	estar	saber	decir	ir
yo		estuve		dije	
nosotros	quisimos		supimos		fuimos
tú		estuviste		dijiste	fuiste
ustedes	quisieron		supieron		
él			supo		fue
ellos	quisieron	estuvieron			

LEER • ESCRIBIR

6 Lee. Luego cambia **En este momento** a **Ayer** y haz todos los cambios necesarios.

En este momento estoy en el mercado de Otavalo en Ecuador. Mi amigo Ramón está conmigo. Andamos por el mercado pero no podemos comprar nada. Qué lástima porque vemos muchas cosas que queremos comprar pero no podemos. ¿Por qué no? Porque vamos al mercado sin un peso.

Comunicación

7 En tus estudios del español leíste sobre unos viajes interesantes en tren: el viaje de Cuzco a Machu Picchu, el viaje por el Cañón del Cobre en México, el viaje a lo largo del canal de Panamá. Imagínate que hiciste uno de estos viajes y cuenta todo lo que «hiciste» y «viste».

8 Mira este dibujo de una escena que tuvo lugar en un aeropuerto ya hace algunos años. Relata todo lo que hicieron los pasajeros en el aeropuerto.

Decoraciones navideñas en Medellín, Colombia

REPASO D

De compras y fiestas

Objetivos

In this chapter you will review:

- vocabulary related to shopping and celebrations
- the imperfect of regular and irregular verbs
- the verbs **interesar, aburrir, gustar**
- indirect object pronouns

QuickPass

Go to glencoe.com
For: **Online book**
Web code: **ASD7844rc**

QuickPass

Go to glencoe.com
For: **Vocabulary practice**
Web code: **ASD7844rc**

Vocabulario 🎧

el camposanto

la tumba

Cuando Guadalupe era niña, vivía en México.
El primero de noviembre siempre iba al
cementerio.
Celebraba el Día de los Muertos en honor de
sus parientes difuntos.

un disfraz

el hueso

un cráneo

una máscara

La familia desfilaba hacia el cementerio.
Algunos llevaban máscaras o disfraces.
A veces todos comían en el cementerio.

un bizcocho

A los niños les gustaba comer
bizcochos en forma de cráneos
o esqueletos.

un puesto

Antes del Día de los Muertos, Guadalupe iba
al mercado con su abuela.
Iban de un puesto a otro.
Su abuela compraba todo lo que necesitaba
para preparar la comida para la fiesta.

el cordero

la carne de res

el jamón

los huevos, los blanquillos

el pan

el jugo de naranja

la naranja

la manzana

las uvas

la leche

la mantequilla

el yogur

los guisantes

las habichuelas, los frijoles

los tomates

la lechuga

el flan

las galletas

REPASO D

una camisa

la talla

los tenis

el número

Los amigos de José están en el centro comercial.
Hay muchas tiendas en el centro comercial.

Felipe está en la tienda de ropa.
Se pone una chaqueta.
No le queda bien.
Necesita una talla más grande.

una camiseta

una blusa

un pantalón

una falda

Práctica

HABLAR

 1 ¿Sí o no?

1. Cuando Guadalupe era niña, vivía en Perú.
2. El primero de noviembre la familia de Guadalupe celebraba el Día de los Muertos.
3. En ese día rendían honor a sus parientes difuntos (muertos).
4. Todos los parientes iban al centro comercial.
5. La familia desfilaba hacia el camposanto.
6. Ellos comían en el camposanto.
7. Algunos llevaban disfraces.
8. Los niños comían bizcochos en forma de cráneos y esqueletos.

 Comunicación

 2 Has aprendido como se celebran otras fiestas en el mundo hispanohablante. Trabaja con un(a) compañero(a). Cada uno va a describir una fiesta diferente.

HABLAR • ESCRIBIR

 3 Identifica.

1. tantas frutas posibles
2. tantas legumbres posibles
3. tantas carnes posibles
4. tantos postres posibles
5. tantas bebidas posibles

CULTURA

Un joven llevaba disfraz mientras celebraba el Día de los Muertos.

Repaso D

Más práctica

Workbook, pp. R.22–R.23
StudentWorks™ Plus

LEER

4 Escoge.

1. Teresa quiere comprar una blusa verde.
   a. Va al mercado.
   b. Va a la verdulería.
   c. Va a la tienda de ropa.

2. ¿Dónde hay muchos puestos diferentes?
   a. en el mercado
   b. en el camposanto
   c. en el centro comercial

3. ¿Dónde hay muchas tiendas diferentes?
   a. en los tenderetes
   b. en el mercado
   c. en el centro comercial

4. ¿Dónde ponía la gente coronas de flores?
   a. en la florería
   b. en los puestos del mercado
   c. en las tumbas en el camposanto

5. ¿Qué bebías cuando eras bebé?
   a. mucha leche
   b. mucho café
   c. muchas bebidas diferentes

6. No me queda bien.
   a. Es verdad. Necesitas una talla más grande.
   b. ¿No? Lo siento mucho.
   c. Es tu talla.

CULTURA

Mucha gente hizo sus compras en el famoso mercado indígena en Otavalo, Ecuador.

 Comunicación

5 Trabajen en grupos de tres a cuatro. Imaginen que fueron a uno o más de los siguientes tipos de tiendas para hacer las compras. Preparen una conversación entre ustedes y no olviden que uno(a) será el/la empleado(a) o el/la vendedor(a).

un mercado indígena
un mercado municipal
una bodega o un colmado
una tienda en un centro comercial

Conversación 🎧

De compras

Felipe	Quiero comprarme una camisa nueva para la fiesta de Maricarmen.
José	Y yo necesito un pantalón. ¿Por qué no vamos juntos a la tienda?
Felipe	Buena idea. ¡Vamos!
	(En la tienda de ropa)
Empleada	¿En qué puedo servirles, señores?
Felipe	Yo estoy buscando una camisa.
Empleada	¿Qué talla usa usted?
Felipe	36.
Empleada	¿Por qué no se pone usted esta?
Felipe	José, ¿qué piensas? ¿Te gusta?
José	Pues, me gusta la camisa pero me parece que no te queda bien. Te queda grande.
Empleada	Sí, sí. Necesita usted una talla más pequeña.
	(Felipe se pone otra camisa y la compra.)
Empleada	Y usted, señor. ¿Quiere un pantalón largo o corto?
José	Largo, por favor. Uso la talla 40.
Empleada	¿Le gusta más un pantalón azul o beige?
José	Beige.
	(José se pone un pantalón beige que le gusta. Le queda bien y lo compra.)

¿Comprendes?

A Contesta.

1. ¿Adónde van los dos muchachos?
2. ¿Con quién hablan?
3. ¿Qué necesita cada uno?
4. ¿Cuál es el problema que tiene Felipe con la camisa que se prueba?
5. El pantalón que compra José, ¿cómo es?

B ¿Quién lo dice?

	José	Felipe	la empleada
1. ¿En qué puedo servirles?			
2. Quiero una camisa, talla 36.			
3. Me gusta más el beige.			
4. Necesito un pantalón.			
5. Me gusta la camisa pero esta no te queda bien.			
6. Quiero un pantalón largo.			

C **Resumiendo** Resume la conversación entre José, Felipe y la empleada en tus propias palabras.

chandals

P	M	G	XG	XXG	TALLAS ESPAÑOLAS
48	52	54	56	58	
P	M	L	XL	XXL	TALLAS INGLESAS

QuickPass

Go to glencoe.com
For: **Grammar practice**
Web code: **ASD7844rc**

Gramática

El imperfecto

1. Review the forms of the imperfect tense of regular verbs. Note that the endings of **-er** and **-ir** verbs are the same.

	hablar	comer	vivir
	habl-	com-	viv-
yo	hablaba	comía	vivía
tú	hablabas	comías	vivías
Ud., él, ella	hablaba	comía	vivía
nosotros (as)	hablábamos	comíamos	vivíamos
vosotros (as)	*hablabais*	*comíais*	*vivíais*
Uds., ellos, ellas	hablaban	comían	vivían

2. The following are the only verbs that are irregular in the imperfect.

	ir	ser	ver
yo	iba	era	veía
tú	ibas	eras	veías
Ud., él, ella	iba	era	veía
nosotros(as)	íbamos	éramos	veíamos
vosotros(as)	*ibais*	*erais*	*veíais*
Uds., ellos, ellas	iban	eran	veían

CULTURA

Mucha gente patinaba en línea y disfrutaba del buen tiempo que hacía en el Parque Palermo en Buenos Aires.

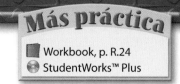
Más práctica

■ Workbook, p. R.24
● StudentWorks™ Plus

3. The imperfect of **hay** is **había**.

Había fuegos artificiales durante la fiesta.

4. The imperfect is used to express repeated, habitual actions or events in the past.

Él lo hacía con frecuencia.
Abuelita iba al mercado todos los días.
Celebrábamos la fiesta cada año.

CULTURA

Los niños se divertían con sus caras pintadas durante una fiesta en Cotacachi, Ecuador.

5. The imperfect is also used to describe persons, places, events, weather, and time in the past. It is also used to describe mental processes such as **creer, querer, saber.**

La muchacha era alta y fuerte.
Tenía dieciséis años.
Siempre estaba contenta.
Ella jugaba fútbol y siempre quería ganar.

Comunidades

¿Cuáles son unas fiestas que se celebran cerca de donde tú vives? ¿Te gusta tomar parte en las festividades? Describe una de las fiestas.

Práctica

HABLAR

1 Contesta.

1. ¿Vivía Isabel en México cuando era niña?
2. ¿Celebraba su familia el Día de los Muertos?
3. ¿Adónde iba la familia para celebrar el Día de los Muertos?
4. ¿Cómo iban todos?
5. ¿Qué llevaban algunos?
6. ¿Qué comían los niños?

HABLAR • ESCRIBIR

2 Personaliza. Da respuestas personales.

1. ¿Dónde vivías cuando eras niño(a)?
2. ¿Dónde vivían tus abuelos?
3. ¿Visitabas con frecuencia a tus abuelos?
4. ¿Estaban contentos cuando los visitabas?
5. ¿A qué escuela asistías cuando tenías ocho años?
6. ¿Participabas en un equipo deportivo con tus amigos?
7. ¿Qué deporte jugaban?
8. ¿Siempre querían ganar?

LEER • ESCRIBIR

3 Completa.

Cuando Ramona __1__ (tener) cuatro años, ella __2__ (vivir) en el campo. Los padres de Ramona __3__ (tener) una hacienda con muchos animales. Ramona __4__ (divertirse) mucho en el campo. Ella __5__ (tener) muchas amiguitas imaginarias. Ella les __6__ (servir) café a sus amiguitas. Las amigas la __7__ (querer) mucho a Ramona. Los padres no __8__ (poder) ver a las amiguitas, pero ellos __9__ (saber) que, para Ramona, las amiguitas sí __10__ (existir). Y Ramona nunca __11__ (aburrirse).

CULTURA

Un gaucho contemporáneo en su caballo en las pampas argentinas

Comunicación

4 Trabaja con un(a) compañero(a) de clase. Dile todo lo que hacías con frecuencia cuando eras muy joven. Luego tu compañero(a) te dirá lo que él o ella hacía. Comparen sus actividades.

5 Describe una fiesta que tu familia celebraba cuando eras niño(a). ¿Te gustaba? ¿Por qué?

Interesar, aburrir, gustar

1. The verbs **interesar** and **aburrir** function the same in English and Spanish.

> **¿Te aburre el béisbol?**
> **No, el béisbol me interesa.**
> **La verdad es que me interesan todos los deportes.**

2. The verb **gustar** functions the same as **interesar** and **aburrir**. **Gustar** conveys the meaning *to like* but its true meaning is *to please*. Note that these verbs are used with an indirect object pronoun.

> **Me gusta el helado.**
> **Te gustan las legumbres, ¿no?**
> **A José le gustan las frutas.**
> **Nos gustan los postres.**
> **A ellos les gusta el café.**

3. The indirect object pronouns are:

me	nos
te	*os*
le (a usted, a él, a ella)	les (a ustedes, a ellos, a ellas)

> **A él le gusta hablar y yo le hablo mucho.**

4. Gustar is often followed by an infinitive.

> **Me gusta nadar.**
> **A todos mis amigos les gusta nadar.**

La gente toma refrescos y meriendas en este café típico en la plaza Dorrego en San Telmo en Buenos Aires, Argentina.

Práctica

6 Contesta según el modelo.

MODELO —¿**Te gusta la ensalada?**
—**Sí, me gusta y como mucha.**

1. ¿Te gustan las hamburguesas?
2. ¿Te gusta la carne?
3. ¿Te gustan los cereales?
4. ¿Te gusta el helado?
5. ¿Te gustan las frutas?
6. ¿Te gusta el arroz?

7 Crea una conversación.

MODELO la gorra →
—¿**Te gusta mi gorra?**
—**Sí, a mí me gusta. La verdad es que te queda bien.**

1. la camisa
2. la blusa
3. los tenis
4. el pantalón
5. la camiseta
6. la falda
7. los zapatos
8. el suéter

8 Contesta con pronombres.

1. ¿Les enseña la empleada las camisas a los clientes?
2. ¿Le dice un cliente la talla que lleva?
3. ¿Le da el cliente el dinero a la empleada en la caja?
4. ¿Les da buen servicio a sus clientes la cajera?

Comunicación

9 Trabaja con un(a) compañero(a) de clase. Discutan algunas cosas que les gustan y que no les gustan. Pueden incluir las siguientes categorías. Luego comparen sus gustos.

comida   ropa   cursos

deportes   actividades

Una plaza en el centro de La Paz, Bolivia, la capital más alta del mundo

REPASO E

Ciudad y campo

Objetivos

In this chapter you will review:

- vocabulary related to city and country
- direct object pronouns
- uses of the preterite and imperfect

Go to glencoe.com
For: **Online book**
Web code: **ASD7844rc**

QuickPass

Go to glencoe.com
For: **Vocabulary practice**
Web code: **ASD7844rc**

Vocabulario 🎧

la ciudad
el semáforo
la esquina
el cruce de peatones

Los peatones cruzaban la calle.
Empezaron a correr porque cambió
el semáforo.

la parada de autobús

Había una cola larga en la parada de
autobús.
Mucha gente esperaba.
Cuando llegó el autobús estaba completo
y nadie pudo subir.

cultivar la tierra
el campo
una finca, una granja

Cuando José era joven, sus primos vivían
en el campo.
Tenían una finca.
José los visitó dos veces.

la autopista, la autovía
el carril

En la autopista hay varios carriles en cada
sentido (dirección).
Un carro pasó (adelantó) otro que andaba
más despacio.
Lo rebasó en el carril izquierdo.

Más práctica

📖 Workbook, pp. R.27–R.28
🌐 StudentWorks™ Plus

Repaso

Práctica

HABLAR

① Indica si describe la ciudad o el campo.

	la ciudad	el campo
1. Hay muchas calles peatonales.		
2. Los campesinos cultivan el trigo.		
3. Hay una parada de autobús en casi cada esquina.		
4. Los caballos corren por el corral.		
5. Las gallinas ponen huevos.		
6. Es muy difícil encontrar un lugar donde se puede estacionar (aparcar) el carro.		

HABLAR • ESCRIBIR

② Contesta.

1. ¿Cruzaba la gente la calle en el cruce de peatones?
2. ¿Por qué empezaron a correr mientras cruzaban la calle?
3. ¿Qué había en la parada de autobús?
4. ¿Por qué no pudo nadie subir al autobús?
5. ¿Se permite el tráfico vehicular en una calle peatonal?
6. Cuando José era joven, ¿vivía en la ciudad? ¿Dónde vivían sus primos?
7. ¿Qué tenían ellos en el campo?
8. ¿Cuántas veces los visitó José?

CULTURA

Un pueblo en el campo cerca de Mérida, Venezuela

QuickPass

Go to glencoe.com
For: **Conversation practice**
Web code: **ASD7844rc**

Conversación

El otro día en la ciudad

Elena	El otro día estuve en la ciudad y no sé lo que pasaba pero el tráfico era horrible.
Teresa	¿Qué hacías en la ciudad?
Elena	Leí en el periódico que había una exposición de arte latinoamericano en el Museo Metropolitano y la quería ver.
Teresa	¿La viste?
Elena	Sí, pero como había tanto tráfico no pude tomar el bus. Tomé el metro.
Teresa	¿Qué tal te gustó la exposición?
Elena	Me gustó mucho. Había muchos cuadros con escenas rurales.

¿Comprendes?

A Contesta.

1. ¿Cuándo estuvo Elena en la ciudad?
2. ¿Qué había?
3. ¿Qué leyó Elena en el periódico?
4. ¿Qué quería ver?
5. ¿La vio?
6. ¿Le gustó?
7. ¿Qué había en muchos de los cuadros en la exposición?

Gramática

Pronombres de complemento directo

1. The direct object is the direct receiver of the action of the verb.

¿El peaje?	Ella lo pagó.
¿Los boletos?	Los compraron.
¿La llave?	La tengo.
¿Te vio?	Sí, me vio.

2. Review the forms of the direct object pronouns.

me	nos
te	*os*
lo	los
la	las

Práctica

ESCUCHAR • HABLAR • ESCRIBIR

1 Sigue el modelo.

MODELO el ticket para el autobús →
Aquí lo tienes.

1. el ticket para el metro
2. las entradas para el museo
3. el dinero para el peaje
4. la llave del carro
5. las fotografías de su finca
6. los boletos para el avión

36725

100 🍵 2007.
CENTENARI DE LA CASA BATLLÓ
ANTONI GAUDÍ. BARCELONA

CASA BATLLÓ
Patrimoni Mundial
UNESCO, 2005

Pg. de Gràcia, 43 • 08007 Barcelona
tel: +34 93 216 03 06
www.casabatllo.es
NIF 8-60.719.051
Precio: 13,20€ (IVA INCLUIDO)

BARCELONA
BUS TURISTIC

2
Dies/Días/Days
Consecutius/Consecutivos/
Consecutive

Data/Fecha/Date
20-05-09

085 00018   01 / 01 402 01

Preu/Precio/Price
23,00 €
Incl. IVA i AOV
C.I.F. A-08016081

57014 / 144

LEER • ESCRIBIR

2 Completa las conversaciones.

1. —Teresa, ¿_____ invitó Elena a su fiesta?
   —Claro que _____ invitó. Ella y yo somos muy buenas
   amigas. ¿_____ invitó a ti también?
   —No, no _____ invitó porque sabe que tengo que
   trabajar.

2. —José, ¿viste a Luisa en el concierto?
   —Sí, _____ vi pero ella no _____ vio.
   —¿Cómo es que tú _____ viste pero ella no _____ vio?
   —Pues, no _____ pudo ver porque estaba sentada
   unas veinte filas delante de nosotros.

El pretérito y el imperfecto

1. Remember that you use the preterite to express actions or events that began and ended at a specific time in the past.

> **Carlos fue a la ciudad ayer.**
> **En la ciudad vio una exposición de arte.**

2. You use the imperfect to talk about a continuous, habitual, or frequently repeated action in the past.

> **Carlos iba a la ciudad con mucha frecuencia.**
> **Casi cada vez que estaba en la ciudad iba al museo donde veía una exposición de arte.**

CULTURA

El joven admiraba un cuadro abstracto en el museo de la Fundación Joan Miró en Barcelona, España.

3. Often a sentence will have two or more verbs in the past. Quite often one verb indicates what was going on when something happened or took place. What was going on—the background—is expressed by the imperfect. What happened or took place is in the preterite.

> **Un carro iba muy despacio y José lo rebasó.**
> **Los peatones cruzaban la calle cuando cambió el semáforo.**

Práctica

3 Contesta.

1. ¿Visitaste a tus abuelos la semana pasada?
   ¿Cuándo visitaste a tus abuelos?
   ¿Visitabas a tus abuelos cada semana?
   ¿Cuándo visitabas a tus abuelos?
2. ¿Fuiste al campo el año pasado?
   ¿Cuándo fuiste al campo?
   ¿Ibas al campo muy a menudo?
   ¿Cuándo ibas al campo?

LEER • ESCRIBIR

4 Completa.

1. Una vez ellos _____ al campo y _____ a caballo.
   (ir, andar)
2. Ellos siempre _____ al campo donde _____ a caballo.
   (ir, andar)
3. Yo _____ el invierno pasado pero Elena _____ todos
   los inviernos. (esquiar, esquiar)
4. Los turistas _____ una semana en la capital y _____
   el casco antiguo. (pasar, visitar)

CULTURA
Una estancia en las pampas argentinas

HABLAR • ESCRIBIR

5 Contesta.

1. ¿Esperaba mucha gente en la parada cuando llegó el autobús?
2. ¿Cruzaban la calle los peatones cuando la luz del semáforo cambió?
3. ¿Vivían los primos de José en el campo cuando él los visitó?
4. ¿Conducía Elena el coche cuando ocurrió el accidente?

CULTURA

Aquí ves un rótulo en una esquina de Quito, Ecuador. ¿Cómo se dice «sentido único» en Ecuador?

LEER • ESCRIBIR

6 Completa para formar frases completas.

1.

Yo estudiaba cuando
a.
b.
c.
d.
e.

2.

Mis amigos	
a.	
b.	
c.	cuando yo llegué.
d.	
e.	

Más práctica

Workbook, pp. R.29–R.30
StudentWorks™ Plus

Repaso

HABLAR • ESCRIBIR

 7 Contesta según se indica.

1. ¿Qué enviaba Manuel cuando sonó su móvil? (un correo electrónico)
2. ¿Quién lo llamó? (un amigo que tiene una finca en el campo)
3. ¿Qué estaba pasando mientras hablaban? (estaba cortando)
4. Por fin, ¿se les cortó la línea? (sí)
5. ¿Qué hizo el amigo de Manuel? (volvió a llamar)
6. ¿Sonó el móvil de Manuel? (no)
7. ¿Por qué no sonó? (él también trataba de llamar)

 Comunicación

8 Cuando eras niño(a), ¿vivías en una ciudad, un suburbio o en el campo? Describe la ciudad o el pueblo donde vivías. Habla de todo lo que hacías allí. ¿Te divertías?

9 ¿Cuántas veces en un solo día estás haciendo algo cuando algo o alguien te interrumpe? Piensa en algunas cosas que hacías ayer cuando algo te interrumpió. Cuenta lo que estabas haciendo y lo que pasó.

CULTURA

A estos dos niños les encanta vivir en el campo en Argentina. Un pasatiempo favorito es el de subir árboles.

El hotel y el restaurante

Objetivos

In this chapter you will review:

- vocabulary related to hotels and restaurants
- double object pronouns
- the present perfect tense
- regular and irregular past participles

◄ A muchas familias les gusta comer los domingos en un restaurante como este en Alajuela, Costa Rica.

QuickPass

Go to glencoe.com
For: **Online book**
Web code: **ASD7844rc**

QuickPass

Go to glencoe.com
For: **Vocabulary practice**
Web code: ASD7844rc

Vocabulario

el hotel
la llave
la recepción

Las amigas han llegado al hotel.
Están en la recepción.
El recepcionista les ha dado sus llaves.

la percha, el colgador
el armario

Anita ha colgado su ropa en el armario.

una toalla limpia
la cama
una toalla sucia

La camarera ha limpiado el cuarto.
Ha hecho la cama.

el restaurante
el mesero
el menú

El padre y su hija están en el restaurante.
Han leído el menú y han escogido lo que van
   a comer.
¿Le ha devuelto el señor el menú al mesero?
No, no se lo ha devuelto pero se lo va a
   devolver.

Práctica

LEER • ESCRIBIR

1 Escoge.

1. (Los huéspedes / Los recepcionistas) han llegado al hotel.
2. El recepcionista les ha dado (sus maletas / sus llaves).
3. Los amigos han subido a (su cuarto / su armario).
4. La camarera ha hecho (la cama / la almohada).
5. Ella ha cambiado las toallas (limpias / sucias).
6. El mesero les ha traído (la mesa / el menú).
7. La ducha y la bañera están en el cuarto de (baño / lavabo).
8. El cliente va a salir y ha (abandonado / reservado) su cuarto.

CULTURA
Un hotel bonito en el centro de la Ciudad de México

Repaso F

Más práctica

Workbook, pp. R.32–R.33
StudentWorks™ Plus

HABLAR • ESCRIBIR

2 Describe.

1. un desayuno continental
2. un desayuno americano

HABLAR • ESCRIBIR

3 Contesta.

1. Vas a poner la mesa. ¿Qué necesitas?
2. Vas a hacer la cama. ¿Qué necesitas?
3. Llegas a un hotel. ¿Qué le dices a la recepcionista?
4. Estás en un restaurante y quieres comer tu comida favorita. ¿Qué vas a pedir?
5. Has terminado la comida. ¿Qué le pides al mesero?

Comunicación

4 Describe el dibujo.

QuickPass

Go to glencoe.com
For: **Conversation practice**
Web code: **ASD7844rc**

Conversación 🎧

¿Comprendes?

A Corrige.

1. Los amigos de José han llegado.
2. José los ha llevado a su hotel.
3. Ellos no han reservado un cuarto en ningún hotel.
4. Los amigos tienen sueño después de su viaje pero no tienen hambre.
5. Ya han comido.
6. José y Beatriz han estado en el nuevo Rincón Argentino.

B Analizando Contesta.

Si José y Beatriz nunca han comido en el Rincón Argentino, ¿por qué han decidido ir a comer allí con los amigos de Beatriz?

QuickPass

Go to glencoe.com
For: **Grammar practice**
Web code: **ASD7844rc**

Gramática
Dos complementos en una frase

1. Many sentences have both a direct and an indirect object pronoun. The indirect object pronoun always precedes the direct object and both objects precede the conjugated form of the verb.

   ¿Quién les ha servido el postre?
   El mesero nos lo ha servido.

   ¿Quién te dio las llaves?
   El recepcionista me las dio.

2. The indirect object pronouns **le** and **les** change to **se** when used with **lo, la, los,** or **las.**

   El mozo le subió el equipaje.
   El mozo se lo subió.

   El mesero les sirvió la comida.
   El mesero se la sirvió.

3. **Se** is often clarified with a prepositional phrase.

   Yo se lo di ⎰ a él.
   a ella.
   a usted.
   a ellos.
   a ellas.
   a ustedes.

CULTURA

Muchos hoteles de lujo ofrecen servicio a cuartos. Aquí el mozo va a servir el desayuno en el cuarto de los huéspedes.

Práctica

HABLAR • ESCRIBIR

1 Sigue el modelo.

   MODELO   la percha →
             —¿Quién te dio la percha?
             —La camarera me la dio.

   1. la almohada   4. las toallas
   2. la manta   5. el papel higiénico
   3. el jabón   6. las perchas

LEER • ESCRIBIR

2 Contesta con **la camarera** o **el mesero** usando pronombres.

1. ¿Quién te ha dado el menú?
2. ¿Quién te ha cambiado las toallas?
3. ¿Quién te ha servido el desayuno?
4. ¿Quién te ha traído la manta?

LEER • ESCRIBIR

3 Cambia los sustantivos (nombres) a pronombres.

1. Abordo del avión el asistente de vuelo les sirvió la comida a los pasajeros.
2. En clase la profesora les explicó las reglas a los alumnos.
3. En la tienda de ropa el empleado le vendió el pantalón a José.
4. En el restaurante el mesero les trajo los platos a los clientes.
5. Elena le dejó la propina para el mesero.

CULTURA

El mesero ha servido un gran plato de mariscos en este restaurante en Punta Cana en la República Dominicana.

El presente perfecto

1. The present perfect tense is formed by using the present tense of the verb **haber** and the past participle. Review the forms of the present perfect.

	hablar	comer	subir
yo	he hablado	he comido	he subido
tú	has hablado	has comido	has subido
Ud., él, ella	ha hablado	ha comido	ha subido
nosotros(as)	hemos hablado	hemos comido	hemos subido
vosotros(as)	*habéis hablado*	*habéis comido*	*habéis subido*
Uds., ellos, ellas	han hablado	han comido	han subido

2. Review the following verbs that have an irregular past participle.

decir	→	dicho	abrir	→	abierto
hacer	→	hecho	cubrir	→	cubierto
escribir	→	escrito	poner	→	puesto
freír	→	frito	morir	→	muerto
romper	→	roto	volver	→	vuelto
ver	→	visto	devolver	→	devuelto

3. The present perfect tense describes an action completed in the very recent past. Review some expressions that are frequently used with the present perfect.

ya
todavía no
hasta ahora
jamás
nunca

—En tu vida, ¿has estado en México?
—No, no he ido nunca a México.
—Yo, sí. Ya he estado tres veces.

CULTURA

Es tarde y mucha gente ya ha terminado de comer en este restaurante en la Ciudad de México.

Más práctica

📕 Workbook, pp. R.35–R.36
💿 StudentWorks™ Plus

Repaso

Práctica

4 Contesta con **sí**.

1. ¿Han llegado los amigos al hotel?
2. ¿Han ido a la recepción?
3. ¿Les ha ayudado el recepcionista?
4. ¿Han reservado ellos un cuarto?
5. ¿Les ha dado sus llaves el recepcionista?
6. ¿Han subido los amigos a su cuarto?
7. ¿Han subido en el ascensor?

5 Personaliza. Da respuestas personales.

1. ¿Has comido en un restaurante mexicano?
2. ¿Jamás has comido tacos y enchiladas?
3. En tu vida, ¿has viajado en avión?
4. ¿Cuántos vuelos has tomado?
5. ¿Te has hospedado en un albergue juvenil?

6 Sigue el modelo.

MODELO —¿Van a verlo?
—Pero, ya lo hemos visto.

1. ¿Van a abrirlo?
2. ¿Van a hacerlo?
3. ¿Van a devolverlo?
4. ¿Van a escribirlo?
5. ¿Van a decirlo?

TACOS		BURRITOS	
CARNE ASADA	2.80	CARNE ASADA	4.25
POLLO ASADO	2.49	POLLO ASADO	3.71
CARNITAS	2.49	CARNITAS	3.71
3 CARNE ASADA	4.25	MACHACA	3.50
3 POLLO ASADO	3.71	CHORIZO	3.50
3 ADOVADA	3.71	CHILE RELLENO	3.50
3 CABEZA	3.71	PANCHOS BURRITO	4.50
3 BUCHE	3.71		
TORTAS		QUESADILLAS	
CARNE ASADA	4.25	CARNE ASADA	4.25
POLLO ASADO	3.71	POLLO ASADO	3.71
MACHACA	3.50		
CHORIZO	3.50		

✿ Comunicación

7 ¿Te has hospedado o has pasado unas vacaciones en un hotel? ¿En qué hotel? Describe tu experiencia.

8 ¿Has tenido una experiencia buena en un restaurante? Describe la experiencia.

9 Discute con un(a) amigo(a) las cosas que todavía no han hecho pero que quieren hacer algún día.

Cocina hispana

Vamos a comparar Ya has aprendido que las sobras son la comida que queda después de comer. Has aprendido también que las sobras de una comida en un restaurante de Latinoamérica o España no se llevan a casa «para el perrito». Ahora vamos a ver si las familias hispanas elaboran unos platos sirviéndose de las sobras en vez de botarlas. Y en tu casa, ¿hay unos platos que llevan sobras?

◄ Estas señoras están elaborando una deliciosa comida mexicana en Guadalajara, México.

Objetivos

You will:

- talk about foods and food preparation
- talk about a Hispanic recipe

You will use:

- the subjunctive
- formal commands
- negative informal commands

QuickPass

Go to glencoe.com
For: **Online book**
Web code: **ASD7844c1**

Introducción al tema
Cocina hispana

Mira estas fotos para familiarizarte con el tema de este capítulo—la cocina hispana. Al mirar las fotos, ¿qué piensas? Hay una gran variedad de platos. ¿Hay algunos que quieres probar?

México La señora está preparando unas tortillas con salsa y frijoles refritos en Mérida. ▶

◀ **España** En unos restaurantes antiguos de España hay hornos de barro en que asan el cordero y el cochinillo, o como dicen en Latinoamérica «el lechón».

▲ **México** Un plato de chiles rellenos acompañado de arroz y aguacate en un restaurante en Tepoztlán

Los pimientos se usan en la cocina de muchos países hispanos. Hay muchos tipos de pimientos—unos picantes y otros dulces—que llevan muchos nombres diferentes: pimientos, ajíes, chiles, chipotles, etc. ▼

▲ **España** El cocinero está asando pollos en una parrilla a la entrada de un restaurante en Barcelona.

THE BEST OF SPAIN

LA PAELLA

INGREDIENTES

3 tomates
2 cebollas grandes
2 pimientos (uno verde y uno rojo)
4 dientes de ajo
1/2 kilo de camarones

4 calamares
12 almejas
12 mejillones
langosta (opcional)
1 pollo en partes
3 chorizos

1 paquete de guisantes congelados
1 bote de pimientos morrones
1 1/2 tazas de arroz
3 tazas de consomé de pollo
4 pizcas de azafrán
1/4 taza de aceite de oliva

PREPARACIÓN

1. Pique los tomates, los pimientos, las cebollas y el ajo.
2. Lave las almejas y los mejillones en agua fría.
3. Limpie y pele los camarones.
4. Limpie y corte en rebanadas los calamares.
5. Corte en rebanadas los chorizos.
6. Fría o ase el pollo aparte.

▲ **España** Una receta para la paella en un libro de cocina española

▲ **Estados Unidos** El señor prepara pinchos y maíz en una parrilla durante el festival cubano de la Calle Ocho en la Pequeña Habana de Miami.

◀ **Argentina** El cocinero asa el famoso bife argentino en un restaurante de Buenos Aires.

Puerto Rico La señora vende empanadas, piononos, alcapurrias y pescado frito en su restaurante en San Juan. ▼

La cocina

el congelador

el refrigerador, la nevera

el horno

el horno de microondas

la estufa, la cocina

el lavaplatos

freír las papas

el/la sartén

hervir el agua

la tapa

la olla, la cacerola

asar la carne

la parrilla

la cazuela

revolver la salsa

Para conversar

¿Quiere usted que yo ase el pollo o que lo fría?

Fríalo, por favor. Me gusta el pollo frito.

VIDEO To practice your new words, watch **Vocabulario en vivo.**

SOPA DE POLLO

una receta

INGREDIENTES
1 taza de cebolla picada
1 taza de apio
1 taza de zanahorias
cortadas en rebanadas
3 dientes de ajo machacados
½ cucharadita de
pimienta negra
10 tazas de caldo de pollo
1½ tazas de pollo cortado
en cubitos (¾ de una libra)

RECETA
Poner la cebolla, el apio, las zanahorias, el ajo y el caldo de pollo en un horno holandés. Poner a hervir; remover una o dos veces. Baje el fuego y déjelo cocer a fuego lento sin tapar por 15 minutos. Añadir el pollo; dejar cocer a fuego lento de 5 a 10 minutos.

la cebolla

el aguacate

los pimientos

el pepino

el ajo

las zanahorias

cortar en pedacitos

cortar en rebanadas

picar

Pique usted el ajo.

pelar

Pele usted las zanahorias.

la chuleta de cerdo

el muslo de pollo

las alitas

el escalope de ternera

la pechuga de pollo

Para conversar

¿Quiere usted que yo ponga la cacerola al fuego?

Sí, póngala, por favor. Pero, cocínela (cuézala) a fuego lento. No quiero que se queme.

Cuando el cocinero cocina algo tiene que añadir condimentos.
Los condimentos le dan sabor a la comida.

En otras partes

- **El aguacate** is **la palta** in Chile.
- There are many terms that mean *slice*. Some general guidelines are:
  rebanada (de pan, pastel)
  tajada (de carne)
  lonja, loncha (de jamón)
  rodaja (de limón, pepino)
  raja (de melón)
- **Pedazos** and **trozos (trocitos)** refer to pieces.

práctica

QuickPass

Go to glencoe.com
For: **Vocabulary practice**
Web code: **ASD7844c1**

ESCUCHAR

1 Escucha cada frase y decide si la información es correcta o no. Usa una tabla como la de abajo para indicar tus respuestas.

correcta	incorrecta

LEER

2 Escoge.

1. Antes de hervirlas, debes (freír, pelar) las zanahorias.
2. Puedes freír las pechugas de pollo en (una cacerola, una sartén).
3. Tienes que (revolver, asar) la salsa.
4. Favor de poner los vasos sucios en (la nevera, el lavaplatos).
5. Si lo quieres cocinar rápido lo debes poner en (el horno, el horno de microondas).
6. ¿Quiere usted que yo ponga la olla (al agua, al fuego)?
7. ¿Quiere usted que yo pele (las zanahorias, los pimientos)?
8. Voy a cortar el pan en (rebanadas, pedacitos).

ESCRIBIR

3 **¡Manos a la obra!** Good nutrition is an important part of staying healthy. Working in groups, use a piece of poster board and markers to make a food pyramid. Label the pyramid with each of the food groups: grains, vegetables, fruits, oils, milk, and meat/beans. Within each food group, write the names of foods that you know. Then present your pyramid to the class and suggest a healthy meal based on the foods you listed in each group.

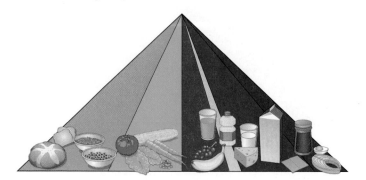

Conexiones

Las matemáticas

Si lees una receta en español tienes que comprender los pesos métricos. La onza, la libra y la tonelada no existen en el sistema métrico que es un sistema decimal. Las medidas para el peso se basan en el kilogramo o kilo. Hay mil gramos en un kilo. El kilo es igual a 2, 2 libras. Una libra inglesa o estadounidense es un poco menos de medio kilo.

Más practica

▪ Workbook, pp. 1.3–1.6
● StudentWorks™ Plus

HABLAR • ESCRIBIR

4 Personaliza. Da respuestas personales.

1. Cuando comes pollo, ¿prefieres el muslo o la pechuga?
2. ¿Te gusta más una chuleta de cerdo o un escalope de ternera?
3. ¿Prefieres el pescado asado o frito?
4. ¿Prefieres tus legumbres muy cocidas o casi crudas?
5. ¿Te gusta la carne con una salsa o sin salsa?
6. ¿Te gusta la comida salada o no? ¿Añades mucha sal?

LEER

5 Usa una tabla como la de abajo para indicar si se puede poner los siguientes ingredientes en una ensalada.

CULTURA

El señor está asando carne en un puesto de comida en una calle de la Ciudad de Panamá.

sí	no

1. la lechuga
2. el ajo
3. la carne cruda
4. el aguacate
5. las zanahorias
6. el aceite
7. el café
8. una cebolla

HABLAR • ESCRIBIR

6 Describe.

1. tu comida favorita
2. las legumbres que te gustan
3. los ingredientes de una buena ensalada
4. algunos alimentos que pones en el refrigerador
5. unas cosas que se preparan a la parrilla
6. una cocina moderna

▲ Unos platos populares ▼

 Comunicación

7 Trabajen en grupos de cuatro y discutan sus platos o comidas favoritas. ¿Tienen ustedes los mismos gustos o no?

QuickPass

Go to glencoe.com
For: **Grammar practice**
Web code: **ASD7844c1**

El subjuntivo

1. All verbs you have learned so far are in the indicative mood. The indicative mood is used to express actions that actually do, did, or will take place. The indicative is used to express real events.

> **Juan es un alumno bueno.**
> **Estudia mucho.**
> **Recibe buenas notas.**

All the preceding information is factual.

> *John is a good student, he studies a lot, and he gets good grades.*

2. You are now going to learn the subjunctive mood. The subjunctive is used to express something that is not necessarily factual or real. It expresses things that might happen. Compare the following.

> **Juan estudia mucho y recibe buenas notas.**
> **Los padres de Juan quieren que él estudie mucho y que reciba buenas notas.**

The first sentence tells you that Juan studies a lot and gets good grades. The information is factual, and for this reason you use the indicative. The second sentence states that Juan's parents want him to study a lot and get good grades, but that doesn't mean that Juan will actually do it even though his parents want him to. The second sentence tells what may happen. It does not present facts, and for this reason you must use the subjunctive in the clause that depends upon **quieren.** Such a clause is called a dependent clause.

3. To form the present tense of the subjunctive of regular verbs, you drop the **o** ending of the **yo** form of the present indicative. This is also true for verbs that have an irregular form in the present tense of the indicative. Add **e** endings to all **-ar** verbs and **a** endings to all **-er** and **-ir** verbs.

INFINITIVE	PRESENT (YO)	STEM	PRESENT SUBJUNCTIVE (YO)
mirar	miro	mir-	mire
comer	como	com-	coma
vivir	vivo	viv-	viva
salir	salgo	salg-	salga
hacer	hago	hag-	haga
decir	digo	dig-	diga
conducir	conduzco	conduzc-	conduzca

La profesora ayuda a una alumna porque quiere que salga bien en su examen y que tenga éxito.

4. Study the forms for the present tense of the subjunctive.

	mirar	comer	vivir	salir
yo	mire	coma	viva	salga
tú	mires	comas	vivas	salgas
Ud., él, ella	mire	coma	viva	salga
nosotros(as)	miremos	comamos	vivamos	salgamos
vosotros(as)	*miréis*	*comáis*	*viváis*	*salgáis*
Uds., ellos, ellas	miren	coman	vivan	salgan

5. The following are the only verbs that do not follow the regular pattern for the formation of the present subjunctive.

	dar	estar	ir	saber	ser
yo	dé	esté	vaya	sepa	sea
tú	des	estés	vayas	sepas	seas
Ud., él, ella	dé	esté	vaya	sepa	sea
nosotros(as)	demos	estemos	vayamos	sepamos	seamos
vosotros(as)	*deis*	*estéis*	*vayáis*	*sepáis*	*seáis*
Uds., ellos, ellas	den	estén	vayan	sepan	sean

Práctica

ESCUCHAR • HABLAR • ESCRIBIR

① Sigue el modelo.

MODELO estudiar mucho →
   **Los padres de Mateo quieren que
      él estudie mucho.**

1. trabajar
2. leer mucho
3. comer bien
4. aprender mucho
5. asistir a la universidad
6. recibir buenas notas
7. hacer el trabajo
8. poner todo en orden
9. salir bien en todo
10. ir a clase
11. estar aquí
12. ser bueno

CULTURA

Los señores están preparando una paella grande en Tenerife, España. Quieren que salga deliciosa y que a todos les guste.

CULTURA

La señora está haciendo pupusas en un restaurante en San Salvador, El Salvador.

LEER • ESCRIBIR

2 Forma una frase completa usando el subjuntivo.

Yo quiero que Luis...

1. preparar la comida
2. cortar las cebollas
3. asar la carne
4. leer la receta
5. pelar los tomates
6. picar el ajo
7. poner la mesa
8. hacer una ensalada

HABLAR • ESCRIBIR

3 Completa la frase con tus propias ideas usando los siguientes nombres y pronombres.

Yo quiero que...

1. tú
2. Justina y Roberto
3. todos ustedes
4. ella
5. todos nosotros
6. mi profesor

LEER • ESCRIBIR

4 Completa con la forma apropiada del verbo.

1. Yo quiero que tú le _____ y ellos quieren que nosotros le _____. (hablar)
2. Yo quiero que él _____ el postre y él quiere que yo lo _____. (comer)
3. Ellos quieren que yo _____ el paquete y yo quiero que ellos lo _____. (abrir)
4. Tú quieres que yo lo _____ y yo quiero que tú lo _____. (hacer)
5. Ellos quieren que nosotros _____ la mesa y nosotros queremos que ellos la _____. (poner)
6. Él quiere que yo lo _____ pero no quiere que tú lo _____. (saber)
7. Ellos quieren que tú _____ pero no quieren que yo _____. (ir)
8. Yo quiero que ustedes se lo _____ y ellos quieren que nosotros se lo _____. (dar)

GeoVistas

To learn more about El Salvador, take a tour on pages SH44–SH45.

InfoGap For more practice with the subjunctive, do Activity 1 on page SR2 at the end of this book.

Comunicación

5 Trabajen en grupos y discutan todo lo que tu profesor(a) de español quiere que ustedes hagan.

El imperativo formal

Más práctica

Workbook, pp. 1.9–1.10
StudentWorks™ Plus

1. The formal commands (**usted, ustedes**), both affirmative and negative, use the subjunctive form of the verb.

(no) prepare usted	(no) preparen ustedes
(no) lea usted	(no) lean ustedes
(no) sirva usted	(no) sirvan ustedes
(no) haga usted	(no) hagan ustedes
(no) salga usted	(no) salgan ustedes
(no) conduzca usted	(no) conduzcan ustedes
(no) vaya usted	(no) vayan ustedes
(no) sea usted	(no) sean ustedes

2. You have already learned that object pronouns can be attached to an infinitive or gerund or come before the helping verb. In the case of commands, the object pronouns must be added to the affirmative command, as you already know from the **tú** commands. They must come before the negative command.

AFFIRMATIVE	NEGATIVE
Háblele.	**No le hable usted.**
Démelo.	**No me lo dé usted.**
Levántense.	**No se levanten ustedes.**

CULTURA

En un parque en San Pablo, Ecuador

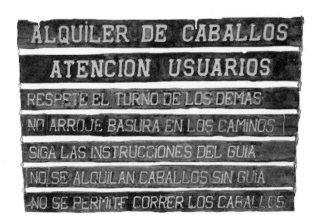

Práctica

ESCUCHAR • HABLAR • ESCRIBIR

6 Contesta según el modelo.

MODELO —¿**Preparo la comida?**
—**Sí, prepare usted la comida.**

1. ¿Preparo el postre?
2. ¿Aso la carne?
3. ¿Pelo los tomates?
4. ¿Pico el ajo?
5. ¿Frío el pollo?
6. ¿Pongo la mesa?
7. ¿Hago la ensalada?
8. ¿Pongo la cacerola al fuego?

FOLDABLES®
Study Organizer

PROJECT BOARD WITH TABS
See page SH30 for help with making this foldable. Think of the food words you know in Spanish and use them to create a recipe of your own. Draw a small picture of each ingredient on the front of each tab in the order you will use it. Next, lift each tab and write instructions about how to prepare your recipe using formal commands.

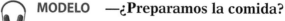

El señor está asando carne en Tikal, Guatemala. ¿Quieres que él te prepare la carne bien hecha o a término medio?

¿Te acuerdas?

Remember other polite ways you learned to express a command.

Favor de pasarme la sal.

¿Me pasaría usted la sal, por favor?

Gramática

ESCUCHAR • HABLAR • ESCRIBIR

7 Contesta según el modelo.

MODELO —¿Preparamos la comida?
—No, no preparen ustedes la comida.
Yo la voy a preparar.

1. ¿Preparamos el postre?
2. ¿Lavamos la lechuga?
3. ¿Pelamos las papas?
4. ¿Cortamos el pepino?
5. ¿Hacemos la ensalada?
6. ¿Ponemos la mesa?

ESCUCHAR • HABLAR • ESCRIBIR

8 Contesta según el modelo.

MODELO —¿Quiere usted que yo ase la chuleta?
—No, no la ase usted. Fríala.

1. ¿Quiere usted que yo ase el pollo?
2. ¿Quiere usted que yo ase las papas?
3. ¿Quiere usted que yo ase las chuletas de cordero?
4. ¿Quiere usted que yo ase los pimientos?
5. ¿Quiere usted que yo ase el pescado?
6. ¿Quiere usted que yo ase los camarones?

ESCUCHAR • HABLAR • ESCRIBIR

9 Sigue el modelo.

MODELO Páseme la sal, por favor. →
Pásemela, por favor.

1. Páseme la pimienta, por favor.
2. Páseme el pan, por favor.
3. Páseme la ensalada, por favor.
4. Páseme los platos, por favor.
5. Páseme el tenedor, por favor.
6. Páseme las zanahorias, por favor.

LEER • ESCRIBIR

10 Completa la tabla.

sí	no
Démelo.	
	No me lo diga usted.
Cocínelo a fuego lento.	
	No la revuelva usted.
Léamela.	

El imperativo familiar—formas negativas

1. The negative **tú** or informal command uses the **tú** form of the verb in the subjunctive.

No hables más.	No salgas.
No comas más.	No vayas.
No sirvas más.	No conduzcas.

2. As with the formal commands, object pronouns are added to the affirmative command and come before the negative command.

Háblame.	No me hables.
Dímelo.	No me lo digas.

Práctica

ESCUCHAR • HABLAR • ESCRIBIR

 Contesta según el modelo.

 MODELO —¿Miro ahora o no?
—No, no mires ahora.

1. ¿Hablo ahora o no?
2. ¿Como ahora o no?
3. ¿Subo ahora o no?
4. ¿Sirvo ahora o no?
5. ¿Salgo ahora o no?
6. ¿Voy ahora o no?

LEER • ESCRIBIR

 Completa la tabla.

sí	no
Ponlo allí.	
Dámelo.	
Dímelo.	
	No me hables.
	No lo hagas.
Llámala.	

Comunicación

 Acabas de recibir un gatito para tu cumpleaños. Como todos los gatitos, es muy curioso. Dale un nombre al gatito y dile que no haga cosas peligrosas y destructivas.

¿Te acuerdas?
You have already learned the familiar **tú** command in the affirmative.

Refrán
Can you guess what the following proverb means?

Espinacas, cómelas a sacas.

¡Bravo!
You have now learned all the new vocabulary and grammar in this chapter. Continue to use and practice all that you know while learning more cultural information. ¡Vamos!

¿Yo? ¿En la cocina?

Alicia, ¿te gusta cocinar?

A mí, ¿cocinar? ¿Hablas en serio, Jorge? En la cocina soy un desastre. ¿A ti te gusta cocinar?

Sí, bastante. La verdad es que algún día me gustaría ser cocinero.

¿De veras? Dame una idea de lo que sabes preparar.

Muchas cosas, pero mi plato favorito es la paella.

La paella, dices. ¿Qué es?

Pues, es una especialidad española, de Valencia. Lleva muchos ingredientes—mariscos, arroz. Algún día, ¿quieres que yo te prepare una paella?

Sí, pero no sé si me gustarán los mariscos.

Pues, nosotros los españoles comemos mucho pescado y mariscos. Pero ahora se están poniendo muy caros.

¿Comprendes?

VIDEO To prepare an Argentine meal, watch **Diálogo en vivo.**

A Contesta según la información en la conversación.

1. ¿A quién le gusta cocinar?
2. ¿Quién es un desastre en la cocina?
3. Algún día, ¿qué quiere ser Jorge?
4. ¿Cuál es el plato que más le gusta preparar?
5. ¿De qué región de España es la paella una especialidad?
6. ¿A Alicia le va a gustar una paella?
7. ¿Son caros los mariscos?

B Identifica quien lo dice.

	Jorge	Alicia
1. Le gusta cocinar y sabe cocinar.		
2. No sabe si le gustan los mariscos.		
3. Es un desastre en la cocina.		
4. Come mariscos.		

C **Analizando** Contesta.

1. ¿De qué país es Jorge? ¿Cómo lo sabes?
2. ¿Es Alicia de España?

D **Personalizando** ¿Qué piensas? ¿A ti te gustaría la paella o no? ¿Por qué?

CULTURA

En esta tienda en Valencia, España, se venden utensilios para elaborar una buena paella.

COCINA HISPANA

Antes de leer

Dale una ojeada a la receta para familiarizarte con los ingredientes y la preparación.

Durante la lectura

Al leer asegúrate que comprendes el orden de cada procedimiento durante la elaboración del plato.

✓ Reading Check

¿Por qué es amarillo el arroz?

Una receta hispana ♻

Otro plato delicioso y muy apreciado en España y otros países hispanohablantes es el arroz con pollo. Hay muchas variaciones en las recetas para elaborar un buen arroz con pollo pero aquí tiene usted una receta bastante sencilla. Decida si a usted le gustaría comer este plato delicioso.

Antes de leer la receta hay que saber algo más. El arroz en el arroz con pollo igual que el arroz en una paella es amarillo. Es el azafrán, una hierba de origen árabe, que le da al arroz el color amarillo. Pero el azafrán es muy caro y como colorante se puede usar bujol. El bujol se vende en muchos supermercados.

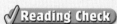

Los ingredientes para hacer arroz con pollo

Después de leer

Trata de contar la receta de la manera más detallada posible a un(a) compañero(a) de clase.

Arroz con pollo

Ingredientes
3 tomates
2 cebollas grandes
2 pimientos (uno verde y uno rojo)
4 dientes[1] de ajo
1 pollo en partes
3 chorizos[2]
1 paquete de guisantes congelados
1 frasco de (pimientos) morrones (rojos)
1 ½ tazas de arroz
3 tazas de consomé de pollo
unas pizcas[3] de azafrán o bujol
¼ (una cuarta) taza de aceite de oliva
una pizca de sal y pimienta

Preparación
1. Pique los tomates, pimientos, cebollas y ajo.
2. Corte en rodajas los chorizos.
3. Fría o ase el pollo aparte (se puede preparar el pollo en partes [muslos, media pechuga, piernas] o se puede cortarlo en pedazos deshuesados[4]).

Elaboración
Se usa una sartén o una olla grande.
1. Fría ligeramente[5] en el aceite los pimientos y las cebollas picadas.
2. Agregue (Añada) a la misma sartén el ajo y los tomates y fría ligeramente a fuego lento unos dos o tres minutos.
3. Agregue el arroz.
4. Revuelva el arroz con los tomates, cebollas, morrones y ajo.
5. Añada el pollo.
6. Agregue el consomé de pollo y llévelo a la ebullición[6].
7. Agregue el azafrán o bujol.
8. Ponga sal y pimienta a su gusto.
9. Tape[7] la sartén o la olla y cocine a fuego lento encima de la estufa unos treinta minutos.
10. Al final agregue los guisantes y pimientos morrones.

[1]dientes *cloves*
[2]chorizos *Spanish sausage*
[3]pizcas *pinches*
[4]deshuesados *deboned*

[5]ligeramente *lightly*
[6]a la ebullición *to a boil*
[7]tape *cover*

¿Comprendes?

Más práctica

■ Workbook, pp. 1.13–1.14
● StudentWorks™ Plus

A Buscando palabras específicas ¿Cuál es la palabra?
Completa según la receta.

    1. una _____ para hacer (elaborar) arroz con pollo
    2. un _____ de guisantes congelados
    3. cuatro _____ de ajo
    4. una _____ de sal
    5. tres _____ de consomé de pollo

B Recordando detalles importantes Lee la receta una vez más.
Luego, sin consultar la receta, escribe una lista de todos los
ingredientes necesarios. Luego consulta la receta para verificar
si has omitido algo.

C Confirmando información Verifica. ¿Sí o no?

	sí	no
1. Se puede cocinar el arroz con pollo encima de la estufa.		
2. El arroz con pollo lleva muchas papas.		
3. Hay muchos mariscos en un arroz con pollo.		
4. El arroz se pone amarillo.		
5. El chorizo es un tipo de salchicha española.		

Antes de leer

A veces no podemos comer todo lo que está en nuestro plato. Lo que no comemos y dejamos en el plato son «las sobras». Piensa en unas recetas que tiene tu familia en que se usan las sobras.

Una receta para «la ropa vieja» ♻

Aquí tienes otra receta para un plato que es popular en muchas partes de Latinoamérica—sobre todo en Cuba. Se llama «ropa vieja»—un nombre divertido, ¿no? Se llama «ropa vieja» porque se puede elaborar con muchas sobras. Este plato tan conocido se originó en las islas Canarias.

Ropa vieja

Ingredientes

½ kg de carne (de ternera, bife) picada
1 cebolla
1 pimiento verde y un pimiento rojo
3 dientes de ajo
1 cucharadita de orégano

una pizca de pimienta
½ taza de tomate cocido (o enlatado)
3 cucharadas de aceite de oliva
½ taza de caldo (consomé de pollo)

Preparación o cocción

Corte los pimientos, las cebollas y los ajos en trocitos. Fría los pimientos, las cebollas y los ajos en el aceite de oliva con una pizca de pimienta y el orégano. Añada la carne picada y revuelva todos los ingredientes (unos dos minutos). Añada el caldo y cueza (cocine) a fuego mediano hasta que se evapore el caldo. Sirva con arroz blanco.

¿Comprendes?

VIDEO To learn more about a staple of Mexican cuisine, watch **Cultura en vivo.**

Escoge o completa.

1. La ropa vieja viene de _____.
   a. Latinoamérica
   b. Cuba
   c. las islas Canarias

2. Se llama «ropa vieja» porque se puede elaborar (hacer) con _____.
   a. ropa
   b. comida que queda
   c. ingredientes divertidos

3. _____ es una cantidad muy pequeña.

4. Hay que _____ los pimientos verdes y rojos, la cebolla y los dientes de ajo en trocitos.
   a. cortar
   b. picar
   c. freír

5. Dos especias que lleva el plato son _____ y _____.

6. Cueza los ingredientes hasta que se evapore _____.
   a. el aceite
   b. el tomate
   c. el caldo

7. La ropa vieja se sirve acompañada de
   a. caldo
   b. azafrán
   c. arroz blanco

8. Un amigo vegetariano comerá la ropa vieja si no pones _____.

Vocabulario

1 **Parea.**

1. hervir
2. freír
3. revolver
4. pelar
5. cortar en rebanadas
6. añadir

a. la salsa
b. el pan
c. las zanahorias
d. el agua
e. sal y pimienta
f. el pollo

 To review **Vocabulario,** turn to pages 4–5.

2 **Identifica.**

7.

8.

9.

10.

11.

12.

Gramática

3 **Completa.**

13–14. Él quiere que yo _____ y yo quiero que él _____. (hablar)

15–16. Tú quieres que nosotros lo _____ y nosotros queremos que tú lo _____. (leer)

17–18. Yo quiero que tú lo _____ y tú quieres que yo lo _____. (escribir)

19–20. Tú quieres que yo lo _____ y él quiere que tú lo _____. (hacer)

21–22. Nosotros queremos que ellos _____ y ellos quieren que nosotros _____. (ir)

To review **el subjuntivo,** turn to pages 8–9.

4 **Completa con el imperativo formal.**

23. _____ usted la comida. (preparar)

24. _____ usted la receta. (leer)

25. _____ usted la lata. (abrir)

26. _____ usted ahora. (salir)

27. Y _____ usted mañana. (regresar)

28. No me lo _____ usted. (decir)

29. No _____ usted más. (añadir)

To review **el imperativo formal,** turn to page 11.

5 **Escribe con el pronombre.**

30. Prepare usted *la ensalada.*

31. No prepare usted *el postre.*

32. Déme *las direcciones.*

6 **Escribe en la forma negativa.**

33. Luis, habla.

34. Jacinta, come más.

35. Carlos, levántate.

36. Teresa, ven.

To review **las formas negativas del imperativo familiar,** turn to page 13.

Cultura

7 **Contesta.**

37–40. ¿Cuáles son algunos ingredientes que lleva el arroz con pollo?

To review this cultural information, turn to page 16.

1 **Yo en la cocina**

✓ *Talk about cooking*

Habla con un(a) compañero(a) de clase. Dile si te gusta cocinar o no. Explícale por qué. Luego verifica si tu compañero(a) tiene las mismas opiniones que tú.

2 **Comidas étnicas**

✓ *Discuss and describe a restaurant and the food it serves*

¿Hay restaurantes étnicos, restaurantes que sirven comida de otras partes del mundo, en tu comunidad? Si hay, con un(a) compañero(a) preparen una lista de estos restaurantes y el tipo de comida que sirven. Luego describan un plato típico de uno de los restaurantes que les gusta.

3 **¡Qué comida más deliciosa!**

✓ *Describe a delicious meal*

Estás viajando por México. Anoche fuiste a cenar en un restaurante y pediste algo que salió delicioso, muy rico. Te gustó mucho. Llama a tus padres y descríbeles el restaurante y el plato que te gustó tanto. Si puedes, explícales como crees que el cocinero preparó el plato.

4 **Simón dice**

✓ *Give and receive commands*

Trabajen ustedes en grupos de cinco. Van a jugar «Simón dice». Cada líder dará cinco órdenes a todos los miembros del grupo y luego escogerá a otro líder.

CULTURA

La gente está sentada en la terraza de un café en Puebla, México.

5 **Mis padres**

✓ *Discuss what your parents want you to do*

Tus padres quieren que hagas muchas cosas, ¿no? Dile a un(a) compañero(a) todo lo que quieren tus padres que hagas. Tu compañero(a) te dirá si sus padres quieren que él o ella haga las mismas cosas.

Tarea

Your teacher wants to know the recipe for the warm quesadillas and chilled fresh tomato salsa that you brought to the last Spanish Club meeting. Use the ingredients listed below and additional vocabulary from the chapter to give your teacher instructions on how to make this delicious, easy-to-prepare Mexican snack.

Quesadillas	Salsa de tomate
unas tortillas de harina	tomates
queso triturado	pimientos verdes
(shredded cheese)	cebolla
aceite de oliva	chiles jalapeños
	ajo
	cilantro
	jugo de lima

Writing Strategy

Giving Instructions When giving instructions, it is important to present the details accurately, clearly, and in logical order. This is especially true when writing a recipe because directions that are incorrect, unclear, or out of order could cause the dish to taste bad or be ruined altogether.

❶ Prewrite

Make a list of the steps for completing the recipe and put them in chronological order. Also think about what utensils and/or appliances will be used, and remember that timing and presentation are very important. What should be prepared first? What should be prepared last? How will the dish be served?

❷ Write

- Use formal commands since this is a recipe for your teacher.
- Make sure all of the steps follow a logical order.
- Use transition words to help you present your information in an organized way.
- Remember to stick to vocabulary you already know and don't attempt to translate from English to Spanish.

Evaluate

Your teacher will evaluate you on accurate and logical presentation of details, correct use of vocabulary and grammar, and completeness of information.

Repaso del Capítulo 1

Gramática

- **El subjuntivo** *(pages 8–9)*

  The subjunctive expresses that which is not necessarily factual or real. It expresses things that might happen.

  El profesor quiere que los alumnos lean el libro.

  Review the following forms of the present subjunctive.

hablar	beber	escribir	poner
hable	beba	escriba	ponga
hables	bebas	escribas	pongas
hable	beba	escriba	ponga
hablemos	bebamos	escribamos	pongamos
habléis	*bebáis*	*escribáis*	*pongáis*
hablen	beban	escriban	pongan

  Review the following irregular verbs in the present subjunctive.

dar	estar	ir	saber	ser
dé	esté	vaya	sepa	sea
des	estés	vayas	sepas	seas
dé	esté	vaya	sepa	sea
demos	estemos	vayamos	sepamos	seamos
deis	*estéis*	*vayáis*	*sepáis*	*seáis*
den	estén	vayan	sepan	sean

- **El imperativo** *(pages 11 and 13)*

  The affirmative and negative formal commands and the negative familiar commands use the subjunctive form of the verb.

(no) mire usted	(no) miren ustedes	no mires
(no) coma usted	(no) coman ustedes	no comas
(no) asista usted	(no) asistan ustedes	no asistas
(no) salga usted	(no) salgan ustedes	no salgas
(no) vaya usted	(no) vayan ustedes	no vayas

  Object pronouns are attached to affirmative commands but must come before negative commands. Review the following sentences.

Mírelo.	No lo mire usted.	No lo mires.
Démelas.	No me las dé usted.	No me las des.
Levántenlas.	No las levanten ustedes.	No las levantes.

There are a number of cognates in this list. See how many you and a partner can find. Who can find the most? Compare your list with those of your classmates.

Vocabulario

Talking about some kitchen appliances and utensils

la cocina
el refrigerador,
  la nevera
el congelador
la estufa, la cocina

el horno
el horno de
  microondas
el lavaplatos
el/la sartén

la olla, la cacerola
la tapa
la cazuela
la parrilla

Talking about food preparation

la receta
el/la cocinero(a)
el sabor
pelar
picar

cortar
  en pedacitos
  en rebanadas
añadir
poner al fuego
cocinar, cocer
  a fuego lento

quemarse
hervir
freír
asar
revolver

Identifying more foods

la chuleta de cerdo
el escalope de
  ternera
el muslo de pollo
las alitas de pollo

la pechuga de pollo
la cebolla
la zanahoria
el pepino
el pimiento

el aguacate
el ajo
el condimento

Repaso cumulativo

Repasa lo que ya has aprendido

These activities will help you review and remember what you have learned so far in Spanish.

 Escucha las frases. Indica en una tabla como la de abajo si la información en cada frase es correcta o no.

sí	no

 Identifica.

1. todas las legumbres que ya conoces en español
2. todas las carnes que ya conoces en español
3. todo lo que necesitas para poner la mesa
4. la diferencia entre un desayuno continental y un desayuno americano

 Completa con el presente.

1. Yo _____ bife y Anita _____ pescado y nosotros dos _____ flan. (pedir)
2. Nosotros no nos _____. El mesero nos _____. (servir)
3. Yo _____ esto y él _____ el otro. Nosotros nunca _____ la misma cosa. (preferir)

 Describe las siguientes fiestas.

1. el Día de los Muertos
2. el Día de los Reyes
3. el Cuatro de Julio en Estados Unidos

 Completa con el imperativo.

1. José, _____ más. (comer)
2. Rosario, _____ el correo electrónico. (leer)
3. Manuel, _____ tu regalo. (abrir)
4. Adela, _____ acá. (venir)
5. Alberto, _____ pronto. (volver)
6. Federico, _____ la mesa. (poner)
7. Magda, _____ la verdad. (decir)
8. Gabriel, _____ la comida. (servir)

CULTURA

Una barbacoa para celebrar el 4 de Julio en Estados Unidos

6 Categoriza según el deporte.

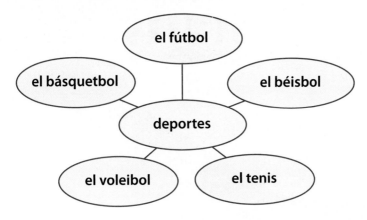

el fútbol

el básquetbol

el béisbol

deportes

el voleibol

el tenis

1. Un jugador lanza el balón y quiere que entre en la portería.

2. El portero no pudo bloquear el balón y el balón entró en la portería.

3. Un jugador corre de una base a otra.

4. Para marcar un tanto hay que meter el balón en el cesto.

5. El jugador corre y dribla con el balón.

6. La jugadora atrapa la pelota con el guante.

7. El balón o la pelota tiene que pasar por encima de la red.

8. Podemos jugar dobles o individuales.

9. Los jugadores juegan con un balón.

10. Los jugadores juegan con una pelota.

7 Usa las siguientes palabras en frases originales.

el campo   la cancha   el balón

la pelota   el segundo tiempo   marcar

el tanto   lanzar   devolver

CULTURA

Un mercado en Tepoztlán, México

8 Prepara una lista de lo que tienes que comprar para preparar un plato favorito. Da las cantidades también.

2

¡Cuídate bien!

Aquí y Allí

Vamos a comparar Hoy en día todos quieren cuidarse bien y mantenerse en forma. No importa que sea aquí en Estados Unidos o en España o Latinoamérica—todos van a un parque o gimnasio para hacer ejercicios. Pero, a veces, ¿qué tenemos? ¡Un accidente pequeño!

◀ **Esta joven se mantiene en forma corriendo delante del museo de Artes y Ciencias en Valencia, España.**

Objetivos

You will:

- identify more parts of the body
- talk about exercise
- talk about having a little accident and a trip to the emergency room
- discuss physical fitness

You will use:

- the subjunctive with impersonal expressions
- ojalá, quizás, tal vez
- the subjunctive of stem-changing verbs
- the comparison of like things

QuickPass

Go to glencoe.com
For: **Online book**
Web code: **ASD7844c2**

Introducción al tema
¡Cuídate bien!

Mira estas fotos para familiarizarte con el tema de este capítulo—cuídate bien. ¿Qué haces para cuidarte? ¿Hay algunas actividades que ves aquí que tú también practicas o que te gustan? Y, ¿puedes simpatizar con el joven ecuatoriano que ha tenido un accidente?

▲ **Chile** El joven anda en bici por las montañas. Nota que él también lleva casco. La seguridad siempre es importante, ¿no?

Ecuador Estos jóvenes van a jugar fútbol en un parque en Quito. ▼

▲ **Argentina** Mucha gente toma agua mineral porque la consideran buena para la salud.

◄ **México** La muchacha hace ejercicios en un gimnasio en la Ciudad de México.

▲ **España** El joven está practicando el monopatín en Barcelona. ¿Qué piensas? ¿Debe llevar casco?

▲ **Guatemala** Una ambulancia en Antigua, Guatemala

◀ **Ecuador** Uno de estos estudiantes de la Universidad Católica en Quito ha tenido un accidente y tiene que andar con muletas. Pero no es nada serio. No se ha hecho mucho daño.

▲ **México** Un hospital privado en Oaxaca, México

◀ **España** Esta familia en Barcelona patina en línea. Es un ejercicio bastante duro. Y nota que llevan casco para protegerse en caso de un accidente.

Más partes del cuerpo

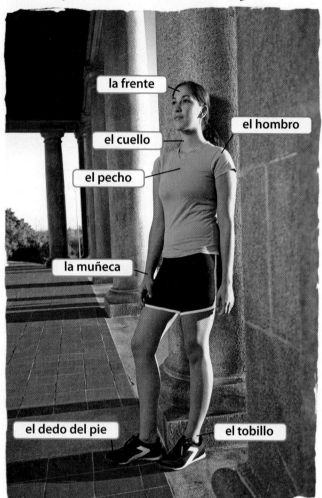

la frente

el cuello

el hombro

el pecho

la muñeca

el dedo del pie

el tobillo

Los amigos están practicando yoga.
Hacen ejercicios de respiración.
Hacen movimientos lentos.
Liberan su espíritu de tensiones.

En el gimnasio

estirarse los brazos

hacer planchas

levantar pesas

La muchacha está haciendo
 ejercicios.
El señor anda en bicicleta.
El muchacho levanta pesas.
Es necesario que él tenga
 cuidado.
Es importante que todos
 hagamos ejercicios.

el casco

las rodilleras

el monopatín

un buzo

descansar

hacer jogging

Las jóvenes están patinando
en línea.
Es importante que lleven
casco y rodilleras.

Los corredores participan en un maratón.

Están corriendo una carrera de relevos.
Cada corredora corre una vuelta.

Es una carrera a campo traviesa.
Una carrera a campo traviesa es de larga distancia.

QuickPass

Go to glencoe.com
For: **Vocabulary practice**
Web code: **ASD7844c2**

ESCUCHAR

 1 Escucha las frases. Parea cada frase con la foto que describe.

a. b. c.

ESCUCHAR • HABLAR

 2 Personaliza. Da respuestas personales.

1. ¿Haces muchos ejercicios?
2. ¿Haces ejercicios aeróbicos o abdominales?
3. ¿Te estiras los brazos y las piernas?
4. ¿Levantas pesas?
5. ¿Andas en bicicleta?
6. ¿Haces jogging?
7. ¿Participas en carreras?
8. ¿Corres vueltas?
9. ¿Practicas yoga?
10. ¿Has participado en un maratón?

LEER • ESCRIBIR

 3 Completa con una palabra apropiada.

1. Uno se pone _____ cuando va al gimnasio o cuando hace jogging.
2. Es importante ponerse _____ para proteger el cráneo al andar en bicicleta.
3. Es importante llevar _____ al patinar en línea.
4. ¿Cuántas _____ puedes correr sin descansar?
5. El yoga ayuda a liberar el espíritu de _____.
6. Muchas ciudades y organizaciones tienen _____ que son carreras de muy larga distancia.
7. Dos tipos de carreras son _____ y _____.

LEER • ESCRIBIR

 4 Pon las siguientes partes del cuerpo en orden desde la parte más alta del cuerpo hasta la más baja.

el pecho la mano el dedo del pie
la frente
el tobillo el cuello el hombro la rodilla

Conexiones

La anatomía
La anatomía es el estudio de la estructura del cuerpo de un ser viviente y de sus órganos. Ya sabemos las partes del cuerpo humano pero son aun más importantes los órganos vitales—el corazón, los pulmones, los riñones, el hígado y el páncreas.

Más practica

Workbook, pp. 2.3–2.5
StudentWorks™ Plus

HABLAR

5 Dramatiza. Trabajen en grupos. Escojan a un líder. El líder va a dramatizar un ejercicio o un deporte. Los otros miembros del grupo adivinarán la actividad. Cambien de líder.

HABLAR • ESCRIBIR

6 Usa las siguientes expresiones en frases originales.

hacer ejercicios	patinar en línea	hacer jogging
practicar yoga	correr vueltas	hacer planchas

CULTURA
Equipo para hacer ejercicios en un gimnasio en un hotel en Montelimar, Nicaragua

ESCRIBIR

7 Completa con lo que falta.

1. el cue_o
2. las rodi_eras
3. el tobi_o
4. el _imnasio

5. los _óvenes
6. un bu_o
7. el bra_o

Comunicación

8 Trabajen en grupos y discutan las actividades que practican en su clase de educación física. Indiquen las actividades que les gustan y que no les gustan. Expliquen por qué.

Unos accidentes

una herida

Pilar se cortó el dedo.
Tiene una herida.
Pero no es seria. No se ha hecho mucho daño.

José corría y se torció el tobillo.
El tobillo está hinchado.
Le duele mucho.

El joven se cayó.
¿Se rompió (Se quebró) la pierna?

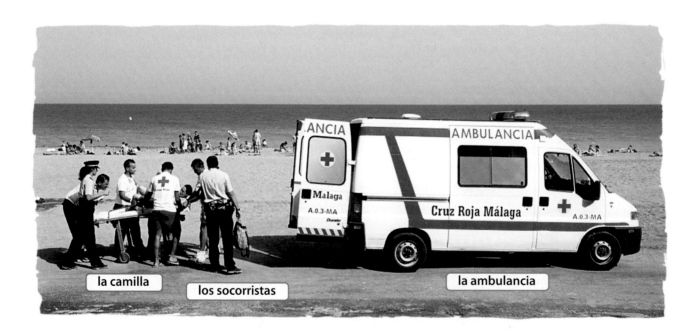

la camilla

los socorristas

la ambulancia

En la sala de emergencia

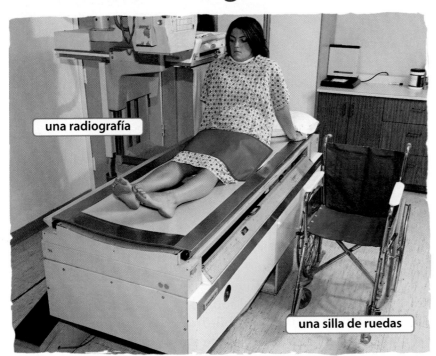

una radiografía

una silla de ruedas

Nota

In addition to **hacerse daño,** you will hear **lastimarse.** Another term for **radiografía** is **rayos equis.**

Le toman (hacen) una radiografía.

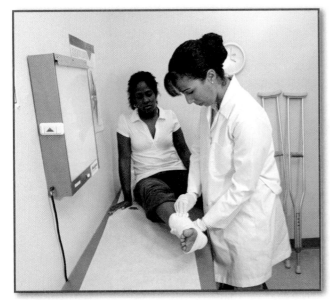

La cirujana ortopédica le ha reducido (acomodado) el hueso.
Le ha puesto la pierna en un yeso.
Paula tendrá que andar con muletas.

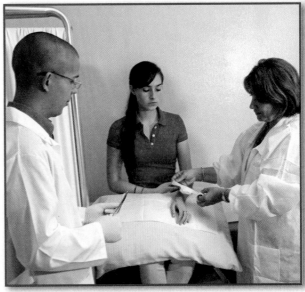

Es necesario que el médico cierre la herida.
El médico pone unos puntos (unas suturas).
La enfermera le va a poner una venda.

ESCUCHAR

 1 Escucha cada frase y decide si la información es correcta o no. Usa una tabla como la de abajo para indicar tus respuestas.

correcta	incorrecta

HABLAR • ESCRIBIR

 2 Contesta sobre un accidente que tuvo Mariana.

1. Mariana ha tenido un accidente. ¿Se cayó ella?
2. ¿Se torció el tobillo?
3. ¿Le duele mucho el tobillo?
4. ¿Está hinchado el tobillo?
5. ¿Le duele mucho cuando anda a pie?
6. ¿Tendrá que andar con muletas?
7. ¿Se ha hecho mucho daño o no?

EXPANSIÓN

Ahora, sin mirar las preguntas, cuenta la información en tus propias palabras. Si no recuerdas algo, un(a) compañero(a) te puede ayudar.

ESCUCHAR • HABLAR • ESCRIBIR

 3 Contesta según se indica.

1. ¿Qué tuvo Tomás? (un accidente serio)
2. ¿Qué le pasó? (se quebró la pierna)
3. ¿Qué le causó la pierna quebrada? (mucho dolor)
4. ¿Adónde fue? (a la sala de emergencia)
5. ¿Cómo fue? (en ambulancia)
6. ¿Quiénes lo ayudaron? (los socorristas)
7. ¿En qué lo pusieron? (una camilla)
8. ¿Qué le tomaron en el hospital? (radiografías)
9. ¿A qué médico llamaron? (al cirujano ortopédico)
10. Al salir del hospital, ¿qué necesitará Tomás? (una silla de ruedas)

EXPANSIÓN

Ahora, sin mirar las preguntas, cuenta la información en tus propias palabras. Si no recuerdas algo, un(a) compañero(a) te puede ayudar.

CULTURA

Un hospital grande y moderno en Barcelona, España

HABLAR • ESCRIBIR

④ Trabajen en grupos. Describan unas actividades que tienen lugar en esta sala de emergencia.

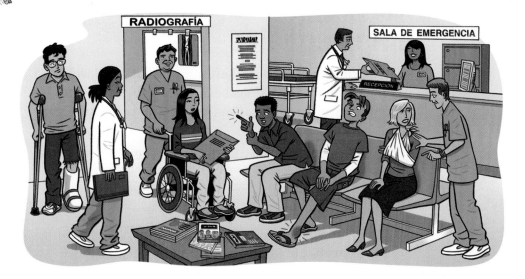

ESCRIBIR

⑤ Completa con lo que falta.

1. una _erida
2. un tobi_o _inchado
3. el _ospital
4. la cami_a y la si_a de ruedas
5. se ca_ó
6. el _eso
7. el _ueso
8. una _enda

CULTURA

Los socorristas ayudan a un herido en una ambulancia en Madrid.

ESCRIBIR

⑥ **Rompecabezas**

Pon las palabras en orden para formar frases. Luego, pon las frases en orden para crear una historia.

1. dijo no que le la necesitaba enfermera suturas
2. corrió la de cerca bicicleta perro muy un
3. calle la andaba por en Catalina bicicleta
4. de sala fue la a emergencia
5. rodilla enfermera venda la le en la puso una
6. ella perro a le cayó el se sorprendió y Catalina
7. rodilla cayó cortó se se la cuando

InfoGap For more practice with your new vocabulary, do Activity 2 on page SR3 at the end of this book.

Gramática

El subjuntivo con expresiones impersonales

The subjunctive is used after each of the following impersonal expressions because it is not known if the information in the clause that follows will actually take place. It may or may not.

es importante	es fácil
es necesario	es difícil
es imposible	es bueno
es posible	es probable
es mejor	es improbable

Es probable que él esté bien.
Pero es necesario que vea al médico.
Es importante que sepa lo que tiene.

Práctica

Papi corre en un maratón con sus dos niños en Tenerife en las islas Canarias. Es posible que ganen, ¿no?

ESCUCHAR • HABLAR • ESCRIBIR

1 Sigue el modelo.

MODELO **Tú haces ejercicios. →**
Es necesario que tú hagas ejercicios.

1. Hablas con el entrenador.
2. Vas al gimnasio.
3. Haces jogging.
4. Corres por lo menos cinco vueltas.
5. Participas en el maratón.

HABLAR • ESCRIBIR

2 Prepara una lista de cosas que es probable que tú hagas con frecuencia porque es fácil hacerlas. Prepara otra lista que indica lo que es difícil que tú hagas. Luego compara tus listas con las listas que ha preparado un(a) compañero(a).

LEER • ESCRIBIR

3 Sigue el modelo.

MODELO **es necesario / saber la receta →**
Es necesario que el cocinero sepa la receta.

1. es importante / lavar las ollas
2. es fácil / pelar las papas
3. es probable / freír el pescado
4. es mejor / asar el cordero
5. es posible / servir la comida

¿Es posible que el cocinero esté aprendiendo a cocinar algo en esta escuela culinaria en España?

HABLAR

4 Contesta.

1. ¿Es importante que los jóvenes de Estados Unidos estudien una lengua?
2. ¿Es necesario que ellos sepan hablar otra lengua?
3. ¿Es bueno que ellos hablen otra lengua?
4. ¿Es necesario que ellos conozcan otra cultura?
5. ¿Es posible que algún día ellos tengan la oportunidad de visitar otros países?
6. ¿Es probable que ellos vayan a otros países?

EXPANSIÓN

Ahora, sin mirar las preguntas, cuenta la información en tus propias palabras. Si no recuerdas algo, un(a) compañero(a) te puede ayudar.

LEER • ESCRIBIR

5 Completa.

Abuelito está un poco nervioso. Es posible que sus nietos __1__ (llegar) mañana por la mañana. Es importante que abuelito __2__ (saber) cuándo van a llegar. Pero es difícil que abuelita le __3__ (decir) la hora precisa de la llegada de los nietos. Es posible que mañana __4__ (hacer) mal tiempo. Como los nietos vienen en carro será necesario que __5__ (conducir) despacio y con mucho cuidado si hay nieve. Es mejor que ellos __6__ (llegar) un poco tarde. Abuelito no quiere que ellos __7__ (tener) un accidente. Es mejor que __8__ (llegar) tarde pero sanos y salvos.

FOLDABLES®
Study Organizer

TAB BOOK
See page SH24 for help with making this foldable. Use this study organizer to help you practice the subjunctive. On the top of each tab, write an expression that requires the subjunctive, for example **Es imposible que...** Then open each tab and write a sentence using that expression with the subjunctive.

Comunicación

6 Trabaja con un(a) compañero(a) de clase. Dile cosas que haces. Tu compañero(a) te dará su opinión sobre las cosas que haces usando las siguientes expresiones: **es importante, es bueno, es necesario, es mejor.**

¡Ojalá! ¡Quizás! ¡Tal vez!

The expression **¡Ojalá!** or **¡Ojalá que!** comes from Arabic and it means *Would that . . .* Since the information that follows **ojalá** may or may not happen, it is followed by the subjunctive. The expressions **¡Quizás!** and **¡Tal vez!** mean *perhaps* or *maybe* and can also be followed by the subjunctive.

> **¡Ojalá que vengan!**
> **¡Quizás lleguen mañana!**
> **¡Tal vez estén aquí!**

Práctica

ESCUCHAR • HABLAR

7 Contesta con **quizás** según el modelo.

MODELO ¿Carla lo va a saber? →
¡Quizás lo sepa!

1. ¿Carla va a estar aquí?
2. ¿Va a ir al parque?
3. ¿Va a participar en la carrera?
4. ¿Va a salir primero?
5. ¿Va a romper un récord?
6. ¿Va a ganar un trofeo?

LEER • ESCRIBIR

8 Sigue el modelo.

MODELO tener cuidado →
¡Ojalá que tengan cuidado!

1. prestar atención
2. no tomar una decisión ridícula
3. ponerse el casco
4. llevar rodilleras
5. no tener ningún accidente
6. no ir al hospital

CULTURA

Esta joven que anda con muletas acaba de salir de un centro médico en Trelew, Argentina. ¡Ojalá que se mejore pronto!

✿ Comunicación

9 Trabaja con un(a) compañero(a). Los dos van a hablar de eventos que quieren que ocurran durante su vida. Introduzcan sus ideas con **¡ojalá!**

Gramática

El subjuntivo de los verbos de cambio radical

1. Verbs that have a stem change in the present indicative also have a stem change in the present subjunctive.

E → IE			
cerrar			
yo	cierre	nosotros(as)	cerremos
tú	cierres	*vosotros(as)*	*cerréis*
Ud., él, ella	cierre	Uds., ellos, ellas	cierren

O → UE			
encontrar			
yo	encuentre	nosotros(as)	encontremos
tú	encuentres	*vosotros(as)*	*encontréis*
Ud., él, ella	encuentre	Uds., ellos, ellas	encuentren

> **Nota**
>
> - Other verbs with the **e → ie** stem change like **cerrar** are: **perder, sentarse, comenzar, empezar, pensar.**
> - Other **o → ue** verbs like **encontrar** are: **acostarse, recordar, poder, volver.**
> - **Sentir** is conjugated like **preferir.**
> - Other verbs with the **e → i** stem change like **pedir** are: **repetir, freír, seguir, servir.**

2. The verbs **preferir (e → ie), dormir (o → ue),** and **pedir (e → i)** have a stem change in every person of the present subjunctive.

	E → IE, I	O → UE, U	E → I
	preferir	**dormir**	**pedir**
yo	prefiera	duerma	pida
tú	prefieras	duermas	pidas
Ud., él, ella	prefiera	duerma	pida
nosotros(as)	prefiramos	durmamos	pidamos
vosotros(as)	*prefiráis*	*durmáis*	*pidáis*
Uds., ellos, ellas	prefieran	duerman	pidan

HABLAR • ESCRIBIR

10 Contesta.

1. ¿Dónde quieres que yo me siente?
2. ¿Es importante que yo no pierda el juego?
3. ¿Quieres que yo vuelva temprano?
4. ¿Es posible que yo duerma aquí?
5. ¿Es necesario que yo se lo repita?

Según los jóvenes, es importante que todos sigamos una dieta sana.

VIDEO Want help with the subjunctive? Watch **Gramática en vivo.**

Práctica

LEER • ESCRIBIR

11 Sigue el modelo.

MODELO **Quiere que tú lo cierres.** →
Quiere que nosotros lo cerremos.

1. Quiere que te sientes aquí.
2. Quiere que tú pierdas.
3. Quiere que tú lo encuentres.
4. Quiere que tú vuelvas pronto.
5. Quiere que duermas aquí.
6. Quiere que lo pidas.
7. Quiere que lo sigas.
8. Quiere que tú no lo repitas.

HABLAR • LEER • ESCRIBIR

12 Cambia el segundo verbo al verbo indicado.

1. Yo quiero que ellos lo cierren. (empezar, perder, encontrar, recordar, devolver, preferir, pedir, repetir)
2. Es posible que yo lo encuentre. (cerrar, perder, recordar, devolver, servir, pedir, repetir)
3. Es necesario que nosotros volvamos. (comenzar, sentarnos, recordar, dormir, seguir)

Comparación de igualdad

1. In Spanish you use **tanto… como** to compare quantities. Because **tanto** is an adjective, it has to agree with the noun it modifies.

> **Elena tiene tanta energía como yo.**
> **Pero ella no tiene tantos accidentes como yo.**

2. In Spanish you use **tan… como** to compare qualities with either an adjective or adverb.

> **Él está tan enfermo como su amiga.**
> **Él se va a curar tan rápido como ella.**

3. The subject pronoun always follows the comparison of equality.

> **Él es tan bueno como tú.**
> **Y tiene tanto dinero como yo.**

Conexiones

El inglés

To compare equal quantities in English you use:
> *as much money as I*
> *as many problems as I*

To compare equal qualities you use:
> *as smart as she*
> *as tall as he*

Práctica

HABLAR

13 Personaliza. Da respuestas personales.

1. ¿Eres tan inteligente como tus amigos?
2. ¿Eres tan cómico(a) como tus amigos?
3. ¿Eres tan ambicioso(a) como tus amigos?
4. ¿Eres tan aficionado(a) a los deportes como tus amigos?
5. ¿Tienes tanta paciencia como tus amigos?
6. ¿Tienes tanto éxito como tus amigos?
7. ¿Tienes tanto trabajo como tus amigos?
8. ¿Tienes tantas ambiciones como tus amigos?

LEER • ESCRIBIR

14 Completa con **tan** o **tanto como**.

1. Ella corre en _____ carreras _____ yo.
2. Y ella va _____ rápido _____ yo.
3. Él puede levantar _____ pesas _____ yo.
4. Pero él no es _____ fuerte _____ yo.
5. Yo no hago _____ ejercicios _____ tú.
6. Yo no soy _____ aficionado(a) a los ejercicios físicos _____ tú.

Refrán

Can you guess what the following proverb means?

La mejor almohada es la conciencia sana.

CULTURA

Un grupo de gente mayor (de la tercera edad) está jugando voleibol en un gimnasio en Oaxaca, México.

Comunicación

15 Trabaja con un(a) compañero(a). Piensen en algunas personas que ustedes conocen que, en su opinión, tienen mucho en común o que tienen las mismas características físicas. Comparen a estas personas.

¡Bravo!

You have now learned all the new vocabulary and grammar in this chapter. Continue to use and practice all that you know while learning more cultural information. ¡Vamos!

QuickPass

Go to glencoe.com
For: **Conversation practice**
Web code: **ASD7844c2**

UN ACCIDENTE

¿Comprendes?

VIDEO To see how one friend helps another after a skateboarding accident, watch **Diálogo en vivo.**

A Contesta según la información en la conversación.

1. ¿Qué hacía Enrique cuando se cayó?
2. ¿Qué le duele?
3. ¿Cómo está el tobillo?
4. ¿Qué crees? ¿Quiere Enrique que Catalina lo lleve a la sala de emergencia? ¿Le gusta la idea?
5. Según Catalina, ¿por qué debe ir Enrique a la sala de emergencia?
6. ¿Es posible que no tenga el tobillo quebrado?

B **Resumiendo** Cuenta todo lo que pasó en la conversación en tus propias palabras.

C **Prediciendo** Predice lo que va a pasar a Enrique y Catalina en la sala de emergencia. Prepara una conversación que tiene lugar en el hospital. Debes incluir a otros en la conversación como el médico o el enfermero. ¡Usa tanta imaginación posible!

Entrada a la sala de emergencias en un hospital en la Ciudad de Panamá

CULTURA

EMERGENCIAS →

HOSPITAL PUNTA PACIFICA
Afiliado a Johns Hopkins Medicine International

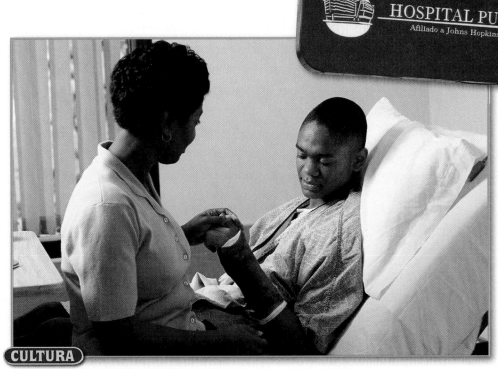

CULTURA

Es necesario que él se cuide bien.
Es posible que le duela mucho el brazo, ¿no?

Antes de leer

Dale una ojeada a la lectura y busca palabras que consideres desconocidas. No habrá muchas.

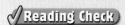
CULTURA

Están haciendo ejercicios aeróbicos en un gimnasio en Buenos Aires, Argentina.

✓ **Reading Check**

¿Qué hacen todos en el gimnasio?

Durante la lectura

Busca clarificaciones—si hay una palabra que no sabes, tal vez haya un sinónimo en la frase.

✓ **Reading Check**

¿Cuál es la ventaja de los parques?

Vida activa y buena salud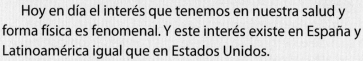

Hoy en día el interés que tenemos en nuestra salud y forma física es fenomenal. Y este interés existe en España y Latinoamérica igual que en Estados Unidos.

Como es importante que uno haga ejercicios a lo menos tres veces a la semana, hay una gran proliferación de gimnasios. Estos gimnasios tienen muchos socios[1]. En el gimnasio hacen ejercicios aeróbicos y abdominales. Se estiran los brazos y las piernas. Hacen planchas. Algunos levantan pesas. ¡Todo para mantenerse en forma!

Además de los gimnasios los parques son inmensamente populares, y para ir a un parque no hay que ser socio o miembro. Un parque es un buen lugar para hacer jogging o correr unas vueltas. A muchos les gusta dar un paseo por el parque en bicicleta. Andar en bicicleta es una forma excelente de ejercicio. Otros se sientan en un lugar aislado del parque donde disfrutan del silencio y de la tranquilidad. Se relajan practicando yoga y meditando.

[1]socios   *members*

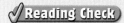
CULTURA

El ciclista está haciendo ejercicios en un parque en Viña del Mar, Chile.

Muchas ciudades tienen un maratón a lo menos una vez al año. Muchos maratones tienen un propósito benévolo[2] y atraen a muchos participantes. Además atraen a muchos espectadores que animan a los corredores que tienen que correr largas distancias.

Entre los jóvenes el patinaje en línea y el monopatín son muy apreciados. Tienen muchos aficionados. Pero, una advertencia[3]—al practicar estas formas de patinaje hay que tener mucho cuidado porque puedes lastimarte fácilmente. Siempre tienes que llevar casco y rodilleras. Nadie quiere que te hagas daño y que te encuentres en una sala de emergencia.

[2]propósito benévolo   *charitable purpose*   [3]advertencia   *warning*

¿Comprendes?

A **Categorizando** Completa la tabla según la información en la lectura.

actividades en un gimnasio	actividades en el parque	actividades durante un maratón	actividades populares entre los jóvenes

B **Personalizando** Contesta.

¿En qué actividades de la Actividad A participas? Explica por qué te gustan.

C **Analizando** Contesta.

¿Por qué son populares los gimnasios y los parques?

Más práctica

- Workbook, pp. 2.15–2.18
- StudentWorks™ Plus

✓ **Reading Check**

¿Quiénes animan a los corredores en el maratón?

✓ **Reading Check**

¿Qué hay que tener al practicar el patinaje o el monopatín? ¿Por qué?

Después de leer

Prepara una lista de palabras aparentadas que encontraste en la lectura.

CULTURA
Los jóvenes están patinando en línea en Barcelona, España.

Antes de leer

Piensa en unas organizaciones benévolas o caritativas donde vives. ¿Qué tipo de trabajo hacen? ¿Has oído de Médicos Sin Fronteras, una famosa organización internacional?

Médicos Sin Fronteras 🎧♻️

Hay gente que se cuida bien y también hay gente que cuida de otros como los Médicos Sin Fronteras. La organización Médicos Sin Fronteras tuvo su origen en Francia en 1971. Un grupo de médicos y periodistas franceses fueron a África con la Cruz Roja donde vieron morir a millones de biafranos[1] de guerra[2] y de hambre. Su situación fue tan desesperada que a su regreso a Francia este grupo de médicos creó una organización pequeña, *Médecins Sans Frontières*. Hoy es una organización internacional independiente con más de dos mil quinientos benévolos (voluntarios) presentes en más de setenta países, incluyendo unos en Latinoamérica. La organización tiene proyectos en zonas de guerra, campos de refugiados y en regiones devastadas por desastres naturales o epidemias de enfermedades como el sida[3].

Entre los benévolos hay médicos, cirujanos, enfermeros y técnicos. Hay también personas que se responsabilizan por los materiales que necesitan y la administración de los proyectos. Todos reciben muy poco dinero por el trabajo maravilloso que hacen.

En 1999 Médicos Sin Fronteras ganó el prestigioso Premio Nobel de la Paz.

[1]biafranos   *people from Biafra*   [3]sida   *AIDS*
[2]guerra   *war*

¿Comprendes?

Escoge.

1. Los Médicos Sin Fronteras _____.
   a. se cuidan bien
   b. cuidan de otros
   c. no tienen país
   d. son todos franceses

2. La organización Médicos Sin Fronteras tuvo su origen en _____.
   a. Francia
   b. Biafra, África
   c. la Cruz Roja
   d. una situación desesperada

3. ¿Quiénes establecieron la organización?
   a. miembros de la Cruz Roja
   b. un grupo internacional independiente
   c. un grupo de médicos y periodistas franceses
   d. un grupo de benévolos

4. Los biafranos morían _____.
   a. de un desastre natural
   b. de una epidemia
   c. de malnutrición y guerra
   d. a causa del calor

5. Por lo general, ¿quiénes toman refugio en los campos de refugiados?
   a. las víctimas de guerra
   b. los benévolos
   c. los enfermos
   d. los soldados

6. Los benévolos que trabajan con la organización _____.
   a. son todos personal médico
   b. tienen un salario
   c. reciben muy poco dinero
   d. viven de proyectos

CULTURA

Un médico de la organización Médicos Sin Fronteras da atención médica a una familia hondureña después de un huracán.

Vocabulario

1 **Identifica.**

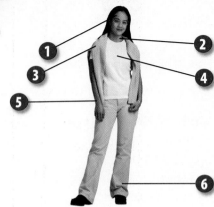

To review **Vocabulario 1,** turn to pages 32–33.

2 **Corrige.**

7. Es importante que uno lleve casco y rodilleras si levanta pesas.

8. A mucha gente le gusta andar en monopatín en el hospital.

9. Un maratón es una carrera de corta distancia.

10. Antes de correr, los corredores se estiran los dedos y los pies.

11. Cuando practicas yoga, haces muchas planchas.

3 **Identifica.**

12.

13.

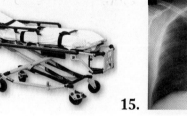

14.

15.

To review **Vocabulario 2,** turn to pages 36–37.

4 **Completa.**

16. El niño se _____ el tobillo y lo tiene muy hinchado.

17. Se _____ la pierna y el cirujano ortopédico la tiene que poner en un yeso.

18. Los socorristas pusieron a la víctima en una camilla y la llevaron al hospital en _____.

19. José necesita ayuda para andar. Anda con _____.

Gramática

5 **Completa.**

20. Es importante que nosotros _____ ejercicios. (hacer)
21. Es necesario que ellos nos _____. (acompañar)
22. Es posible que ella _____. (estar)
23. Es probable que yo _____. (ir)
24. Es imposible que tú lo _____. (saber)

To review **el subjuntivo con expresiones impersonales,** turn to page 40.

6 **Completa formando una frase.**

25. Es necesario que…
26. Es posible que…
27. Es difícil que…

7 **Completa.**

28. ¡Ojalá _____ su equipo! (ganar)
29. ¡Quizás _____ ellos! (venir)
30. ¡Tal vez _____ (ellos) en el gimnasio! (estar)
31. ¡Ojalá _____ (tú) los resultados mañana! (tener)

To review **ojalá, quizás, tal vez,** turn to page 42.

8 **Completa las frases con nosotros.**

32. Ellos quieren que tú se lo pidas a Javier.
    Ellos quieren que nosotros…
33. Ella quiere que yo me siente aquí.
    Ella quiere que nosotros…

To review **el subjuntivo de los verbos de cambio radical,** turn to page 43.

9 **Completa con tan… como o tanto… como.**

34. A veces los hospitales en las zonas rurales no son _____ buenos _____ los de las grandes ciudades.
35. Esta clínica es _____ moderna _____ la otra.
36. Ella tiene _____ paciencia _____ yo.
37. Yo hago _____ ejercicios _____ tú.

To review **la comparación de igualdad,** turn to page 44.

Cultura

10 **Contesta.**

38. ¿Por qué hay gimnasios que tienen muchos socios?
39. ¿Cuáles son algunas actividades atléticas que practica la gente en un parque?
40. ¿Qué propósito tienen muchos maratones?

To review this cultural information, turn to pages 48–49.

1 **Actividades atléticas**

✔ *Discuss which sports you play*

Trabajen en grupos de tres o cuatro. Discutan todas las actividades atléticas en que participan ustedes. Determinen si tienen los mismos intereses o no.

EL DEPORTE LE PIDE MINERALES A TU CUERPO.

Villavicencio. Tu vida necesita minerales.

2 **Peligros**

✔ *Talk about avoiding danger*

Las actividades atléticas pueden ser buenas para la salud pero cuando practicas ciertas actividades hay que tener cuidado de no lastimarte. ¿Cuáles son algunas cosas que debes hacer para evitar (no tener) accidentes?

3 **Un accidente**

✔ *Describe an accident you had when you were young*

Explica si tú eres propenso(a) a accidentes o si lo eras de niño(a). ¿Has tenido unos accidentes? Descríbelos. Si nunca has tenido un accidente explica como es posible que tengas tanta suerte.

4 **Importante y necesario**

✔ *Talk about what is important for you to do and what is necessary for you to do*

Completa una tabla como la de abajo y presenta la información a tu clase.

Es importante que yo	Y es necesario que yo
porque	

5 **En la sala de emergencia**

✔ *Helping someone out after an accident*

Estás en la sala de espera de la sala de emergencia en un hospital. Entran los padres con su hijo que ha tenido un accidente y se ha hecho daño. Los padres están nerviosos y solo hablan español. Ayúdalos.

Tarea

You have learned about many sports in Spanish. You have also learned about the parts of the body and physical fitness. Now you are going to write a research paper that discusses the physical benefits of some sports. Use the library and the Internet to find out more about how your body stays fit by doing each sport. Be sure to cite your sources.

Writing Strategy

Researching As you prepare to write your research paper, you will be consulting many sources for information. It is important that your sources be reliable, especially when they are found on the Internet. It is advisable to consult more than one source for any fact you present. If your two sources disagree, consult a third.

CULTURA

El andinista venezolano tiene todo el equipo necesario para escalar montañas.

❶ Prewrite

- Before you begin your research, create a rough outline of your paper. This will help you identify the topics you need to research.

	Título
	A. El fútbol
	1. ¿Cómo se mantiene uno en forma jugando fútbol?
	a.
	b.
	2. ¿Cuáles son algunas desventajas o peligros del fútbol?
	a.
	b.
	B. El jogging
	1. ¿Cómo se mantiene uno en forma haciendo jogging?

- As you research, fill the holes in your outline.

❷ Write

- Use your outline as a guide while you write. It will ensure your information is organized and that nothing is omitted.
- It is very important to cite the sources you used to obtain information. This will add validity to your paper and it will also ensure that you do not plagiarize.

Evaluate

Your teacher will evaluate you on organization of information, correctness of grammar, and proper citation.

Repaso del Capítulo 2

Gramática

- ### El subjuntivo con expresiones impersonales *(page 40)*
  The subjunctive is used after many impersonal expressions when it is not known if the information that follows will or will not take place.

    Es importante que tengas cuidado cuando levantas pesas.
    Es necesario que la niña lleve casco cuando anda en bicicleta.
    Es probable que ellos lleguen a tiempo.

- ### ¡Ojalá! ¡Quizás! ¡Tal vez! *(page 42)*
  The expressions **¡Ojalá!**, **¡Quizás!**, and **¡Tal vez!** are also followed by the subjunctive. Review the following sentences.

    ¡Ojalá no te hagas daño!
    Quizás vengan mañana.

- ### El subjuntivo de los verbos de cambio radical *(page 43)*
  Verbs that have a stem change in the present indicative also have a stem change in the present subjunctive.

cerrar		encontrar	
cierre	cerremos	encuentre	encontremos
cierres	*cerréis*	encuentres	*encontréis*
cierre	cierren	encuentre	encuentren

  Preferir and **sentir (e → ie, i), dormir (o → ue, u),** and **pedir, repetir, freír, seguir,** and **servir (e → i, i)** have a stem change in every person of the subjunctive. Review the following forms.

preferir		dormir		pedir	
prefiera	prefiramos	duerma	durmamos	pida	pidamos
prefieras	*prefiráis*	duermas	*durmáis*	pidas	*pidáis*
prefiera	prefieran	duerma	duerman	pida	pidan

- ### Comparación de igualdad *(page 44)*
  You use **tanto... como** to compare like quantities and **tan... como** to compare like qualities.

    Yo tengo tanta paciencia como mi padre.
    Anita hace tantos ejercicios como yo.

    La señora Mayo es tan simpática como la señora Hernández.
    Manolo corre tan rápido como tú.

CULTURA

Los jóvenes están haciendo jogging en Barcelona, España.

There are a number of cognates in this list. See how many you and a partner can find. Who can find the most? Compare your list with those of your classmates.

Vocabulario

Identifying more parts of the body

la frente	el hombro	la muñeca	el dedo del pie
el cuello	el pecho	el tobillo	

Talking about physical fitness

el gimnasio	las pesas	una carrera	estirarse
el buzo	el movimiento	de relevos	patinar
el casco	la respiración	a campo traviesa	en línea
las rodilleras	el monopatín	de larga distancia	practicar yoga
los ejercicios	el jogging	una vuelta	descansar
las planchas	el/la corredor(a)	un maratón	liberar

Talking about an accident

una herida	cortarse	caerse	doler
hinchado(a)	torcerse	romperse, quebrarse	hacerse daño

Talking about medical emergencies and a hospital

la ambulancia	la sala de	la silla de ruedas
el/la socorrista	emergencia	andar con muletas
la camilla		

Talking about medical care

el/la cirujano(a) ortopédico(a)	una radiografía	los puntos, las suturas	reducir, acomodar
el/la enfermero(a)	un yeso	una venda	
	un hueso		

Other useful words and expressions

el espíritu	lento(a)
la tensión	

Repaso cumulativo

Repasa lo que ya has aprendido

These activities will help you review and remember what you have learned so far in Spanish.

 1 Escucha las frases. Indica en una tabla como la de abajo a quien habla el joven en cada frase.

a un(a) amigo(a)	a su profesor(a)	a sus padres

 2 Sigue el modelo.

MODELO   —Son mis zapatos nuevos.
             —¿Quién te los compró?

1. Es mi cámara nueva.
2. Es mi casco nuevo.
3. Son mis gafas nuevas.
4. Son mis esquís nuevos.
5. Son mis botas nuevas.

 3 Completa con los pronombres.

1. Yo le di los CDs a Anita.
   Yo _____ di a ella.
2. Carlos le devolvió el dinero a Juan.
   Carlos _____ devolvió a él.
3. Sara le dio las direcciones a usted.
   Sara _____ dio.
4. Yo le leí la receta a Susana.
   Yo _____ leí a ella.
5. Yo no le preparé la comida.
   Yo no _____ preparé.

4 Completa cada serie de frases en el presente, el pretérito y el imperfecto.

hablar

1. a. Yo _____ con Juan todos los días.

   b. Yo _____ con Juan ayer.

   c. Yo _____ mucho con Juan cuando éramos niños.

vender

2. a. Mi padre _____ carros.

   b. Ayer él _____ dos.

   c. Pero cuando yo era niño él no _____ carros.

escribir

3. a. Ahora nosotros le _____ un correo electrónico todos los días.

   b. Nosotros le _____ un correo electrónico el otro día.

   c. Nosotros le _____ correos electrónicos casi a diario cuando estaba en España.

hacer

4. a. No lo _____ yo.

   b. No lo _____ yo ayer.

   c. Yo no lo _____ nunca.

poner

5. a. ¿Por qué no _____ (tú) las maletas en la maletera?

   b. ¿Por qué no _____ (tú) las maletas en la maletera cuando fuiste al aeropuerto?

   c. Cada vez que hacías un viaje _____ las maletas en la maletera.

decir

6. a. Yo siempre _____ la verdad.

   b. Yo no te _____ una mentira. Fue la verdad.

   c. Yo nunca _____ mentiras—siempre la verdad.

poder

7. a. Ellos _____ hacerlo ahora.

   b. Ellos intentaron pero no _____ hacerlo.

   c. Ellos _____ hacerlo cuando eran más jóvenes.

CULTURA

El señor compraba el periódico cada día en el mismo quiosco en Buenos Aires, Argentina.

Pasajes de la vida

Vamos a comparar En todas las sociedades y culturas hay ceremonias y fiestas que acompañan los eventos importantes en la vida de una persona. Piensa en las ceremonias y fiestas que celebran tu familia y las familias de tus amigos.

Objetivos

You will:

- talk about passages of life: weddings, baptisms, birthdays, and funerals
- read a poem by the Peruvian writer Abraham Valdelomar

You will use:

- the subjunctive to express wishes
- the subjunctive to express emotions
- possessive pronouns

Los recién casados salen de la iglesia después de la ceremonia nupcial en Málaga, España.

QuickPass

Go to glencoe.com
For: **Online book**
Web code: **ASD7844c3**

Introducción al tema
Pasajes de la vida

Los pasajes de la vida son los eventos importantes que tienen lugar en la vida de todos nosotros desde el momento de nuestro nacimiento hasta la muerte. En este capítulo tendrás la oportunidad de observar unos de los ritos que acompañan los pasajes de la vida en las sociedades latinas.

◀ **México**
Es una máscara o disfraz que se lleva durante las celebraciones para el Día de los Muertos en varios países latinos—sobre todo en México.

Estados Unidos
Una gran fiesta siempre acompaña el día que una muchacha latina cumple sus quince años. Esta quinceañera elegante celebra la ocasión rodeada de sus amigos y familiares en Miami. ▶

Costa Rica No hay duda que Abuelito adora a su nieta recién nacida. ▼

▲ **República Dominicana** Esta quinceañera dominicana entra en la iglesia al brazo de su hermano. Además de una fiesta, un rito religioso puede acompañar las celebraciones.

◀ **España** Un amigo saca una fotografía de los novios en los jardines del Alcázar de los Reyes Cristianos en Córdoba.

▲ **México** El cura bautiza al bebé en una iglesia de la Ciudad de México.

◀ **España** A veces el novio español le da a la novia flores del naranjo que, según tradición, les traerán mucha felicidad.

▲ **México** La pareja llega para la ceremonia nupcial en Pátzcuaro.

▲ **Argentina** Es la placa en la tumba de Eva Perón en el cementerio de la Recoleta en Buenos Aires.

Puerto Rico Es el cementerio de San Juan en el Viejo San Juan. En el fondo se puede ver la fortaleza del Morro. En las tumbas se ven muchas ofrendas de flores. ▼

EVA PERON

1952 - 26 DE JULIO - 1952
SUS DISCIPULAS

El matrimonio

La pareja se casa.
La ceremonia tiene lugar en la iglesia.
No le sorprende a nadie que ellos se casen.
Todos sus amigos esperan que pasen muchos años juntos.
Y todos quieren que sean felices.

Nota

- Another commonly used word for **anillo** is **sortija.**
- **El novio/La novia** can mean both *fiancé (fiancée)* and *groom/bride.* **Los novios** are the bride and groom.
- **El padrino** can mean *godfather* as well as *best man.*

Durante la ceremonia nupcial, el novio y la novia intercambian los anillos de boda.

el ayuntamiento

la alcaldesa

el registro de matrimonio

REGISTRO CIVIL

Esta pareja se casa por (el, lo) civil.
Se casan en el ayuntamiento.
La alcaldesa los casa.

Durante la ceremonia civil es necesario
que los novios firmen el registro de
matrimonio.

La recepción

¡Enhorabuena!

el anuncio nupcial

Ana Cristina y Anton

UNIÉNDONOS CON AMOR Y POR SIEMPRE CON
LA BENDICIÓN DE NUESTROS PADRES

Delia Aurora Aparicio de Lois
Carlos Estuardo Lois Rosado

Elena Marisol Gutiérrez de Ochoa
César David Ochoa Hernández

DESEAMOS COMPARTIR EL MOMENTO EN QUE
REAFIRMAREMOS NUESTRO AMOR INVITÁNDOLES A LA
CEREMONIA RELIGIOSA QUE SE REALIZARÁ EL DÍA VIERNES 25
DE MAYO A LAS 7.30 DE LA NOCHE EN LA IGLESIA
SAN FRANCISCO DE ASÍS CASTILLA 842 - SAN MIGUEL

SEVILLA, MAYO

AL CULMINAR LA CEREMONIA
LES ESPERAMOS EN LOS SALONES
DE LA VICARIA.

Hay una recepción en honor de los novios (recién casados).
Hay una cena (un banquete, un bufé).
Los novios reciben muchos regalos.

ESCUCHAR

1 Escucha. Escoge la frase correcta. Usa una tabla como la de abajo para indicar tus respuestas.

a	b

HABLAR • ESCRIBIR

2 Personaliza. Da respuestas personales.

1. ¿Has asistido una vez a una boda?
2. ¿Quiénes se casaron?
3. ¿Cómo se vistió la novia?
4. ¿Fue una ceremonia religiosa o civil?
5. ¿Dónde tuvo lugar la boda?
6. ¿Quiénes fueron el padrino y la dama de honor?
7. ¿Había un banquete?
8. ¿Fuiste a la recepción?

EXPANSIÓN

Ahora, sin mirar las preguntas, cuenta la información en tus propias palabras. Si no recuerdas algo, un(a) compañero(a) te puede ayudar.

LEER • HABLAR

3 Con un(a) compañero(a) de clase, mira el anuncio nupcial. Hablen juntos haciendo y contestando preguntas sobre la información en el anuncio.

Ana Cristina
y Antonio

UNIÉNDONOS CON AMOR Y POR SIEMPRE CON
LA BENDICIÓN DE NUESTROS PADRES

Delia Aurora Aparicio de Lois
Carlos Estuardo Lois Rosado

Elena Marisol Gutiérrez de Ochoa
César David Ochoa Hernández

DESEAMOS COMPARTIR EL MOMENTO EN QUE
REAFIRMAREMOS NUESTRO AMOR INVITÁNDOLES A LA
CEREMONIA RELIGIOSA QUE SE REALIZARÁ EL DÍA VIERNES 25
DE MAYO A LAS 7.30 DE LA NOCHE EN LA IGLESIA
SAN FRANCISCO DE ASÍS CASTILLA 842 - SAN MIGUEL.

SEVILLA, MAYO

AL CULMINAR LA CEREMONIA
LES ESPERAMOS EN LOS SALONES
DE LA VICARIA.

CULTURA

Los recién casados salen de la iglesia en Madrid y van a su recepción en una limusina antigua.

LEER • ESCRIBIR

4 Completa con una palabra apropiada.

1. Una boda religiosa tiene lugar en una _____ o un templo.
2. Una _____ suele llevar un velo.
3. Un novio y una novia forman una _____.
4. Una boda civil tiene lugar en el _____.
5. En los países hispanos, el _____ casa a una pareja en una ceremonia civil.
6. Durante la ceremonia civil los novios tienen que _____ el registro nupcial.
7. Después de la ceremonia nupcial hay una _____.

✿ Comunicación

5 En tus propias palabras describe una boda a la que asististe.

FOLDABLES®
Study Organizer

POCKET BOOK
See page SH23 for help with making this foldable. Use this foldable to categorize the vocabulary and information you have learned that is related to passages of life. Make a pocket book for each passage of life that you study. Each time you read something about a passage of life, make a card and file it in the appropriate pocket book.

Estudio de palabras

casarse Ellos van a casarse en junio.

el casamiento El casamiento tendrá lugar en la iglesia.

los casados Los recién casados están muy contentos.

alegrarse Ellos se alegran de ver a todos sus amigos.

alegre Todos están muy alegres (contentos).

la alegría Hay mucha alegría.

Escribe con el contrario.
1. Ellos *se entristecen*.
2. Todos están *tristes*.
3. Se ve que hay mucha *tristeza*.
4. Ellos van a *divorciarse*.
5. No sé cuándo tendrá lugar *el divorcio*.
6. Sé que los recién *divorciados* están contentos.

CULTURA

Los recién casados con sus familiares y amigos delante de la catedral en Jerez de la Frontera en España

El bautizo

El cura bautiza al recién nacido.

El cumpleaños

Anita nació el ocho de noviembre.
Hoy cumple dieciséis años.
Ella está contenta que todas sus amigas vengan
 a celebrar su cumpleaños con ella.
Se alegra de que todas ellas se diviertan.

El velorio

una esquela

Ha fallecido el señor

José Hernández

Falleció el día lunes 29-10. Su viuda, María Eugenia; sus hijas: Eugenia, Saeli; su yerno, Miguel González; su nieto, Mikel; su hermano, Constantino y señora; sus cuñados, sobrinos, demás familiares y amigos, invitan al acto del sepelio que se efectuará hoy a las 4:00 pm, en el Cementerio del Este.

El cortejo fúnebre partirá desde la Capilla CENTRAL de Funeraria Vallés.

Caracas, 30 de septiembre

el ataúd

Los amigos y familiares del difunto asisten al velorio.

El cementerio, El camposanto

la viuda del difunto

El cortejo fúnebre llega al cementerio.
El entierro tiene lugar en el cementerio.

Nota

- **El entierro** is often referred to as **el sepelio.** The corresponding verbs are **enterrar** and **sepultar.**
- The most common term is **la esquela** but you will also see and hear **el obituario.**

QuickPass

Go to glencoe.com
For: **Vocabulary practice**
Web code: **ASD7844c3**

ESCUCHAR

1 Escucha y determina si la información que oyes es correcta o no. Usa una tabla como la de abajo para indicar tus respuestas.

correcta	incorrecta

ESCUCHAR • HABLAR • ESCRIBIR

2   Personaliza. Da respuestas personales.

1. ¿Cuándo es tu cumpleaños?
2. ¿Cuándo naciste?
3. ¿Te preparan un pastel para tu cumpleaños?
4. ¿Cuántas velas habrá en tu próximo pastel?
5. ¿Te darán una fiesta para tu cumpleaños?
6. ¿Quiénes asistirán a la fiesta?
7. ¿Recibirás muchos regalos?
8. ¿Cuántos años cumplirás?

EXPANSIÓN

Ahora, sin mirar las preguntas, cuenta la información en tus propias palabras. Si no recuerdas algo, un(a) compañero(a) te puede ayudar.

LEER • ESCRIBIR

3 Da otra palabra o expresión que significa la misma cosa.

1. un pastel
2. alegre
3. el obituario
4. el cementerio
5. el entierro
6. un cadáver, una persona muerta

Misa y Agradecimiento

Con motivo de cumplirse Diez y Ocho años de la partida de nuestra amada e inolvidable

JULIA MARÍA HERNÁNDEZ
(Q.E.P.D.)

Sus familiares Victor Lucena, sus hijas Cristina, Eucari, Miligros, Gregoria; sus nietos, bisnietos y amigos invitan para compartir su recuerdo a las misas de los días 9 de Noviembre y 10 de Noviembre a las 6:00 p.m. en la Iglesia de Nuestra Señora de la Chiquinquirá, Av. Andrés Bello, La Florida.

Caracas, 9 de Noviembre

 Comunidades

4   En un grupo hagan una encuesta sobre los diferentes ritos que acompañan los pasajes de la vida de los miembros de su comunidad. ¿Varían los ritos o celebraciones según la etnia de las personas? ¿Son muchos de índole religiosa? Preparen una lista de las celebraciones y el (los) grupo(s) que las celebra(n). Presenten sus resultados a la clase.

LEER • ESCRIBIR

5 Completa con una palabra apropiada.

1. El _____ bautiza al recién _____ en la _____.
2. El agua está en una _____.
3. Los _____ están presentes durante el bautizo.
4. Se le murió el esposo. Ella es _____.
5. Antes de ir al cementerio, los amigos y familiares del _____ asisten al velorio.
6. El _____ fúnebre llega al cementerio para el sepelio.
7. La novia lleva un traje de novia y un _____.
8. Hay _____ en un pastel de cumpleaños.

GeoVistas

To learn more about Chile, take a tour on pages SH52–SH53.

CULTURA

El camposanto en el desierto de Atacama en Poconchile, Chile

ESCRIBIR

6 Completa con la letra que falta.

1. el cemente__io
2. el velo__io
3. el entie__o
4. el obitua__io
5. el cu__a
6. la __ecepción
7. la pa__eja
8. ¡Enho__abuena!
9. la ce__emonia
10. lo entie__an en un ataúd

 Comunicación

7 Con un(a) compañero(a) de clase hablen juntos haciendo y contestando preguntas sobre la información en la esquela.

Ha fallecido el señor

José Hernández

Falleció el día lunes 29-10. Su viuda, María Eugenia; sus hijas: Eugenia, Saeli; su yerno, Miguel González; su nieto, Mikel; su herma Constantino y señora; sus cuñados, sobri demás familiares y amigos, invitan al acto sepelio que se efectuará hoy a las 4:00 pm en el Cementerio del Este.

El cortejo fúnebre partirá desde la Capilla CENTRAL de Funeraria Vallés.

Caracas, 30 de septiembre

QuickPass

Go to glencoe.com
For: **Grammar practice**
Web code: **ASD7844c3**

El subjuntivo con deseos

Conexiones

El inglés

The subjunctive is now rarely used in English. With many of these expressions, however, many speakers of English continue to use the subjunctive.

They insist that he do it.
I prefer that she know.

1. You already know that the subjunctive is used in a clause that follows the verb **querer** because even though someone wants another person to do something, it is not certain that he or she will really do it. The information in the clause is not factual. It may or may not happen and for this reason you must use the subjunctive.

> **Quiero que mis amigos vayan a la fiesta.**

2. For the same reason, the subjunctive is used in clauses introduced by each of the following expressions, since the information in the dependent clause is not definite.

desear	mandar *(to order)*
esperar	temer *(to fear)*
preferir	tener miedo de
insistir en	

> **Espero que no lleguen tarde.**
> **¿Insistes en que yo se lo diga?**
> **Tengo miedo de que él no me haga caso**
> **(que no me preste atención).**

Quiero que mi amigo suba conmigo en esta montaña rusa en el parque de atracciones en el Bosque de Chapultepec en México. Espero que no tenga miedo pero la verdad es que temo que le dé miedo.

Práctica

ESCUCHAR • HABLAR

1 Conversa con un(a) compañero(a) según el modelo.

MODELO ¿Hacerlo? →
—¿Quién? ¿Yo?
—Sí, él prefiere que tú lo hagas.

1. ¿Aceptar la invitación?
2. ¿Asistir a la ceremonia?
3. ¿Comprar el regalo?
4. ¿Ir con él?
5. ¿No decir nada a nadie?

El escaparate de una tienda para novias en Barcelona, España

HABLAR • ESCRIBIR

2 Imagina que tienes unos amigos que se van a casar. Contesta.

1. ¿Prefieres que ellos se casen?
2. ¿Esperas que ellos sean felices?
3. ¿Deseas que te inviten a la boda?
4. ¿Deseas que ellos tengan una vida larga juntos?
5. ¿Temes que sea posible que tengan algunos problemas?

 Comunicación

3 Con un(a) compañero(a), discutan lo que ustedes quieren que sus amigos hagan y lo que prefieren que no hagan.

HABLAR • ESCRIBIR

4 Personaliza. Da respuestas personales.

1. ¿Insiste el/la profesor(a) en que ustedes le presten atención?
2. ¿Insiste en que ustedes escuchen cuando él/ella habla?
3. ¿Insiste en que ustedes hagan sus tareas?
4. ¿Insiste en que ustedes sepan las reglas de gramática?
5. ¿Insiste en que ustedes lleguen a clase a tiempo?

LEER • ESCRIBIR

5 Completa con la forma apropiada del verbo.

Yo no sé lo que vamos a hacer esta noche. Pablo quiere que nosotros __1__ (ir) al cine. Él insiste en que nosotros __2__ (ver) la película en el cine Apolo. Carlota teme que mañana __3__ (ser) el último día. Tiene miedo de que ellos __4__ (cambiar) las películas los sábados. Y tú, ¿quieres que nosotros __5__ (ir) al cine o que __6__ (hacer) otra cosa? ¿Qué me dices? Que Felipe quiere que ustedes __7__ (quedarse) en casa. ¿Por qué? Ah, él quiere que todo el grupo __8__ (ir) a su casa. Él prefiere que nosotros __9__ (escuchar) música y que __10__ (bailar). ¡Buena idea!

CARTELERA DE CINE

AMOR CIEGO
(Todo público)

San Pedro 5	2-4:30-6:45-9:15 p.m.	*¢1.100 **¢600
Internacional 3	2-4:30-6:45-9:15 p. m	*¢1.100 **¢600
Cariari 6	2-4:30-6:45-7-9:15 p.m.	*¢1.100 **¢600
Cinemark	1:20-4:05-7:20-9:55 p.m.	*¢1.300 **¢1.000

LOS OTROS
(May. de 16 años)

San Pedro 4	2-4-7-9 p.m.	*¢1.100 **¢600

MONSTER, INC
(Todo público)

San Pedro 2	9 p.m. (inglés)	*¢1.200 **¢600
San Pedro 2	1:15-3:10-5:05-7 p.m.	*¢1.200 **¢600
Internacional 2	11:25-3:20-5:15-7:10-9:05 p.m.	*¢1.100 **¢600
Cariari 5	1:25-3:20-5:15-7:10-9:05 p.m.	*¢1.100 **¢600
Cinemark	1:25-3:40-6:45-9 p.m.	*¢1.300 **¢1.000
Cinemark	2-4:15 p.m. (inglés)	*¢1.300 **¢1.000

Comunicación

6 Trabaja con un(a) compañero(a). Cada uno(a) de ustedes va a preparar una lista de características que ustedes quieren, prefieren o esperan que tenga su mejor amigo(a). Luego comparen sus listas y determinen las características que ustedes dos buscan en su mejor amigo(a).

El subjuntivo con expresiones de emoción

1. The subjunctive is used in a clause that is introduced by a verb or expression that conveys an emotion. Study the following sentences.

> **Me alegro de que él esté.**
> **Pero siento que su hermano no pueda asistir.**

One can argue that the information in the clause is factual. Such may be the case. Why then is the subjunctive used? It is used because the information in the clause is very subjective. I may be happy that he is here, but someone else may not be. I am sorry that his brother cannot attend, but someone else may be glad.

2. The following are verbs and expressions that convey emotion. They are all followed by the subjunctive.

alegrarse de	gustar
estar contento(a), triste	sentir
sorprender	ser una lástima (pena)

InfoGap For more practice with the subjunctive used to express wishes and emotions, do Activity 3 on page SR4 at the end of this book.

Práctica

ESCUCHAR • HABLAR • ESCRIBIR

7 Contesta según se indica sobre una boda.

1. ¿Te sorprende que ellos se casen? (sí)
2. ¿Le sorprende a Elena que ellos se casen? (no)
3. ¿Te sorprende que ellos te inviten a la boda? (sí)
4. ¿Le sorprende a Elena que ellos la inviten a la fiesta? (no)
5. ¿Estás contento(a) que José reciba una invitación? (sí)
6. ¿Está contenta Julia que él reciba una invitación? (no)
7. ¿Siente Julia que José asista a la fiesta? (no)

HABLAR • ESCRIBIR

8 Completa.

1. Me alegro de que ellos...
2. Sentimos mucho que...
3. Es una pena que...
4. ¿Te sorprende que...
5. Ellos están contentos que...
6. Me gusta que...

CULTURA

La señorita se va a casar y entra en la iglesia al brazo de su padre en Ajijic, México.

Comunicación

9 Trabaja con un(a) compañero(a). Van a hablar de su escuela y de su vida escolar. Es cierto que en la escuela hay cosas que les ponen contentos y hay otras cosas que les ponen tristes. Al hablar de su vida escolar usen las expresiones **Me alegro de que, Siento que, Estoy contento(a) que, Estoy triste que** y den sus opiniones.

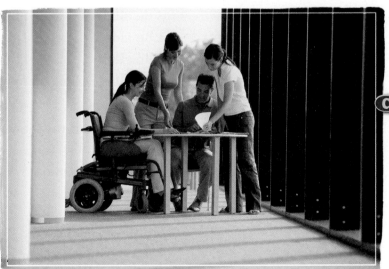

CULTURA

¡Qué pena! Es una lástima que los amigos tengan que pasar el fin de semana estudiando. Pero me sorprende que estén tan alegres.

Los pronombres posesivos

1. A possessive pronoun replaces a noun that is modified by a possessive adjective.

> mi carro → el mío
> mi casa → la mía
> mis amigos → los míos

Note that the possessive pronoun must agree in number and gender with the noun it replaces. Possessive pronouns are accompanied by definite articles.

2. Study the following.

> POSSESSIVE PRONOUNS
>
> el mío, la mía, los míos, las mías
> el tuyo, la tuya, los tuyos, las tuyas
> el nuestro, la nuestra, los nuestros, las nuestras
> *el vuestro, la vuestra, los vuestros, las vuestras*
> el suyo, la suya, los suyos, las suyas
>
> Yo tengo mis regalos, no los tuyos.
> Y él tiene sus regalos, no los nuestros.

3. Since the forms of **el suyo** can refer to so many different people, the meaning of **el suyo** is not always clear.

> Elena tiene el suyo.   *Elena has hers.*
> Elena tiene el de él.   *Elena has his.*

Whenever it is unclear to whom the possessive pronoun refers, a prepositional phrase replaces it for clarification.

EL SUYO	LA SUYA	LOS SUYOS	LAS SUYAS
el de Ud.	la de Ud.	los de Ud.	las de Ud.
el de él	la de él	los de él	las de él
el de ella	la de ella	los de ella	las de ella
el de Uds.	la de Uds.	los de Uds.	las de Uds.
el de ellos	la de ellos	los de ellos	las de ellos
el de ellas	la de ellas	los de ellas	las de ellas

4. Note that the definite article is often omitted after the verb **ser**. The article can be used, however, for emphasis.

> Estos libros son de Marta. Son suyos. No son míos.
> Estos son los míos y aquellos son los tuyos.

CULTURA

Les sorprende a la joven y a su amigo que haya una mesa libre en el café.

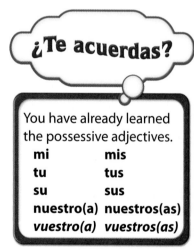

¿Te acuerdas?

You have already learned the possessive adjectives.

mi	mis
tu	tus
su	sus
nuestro(a)	nuestros(as)
vuestro(a)	*vuestros(as)*

Práctica

ESCUCHAR • HABLAR

10 Practica con un(a) compañero(a) según el modelo.

MODELO   mi casa y tu casa →
          la mía y la tuya

1. mi carro y tu carro
2. mi maleta y la maleta de Enrique
3. tu boleto y mis boletos
4. la lista de Elena y tu lista
5. nuestras ideas y las ideas de ustedes
6. mis profesores y los profesores de mi hermano

ESCUCHAR • HABLAR • ESCRIBIR

11 Sigue el modelo.

MODELO   ¿Tienes tu boleto? →
          ¡Ojalá tenga el mío!

1. ¿Tienes tu carro?
2. ¿Tienes nuestras maletas?
3. ¿Tienes tu pasaporte?
4. ¿Tienes mi pasaporte también?
5. ¿Tienes la dirección de Elena?
6. ¿Tienes el número del móvil de José?

LEER • ESCRIBIR

12 Emplea el pronombre posesivo en cada frase.

1. *Mi dama de honor* fue mi madre y *la dama de honor de Alicia* fue su mejor amiga.
2. *Mi ceremonia* tuvo lugar en la iglesia y *tu ceremonia* tuvo lugar en el ayuntamiento.
3. *Nuestra recepción* fue en un salón de banquetes y *la recepción de María y Carlos* fue en un restaurante.
4. *Tu cumpleaños* es el doce y *mi cumpleaños* es el trece del mismo mes.

Refrán

Can you guess what the following proverb means?

El casado casa quiere.

¡Bravo!

You have now learned all the new vocabulary and grammar in this chapter. Continue to use and practice all that you know while learning more cultural information. ¡Vamos!

CULTURA

El joven lleva a los perros a pasear por un parque en Buenos Aires. Todos estos perros no son suyos. Son de sus clientes.

¿Habrá una boda?

Adela	¿Te sorprende que se casen Cecilia y Enrique?
Carolina	De ninguna manera. Ya hace mucho tiempo que están saliendo juntos.
Adela	Hacen una buena pareja. Espero que sean felices y que tengan una buena vida.
Carolina	Yo también. Cecilia quiere que yo la ayude a escoger su traje de novia.
Adela	No compré el mío. Cuando me casé llevé el de mi mamá. A propósito, ¿vas a ser la dama de honor?
Carolina	No lo creo. Cecilia quiere que su madre sirva de dama de honor.
Adela	¿Cuándo será la boda? ¿Han fijado una fecha?
Carolina	¡Por supuesto! Dentro de poco van a enviar las invitaciones.

¿Comprendes?

VIDEO To view a family planning a wedding, watch **Diálogo en vivo.**

A Identifica quien lo dice.

	Adela	Carolina
1. Es posible que le sorprenda que Cecilia y Enrique se casen.		
2. No le sorprende que Cecilia y Enrique se casen.		
3. Va a ayudar a Cecilia a escoger su traje de novia.		
4. No compró un traje de novia. Llevó el de su madre.		
5. Cecilia quiere que su madre sea la dama de honor.		
6. La pareja va a enviar las invitaciones dentro de poco.		

B Contesta.

1. ¿Por qué no le sorprende a Carolina que Cecilia y Enrique se casen?
2. ¿Qué esperan Adela y Carolina?
3. ¿Qué quiere Cecilia que haga Carolina?
4. ¿Por qué no compró un traje de novia Adela?
5. ¿Quién va a servir de dama de honor en la boda?
6. ¿Han fijado los novios una fecha para la boda?

C Resumiendo Con un(a) compañero(a) de clase discutan lo que aprendieron de la boda de Cecilia y Enrique según la conversación de Adela y Carolina.

Fidel Antonio Sánchez Rodríguez
María Eugenia Acosta Ardila

Filadelfo García Martínez
María del Refugio Martínez Lara

María Carolina y Alonso

Participan el enlace matrimonial de sus hijos y tienen el honor de invitarles a la ceremonia religiosa que se celebrará el día 22 de diciembre del presente en punto de las 18:30 horas, en la Capilla de Nuestra Señora del Rosario, Templo de Santo Domingo ubicada en calle 5 de Mayo y 4 Poniente, Centro Histórico

Puebla, Pue. Diciembre de 2012.

Celebraciones y ritos de pasaje 🎧♻

Antes de leer

Piensa en celebraciones y ritos de pasaje en tu familia. ¿Cómo celebra tu familia? ¿Cuáles son algunas tradiciones o costumbres típicas?

✓ Reading Check

¿Qué tipo de relación existe entre los padrinos y la familia del bebé?

Los pasajes de la vida empiezan con el nacimiento y terminan con la muerte o el fallecimiento de la persona. Casi todos los pasajes de la vida van acompañados de una ceremonia y en muchas ocasiones de una celebración. La mayoría de las ceremonias son de índole[1] religiosa.

El bautizo En los países hispanos donde la tradición católica es bastante fuerte, la primera ceremonia o rito de pasaje es el bautizo. Antes del bautizo los padres del bebé escogen a miembros de la familia o amigos íntimos para servir de padrinos. Una relación casi parentesca existe entre los padrinos y la familia del bebé. Esta relación empieza con la ceremonia del bautizo y perdura durante toda la vida. Se espera que los padrinos puedan ayudar a su ahijado(a) en el futuro y si es necesario sustituir a los padres naturales en el caso de la muerte, por ejemplo.

[1]índole   *kind, sort*

CULTURA
El cura bautiza al bebé en una iglesia en México. Los padres y los padrinos están muy orgullosos.

Otros ritos A los seis o siete años de edad el niño o la niña católica recibe su primera comunión. Tanto para los católicos como para los protestantes la confirmación tiene lugar entre los doce y catorce años. Un joven judío recibe su bar mitzvah a los trece años. Para la muchacha es el bat mitzvah o el bas mitzvah. Una fiesta o cena suele² seguir cada una de estas ceremonias religiosas.

✓ **Reading Check**

¿Qué se recibe a los trece años?

CULTURA
Un joven judío recibe su bar mitzvah en una sinagoga en la Ciudad de México. Durante la ceremonia lee del *Torá*.

CULTURA
Esta niña va a recibir su primera comunión.

El matrimonio La edad legal para contraer matrimonio varía de un país a otro. Hoy en día en España y Latinoamérica las parejas no se están casando tan jóvenes como antes. Los novios pueden casarse por la Iglesia o por (el, lo) civil. En algunos países el matrimonio civil es obligatorio. Durante la ceremonia civil en el ayuntamiento, los novios, acompañados de los testigos³, tienen que firmar el registro nupcial. La ceremonia religiosa puede tener lugar el mismo día o uno o dos días después. Para la ceremonia religiosa los convidados (invitados) toman sus asientos en la iglesia donde esperan la llegada de la novia que entra al brazo de su padre. La procesión nupcial consiste en la dama de honor, el padrino y los pajes. No siempre, pero en muchas ocasiones, la madre de la novia sirve de dama de honor y el padre del novio sirve de padrino. Los pajes suelen ser niños—en muchas ocasiones sobrinos de los novios. Durante la ceremonia los novios intercambian alianzas (anillos de matrimonio).

²suele *tends to*   ³testigos *witnesses*

✓ **Reading Check**

Típicamente, ¿quiénes sirven de dama de honor y padrino?

Después de la ceremonia hay una recepción con una gran cena o bufé. Todos los invitados bailan al ritmo de una orquesta o al son de un DJ. Todos los presentes les dan la enhorabuena a los recién casados.

El joven baila con su madre durante la recepción que sigue la ceremonia nupcial en Panamá.

Siguen los pasajes. Los hijos tienen hijos. Los nietos crecen[4]. Hay aniversarios de boda—bodas de plata y bodas de oro. Y un día llega el último pasaje—la muerte.

El sepelio En los países hispanos el velorio en casa era tradicional, con el cuerpo presente. Hoy en día el velorio en casa es menos frecuente. En el caso de un difunto católico hay una misa en la iglesia. Después de la misa los amigos y parientes del difunto forman un cortejo para ir al cementerio donde se efectúa el entierro o el sepelio—frecuentemente en la tumba familiar. Se publica una esquela en el periódico avisando del fallecimiento del difunto.

[4]crecen *grow up*

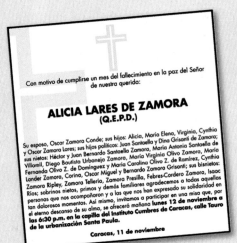

Con motivo de cumplirse un mes del fallecimiento en la paz del Señor de nuestra querida:

ALICIA LARES DE ZAMORA
(Q.E.P.D.)

Su esposo, Oscar Zamora Conde; sus hijos: Alicia, María Elena, Virginia, Cynthia y Oscar Zamora Lares; sus hijos políticos: Juan Santaella y Dina Grisanti de Zamora; sus nietos: Héctor y Juan Bernardo Santaella Zamora, María Antonia Santaella de Villamil, Diego Bautista Urbaneja Zamora, María Virginia Olivo Zamora, María Fernanda Olivo Z. de Domínguez y María Carolina Olivo Z. de Ramírez, Cynthia Lander Zamora, Corina, Oscar Miguel y Bernardo Zamora Grisanti; sus bisnietos: Zamora Ripley, Zamora Tellería, Zamora Presilla, Febres-Cordero Zamora, Isaac Ríos; sobrinos nietos, primos y demás familiares agradecemos a todas aquellas personas que nos acompañaron y a las que nos han expresado su solidaridad en tan dolorosos momentos. Así mismo, invitamos a participar en una misa que, por el eterno descanso de su alma, se ofrecerá mañana **lunes 12 de noviembre a las 6:30 p.m. en la capilla del Instituto Cumbres de Caracas, calle Tauro de la urbanización Santa Paula.**

Caracas, 11 de noviembre

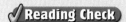 **Reading Check**

¿Qué hacen los amigos y parientes del difunto después de la misa?

¿Comprendes?

A Confirmando información Corrige las frases erróneas.

1. Los pasajes de la vida empiezan con la muerte y terminan con el nacimiento.
2. Un rito o ceremonia acompaña casi todos los pasajes de la vida.
3. Hay muy poca tradición católica en los países hispanos.
4. El bautizo es una ceremonia para el recién casado.
5. Los padres del bebé escogen a los padrinos después del bautizo.

B Analizando Analiza la importancia de los padrinos en la vida del recién nacido.

C Recordando hechos Contesta.

1. ¿Cuál es la edad legal para contraer matrimonio en los países hispanos?
2. ¿Se casan muy jóvenes los españoles y latinoamericanos?
3. ¿Cómo pueden casarse las parejas?
4. ¿Dónde tiene lugar la ceremonia religiosa?
5. ¿Dónde tiene lugar la ceremonia civil?
6. ¿Con quién entra en la iglesia la novia?
7. Con frecuencia, ¿a quién escoge la novia como dama de honor?
8. ¿A quién escoge el novio como padrino?
9. ¿Quiénes suelen ser los pajes?
10. ¿Qué intercambian los novios durante la ceremonia nupcial?

D Comparando y contrastando Compara unas costumbres tradicionales hispanas sobre las bodas con las costumbres de tu familia.

E Organizando Pon las siguientes oraciones en el orden apropiado.

1. El cortejo fúnebre sale para el camposanto.
2. A veces hay un velorio con el cuerpo presente.
3. El sepelio tiene lugar en el camposanto.
4. Según la tradición católica, hay una misa en la iglesia.

VIDEO To visit a famous cemetery in Argentina, watch **Cultura en vivo.**

CULTURA

Un camposanto en la Ciudad de Guatemala

Cultura

Aquí vemos una boda que tiene lugar en México. Como en muchas bodas latinas, los pajes son sobrinos de los novios. Un grupo de mariachis están ayudando a los novios a celebrar después de la ceremonia nupcial.

Literatura

El hermano ausente en la cena de Pascua

de Abraham Valdelomar

▲ Ayacucho, Perú, ciudad en que murió Abraham Valdelomar en 1919

Vocabulario

el afán un deseo fuerte

el pincel un instrumento que se usa para pintar

la miel una sustancia dulce del néctar de las flores

la criada una persona que hace tareas domésticas por un salario

musitar murmurar

antaño de tiempos pasados

vacío(a) no ocupado, libre

acaso quizás

Práctica

Completa con una palabra apropiada.

1. No hay nada en el vaso. Está _____.
2. Tengo mucho _____ de ayudar a los menos afortunados.
3. Mucha gente pone _____ en su té en vez de azúcar.
4. El artista que pinta usa un _____.
5. _____ limpia la casa y recibe un sueldo.
6. No son cosas de hoy. Son cosas de _____.
7. No oigo bien lo que dice porque siempre _____.

INTRODUCCIÓN

Abraham Valdelomar (1888–1919) nació en Ica, Perú y murió en Ayacucho. Escribió cuentos regionales y poesías. Uno de los temas favoritos de su poesía es la vida familiar.

La laguna de Huacachina en Ica, Perú, ciudad natal de Abraham Valdelomar

El hermano ausente en la cena de Pascua 🎧

La misma mesa antigua y holgada[1], de nogal[2]
y sobre ella la misma blancura del mantel
y los cuadros de caza[3] de anónimo pincel
y la oscura alacena[4], todo, todo está igual...

5 Hay un sitio vacío en la mesa hacia el cual
mi madre tiende a veces su mirada de miel
y se musita el nombre del ausente; pero él
hoy no vendrá a sentarse en la mesa pascual.

La misma criada pone, sin dejarse sentir,
10 la suculenta vianda[5] y el plácido manjar[6]
pero no hay la alegría ni el afán de reír[7]

que animaran antaño la cena familiar;
y mi madre que acaso algo quiere decir,
ve el lugar del ausente y se pone a llorar.

[1] holgada *cómoda*
[2] nogal *tipo de madera*
[3] caza *hunting*
[4] alacena *cupboard*

[5] vianda *comida*
[6] manjar *meal*
[7] reír *laugh*

Antes de leer

Reflexiona sobre el amor que tiene una madre por su hijo(a). No hay amor más sincero que el amor maternal. Piensa en lo que le trae mucha felicidad a la madre. Piensa también en lo que le puede traer tristeza y pena.

Durante la lectura

¿Qué información te da el título del poema? ¿Qué tendrá que ver con el estado de ánimo de la madre?

Después de leer

Forma tus opiniones sobre las razones del estado de ánimo de la madre.

CULTURA

Un comedor en una casa de Perú

¿Comprendes?

A **Parafraseando** ¿Cómo lo dice el poeta?

1. La misma mesa vieja y cómoda, de madera
2. y sobre la mesa el mismo mantel blanco
3. y las pinturas de caza de un artista desconocido
4. mi madre fija de vez en cuando su mirada dulce
5. pero no hay la felicidad ni el fuerte deseo de reír

B **Describiendo** Describe el comedor de la familia.

C **Recordando hechos** Contesta.

1. ¿Qué hay en la mesa?
2. ¿Quién mira hacia el sitio vacío?
3. ¿Qué se musita?
4. ¿Vendrá él hoy?

D **Explicando** Contesta.

¿Por qué es tan diferente esta cena familiar de las de antaño?

E **Llegando a conclusiones** Contesta.

¿Dónde estará el hermano ausente?

CULTURA

¿Es en esta casa que vive la familia que celebra la cena de Pascua?

Vocabulario

1 **Completa con la palabra apropiada.**

1. Muchos trajes de novia tienen _____.
2. La novia y el novio son una _____.
3. Ellos quieren una ceremonia religiosa y van a casarse en la _____.
4. Durante la ceremonia nupcial los novios intercambian _____ de boda.
5. Una ceremonia civil tiene lugar en el _____.
6. Después de la ceremonia nupcial hay una _____.
7. Todos les dicen «_____» a los recién casados.
8. Durante la recepción hay un _____.
9. Un recién nacido católico recibe el _____.
10. El _____ bautiza al niño.
11. El _____ fúnebre va de la iglesia al cementerio.
12. El _____ tiene lugar en el cementerio.

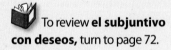 To review **Vocabulario 1** and **Vocabulario 2,** turn to pages 64–65 and 68–69.

Gramática

2 **Sigue el modelo.**

MODELO   desear / hacerlo →
         Deseo que tú lo hagas.

13. esperar / saberlo
14. preferir / tenerlo
15. insistir en / leerlo
16. temer / recordarlo
17. tener miedo de / perderte

To review **el subjuntivo con deseos,** turn to page 72.

3 **Completa con la forma apropiada del verbo.**

18. El profesor insiste en que nosotros _____. (aprender)
19. Yo espero que ustedes _____ buenos resultados. (tener)
20. Ellos desean que nosotros _____ felices. (ser)
21. Él prefiere que tú _____ conmigo. (ir)
22. Tememos que ellos _____ enfermos. (estar)

4 **Completa las siguientes frases.**

23. Me sorprende que tú _____.

24. Ellos se alegran de que nosotros _____.

25. Yo siento que ellos _____.

26. Ella está contenta que tú _____.

27. Es una lástima que yo _____.

To review **el subjuntivo con expresiones de emoción,** turn to page 74.

5 **Emplea el pronombre posesivo apropiado.**

28–29. *Mi carro* es nuevo y *tu carro* es viejo.

30–31. *Nuestros amigos* pueden asistir pero *los amigos de José* no quieren asistir.

32–33. Yo he recibido *mi invitación.* ¿Has recibido *tu invitación*?

34–35. Tenemos *nuestros regalos* pero no tenemos *los regalos de ustedes.*

To review **los pronombres posesivos,** turn to page 76.

Cultura

6 **Corrige las frases falsas.**

36. La mayoría de las celebraciones o ritos que marcan los pasajes de la vida son de índole civil.

37. El bautizo es una ceremonia hebrea y el bat mitzvah es una ceremonia cristiana.

38. La edad legal para contraer matrimonio es la misma en todos los países hispanos.

To review this cultural information, turn to pages 80–82.

7 **Contesta.**

39. En los países hispanos ¿dónde se casan muchas parejas?

40. ¿Cuál es el último pasaje de la vida?

BODA CAMPESTRE

CON DOS "COHETONES" ANUNCIAN LA SALIDA DE LA IGLESIA.
DELANTE VA EL CURA, SIGUE EL ALCALDE LE DEZMA,

1 **Una boda**

✓ *Discuss weddings you have attended*

Trabaja con un(a) compañero(a). Cada uno(a) de ustedes va a describir una boda a la que has asistido. Luego comparen las dos bodas. ¿Había algunas diferencias entre las dos? ¿Cuáles eran las diferencias?

2 **Mi boda**

✓ *Talk about the type of wedding you prefer*

¿Has pensado alguna vez en tu boda? ¿Qué tipo de boda quieres tener? ¿Prefieres una gala o algo sencillo?

3 **Pasajes de la vida**

✓ *Discuss passages of life*

Con un grupo de compañeros, discute los ritos o ceremonias de pasajes de vida que ustedes han experimentado. ¿Han tenido experiencias diferentes? ¿Juega la religión un papel (rol) importante en estas ceremonias? ¿Juega su ascendencia cultural o étnica un papel en las ceremonias?

4 **Una fiesta**

✓ *Describe a celebration*

Describe tu fiesta favorita. ¿Qué celebra o conmemora? ¿Cuáles son algunas cosas que hacen los invitados durante la fiesta? ¿Hay ciertas costumbres tradicionales? ¿Cuáles son? ¿Son étnicas o religiosas?

5 **Los deseos de mis padres**

✓ *Discuss what your parents want you to do*

Trabajen en grupos de cuatro y discutan lo que desean sus padres que ustedes hagan. Comparen los resultados y determinen si sus padres tienen los mismos deseos.

CULTURA

Decoraciones de Navidad en Madrid

Tarea

In as much detail as possible, describe either your dream wedding or your ideal eighteenth birthday party. In addition to describing the scene, you should also discuss your hopes and wishes as well as your emotions. Your goal will be to create a description that is so vivid that the reader feels as if he or she is present at the event.

Writing Strategy

Visualizing A vivid description should draw the reader into the writer's world. In order to recreate this world, you must first have an image of it in your head. Before you begin to write, take some time to imagine the picture you want to capture and relay to the reader.

Close your eyes and visualize the scene that you will translate into words. Think about everything that your senses might perceive during this special occasion in your life.

- Who will be there and why? What are they wearing, saying, and doing?
- What emotions are you feeling and why?
- What is the atmosphere like? How does the scene appear and what is the mood?
- What is happening? How do you react, respond, or feel as a result of your surroundings?
- What do you hope will happen? Who do you hope will be there? What do you wish to occur?

❶ Prewrite

First use the diagram to help you decide what you would like to include in your description. Then, as you consider the different aspects of your description, think of more specific questions, such as:

❷ Write

- Set the stage by identifying the event and describing the scene that surrounds it.
- Write about the event in chronological order, focusing on those aspects that will interest the reader.
- Remember to incorporate new vocabulary that you have learned from the chapter.
- Be sure to show your understanding of the use of the subjunctive to express wishes and emotions.

Evaluate

Your teacher will evaluate you on your ability to write a vivid description as well as on the correct use of vocabulary and grammar.

Repaso del Capítulo 3

Gramática

- ### El subjuntivo con deseos *(page 72)*

  The subjunctive is used in clauses introduced by each of the following expressions, since the information in the dependent clause is not definite.

desear	mandar
esperar	temer
preferir	tener miedo de
insistir en	

  Espero que no lleguen tarde.

- ### El subjuntivo con expresiones de emoción *(page 74)*

  The subjunctive is used in a clause that is introduced by a verb or expression that conveys an emotion.

  Me alegro de que él esté.

  The following are verbs and expressions that convey emotion.

alegrarse de	gustar
estar contento(a), triste	sentir
sorprender	ser una lástima (pena)

- ### Los pronombres posesivos *(page 76)*

  A possessive pronoun replaces a noun modified by a possessive adjective. As with any pronoun, it must agree in number and gender with the noun it modifies.

  el mío, la mía, los míos, las mías
  el tuyo, la tuya, los tuyos, las tuyas
  el nuestro, la nuestra, los nuestros, las nuestras
  el vuestro, la vuestra, los vuestros, las vuestras
  el suyo, la suya, los suyos, las suyas

Estas jóvenes chilenas están contentas que no haya más clases hoy y que puedan disfrutar de un rato libre.

Vocabulario

Talking about a wedding

la ceremonia	la iglesia	el/la recién casado(a)	el velo
el anuncio nupcial	el cura	la dama de honor	el anillo de boda
el matrimonio, el casamiento	la novia	el padrino	casarse
	el novio	el paje	
la boda	la pareja	el traje de novia	

Talking about a civil ceremony

la ceremonia civil	el ayuntamiento	firmar
el registro de matrimonio	el alcalde, la alcaldesa	por (el, lo) civil

Talking about a wedding reception

una recepción	un banquete, un bufé	un regalo	¡Enhorabuena!
una cena		en honor de	

Talking about a baptism

el bautizo	el padrino	la pila
el recién nacido	la madrina	bautizar

Talking about a birthday party

el cumpleaños	el bizcocho	la vela	cumplir… años
el pastel	la torta, la tarta	nacer	celebrar

Talking about a funeral

una esquela, un obituario	el ataúd	el cementerio, el camposanto	el entierro, el sepelio
el velorio	la viuda del difunto	el cortejo fúnebre	

Other useful words and expressions

los pasajes de la vida	alegre	esperar
la alegría	alegrarse	intercambiar
	sorprender	tener lugar

The words listed below come from this chapter's literary selection, *El hermano ausente en la cena de Pascua*. They were selected to become part of your active vocabulary because of their relatively high frequency.

el afán	la criada	vacío(a)
el pincel	musitar	acaso
la miel	antaño	

Repaso cumulativo

Repasa lo que ya has aprendido

These activities will help you review and remember
what you have learned so far in Spanish.

1 Escucha las frases. Indica si cada frase es correcta según
lo que ves en el dibujo.

La familia López

Ana Antonio
Carlos
Marisa
Juan
Maja
Elisa
Chispa

2 Completa con el adjetivo posesivo.

1. El otro hijo de mi padre es ____ hermano.
2. El hermano de mi padre es ____ tío y ____ hijos
   son ____ primos.
3. El esposo de mi tía Sandra es Alejandro. ____
   esposo es ____ tío.
4. ¿Quieres que yo vaya a ____ casa esta tarde?
   ¿Dónde está ____ casa? Es necesario que tú me
   dés el número de ____ móvil.
5. Nosotros vivimos en San Luis. ____ casa tiene dos
   pisos y alrededor de ____ casa tenemos un jardín.
   ____ jardín es muy bonito.
6. Susana va a visitar a ____ abuelos. ____ abuelos
   viven bastante lejos de aquí y siempre están
   contentos de ver a ____ querida nieta.

3 Contesta.
Dentro de poco tu familia va a comer. Una tarea tuya es la
de poner la mesa. ¿Qué vas a poner en la mesa?

4 Completa con el mandato de tú.

1. ____ más. (comer)
2. ____ la sal. (pasar)
3. ____ el postre. (servir)
4. ____ la mesa. (poner)
5. ____ conmigo a la cocina. (venir)
6. ____ los platos. (lavar)
7. ____ la mesa. (limpiar)

Pon las frases de la Actividad 4 en la forma negativa.

 Cambia a la forma negativa.

1. Levántate.
2. Acuéstate.
3. Háblame.
4. Dámelo.
5. Pásamelo.
6. Dímelo.

 Prepara una lista de ingredientes que lleva el arroz con pollo.

 Personaliza. Da respuestas personales.

1. ¿Has estado en la Florida?
2. Si has estado en la Florida, ¿qué ciudades has visitado en este estado?
3. Si no has estado en la Florida, ¿cuál es otro estado que has visitado?
4. ¿Has conocido a mucha gente?
5. ¿Has vuelto a visitar a tus amigos?

Escoge del banco de palabras y completa.

| abierto | vuelto | dicho |
| hecho | puesto | visto |

1. Nosotros hemos _____ el viaje.
2. ¿Quién ha _____ la puerta?
3. ¿Dónde has _____ los boletos?
4. Ellos no han _____.
5. Yo he _____ la exposición en el museo.
6. ¿Quién te ha _____ tal cosa?

CULTURA
La Plaza Mayor en el Viejo Madrid

Quehaceres

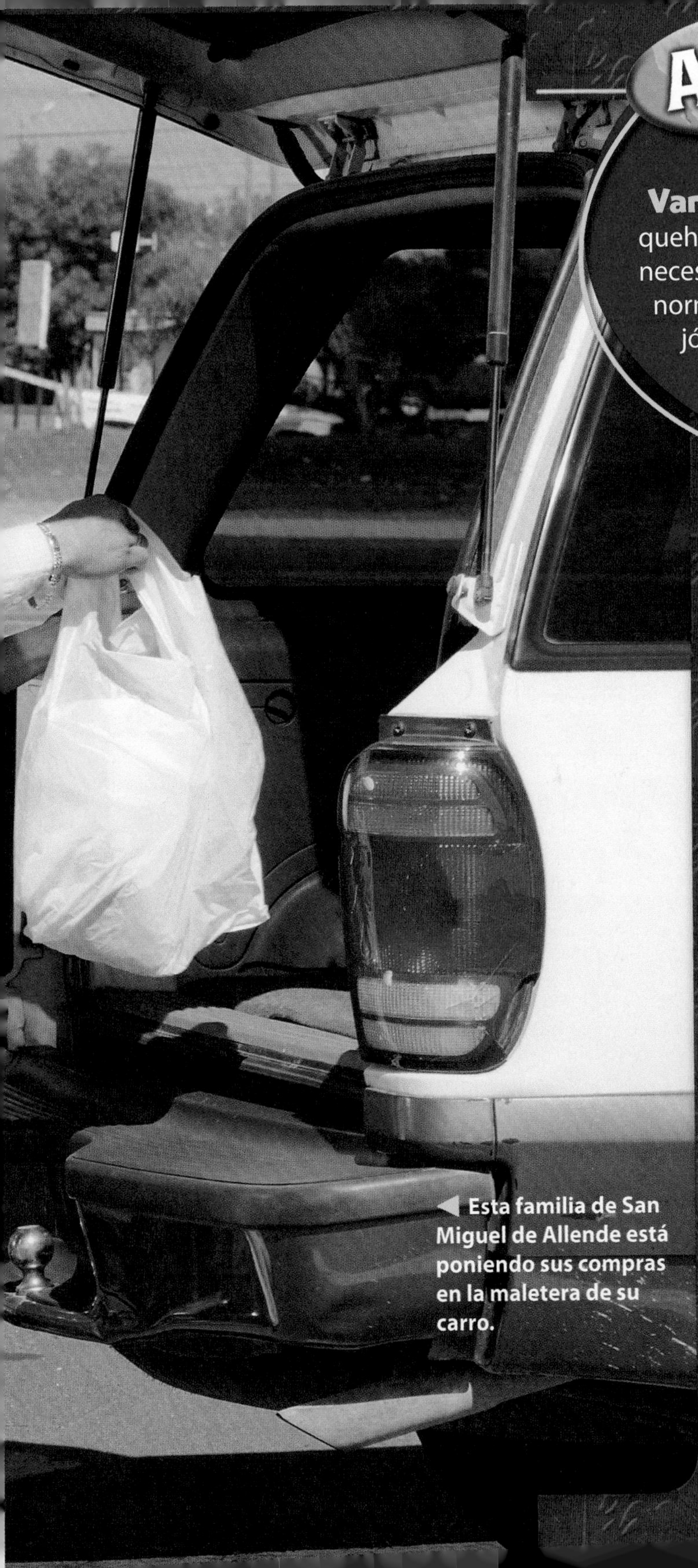

Aquí y Allí

Vamos a comparar Todos tenemos quehaceres—tareas rutinarias pero necesarias para llevar un tren de vida normal. Vamos a pasar un rato con unos jóvenes españoles que cumplen sus quehaceres antes de salir de vacaciones.

Objetivos

You will:

- talk about errands
- discuss preparing for a trip through Andalusia
- read a short story from Argentina

You will use:

- the subjunctive with expressions of doubt
- the subjunctive with adverbial clauses
- the pluperfect, conditional perfect, and future perfect tenses

◀ Esta familia de San Miguel de Allende está poniendo sus compras en la maletera de su carro.

QuickPass

Go to glencoe.com
For: **Online book**
Web code: **ASD7844c4**

Introducción al tema
Quehaceres

Mira las fotos para familiarizarte con el tema de este capítulo—los quehaceres. Pero, ¿qué son los quehaceres? Como indica la palabra misma son las tareas que tenemos que hacer—ir al banco, a la lavandería, a la peluquería, etc.

▲ **Nicaragua** Hoy en día la mayoría de las peluquerías son unisex como esta que vemos en un centro comercial en Managua.

México Cuando uno tiene muchos quehaceres, a veces no tiene tiempo para comer y se aprovecha de un puesto de comida como este en la Ciudad de México. Puede comer algo muy rápido y no perder tiempo. ▶

España ¿Es un palacio? Pues, sí y no. Es el Palacio de Telecomunicaciones en Madrid. Sirve de casa de correos. Es un lugar elegante adonde ir para echar una carta, ¿no? ▼

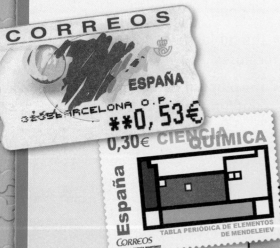

Puerto Rico Las instrucciones que salen en la pantalla de un cajero automático te facilitan el uso de la máquina. ▶

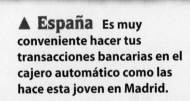

▲ **Argentina** A veces las lavanderías, que se llaman también lavaderos, están abiertas de noche como esta en Buenos Aires.

▲ **España** Es muy conveniente hacer tus transacciones bancarias en el cajero automático como las hace esta joven en Madrid.

◀ **Europa** El euro es la moneda de todos los países de la Unión Europea. Si viajas por España tienes que cambiar tus dólares en euros.

Costa Rica Esta familia costarricense respeta su responsabilidad y obligación de reciclar. ▶

La peluquería

José está muy apresurado.
Tiene mucho que hacer.

José va a la peluquería.
El peluquero no le hizo un corte de pelo.
José quería solo un recorte.

un corte de pelo

un recorte

La lavandería

la ropa sucia (para lavar), el lavado

José está en la lavandería automática.
Pone su ropa sucia en la lavadora.

el detergente, el jabón en polvo

Luego él añade un paquete de
jabón en polvo.

la secadora

una camisa arrugada

Cuando la ropa sale de la secadora
está muy arrugada.
Pero José la va a planchar.

El correo

el buzón

la tarjeta postal

Saludos de México

el sobre

el sello, la estampilla

María fue al correo.

No tuvo que esperar en fila porque ya había puesto los sellos en la tarjeta.

Por eso la echó enseguida en el buzón.

No se puede echar una carta sin sellos.

El banco

el dinero en efectivo   los billetes

el suelto   una moneda

Es necesario endosar un cheque antes de cobrarlo.

No puedes pagar con cheque sin que tengas una cuenta corriente.

Es necesario mantener un saldo (una cantidad de dinero en la cuenta).

el cajero automático

Es posible depositar y retirar fondos electrónicamente.

Tasa de interés 5%

Susana pide un préstamo estudiantil para pagar la matrícula universitaria.

Un préstamo estudiantil es un préstamo a largo plazo, no a corto plazo.

La tasa de interés de un préstamo a largo plazo es más baja.

QuickPass

Go to glencoe.com
For: **Vocabulary practice**
Web code: **ASD7844c4**

ESCUCHAR

1 Escucha y determina si la información que oyes es correcta o no. Usa una tabla como la de abajo para indicar tus respuestas.

correcta	incorrecta

¡Así se dice!

Habría de is a useful expression that means *I was supposed to.*
> **Habría de ir al banco y no fui.**

HABLAR • ESCRIBIR

2 Personaliza. Da respuestas personales.

1. ¿Tienes muchos quehaceres?
2. ¿Cuándo vas a la peluquería?
3. ¿Lavas tu propia ropa sucia, o la lava otra persona? ¿Quién?
4. ¿Mandas cartas de vez en cuando?
5. ¿Envías muchos correos electrónicos?
6. ¿Te importa que tu camisa o pantalón esté arrugado?
7. ¿Tienes una cuenta corriente en el banco?
8. ¿Tienes una tarjeta de crédito?

EXPANSIÓN

Ahora, sin mirar las preguntas, cuenta la información en tus propias palabras. Si no recuerdas algo, un(a) compañero(a) te puede ayudar.

LEER

3 Escoge la frase correcta.

1. **a.** Un préstamo estudiantil es para pagar la matrícula y otros gastos universitarios.
   b. Un préstamo estudiantil es para comprar un carro.
2. **a.** Una hipoteca es un préstamo para comprar una casa. Una hipoteca es un préstamo a corto plazo.
   b. Una hipoteca es un préstamo para comprar una casa. Una hipoteca es un préstamo a largo plazo.
3. **a.** La tasa de interés es más baja para un préstamo a largo plazo.
   b. La tasa de interés es más baja para un préstamo a corto plazo.
4. **a.** Es necesario endosar un cheque.
   b. Es necesario endosar el dinero en efectivo.
5. **a.** Cuando necesitas dinero lo depositas en el banco.
   b. Cuando necesitas dinero lo retiras del banco.

Nota

El cambio is a general word that means *change* or *exchange*. **El suelto** is *loose change*. **El vuelto,** sometimes **la vuelta,** is *change from a sale.*

Más practica

■ Workbook, pp. 4.3–4.5
● StudentWorks™ Plus

LEER • ESCRIBIR

4 Completa con la palabra apropiada.

1. Los billetes y las monedas son _____.
2. Solo tengo billetes y necesito una moneda para el parquímetro. ¿Tienes _____?
3. Hay que _____ un cheque antes de cobrarlo.
4. Puedes depositar o _____ fondos electrónicamente.
5. Es necesario mantener un _____ en la cuenta corriente.
6. Por lo general la ropa que sale de la secadora está bastante _____ y es posible que la quieras _____.

CULTURA

Este banco está en una esquina de la ciudad de Punta Arenas en la Patagonia chilena.

5 Rompecabezas

Indica la expresión «intrusa».

1. a. poner sellos en la tarjeta
   b. echar una carta en el buzón
   c. buscar un cajero automático
   d. mandar una tarjeta postal

2. a. pedir un préstamo
   b. depositar fondos
   c. endosar un cheque
   d. ir por un corte de pelo

3. a. lavar la ropa sucia
   b. ir al correo
   c. añadir el detergente
   d. tener ropa arrugada

Estudio de palabras

cortar El barbero le corta el pelo.

el corte Tiene el pelo muy largo. Necesita un corte.

el recorte Le corta un poco. Le da solo un recorte.

corto Ahora tiene el pelo corto.

lavar Voy a lavar la ropa.

el lavado Tengo mucha ropa sucia. Tengo mucho lavado.

la lavadora Lo voy a lavar en la lavadora.

la lavandería Hay muchas lavadoras en la lavandería.

Completa con las palabras apropiadas.

1. No tengo el pelo _____. Lo tengo muy largo. No hay duda que necesito _____. Tendré que ir a la peluquería donde el peluquero me puede _____ el pelo.
2. Catalina es una estudiante universitaria. Vive en el dormitorio. Cuando tiene mucha ropa sucia, o sea mucho _____, no lo puede _____ en el dormitorio porque en el dormitorio no hay _____. Catalina tiene que ir a _____.

InfoGap For more practice using your new vocabulary, do Activity 4 on page SR5 at the end of this book.

QUEHACERES

ciento tres **103**

El subjuntivo con expresiones de duda

1. The subjunctive is always used after verbs or expressions that imply doubt or uncertainty.

> **Dudo que él vaya por un corte de pelo.**
> **No creo que vaya por un corte de pelo.**

2. If the verb or expression implies certainty, however, it is followed by a verb in the indicative, rather than in the subjunctive. The verb is frequently in the future tense.

> **No dudo que él irá a la peluquería.**
> **Creo que él irá a la peluquería.**

3. Study the following verbs and expressions of doubt and certainty.

DOUBT → SUBJUNCTIVE	CERTAINTY → INDICATIVE
dudar	no dudar
es dudoso	no es dudoso
no estar seguro(a)	estar seguro(a)
no creer	creer
no es cierto	es cierto

CULTURA

¿Crees que las motos son populares entre los jóvenes en España? Las motos estacionadas aquí están en una calle de Málaga.

Práctica

VIDEO Want help with the subjunctive with emotions, wishes, and doubts? Watch **Gramática en vivo.**

LEER • HABLAR • ESCRIBIR

 Expresa tu opinión con **creo** o **no creo.** Usa el indicativo o subjuntivo como necesario.

1. Cuesta mucho asistir a la universidad.
2. Hoy en día la gente escribe y envía muchas cartas.
3. La gente recibe y envía muchos correos electrónicos.
4. Las bicicletas contaminan el aire.
5. Sirven comida excelente en la cafetería.
6. Ellas son más inteligentes que ellos.

ESCUCHAR • HABLAR

 Conversa con un(a) compañero(a) según el modelo.

MODELO —Creo que iré por un corte de pelo.
—No, Martín. No creo que vayas por un corte de pelo.

1. Creo que tendré una manicura.
2. Creo que les mandaré una tarjeta postal.
3. Creo que llevaré el lavado a la lavandería.
4. Creo que me queda bastante dinero.
5. Creo que tengo el suelto exacto.

LEER • ESCRIBIR

 Introduce con **creo** o **dudo** y haz los cambios necesarios.

1. Mi mejor amigo(a) se casa pronto.
2. Me invita a la recepción.
3. La recepción será en un gran hotel.
4. La orquesta tocará música clásica.
5. Yo le regalo un carro.
6. Los novios viajan a Cancún.

CULTURA

Creo que esta pareja en Oaxaca, México, se va a casar.

Comunicación

 Habla con un(a) amigo(a) y dile todo lo que crees que harás mañana y todo lo que dudas que hagas mañana.

 Trabajen en grupos de cuatro o cinco. Hablen de todo lo que creen que sucederá (ocurrirá) en sus vidas y lo que dudan o no creen que suceda (ocurra). Si es posible, expliquen por qué.

El subjuntivo en cláusulas adverbiales

The subjunctive is used after the following conjunctions because the information that they introduce is not necessarily real. It may or may not occur.

para que   *so that*
de modo que   *so that, in such a way that*
de manera que   *so that, in such a way that*
con tal de que   *provided that*
sin que   *unless, without*
a menos que   *unless*

Marta no irá a menos que vayas tú.
Yo les voy a escribir para que sepan lo que está pasando.
Él no podrá pagar la matrícula a menos que le den un préstamo estudiantil.

CULTURA

Estos policías vigilan para que no se cometan crímenes en las calles de Málaga, España.

Práctica

ESCUCHAR • HABLAR • ESCRIBIR

6 Contesta con **sí.**

1. ¿Terminará el trabajo con tal de que tú lo ayudes?
2. ¿Te lo explicará de modo que lo entiendas?
3. ¿Pedirás un préstamo sin que ellos lo sepan?
4. ¿Lo lavarás para que esté muy limpio?
5. ¿Tendrás que ir al banco para que te cambien los billetes grandes?

 Comunidades

7 Un servicio de suma importancia que tiene que proveer un municipio a sus ciudadanos es el de la seguridad. Cada ciudad o pueblo tiene su departamento policial. En muchas ciudades de España y Latinoamérica hay policías de turismo sobre todo en los cascos históricos que frecuentan los turistas. Están para su seguridad y también para contestar sus preguntas o ayudarles con cualquier problema. En grupos de cuatro, discutan las obligaciones y responsabilidades que tienen los policías en su municipio y el trabajo que hacen. Presenten los resultados a la clase.

LEER • ESCRIBIR

8 Completa con la forma apropiada del verbo indicado.

1. El profesor presenta la lección de modo que todos nosotros _____. (comprender)
2. Él sabe que nadie va a entender a menos que él la _____ de una manera clara. (presentar)
3. Explica todo de manera que _____ bien claro. (estar)
4. Nos enseña de manera que todos (nosotros) _____ aprender más. (querer)
5. Él ayudará a sus alumnos con tal de que le _____ atención. (prestar)
6. No te ayudará sin que _____ un esfuerzo. (hacer)

EXPANSIÓN

Ahora, sin mirar las preguntas, cuenta la información en tus propias palabras. Si no recuerdas algo, un(a) compañero(a) te puede ayudar.

CULTURA

Este profesor en Caracas, Venezuela, ¿presenta la lección de manera que sus alumnos la entiendan?

Comunicación

9   Dile a un(a) compañero(a) lo que vas a hacer después de las clases. Tu compañero(a) te va a preguntar por qué. Explícale por qué usando algunas de las expresiones siguientes: **para que, de modo que, de manera que, con tal de que, sin que, a menos que.**

Otros tiempos compuestos
El pluscuamperfecto, el condicional perfecto y el futuro perfecto

1. The pluperfect tense is formed by using the imperfect of the verb **haber** and the past participle. The conditional perfect is formed by using the conditional of the verb **haber** and the past participle.

	pluscuamperfecto salir	condicional perfecto volver
yo	había salido	habría vuelto
tú	habías salido	habrías vuelto
Ud., él, ella	había salido	habría vuelto
nosotros(as)	habíamos salido	habríamos vuelto
vosotros(as)	habíais salido	habríais vuelto
Uds., ellos, ellas	habían salido	habrían vuelto

2. The pluperfect is used the same way in Spanish as it is in English—to state an action in the past that was completed prior to another past action.

   Yo ya había salido cuando él llegó.
   Ellos ya habían terminado cuando nosotros empezamos.

3. The conditional perfect is used in Spanish, as it is in English, to state what would have taken place had something else not interfered or made it impossible.

   Yo habría ido pero no pude porque tuve que trabajar.
   Yo te habría dado cambio pero no me lo pediste.

4. The future perfect is a tense that is hardly ever used. It is formed by using the future of **haber** and the past participle. It expresses a future action completed prior to another future action.

	terminar	ver
yo	habré terminado	habré visto
tú	habrás terminado	habrás visto
Ud., él, ella	habrá terminado	habrá visto
nosotros(as)	habremos terminado	habremos visto
vosotros(as)	habréis terminado	habréis visto
Uds., ellos, ellas	habrán terminado	habrán visto

¿Te acuerdas?

Remember the following verbs have an irregular past participle.

decir	dicho
hacer	hecho
ver	visto
escribir	escrito
romper	roto
poner	puesto
volver	vuelto
morir	muerto
abrir	abierto
cubrir	cubierto

VIDEO To visit a **peluquería** in Madrid, watch **Cultura en vivo.**

Más práctica
- Workbook, pp. 4.8–4.10
- StudentWorks™ Plus

Práctica

ESCUCHAR • LEER • ESCRIBIR

10 Cambia cada frase al pluscuamperfecto.

1. José ha ido a la peluquería.
2. El peluquero le ha cortado el pelo.
3. José ha salido de la peluquería.
4. María ha estado en la lavandería.
5. Su amigo ha puesto la ropa sucia en la lavadora.
6. Yo he lavado el pantalón con detergente en agua fría.
7. Le he pedido suelto.
8. Elena ha solicitado un préstamo.

ESCUCHAR • HABLAR • ESCRIBIR

11 Haz una sola frase según el modelo.

MODELO **Ellos salieron. Yo salí después. →**
Ellos ya habían salido cuando yo salí.

1. Ellos fueron a la peluquería. Yo los llamé después.
2. Ellos pidieron un préstamo. Yo fui al banco después.
3. Ellos pagaron. Yo pagué después.
4. Ellos cambiaron su dinero. Yo cambié el mío después.
5. Ellos volvieron a casa. Yo los vi después.

HABLAR • ESCRIBIR

12 Completa la siguiente tabla para indicar las cosas que ya habías hecho cuando tenías solo ocho años.

Yo ya		cuando tenía ocho años.

CULTURA
Una peluquería en Pisco, una ciudad en el sur de Perú

CULTURA
Una plaza en Baños, Ecuador

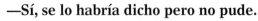

VIDEO Want help with compound tenses? Watch **Gramática en vivo.**

¿Por qué no habrían jugado los niños a la pelota en esta calle peatonal de Estepona, España?

 ESCUCHAR • HABLAR

13 Contesta según el modelo indicando lo que habrías hecho pero no pudiste.

MODELO —¿Se lo habrías dicho?
—Sí, se lo habría dicho pero no pude.

1. ¿Habrías ido?
2. ¿Le habrías hablado?
3. ¿Les habrías ayudado?
4. ¿Lo habrías visto?
5. ¿Le habrías dicho algo?
6. ¿Habrías hecho algo?

 LEER • ESCRIBIR

14 Completa con el condicional perfecto.

1. Ellos _____ pero no tenían hambre. (comer)
2. Ellos _____ algo pero no tenían sed. (tomar)
3. Ellos _____ pero no tenían sueño. (dormir)
4. Nosotros lo _____ pero no teníamos bastante dinero. (comprar)
5. Nosotros lo _____ pero la verdad es que teníamos miedo. (hacer)
6. Nosotros le _____ algo pero no lo vimos. (decir)
7. Sé que tú _____ éxito pero no fuiste. (tener)
8. Tú _____ pero sonó el teléfono. (salir)

 HABLAR • ESCRIBIR

15 Explica por qué completando la siguiente tabla.

	ido	
	asistido	
	jugado	
Yo sé que Tomás habría	salido	pero...
	estudiado	
	vuelto	
	estado	

16 Completa con el condicional perfecto y el pretérito.

1. Ellos _____ pero no _____ porque empezó a llover. (salir)
2. Nosotros _____ a la playa pero no _____ porque hacía mal tiempo. (ir)
3. Él me _____ el dinero pero no me lo _____ porque no lo tenía. (dar)
4. Yo te lo _____ pero no te lo _____ porque no sabía los resultados. (decir)
5. Ella _____ en la ciudad pero no _____ en la ciudad porque costaba demasiado. (vivir)

 Comunicación

17 Trabajen en grupos de tres o cuatro y comenten sobre lo que cada uno(a) de ustedes habría hecho pero no pudo porque tuvo que hacer otra cosa.

Refrán

Can you guess what the following proverb means?

La ropa limpia no necesita jabón.

CULTURA

Me habría gustado pasar unos días en esta playa de la Costa del Sol en España.

¡Bravo!

You have now learned all the new vocabulary and grammar in this chapter. Continue to use and practice all that you know while learning more cultural information. ¡Vamos!

Conversación

QuickPass

Go to glencoe.com
For: **Conversation practice**
Web code: ASD7844c4

¿Comprendes?

VIDEO To watch some busy friends run errands in Argentina, watch **Diálogo en vivo.**

A Contesta.
1. ¿Por qué está muy apresurada Julia?
2. ¿Cuándo habría de salir para Puerto Rico?
3. ¿Por qué no salió?
4. ¿Cuándo va a salir?
5. ¿Por qué tiene que ir a la lavandería?
6. ¿Por qué no va a ir a la peluquería?
7. ¿Por qué es importante que ella vaya al banco?
8. ¿Por qué no le importa que salga su ropa arrugada de la secadora?

B **Analizando** Contesta.
1. Isabel es una amiga buena. ¿Por qué? ¿Tienes un(a) amigo(a) como ella? ¿Lo (La) aprecias?
2. De todas las cosas que tiene que hacer Julia, una es muy importante. ¿Cuál es? ¿Por qué?

C **Personalizando** ¿Tienes quehaceres que son similares a los de Julia? ¿Cuáles?

FOLDABLES®
Study Organizer

MINIBOOK
See page SH26 for help with making this foldable. Use this foldable to talk about errands. On each page, illustrate someone running an errand. Under each illustration, write about what each person is doing.

CULTURA

¿Cuáles son algunos servicios que ofrece esta lavandería en la Ciudad de Panamá? Se pone una colcha en la cama y es importante no manchar el mantel de café o salsa de tomate cuando tomas o comes algo. ¿Qué significarán «colcha» y «mancha»?

Conversación

Los preparativos para un viaje

Antes de leer

Todos tenemos una lista de quehaceres típicos. Pero, piensa en unas cosas especiales que tienes que hacer en poco tiempo si decides salir por unas semanas.

✓ Reading Check

¿Quiénes ocuparon España y por cuánto tiempo?

✓ Reading Check

¿Qué tienen que hacer Gregorio y Maricarmen antes de salir?

✓ Reading Check

¿Cómo se puede cambiar dólares en otras monedas en el extranjero?

Gregorio y unos amigos de su colegio en Madrid decidieron hacer un viaje por el sur de España—por Andalucía. Querían visitar Andalucía porque habían visto muchas fotografías de los famosos monumentos de los musulmanes: la Mezquita de Córdoba, la Alhambra de Granada y el Alcázar de Sevilla. De sus cursos de historia ya sabían que los árabes habían ocupado España por unos ocho siglos de 711 a 1492.

Como les quedan solo unos días antes de salir para Andalucía, cada uno tiene muchos quehaceres. Gregorio tiene el pelo bastante largo y quiere ir a la peluquería. Sabe que en agosto va a hacer mucho calor en Andalucía y sin duda van a pasar unos días en una playa de la Costa del Sol. Es mejor tener el pelo corto si va a ir al mar, ¿no?

Maricarmen tiene un montón de ropa sucia que tiene que llevar a la lavandería. Es una tarea que no le gusta nada pero no importa si sus pantalones, blusas y camisetas salen arrugadas porque todo se arrugará de nuevo en su mochila.

¡El dinero! Todos tienen que ir al banco porque sin dinero no se puede hacer nada. Pero en el banco todo es muy conveniente porque se puede usar el cajero automático a menos que uno no tenga una cuenta corriente.

¡Un detalle importante para ti! Si algún día decides viajar al extranjero[1] puedes usar el cajero automático para cambiar dinero. En España entras la cantidad de euros que quieres y en México la cantidad de pesos. Te saldrán los euros o pesos. Se convierten en dólares que enseguida se retiran electrónicamente de tu cuenta corriente. Es una transacción sencilla a menos que no tengas suficiente saldo en tu cuenta. ¡Cuidado!

[1]extranjero *abroad*

CULTURA
Una vista de Córdoba

¿Comprendes?

Más práctica

■ Workbook, p. 4.11
● StudentWorks™ Plus

A Analizando Contesta.

1. ¿Por qué tiene que ir a la peluquería Gregorio?
2. ¿Por qué tiene que ir a la lavandería Maricarmen?
3. ¿Por qué no le importa que salga su ropa arrugada?
4. ¿Por qué tienen que ir todos al banco?
5. ¿Por qué será muy conveniente?

B Explicando Explica como puedes usar el cajero automático si viajas a un país extranjero donde no se usan dólares.

C Conectando con la historia Contesta.

Haz unas investigaciones sobre la enorme influencia de los árabes (los musulmanes) en la historia de España.

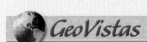

GeoVistas

To learn more about Spain, take a tour on pages SH40–SH41.

CULTURA

Una vista de Olvera, un pueblo pequeño cerca de la ciudad de Cádiz en Andalucía

El mensajero de San Martín

de autor anónimo

▲ Una vista del Parque Nacional Torres del Paine en Chile

Vocabulario

el despacho   la oficina

un puñado   cantidad pequeña que cabe en la mano

el ejército   un grupo de soldados o militares

la choza   una casa muy humilde

apoderarse de   hacerse dueño de una cosa por la fuerza

encargar   poner una cosa al cuidado de otro; darle la responsabilidad a alguien de hacer algo

huir (huye)   escapar

sujetar   dominar a alguien

Práctica

Expresa de otra manera.

1. No quiero mucho. Necesito *solo un poco*.
2. Era imposible *dominar* al caballo.
3. Él *se hizo dueño* de todo el territorio.
4. ¿Por qué no pudo *escapar*?
5. Salió de su *oficina* apresuradamente.
6. Entró *el grupo de soldados*.
7. Hay *casas humildes* en los barrios pobres.

INTRODUCCIÓN

Hay muchos quehaceres que la gente tenía que hacer casi a diario que hoy no tenemos que hacer casi nunca. Muchos de nosotros no vamos ni al correo para comprar sellos porque nos comunicamos casi exclusivamente por correo electrónico, mensaje de texto y mensaje instantáneo. Pero una vez era un mensajero el que tenía que viajar a pie o a caballo para transportar una comunicación. Y así fue el caso del joven Miguel quien se encargó de servir de mensajero al general San Martín.

FONDO HISTÓRICO

El general José de San Martín luchó por la independencia de Sudamérica. Era un hombre de mucha experiencia militar. San Martín ya había luchado en las guerras contra Napoleón en España y sabía que era imposible invadir Perú sin tomar la ruta que pasa por Chile. En 1817 cruzó la cordillera con su Ejército de los Andes y derrotó a (salió victorioso contra) los españoles en la batalla de Chacabuco. Esta derrota de las fuerzas españolas permitió al ejército de San Martín entrar triunfante en Santiago de Chile.

CULTURA

Monumento al libertador General San Martín en la Plaza San Martín en Buenos Aires

Identificándose con los personajes Al leer un cuento hay que fijarte en la personalidad, el comportamiento y las acciones de los protagonistas. Poder precisar las razones por su conducta y acciones en muchas ocasiones te permitirá entender y seguir el desarrollo del argumento del cuento.

CULTURA

Lo viejo y lo moderno en Santiago de Chile

Antes de leer

Reflexiona sobre tu reacción personal si algún día te encuentras en una situación que te hace salir de casa para hacer algo patriótico y peligroso.

fusilarán *they will shoot*

arrieros *los que guardan animales*

halló *he found*
abogado *lawyer*

El mensajero de San Martín

El general don José de San Martín leía unas cartas en su despacho. Terminada la lectura, se volvió para llamar a un muchacho de unos dieciséis años que esperaba de pie junto a la puerta.

—Voy a encargarte una misión difícil y honrosa. Te conozco bien; tu padre y tres hermanos tuyos están en mi ejército y sé que deseas servir a la patria. ¿Estás resuelto a servirme?

—Sí, mi general, sí—contestó el muchacho.

—Debes saber que en caso de ser descubierto te fusilarán°—continuó el general.

—Ya lo sé, mi general.

—Muy bien. Quiero enviarte a Chile con una carta que no debe caer en manos del enemigo. ¿Has entendido, Miguel?

—Perfectamente, mi general—respondió el muchacho.
Dos días después, Miguel pasaba la cordillera de los Andes en compañía de unos arrieros°.

Llegó a Santiago de Chile; halló° al abogado° Rodríguez, le entregó la carta y recibió la respuesta, que guardó en su cinturón secreto.

—Mucho cuidado con esta carta—le dijo también el patriota chileno.

—Eres realmente muy joven; pero debes ser inteligente y buen patriota.

Miguel volvió a ponerse en camino lleno de orgullo°. Había hecho el viaje sin dificultades, pero tuvo que pasar por un pueblo cerca del cual se hallaba una fuerza realista al mando del coronel Ordóñez.

Alrededor se extendía el hermoso paisaje chileno. Miguel se sintió impresionado por aquel cuadro mágico; pero algo inesperado vino a distraer su atención.

Dos soldados, a quienes pareció sospechoso° ese muchacho que viajaba solo y en dirección a las sierras, se acercaron a él a galope. En la sorpresa del primer momento, Miguel cometió la imprudencia° de huir.

—¡Hola!—gritó uno de los soldados sujetándole el caballo por las riendas°.—¿Quién eres y adónde vas?

Miguel contestó humildemente que era chileno, que se llamaba Juan Gómez y que iba a la hacienda de sus padres.

Lo llevaron sin embargo a una tienda de campaña donde se hallaba, en compañía de varios oficiales, el coronel Ordóñez.

—Te acusan de ser agente del general San Martín—dijo el coronel.—¿Qué contestas a eso?

Miguel habría preferido decir la verdad, pero negó la acusación.

—Oye, muchacho,—añadió el coronel—más vale que confieses francamente, así quizá puedas evitarte el castigo°, porque eres muy joven. ¿Llevas alguna carta?

—No—contestó Miguel, pero cambió de color y el coronel lo notó.

Dos soldados se apoderaron del muchacho, y mientras el uno lo sujetaba, el otro no tardó en hallar el cinturón con la carta.

—Bien lo decía yo—observó Ordóñez, mientras abría la carta. Pero en ese instante Miguel, con un movimiento brusco, saltó como un tigre, le arrebató° la carta de las manos y la arrojó en un brasero° allí encendido.

—Hay que convenir en que eres muy valiente—dijo Ordóñez. —Aquél que te ha mandado sabe elegir su gente. Ahora bien, puesto que eres resuelto, quisiera salvarte y lo haré si me dices lo que contenía la carta.

—No sé, señor.

—¿No sabes? Mira que tengo medios de despertar tu memoria.

—No sé, señor. La persona que me dio la carta no me dijo nada.

orgullo *pride*

sospechoso *suspicious*

imprudencia *mistake*

riendas *reins*

castigo *punishment*

arrebató *grabbed*
la arrojó en un brasero *tossed it in a brasier*

Durante la lectura

Para seguir la acción, presta atención a los detalles. Identifícate con las acciones de Miguel y reflexiona sobre lo que tú habrías hecho en la misma situación.

jurado *sworn*

azotes *lashes*

El coronel meditó un momento.

—Bien—dijo—te creo. ¿Podrías decirme al menos de quien era y a quien iba dirigida?

—No puedo, señor.

—¿Y por qué no?

—Porque he jurado°.

El coronel admiró en secreto al niño pero no lo demostró. Abriendo un cajón de la mesa, tomó un puñado de monedas de oro.

—¿Has tenido alguna vez una moneda de oro?—preguntó a Miguel.

—No, señor—contestó el muchacho.

—Bueno, pues, yo te daré diez. ¿Entiendes? Diez de éstas, si me dices lo que quiero saber. Y eso, con sólo decirme dos nombres. Puedes decírmelo en voz baja—continuó el coronel.

—No quiero, señor.

—A ver—ordenó—unos cuantos azotes° bien dados a este muchacho.

CULTURA

Es la réplica de la casa en que vivió San Martín durante su exilio en el norte de Francia. La casa se encuentra en la zona de Palermo en Buenos Aires.

CULTURA

Un corral en Villa Tehuelches, Chile

En presencia de Ordóñez, de sus oficiales y de muchos soldados, dos de éstos lo golpearon sin piedad. El muchacho apretó los dientes para no gritar. Sus sentidos comenzaron a turbarse° y luego perdió el conocimiento°.

—Basta—dijo Ordóñez—enciérrenlo por esta noche. Mañana confesará.

Entre los que presenciaron los golpes se encontraba un soldado chileno que, como todos sus compatriotas, simpatizaba con la causa de la libertad. Tenía dos hermanos, agentes de San Martín, y él mismo esperaba la ocasión favorable para abandonar el ejército real. El valor del muchacho le llenó de admiración.

A medianoche el silencio más profundo reinaba en el campamento. Los fuegos estaban apagados y sólo los centinelas° velaban con el arma en el brazo.

Miguel estaba en una choza, donde lo habían dejado bajo cerrojo°, sin preocuparse° más de él.

Entonces, en el silencio de la noche, oyó un ruido como el de un cerrojo corrido° con precaución. La puerta se abrió despacio y apareció la figura de un hombre. Miguel se levantó sorprendido.

turbarse *to become confused*
perdió el conocimiento *he lost consciousness*

centinelas *guardias*

cerrojo *lock*
preocuparse *worrying*
corrido *opened, unbolted*

CULTURA

Una estatua del general San Martín con sus nietas en el parque de Palermo en Buenos Aires.

—¡Quieto!—murmuró una voz.—¿Tienes valor para escapar?

De repente Miguel no sintió dolores, cansancio°, ni debilidad; estaba ya bien, ágil y resuelto a todo. Siguió al soldado y los dos andaban como sombras° por el campamento dormido, hacia un corral donde se hallaban los caballos del servicio. El pobre animal de Miguel permanecía ensillado° aún y atado a un poste.

—Éste es el único punto por donde puedes escapar,—dijo el soldado—el único lugar donde no hay centinelas. ¡Pronto, a caballo y buena suerte!

El joven héroe obedeció°, despidiéndose de su generoso salvador con un apretón de manos y un ¡Dios se lo pague! Luego, espoleó° su caballo sin perder un minuto y huyó en dirección a las montañas.

Huyó para mostrar a San Martín, con las heridas de los golpes que habían roto sus espaldas, cómo había sabido guardar un secreto y servir a la patria.

cansancio *tiredness*

sombras *shadows*

ensillado *saddled*

obedeció *obeyed*

espoleó *he spurred*

¿Comprendes?

A **Recordando hechos** Contesta.

1. ¿Qué misión le encargó San Martín al joven Miguel?
2. ¿Adónde fue Miguel?
3. ¿Dónde guardó la respuesta a la carta que le dio el abogado?
4. Al llegar los dos soldados enemigos, Miguel hizo algo erróneo, algo que no habría debido hacer. ¿Qué hizo?
5. ¿Adónde llevaron a Miguel y de qué le acusaron?
6. ¿Qué hizo Miguel cuando uno de los soldados halló su cinturón secreto?
7. ¿Cómo trataron de hacerle confesar?
8. ¿Qué le ofreció Ordóñez a Miguel para convencerle a hablar?
9. ¿Quién ayudó a Miguel?
10. ¿Cómo huyó Miguel?

Después de leer

Piensa en todo lo que hizo Miguel y determina si tú lo consideras un héroe o no. ¿Por qué?

B **Describiendo** Describe como el autor presenta la severidad con la que golpearon al pobre Miguel.

C **Resumiendo** Da un resumen de todo lo que hizo el joven Miguel para demostrar su heroísmo.

D **Personalizando** Acabas de leer sobre el heroísmo de un joven chileno. A tu juicio, ¿qué es una persona heroica? Escribe tu percepción personal del heroísmo.

E **Analizando** El clímax de un cuento es el punto de mayor interés o suspenso en el cuento. Para ti, ¿cuál es el clímax de este cuento?

CULTURA

La tumba de San Martín en la Catedral Metropolitana de Buenos Aires

Prepárate para el examen
Self-check for achievement

Vocabulario

1 Identifica.

1. _____

2. _____

3. _____

4. _____

5. _____

To review **Vocabulario**, turn to pages 100–101.

2 Completa con una palabra apropiada.

6. El peluquero le hace un _____ de pelo. No lo quiere muy corto.

7. El muchacho pone su ropa sucia en la _____.

8. Él tiene solo billetes grandes; necesita _____.

9–10. Se puede _____ y _____ fondos de una cuenta bancaria. Se puede hacer estas transacciones electrónicamente.

11. Un _____ estudiantil te puede ayudar a pagar la matrícula y otros gastos universitarios.

Gramática

To review **el subjuntivo con expresiones de duda,** turn to page 104.

3 Introduce la frase con **no** y haz los cambios necesarios.

12. Creo que él vendrá.

13. Dudo que él esté.

14. Creo que Susana lo conoce.

15. Dudo que él sea más inteligente que su hermana.

16. José cree que yo iré.

To review **el subjuntivo en cláusulas adverbiales,** turn to page 106.

4 Completa con la forma apropiada del verbo indicado.

17. Él no podrá terminar el trabajo a menos que tú le _____. (ayudar)

18. Tenemos que mandarles un correo electrónico para que _____ lo que está pasando. (saber)

19. No le voy a molestar de manera que él _____ terminar con sus quehaceres. (poder)

20. Yo creo que él irá con tal de que nosotros _____ también. (ir)

⑤ Completa con el pluscuamperfecto.

21. Ella ya _____ cuando nosotros llegamos. (salir)

22. Ellos lo _____ y yo no lo sabía. (ver)

23. Ellos no sabían que yo le _____. (hablar)

24. Él ya te lo _____ cuando me lo dijo a mí. (decir)

To review **el pluscuamperfecto,** turn to page 108.

⑥ Contesta y completa.

25–26. ¿Habrías ido?
Sí, _____ pero no pude porque _____.

27–28. ¿Habrían hecho ellos el trabajo?
Sí, lo _____ pero no pudieron porque _____.

29–30. ¿Habrían ustedes comido algo?
Sí, (nosotros) _____ algo pero no comimos nada porque _____.

31–32. ¿Lo habría hecho Enrique?
Sí, lo _____ pero no lo hizo porque _____.

33–34. ¿Lo habrían comprado ustedes? Sí, lo _____ pero no lo compramos porque _____.

To review **el condicional perfecto,** turn to page 108.

⑦ Escoge la forma apropiada del verbo.

35. Tengo un montón de cosas que hacer sin que nadie me _____.

   a. ayuda   **b.** ayude

36. Él _____ hoy para Puerto Rico pero no pudo porque tenía mucho que hacer.

   a. habría salido   **b.** había salido

37. Gregorio y un grupo de amigos ya _____ que iban a hacer un viaje a Andalucía.

   a. habrían decidido   **b.** habían decidido

38. Quiere ir a la peluquería para que el peluquero le _____ el pelo.

   a. corte   **b.** corta

CULTURA

Plaza de España, Sevilla

Cultura

⑧ Contesta.

39. ¿Por qué quieren ir a Andalucía Gregorio y sus amigos?

40. ¿Cuáles son algunos monumentos famosos que van a ver en Andalucía?

To review this cultural information, turn to page 114.

1 **Algunos quehaceres**

Discuss chores or duties you like and dislike

Todos tenemos quehaceres. Algunos son tareas que nos gusta hacer y otros son tareas que no nos gusta hacer. Habla con un(a) compañero(a) de clase de sus quehaceres. Compárenlos y den las opiniones que tienen de ellos.

2 **Una tabla de quehaceres**

Talk about chores

Toma los quehaceres mencionados en la Actividad 1 y organízalos en una tabla con los siguientes subtítulos. Preséntalos a la clase.

siempre	con frecuencia	nunca	me gusta	no me gusta

3 **En mi futuro**

Discuss what you may or may not do in the future

Habla con un(a) compañero(a) de clase. Dile todo lo que crees que harás algún día y todo lo que dudas que hagas. Sigue hablando de un(a) hermano(a) o buen(a) amigo(a) y di lo que crees que él o ella hará o no hará.

CULTURA

¿Habría sido necesario ir a recoger tu ropa de esta lavandería en Málaga?

4 **Lo habría hecho pero no pude**

Talk about what you would have done but couldn't

No hay duda que hay cosas que te habría gustado hacer pero no las hiciste porque por una razón u otra no pudiste. Di todas las cosas que habrías hecho y explica por qué no pudiste hacerlas.

5 **Preparativos para un viaje—muchos quehaceres**

Talk about preparing for a trip

Antes de salir por una semana o más hay que organizar muchas cosas. Imagina que por un motivo u otro vas a pasar una semana fuera de casa. Explica todo lo que tienes que hacer antes de salir.

Tarea

Write a personal letter to a close friend or family member describing your experience living with a host family while studying abroad in a Spanish-speaking country. Discuss some memorable things that you did there, using vocabulary and grammar from this chapter.

Writing Strategy

Composing a personal letter Although the guidelines for writing a personal letter are not as strict as those of a formal letter, establishing a logical structure will make it easier to organize your thoughts while also making your message more enjoyable to the reader. The overall structure of a letter generally follows the basic pattern of starting with an introduction that describes the setting and sets the tone, followed by the body of the letter in which you use detailed descriptions to expand on different themes, then ending with a brief conclusion that ties everything together.

❶ Prewrite

- Before you compile the details that you wish to include in your letter, create an informal outline with the following headings.

  I. Introduction

  II. Things I have done and things I would have done but couldn't

  III. My daily or weekly routine

  IV. My host family and what it's like to live with them

  V. How my host family compares with my family at home

  VI. Conclusion

❷ Write

- Be sure to begin your letter with the date and the proper greeting (**Querido(a)** _____,).
- As you write, stick to language that you already know and try to incorporate as much vocabulary from this chapter as possible.
- Before signing off, don't forget the closing (**Atentamente, Besitos, Un abrazo,** etc.)

Evaluate

Your teacher will evaluate you based on your ability to incorporate appropriate vocabulary and correct grammar, as well as on the logical structure of your letter, the overall quality of the content, and the completeness of information.

Repaso del Capítulo 4

Gramática

- ### El subjuntivo con expresiones de duda *(page 104)*
  The subjunctive is always used after expressions that imply doubt or uncertainty. Review the following examples.

  Dudo que él lo haga.
  No creo que él lo haga.

  If the statement implies certainty, however, the indicative rather than the subjunctive is used. The verb is frequently in the future tense.

  No dudo que él lo hará.
  Creo que él lo hará.

- ### El subjuntivo en cláusulas adverbiales *(page 106)*
  The subjunctive is used after the following conjunctions: **para que, de modo que, de manera que, con tal de que, sin que, a menos que.**

  Marta irá con tal de que tú vayas.
  Marta no irá a menos que vayas tú.

- ### El pluscuamperfecto, el condicional perfecto y el futuro perfecto *(page 108)*
  Review the following forms of the pluperfect, conditional perfect, and future perfect.

	pluperfect	conditional perfect	future perfect
	salir	hacer	volver
yo	había salido	habría hecho	habré vuelto
tú	habías salido	habrías hecho	habrás vuelto
Ud., él, ella	había salido	habría hecho	habrá vuelto
nosotros(as)	habíamos salido	habríamos hecho	habremos vuelto
vosotros(as)	*habíais salido*	*habríais hecho*	*habréis vuelto*
Uds., ellos, ellas	habían salido	habrían hecho	habrán vuelto

The pluperfect is used to state what had happened in the past prior to another event. The conditional perfect is used to express what would have happened. The future perfect is very seldom used.

Yo había salido y ellos llegaron después.
Yo lo habría comprado pero no lo compré porque iba a costar demasiado.

Vocabulario

Talking about the hair salon

la peluquería	un corte de pelo	corto(a)
el/la peluquero(a)	un recorte	cortar

Talking about the laundromat

la lavandería	el jabón en polvo,	la secadora	planchar
la ropa sucia (para	el detergente	arrugado(a)	
lavar), el lavado	la lavadora	lavar	

Talking about the post office

el correo	el sobre	el buzón
la tarjeta postal	el sello, la	echar una carta
la carta	estampilla	

Talking about the bank

el banco	la cuenta corriente	el préstamo	cobrar
el dinero en efectivo	el saldo	a largo (corto)	depositar
los billetes	el cajero automático	plazo	retirar
la moneda	los fondos	la tasa de interés	
el suelto		endosar	

Other useful words and expressions

la matrícula	apresurado(a)
universitaria	habría de + *infinitivo*

The words listed below come from this chapter's literary selection, *El mensajero de San Martín*. They were selected to become part of your active vocabulary because of their relatively high frequency.

el despacho	la choza	huir
un puñado	apoderarse de	sujetar
el ejército	encargar	

Repaso cumulativo

Repasa lo que ya has aprendido

These activities will help you review and remember what you have learned so far in Spanish.

 1 Escucha las frases. Indica si la frase describe el dibujo o no.

 2 Parea el infinitivo con el pretérito.

1. decir
2. poner
3. estar
4. venir
5. tener
6. querer
7. hacer
8. andar
9. ir

a. estuve
b. fui
c. anduve
d. puse
e. quise
f. dije
g. vine
h. tuve
i. hice

 3 Completa con el pretérito del verbo indicado.

1. Yo _____ muchos quehaceres. (tener)
2. Ellos _____ mucho pero no me _____. (hacer, ayudar)
3. Yo _____ que él no vendría pero ustedes _____ que vendría. (decir, decir)
4. Yo no _____ hacerlo y no _____ hacerlo. (querer, poder)
5. Tú lo _____ con cuidado, ¿no? (hacer)

Peatones en una calle de La Palma en las islas Canarias

6. Yo _____ y ella _____ también. (ir, ir)

7. Ellos _____ en carro y _____ todo su equipaje en la maletera. (venir, poner)

8. Ellos no saben por qué no _____ nosotros. (estar)

Cambia cada frase al pretérito.

1. Ellos hablan.

2. Mis hermanos trabajan.

3. Los niños comen.

4. Ellos beben leche.

5. Mis abuelos no viven aquí.

6. Ellos me escriben.

7. Los alumnos leen mucho.

8. Ellos oyen las noticias.

CULTURA

Los mochileros pasaron unos días fantásticos en Oaxaca, México.

Trabaja con un(a) amigo(a). Cada uno dirá lo que hizo la semana pasada. Comparen lo que hicieron y decidan quién tuvo la semana más interesante.

Escoge el artículo apropiado.

1. _____ leche es buena para la salud.

   a. El   b. La

2. _____ coche es nuevo.

   a. El   b. La

3. _____ clase es grande.

   a. El   b. La

4. ¿Dónde está _____ jabón en polvo?

   a. el   b. la

5. Es necesario endosar _____ cheque.

   a. el   b. la

6. Ellos viven en _____ ciudad.

   a. el   b. la

7. Están decorando _____ árbol de Navidad.

   a. el   b. la

8. _____ traje de novia es muy bonito.

   a. El   b. La

¿Buenos o malos modales?

Aquí y Allí

Vamos a comparar En todas las sociedades y culturas hay comportamiento que se considera apropiado e inapropiado. Lo que se consideran buenos modales dentro de un grupo cultural pueden considerarse malos dentro de otro. Vamos a observar unas costumbres hispanas que se consideran buenos modales. Determina si estas costumbres son las mismas que tus costumbres o no.

◄ Estos amigos tienen buenos modales. Todos comparten el trabajo de descargar su equipaje de la camioneta al llegar a un albergue en Bariloche, Argentina.

Objetivos

You will:

- discuss manners

- compare manners in Spanish-speaking countries to manners in the United States

- read a famous episode from *El conde Lucanor* by Don Juan Manuel

You will use:

- the imperfect subjunctive

- the subjunctive vs. the infinitive

- suffixes

Go to glencoe.com
For: **Online book**
Web code: **ASD7844c5**

Introducción al tema

¿Buenos o malos modales?

En este capítulo vas a estudiar unas costumbres de cortesía y lo que se consideran buenos o malos modales en las culturas latinas. Al mirar estas fotos, observa si hay unas cosas que tú también sueles hacer cuando saludas a un(a) amigo(a) o si te despides de un(a) amigo(a).

NO SE PERMITE EL USO DEL MOVIL

▲ **Estados Unidos** Estos jóvenes están en Estados Unidos. Observa que los muchachos se dan la mano y las muchachas se dan un besito en las mejillas. Es una costumbre latina que están adoptando muchos estadounidenses.

México Los amigos se dan un besito en esta plaza en San Miguel de Allende. ¿Qué piensas? ¿Se están saludando o se están despidiendo el uno de la otra? ▶

▲ **México** Los dos señores se dan el abrazo típico con unas palmadas en la espalda.

▲ **Argentina** Estas muchachas en Buenos Aires se dan el besito típico cuando se saludan y también cuando se despiden.

Ecuador En todas partes cuidar de los parques y jardines se considera buen comportamiento como indica este aviso en un parquecito de Baños. ▶

Panamá A mucha gente hispanohablante le gusta una conversación animada. Pero estos jóvenes en un cine en la Ciudad de Panamá no quieren que sus vecinos hablen durante la película. Con un gesto el joven les dice que se callen. ▼

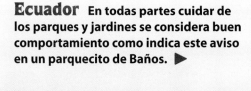

▲ **España** Estos jóvenes están conversando en un pueblo de España. Los españoles, igual que los latinoamericanos, suelen tocar a sus amigos y mantenerse cerca los unos de los otros cuando hablan juntos— y no es necesario que estén enamorados.

Saludos

Todos estaban sentados en la sala.
Llegó un invitado.

Cuando el invitado llegó, todos se levantaron.
Saludaron al recién llegado.
Para ser corteses, todos se pusieron de pie.

Un joven le dio la mano.
Es probable que los jóvenes y el invitado no se conozcan bien.
Pero no importa. Se da la mano a un amigo igual que a un conocido.

Despedidas

Las dos jóvenes se dieron un besito.
Se dieron un besito en cada mejilla.

Los dos jóvenes se dieron un abrazo.
Se abrazaron cuando se despidieron.
Los dos jóvenes son amigos.

Jaime me invitó a cenar.
Cuando llegó la cuenta, no quería que yo pagara.
Insistió en que yo no pagara.
Él quería pagar porque me había invitado.

En otras partes

You will also hear **portarse,** as well as **comportarse,** in quite a few areas of Latin America.

Comportamiento

El chico no se había comportado bien.
Su madre se enfadó.
Se enfadó porque el chico no se comportaba bien.
Lo castigaba porque quería que tuviera buenos modales.

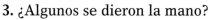

QuickPass

Go to glencoe.com
For: **Vocabulary practice**
Web code: **ASD7844c5**

ESCUCHAR

1 Escucha. Escoge la frase correcta. Usa una tabla como la de abajo para indicar tus respuestas.

a	b

ESCUCHAR • HABLAR

2 Contesta con **sí.**

1. ¿Se levantaron todos de la mesa?
2. ¿Se levantaron cuando los otros llegaron?
3. ¿Algunos se dieron la mano?
4. ¿Algunos se dieron un besito?
5. ¿Se besaron en la mejilla?
6. ¿Se abrazaron los señores?

HABLAR • ESCRIBIR

3 Personaliza. Da respuestas personales.

1. Cuando estás sentado(a) y llega otra persona, ¿te levantas?
2. Cuando ves a un(a) amigo(a), ¿le das la mano?
3. Si eres un muchacho, ¿le das un abrazo a un amigo?
4. Si eres una muchacha, ¿le das un besito a una amiga?
5. Si tú invitas a alguien a ir a una película, ¿pagas?
6. Si estás haciendo cola y alguien se pone delante de ti, ¿te enfadas?
7. ¿Quiénes se conocen mejor? ¿Los amigos o los conocidos?

GeoVistas

To learn more about Uruguay, take a tour on pages SH52–SH53.

Comunicación

4 Dile a un(a) amigo(a) lo que haces que consideras buenos modales. Sigue diciéndole lo que consideras malos modales. ¿Cuáles son algunos comportamientos que te enfadan?

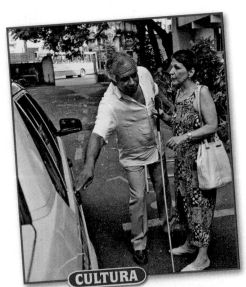

CULTURA

El señor ayuda a una señora ciega a subir al taxi en su pueblo en Uruguay.

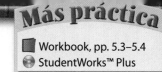

Vocabulario

LEER • ESCRIBIR

5 Da una palabra relacionada.

1. abrazar
2. besar
3. invitar
4. el brazo
5. el comportamiento

ESCRIBIR

6 Da la palabra cuya definición sigue.

1. una persona que acaba de llegar
2. un beso pequeño
3. una parte de la cara
4. un niño

EXPANSIÓN

Usa cada expresión en una frase original.

7 **Juego** Cambia una letra en cada palabra para formar una palabra nueva.

1. chino
2. casa
3. cuesta
4. sano
5. cuanto

Estudio de palabras

el amor El amor es una cosa divina.

enamorarse Los jóvenes se están enamorando.

enamorado(a) Ellos están enamorados y se van a casar.

malentender Ellos no lo entendieron bien. Lo malentendieron.

el malentendido Tenían un pequeño malentendido, pero nada serio.

Completa con la palabra apropiada.

Se ve el _____ en su cara. No hay duda que se están _____ si no están ya _____. Es evidente que no hay ningún _____ entre ellos.

Conexiones

La sociología
Los hablantes de todas las lenguas tienen sus gestos particulares. Aquí tienes dos que usan muchos hispanohablantes.

¡Estupendo!

¡Cuidado! ¡Mucho ojo!

¿Te acuerdas?

Remember that the preterite tense was reviewed in the previous chapter. See pages 130–131.

El imperfecto del subjuntivo

1. The imperfect subjunctive of all verbs is formed by dropping the **-on** from the ending of the third person plural, **ellos(as),** form of the preterite tense of the verb.

PRETERITE	hablaron	comieron	pidieron	tuvieron	dijeron
STEM	hablar-	comier-	pidier-	tuvier-	dijer-

2. To this stem, you add the following endings:
-a, -as, -a, -amos, *-ais,* -an.

	hablar	comer	pedir	tener	decir
yo	hablara	comiera	pidiera	tuviera	dijera
tú	hablaras	comieras	pidieras	tuvieras	dijeras
Ud., él, ella	hablara	comiera	pidiera	tuviera	dijera
nosotros(as)	habláramos	comiéramos	pidiéramos	tuviéramos	dijéramos
vosotros(as)	*hablarais*	*comierais*	*pidierais*	*tuvierais*	*dijerais*
Uds., ellos, ellas	hablaran	comieran	pidieran	tuvieran	dijeran

3. The same rules that apply to the use of the present subjunctive apply to the use of the imperfect subjunctive. The tense of the verb in the main clause determines whether the present or imperfect subjunctive must be used in the dependent clause. If the verb of the main clause is in the present or future tense, the present subjunctive is used in the dependent clause.

> **Quiero que ellos se comporten bien.**
> **Será necesario que tengan buenos modales.**

¡Ojo!

Quisiera and pudiera can be used on their own to express *would like* and *could.*

Quisiera ir con ellos.
Nosotros pudiéramos.

4. If the verb of the main clause is in the preterite, imperfect, or conditional, the imperfect subjunctive must be used in the dependent clause.

> **Él habló así para que comprendiéramos.**
> **Me sorprendió que ellos no se dieran la mano.**
> **Ella no quería que yo pagara.**
> **Sería imposible que él no lo supiera.**

5. The following is the sequence of tenses for using the present and imperfect subjunctive.

present ⎫
        ⎬ present subjunctive
future ⎭

preterite   ⎫
imperfect   ⎬ imperfect subjunctive
conditional ⎭

Práctica

ESCUCHAR • HABLAR • ESCRIBIR

1 Sigue el modelo para hacer una frase completa.

MODELO   invitarlo →
               Él quería que yo lo invitara.

1. tenerlo
2. saberlo
3. comprarlo
4. hacerlo
5. devolverlo
6. leerlo

7. comerlo
8. escribirlo
9. ponerlo
10. buscarlo
11. decirlo
12. pedirlo

HABLAR

2 Contesta con **sí** o **no** según tu opinión.

1. ¿Te sorprendería que tus amigos te dieran la mano?
2. ¿Te sorprendería que una amiga te diera un besito en la mejilla?
3. ¿Te sorprendería que tus amigos se levantaran para saludarte?
4. ¿Te sorprendería que ellos se abrazaran?
5. ¿Te sorprendería que tus amigos tuvieran buenos modales?
6. ¿Te sorprendería que ellos se comportaran bien?
7. ¿Te sorprendería que hubiera un malentendido entre tus amigos?

CULTURA

Abuelita quería que su nieta le diera la mano para ayudarla a bajarse del metro.

Nota

Verbs with **y** are spelled the same as those with **j**.

leyera   dijera
oyera   trajera

Comunicación

3 Trabajen en grupos pequeños y hablen de todo lo que les gustaría, lo que no les gustaría o lo que les sorprendería que pasara. Si es posible expliquen por qué.

ESCUCHAR • HABLAR • ESCRIBIR

4 Contesta según el modelo.

MODELO   hablar español →
               El profesor insistió en que habláramos español.

1. hablar mucho
2. pronunciar bien
3. llegar a clase a tiempo
4. aprender la gramática

5. escribir composiciones
6. leer novelas
7. trabajar mucho
8. hacer nuestras tareas

InfoGap For more practice using the imperfect subjunctive, do Activity 5 on page SR6 at the end of this book.

VIDEO Want help with the imperfect subjunctive? Watch **Gramática en vivo.**

CULTURA

El entrenador insistió en que los miembros de su equipo jugaran bien.

FOLDABLES®
Study Organizer

LARGE SENTENCE STRIPS

See page SH29 for help with making this foldable. Use this foldable to practice using the imperfect subjunctive with a partner. On the front of each strip, use the verbs **querer, insistir, esperar,** and **dudar** to write a sentence in the present tense. Then have your partner rewrite each sentence on the back of each strip using the imperfect subjunctive. When you're finished, switch roles.

LEER • ESCRIBIR

5 Completa con la forma apropiada del verbo indicado.

1. Yo tenía miedo de que ellos no ____ a tiempo. (llegar)
2. Estaban contentos que tú ____ para ayudarles. (estar)
3. No me sorprendió que ellos ____. (casarse)
4. Tenían miedo de que yo no ____ asistir a la recepción. (poder)
5. Durante la ceremonia civil, fue necesario que la pareja ____ el registro de matrimonio. (firmar)

ESCRIBIR

6 Escribe la frase de nuevo. Haz los cambios necesarios.

1. Ella quiere que yo llegue a tiempo.
   Ella quería ____.
2. Ella insiste en que seas cortés.
   Ella insistió ____.
3. Ella insistirá en que lo hagas correctamente.
   Ella insistiría ____.
4. Ella duda que ellos tengan razón.
   Ella dudó ____.
5. Ella quiere que hablemos con nuestros padres.
   Ella quería ____.

CULTURA

La familia de la novia insistió en que ella tuviera una boda tradicional en Ibiza, una de las islas Baleares de España.

Subjuntivo o infinitivo

Más práctica

📖 Workbook, p. 5.8
💿 StudentWorks™ Plus

1. If the subject of the main clause is different from the subject of the dependent clause, the subjunctive is used.

MAIN CLAUSE		DEPENDENT CLAUSE
¿Tú quieres	que	yo vaya?
Nosotros preferimos	que	ustedes se lo digan.
Era necesario	que	tú lo supieras.

2. If there is no change of subject, the infinitive is used.

¿Tú quieres ir?
Preferimos decírselo.
Era necesario saberlo.

Práctica

ESCUCHAR • HABLAR • ESCRIBIR

7 Contesta con **sí**. Presta atención a los sujetos.

1. ¿Quieres decírselo?
2. ¿Quieres que yo se lo diga?
3. ¿Quieres sentarte?
4. ¿Quieres que ellos se sienten?
5. ¿Prefieres salir con ellos?
6. ¿Prefieres que yo salga con ellos?
7. ¿Prefieres pagar?
8. ¿Prefieres que ellos paguen?

ESCRIBIR

8 Forma frases.

MODELO yo / esperar / él / ir →
            Yo espero que él vaya.

1. yo / esperar / ustedes / venir pronto
2. yo / esperar / venir
3. ellos / esperar / nosotros / llegar
4. nosotros / esperar / tú / divertirte
5. yo / esperar / divertirme

CULTURA

¿Quieres dar un paseo por los bonitos jardines del Palacio Real en Madrid?

CULTURA

Estos jóvenes esperan pasar un buen día en Zaragoza, España. Están mirando la vista de la Basílica de Nuestra Señora del Pilar desde el puente de Piedra sobre el río Ebro.

🎴 Comunicación

9 Pregúntale a tu compañero(a) lo que él o ella quiere hacer este fin de semana. Después, pregúntale lo que sus padres quieren que él o ella haga. Decidan si ustedes quieren hacer las mismas cosas que sus padres quieren que hagan o no.

Gramática

Sufijos

En otras partes

Diminutive endings can vary in different parts of the Spanish-speaking world. The two most common are probably **-ito** and **-illo,** but you will also hear **-ico.**

1. A suffix is an ending you add to a word. You can add the suffixes **-ito** or **-illo** to a Spanish noun to form what is called the "diminutive" form of the noun. The meaning of the diminutive may refer to the actual physical size or it may convey a favorable emotional quality on the part of the speaker.

| la casa | la casita | la chica | la chiquita |
| el beso | el besito | el perro | el perrito |

2. If the noun ends in **-n** or the vowel **-e,** the suffix **-cito** is added.

| el ratón | el ratoncito |
| el café | el cafecito |

3. You can add the suffix **-ísimo** to an adjective to convey the meaning *very* or *most*. Remember that the adjective must agree with the noun it modifies.

| un joven guapísimo | una joven guapísima |
| unos jóvenes guapísimos | unas jóvenes guapísimas |

Note that an adjective that ends in a vowel drops the vowel before adding **-ísimo.**

bueno → buenísimo
grande → grandísimo

Práctica

LEER • ESCRIBIR

10 Da la forma diminutiva.

1. el vaso
2. la casa
3. el beso
4. el perro
5. el plato
6. el amigo
7. la abuela
8. el hijo
9. la botella
10. la caja

LEER • ESCRIBIR

11 Da la forma diminutiva.

1. el coche
2. el café
3. el parque
4. el ratón
5. la calle
6. el limón

CULTURA

Una casita bellísima en Cadaqués, España

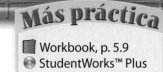
Gramática

LEER • ESCRIBIR

12 Emplea **-ísimo** con el adjetivo.

1. Es una comida buena.
2. Son animales grandes.
3. Es una lección difícil.
4. Tienen dos niños preciosos.
5. Tiene una prima bella.

13 **Trabalenguas** Lee con cuidado. ¡Diviértete!

1. Abuelita toma un cafecito y un platito de pastelitos en su cafecito favorito en el parquecito.
2. Los amiguitos juegan con su perrito en el jardincito de su casita.
3. Los gatitos y los perritos son animalitos preciosísimos.

14 **Juego** Work in groups. Make up as many words with **-ito, -ico, -illo** as possible in two minutes. See who wins.

CULTURA
Un cochecito en Sevilla

Refrán

Can you guess what the following proverb means?

A chico pajarillo, chico nidillo.

¡Bravo!

You have now learned all the new vocabulary and grammar in this chapter. Continue to use and practice all that you know while learning more cultural information. ¡Vamos!

¡UN PEQUEÑO MALENTENDIDO!

YO VI A TU PRIMA EL OTRO DÍA EN EL CAFÉ SOL Y SOMBRA.

¿AH, SÍ?

SÍ, Y TU PRIMA ES UNA BELLEZA. CREO QUE ESTÁ ENAMORADA DE MÍ.

¿JULIA? ¿ENAMORADA DE TI? PERO, BILL, ¿POR QUÉ DIRÍAS TAL COSA? ¡QUÉ TONTERÍA!

PUES, ¿SABES LO QUE HIZO? CUANDO ME VIO EN EL CAFÉ SE ACERCÓ Y ME BESÓ— Y NO SOLO UNA VEZ SINO DOS VECES. ¿CÓMO ME DARÍA DOS BESITOS SIN QUE YO TUVIERA SOSPECHAS DE QUE ME QUIERE?

BILL, ESTOS BESITOS NO TIENEN IMPORTANCIA. ES UNA COSTUMBRE NUESTRA. ELLA TE BESÓ EN CADA MEJILLA COMO SEÑAL DE CARIÑO Y AMISTAD. NO TIENE NADA QUE VER CON EL AMOR.

NO ME QUEDO CONVENCIDO, YOLANDA.

NO TE QUEDAS CONVENCIDO PORQUE PREFERIRÍAS QUE TE DIJERA QUE JULIA TE QUIERE. PERO, ¿QUIERES QUE YO TE DIGA LO QUE PIENSO YO?

YO CREO QUE ERES TÚ QUIEN TE ESTÁS ENAMORANDO DE JULIA.

¿Comprendes?

VIDEO To learn about a Mexican custom, watch **Cultura en vivo.**

A Contesta según la información en la conversación.

1. ¿Quiénes hablan?
2. ¿Cómo se llama la prima de Yolanda?
3. ¿Quién la vio?
4. ¿Cómo la describió?
5. ¿Qué cree Bill?
6. ¿Por qué cree tal cosa?

B Explicando Contesta.

1. ¿Qué le explica Yolanda a Bill?
2. ¿Puede ella convencer a Bill?
3. ¿Qué cree Yolanda?

C Llegando a conclusiones ¿Qué piensas? ¿Estás de acuerdo con Bill o con Yolanda?

D Interpretando El título de la conversación es «¡Un pequeño malentendido!» ¿Por qué lleva tal título?

E Analizando How do such **malentendidos culturales** take place? Have you ever experienced one?

¿Qué crees? ¿Tiene razón Bill o hay un malentendido?

Antes de leer

Con tus compañeros, discute las convenciones de cortesía que se practican en tu familia y en tu comunidad.

 Reading Check

El mundo hispano goza de muchas influencias culturales diferentes. ¿Cuáles son algunas?

¿Buen comportamiento o mal comportamiento? 🎧 ♻️

Costumbres diferentes Cada cultura tiene sus propias tradiciones y costumbres. Además cada sociedad tiene sus convenciones de cortesía que dictan lo que son buenos y malos modales. Si uno quiere relacionarse bien con gente de otras culturas tiene que aprender y entender sus tradiciones sociales. Y siempre hay que tomar en cuenta que «diferente» no es sinónimo de «inferior» ni «superior» porque cada sociedad tiene distintas normas de buen comportamiento.

Ya sabes que el mundo hispano es muy grande, y no hay una sola cultura hispana. Los muchos países que componen el mundo hispano gozan de[1] muchas influencias culturales diferentes—indígena, español-mediterránea, africana. Y ahora vamos a explorar algunos modales que se consideran buenos o malos en casi todas las naciones hispanohablantes.

Si una persona o un grupo de personas está sentado en un café, una oficina o aun en casa y llega otra persona, todos suelen levantarse y darle la mano al recién llegado para saludarlo. Es una costumbre que se practica igual entre los jóvenes.

[1]gozan de   *enjoy*

CULTURA

Un besito entre amigos en la mejilla no es señal de amor.

El abrazo El abrazo es otra costumbre muy hispana. Son los hombres que se conocen bien que se abrazan. Un señor rodea a un amigo con los brazos mientras le da unos golpes en la espalda. Los hombres se abrazan así cuando se encuentran[2] o cuando se despiden[3] el uno del otro.

El besito Las mujeres no se abrazan. Se dan un besito. Le dan el besito a una amiga o a un amigo que conocen bien. Dan el besito en cada mejilla, y la verdad es que las mejillas y los labios no se tocan. El besito va al aire. El abrazo o el besito es una señal de cariño y amistad entre amigos y parientes y nada más.

«Tú» y «usted» Hay que tener mucho cuidado con el uso de «tú» y «usted» y no hay siempre normas claras porque el uso de «tú» y «usted» puede variar de un país a otro o de una clase social a otra. El uso de «tú» se llama «el tuteo», y hablar con alguien en la forma de «tú» es «tutearlo». ¿Cuándo puedes tutear a una persona? Pues, es casi siempre aceptable tutear a una persona que tiene la misma edad que tú. En otras circunstancias debes esperar a que el individuo con quien hablas te invite a tutearlo. En general se tutea entre amigos, parientes y jóvenes. En los otros casos se usa «usted».

El voseo Ya sabes que el plural de «tú» en España es «vosotros». En Latinoamérica es «ustedes». Pero hay que señalar algo importantísimo. No en todas partes, pero en muchas partes de Latinoamérica en vez de decir «tú» la gente usa «vos», llamado «el voseo». Algunos ejemplos del voseo son:

> **Vos estás bien.**
> **Vos podés hacerlo.**
> **Vos tenés tiempo.**
> **¿Vos te sentís mejor?**
> **¿A qué hora vos te acostás?**

[2]se encuentran *they meet*
[3]se despiden *they take leave*

✓ **Reading Check**
¿Cuándo se abrazan los hombres?

✓ **Reading Check**
¿Cuándo es aceptable tutear a una persona?

✓ **Reading Check**
¿Qué es «el voseo»?

CULTURA
Un saludo típico entre dos amigas en San Juan de Puerto Rico

Títulos Como señal de respeto, los hispanos suelen usar el título de una persona. Por ejemplo, el doctor es siempre «doctor(a) López», el abogado[4] es «abogado(a) Salas», el profesor «profesor(a) Iglesias» en vez de señor o señora. Si la persona tiene la licenciatura[5], se usa el título «licenciado(a)».

CULTURA

Observa el uso de títulos en este aviso delante de un despacho (oficina) en la isla de Vieques, Puerto Rico. ¿De qué será la abreviatura **Lcda.?**

> Lcda. Aurora Padilla Morales
> Abogado-Notario
> Servicios Notariales
> CasosCivilesyCriminales

✓ **Reading Check**

¿Cuál es la diferencia entre un amigo y un conocido?

Amigos o conocidos En unas culturas la gente se refiere a casi todos los que conocen como «amigos». Pero no es así en las culturas latinas. Un «amigo» es «un amigo»—una persona a quien conoces bien y en quien tienes confianza. Una persona a quien conoces pero no muy bien es un «conocido». En las culturas latinas uno tiene muchos conocidos y menos amigos. En otras culturas uno tiene muchos amigos y menos conocidos.

✓ **Reading Check**

¿Cuál es una diversión que les gusta a muchos hispanohablantes?

Conversaciones y tertulias Para mucha gente hispanohablante no hay nada mejor que una buena conversación animada en que todos ofrecen sus opiniones o ideas con mucho entusiasmo. Si buscas la palabra «tertulia» en un diccionario bilingüe, es posible que encuentres la definición *party,* pero es en realidad una reunión de personas que se juntan con frecuencia. ¿Para qué? Para pasarlo bien pero aún más importante para conversar.

[4]abogado   *lawyer*
[5]licenciatura   *degree more or less equivalent to a master's degree*

CULTURA

Varias tertulias en un restaurante de un pueblecito vasco. Estos mismos señores se reúnen habitualmente para conversar de todo.

¿Comprendes?

Más práctica

📖 Workbook, pp. 5.10–5.12
🔵 StudentWorks™ Plus

A Analizando Contesta.

💡 ¿Por qué es importante tomar en cuenta que «diferente» no es sinónimo de «inferior» ni «superior»?

B Recordando hechos Contesta.

¿Cuáles son tres culturas que tienen una influencia en las culturas hispanas?

C Describiendo Describe.

1. lo que hacen los hispanos cuando están sentados y llega(n) otra(s) persona(s)
2. un abrazo entre hombres
3. el besito que se dan los hispanos

D Explicando

1. Explica la diferencia entre el uso de «tú» y «usted». Explica también por qué es importante distinguir entre el uso de «tú» y «usted».
2. Explica lo que es «el voseo».

E Confirmando información Escoge según lo que has aprendido sobre las costumbres hispanas.

CULTURA

Tommy Robredo y Martina Hingis practican buena conducta y buenos modales durante un partido de tenis en una playa de España.

	buenos modales	malos modales
1. no usar el título de la persona con quien hablas		
2. invitar a una persona a hacer algo y no pagar		
3. quedarse sentado(a) cuando llega alguien		
4. tutear a una persona que no conoces bien		
5. darle un besito a una amiga en las mejillas		

El conde Lucanor
de don Juan Manuel

▲ El pueblo medieval de Pedraza cerca de Segovia

Estrategia

Simplificando el texto Cuando lees una obra literaria antigua, es necesario simplificar el lenguaje porque el estilo ha cambiado mucho durante los siglos. Una sola frase puede ser larga y contener mucha información. Una estrategia importante es la de dividir las frases en segmentos más cortos mientras lees. Esto te ayuda a seguir el texto y recordar los detalles.

Vocabulario

la villa   ciudad, población

los demás   otras personas

el apodo   otro nombre que toma una persona o que se le da a la persona

el mozo   el joven

el provecho   el beneficio

sabio(a)   muy inteligente

mejorar   hacer mejor

suceder   ocurrir, pasar, tener lugar

olvidar   no recordar

hacerle caso   prestar atención

Práctica

1 Parea los contrarios.

1. los demás
2. una villa
3. mejorar
4. suceder

a. no pasar nada
b. un pueblo pequeño
c. empeorar
d. nosotros mismos

2 Usa cada palabra de la Actividad 1 en una frase original.

3 Da otra palabra o expresión.

1. ciudad o población
2. no tener en la memoria
3. un muchacho
4. prestar atención; fijarse en
5. de mucha inteligencia
6. los otros (refiriéndose a gente)

4 Expresa de otra manera.

1. Tenemos que proteger los derechos de *los otros*.
2. ¿Qué *pasa*?
3. Tienes que *prestarle atención* porque es *muy inteligente*.
4. Él tiene *varios nombres*.
5. Hay que sacar *beneficio* de la oportunidad.

INTRODUCCIÓN

El autor de *El conde Lucanor* es don Juan Manuel (1282–1349?), el sobrino del rey Alfonso X que tenía el apodo Alfonso X el Sabio. El plan del libro es sencillo. El conde Lucanor consulta a su consejero Patronio cada vez que tiene que enfrentar una situación difícil. Patronio le relata un cuento que le puede servir de guía al conde en la decisión que tiene que tomar. La moraleja del cuento se resume al final en unos versos cortitos.

Antes de leer

Es casi imposible tomar decisiones y hacer cosas sin que nadie te critique. ¿Es posible que tengas un amigo o pariente que casi siempre está en contra de lo que quieres hacer? Piensa en tal persona al leer este capítulo de El conde Lucanor.

El conde Lucanor 🎧

Capítulo XXIV

De lo que conteció° a un buen hombre con su hijo

conteció *sucedió*

En una ocasión ocurrió que el conde Lucanor le hablaba a Patronio, su consejero, y le dijo que estaba muy ansioso sobre una cosa que quería hacer. Estaba ansioso porque sabía que no importaba que lo hiciera o que no lo hiciera, habría quien lo criticara. El conde Lucanor quería que Patronio le diera consejos y Patronio le relató el siguiente cuento.

Ocurrió que un labrador bueno y honrado tenía un hijo joven y muy inteligente pero cada vez que el padre quería hacer algo para mejorar su hacienda° el hijo le contaba un montón de cosas negativas que podrían suceder. Después de un tiempo el buen labrador se puso enfadado porque sabía que estaba sufriendo daños en su negocio° porque siempre le hacía caso a lo que le decía su hijo. Por fin decidió que tenía que enseñarle una lección.

hacienda *estate, income*

negocio *business*

El buen hombre y su hijo eran labradores que vivían cerca de una villa. Un día fueron al mercado de la villa para comprar algunas cosas que necesitaban. Los dos se pusieron de acuerdo° que llevarían un asno para cargar° las compras. Los dos iban al mercado a pie y el asno no llevaba ninguna carga. Encontraron a unos hombres que volvían de la villa. Estos hombres empezaron a hablar entre sí°. El labrador oyó que decían que no les parecía muy prudente que los dos iban a pie mientras el asno andaba descargado. El padre le preguntó a su hijo lo que pensaba de los comentarios de

se pusieron de acuerdo *agreed*
cargar *carry, load*

entre sí *among themselves*

*Identifica el problema
que tiene el padre con su
hijo. No olvides de que lo
que sucede en el cuento
tiene lugar en el siglo XIV.
¿Podría suceder hoy?*

*Al leer fíjate en lo que
hace o dice el hijo que le
enfada al padre.*

tierno *tender*

CULTURA

Un burro con su carga de canastas
en Segovia. Es una escena poco
frecuente hoy en día.

fiel *faithful*

no dejes *don't stop*

aquellos hombres. El hijo dijo que le parecía que decían
la verdad. Entonces el buen hombre mandó a su hijo que
subiera en el (al) asno.

Seguían por el camino cuando encontraron a otros
hombres que al verlos dijeron que no les parecía normal
que un labrador viejo y cansado anduviera a pie (caminara)
y que un joven fuerte anduviera montado en el asno. Una
vez más el padre le preguntó a su hijo lo que pensaba de
lo que decían estos. El hijo creyó que tenían razón y el
padre mandó a su hijo que se bajara del asno para que él lo
subiera.

A poca distancia encontraron una vez más a otros
hombres. Estos dijeron que el buen hombre hacía muy mal
porque él estaba acostumbrado a las fatigas del trabajo y
él, y no el hijo pequeño y tierno°, debía andar a pie. El
buen hombre le preguntó a su hijo qué le parecía de esto
que aquellos hombres decían. El mozo contestó que estaba
de acuerdo con ellos. Entonces el padre mandó a su hijo que
él también subiera al asno de manera que ninguno de los
dos anduviera a pie.

Después de poco encontraron a otros hombres que
comenzaron a decir que aquella bestia en que iban era
tan flaca que era cruel que los dos caballeros anduvieran
montados en ella.

El padre le habló a su hijo:

—Mi hijo, ¿qué quieres que yo haga para que nadie me
critique? Ya ves que todos nos han criticado—si los dos
vamos a pie, si tú vas a pie, si yo voy a pie o si ninguno de los
dos va a pie. Y cada vez que nos han criticado tú has estado
de acuerdo con lo que decían. Espero que esto te sirva de
lección. No puedes hacer nada que les parezca bien a todos.
Hay que hacer lo que te sea conveniente con tal de que no
sea malo. No puedes tener miedo de que alguien te critique
porque la gente siempre habla de las cosas de los demás.
Hay que aceptar el «lo que dirán».

—Y tú, señor conde, tienes que considerar el daño o
el provecho que puedes sacar de algo. Si no tienes total
confianza en lo que quieres hacer, debes buscar el consejo
de gente inteligente y fiel°. Y si no encuentras tal consejero
debes esperar a lo menos un día y una noche antes de
resolver lo que quieres hacer. Y no dejes nunca de hacer lo
que quieres hacer por miedo de lo que puede decir la gente
de ello.

La moraleja es:

*Por miedo a lo que dirá la gente, no dejes° de hacer lo que
más apropiado y conveniente te parece ser.*

¿Comprendes?

A **Recordando hechos** Contesta.

1. ¿Cuál fue el problema que tenía el buen labrador con su hijo?
2. ¿Por qué decidió que tenía que enseñarle una lección?
3. ¿Dónde vivían el labrador y su hijo?
4. ¿Adónde iban? ¿Por qué?
5. ¿Sobre qué se pusieron de acuerdo los dos?

B **Describiendo** Describe lo que pasó cuando...

1. ninguno de los dos iba en el asno.
2. solo el hijo iba en el asno.
3. solo el padre iba en el asno.
4. los dos iban en el asno.

C **Analizando** Discute.

1. el por qué de los comentarios de los cuatro grupos de hombres que el padre y el hijo encontraron
2. la razón por la cual el padre se enfadó con su hijo

D **Resumiendo**

En tus propias palabras da un resumen de la conclusión del cuento.

Después de leer

Piensa en los consejos y la moraleja del cuento. ¿Estás de acuerdo con la conclusión o no? ¿La puedes relacionar con tu propia vida? ¿Cómo?

CULTURA

Cuadro de un mercado en Segovia por Edward Angelo Goodall—siglo XIX

¿BUENOS O MALOS MODALES?

Prepárate para el examen
Self-check for achievement

To review **Vocabulario,** turn to pages 136–137.

Vocabulario

1 Completa.

1. Ellos no se quedaron sentados. Se ____.
2. Ellas se dieron un besito en la ____.
3. Dos señores que son amigos se dan ____ cuando se ven.
4. Él siempre se comporta bien. Tiene buenos ____.
5. Los dos están ____ y se van a casar pronto.

2 Da otra palabra o expresión.

6. ponerse de pie
7. darse la mano
8. darse un abrazo
9. salir y decir «adiós»

Gramática

3 Completa.

10. Era necesario que ellos ____. (levantarse)
11. Me sorprendió que tú no le ____ la mano. (dar)
12. A mi parecer, sería imposible que él no ____ nada del asunto. (saber)
13. Ellos no querían que yo ____. (pagar)
14. Yo no lo haría a menos que lo ____ tú. (hacer)
15. Ellos salieron sin que nadie los ____. (ver)
16. Ella preferiría que Uds. no se lo ____ a nadie. (decir)
17. Me gustaría que él le ____ el regalo a mi hermano. (dar)

To review **el imperfecto del subjuntivo,** turn to page 140.

4 Escribe de nuevo.

18. Yo espero que tú lo hagas.
    Yo esperaba que ____.
19. Ellos quieren que yo vaya.
    Ellos querían que ____.
20. Ellos prefieren que lo sepamos.
    Ellos preferirían que ____.

21. Es imposible que vengan.
Sería imposible que _____.

22. Insisto en que asistas a la fiesta.
Insistí en que _____.

To review **subjuntivo o infinitivo,** turn to page 143.

5 **Completa.**

23. Es necesario que nosotros le _____. (hablar)

24. Es necesario _____ con él. (hablar)

25. Ellos no quieren que tú lo _____. (hacer)

26. Y ellos no lo quieren _____ tampoco. (hacer)

27. Es importante _____ a tiempo. (llegar)

28. Prefiero _____ ahora. (salir)

To review **sufijos,** turn to page 144.

6 **Da la palabra apropiada usando un sufijo.**

29. mi hijo querido

30. una casa pequeña

31. un coche pequeño

32. nuestro perro adorable

33. un café pequeño

7 **Emplea -ísimo con el adjetivo.**

34. Tengo dos cursos aburridos.

35. Es una muchacha guapa.

To review this cultural information, turn to pages 148–150.

Cultura

8 **¿Sí o no?**

36. En los países hispanos todos se quedan sentados cuando llega o entra otra persona.

37. En las sociedades hispanas las mujeres siempre se abrazan cuando se encuentran.

38. En las sociedades hispanas los señores y las señoras que se conocen bien se dan un besito en la mejilla cuando se encuentran.

39. En los países hispanos son solo los mayores que se levantan cuando llega otra persona.

40. El voseo se usa en muy pocos países.

CULTURA

Los jóvenes se encontraron y se saludaron en un centro comercial en San Juan, Puerto Rico. ¿Son amigos o conocidos?

1 **Buenos y malos modales**

✔ *Discuss good and bad manners*

Trabajen en grupos de cuatro. Den algunos ejemplos de lo que ustedes consideran buenos y malos modales.

2 **Diferencias**

✔ *Discuss some customs that are different*

Discute con un(a) compañero(a) de clase algunas diferencias entre costumbres sociales hispanas y costumbres que son «típicas» aquí en Estados Unidos. ¿Cuáles son algunas reglas de cortesía que existen en España y Latinoamérica que no existen aquí y viceversa?

CULTURA

Un saludo tailandés típico. El saludo se llama *wai* y es un aspecto importante de la cultura tailandesa.

3 **Entrevista**

✔ *Interview a classmate*

Si en tu escuela hay alumnos de unos países latinos, entrevístalos para determinar cuáles son algunas costumbres de cortesía y ejemplos de buenos modales que ellos practican que no se practican aquí y viceversa.

4 **Mi querida familia**

✔ *Discuss what your family would like you to do*

Habla con un(a) compañero(a) de clase. Dile todo lo que tu familia quisiera que tú hicieras. A tu parecer, ¿son exigentes (estrictos) o no? ¿Quisiera la familia de tu compañero(a) que él/ella hiciera más o menos las mismas cosas?

5 **Un(a) niño(a) mal educado(a)**

✔ *Describe an ill-behaved child*

Describe el comportamiento de un(a) niño(a) mal educado(a). Sé lo más original posible.

Tarea

You have been asked to interview several people and then write a short essay for an upcoming program on manners around the world. Your short essay should focus not only on what are considered good and bad manners in your home, school, and community, but also on what you have learned about proper conduct in Spanish-speaking cultures. Be sure to incorporate vocabulary and grammar learned in this chapter.

Writing Strategy

Conducting an interview Interviewing a variety of individuals about a given topic can help to make your writing more authentic and convincing because it allows you to present several different perspectives while comparing and contrasting them with your own. By using multiple perspectives to elaborate on your theme, you provide the reader with more than one option, thus increasing the chances that he or she will relate to what you have written. Always prepare your questions ahead of time, and as you do so, think about the person you will be interviewing. It is also very important to take good notes during the interview process.

❶ Prewrite

- Decide whom you will be interviewing and arrange to meet them at a convenient time and place. Inform them that you will be asking what they think constitutes good and bad manners and what they know about manners around the world.

- Prepare at least five good questions for each separate interview.

❷ Write

- As you piece together the different elements of your short essay, think about the vocabulary you will be using.

- When considering how you are going to use the chapter's main grammar points, you should keep in mind that you will need to use other previously learned grammatical structures in order for your essay to be informative and meaningful.

Evaluate

Your teacher will evaluate you based on the proper use of vocabulary, correctness of grammar, logical structure, and completeness of information.

Repaso del Capítulo 5

Gramática

- ### El imperfecto del subjuntivo *(page 140)*
  If the verb of the main clause is in the present or future tense, the present subjunctive is used in the dependent clause. If the verb of the main clause is in the preterite, imperfect, or conditional, the imperfect subjunctive is used in the dependent clause.

  Será imposible que él no lo sepa.
  Sería imposible que él no lo supiera.

  Él habla así para que comprendamos.
  Él habló así para que comprendiéramos.

  Ellos no quieren que él hable así.
  Ellos no querían que él hablara así.

- ### Subjuntivo o infinitivo *(page 143)*
  When there is no change of subject, the infinitive is used.

  Yo quiero ir. Y ellos no quieren que yo vaya.

- ### Sufijos *(page 144)*
  You add the suffixes **-ito** or **-illo** to a noun to form the diminutive form of the noun.

  la casa   la casita   la chica   la chiquita

  If the noun ends in **-n** or the vowel **-e**, the suffix **-cito** is added.

  el ratón   el ratoncito

  To express *very* or *most,* add the suffix **-ísimo** to an adjective.

  un joven guapísimo
  una joven guapísima

CULTURA

Este jovencito trabaja de mesero en un café en Buenos Aires y da un servicio buenísimo.

There are a number of cognates in this list. See how many you and a partner can find. Who can find the most? Compare your list with those of your classmates.

Vocabulario

Discussing manners

el/la recién llegado(a)	el comportamiento	despedirse	comportarse
el/la invitado(a)	la mejilla	ponerse de pie	enfadarse
un besito	cortés	darse la mano	
un abrazo	formal	besar	
los modales	saludar(se)	abrazar(se)	

Other useful words and expressions

el/la conocido(a)	el amor	castigar
el/la chico(a)	enamorarse	¡Cuidado!
el malentendido	malentender	¡Mucho ojo!

 The words listed below come from this chapter's literary selection, *El conde Lucanor*. They were selected to become part of your active vocabulary because of their relatively high frequency.

la villa	el provecho	olvidar
los demás	sabio(a)	hacerle caso
el apodo	mejorar	
el/la mozo(a)	suceder	

Repaso cumulativo

Repasa lo que ya has aprendido

These activities will help you review and remember what you have learned so far in Spanish.

 Escucha las frases. Indica en una tabla como la de abajo si describe un viaje en avión o en tren.

en avión	en tren

 Forma frases.

1. pasajeros / los / equipaje / el / facturan / el / en / mostrador
2. sale / número / vuelo / el / cincuenta / destino / con / a / Caracas
3. pasajeros / esperan / vuelo / los / salida / la / su / de
4. tienen / pasar / que / pasajeros / por / control / el / seguridad / de / los
5. necesario / tener / es / embarque / de / una / antes de / abordar / tarjeta / avión / el

 Identifica.

CULTURA

Dos AVES en la estación de Santa Justa en Sevilla, España

4 **Parea los contrarios.**

1. procedente de	**a.** la llegada
2. aterrizar	**b.** abordar
3. tarde	**c.** despegar
4. la salida	**d.** a tiempo
5. desembarcar	**e.** con destino a
6. sencillo	**f.** de ida y vuelta

5 **Parea los sinónimos.**

1. el boleto	**a.** con un retraso
2. la tarjeta de embarque	**b.** de ida y regreso
3. con una demora	**c.** el billete
4. embarcar	**d.** el coche
5. el vagón	**e.** el pasabordo
6. de ida y vuelta	**f.** abordar

6 **Completa con un verbo apropiado en el presente.**

1. Los pasajeros _____ un viaje en tren.

2. Yo _____ mi ropa en mi mochila.

3. El tren _____ del andén cinco.

4. Estamos en la estación de ferrocarril y no necesitamos un carrito porque _____ solamente dos mochilas.

5. Los pasajeros _____ cola delante de la ventanilla.

6. Ellos _____ su equipaje en la maletera del carro.

7 **Pon las frases de la Actividad 6 en el pretérito.**

8 **Describe todo lo que ves en los dibujos sobre un fin de semana que la familia Núñez pasó en el camping.**

Viajes

Aquí y Allí

Vamos a comparar Muchos dicen que no hay nada más interesante que el viajar. No hay duda que viajando se aprende mucho. Pero también hay que saber mucho para viajar—hay muchas cosas que uno tiene que hacer como observarás en este capítulo.

Objetivos

You will:

- discuss several modes of travel
- talk about a trip to Bolivia
- read a short story by the Spanish author Emilia Pardo Bazán

You will use:

- the subjunctive with conjunctions of time
- the subjunctive to express suggestions and advice
- irregular nouns

◀ La madre y su hijo, como muchos otros pasajeros, están esperando la salida de su vuelo en el aeropuerto en Cancún, México. Desgraciadamente hay una demora.

Go to glencoe.com
For: **Online book**
Web code: **ASD7844c6**

Introducción al tema
Viajes

Cada día hay miles de personas que están viajando. Hay muchos motivos para hacer un viaje—vacaciones, negocios, visitas familiares, etc. Como vas a observar en este capítulo, hay más de una manera de viajar y de vez en cuando es necesario cambiar de planes al último momento.

▲ **República Dominicana**
Este señor tiene que hacer un viaje importante y no importa que tenga una pierna quebrada. Una agente de la línea aérea le puede ayudar en el aeropuerto.

◄ **Guatemala** Estas dos jóvenes están de vacaciones en Guatemala. Acaban de visitar las famosas ruinas en Tikal y ahora están llegando al aeropuerto de Santa Elena.

España ¿Es una cafetería en un parque tropical? No. Está en la sala de espera de la estación de ferrocarril Atocha en Madrid. ▶

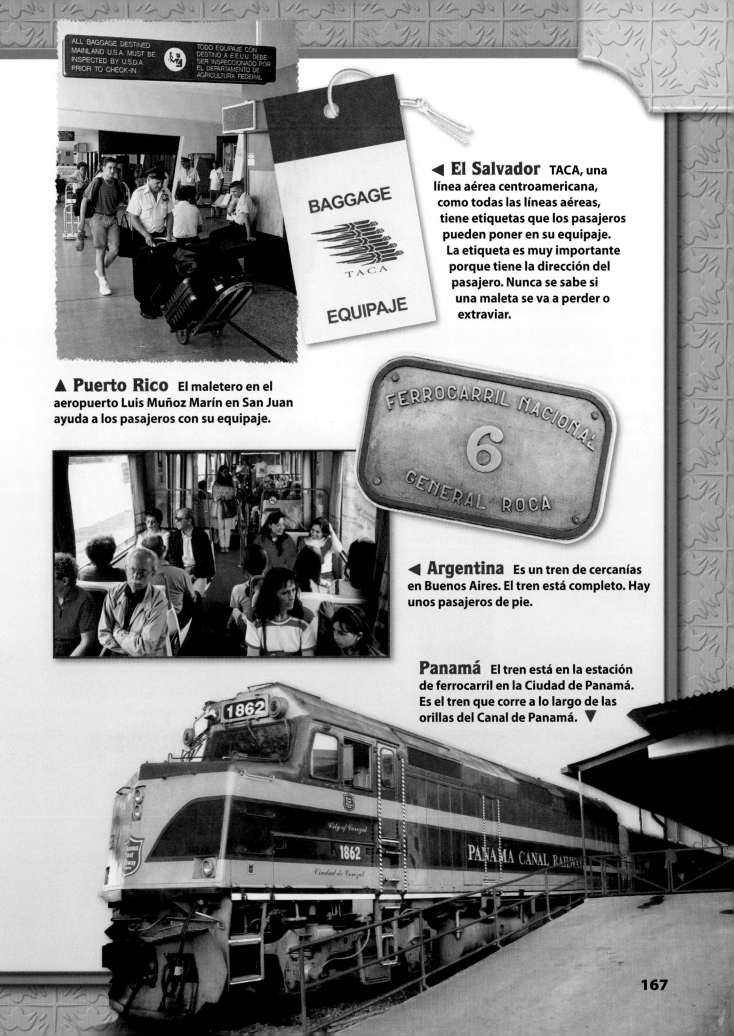

◀ El Salvador TACA, una línea aérea centroamericana, como todas las líneas aéreas, tiene etiquetas que los pasajeros pueden poner en su equipaje. La etiqueta es muy importante porque tiene la dirección del pasajero. Nunca se sabe si una maleta se va a perder o extraviar.

ALL BAGGAGE DESTINED MAINLAND U.S.A. MUST BE INSPECTED BY U.S.D.A. PRIOR TO CHECK-IN

TODO EQUIPAJE CON DESTINO A EE.UU. DEBE SER INSPECCIONADO POR EL DEPARTAMENTO DE AGRICULTURA FEDERAL

BAGGAGE

TACA

EQUIPAJE

▲ Puerto Rico El maletero en el aeropuerto Luis Muñoz Marín en San Juan ayuda a los pasajeros con su equipaje.

FERROCARRIL NACIONAL **6** GENERAL ROCA

◀ Argentina Es un tren de cercanías en Buenos Aires. El tren está completo. Hay unos pasajeros de pie.

Panamá El tren está en la estación de ferrocarril en la Ciudad de Panamá. Es el tren que corre a lo largo de las orillas del Canal de Panamá. ▼

1862

City of Corozal

1862

Ciudad de Corozal

PANAMA CANAL RAILWAY

En el aeropuerto

El talón indica hasta donde está facturado el equipaje—el destino.

La etiqueta lleva el nombre y la dirección del pasajero.

Hay un límite de peso. Una maleta no puede pesar más de 22 kilos.

No puede exceder el límite.

Los vuelos a Barcelona y a Pamplona no hacen escala.

Son vuelos sin escala.

Un vuelo directo hace escala antes de continuar a su destino.

El vuelo no está completo.

Hay unos asientos disponibles.

El vuelo no va a salir debido a un problema técnico (mecánico).

La línea tendrá que confirmar a los pasajeros en otro vuelo.

La pareja perdió su vuelo.

El vuelo ya había salido antes de que ellos llegaran a la puerta de salida.

el reclamo de equipaje

la correa

Los pasajeros podrán reclamar (recoger) su equipaje
facturado cuando lleguen a su destino.
El equipaje del vuelo 125 está llegando en la correa F.
Los pasajeros están reclamando (recogiendo) su equipaje.
Tienen que esperar hasta que vean sus maletas en la correa.

la inmigración

la aduana

el control de pasaportes

Los pasajeros en un vuelo internacional tienen que
pasar por el control de pasaportes.
Tienen que pasar por la aduana también.

ESCUCHAR

1 Escucha y determina si la información que oyes es correcta o no. Usa una tabla como la de abajo para indicar tus respuestas.

correcta	incorrecta

HABLAR • ESCRIBIR

2 Identifica.

1.

2.

3.

4.

5.

6.

HABLAR • ESCRIBIR

3 Contesta sobre un viaje en avión.

1. ¿Qué información hay en una etiqueta?
2. ¿Cuántos kilos no puede exceder una maleta sin que el pasajero tenga que pagar un suplemento?
3. ¿Hace un vuelo directo una escala antes de llegar a su destino final?
4. ¿Qué tienen que hacer las líneas aéreas si anulan un vuelo?
5. ¿Te gustaría más tener un asiento en la ventanilla o en el pasillo?
6. ¿Por dónde tienen que pasar los pasajeros que llegan en un vuelo internacional?
7. Como siempre hay una fila larga en el control de seguridad, ¿es posible perder tu vuelo si no llegas al aeropuerto bastante temprano?

LEER

4 Parea los sinónimos.

1. completo
2. anulado
3. una demora
4. el asiento
5. reclamar

a. recoger
b. lleno
c. la plaza
d. cancelado
e. un retraso

LEER • ESCRIBIR

5 Identifica donde.

1. donde puedes verificar (chequear) las salidas y llegadas de los vuelos
2. de donde salen los vuelos
3. donde llega el equipaje que descargan del avión después de un vuelo
4. donde inspeccionan el equipaje de los pasajeros que llegan en vuelos internacionales
5. donde revisan los pasaportes de los pasajeros internacionales

Estudio de palabras

disponer Ellos disponen de muchas oportunidades.

disponible Hay muchas oportunidades disponibles.

disposición Ellos tienen muchas oportunidades a su disposición.

pasar José, favor de pasar la sal.
Pásame la sal, por favor.

el paso El niño tomó su primer paso.

el pasillo En el avión hay asientos en el pasillo y en la ventanilla.

el pase Él tiene un pase para poder entrar en la zona restringida.

Contesta. Da respuestas personales.

1. ¿Cuáles son algunas actividades disponibles en tu escuela?
2. ¿Cuáles son algunas ventajas o cosas beneficiosas que tú crees tener a tu disposición?
3. A veces para ser cortés, ¿le permites a alguien pasar delante de ti?
4. ¿Hay muchos pasillos en tu escuela?
5. ¿Necesitas un pase para poder entrar en tu escuela?

La estación de tren (ferrocarril)

El tren de cercanías va a los suburbios—a las afueras de una ciudad.

cambiar de tren, transbordar

Los pasajeros tienen que cambiar de tren en Sevilla.

En Sevilla tienen que bajar(se) del tren de cercanías y tomar el tren de largo recorrido.

El tren de largo recorrido enlaza ciudades grandes pero no muy cercanas.

La agencia de alquiler

En otras partes

Alquilar is universally understood, but **rentar** and **arrendar** are used in many areas of Latin America.

Beatriz quiere alquilar (rentar, arrendar) un coche (un carro).
Quiere un coche con transmisión manual.

un mapa

los seguros contra todo riesgo

el contrato

Rafaela firma el contrato.
Declinó los seguros porque tiene su propia póliza.
La tarifa incluye kilometraje ilimitado.
La agente le da un mapa.

el retrovisor

los limpiaparabrisas

el neumático

el tanque lleno

una abolladura

un rayón

Rafaela verifica (chequea) la condición del vehículo antes de aceptarlo.
Hay que devolver el carro a la agencia con el tanque lleno.

ESCUCHAR

1 Escucha. Escoge la respuesta correcta. Usa una tabla como la de abajo para indicar tus respuestas.

a	b	c

HABLAR • ESCRIBIR

2 Identifica.

1.

2.

3.

4.

5.

6.

LEER

3 Parea los contrarios.

1. de cercanías
2. las afueras
3. transmisión manual
4. declinar
5. lleno

a. el centro
b. aceptar
c. vacío
d. de largo recorrido
e. transmisión automática

HABLAR • ESCRIBIR

4 ¡Te toca a ti! Usa cada palabra de la Actividad 3 en una frase original.

CULTURA

Las señoras están sacando sus billetes de una máquina automática de ventas y al mismo tiempo están verificando la hora de salida de su tren.

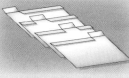

Vocabulario 2

HABLAR • ESCRIBIR

 5 Contrasta. Explica la diferencia entre un tren de largo recorrido y un tren de cercanías.

LEER

6 Indica si la información es correcta o no.

1. Debes mirar en el retrovisor antes de rebasar otro carro.
2. Mucha gente va a una agencia de alquiler para comprar un carro.
3. Si una persona no tiene un permiso de conducir, no puede arrendar un carro.
4. Después de un accidente o choque, es posible que el carro tenga unos rayones y abolladuras.
5. No debes conducir un carro si no tienes una póliza de seguros.

FOLDABLES®
Study Organizer

PAPER FILE FOLDER
See page SH27 for help with making this foldable. Use this study organizer to talk about travel with a partner. Label each tab with the name of a city or country you would like to visit. Describe how you would travel to each destination, who you would travel with, and what you would do there.

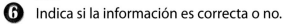
Comunicación

 7 Con un(a) compañero(a), habla de los trenes que hay donde vives. ¿Hay un tren de cercanías? ¿Y un tren de largo recorrido? ¿Tienen muchos usuarios o no?

 ¿Has viajado en tren alguna vez? Describe tus experiencias.

Estudio de palabras

acercarse a El tren se acerca a la estación.

cerca La estación está cerca del centro.

las cercanías Las cercanías están cerca de la ciudad.

cercano(a) El tren de cercanías sirve los pueblos cercanos.

 1 Da los contrarios.
1. lejos de
2. lejano
3. las lejanías
4. alejarse de

2 Usa cada palabra de la Actividad 1 en una frase original.

CULTURA

Los jóvenes están esperando el tranvía en Bilbao, Euskadi. El tranvía, que es un medio de transporte popular en muchas ciudades de Europa y Latinoamérica, se está acercando a la estación.

Gramática

QuickPass

Go to glencoe.com
For: **Grammar practice**
Web code: **ASD7844c6**

El subjuntivo con conjunciones de tiempo

1. The subjunctive is used with adverbial conjunctions of time when the verb of the main clause conveys a future time, since it is uncertain if the action in the adverbial clause will really take place. When the verb in the main clause is in the past, however, the indicative is used because the action of the clause has already taken place and is a reality.

> **FUTURO**
> **Ella nos hablará cuando lleguemos.**
>
> **PASADO**
> **Ella nos habló cuando llegamos.**

2. Some frequently used adverbial conjunctions of time that follow the same pattern are:

cuando	*when*	**hasta que**	*until*
en cuanto	*as soon as*	**después de que**	*after*
tan pronto como	*as soon as*		

3. The conjunction **antes de que,** *before,* is an exception. **Antes de que** is always followed by the subjunctive. The imperfect subjunctive is used after **antes de que** when the verb of the main clause is in the past or in the conditional.

> **Ellos saldrán antes de que nosotros lleguemos.**
> **Ellos salieron antes de que nosotros llegáramos.**
> **Ellos saldrían antes de que nosotros llegáramos.**

Práctica

ESCUCHAR • HABLAR • ESCRIBIR

① Contesta según se indica. Presta atención a la forma del segundo verbo.

1. ¿Pasará Julia unos días en La Paz cuando esté en Bolivia? (sí)
2. ¿Arrendará su hermana un jeep en cuanto lleguen a La Paz? (no)
3. ¿Esperará hasta que salgan para el lago Titicaca? (sí)
4. ¿Inspeccionará Julia el jeep antes de que salgan de la agencia? (sí)
5. ¿Devolverá el jeep después de que vuelvan de su excursión a Titicaca? (sí)

CULTURA

La pobre pareja perdió su tren porque ya había salido antes de que ellos llegaran a la estación en Sitges.

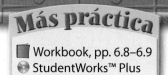
ESCUCHAR • HABLAR • ESCRIBIR

2 Contesta según se indica. Presta atención a la forma del segundo verbo.

1. Julia ha vuelto de Bolivia. ¿Pasó ella unos días en La Paz cuando estaba en Bolivia? (sí)
2. ¿Arrendó su hermana un jeep en cuanto llegaron a La Paz? (no)
3. ¿Esperó ella hasta que salieron para el lago Titicaca? (sí)
4. ¿Inspeccionó Julia el jeep antes de que salieran de la agencia? (sí)
5. ¿Devolvió el jeep a la agencia después de que volvieron de su excursión a Titicaca? (sí)

EXPANSIÓN

Ahora, sin mirar las preguntas, cuenta la información en tus propias palabras. Si no recuerdas algo, un(a) compañero(a) te puede ayudar.

LEER • ESCRIBIR

3 Completa con la forma apropiada del verbo indicado.

1. Ellos quieren salir en cuanto _____. (poder)
2. Van a salir cuando Carlos _____. (volver)
3. Luego tendrán que esperar hasta que él _____ las maletas en el baúl del carro. (poner)
4. Ellos salieron en cuanto _____. (poder)
5. Salieron en cuanto él _____. (volver)

LEER • ESCRIBIR

4 Completa con la forma apropiada del verbo indicado.

1. Ellos estarán aquí antes de que yo _____. (salir)
2. Ellos estuvieron aquí antes de que yo _____. (salir)
3. Yo lo sabré antes de que ustedes lo _____. (saber)
4. Yo lo sabía antes de que ustedes lo _____. (saber)
5. Ella me lo dirá antes de que yo te _____. (ver)
6. Ella me lo dijo antes de que yo te _____. (ver)

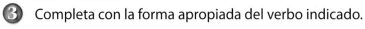

CULTURA

Una vista del lago Titicaca no muy lejos de La Paz, Bolivia

InfoGap For more practice with the subjunctive used with conjunctions of time, do Activity 6 on page SR7 at the end of this book.

CULTURA

Unos excursionistas en su SUV viajando por los Andes en Bolivia

El subjuntivo con verbos especiales

1. Some verbs state or imply a command, advice, or suggestion. Such verbs are followed by the subjunctive because, even though we ask, tell, advise, or suggest that someone do something, it is not certain that the person will actually do it.

2. Some frequently used verbs that state or imply a command, an order, advice, or a suggestion are:

decir	*to tell*	**exigir**	*to demand*
escribir	*to write*	**aconsejar**	*to advise*
pedir	*to ask, request*	**recomendar**	*to recommend*
rogar	*to beg, plead*	**sugerir**	*to suggest*
mandar	*to order*		

3. Observe and analyze the following sentences.

Te digo que no llegues tarde.
Te dije que no llegaras tarde.

Les aconsejo que salgan juntos.
Les aconsejé que salieran juntos.

These verbs often take an indirect object pronoun in the main clause. The indirect object of the main clause is the subject of the dependent clause.

▲ El agente de policía le dice a la señora que siga derecho.

4. Note that the subjunctive follows the verbs **decir** and **escribir** only when they imply a command. If someone is simply giving information, the subjunctive is not used. Observe the following sentences.

Ella me dice que viene mañana.
She tells me that she's coming tomorrow.

Ella me dice que venga mañana.
She tells me to come tomorrow.

Más práctica

Workbook, pp. 6.9–6.10
StudentWorks™ Plus

Práctica

HABLAR

5 Contesta.

1. ¿Le recomiendas a Julia que alquile un jeep?
2. ¿Les aconsejas a tus amigos que no hagan muchos ejercicios en cuanto lleguen a La Paz?
3. ¿Te rogó tu amigo que lo esperaras en el aeropuerto?
4. ¿Te sugirió que llegaras temprano al aeropuerto?

CULTURA

Vista de una calle pintoresca en La Paz

ESCUCHAR • HABLAR

6 Sigue el modelo.

MODELO —¿Qué les pidió Pedro?
esperar
—Él nos pidió que esperáramos.

1. no salir sin él
2. ir en metro
3. comprar los boletos para el avión
4. llegar temprano

LEER • ESCRIBIR

7 Forma oraciones con **que.**

1. su abuela le escribe / ser bueno
2. su abuela le escribe / estar bien
3. su abuela le escribe / tratar bien a su hermanita
4. su abuela le escribe / querer verlo
5. su abuela le escribe / cuidarse

CULTURA

Abuelita vive en Santo Domingo y está muy contenta cuando sus nietos le escriben y le dicen todo lo que están haciendo. Abuelita les dice que le escriban muy a menudo.

Sustantivos irregulares

1. Feminine nouns that begin with a stressed **a** or the silent **h** followed by a stressed **a** take the masculine definite article **el** or the indefinite article **un**. The reason such nouns take the articles **el** and **un** is that it would be difficult to pronounce the two vowels—**la a, una a**—together. Since the nouns are feminine, the plural articles **las** and **unas** are used and any adjective modifying the noun is in the feminine form.

el agua	las aguas	*water(s)*
el/un águila	las águilas	*eagle(s)*
el/un área	las áreas	*area(s)*
el/un arma	las armas	*weapon(s)*
el/un hacha	las hachas	*ax(es)*
el/un ala	las alas	*wing(s)*
el hambre		*hunger*

El agua limpia es buena para la salud.
Las aguas turbulentas del mar pueden ser peligrosas.

2. There are several nouns in Spanish that end in **a** but are masculine. These are nouns derived from Greek roots. They take the definite article **el** and the indefinite article **un.**

el clima	el poema
el día	el programa
el drama	el sistema
el mapa	el telegrama
el planeta	el tema

3. Note that the noun **la mano** is irregular. Even though **la mano** ends in **o**, it is feminine—**la mano. La foto** is also used as a shortened version of **la fotografía.** The noun **radio** can be either **la radio** or **el radio.**

CULTURA

Las aguas del mar abierto pueden ser turbulentas y peligrosas.

CULTURA

¿Cuántos alumnos han levantado la mano? El aula es moderna, ¿no?

Práctica

ESCUCHAR • HABLAR

8 Contesta según se indica.

1. ¿Cuál es el arma que lleva don Quijote? (la lanza)
2. ¿Has leído los poemas de Rubén Darío? (no)
3. ¿Dónde pasaste el día? (en la escuela)
4. En clase, ¿qué tienes que levantar cuando tienes una pregunta? (la mano)
5. ¿Cuál es el tema de este capítulo? (los problemas que podemos encontrar cuando viajamos)
6. ¿Se envían muchos telegramas hoy en día? (no)

LEER • ESCRIBIR

9 Completa con el artículo definido.

1. _____ agua es buena para la salud.
2. Vamos a necesitar _____ mapa porque no somos de aquí y no conocemos _____ área.
3. El aire debajo de _____ alas del avión levanta el avión cuando despega.
4. _____ sistema de ferrocarriles en España es muy bueno.
5. Creo que _____ águila tiene _____ ala rota.
6. _____ hambre es _____ problema número uno en varias partes del mundo.
7. _____ aguas del Mediterráneo son más calmas que _____ aguas del Atlántico.
8. Tenemos que proteger _____ planeta Tierra.

Refrán

Can you guess what the following proverb means?

Todos los caminos conducen a Roma.

CULTURA

Un ave exótica en una selva tropical de Ecuador

¡Bravo!

You have now learned all the new vocabulary and grammar in this chapter. Continue to use and practice all that you know while learning more cultural information. ¡Vamos!

QuickPass

Go to glencoe.com
For: **Conversation practice**
Web code: **ASD7844c6**

¡Qué lío!

Anita	Tengo malas noticias.
Mara	¿Qué? Dime.
Anita	Hay un problema mecánico y han anulado nuestro vuelo pero nos han confirmado en otro.
Mara	¿Cuándo sale?
Anita	¿Quieres que yo te lo diga? En cuatro horas.
Mara	¡Cuatro horas! Y además, ¿quién sabe si habrá otra demora? ¿Qué vamos a hacer cuando lleguemos tan tarde a Barcelona? Vamos a perder nuestro tren para Tarragona, ¿no?
Anita	Sí, el último tren sale antes de que llegue nuestro vuelo. Y además sería necesario ir del aeropuerto a la estación de tren.
Mara	¡Qué lío! En ese caso tendremos que buscar un hotel, ¿no?
Anita	No. No quiero tener que ir a un hotel.
Mara	Ni yo tampoco. ¿Por qué no alquilamos un coche? ¿Qué te parece?
Anita	¡Buena idea! Pero tenemos que pedir un mapa en la agencia de alquiler porque no conocemos el área.

¿Comprendes?

VIDEO To take an interesting flight from Argentina to Venezuela, watch **Diálogo en vivo.**

A Completa según la información en la conversación.

1. Anita tiene _____.
2. Han anulado el vuelo porque _____.
3. La línea aérea ha confirmado a Anita y a Mara _____.
4. El vuelo sale _____.
5. Ellas van a llegar _____.
6. Van a perder _____.
7. Lo van a perder porque _____.
8. Ninguna de las dos quiere _____.
9. Deciden que van a _____.

B **Resumiendo** Cuenta toda la información en la conversación en tus propias palabras.

C **Analizando** Contesta.

¿Por qué deciden Anita y Mara que deben alquilar un coche?

Cultura

Si algún día decides rentar un vehículo en un país extranjero, es necesario inspeccionar bien el carro para determinar si tiene abolladuras o rayones y que el agente los anote. ¿Por qué? Porque, cuando devuelvas el vehículo, el agente lo inspeccionará por cualquier daño que encuentre.

¡A Bolivia ya! 🎧♻

¿Quieres hacer un viaje algún día a Bolivia? No hay duda que sería una experiencia estupenda. Pero hay unas cosas interesantes que debes saber antes de llegar. ¡Número uno! La palabra «alto» es importante.

Hasta el aeropuerto que sirve La Paz se llama «El Alto». Lleva este nombre porque es el aeropuerto comercial más alto del mundo a una altura de 13.450 pies o 4.100 metros. A estas alturas hay menos oxígeno que al nivel del mar. Por eso, tendrás que tener cuidado cuando desembarques del avión. No es raro que un recién llegado tenga dificultad en respirar por la falta de oxígeno, pero el aeropuerto siempre tiene tanques de oxígeno disponibles.

Durante el aterrizaje tendrás una vista magnífica de La Paz porque está a 1.000 metros más abajo del aeropuerto. Parece estar en un cráter, y la belleza del claro cielo azul paceño es inolvidable—sobre todo en el invierno.

Y cuando salgas, tendrás otra experiencia que no vas a olvidar. Tu avión despegará de una de las pistas más largas del mundo. A esta altura el aire tiene muy poca densidad por falta de oxígeno y es difícil sostener el peso del avión. Así tiene que alcanzar una gran velocidad para poder despegar y continuar subiendo.

Cuando estés en Bolivia tienes que ir al lago Titicaca en la frontera entre Bolivia y Perú. Una vez más la palabra «alto». El lago Titicaca es el lago navegable más alto del mundo. A lo largo de las orillas[1] peruanas viven los quechua y a las orillas bolivianas los aymara. Estos grupos indígenas vestidos en trajes tradicionales cultivan papas y habichuelas y pescan trucha en sus barquitos o balsas de junco[2].

[1]orillas   *shores*
[2]junco   *reed*

Antes de leer

Antes de leer esta lectura sobre un viaje que van a hacer unas amigas a Bolivia, piensa en lo que ya sabes de los efectos de la altitud.

✓ **Reading Check**

¿Por qué tendrás que tener cuidado cuando desembarques del avión?

✓ **Reading Check**

¿Por qué tiene que ser muy larga la pista?

✓ **Reading Check**

¿Dónde viven los quechua y los aymara?

GeoVistas

To learn more about Bolivia, take a tour on pages SH50–SH51.

CULTURA

Plaza Murillo en La Paz

¿Comprendes?

A Recordando hechos Contesta.

1. ¿Cuál es el aeropuerto comercial más alto del mundo?
2. ¿Por qué tienen problemas unos recién llegados?
3. ¿Qué hay siempre a su disposición en el aeropuerto?
4. ¿Cómo es la pista en el aeropuerto de La Paz?
5. Durante el aterrizaje, ¿dónde parece estar La Paz?

B Identificando Identifica.

1. los aymara
2. los quechua

C Analizando Contesta.

1. ¿Por qué lleva el nombre «El Alto» el aeropuerto que sirve La Paz?
2. ¿Por qué pueden muchos recién llegados tener dificultad en respirar?
3. ¿Por qué tiene que ser tan larga la pista en el aeropuerto El Alto?

D Describiendo Describe.

1. la vista de la ciudad de La Paz desde la ventanilla de un avión
2. el lago Titicaca

VIDEO To take a trip through another Andean country, watch **Cultura en vivo.**

CULTURA

Una familia indígena en su balsa de junco en el lago Titicaca

CULTURA

Una joven con su alpaca en la isla del Sol en el lago Titicaca

Temprano y con sol
de Emilia Pardo Bazán

▲ La Coruña, la provincia natal de Pardo Bazán en Galicia

Vocabulario

la manía preocupación exagerada; deseo desordenado

la criada señora que trabaja haciendo tareas domésticas por dinero

el oído el aparato que sirve para la audición, que nos permite oír

el/la novio(a) amigo con quien uno sale con frecuencia y a quien le expresa cariño

el mozo el joven, el muchacho

el reloj aparato que nos indica la hora

entregar dar

echar a empezar a, ponerse a

avisar informarle a alguien de algo; dejarle a uno saber algo

Práctica

1 Completa con una palabra apropiada.

1. No sé la hora porque mi _____ no anda.
2. No quería que nadie oyera lo que me decía. Así es que lo murmuró en mi _____.
3. Él tiene muchas _____. A veces yo no comprendo lo que hace.
4. Hace tiempo que los _____ están saliendo. Creo que se están enamorando.
5. Mucha gente de las clases altas pagan a una _____ para limpiar la casa.
6. El hijo de los López es un buen _____.

2 Expresa de otra manera.

1. Lo necesitan. ¿Cuándo se lo vas a *dar*?
2. El niño tenía miedo y *se puso a* correr.
3. Es necesario que lo sepan. ¿Por qué no les *informan* de lo que está pasando?
4. Es *un muchacho* inteligente y simpático.
5. Es *una obsesión* que tiene.

▲ Emilia Pardo Bazán (1852–1921), una ilustre autora española

INTRODUCCIÓN

Emilia Pardo Bazán, la condesa de Pardo Bazán, es considerada una de los novelistas más importantes de la literatura española. Nació en La Coruña, Galicia, de una familia aristócrata. Fue una mujer culta de gran curiosidad intelectual y talento creativo.

Su obra incluye varias novelas psicológicas y regionales. En dos de sus novelas importantes estudia y describe la decadencia de la aristocracia gallega.

Pardo Bazán cultivó el cuento también y se le considera una maestra de este género literario.

Temprano y con sol

duros *antiguas monedas españolas*

dando una patada *stamping her feet*

El empleado que vendía billetes en la oficina de la estación quedó sorprendido al oír una voz infantil que decía:

—¡Dos billetes, de primera clase, para París!...

Miró a una niña de once o doce años, de ojos y pelo negros, con un rico vestido de color rojo y un bonito sombrerillo. De la mano traía a un niño casi de la misma edad que ella, el cual iba muy bien vestido también. El chico parecía confuso; la niña muy alegre. El empleado sonrió y murmuró paternalmente:

—¿Directo, o a la frontera? A la frontera son ciento cincuenta pesetas, y...

—Aquí está el dinero—contestó la niña, abriendo su bolsa. El empleado volvió a sonreír y dijo:

—No es bastante.

—¡Hay quince duros° y tres pesetas!—exclamó la niña.

—Pero no es suficiente. Si no lo creen, pregunten ustedes a sus papás.

El niño se puso rojo, y la niña, dando una patada° en el suelo, gritó:

—¡Bien... , pues... , dos billetes más baratos!

—¿A una estación más próxima? ¿Escorial; Ávila?...

—¡Ávila, sí... , Ávila!...—respondió la niña.

Vaciló el empleado un momento; luego entregó los dos billetes. Subieron los dos chicos al tren y, al verse dentro del coche, comenzaron a bailar de alegría.

La bella ciudad amurallada de Ávila, España

¿Cómo empezó aquel amor apasionado? Pues comenzó del modo más simple e inocente. Comenzó por la manía de los dos chicos de formar colecciones de sellos.

El papá de Finita y la mamá de Currín, ya enviudados° los dos, apenas° se conocían, aunque vivían en el mismo edificio. Currín y Finita, en cambio, se encontraban siempre en la escalera, cuando iban a la escuela.

Una mañana, al bajar la escalera, Currín notó que Finita llevaba un objeto, un libro rojo, ¡el álbum de sellos! Quería verlo. La colección estaba muy completa y contenía muchos sellos de varios países. Al ver un sello muy raro de la república de Liberia, exclamó Currín:

—¿Me lo das?

—Toma—respondió Finita.

—Gracias, hermosa—contestó Currín.

Finita se puso roja y muy alegre.

—¿Sabes que te he de decir una cosa?—murmuró el chico.

—Anda, dímela.

—Hoy no.

Ya era tarde y la criada que acompañaba a Finita la llevó a la escuela. Currín se quedó admirando su sello y pensando en Finita. Currín era un chico de carácter dulce, aficionado a los dramas tristes, a las novelas de aventuras y a la poesía. Soñaba con° viajes largos a países desconocidos. Verdad es que, aquella noche, soñó que Finita y él habían hecho una excursión a una tierra lejana.

Al día siguiente, nuevo encuentro en la escalera. Currín tenía unos sellos que iba a dar a Finita. Finita sonrió y se acercó a Currín, con misterio, diciendo:

—Dime lo que me ibas a decir ayer…

—No era nada…

—¡Cómo nada!—exclamó Finita, furiosa.—¡Qué idiota! Nada, ¿eh?

Currín se acercó al oído de la niña y murmuró:

—Sí, era algo…. Quería decirte que eres… ¡muy guapita!

Al decir esto, echó a correr escalera abajo.

Currín escribía versos a Finita y no pensaba en otra cosa más que en ella. Al fin de la semana eran novios.

Cierta tarde creyó el portero del edificio que soñaba. ¿No era aquélla la señorita Finita? ¿Y no era aquél el señorito Currín? ¿Y no subían los dos a un coche que pasaba? ¿Adónde van? ¿Deberé avisar a los padres?

—Oye—decía Finita a Currín, cuando el tren se puso en marcha.—Ávila, ¿cómo es? ¿Muy grande? ¿Bonita, lo mismo que París?

—No—respondió Currín.—Debe de ser un pueblo de pesca°.

enviudados *widowed*
apenas *scarcely*

Durante la lectura

Reflexiona sobre tu niñez y contesta las siguientes preguntas. ¿Recuerdas cuando eras niño(a)? ¿Imaginabas que tenías novio(a)? ¿Quién era? ¿Cómo se conocieron?

Soñaba con *He dreamed of*

pueblo de pesca *fishing village*

CULTURA

El famoso Arco de Triunfo en
el París de los años 1920

—Yo quiero ver París; y también quiero ver las pirámides de Egipto.

—Sí... —murmuró Currín,— pero... ¿y el dinero?

—¿El dinero?—contestó Finita.—Eres tonto. ¡Se puede pedir prestado°!

—¿Y a quién?

—¡A cualquier persona!

—¿Y si no nos lo quieren dar?

—Yo tengo mi reloj que empeñar°. Tú también. Y puedo empeñar mi abrigo° nuevo. Si escribo a papá, nos enviará dinero.

—Tu papá estará furioso... ¡No sé qué haremos!

—Pues voy a empeñar mi reloj y tú puedes empeñar el tuyo. ¡Qué bien vamos a divertirnos en Ávila! Me llevarás al café... y al teatro... y al paseo....

Cuando llegaron a Ávila, salieron del tren. La gente salía y los novios no sabían a dónde dirigirse.

—¿Por dónde se va a Ávila?—preguntó Currín a un mozo que no les hizo caso. Por instinto se encaminaron a una puerta, entregaron sus billetes y, cogidos por un solícito agente de hotel, se metieron en el coche, que los llevó al Hotel Inglés.

Entretanto el gobernador de Ávila recibió un telegrama mandando la captura de los dos enamorados. Los fugitivos fueron llevados a Madrid, sin pérdida de tiempo. Finita fue internada en un convento y Currín quedó en una escuela, de donde no fueron permitidos salir en todo el año, ni aun los domingos.

Como consecuencia de aquella tragedia, el papá de Finita y la mamá de Currín llegaron a conocerse muy bien, y creció su mutua admiración de día en día. Aunque no tenemos noticias exactas, creemos que Finita y Currín llegaron a ser... hermanastros.

pedir prestado *borrow*

empeñar *pawn*
abrigo *overcoat*

Después de leer

¿Qué opinión tienes de este cuento? ¿Te parece verosímil o no? ¿Tiene un final feliz? ¿Por qué?

¿Comprendes?

A **Parafraseando** Parea.

1. dio una sonrisa
2. dijo en voz muy baja
3. como un padre
4. de un niño
5. suficiente
6. tonto
7. solícito
8. entregar

a. murmuró
b. estúpido
c. paternalmente
d. sonrió
e. dar
f. infantil
g. diligente
h. bastante

B **Recordando hechos** Contesta.

1. ¿Qué compraba la niña? ¿Dónde?
2. ¿Adónde quería ir?
3. ¿Qué no tenía la niña?
4. ¿Para dónde sacó los billetes?
5. ¿Cómo se pusieron los dos niños cuando subieron al tren?
6. ¿Qué coleccionaban los niños?
7. ¿Dónde vivían ellos?
8. ¿Se conocían sus padres?
9. ¿Habían enviudado sus padres?

C **Describiendo** Describe.

1. Da una descripción de Finita.
2. Da una descripción de Currín.

D **Interpretando** El final del cuento dice: «Aunque no tenemos noticias exactas, creemos que Finita y Currín llegaron a ser… hermanastros». Explica como será posible esto.

CULTURA
El Escorial

Vocabulario

1 **Indica si la información es correcta o no.**

1. Un vuelo internacional despega en un país y aterriza en otro.

2. La línea aérea ha anulado el vuelo. Sale a tiempo.

3. Ellos perdieron su vuelo porque llegaron tarde al aeropuerto.

4. Los pasajeros pueden reclamar su equipaje en inmigración.

5. No somos de aquí y necesitamos un mapa.

6. Las abolladuras son el resultado de un accidente.

 To review **Vocabulario 1** and **Vocabulario 2,** turn to pages 168–169 and 172–173.

2 **Escoge.**

7. (La maleta, El talón) indica hasta donde está facturado el equipaje.

8. Un vuelo entre Miami y Lima con una escala en Guayaquil es un vuelo (sin escala, internacional).

9. El avión no va a salir porque (hay una demora, está anulado).

10. El vuelo está completo y no hay asientos (disponibles, en la fila).

11. Los pasajeros (hacen, reclaman) su equipaje después del vuelo.

12. No soy de aquí y no conozco la región. Tendré que consultar (mi contrato, el mapa).

13. ¿Ha tenido este carro un accidente? Mira este (retrovisor, rayón).

14. Si alquilas un carro lo tienes que (reclamar, devolver) con el tanque lleno.

Gramática

To review **el subjuntivo con conjunciones de tiempo,** turn to page 176.

3 **Completa con la forma apropiada del verbo.**

15. Él me habló en cuanto me _____. (ver)

16. Él me hablará en cuanto me _____. (ver)

17. Ellos saldrán después de que nosotros _____. (llegar)

18. Ellos salieron después de que nosotros _____. (llegar)

19. Tú lo sabrás antes de que lo _____ yo. (saber)

20. Tú lo sabías antes de que lo _____ yo. (saber)

21. Él no comprará el billete hasta que ustedes lo _____. (pagar)

22. Él no compró el billete hasta que ustedes lo _____. (pagar)

23. Marta volverá a casa en cuanto _____. (poder)

24. Marta volvió a casa en cuanto _____. (poder)

25. Te llamaré tan pronto como _____ del aeropuerto. (volver)

26. Te llamé tan pronto como _____ del aeropuerto. (volver)

4 **Completa.**

27. Él me dijo que (yo) _____. (salir)

28. Ellos te dirán que lo _____. (hacer)

29. Ella nos aconseja que _____ atención. (prestar)

30. Yo les pedí que _____ a tiempo. (llegar)

31. Mi abuela me dice que _____ enferma pero no sabe lo que tiene. (estar)

5 **Completa con el artículo definido.**

32. Levanta _____ mano si tienes una pregunta.

33. No puedes beber _____ agua. No es potable.

34. Tenemos que proteger _____ planeta Tierra.

35. ¿Vas a ver _____ programa?

36. _____ aves tienen alas.

Cultura

6 **Contesta.**

37. ¿Qué es El Alto?

38. ¿Por qué tiene dificultad en respirar mucha gente que acaba de llegar a La Paz?

39. ¿Cuál es el lago navegable más alto del mundo?

40. ¿Quiénes viven a las orillas de este lago?

To review **el subjuntivo con verbos especiales,** turn to page 178.

To review **sustantivos irregulares,** turn to page 180.

To review this cultural information, turn to page 184.

CULTURA

Laguna Verde y el volcán Licancabur en Bolivia

1 **En el aeropuerto**

Check in at the airport

Imagínate que estás en el aeropuerto. Estás saliendo para una ciudad latinoamericana. Tienes que facturar tu equipaje, conseguir (obtener) tu tarjeta de embarque, etc. Ten una conversación con el/la agente de la compañía de aviación (tu compañero[a]).

2 **Un vuelo anulado**

Get help when a flight's been cancelled

Trabajen en grupos de tres. Dos de ustedes son pasajeros y uno(a) es el/la agente de la línea aérea. El/La agente acaba de informarles que han anulado su vuelo. Tengan una conversación con el/la agente para determinar lo que va a hacer la línea aérea para acomodarlos.

3 **En una agencia de alquiler**

Rent a car

Quieres alquilar un carro. Estás en la agencia. Ten una conversación con el/la empleado(a) de la agencia (tu compañero[a]).

4 **¿Qué tal el viaje?**

Tell what you did before and after your trip

Imagínate que has hecho un viaje con unos amigos. Di todo lo que tú o ellos hicieron antes de que salieran y di todo lo que hiciste o hicieron todos ustedes en cuanto volvieron a casa.

CULTURA

Estos pasajeros están para salir en un vuelo del aeropuerto de la Ciudad de México.

Tarea

You have recently been hired as a part-time travel agent for a local travel agency that specializes in booking and planning vacations to Spain and Latin America, and your first major assignment is to create a newsletter to be sent out to customers that will give them advice on traveling and tips on how to have a successful trip.

Writing Strategy

Creating a newsletter A newsletter from a travel agency serves two main purposes: first, to provide customers with useful information about their upcoming travel experience, and second, to promote the continued use of services offered by the company. Your newsletter should be clear and concise, as well as useful and inviting to your reader. In addition to including informative details, you should also think about style or layout, making sure that your newsletter is as visually appealing as it is easy to understand.

❶ Prewrite

- Give the travel agency a catchy name. Then choose three popular travel destinations in the Spanish-speaking world that you would like to visit and make them the focus of your newsletter.
- Use the diagram for each of your destinations to help you decide which ones to talk about when discussing the three different subtopics of this chapter: traveling by plane, by train, and by car. You should also include additional information about the main tourist attractions, hotel accommodations, and typical cuisine of each area, as well as any tips or advice

that travelers to each destination might find useful.

- Once you have filled in your diagram, you may find it necessary to eliminate some details because you do not want to overwhelm the reader with too much information. Remember that you want your newsletter to be both informative and enjoyable.

❷ Write

- Before you begin arranging the final version, write each part of your newsletter separately. Once you have written all of the parts, read over each of them to check for correct spelling and grammar, proper use of vocabulary, and the completeness as well as the usefulness of information.
- In addition to using vocabulary from the textbook, be sure to incorporate the main grammar points from this chapter—the subjunctive with conjunctions of time and the subjunctive to express commands, orders, advice, and suggestions.

Evaluate

Your teacher will evaluate you based on the style or design of your newsletter, the proper use of vocabulary, the correctness of spelling and grammar, and the completeness and usefulness of information.

Repaso del Capítulo 6

Gramática

- ### El subjuntivo con conjunciones de tiempo *(page 176)*
  Adverbial conjunctions of time such as **cuando, en cuanto, tan pronto como, hasta que,** and **después de que** are followed by the indicative when the action is in the past and by the subjunctive when it is in the future.

PASADO	FUTURO
Ella nos habló cuando llegamos.	**Ella nos hablará cuando lleguemos.**

  Note that the conjunction **antes de que** is always followed by the subjunctive.

  > **Ellos saldrán antes de que lleguemos.**
  > **Ellos salieron antes de que nosotros llegáramos.**

- ### El subjuntivo con verbos especiales *(page 178)*
  Verbs that state or imply a command, advice, or suggestion are followed by the subjunctive. Note also that they are usually used with an indirect object pronoun.

  > **Ellos te dicen que lo hagas.**
  > **Ellos me aconsejaron que (yo) lo hiciera también.**
  > **Ellos nos sugirieron a todos que lo hiciéramos.**

- ### Sustantivos irregulares *(page 180)*
  Feminine nouns that begin with a stressed **a (ha)** take the masculine definite article **el** or the indefinite article **un** for the sake of pronunciation. However, they are feminine.

el/un águila	**las águilas**
el/un hacha	**las hachas**

  Many nouns that end in **-ma** have a Greek root and they are masculine—**el poema, el drama, el tema, el clima.** Note also that **el planeta** is masculine.

  Remember that **la mano** and **la foto** are feminine. **Radio** can be either **la radio** or **el radio.**

Un Águila imperial de España

Vocabulario

Getting around an airport

el aeropuerto	el peso	el reclamo de	la inmigración
la maleta	la correa	equipaje	la aduana
el equipaje	la pantalla	el control de	pesar
el talón	la puerta de salida	pasaportes	reclamar, recoger
la etiqueta			

Talking about flights

un vuelo	una demora	la ventanilla	anular
directo	un asiento, una	la fila	confirmar
sin escala	plaza	completo(a)	hacer escala
el destino	el pasillo	disponible	perder el vuelo

Getting around a train station

la estación de tren	el tren	cercano(a)	cambiar de tren,
(ferrocarril)	de cercanías	enlazar	transbordar
	de largo recorrido		

Talking about renting a car

la agencia de	los seguros	un rayón	firmar
alquiler	contra todo riesgo	una abolladura	aceptar
el/la agente	la tarifa	ilimitado(a)	declinar
el contrato	el kilometraje	alquilar, rentar,	incluir
la póliza	el mapa	arrendar	verificar, chequear

Identifying some car parts

la transmisión	el retrovisor	el neumático
manual	los limpiaparabrisas	el tanque

Other useful words and expressions

los suburbios, las	acercarse a	¡Qué lío!
afueras	debido a	

 The words listed below come from this chapter's literary selection, *Temprano y con sol*. They were selected to become part of your active vocabulary because of their relatively high frequency.

la manía	el/la novio(a)	entregar
la criada	el/la mozo(a)	echar a
el oído	el reloj	avisar

Repaso cumulativo

Repasa lo que ya has aprendido

These activities will help you review and remember
what you have learned so far in Spanish.

 **Escucha las frases. Indica en una tabla como la de
abajo si la acción ocurre en el pasado, el presente o el
futuro.**

en el pasado	en el presente	en el futuro

 Cambia el futuro al condicional.

1. Iré en avión.
2. Ellos tomarán el tren.
3. ¿Pondrás el equipaje en la maletera?
4. Haremos el viaje juntos.
5. ¿Llegarán ustedes a tiempo?
6. ¿No comerás durante el vuelo?
7. No subiré la escalera.
8. Tomaré el ascensor.

 Contesta.

1. Algún día, ¿irás a México?
2. ¿Pasarás unos días en la capital?
3. ¿Visitarás el museo de Antropología?
4. ¿Harás una excursión a Xochimilco?
5. ¿Verás los jardines flotantes?

CULTURA

La Torre Latinoamericana en la
Ciudad de México

Completa con el condicional.

1. Él lo _____ pero yo no lo _____. (hacer)

2. Ellos lo _____ pero tú no lo _____. (saber)

3. Nosotros lo _____ pero ellos no lo _____. (decir)

4. Yo _____ pero mi hermano no _____. (salir)

5. Yo sé que tú lo _____ pero yo no lo _____. (devolver)

 Parea el infinitivo con el participio pasado.

1. hacer	**a.** abierto
2. decir	**b.** puesto
3. poner	**c.** vuelto
4. volver	**d.** cerrado
5. romper	**e.** visto
6. abrir	**f.** comido
7. cerrar	**g.** hecho
8. vivir	**h.** roto
9. comer	**i.** dicho
10. ver	**j.** vivido

 Contesta según el modelo.

MODELO —¿Lo habrían hecho ustedes?

—Sí, lo habríamos hecho pero no pudimos.

1. ¿Habrían ido ustedes?

2. ¿Se lo habrías dicho a José?

3. ¿Habría vuelto tu hermano?

4. ¿Habrías firmado el contrato?

5. ¿Ella te habría devuelto el dinero?

Completa la siguiente tabla.

infinitivo	participio presente	participio pasado
hablar		
	comiendo	
		recibido
abrir		
		vuelto
pedir		
	leyendo	

Arte y literatura

Vamos a comparar La gente del mundo hispanohablante aprecia mucho la literatura y las artes plásticas. No es raro que durante una fiesta alguien se levante para recitar una poesía bonita. ¿Consideras importantes las artes? ¿Te interesan mucho?

Objetivos

You will:

- discuss fine art and literature
- talk about a mural by the Mexican artist Diego Rivera
- read a sonnet by the Spaniard Federico García Lorca
- read a poem by the Cuban poet Nicolás Guillén

You will use:

- the present perfect and pluperfect subjunctive
- **si** clauses
- adverbs ending in **-mente**

◀ Mural de tema prehistórico en Pinar del Río, Cuba

QuickPass

Go to glencoe.com
For: **Online book**
Web code: **ASD7844c7**

Introducción al tema
Arte y literatura

Mira las fotos para averiguar lo mucho que tiene que ofrecer el mundo hispanohablante en cuanto a las artes visuales y literarias.

▲ **España** Un manuscrito antiguo en el Museo de Arte en Girona

▲ **Colombia** El famoso escultor y pintor colombiano Fernando Botero

México La casa de Frida Kahlo en Coyoacán, un suburbio de la Ciudad de México, es hoy un museo. ▼

◀ **España** El busto del renombrado poeta andaluz Federico García Lorca en el jardín de su casa natal en Fuentevaqueros en la provincia de Granada

▲ **España** Una joven en el museo de la Fundación Joan Miró en Barcelona

▲ **Honduras** Una estela en las magníficas ruinas mayas de Copán

España Las fallas es una fiesta que tiene lugar en marzo en Valencia. Se hacen figuras de cartón de personajes conocidos que se exhíben por una semana por toda la ciudad. Estas figuras se llaman «ninots» en valenciano. La noche del 19 de marzo se queman y a la medianoche los fuegos iluminan la ciudad entera. El «ninot» que vemos aquí es del artista surrealista Salvador Dalí. ▼

203

El arte

La pintura

la pintora, la artista

el lienzo

el caballete

las acuarelas

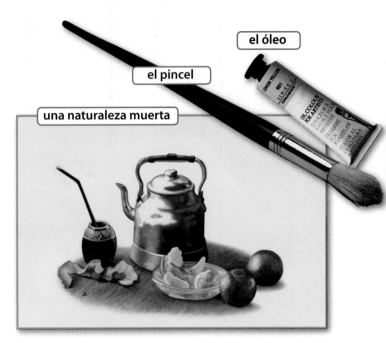

el óleo

el pincel

una naturaleza muerta

La artista pone el lienzo en un caballete.
Pinta con un pincel.

una obra abstracta

una superficie plana

una obra figurativa

el fondo

la perspectiva

el primer plano

Es un cuadro famoso de Velázquez.
En el fondo hay una puerta abierta.
En el primer plano vemos al artista mismo.
Tiene su pincel en la mano.
Vemos también la parte trasera del caballete.

La escultura

el taller

el escultor

la estatua, la escultura

el cincel

El escultor talla con un cincel.
Trabaja en un taller.

una estatua de bronce

una estatua de madera

una cerámica de yeso

ESCUCHAR

1 Escucha y determina si la información que oyes es correcta o no. Usa una tabla como la de abajo para indicar tus respuestas.

correcta	incorrecta

HABLAR • ESCRIBIR

2 Contesta sobre el trabajo de los artistas.

1. ¿En qué pone el artista el lienzo?
2. ¿Con qué aplica el artista los óleos al lienzo?
3. ¿Con qué talla un escultor?
4. ¿Qué materias puede usar el escultor?
5. ¿Dónde trabajan un artista y un escultor?
6. ¿Es una cerámica de yeso, de madera o de bronce?

LEER • ESCRIBIR

3 Categoriza las palabras.

	pintura	escultura
1. el cincel		
2. el pincel		
3. el lienzo		
4. el bronce		
5. el caballete		
6. tallar		
7. pintar		
8. una superficie plana		
9. acuarelas y óleos		
10. cerámicas		

CULTURA

El artista está pintando una vista playera en Calella de Palafrugell en la Costa Brava de España.

LEER

4 ¿Sí o no? Determina si la información es correcta o no.

1. Una obra de arte figurativa presenta una interpretación literal o realista de la materia que pinta el artista.
2. La materia que pinta el artista es el tema o motivo de la obra.
3. Dos medios que emplean los pintores son la acuarela y el óleo. Hay un tercero—el acrílico.
4. Un artista nunca pinta sobre una superficie plana (llana).
5. La perspectiva es la representación de los objetos en tres dimensiones—alto, ancho, profundidad—sobre una superficie plana.
6. Una naturaleza muerta tiene mucha acción y movimiento.

 Comunicación

5 Trabaja con un(a) compañero(a) y en sus propias palabras describan las diferencias entre un cuadro abstracto, un cuadro figurativo y una naturaleza muerta. Por lo general, ¿qué tipo de cuadro les atrae más?

Conexiones

Las Bellas Artes

Frida Kahlo es una de las más renombradas artistas del siglo veinte. Su padre era de ascendencia judío-húngara y su madre una señora mexicana quien persuadió a su esposo ser fotógrafo. La madre dio a sus hijas una educación tradicional mexicana pero Frida siempre tenía cierto espíritu rebelde. Decidió estudiar arte. Un día al regresar a casa el camión (bus) que tomaba chocó con un tranvía. Frida recibió numerosas heridas y sufrió de profundos dolores durante toda su vida. Pero su sufrimiento no la prohibió producir una obra cautelosa (grande).

Estudio de palabras

pintar El artista pinta.

el pintor El que pinta es pintor.

la pintura El pintor usa pintura.

pintoresco Ella pinta una escena pintoresca.

Completa el párrafo.

El _____ _____. Aplica la _____ al lienzo con un pincel. _____ una escena _____.

CULTURA

Una galería del famoso museo Guggenheim en Bilbao, España

La literatura

La novela

Es una novela famosa, *El Quijote*.

La novela es una forma literaria narrativa.

Don Quijote y Sancho Panza son los protagonistas de la novela.

Los protagonistas son los personajes más importantes de la obra.

La novela *El Quijote* tiene lugar en La Mancha.

La acción en la novela es el argumento.

El lugar y el ambiente en que se desarrolla el argumento es La Mancha.

Un libro se divide en capítulos.

El cuento

HORACIO QUIROGA

CUENTOS DE LA SELVA

LA ABEJA HARAGANA
LA TORTUGA GIGANTE
LAS MEDIAS DE LOS FLAMENCOS
LA GAMA CIEGA
EL POTRO SALVAJE
EL PASO DEL YABEBIRI
EL LORO PELADO
LA GUERRA DE LOS YACARES
LA HISTORIA DE DOS CACHORROS DE
COATI Y DOS CACHORROS DE HOMBRE

Es un libro de cuentos de Horacio Quiroga.
Un cuento es más corto que una novela.
Un cuento, igual que una novela, es prosa.

Si yo tuviera talento, escribiría un cuento.

La poesía

el poeta

La poesía es un género literario.
El poeta escribe poesías.

Verde que te quiero verde.
Verde viento. Verdes ramas.
El barco sobre la mar
y el caballo en la montaña.
Sobre el rostro del aljibe,
se mecía la gitana.
Verde carne, pelo verde,
con ojos de fría plata.
Un carámbano de luna
la sostiene sobre el agua.

Verde que te quiero verde.
Verde viento. Verde ramas.
¿No veis la herida que tengo
desde el pecho a la garganta?
Dejadme subir al menos
hasta las altas barandas,
¡dejadme subir!, dejadme
hasta las verdes barandas.
Barandales de la luna
por donde retumba el agua.
F. García Lorca

Cada línea de un poema es un verso.
Cada serie de versos es una estrofa.
Muchos poemas o poesías tienen rima,
    pero no todos.

CULTURA

Un azulejo en la puerta de Bisagra
en Toledo, España

ESCUCHAR • HABLAR

1 Contesta sobre un género literario.

1. ¿Es una novela prosa o poesía?
2. ¿En qué se divide una novela?
3. ¿Tiene personajes una novela?
4. ¿Quiénes son los personajes más importantes?
5. ¿Es una novela más larga o más corta que un cuento?
6. ¿Tiene un cuento un argumento igual que una novela?

LEER • ESCRIBIR

2 Identifica.

1. los personajes más importantes de una novela
2. la acción en una novela
3. donde se desarrolla o sucede la acción de la novela
4. forma literaria a la cual pertenecen la novela y el cuento

LEER • ESCRIBIR

3 Completa con palabras apropiadas.

La ___1___ y la prosa son dos géneros literarios. Cada línea de un poema es un ___2___ y cada serie de versos es una ___3___. Muchas ___4___ tienen ___5___ pero no todas.

HABLAR

4 Personaliza. Da respuestas personales.

1. ¿Prefieres la poesía o la prosa?
2. ¿Prefieres leer una novela o un cuento?
3. ¿Lees mucho?
4. ¿Cuál es tu novela favorita?
5. ¿Quién es tu novelista favorito(a)?
6. ¿Quién es tu poeta favorito(a)?
7. ¿Prefieres mirar un cuadro o leer un libro?

EXPANSIÓN

Trabaja con un(a) compañero(a). Compartan sus respuestas y compárenlas.

LEER • ESCRIBIR

5 Completa.

	novelas que he leído	cuentos que he leído	poesías que he leído
en inglés			
en español			

Más practica

■ Workbook, pp. 7.5–7.6
● StudentWorks™ Plus

VIDEO To watch a performance of a scene from *Don Quijote*, watch **Diálogo en vivo.**

LEER

6 Escoge. Indica tus preferencias en cada categoría de uno a tres. Uno—te gusta mucho, tres—no te gusta.

	1	2	3
1. novelas románticas			
2. novelas históricas			
3. novelas de ficción, novelas ficticias			
4. novelas policíacas			
5. novelas de ciencia-ficción			
6. biografías			
7. autobiografías			

Comunicación

7 Trabajando en grupos de tres o cuatro, van a preparar una encuesta. Cada grupo informará a los otros grupos los resultados de su grupo al completar el cuestionario en la Actividad 6. Luego van a compilar los resultados y determinar el orden de las preferencias de todos los miembros de la clase.

CULTURA

La biblioteca de El Escorial, un palacio y monasterio cerca de Madrid, construido en el siglo dieciséis.

ARTE Y LITERATURA

QuickPass

Go to glencoe.com
For: **Grammar practice**
Web code: **ASD7844c7**

El subjuntivo
Presente perfecto, pluscuamperfecto

1. The present perfect subjunctive is formed by using the present subjunctive of the auxiliary verb **haber** and the past participle. Study the following forms.

	hablar	comer	vivir
yo	haya hablado	haya comido	haya vivido
tú	hayas hablado	hayas comido	hayas vivido
Ud., él, ella	haya hablado	haya comido	haya vivido
nosotros(as)	hayamos hablado	hayamos comido	hayamos vivido
vosotros(as)	*hayáis hablado*	*hayáis comido*	*hayáis vivido*
Uds., ellos, ellas	hayan hablado	hayan comido	hayan vivido

¿Te acuerdas?

You reviewed the irregular past participles in the previous chapter on page 199.

2. The present perfect subjunctive is used when the action in a dependent clause that takes the subjunctive occurred before the action in the main clause.

Has venido.	Me alegro de que hayas venido.
Lo han visto.	Dudo que lo hayan visto.
Lo hemos hecho.	Es imposible que lo hayamos hecho.

3. The pluperfect subjunctive is formed with the imperfect subjunctive of the verb **haber** and the past participle.

	hablar	comer	vivir
yo	hubiera hablado	hubiera comido	hubiera vivido
tú	hubieras hablado	hubieras comido	hubieras vivido
Ud., él, ella	hubiera hablado	hubiera comido	hubiera vivido
nosotros(as)	hubiéramos hablado	hubiéramos comido	hubiéramos vivido
vosotros(as)	*hubierais hablado*	*hubierais comido*	*hubierais vivido*
Uds., ellos, ellas	hubieran hablado	hubieran comido	hubieran vivido

4. The pluperfect subjunctive is used after a verb in the past tense or conditional when the action of the verb in the subjunctive occurred prior to the action in the main clause.

Estaba convencido de que ellos lo habían hecho.
Pero me sorprendió que ellos lo hubieran hecho.
Me dijeron que él lo había dicho.
Nunca habría (yo) creído que él lo hubiera dicho.

Práctica

ESCUCHAR • HABLAR

1 Contesta.

1. ¿No crees que ellos hayan llegado?
2. ¿Es posible que hayan salido tarde?
3. Es imposible que se hayan perdido, ¿no?
4. Es raro que Roberto no te haya llamado, ¿no?
5. ¿Temes que les haya pasado algo?
6. ¿Es posible que ellos te hayan llamado y que no haya sonado tu móvil?

> No puedo creer que no hayan llegado todavía. Es posible que me hayan enviado un mensaje.

LEER • ESCRIBIR

2 Completa la siguiente tarjeta postal con el presente perfecto del subjuntivo.

Querida Susana,

¿Es posible que ya ___1___ (terminar) tus vacaciones? No creo que los quince días ___2___ (pasar) tan rápido. Espero que tú lo ___3___ (pasar) bien en México y que ___4___ (divertirse). Me alegro de que ___5___ (tener) la oportunidad de visitar la casa de Diego Rivera y Frida Kahlo en Coyoacán. Y me alegro de que ___6___ (poder) visitar el país de tus abuelos.

LEER • ESCRIBIR

3 Completa con el pluscuamperfecto del subjuntivo.

1. Francamente yo dudaba que él lo _____. (hacer)
2. Y él dudaba que yo lo _____. (hacer)
3. ¿Cómo era posible que nadie le _____ nada? (decir)
4. Me sorprendió que ustedes no _____ el trabajo. (terminar)
5. Estaba contento que tú _____ la exposición. (ver)

CULTURA

Entrada principal al museo Frida Kahlo en Coyoacán, México. Es en esta casa que nació la famosa artista.

Cláusulas con si

1. Si (*If*) clauses are used to express a contrary-to-fact condition. For these clauses, there is a very definite sequence of tenses. Study the following examples.

GeoVistas

To learn more about Argentina, take a tour on pages SH52–SH53.

> **Si tengo bastante dinero, haré el viaje.**
> *If I have enough money, I will take the trip.*
>
> **Si tuviera bastante dinero, haría el viaje.**
> *If I had enough money, I would take the trip.*
>
> **Si yo hubiera tenido bastante dinero, yo habría hecho el viaje.**
> *If I had had enough money, I would have taken the trip.*

2. Note that the sequence of tenses for **si** clauses is the following:

MAIN CLAUSE	SI CLAUSE
future	present indicative
conditional	imperfect subjunctive
conditional perfect	pluperfect subjunctive

CULTURA

Si yo pudiera ir a Buenos Aires, me encantaría visitar el barrio artístico de La Boca.

VIDEO Want help with the present perfect and pluperfect subjunctive? Watch **Gramática en vivo.**

Más práctica

Workbook, p. 7.9
StudentWorks™ Plus

Práctica

HABLAR

4 Personaliza. Da respuestas personales.

1. Si tienes el dinero, ¿comprarás el cuadro?
2. Si tuvieras el dinero, ¿comprarías el cuadro?
3. Si hubieras tenido el dinero, ¿habrías comprado el cuadro?
4. Si vas a Puerto Rico, ¿visitarás el Museo de Arte en San Juan?
5. Si fueras a Puerto Rico, ¿visitarías el Museo de Arte en San Juan?
6. Si hubieras ido a Puerto Rico, ¿habrías visitado el Museo de Arte en San Juan?

LEER • ESCRIBIR

5 Completa con las formas apropiadas del verbo.

1. **tener**
   Ellos irán si ____ el tiempo.
   Yo también iría si ____ el tiempo.
   Yo sé que tú habrías ido si ____ el tiempo.

2. **dar**
   Yo lo compraré si alguien me ____ el dinero.
   Y él también lo compraría si alguien le ____ el dinero.
   ¿Uds. lo habrían comprado si alguien les ____ el dinero?

3. **ir**
   Yo iré a Córdoba si ____ a España.
   Él iría a Córdoba si ____ a España.
   Yo sé que nosotros habríamos ido a Córdoba si ____ a España.

CULTURA

Museo de Arte en San Juan, Puerto Rico

HABLAR • ESCRIBIR

6 Personaliza. Da respuestas personales.

1. Si alguien te diera mil dólares, ¿qué comprarías?
2. Si tú pudieras hacer un viaje, ¿adónde irías?
3. Si tú estudias mucho, ¿qué notas recibirás?
4. Si tú hubieras estado en España, ¿qué ciudades habrías visitado?

InfoGap For more practice with **si** clauses, do Activity 7 on page SR8 at the end of this book.

Comunicación

7 Trabaja con un(a) compañero(a). Dile todo lo que harías si tuvieras más tiempo. Luego él o ella dirá lo que él o ella haría.

FOLDABLES®
Study Organizer

CATEGORY BOOK

See page SH21 for help with making this foldable. Use this study organizer to practice forming adverbs with a partner. On the front of each tab, write an adjective. Then pass the foldable to your partner who will, on the back of each strip, rewrite the adjective in the form of an adverb. When you're finished, switch roles.

Los adverbios que terminan en -mente

1. An adverb modifies a verb, an adjective, or another adverb. In Spanish, many adverbs end in **-mente.** To form an adverb from an adjective that ends in **-e** or a consonant, you simply add **-mente** to the adjective. Study the following.

ADJECTIVE	+ -mente	ADVERB
enorme		enormemente
reciente		recientemente
principal		principalmente
general		generalmente

2. To form an adverb from an adjective that ends in **-o,** add **-mente** to the feminine **-a** form of the adjective.

FEMININE ADJECTIVE	+ -mente	ADVERB
sincera		sinceramente
cariñosa		cariñosamente

3. When more than one adverb ending in **-mente** modifies a verb, only the last adverb carries the **-mente** ending. Study the following.

> **Él habló lenta y claramente.**
> **Yo se lo digo honesta y sinceramente.**

CULTURA

Córdoba es realmente una ciudad pintoresca.

Práctica

ESCUCHAR • HABLAR • ESCRIBIR

8 Forma adverbios.

1. triste
2. puntual
3. elegante
4. rápido
5. respetuoso

6. humilde
7. loco
8. discreto
9. rico
10. posible

ESCUCHAR • HABLAR • ESCRIBIR

9 Contesta según el modelo.

MODELO ¿Cómo habla Ramón? (lento / claro) →
Ramón habla lenta y claramente.

1. ¿Cómo responde Luisa? (sincero / honesto)
2. ¿Cómo enseña la profesora? (claro / cuidadoso)
3. ¿Cómo se viste ella? (sencillo / elegante)
4. ¿Cómo conduce Pepe? (rápido / peligroso)
5. ¿Cómo se porta el niño? (cortés / respetuoso)

Refrán

Can you guess what the following proverb means?

Allá va Sancho con su rocín.

CULTURA

El niño mira atentamente al payaso que trabaja energéticamente en una plaza de Granada.

¡Bravo!

You have now learned all the new vocabulary and grammar in this chapter. Continue to use and practice all that you know while learning more cultural information. ¡Vamos!

QuickPass

Go to glencoe.com
For: **Conversation practice**
Web code: **ASD7844c7**

¡Ojalá que tuviera el talento!

Carlos	¿Te gustaría ser artista?
Elena	Me gustaría si tuviera algún talento, pero no lo tengo.
Carlos	Ni yo tampoco. Y es una pena porque aprecio mucho el arte.
Elena	Yo también. Pero creo que tú eres aún más aficionado que yo.
Carlos	Creo que he heredado mi afición a las artes de mi madre. Si ella no se hubiera dedicado la vida a una carrera de medicina, le habría gustado ser escritora.
Elena	¿A ella le gusta leer?
Carlos	Mucho. No puedes imaginar cuántas novelas lee en un mes. Con tantos pacientes no sé cómo tiene el tiempo.
Elena	Hablando de novelas me hace pensar en algo que me pasó en una librería en Guatemala.
Carlos	Dime.
Elena	Es un cuento real. Una joven le pidió al empleado que le recomendara una novela.
Carlos	¿Y?
Elena	Él le preguntó qué tipo de novela quería y ella respondió «buena literatura». El empleado no quería ser descortés pero empezó a reír y dijo que lo que es buena literatura para uno no lo es para otro.
Carlos	El empleado tenía razón. No importa que sea una novela, una poesía o un cuadro, yo sé si me gusta o no. Y es posible que lo que a mí me gusta no te guste a ti. ¡Así es!

¿Comprendes?

A Identifica quién según la información en la conversación.

	Carlos	Elena
1. Le gustaría ser artista pero no puede porque no tiene talento artístico.		
2. Aprecia mucho el arte, aún más que el/la otro(a).		
3. Su madre habría querido ser escritora si no se hubiera dedicado a la medicina.		
4. Había estado en una librería en Guatemala.		

B Contesta según la información en la conversación.

1. ¿Qué pidió una joven en una librería de Guatemala?
2. ¿Qué tipo de novela quería?
3. ¿Por qué se rió el empleado?
4. ¿Estás de acuerdo con lo que dijo él?

C Personalizando ¿Cuál es tu reacción al episodio en la librería en Guatemala?

CULTURA

La librería en Antigua, Guatemala, donde tuvo lugar la conversación sobre «la buena literatura»

Las artes 🎧♻️

Antes de leer

¿Cómo afectan tu vida el arte y la literatura? ¿Te interesan? ¿Te importan? ¿Cómo y por qué?

El arte y la literatura están estrechamente relacionadas con la vida porque es la vida misma o la percepción de la vida la que inspira la obra de muchos artistas y escritores. Vamos a tomar como ejemplo la obra del famoso muralista mexicano Diego Rivera. Para comprender su obra hay que saber algo sobre la realidad de la vida mexicana durante la época en que vivía. A principios del siglo veinte reinaban en México la inquietud e inestabilidad políticas. Los peones pobres trataban de mejorar su vida. Querían liberarse de los terratenientes corruptos que los trataban muy mal. En 1911 cayó la dictadura de Porfirio Díaz y estalló (empezó) la Revolución mexicana que duró hasta 1921. Fue durante esta época que vivió Diego Rivera, y lo que vio le inspiró a representar en arte la valiente lucha del peón mexicano.

✓ Reading Check

¿Cómo era la vida mexicana durante la época en que vivía Diego Rivera?

CULTURA
El famoso pintor y muralista Diego Rivera (1886–1957)

La liberación del peón *La liberación del peón* es un fresco sobre yeso. En el primer plano vemos a un grupo de tristes soldados revolucionarios. Están cortando las cuerdas¹ con que está atado² un peón muerto. Tienen una manta para cubrirle el cuerpo desnudo y azotado³. A lo lejos en el fondo se ven las llamas⁴ de una hacienda que está ardiendo⁵. La hacienda en llamas nos indica que el dueño (propietario) de la hacienda que tenía la responsabilidad de la muerte del pobre peón ya ha recibido su castigo⁶. Y ahora, silenciosa y tristemente, los soldados hacen lo que pueden por su compañero caído.

¹cuerdas   *ropes*
²atado   *tied*
³azotado   *beaten*

⁴llamas   *flames*
⁵ardiendo   *burning*
⁶castigo   *punishment*

VIDEO To learn about artisans from Venezuela, watch **Cultura en vivo.**

✓ **Reading Check**

¿A quién cuidan los soldados?
¿Por qué están muy tristes?

CULTURA

La liberación del peón de Diego Rivera

Federico García Lorca A veces es difícil distinguir entre el arte y la literatura. El siguiente poema del célebre autor español Federico García Lorca es un buen ejemplo. Es casi imposible leer esta poesía tan intensamente musical y sensual sin pintar un cuadro mental. Lee la poesía en voz alta.

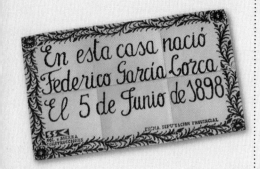

Canción de jinete[7]

Córdoba
Lejana y sola.

Jaca[8] negra, luna grande,
y aceitunas en mi alforja[9].
Aunque sepa los caminos
yo nunca llegaré a Córdoba.

Por el llano[10], por el viento,
jaca negra, luna roja.
La muerte me está mirando
desde las torres de Córdoba.

¡Ay qué camino tan largo!
¡Ay mi jaca valerosa!
¡Ay que la muerte me espera,
antes de llegar a Córdoba!

Córdoba.
Lejana y sola.

Ahora que has leído la poesía piensa en el cuadro mental que viste. ¿Qué animal viste? ¿Qué había en la alforja? ¿Qué había en el cielo? ¿Era grande o no? ¿Iluminaba el camino? ¿Qué viste en el fondo de tu cuadro mental?

García Lorca (1898–1936) vivía en Andalucía cuando estalló la horrible Guerra Civil española en 1936. El joven escritor, artista y músico murió en este mismo año cuando tenía solo treinta y ocho años. Todavía queda vaga y misteriosa la causa de su muerte pero se cree que fue la Guardia Civil quien lo mató. ¿Te parece que el autor presumía su trágico fin al escribir esta poesía?

CULTURA

Murales dedicados a las obras de Federico García Lorca en su pueblo natal de Fuentevaqueros en Granada

[7]jinete   *(horse) rider*
[8]Jaca   *pony*

[9]alforja   *saddle bag*
[10]llano   *plain*

¿Comprendes?

Más práctica

■ Workbook, pp. 7.11–7.12
● StudentWorks™ Plus

A Explicando y analizando Explica en tus propias palabras el significado de la siguiente frase: «El arte y la literatura están estrechamente relacionadas con la vida porque es la vida misma o la percepción de la vida la que inspira la obra de muchos artistas y escritores».

B Recordando hechos Contesta.
1. ¿Cómo fue la situación política en México durante la vida de Diego Rivera?
2. ¿Quiénes querían mejorar su vida?
3. ¿De quiénes querían liberarse?
4. ¿Cuándo estalló la Revolución mexicana?

C Describiendo Describe lo que ves en *La liberación del peón*. ¿Qué sentimientos surgen en ti al mirar el cuadro?

D Visualizando Lee de nuevo *Canción de jinete* y completa lo siguiente sobre tu cuadro mental.
1. la persona en tu cuadro
2. el animal
3. el cielo
4. los ruidos
5. el camino
6. el paisaje

E Personalizando Explica como te sientes al leer esta poesía. ¿Cuál es el elemento de misterio?

F Interpretando Contesta.
1. ¿Qué emoción evoca en ti el pensar en una jaca negra galopeando por un llano ventoso durante una noche oscura bajo una luna llena?
2. Para ti, ¿qué simboliza la luna llena?
3. ¿Quién habla en la poesía? ¿Adónde va? ¿Dónde está? ¿Cómo es?
4. ¿Cuándo llegará a Córdoba? ¿Por qué?
5. Llama a su jaca «valerosa». ¿Quién es realmente el valiente? ¿Por qué?

G Intrepretando ¿Cuál es tu opinión? ¿Presumía García Lorca su trágico fin al escribir esta poesía unos nueve años antes de su muerte?

CULTURA

La torre de la Mezquita de Córdoba

No sé por qué piensas tú

de Nicolás Guillén

▲ Bandera cubana delante del Hotel Nacional en la Habana

▲ Nicolás Guillén

Introducción

Nicolás Guillén (1902–1989) nació en Camagüey, Cuba, de sangre española y africana. Es el más conocido de los poetas cubanos, sobre todo por su poesía negroide. Muchas poesías de Guillén tienen el ritmo sensual y musical africano de uno de los bailes típicos de Cuba, el son, tal como:

¡Mayombe—bombe—mayombé!
¡Mayombe—bombe—mayombé!
¡Mayombe—bombe—mayombé!

En otras poesías Guillén habla de sus preocupaciones sociales, raciales y humanas—sobre todo la explotación socioeconómica de los de ascendencia africana.

Fondo histórico

No te será difícil leer esta poesía tierna y emotiva porque el autor emplea un lenguaje sencillo. Pero antes de leer la poesía tienes que saber algo sobre el fondo histórico.

El jefe del gobierno cubano, Fulgencio Batista, era un dictador cruel. La población civil, o sea el pueblo, odiaba[1] y temía al ejército porque era el ejército que tenía el deber de imponer la política opresiva e injusta del dictador.

[1]odiaba *hated*

No sé por qué piensas tú 🎧

No sé por qué piensas tú
soldado, que te odio yo,
si somos la misma cosa
yo,
5   tú

Tú eres pobre, lo soy yo:
soy de abajo, lo eres tú;
¿de dónde has sacado tú,
soldado, que te odio yo?

10   Me duele que a veces tú
te olvides de quién soy yo;
caramba, si yo soy tú,
lo mismo que tú eres yo.

Pero no por eso yo
15   he de[1] malquererte, tú;
si somos la misma cosa,
yo,
tú,
no sé por qué piensas tú
20   soldado, que te odio yo.

Ya nos veremos yo y tú
juntos en la misma calle,
hombro con hombro, tú y yo,
sin odios ni yo ni tú
25   pero sabiendo tú y yo,
a donde vamos yo y tú…
¡No sé por qué piensas tú,
soldado, que te odio yo!

[1]he de *I am supposed to*

Estrategia

Leyendo en voz alta Lee el poema en voz alta a un(a) compañero(a). El oírlo te ayudará a identificarte mejor con los sentimientos y el estado de ánimo de la persona que habla.

Una vista de La Habana, Cuba

GeoVistas

To learn more about Cuba, take a tour on pages SH46–SH47.

¿Comprendes?

A **Interpretando** En tu opinión ¿qué quiere decir el autor cuando dice…
1. «somos la misma cosa»?
2. «soy de abajo, lo eres tú»?

B **Interpretando** A veces el poeta dice «yo y tú» y otras veces dice «tú y yo». ¿Es posible que tenga una razón para cambiar la posición de los pronombres? ¿Cuál será?

C **Analizando** Contesta.
1. ¿Qué dice el hablante para tratar de convencer al soldado que no lo odia?
2. Según lo que has aprendido sobre el fondo histórico o el ambiente político en que tiene lugar la poesía, ¿por qué sería posible que la persona quien habla lo odiara?

Vocabulario

1 Identifica.

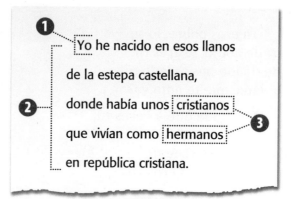

Yo he nacido en esos llanos de la estepa castellana, donde había unos **cristianos** que vivían como **hermanos** en república cristiana.

To review **Vocabulario 1** and **Vocabulario 2,** turn to pages 204–205 and 208–209.

2 Completa.

7. El artista pone el lienzo en un _____.

8. Muchos artistas pintan en un _____.

9. Los escultores tallan con un _____.

10–11. Los escultores pueden tallar estatuas o esculturas de _____ o de _____.

12. La _____ es la representación de los objetos en tres dimensiones sobre una superficie llana.

13. Dos medios que emplean los artistas son acuarelas y _____.

14. Una novela se divide en _____.

15. _____ es el personaje más importante de una novela.

16. _____ es la acción o lo que tiene lugar en una novela.

17–18. Cada línea de una poesía es un _____ y una serie de estos es una _____.

Gramática

3 **Completa con el presente perfecto del subjuntivo.**

19. Es posible que ellos _____ la exposición de las estatuas de Fernando Botero. (ver)

20. Me alegro de que a ti te _____ la exposición. (gustar)

21. Es una lástima que yo no _____ ir. (poder)

22. Dudo que ellos _____ la misma oportunidad. (tener)

To review **el presente perfecto del subjuntivo,** turn to page 212.

4 **Sigue el modelo.**

MODELO   yo / tener tiempo / ir →
Si yo tengo tiempo, iré.
Si yo tuviera tiempo, iría.
Si yo hubiera tenido tiempo, habría ido.

23–25. ellos / poder / visitar a sus abuelos

26–28. tú / prometer hacerlo / yo / no decir nada

29–31. yo / ir / hacer el trabajo

To review **cláusulas con si,** turn to page 214.

5 **Forma el adverbio.**

32. elegante

33. franco

34. cordial

35. sencillo

To review **los adverbios que terminan en -mente,** turn to page 216.

Cultura

6 **Contesta.**

36. ¿Qué tipo de obra refleja la realidad con más precisión—una obra figurativa o una obra abstracta?

37. ¿Cómo fue la situación política mexicana durante la vida de Diego Rivera?

38. ¿Cuáles son algunas cosas que puedes ver en su cuadro *La liberación del peón*?

39. ¿Cuáles son algunas cosas que puedes visualizar al leer la poesía *Canción de jinete* de García Lorca?

40. ¿Cómo murió García Lorca?

To review this cultural information, turn to pages 220–222.

CULTURA

Un mural en un edificio de la Universidad Autónoma de México

1 **¿El arte o la literatura?**

✓ *Discuss fine art and literature*

Trabajen en grupos de cuatro. Discutan si son más aficionados al arte o a la literatura. Den sus razones. Determinen los resultados. ¿Comparten ustedes las mismas opiniones o no? Entre el grupo, ¿hay uno o más que tenga talento artístico? Discutan el talento.

2 **Lecturas**

✓ *Discuss what you like to read*

Trabaja con un(a) compañero(a). Hablen de las cosas que les gusta leer. Si es posible que haya cosas que no les gusta leer, identifíquenlas.

3 **El arte**

✓ *Talk about preferences in art*

Discute el arte con un(a) compañero(a). ¿Eres muy aficionado(a) al arte o no? ¿Prefieres obras de arte figurativo o de arte abstracto? Explica tu preferencia.

4 **Mi cuadro favorito**

✓ *Talk about your favorite painting*

En el Internet, busca unos cuadros. De todos los cuadros que miras decide cuál es tu favorito. Descríbelo de la manera más detallada posible. Explica por qué has escogido este cuadro.

5 **Mi novela o cuento favorito**

✓ *Talk about your favorite novel or short story*

De todas las novelas o cuentos que has leído, ¿cuál es tu favorito(a)? Da una sinopsis de tu obra favorita.

CULTURA

Artistas del futuro estudiando en México

6 **Si tuvieras un millón de dólares...**

✓ *Discuss what you would do*

Piensa en todo lo que harías si tuvieras un millón de dólares. Prepara una lista. Compara tu lista con la de otros miembros de la clase. ¿Hay muchos que harían las mismas cosas? Piensa en tu lista y decide si te indica algo sobre tu personalidad o el tipo de persona que eres. ¿A qué conclusiones has llegado?

Tarea

Write a critique of a poem or work of art. Discuss the scene/setting and the images created by the artist or the author, as well as the emotions and feelings evoked by the artwork or poem.

Writing Strategy

Critiquing Writing a critique of a work of art or of literature does not so much involve criticizing as it does using a critical eye to describe the way in which different elements or aspects of the work function together to give an overall impression. When critiquing a painting or a poem, it often helps to begin with objective information and observations. Then gradually move to subjective statements such as what you like about the work, what the work means to you, why you think the work is important, etc.

1 Prewrite

- Choose the poem or work of art that you would like to critique. Take a few moments to reflect upon the author or artist, the title, and the historical context in which the work was created.
- Use the diagram to help you structure the details you wish to include.

lo objetivo

título, autor o artista, contexto histórico, técnica, materiales, estructura, ambiente

imágenes, personajes, objetos, colores, tono

emociones y sentimientos

interpretación personal

lo subjetivo

- Check your compiled information for correct spelling and proper use of vocabulary before you begin the first draft.

2 Write

- Start off your critique by mentioning the most objective details, such as title and artist or author, historical context, technique, materials used, structure, setting or scene, etc.

- Next describe the different elements of the artwork or poem; then discuss the emotions or feelings evoked by those elements.

- Conclude with your own interpretation and personal reaction.

- Reread what you have written. Double check to see that you have used correct vocabulary, and, if you have not already done so, look for ways to incorporate at least two of the chapter's grammar points.

- Once you have revised your first draft, write the final version.

Evaluate

Your teacher will evaluate you based on correct spelling, proper use of vocabulary and grammar, logical structure, and completeness of information.

Repaso del Capítulo 7

Gramática

- ### Presente perfecto y pluscuamperfecto del subjuntivo
  (page 212)

  The present perfect subjunctive is formed by using the present subjunctive of **haber** and the past participle. The pluperfect subjunctive is formed with the imperfect subjunctive of **haber** and the past participle.

	hablar	
	present perfect	**pluperfect**
yo	haya hablado	hubiera hablado
tú	hayas hablado	hubieras hablado
Ud., él, ella	haya hablado	hubiera hablado
nosotros(as)	hayamos hablado	hubiéramos hablado
vosotros(as)	*hayáis hablado*	*hubierais hablado*
Uds., ellos, ellas	hayan hablado	hubieran hablado

  Note that the present perfect or pluperfect subjunctive is used when the action in the dependent clause occurred prior to the action in the main clause.

    Dudo que ellos lo hayan visto.
    I doubt that they have seen it.

    Me sorprendió que ellos hubieran hecho tal cosa.
    It surprised me that they had (would have) done such a thing.

- ### Cláusulas con si *(page 214)*

  The sequence of tenses for **si** clauses is as follows.

MAIN CLAUSE	SI CLAUSE
future	present indicative
conditional	imperfect subjunctive
conditional perfect	pluperfect subjunctive

    Si tengo bastante dinero, haré el viaje.
    Si tuviera bastante dinero, haría el viaje.
    Si yo hubiera tenido bastante dinero, yo habría hecho el viaje.

- ### Los adverbios que terminan en -mente *(page 216)*

  To form an adverb from an adjective that ends in **-e** or a consonant, add **-mente** to the adjective. If an adjective ends in **-o**, add **-mente** to the feminine **-a** form of the adjective.

    enorme → enormemente   principal → principalmente
    sincera → sinceramente

Vocabulario

Talking about painting

el arte	la pintura	una naturaleza	pintoresco(a)
el/la artista, el/la	el óleo	muerta	plano(a)
pintor(a)	la acuarela	una superficie	pintar
el lienzo	el cuadro	la perspectiva	
el caballete	una obra figurativa	el primer plano	
el pincel	(abstracta)	el fondo	

Talking about sculpture

el/la escultor(a)	la escultura, la	una cerámica de
el taller	estatua	yeso
	de bronce (de	el cincel
	madera)	tallar

Talking about literature and poetry

la literatura	el capítulo	el cuento	la rima
el género	los personajes	la poesía	dividirse
la obra	el/la protagonista	el/la poeta	desarrollarse
la prosa (la	el argumento	el poema	
narrativa)	el lugar	el verso	
la novela	el ambiente	la estrofa	

Other useful words and expressions

el talento	trasero(a)

CULTURA

Una obra del escultor Agustín Ibarrola «Los cubos de la memoria» en Llanes, Asturias. ¿Presentó claramente su motivo el artista?

Repaso cumulativo

Repasa lo que ya has aprendido

These activities will help you review and remember
what you have learned so far in Spanish.

1 Escucha las frases. Indica en una tabla como la de abajo
si cada frase representa buenos o malos modales.

buenos modales	malos modales

2 Escribe cada frase de nuevo con pronombres de
complemento.

1. Compré *el traje de baño*.
2. ¿Pusiste *los boletos* en la maleta?
3. Él me vendió *el carro*.
4. Yo te devolví *el dinero*.
5. Ella me enseñó *las fotografías*.
6. Vimos *los cuadros* ayer.
7. Yo he leído *la novela* dos veces.
8. *Le* mandé *el correo electrónico a Susana*.
9. El médico *le* dio *los medicamentos a Felipe*.
10. El profesor *les* explicó *la lección*.

CULTURA

La muchacha lee claramente en
voz alta delante de su clase en una
escuela en Trinidad, Cuba.

3 Completa con el comparativo o el superlativo.

1. Gabriel García Márquez es _____ conocido _____
   muchos autores contemporáneos.
2. Es posible que él sea _____ conocido _____ todos.
3. Me gusta _____ la obra de Velázquez _____ la de
   Murillo.
4. El Museo de Antropología en la Ciudad de México
   es _____ grande _____ el Palacio de Bellas Artes.
5. Creo que es _____ grande _____ todos los museos
   del país.
6. La obra de García Lorca es _____ extensa _____ la
   obra de Antonio Machado.

Contesta según la información.

José tiene trece años. Sara tiene ocho.

Y Elena tiene diecisiete.

1. ¿Quién es menor que José?

2. ¿Quién es mayor que José?

3. ¿Quién es el/la menor?

4. ¿Quién es el/la mayor?

5. ¿Quiénes son mayores que Sara?

Completa con el comparativo o superlativo.

1. Esta novela es buena pero a mi parecer esa es
   _____. No sé cuál es _____ mejor _____ todas.

2. El comportamiento de este niño es malo pero
   el comportamiento de su hermano es aún _____.
   Es posible que el suyo sea _____ todos.

Haz lo siguiente.

1. Prepara una lista de todos los artículos de ropa
   (las prendas de vestir) que conoces.

2. Prepara una lista de expresiones que necesitas
   si vas de compras en una tienda de ropa.

Conversa. Con un(a) compañero(a) prepara una
conversación que tiene lugar en una tienda de ropa.

◄ ¿Qué piensas? ¿Es uno de estos
hermanos menor que el otro?
O, ¿es posible que sean gemelos?

Latinos en Estados Unidos

Aquí y Allí

Vamos a comparar Hoy en día la población latina consta de más de cincuenta millones de personas. Los latinos o hispanos en Estados Unidos vienen de todos los países hispanohablantes y viven en todas partes de Estados Unidos. Se ve la influencia hispana o latina en muchos aspectos de la vida estadounidense.

◀ Hay un gran desfile para celebrar el día de los dominicanos en la Ciudad de Nueva York.

Objetivos

You will:

- talk about the history of Spanish speakers in the United States
- read a poem by the Puerto Rican poet Julia de Burgos

You will use:

- the subjunctive with **aunque**
- the subjunctive with **-quiera**
- definite and indefinite articles (special uses)
- apocopated adjectives

QuickPass

Go to glencoe.com
For: **Online book**
Web code: ASD7844c8

Introducción al tema
Latinos en Estados Unidos

No importa adonde vayas en Estados Unidos no hay duda que podrás observar la influencia latina. Hoy hay más de cincuenta millones de hispanos o latinos en Estados Unidos. Aunque vienen de todos los países latinos, el grupo mayoritario son de ascendencia mexicana.

◄ **Florida** Como en muchas ciudades de Estados Unidos, las instrucciones en los centros electorales se dan en inglés y español. En este centro electoral en Miami son también en criollo, el idioma de los haitianos.

▲ **Nueva York** Alex Rodríguez, el famoso beisbolista de los Yanquis de Nueva York, nació en Washington Heights de padres dominicanos. Ha vivido también en la República Dominicana y Miami, Florida. Rodríguez donó 3,9 millones de dólares a la Universidad de Miami para la construcción de un estadio de béisbol.

California Salma Hayek juega el papel de Frida Kahlo en la película *Frida*. ▼

▲ **Florida** Este azulejo español está en la entrada de un restaurante en Ybor City en Tampa.

Florida Se venden camisetas durante el Carnaval de la Calle Ocho en la Pequeña Habana en Miami. ▶

◀ **California** Jaime Escalante se considera uno de los educadores más famosos de Estados Unidos. Él nació en La Paz, Bolivia, pero pasó la mayor parte de su carrera como profesor de cálculo en una escuela secundaria en East Los Angeles. Su vida se dramatizó en la película *Stand and Deliver*.

Texas Estatua en honor de los conquistadores españoles en San Antonio ▶

▲ **California** Una celebración para el Cinco de Mayo en la calle Olvera en East Los Angeles

La televisión

una emisora
de televisión

una emisión televisiva, un
programa de televisión

Univisión es una emisora de televisión.
Una emisora es una empresa o compañía.
Se dedica a emisiones de radio y televisión.

Una emisora es también una estación de
televisión, como el canal (la cadena) 7,
por ejemplo.
Hay muchas emisoras latinas en Estados
Unidos.
Aunque están en Estados Unidos, emiten
los programas en español.

un ancla

El ancla (noticiero) da las noticias.
Quienquiera que lo escuche dice que es
un buen noticiero.
Tiene reportajes interesantes.

La prensa

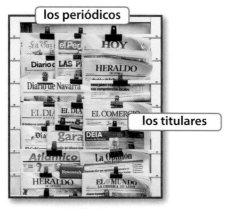

los periódicos

los titulares

los libros de bolsillo

la revista

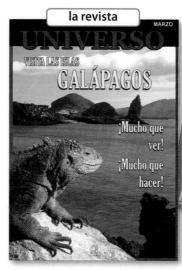

la publicidad, la promoción, la propaganda

La periodista escribe para el periódico.

Los artículos llevan titulares.

Una revista tiene mucha publicidad.

La televisión y la prensa son medios de comunicación.

Más vocabulario

una ojeada mirada rápida

una guerra una serie de luchas o batallas

los soldados los que luchan en las batallas durante una guerra

el sacerdote un cura o padre religioso (católico)

acomodado(a) adinerado, rico, que tiene dinero

ilustre famoso

apoderarse de tomar el poder por fuerza, tomar el control

darse cuenta de llegar a saber, comprender

sobrepasar exceder

tomar en cuenta considerar

lograr obtener (conseguir) lo que se desea

otorgar dar

invertir dar fondos monetarios, hacer inversiones

Vocabulario

práctica

QuickPass

Go to glencoe.com
For: **Vocabulary practice**
Web code: **ASD7844c8**

FOLDABLES®
Study Organizer

FORWARD-BACKWARD BOOK
See page SH22 for help with making this foldable. Use this study organizer to talk to a partner about television and the press. Write **La televisión** on the cover and inside list your favorite television programs. On the other cover, write **La prensa** and inside list your favorite magazines and newspapers. Share your book with your partner and explain why these programs and publications are your favorites. When you're finished, switch roles.

HABLAR • ESCRIBIR

1 Da una(s) palabra(s) relacionada(s).

1. las noticias
2. guerrero
3. emitir
4. la televisión
5. el periódico
6. la inversión
7. el ojo
8. cómodo

HABLAR

2 Personaliza. Da respuestas personales.

1. ¿Cuál es tu canal de televisión favorito?
2. ¿Hay emisoras que emiten en español donde vives?
3. ¿Quién es tu ancla favorito(a)?
4. ¿Hay mucha publicidad en la televisión?
5. ¿Interrumpe las emisiones la publicidad?
6. ¿Qué periódico lees?
7. ¿Qué medio prefieres? ¿La televisión o la prensa?
8. ¿Das una ojeada al periódico todos los días?
9. ¿Lees los titulares?
10. ¿Encabeza o introduce un artículo el titular?

LEER • ESCRIBIR

3 Completa con la palabra o expresión apropiada.

1. Es necesario _____ todas las opiniones disponibles antes de tomar una decisión.
2. Si quieren que el proyecto tenga éxito tendrán que _____ mucho dinero.
3. Espero que ellos tengan éxito y que _____ realizar su objetivo.
4. Él tiene mucho dinero. Es bastante _____.
5. Los dos grupos quieren _____ del mismo territorio y no hay duda que van a luchar.
6. No tienes que leerlo detenida y detalladamente. Es suficiente darle una _____.

LEER • ESCRIBIR

4 Expresa de otra manera.

1. Ella es una poeta *famosa*.
2. Había una *serie de batallas*.
3. Van a *darle* un premio.
4. Es de una familia *adinerada*.
5. No debes *exceder* el límite.
6. Debes *considerar* todas las opciones que tienes a tu disposición.
7. Quieren *tomar control* de la ciudad *por fuerza*.
8. Es *un programa de televisión*.

Estudio de palabras

conquistar Los españoles conquistaron a los indígenas americanos.

el conquistador Los españoles eran los conquistadores.

la conquista La conquista española tuvo lugar en el siglo dieciséis.

colonizar Los españoles colonizaron gran parte de las Américas.

el colonizador Los españoles eran los colonizadores.

la colonia Ellos establecieron muchas colonias.

colonial Las zonas coloniales de las ciudades son pintorescas.

1 Completa.

1. Francisco Pizarro fue el _____ de Perú.
2. Francisco Pizarro _____ Perú y Hernán Cortés _____ México.
3. La _____ era muy cruel.
4. Los sacerdotes españoles establecieron _____ en California.
5. Ellos _____ muchas partes del sudoeste de Estados Unidos.
6. Muchas ciudades latinoamericanas tienen barrios o cascos _____.

2 Contesta sobre la época de la conquista. Fíjate en las palabras aparentadas.

1. ¿Llegaron los conquistadores españoles a las Américas durante el siglo XVI?
2. ¿Vinieron los sacerdotes con los conquistadores?
3. Después de los conquistadores, ¿llegaron los colonizadores?
4. ¿Establecieron ellos colonias?
5. ¿Había luchas entre los españoles y los indígenas?

CULTURA

Misión al norte de San Diego, California

QuickPass

Go to glencoe.com
For: **Grammar practice**
Web code: **ASD7844c8**

El subjuntivo con aunque

The conjunction **aunque** (*although*) may be followed by the subjunctive or the indicative depending upon the meaning of the sentence.

> **Ellos van a salir aunque llueva.**
> **Ellos van a salir aunque llueve.**

In the first example the subjunctive is used to indicate that it is not raining now, but they will go out even if it does rain. In the second example, the indicative is used to indicate that it is raining and they will go out even though it is indeed raining.

Práctica

ESCUCHAR • HABLAR • ESCRIBIR

1 Contesta según el modelo.

MODELO —**Hace mucho calor. ¿Vas a jugar?**
—**Sí, voy a jugar aunque hace mucho calor.**

1. No tienes entrada. ¿Vas al concierto?
2. Podría llover. ¿Vas a salir?
3. No entiendes español. ¿Vas a escuchar el programa?
4. Elena no tiene dinero. ¿Va a hacer el viaje?
5. Es posible que ella no tenga dinero. ¿Va a hacer el viaje?
6. Es posible que haya tráfico. ¿Quieres ir en carro?
7. El avión te cuesta más. ¿Quieres ir en avión?
8. Es posible que el bus tarde más tiempo. ¿Vas a tomar el bus?

Conexiones

El mercado

¿Qué es un mercado? Es cualquier lugar adonde vayamos a comprar algo. Pero el término «el mercado» tiene otro significado. El mercado incluye todos los consumidores, o sea, todos los eventuales compradores de un producto. Como todos no queremos comprar el mismo producto, el mercado tiene segmentos. Algunos ejemplos son los jóvenes, la gente mayor, los hombres, las mujeres, los latinos.

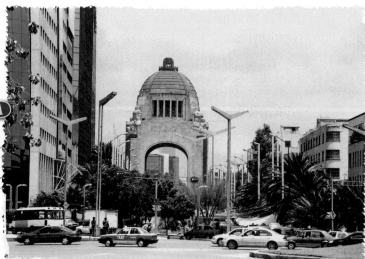

CULTURA

Monumento a la Revolución en la Ciudad de México

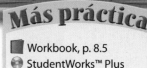

Más práctica

Workbook, p. 8.5

StudentWorks™ Plus

LEER • ESCRIBIR

② Escoge según el contexto.

1. Hoy en día las noticias son malas pero el ancla tiene que dar las noticias aunque (sean, son) malas.

2. Ellos hablan muy bien el español pero contestan en inglés aunque (hablan, hablen) español.

3. Yo no sé si la profesora nos va a dar una tarea pero voy a salir aunque nos (da, dé) una.

4. Se sabe que él tiene mucho dinero pero aunque (es, sea) muy acomodado, es bastante tacaño. No le gusta gastar su dinero.

5. Es posible que él no lo sepa. Pero aunque no lo (sabe, sepa) no le voy a decir nada.

6. El público se opone. Sin embargo el oficial va a seguir con su plan aunque todos (están, estén) en contra.

InfoGap For more practice using the subjunctive with **aunque,** do Activity 8 on page SR9 at the end of this book.

CULTURA

Una empresa latina cubriendo las noticias en Chicago

Comunicación

③ Trabaja con un(a) compañero(a) de clase. Los dos van a discutir unas cosas que van a hacer aunque ocurra algo que lo haga difícil. Luego discutan unas cosas que van a hacer aunque saben que va a ser muy difícil hacerlas. En ambos casos, expliquen por qué.

El subjuntivo con -quiera

Many words are made indefinite by adding **-quiera.** Such words are followed by the subjunctive. **Quiera** is the same as the *ever* in *whoever, wherever.*

quienquiera	**cuandoquiera**	**dondequiera**
comoquiera	**cualquiera**	**adondequiera**

Quienquiera que sea, no nos podrá resolver el problema.
Adondequiera que vayas, oirás el español.

CULTURA

Adondequiera que vayas en las islas Baleares tendrás vistas fabulosas.

Práctica

ESCUCHAR • HABLAR • ESCRIBIR

4 Contesta.

1. ¿Irás cuandoquiera que salgan ellos?
2. ¿Estarás de acuerdo con cualquier idea que tenga él?
3. ¿Los acompañarás adondequiera que vayan?
4. ¿Se lo dirás a quienquiera que te escuche?
5. ¿Lo podrás hacer dondequiera que estés?

LEER • ESCRIBIR

5 Completa con la forma apropiada del verbo.

1. Te prometo que te ayudaré con cualquier problema que _____. (tener)
2. Te daré ayuda cuandoquiera que la _____. (necesitar)
3. Adondequiera que (nosotros) _____ no veremos nada más bello. (ir)
4. Quienquiera que lo _____ hecho, debe confesar. (haber)
5. Comoquiera que ellos lo _____, saldrá bien. (hacer)

Usos especiales del artículo definido

1. Unlike English, the definite article must be used in Spanish with all general or abstract nouns. Compare the Spanish and English in the following examples.

> **La leche es buena para la salud.**
> *Milk is good for the health.*

> **Los programas de televisión pueden ser educativos.**
> *Television programs can be educational.*

> **El amor es una cosa divina.**
> *Love is a divine thing.*

2. The definite article must be used with the title of a person when talking about the person. The article is not used when addressing the person.

> **La doctora González es dentista.**
> **Buenos días, Doctora González.**

> **El licenciado Ugarte es periodista.**
> **Buenas tardes, Licenciado Ugarte.**

3. The definite article, rather than the indefinite article, is used with quantities, weights, and measures.

> **El biftec está a 500 pesos el kilo.**
> *Steak is 500 pesos a kilo.*

> **Los huevos cuestan 1,50 la docena.**
> *Eggs cost 1.50 a dozen.*

4. When the definite article is used with the days of the week, it means *on.*

> **Lunes es el primer día de la semana.**
> *Monday is the first day of the week.*

> **Él sale el sábado.**
> *He leaves on Saturday.*

> **Ella no trabaja los domingos.**
> *She doesn't work on Sundays.*

5. The definite article is used with the season in a general sense.

> **El verano es una estación de calor.**
> > *but*
> **Hace calor en (el) verano.**
> **Julio es un mes de verano.**

Conexiones

Las matemáticas
Los huevos están a 1,17 euros la media docena. El tipo de cambio actual es 1,48 euros a un dólar. Calcula cuánto cuesta media docena de huevos. Luego calcula cuánto costaría una docena.

Manny Díaz, el alcalde de Miami, da una entrevista a un ancla latina.

Carreras

¿Te interesaría tratar de identificar a los consumidores que necesitarían o comprarían cierto producto? Si contestas que sí, es posible que una carrera en marketing te interese. Y una función importante del marketing es la publicidad y la promoción, porque es necesario convencer a los consumidores (al mercado) que deben comprar cierto producto. ¿Te gusta escribir un mensaje en pocas palabras—un mensaje interesante que atrae mucha atención? Si tienes tal talento, debes considerar una carrera en la publicidad. Y como el mercado hispanohablante es tan grande, el español te puede ayudar.

Práctica

HABLAR

6 Personaliza. Da respuestas personales.

1. ¿Cuáles son los vegetales y frutas que te gustan?
2. ¿Cuáles son los deportes que te gustan?
3. ¿Cuáles son los cursos que te interesan?

LEER • ESCRIBIR

7 Completa.

1. _____ guerra es una cosa horrible.
2. _____ periodistas trabajan para un periódico y _____ anclas para emisoras de televisión.
3. _____ tigres y _____ leones son animales salvajes pero _____ perros y _____ gatos son animales domésticos.
4. A _____ niños les gusta _____ leche. _____ leche y _____ legumbres son buenas para la salud.
5. _____ verano es mi estación favorita pero mi amiga prefiere _____ primavera.

LEER • HABLAR • ESCRIBIR

8 Completa con el artículo cuando necesario.

—Buenos días. ¿Está __1__ doctor Salas, por favor?
—Sí, __2__ Señora. ¿De parte de quién?
—De parte de __3__ señora Ochoa.
—Un momentito, __4__ Señora Ochoa. __5__ doctor Salas estará con usted en un momento.
—Buenos días, __6__ Doctor Salas.

HABLAR • ESCRIBIR

9 Contesta.

1. ¿Qué días de la semana tienes clases?
2. ¿Cuál es tu día favorito?
3. ¿Qué día es hoy?
4. ¿Cuáles son los días laborales, los días que tenemos que trabajar?

HABLAR

10 Con un(a) compañero(a) prepara una conversación según el modelo.

MODELO **una lata de atún / 10 pesos →**
   —¿Cuál es el precio del atún?
   —10 pesos la lata.

1. una docena de huevos / 1 euro
2. un kilo de tomates / 500 pesos
3. una botella de agua mineral / 3 quetzales
4. un frasco de mayonesa / 50 pesos

Uso especial del artículo indefinido

1. In Spanish, unlike English, the indefinite article is omitted after the verb **ser** when the noun that follows is not modified.

> **La señora Dávila es periodista.**
> **Don Luis es profesor.**

2. The indefinite article is used, however, in the same way as in English if the noun is modified.

> **Sandra Cisneros es una autora conocida.**
> **Es una autora que ha tenido mucha fama.**
> **Es una autora de mucho renombre.**

Práctica

HABLAR

11 Contesta.

1. ¿Es profesor el señor Gómez?
2. ¿Es un profesor bueno?
3. ¿Era poeta García Lorca?
4. ¿Era un poeta famoso?
5. ¿Es artista Isabel?
6. ¿Es una artista que ha tenido exposiciones de sus cuadros?

CULTURA

La famosa escritora latina Sandra Cisneros da una conferencia durante un festival de libros en Los Ángeles.

LEER • ESCRIBIR

12 Completa con el artículo indefinido cuando necesario.

1. El señor Fernández es _____ periodista.
2. El señor Fernández es _____ periodista conocido que escribe para el *Miami Herald*.
3. Carlos es _____ alumno que estudia mucho.
4. El señor López es _____ cocinero.
5. Es _____ cocinero excelente.

 Comunicación

13 Trabaja con un(a) compañero(a) de clase. Cada uno(a) pensará en una persona que conoce. Dirá qué es y luego dará uno o más detalles. Túrnense. Pueden usar las siguientes palabras.

profesor(a)	actor, actriz	médico(a)	dentista
futbolista	periodista	beisbolista	ancla
artista	escritor(a)		

Adjetivos apocopados

1. Several adjectives in Spanish have a shortened form when they precede a singular masculine noun. The **-o** ending is dropped.

bueno	El Universal es un **buen** periódico.
	Es un periódico bueno.
malo	No es un **mal** periódico.
	No es un periódico malo.
primero	No estamos en el **primer** semestre.
	Estamos en el segundo.
tercero	Estamos en el **tercer** año de español.

2. **Alguno** and **ninguno** also drop the **-o** before a masculine singular noun.

Algún día lo vamos a saber.
No hay **ningún** problema.

3. **Ciento** is shortened to **cien** before a masculine or a feminine noun.

Hay más de **cien** periódicos y **cien** emisoras en español.

4. **Grande** becomes **gran** when it precedes a singular masculine or feminine noun. The form **gran** conveys the meaning of *great* or *famous*. **Grande** after the noun almost always means *big* or *large*.

una **gran** mujer y un **gran** hombre

5. **Santo** becomes **San** before a masculine saint's name unless the name begins with **To-** or **Do-**.

San Pedro	Santo Domingo	Santa María
San Diego	Santo Tomás	Santa Teresa

Práctica

HABLAR

14 Contesta.

1. En tu opinión, ¿cuál es un buen canal de televisión donde tú vives?
2. ¿Conoces una buena emisora en español?
3. En tu opinión, ¿cuál es un buen periódico y cuál es una buena revista?
4. ¿Fue Cervantes un gran autor?
5. ¿Es *El Quijote* una gran novela?

6. ¿Es el español el primer idioma de muchos latinos en Estados Unidos?

7. ¿Es San Diego una ciudad en California?

8. ¿Es Santo Domingo la capital de la República Dominicana?

LEER • ESCRIBIR

15 Completa con la forma apropiada del adjetivo.

1. **primero**
Es la _____ vez que el equipo gana el _____ partido.

2. **tercero**
Tienes que doblar a la derecha en la _____ bocacalle y el edificio que buscas es el _____ edificio a mano izquierda.

3. **grande**
Nueva York es una _____ ciudad y es también una ciudad _____.

4. **alguno, ninguno**
¡Ojalá que _____ día él no tenga _____ problema!

5. **ciento**
La novela tiene más de _____ páginas pero no tiene _____ capítulos.

6. **malo**
Es una _____ situación. Él ha invertido mucho dinero en un _____ negocio.

7. **ninguno**
Desgraciadamente él no tiene _____ experiencia.

Refrán

Can you guess what the following proverb means?

Aunque duela, salga la muela.

Conexiones

La geografía

16 Da la información.
1. la capital de Puerto Rico
2. la capital de El Salvador
3. la capital de Costa Rica
4. la capital de la República Dominicana
5. tres ciudades de California que llevan los nombres de santos

¡Bravo!

You have now learned all the new vocabulary and grammar in this chapter. Continue to use and practice all that you know while learning more cultural information. ¡Vamos!

QuickPass

Go to glencoe.com
For: **Conversation practice**
Web code: ASD7844c8

LOS MEDIOS HAN CAMBIADO

LUIS, ¿TE ACUERDAS QUE SOLO HACE POCO HABÍA POCOS PROGRAMAS LATINOS EN LA TELEVISIÓN?

SÍ, ES ALGO QUE HA CAMBIADO COMPLETAMENTE.

HOY HAY EMISIONES EN ESPAÑOL PARA TODOS LOS GUSTOS— NOTICIEROS, DEBATES, TELENOVELAS, FILMES, JUEGOS INFANTILES, EMISIONES DEPORTIVAS— EN FIN, DE TODO.

AUNQUE YA HAY MUCHAS OPCIONES SIGUE EN AUMENTO EL NÚMERO DE EMISORAS QUE EMITEN EN ESPAÑOL.

YO SÉ QUE UNIVISIÓN TIENE MÁS DE CINCUENTA EMISORAS Y TELEMUNDO TIENE MÁS DE QUINCE Y SIEMPRE ESTÁN AÑADIENDO SOCIOS Y AFILIADOS.

HAY MUCHAS COMPAÑÍAS QUE ESTÁN INVIRTIENDO DINERO EN LA PUBLICIDAD EN ESPAÑOL PORQUE QUIEREN QUE SUS PRODUCTOS LLEGUEN AL ENORME MERCADO LATINO. Y NO HAY MEJOR MEDIO QUE LA TELEVISIÓN.

DE ACUERDO. PERO TAMPOCO SE PUEDE OLVIDAR LA PRENSA. ACTUALMENTE HAY UNA GRAN PROLIFERACIÓN DE PERIÓDICOS Y REVISTAS EN ESPAÑOL.

AUNQUE WASHINGTON, D.C., NO SE CONSIDERA UNA CIUDAD CON UNA GRAN POBLACIÓN HISPANA TIENE MÁS DE VEINTICUATRO PERIÓDICOS DIARIOS Y DOMINICALES EN ESPAÑOL.

NO HAY DUDA QUE DONDEQUIERA QUE ESTÉS EN ESTADOS UNIDOS HAY PROGRAMAS DE TELEVISIÓN Y PERIÓDICOS Y REVISTAS EN ESPAÑOL.

PARTICIPAN 13 MIL CORREDORES

¿Comprendes?

A Prepara una lista de tipos de emisiones televisivas.

B Explica.
Explica lo que son Univisión y Telemundo.

C Contesta según la información en la conversación.
1. ¿Qué está aumentando en los medios en Estados Unidos?
2. ¿Por qué están invirtiendo dinero en la publicidad en español muchas compañías estadounidenses?
3. ¿Por qué es interesante que una ciudad como Washington, D.C., tenga unos veinticuatro periódicos publicados en español?

D **Resumiendo** En tus propias palabras resume toda la información sobre los medios en español.

E **¡En tu tiempo libre!**
Como hay tantas emisoras de televisión y radio en español aquí en Estados Unidos tienes una oportunidad de practicar tu español y divertirte al mismo tiempo. Escucha un programa de radio en español o mira un programa de televisión. Luego dile a la clase lo que oíste o viste. ¿Qué tipo de programa fue? ¿Te gustó? ¿Lo entendiste fácilmente?

Comunidades

¿Hay emisoras de televisión hispanas donde vives? ¿Cuántas? ¿Cuáles son? ¿Hay periódicos o revistas en español? ¿Cuáles?

UNIDOS POR LA SED DE FÚTBOL
COPA MUNDIAL DE LA FIFA
Coca-Cola

◀ Publicidad en español en la ciudad de Chicago

Latinos en Estados Unidos

Antes de leer

Antes de leer esta lectura, piensa en tus antepasados y contesta las siguientes preguntas: ¿De dónde vinieron tus antepasados? ¿De qué país inmigraron? ¿Cuándo? ¿Por qué?

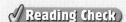
Reading Check

¿Dónde establecieron colonias los españoles?

Todo el mundo sabe que los españoles exploraron y colonizaron la mayor parte de Centroamérica y Sudamérica. Menos conocido es el hecho de que los españoles también exploraron y colonizaron gran parte de la América del Norte. En 1512 Juan Ponce de León, el gobernador de Puerto Rico, llegó a la Florida. Poco después Lucas Vázquez de Ayllón fundó una colonia en la Carolina del Sur mientras Álvaro Núñez Cabeza de Vaca exploraba todo el sudoeste desde Tampa, Florida, hasta el golfo de California.

También vinieron sacerdotes que establecieron misiones que a través de los años dieron sus nombres a pueblos y ciudades como San Antonio, Santa Fe, San Diego y tantas más. Los españoles llegaron a lo que hoy es Estados Unidos mucho antes de que los ingleses fundaran su primera colonia en Jamestown en 1607. Hubo otra ola de inmigración española en 1936 cuando estalló la horrible Guerra Civil española.

Los mexicanoamericanos Ya sabemos que el grupo más grande de latinos o hispanos en Estados Unidos son los mexicanoamericanos. Viven en todas partes del país aunque se concentran en los estados del suroeste entre Texas y California—territorio que una vez fue mexicano. Muchos de ellos nacieron allí antes de que el territorio pasara a manos de Estados Unidos. Luego, después de la Revolución mexicana hubo otra ola de inmigración de gente que salía de México por razones políticas y económicas. Hoy también vienen muchos mexicanos en busca de trabajo con la esperanza de lograr una vida mejor para sus familias.

Entre los inmigrantes más recientes hay quienes no se consideran formalmente mexicanoamericanos porque en muchos casos no se establecen permanentemente en Estados Unidos. Dentro de la comunidad mexicanoamericana hay una gran diversidad social, económica, lingüística y política. Una gran mayoría de los mexicanoamericanos mantienen elementos de la cultura mexicana y la lengua española. Se sienten participantes en dos culturas igualmente importantes—la mexicana y la estadounidense.

CULTURA
Las calles Diez y Once en el centro de Los Ángeles

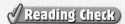
Reading Check

¿Cuáles son los diferentes grupos de mexicanoamericanos?

Los puertorriqueños En 1899 Estados Unidos salió victorioso en una guerra con España. Como consecuencia de esta guerra Cuba ganó su independencia y España cedió Puerto Rico a Estados Unidos. En 1917 el presidente Woodrow Wilson firmó el *Jones Act* otorgándoles a los puertorriqueños la ciudadanía estadounidense. Puerto Rico sigue siendo un Estado Asociado[1] de Estados Unidos. La gran migración hacia el «continente» no se realizó hasta después de la Segunda Guerra mundial. El mayor motivo por esta migración fue económico. Muchos puertorriqueños salieron de su querida Isla del Encanto en busca de trabajo. La mayoría de ellos se establecieron en el nordeste, sobre todo en zonas urbanas de Nueva York y Nueva Jersey. Mucha gente de ascendencia puertorriqueña sigue viviendo en el nordeste pero hoy en día están en todas partes con comunidades bastante numerosas en Illinois, Texas y la Florida.

[1]Estado Asociado *Commonwealth*

VIDEO To learn about a Latino tradition in the United States, watch **Cultura en vivo.**

Reading Check

¿Por qué son ciudadanos de Estados Unidos los puertorriqueños?

CULTURA
El Morro en San Juan de Puerto Rico

Los cubanoamericanos Desde 1868 ha habido colonias cubanas en Estados Unidos. En ese año Vicente Martínez Ybor trasladó su fábrica de tabacos de La Habana a Cabo Cayo, *Key West* en inglés. Poco después otros tabaqueros lo siguieron y se establecieron en Tampa en un barrio que todavía hoy se llama Ybor City. Pero la gran migración de los cubanos empezó en 1959 cuando los guerrilleros bajo Fidel Castro dieron fin a la dictadura de Fulgencio Batista y establecieron en Cuba un gobierno marxista. Muchos cubanos, sobre todo los más acomodados, decidieron abandonar su patria y tomar el duro camino del exilio. Muchos de ellos se dirigieron a Nueva Jersey y la Florida. Aún hoy muchas partes de la ciudad de Miami siguen siendo otra versión de La Habana.

Los nuevos inmigrantes Sigue llegando gente de muchas partes de Latinoamérica añadiendo a la población latina o hispana de este país. Dentro de poco los dominicanos van a sobrepasar la población puertorriqueña en la Ciudad de Nueva York.

La mayoría de los recién llegados—dominicanos, colombianos, ecuatorianos, venezolanos, centroamericanos—vienen por motivos económicos o políticos. A causa de una serie de guerras y conflictos, muchos nicaragüenses, guatemaltecos y salvadoreños han tenido que tomar el camino del exilio.

La comunidad latina de Estados Unidos es una vasta comunidad heterogénea que ha contribuido y sigue contribuyendo con su arte, su talento y su sabor al bienestar y al progreso de la nación entera.

Reading Check
¿Tuvieron motivos diferentes los cubanos que se establecieron en Tampa en el siglo diecinueve que los cubanos que vinieron en los años sesenta del siglo pasado?

GeoVistas
To learn more about Latinos in the United States, take a tour on pages SH54–SH55.

Reading Check
¿A qué contribuye la comunidad latina?

CULTURA
Desfile en la avenida de las Américas en Nueva York para celebrar el Día de la Independencia de la República Dominicana

¿Comprendes?

Más práctica

■ Workbook, pp. 8.8–8.9
● StudentWorks™ Plus

A **Resumiendo** En tus propias palabras resume la información histórica sobre los españoles en la América del Norte.

B **Recordando hechos** Contesta.

1. ¿Cuál es el grupo mayoritario de latinos en Estados Unidos?
2. ¿Dónde viven?
3. ¿Dónde nacieron muchos de ellos?
4. ¿Cuándo hubo otra gran ola de inmigración mexicana?
5. Entre los inmigrantes más recientes de México, ¿por qué hay unos que no se consideran mexicanoamericanos?

C **Explicando** Explica.

1. como es que los puertorriqueños son ciudadanos estadounidenses
2. por qué había grandes migraciones de puertorriqueños hacia el «continente»
3. donde se establecieron la mayoría de los puertorriqueños
4. cuando empezó la gran migración de cubanos a Estados Unidos y por qué
5. de donde vienen los nuevos inmigrantes
6. las razones por las cuales los nuevos inmigrantes deciden venir a Estados Unidos

Conexiones

El inglés
¿Cuáles son algunas palabras que se usan en inglés que son de origen español? Y, ¿cuáles son algunos lugares geográficos en Estados Unidos que tienen nombres españoles? Presenta tu información a la clase.

CULTURA
Un restaurante latino en Hialeah, Florida

A Julia de Burgos
de Julia de Burgos

▲ Universidad de
Puerto Rico en
Río Piedras

Vocabulario

el amo dueño, propietario

el corazón órgano vital que impulsa la sangre

el cura sacerdote

la cifra número, dígito

mentir no decir la verdad, decir mentiras

olfatear percibir olores y aromas

alzarse levantarse

Práctica

Completa con una palabra apropiada.

1. _____ bendice a los que asisten a Misa.
2. El número 10 es una _____ y el número 5 es otra.
3. _____ es un órgano musculoso. Es también un órgano vital.
4. Te voy a decir la verdad. Te prometo que no voy a _____.
5. Yo no sé quién es el _____ del negocio.
6. Ella _____ antes de empezar a hablar a su público.

INTRODUCCIÓN

Julia de Burgos era poeta, dramaturga y educadora puertorriqueña. Era también feminista y una activista política. Nació en Carolina, Puerto Rico, en 1914. Era de una familia grande y pobre pero sus padres insistieron en que sus hijos recibieran una educación buena. Desde niña Julia mostró una gran inteligencia. Ella estudió en la Universidad de Puerto Rico donde recibió el Certificado de Maestra.

Mientras ejercía su profesión de maestra primaria, se dedicaba también a la poesía. En 1940 ella fue a Nueva York donde dio recitales de sus poesías a los puertorriqueños que residían en esta gran ciudad. Salió de Estados Unidos y fue a vivir en Cuba donde continuó a dedicarse a la poesía. En Cuba se descubrió que sufría de cáncer, lo que afectó negativamente a su producción literaria.

Dejó Cuba y se estableció una vez más en Nueva York. Además de sufrir de un cáncer mortífero tuvo una vida turbulenta—varios matrimonios fracasados, problemas psicológicos y una adicción al alcohol. Falleció (murió) trágicamente en Nueva York en 1953 a los 39 años.

CULTURA

Mural de Julia de Burgos en el barrio de East Harlem en la Ciudad de Nueva York

CULTURA

Capitolio Nacional en La Habana, Cuba

Estrategia

Hojeando Antes de leer este poema, dale una ojeada, o sea, léelo rápidamente. Fíjate en el título y determina a quién le estará hablando la poeta. Después de hojearlo, reflexiona sobre su mensaje principal. Luego léelo de nuevo prestando atención a todos los detalles.

A Julia de Burgos 🎧

Ya las gentes murmuran que yo soy tu enemiga
porque dicen que en verso doy al mundo mi yo.
Mienten, Julia de Burgos. Mienten, Julia de Burgos.
La que se alza en mis versos no es tu voz: es mi voz
5   porque tú eres ropaje y la esencia soy yo;
y el más profundo abismo se tiende[1] entre las dos.

Tú eres fría muñeca[2] de mentira social,
y yo, viril destello[3] de la humana verdad.
Tú, miel[4] de cortesanas hipocresías; yo no;
10   que en todos mis poemas desnudo el corazón.

Tú eres como tu mundo, egoísta; yo no;
que en todo me lo juego a ser lo que soy yo.
Tú eres solo la grave señora señorona; yo no,
yo soy la vida, la fuerza, la mujer.

15   Tú eres de tu marido, de tu amo; yo no;
yo de nadie, o de todos, porque a todos, a
todos en mi limpio sentir y en mi pensar me doy.
Tú te rizas[5] el pelo y te pintas; yo no;
a mí me riza el viento, a mí me pinta el sol.

20   Tú eres dama casera[6], resignada, sumisa,
atada a los prejuicios[7] de los hombres; yo no;
que yo soy Rocinante corriendo desbocado[8]
olfateando horizontes de justicia de Dios.

Tú en ti misma no mandas;
25   a ti todos te mandan; en ti mandan tu esposo, tus
padres, tus parientes, el cura, el modista,
el teatro, el casino, el auto, las alhajas[9],
el banquete, el champán, el cielo
y el infierno, y el qué dirán social.
30   En mí no, que en mí manda mi solo corazón,
mi solo pensamiento; quien manda en mí soy yo.

Tú, flor de aristocracia; y yo, la flor del pueblo.
Tú en ti lo tienes todo y a todos se lo debes,
mientras que yo, mi nada a nadie se la debo.
35   Tú, clavada[10] al estático dividendo ancestral,
y yo, un uno en la cifra del divisor social
somos el duelo[11] a muerte que se acerca fatal.

Cuando las multitudes corran alborotadas[12]
dejando atrás cenizas[13] de injusticias quemadas,
40   y cuando con la tea[14] de las siete virtudes,
tras los siete pecados[15], corran las multitudes,
contra ti, y contra todo lo injusto y lo inhumano,
yo iré en medio de ellas con la tea en la mano.

Antes de leer

Basado en lo que sabes de la vida de Julia de Burgos, piensa en lo que serían sus reacciones ante las injusticias e hipocresías sociales.

Durante la lectura

Presta atención al tono del poema. ¿Qué emociones te sientes? ¿Qué dice la poeta de las mujeres?

Después de leer

Reflexiona sobre el «tú» y el «yo» en el poema. ¿A cuál te simpatizas más?

[1]se tiende *spreads out*
[2]muñeca *doll*
[3]destello *sparkle*
[4]miel *honey*
[5]te rizas *curl*
[6]casera *homemaker*
[7]atada a los prejuicios *tied to the prejudices*
[8]desbocado *runaway*
[9]alhajas *jewels*
[10]clavada *stuck*
[11]duelo *sorrow, grief*
[12]alborotadas *excited, noisy*
[13]cenizas *ashes*
[14]tea *torch*
[15]pecados *sins*

¿Comprendes?

A **Analizando** Contesta.

    1. Cuando Julia de Burgos escribe, ¿de quién está hablando en sus versos? ¿De sí misma o de otras?

    2. ¿Qué alusiones hace la autora a la hipocresía y falsedad de la sociedad?

    3. ¿Cómo expresa Julia de Burgos que ella nunca es hipócrita?

    4. ¿A qué se refiere la poeta al decir «el qué dirán social»?

B **Interpretando** ¿Qué simboliza… ?

    1. «ropaje y la esencia»

    2. «fría muñeca de mentira social»

    3. «destello de la humana verdad»

    4. «en todos mis poemas desnudo el corazón»

    5. «tú te rizas el pelo… a mí me riza el viento»

    6. «te pintas; yo no… a mí me pinta el sol»

    7. «tú en ti misma no mandas»

    8. «en mí manda mi solo corazón»

    9. «tú, flor de aristocracia; y yo; la flor del pueblo»

C **Identificando**

    1. Identifica todos los elementos feministas en el poema.

    2. Identifica todas las alusiones al esnobismo.

D **Comparando** Compara todas las características del «tú» y del «yo».

E **Criticando** Critica y da tus opiniones sobre la siguiente interpretación del poema. «Es el conflicto entre ‹la mujer interior› libre y ‹la mujer exterior› sujeta a las restricciones y limitaciones sociales».

F **Personalizando** Contesta.

    1. ¿Es posible que conozcas a una «tú»? Describe a esa persona.

    2. ¿Es posible que conozcas a una «yo»? Describe a esa persona.

    3. ¿Qué opiniones tienes de cada una de esas personas?

CULTURA

Una exhibición de cerámicas en la Galería Taller Boricua en el Centro Cultural Julia de Burgos en East Harlem en la Ciudad de Nueva York

Vocabulario

1 **Da una palabra relacionada.**

1. conquistar
2. emitir
3. guerrero
4. cómodo
5. ojo

2 **Da la palabra cuya definición sigue.**

6. un cura
7. dar, conceder
8. considerar, tomar en consideración
9. famoso
10. el que escribe para un periódico
11. los que luchan en una guerra
12. el que da o anuncia las noticias en la televisión
13. exceder
14. llegar a saber
15. tomar el poder
16. lo que interrumpe los programas de televisión

Gramática

3 **Escribe una sola frase con aunque.**

17. Van a salir. Y está lloviendo.
18. Van a salir. Y parece que va a llover.
19. Él lo terminará. Y sabemos que va a ser difícil.
20. Él lo terminará. No se sabe si será difícil o no.
21. El profesor enseñará. Y no le pagan bien.
22. El profesor enseñará. Y parece que no van a pagarle bien.

4 **Completa.**

23–24. Quienquiera que ＿＿＿ (ser) (tú) y adondequiera que ＿＿＿ (ir), date cuenta de las consecuencias de tus acciones.

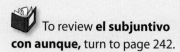 To review **Vocabulario,** turn to pages 238–239.

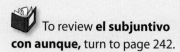 To review **el subjuntivo con aunque,** turn to page 242.

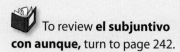 To review **el subjuntivo con -quiera,** turn to page 244.

5 Completa con el artículo definido cuando necesario.

25–26. Tenemos clases ____ lunes pero yo no fui a la escuela ____ lunes pasado.

27. ____ profesor González es un profesor excelente.

28. Buenos días, ____ Doctora Amaral.

29. ____ paciencia es una virtud.

30. Los tomates están a cincuenta ____ kilo.

31–32. En algunos calendarios ____ domingo es el primer día de la semana y en otros ____ lunes es el primer día de la semana.

To review **los artículos definidos,** turn to page 245.

6 Escribe cada frase de nuevo añadiendo los detalles adicionales.

33. Ella es escritora. (buena y famosa)

34. Don José es periodista. (que escribe para el *Miami Herald*)

35. El doctor García es médico. (en el Hospital Metropolitano)

To review **los artículos indefinidos,** turn to page 247.

7 Completa con la forma apropiada del adjetivo.

36. Es un ____ canal de televisión. (bueno)

37. Hay más de ____ páginas en este libro. (ciento)

To review **los adjetivos apocopados,** turn to page 248.

Cultura

8 ¿Sí o no?

38. Muchos mexicanoamericanos nacieron en tierra que una vez fue territorio mexicano.

39. Después de la guerra, en 1899, Cuba cedió Puerto Rico a Estados Unidos.

40. La gran migración de cubanoamericanos tuvo lugar después de la derrota del dictador Fulgencio Batista cuando Fidel Castro estableció un gobierno marxista.

To review this cultural information, turn to pages 252–254.

CULTURA

Celebración para el Cinco de Mayo en Old Town Historic State Park en San Diego, California

1 **Comunidades**

✓ *Interview Latinos in your community*

Trabajen en grupos pequeños. Van a hacer una encuesta. Entrevisten a alumnos en la escuela o a personas que viven en su ciudad o pueblo. Si hay muchos latinos en su comunidad determinen de dónde son. Organicen los resultados de su encuesta y preparen una tabla indicando el número de habitantes de cada grupo—desde el más numeroso hasta el menos numeroso. Si no hay latinos en la comunidad, identifiquen otros grupos étnicos que viven en la comunidad.

CULTURA

Residentes de un barrio latino en Chicago llamado el «Pueblo Pequeño» mirando el desfile para celebrar el Día de la Independencia mexicana

2 **Nuestros antepasados**

✓ *Discuss your ancestors*

En grupos pequeños, hablen de donde vienen o de donde vinieron sus antepasados. Si posible, discutan los motivos que tenían los que emigraron a Estados Unidos. ¿Tenían muchos los mismos motivos?

3 **Costumbres y tradiciones latinas**

✓ *Interview Latino students about their customs and traditions*

Si hay alumnos latinos en la clase de español o en la escuela, habla con ellos de sus costumbres y tradiciones ¿Tienen todos las mismas costumbres y tradiciones o son diferentes aunque todos son latinos?

4 **No me importa. Lo voy a hacer.**

✓ *Talk about what you will do even if it is difficult*

Eres una persona que persevera mucho. Eres tenaz. Di todo lo que vas a hacer aunque pase algo que haga difícil lo que quieres hacer.

Tarea

Write a biographical sketch of a famous Hispanic American who is no longer living. Your biography should include important data that will provide the reader with a snapshot of the person's life and an overview of his or her contributions to society (why he or she is considered a famous historical figure).

Writing Strategy

Biography Writing a biographical sketch involves presenting information about a person's life in a clear, concise, and orderly fashion. Although it is necessary to remain objective when telling another's life story, it is also important to carefully select the facts that you wish to present, because a biography is not just a summary of an individual's life but also a celebration of his or her life accomplishments.

❶ Prewrite

As you begin compiling data, arrange the information in chronological order. It may also be helpful to research the person's life in terms of distinct phases or stages, such as birth, childhood, youth, marriage, parenthood, old age, and death.

You may wish to use the following graphic timeline to organize your information and ideas.

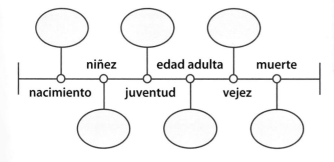

- You should also think about ways to incorporate **aunque** with the subjunctive and/or indicative, as well as the subjunctive with **-quiera,** into your writing.
- Before you begin your biographical sketch, try to estimate how many paragraphs you are going to write and which information you are going to include in each one.

❷ Write

- As you compose your biographical sketch, be sure to structure your writing in a logical fashion. Use transitions to ensure that your writing flows smoothly.
- Be cautious not to plagiarize or copy information word-for-word. You should cite any sources used.
- Do not attempt to translate from English to Spanish.
- Don't be afraid to use the dictionary, but at the same time, don't overuse it. Whenever possible, stick to vocabulary and grammar that you already know.
- After you finish the rough draft, revise it and write the final version. Double check for any unnecessary errors or avoidable mistakes.

Evaluate

Your teacher will evaluate you based on proper use of vocabulary, correct spelling and grammar, logical structure, and completeness and appropriateness of information.

Repaso del Capítulo 8

Gramática

- ### El subjuntivo con aunque *(page 242)*
  The conjunction **aunque** *(although)* may be followed by the subjunctive or the indicative depending upon the meaning of the sentence.

Ellos van a salir aunque llueva.	*They are going out even though it may rain.*
Ellos van a salir aunque llueve.	*They are going out even though it is raining.*

- ### El subjuntivo con -quiera *(page 244)*
  Many words are made indefinite by adding **-quiera**. Such words are followed by the subjunctive. **Quiera** is the same as the *ever* in *whoever, wherever.*

quienquiera	cuandoquiera	dondequiera
comoquiera	cualquiera	adondequiera

  Quienquiera que sea, no nos podrá resolver el problema.

- ### Usos especiales del artículo definido *(page 245)*
  The definite article must be used with all general or abstract nouns, with a title (except in direct address), with quantities, and with days of the week to express the meaning *on.*

La leche es buena para la salud.	*Milk is good for the health.*
La doctora González es dentista.	*Dr. González is a dentist.*
El biftec está a 900 pesos el kilo.	*Steak is 900 pesos a kilo.*
Él sale el sábado.	*He leaves on Saturday.*
Ella trabaja los viernes.	*She works on Fridays.*

▲ La leche es importante para los niños, como vemos en este envase de leche en Guadalajara, México.

- ### Uso especial del artículo indefinido *(page 247)*
  The indefinite article is omitted after the verb **ser** when the noun that follows is not modified. The indefinite article is used if the noun is modified.

  La señora Dávila es periodista.
  Sandra Cisneros es una autora conocida.

- ### Adjetivos apocopados *(page 248)*
  Some adjectives in Spanish have a shortened form when they precede a singular masculine noun.

  un buen libro   **el tercer mes**

  Some adjectives have a shortened form when they precede a masculine or feminine noun.

  una gran mujer   **cien personas**

Vocabulario

Talking about the Spanish conquest of the Americas

el sacerdote	la colonia	la lucha, la batalla	luchar
el conquistador	la guerra	colonial	colonizar
la conquista	el soldado	conquistar	establecer
el colonizador			

Talking about the news media

los medios de comunicación	el ancla, el/la noticiero(a)	la prensa	el artículo
la emisora de televisión	el canal, la cadena	el periódico	el/la radio
la emisión televisiva, el programa de televisión	las noticias	el titular	emitir
	la publicidad, la propaganda, la promoción	la revista	
		el/la periodista	
		el reportaje	

Other useful words and expressions

una ojeada	acomodado(a)	sobrepasar	otorgar
el libro de bolsillo	ilustre	tomar en cuenta	invertir
la empresa, la compañía	apoderarse de	lograr	
	darse cuenta de		

 The words listed below come from this chapter's literary selection, *A Julia de Burgos*. They were selected to become part of your active vocabulary because of their relatively high frequency.

el amo	la cifra	olfatear
el corazón	mentir	alzarse
el cura		

Repaso cumulativo

Repasa lo que ya has aprendido

These activities will help you review and remember what you have learned so far in Spanish.

 Escucha las frases. Indica en una tabla como la de abajo si la acción de cada frase tiene lugar en el pasado, el presente o el futuro.

pasado	presente	futuro

 Completa con la forma apropiada del pretérito o del imperfecto.

1. Él _____ a México el año pasado. (ir)
2. Él _____ a México cada año. (ir)
3. Ella me lo _____ solo una vez. (decir)
4. Ella siempre _____ la misma cosa. (decir)
5. Ellos nos _____ muy a menudo. (visitar)
6. Ellos nos _____ el enero pasado. (visitar)
7. Yo lo _____ ayer. (ver)
8. Yo lo _____ con frecuencia. (ver)

 Escribe las siguientes frases en el pasado.

1. Hace muy buen tiempo.
2. El sol brilla en el cielo.
3. Todos están contentos.
4. El bebé tiene solo dos meses.
5. Es adorable.
6. Tiene ojos grandes y una sonrisa adorable.

CULTURA

Una plaza en Guadalajara, México

4 Completa en el pasado.

1. Yo _____ con José cuando tú me _____. (hablar, interrumpir)

2. Él _____ sus tareas cuando yo _____. (hacer, salir)

3. Ellos _____ en México cuando _____ la noticia. (estar, recibir)

4. Yo _____ durmiendo cuando _____ mi móvil. (estar, sonar)

5. ¿Qué _____ tú cuando ellos _____? (hacer, llegar)

5 Da el artículo definido apropiado.

1. _____ mano
2. _____ mapa
3. _____ planeta
4. _____ tierra
5. _____ clase

6. _____ arma
7. _____ armas
8. _____ dramas
9. _____ agua
10. _____ águilas

6 Trabaja con un(a) compañero(a). Inventen una conversación basada en los dibujos.

Historia de la comida latina

Aquí y Allí

Vamos a comparar Cuando comemos algo es raro que pensemos en el origen, o sea, en la historia de lo que estamos comiendo. La historia de la comida es muy interesante. Vamos a ver las influencias históricas entre unos platos que se comen en Estados Unidos y en los países hispanos.

Objetivos

You will:

- identify more foods
- describe food preparation
- discuss the history of foods from Europe and the Americas
- read a poem by the famous Chilean poet Pablo Neruda

You will use:

- the passive voice
- relative pronouns
- expressions of time with **hace** and **hacía**

◀ Comestibles— unos tienen su origen en Europa y otros en las Américas.

QuickPass

Go to glencoe.com
For: **Online book**
Web code: **ASD7844c9**

Historia de la comida latina

El tema de este capítulo, «La historia de la comida», tiene unos hechos interesantes y sorprendentes. Mira estas fotos y adivina si sabes dónde tienen su origen estos comestibles.

▲ **Guatemala** Este señor está vendiendo mangos, una deliciosa fruta que se cultiva en muchas regiones tropicales de las Américas.

◄ **España** La alcachofa es una legumbre verde. Tiene hojas, algunas de ellas espinosas. La palabra «alcachofa», como casi todas las palabras que empiezan en al-, es del árabe. Los árabes introdujeron las alcachofas en España.

España Los olivares de Andalucía producen muchas olivas o aceitunas de que se produce el famoso aceite español. ▼

España El jamón serrano goza de fama mundial. ▼

FERNANDO

SECADERO DE JAMONES

▲ Perú Aquí vemos un campo de maíz en la región de Arequipa. Como se ve, el maíz no es siempre amarillo. Un campo de maíz en México y Centroamérica es «una milpa». ¿Crees que se come más maíz en las Américas o en Europa?

▲ Perú Estas papas de varios colores están en un supermercado de Estados Unidos pero vienen de Perú. ¿Sabes quiénes son los primeros cultivadores de papas?

◄ Venezuela La familia está disfrutando de un bufé grande que tiene una selección variada de comida de muchas influencias.

Ecuador Los tomates, como vas a aprender, tienen una historia muy interesante. Los tomates, igual que las habichuelas o los frijoles que se ven aquí, se cultivan en Ecuador. La agricultura es una industria importante del país. ▼

Más legumbres y hortalizas

la alcachofa

la col, el repollo

los pimientos

la berenjena

la harina

el trigo

las zanahorias

las vainitas, las judías verdes

las hojas de lechuga, la hoja

una mazorca de maíz

el huerto

En un huerto se cultivan legumbres (hortalizas) o frutas.
Un huerto es más pequeño que una huerta.

la viña

la vid

las uvas

La carne

el cordero

Las especias

el cilantro

la carne de res

el cerdo

el orégano

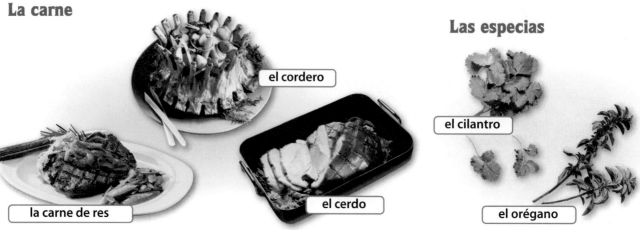

la rodaja

el huevo batido

el pan rallado

Se rebozan las rodajas de berenjena en huevo batido y pan rallado.

el/la sartén

Después se fríen en una sartén con aceite de oliva.

la olla

El que prepara la comida o cocina es el cocinero.
El cocinero que elabora algo delicioso debe estar muy orgulloso.

Se hierve el arroz en una olla.

el picadillo, la carne picada

Los comensales son los que se sientan a la mesa para comer juntos.

Se rellenan los pimientos de carne picada.

QuickPass

Go to glencoe.com
For: **Vocabulary practice**
Web code: ASD7844c9

ESCUCHAR

 1 Escoge la palabra apropiada del banco de palabras.

la zanahoria	el pimiento	la lechuga
el huerto	la especia	el cordero
la viña	los comensales	

HABLAR

2 Contesta.

1. ¿Se puede cultivar frutas y vegetales en un huerto?
2. ¿Qué fruta producen las vides en una viña?
3. ¿Es la manzana una fruta tropical o no?
4. El cilantro es una hierba que se usa mucho en la cocina latina. ¿Conoces el cilantro? ¿Te gusta su sabor?
5. ¿Pones orégano en tu pizza?
6. ¿Se puede rebozar muchos mariscos y pescados en pan rallado antes de freírlos?

LEER • ESCRIBIR

 3 Da otra palabra.

1. las vainitas
2. las legumbres
3. preparar la comida
4. el biftec
5. la carne picada

LEER • ESCRIBIR

 4 Completa con una palabra apropiada.

1. _____ es el producto que resulta del trigo molido (*ground*).
2. _____ y _____ son especias.
3. Se corta la berenjena en _____ antes de freírla.
4. Se reboza la berenjena en _____ y _____ antes de freírla.
5. Se _____ los pimientos de carne picada o de queso.

CULTURA

Una enchilada de carne y una enchilada de queso

InfoGap For more practice using your new vocabulary, do Activity 9 on page SR10 at the end of this book.

LEER • ESCRIBIR

5 Corrige la información falsa.

1. Se hierve el agua en una sartén.
2. Los que preparan la comida son los camareros.
3. Los que comen juntos son los meseros.
4. El que elabora algo que sale riquísimo (delicioso) debe estar deprimido.
5. Una huerta es más pequeña que un huerto.

CULTURA

Se sirve muy buena pizza en este restaurante de Buenos Aires.

 6  **Rompecabezas**

Trata de identificar tantos comestibles que puedas usando las letras en la frase siguiente. Puedes usar la misma letra más de una vez. Compara tu lista con las de tus compañeros.

¡Vamos al Restaurante Valladolid para cenar!

 Comunidades

7 Si hay unos alumnos latinos en la clase de español o algunos latinos que viven en tu comunidad, pregúntales las palabras que ellos usan para los diferentes comestibles. Los nombres cambian mucho de una región a otra. Aquí tienes solo un ejemplo: **judías verdes, ejotes, vainitas, habichuelas y chauchas.**

FOLDABLES®
Study Organizer

SINGLE PICTURE FRAME
See page SH25 for help with making this foldable. Use this study organizer to practice talking about food with a partner. Draw a picture of a meal that includes some of the ingredients and foods you just learned about. Pass the foldable to your partner who will identify the ingredients of the meal and explain how they are prepared. Take turns.

Gramática

La voz pasiva

1. The following are examples of sentences in the active and passive voice.

ACTIVE   *The chef prepared the food.*
               The servers served the meal.

PASSIVE   *The food was prepared by the chef.*
               The meal was served by the servers.

Note that the subject in a sentence in the active voice becomes what is called the "agent" (by whom it was done).

¿Te acuerdas?

You have already learned the **se** construction to express the passive voice.

2. In Spanish, the passive voice is most frequently expressed by using the pronoun **se,** especially when the agent is not expressed.

Se venden legumbres en la verdulería.
Se vende carne en la carnicería.
Se comen muchos frijoles en México.
Se usa mucho aceite de oliva en España.

3. This **se** construction is also used when the subject is indefinite.

¿Cómo se dice en español?
How does one say it in Spanish?
How is it said in Spanish?

Se habla español en muchos países.
They speak Spanish in many countries.
Spanish is spoken in many countries.

4. The true passive is much less commonly used in Spanish than in English. In Spanish, the active voice is preferred. When used, the true passive is formed by using the verb **ser** and the past participle followed by **por.**

ACTIVE   **Los moros conquistaron España**
                 en el siglo ocho.

PASSIVE   **España fue conquistada por los moros**
                 en el siglo ocho.

5. The true passive is frequently found in a shortened form in headlines.

Casa destruida por huracán
Niño herido en accidente de automóvil

CULTURA

Se venden periódicos de todas partes del mundo hispano en este quiosco en la Ciudad de México.

Práctica

ESCUCHAR • HABLAR

1 Contesta.

1. ¿Se abre o se cierra la tienda por la mañana?
2. ¿Qué idioma se habla en México?
3. ¿Se oye mucho español en la ciudad de Miami?
4. ¿Cómo se dice *vegetable* en español?

LEER • ESCRIBIR

2 Completa con la voz pasiva usando **se**.

1. _____ vegetales y frutas en un huerto. (cultivar)
2. _____ mucho pescado en las regiones cerca de la costa. (comer)
3. _____ las rodajas de berenjena en huevos batidos y pan rallado. (rebozar)
4. _____ las alcachofas en una olla. (hervir)
5. _____ la carne con arroz y habichuelas. (servir)
6. _____ el bacón en una sartén. (freír)
7. _____ las compras en una bolsa. (poner)
8. _____ pan en la panadería y _____ dulces y tortas en la pastelería. (vender)

3 **Juego** Trabajando en grupos, hagan tantas frases que puedan con las siguientes expresiones.

se habla   se oye   se come   se dice   se cierra
se escribe   se venden   se abre   se ven

ESCUCHAR • HABLAR • ESCRIBIR

4 Sigue el modelo.

MODELO   **La comida fue preparada por el cocinero.** →
El cocinero preparó la comida.

1. España fue conquistada por los árabes.
2. España fue invadida por los árabes en el siglo ocho.
3. Los árabes fueron expulsados por los españoles en el siglo quince.
4. La mayor parte de Latinoamérica fue colonizada por España.
5. La novela fue escrita por Gabriel García Márquez.
6. La cocinera fue admirada por sus clientes.

HORARIO DE LUNES A VIERNES		
Mañanas	09.30	13.30
Tardes	16.30	20.00
Sábados	10.00	13.00

CULTURA

El horario indica a qué hora se abre y a qué hora se cierra el negocio.

SE PROHIBE
EJERCER EL COMERCIO EN ESTE LUGAR, LA PERSONA QUE SEA SORPRENDIDA SERA CONSIGNADA A LA AUTORIDAD COMPETENTE

CULTURA

Un aviso fuerte sobre algo que se prohíbe en la Ciudad de México

Los pronombres relativos

1. The pronouns **el que, la que, los que,** and **las que** are equivalent to the English *the one who (that)* or *the ones who (that)*. They can be used as subjects or objects and they can replace either persons or things.

> **De todas mis recetas, la que preparo ahora es mi favorita.**
> *Of all my recipes, the one I am preparing now is my favorite.*
>
> **De todos mis hermanos, es José el que tiene más talento.**
> *Of all my brothers, Joe is the one who has the most talent.*

2. The relative pronoun often introduces a sentence. Note the sequence of tenses in the following sentences.

> **El que habla ahora es mi hermano.** *(present / present)*
> **La que hablará mañana es mi hermana.** *(future / present)*
> **Los que hablaron ayer fueron mis primos.** *(preterite / preterite)*

3. **Lo que** is a neuter relative pronoun that replaces a general or abstract idea rather than a specific antecedent.

> **Lo que le hace falta a este plato es más sal.**
> *What this dish needs is more salt.*
>
> **No sé lo que están haciendo en la cocina.**
> *I don't know what they are doing in the kitchen.*

4. The relative adjective **cuyo** is equivalent to the English *whose*. **Cuyo** agrees with the noun it modifies.

> **Es la señora cuyos hijos son los dueños del restaurante.**
> **El cocinero cuyas recetas prefiero trabaja aquí.**

CULTURA

Este joven cuyo padre es dueño de una cafetería en Córdoba, España, está preparando churros.

GeoVistas

To learn more about Mexico, take a tour on pages SH42–SH43.

CULTURA

La cocinera María Solarzano es la que tiene una escuela culinaria de cocina tradicional mexicana en San Miguel de Allende.

Práctica

LEER • HABLAR • ESCRIBIR

5 Sigue el modelo.

MODELO don Pedro / hablar / con el dueño →
El que habla con el dueño es don Pedro.
El que hablará con el dueño es don Pedro.
El que habló con el dueño fue don Pedro.

1. la cocinera / preparar / la comida
2. los comensales / comer / la comida
3. los campesinos / cultivar / las legumbres
4. el dueño / pagar / el salario
5. mis primas / llegar / tarde

LEER • ESCRIBIR

6 Completa.

1. De todos los vegetales _____ prefiero es el repollo.
2. De todas las frutas _____ me gusta más es la manzana.
3. De todos mis profesores _____ me enseñó más fue el señor Centeno.
4. _____ salieron fueron los primeros en llegar.

CULTURA

Las que están tocando instrumentos y cantando delante de su escuela son estudiantes del Liceo 7 en Providencia, una zona de Santiago de Chile.

HABLAR

7 Completa. Da respuestas personales.

1. Lo que necesito es _____.
2. Lo que quiero es _____.
3. Lo que me gusta es _____.
4. Lo que prefiero es _____.
5. Lo que ellos me dicen es _____.

LEER • ESCRIBIR

8 Completa.

1. El restaurante _____ nombre se me escapa es fabuloso.
2. Es el cocinero _____ recetas han ganado premios.
3. Es la señora _____ vides producen las mejores uvas.
4. Es una cocinera _____ fama es mundial.
5. La señora _____ hijo está hablando ahora es la directora de la escuela.

Expresiones de tiempo con hace y hacía

¿Te acuerdas?

You have already learned the time expression with **hace** in the present tense.

1. The present tense is used with **hace** to express an action that began in the past and continues into the present. English uses the present perfect.

> **¿Hace cuánto tiempo que estás aquí?**
> *How long have you been here?*
>
> **Hace dos años que estoy aquí.**
> *I have been here for two years.*

2. The imperfect tense is used with **hacía** to express something that had been going on for some time before something else intervened. You will note from the following examples that in English the pluperfect tense is used.

> **Hacía cinco años que ellos se conocían.**
> *They had known each other for five years.*
>
> **Hacía mucho tiempo que él lo sabía.**
> *He had known it for a long time.*

Práctica

HABLAR

 Personaliza. Da respuestas personales.

1. ¿Hace cuántos años que vives en la misma casa?
2. ¿Tienes una mascota? ¿Tienen tus primos una mascota? ¿Hace cuánto tiempo que tú o tus primos tienen una mascota?
3. ¿Tienes un móvil? ¿Hace cuánto tiempo que tienes tu móvil?
4. ¿Tienes novio(a)? ¿Hace cuánto tiempo que sales con él o ella?

El muchacho quiere a su perro. Hace cinco años que tiene su perro. ▶

LEER • ESCRIBIR • HABLAR

10 Completa cada pregunta y luego contéstala.

   1. ¿Hace cuánto tiempo que tú _____ aquí? (estar)
   2. ¿Hace cuánto tiempo que tú _____ a esta escuela? (asistir)
   3. ¿Hace cuánto tiempo que tú _____ a tu mejor amigo(a)? (conocer)
   4. ¿Hace cuánto tiempo que tú _____ español? (estudiar)
   5. ¿Hace cuánto tiempo que Enrique _____ con Sandra? (salir)
   6. ¿Hace una hora que _____ aquel señor? (hablar)

LEER • ESCRIBIR

11 Completa con la forma apropiada del verbo indicado.

   1. Hacía dos años que ellos _____ allí cuando tuvieron que mudarse. (vivir)
   2. Hacía cinco años que ellos se _____ antes de casarse. (conocer)
   3. Hacía solo cinco días que él _____ enfermo cuando se murió. (estar)
   4. Hacía mucho tiempo que ellos lo _____ sin que dijeran nada a nadie. (saber)
   5. Hacía a lo menos dos años que ella _____ en el mismo restaurante. (trabajar)

Refrán

Can you guess what the following proverb means?

CERRADO

Cuando una puerta se cierra, ciento se abren.

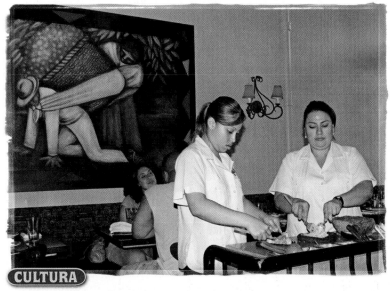

CULTURA

Las dos meseras están preparando guacamole. Hace muchos años que trabajan en este restaurante en Guadalajara, México.

¡Bravo!

You have now learned all the new vocabulary and grammar in this chapter. Continue to use and practice all that you know while learning more cultural information. ¡Vamos!

¡¿Los tomates son venenosos?!

Felipe Joe, ¿qué crees? ¿La papa? ¿Es de Europa o de las Américas?

Joe ¡La papa! Es de Europa. Mi familia es de ascendencia irlandesa y comemos muchas papas.

Felipe Y Teresa. ¿De dónde será el tomate?

Teresa Pues, el tomate también tiene que ser de Europa. Yo lo sé porque mi familia es italiana y en Italia preparamos muchas salsas a base de tomates.

Felipe Les voy a decir una cosa. Ninguno de los dos tiene razón. Están equivocados.

Joe ¡Increíble! ¿Nos estás diciendo que la papa y el tomate son de las Américas?

Felipe Sí. Y lo que es muy interesante es que hasta el siglo veinte había muchos europeos que creían que los tomates eran venenosos y no los comían por nada.

Teresa Felipe, me estás tomando el pelo. No es posible que una vez en Italia no se comieran tomates.

Felipe No. No te estoy tomando el pelo. Es la pura verdad. Y, en su vida, ¿han comido papas azules o negras?

Teresa Nunca.

Felipe Pues, los primeros que cultivaban las papas eran los incas en las regiones frías del altiplano andino y siguen produciéndolas en una gran variedad de colores.

Joe Lo encuentro difícil creer que se estaban comiendo papas en los Andes antes de que las comieran mis antepasados en Irlanda.

¿Comprendes?

A Identifica según la información en la conversación.
1. los errores que cometieron Joe y Teresa
2. información sobre la ascendencia de Joe y Teresa

B **Describiendo** Da algunos detalles sobre estas hortalizas.
1. los tomates
2. las papas

C **Analizando** Contesta.
1. ¿Por qué creían Joe y Teresa que Felipe les estaba tomando el pelo?
2. ¿Te sorprendió la información sobre las papas y los tomates? ¿Por qué?

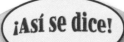

¡Así se dice!

Tomarle el pelo a alguien is a fun expression that is equivalent to the English expression *to pull someone's leg*.

 Cultura

D ¿Cuáles son algunos productos que se usan con frecuencia en la elaboración de platos étnicos de tu grupo cultural?

CULTURA

Ya sabes que se dice «cacahuates» en muchas partes de Latinoamérica y «maní» en Puerto Rico. Nota que se dice «maní» en Argentina también.

Historia de la comida 🎧 ♻

Antes de leer
Piensa en todo lo que te gusta comer. ¿Has pensado jamás en el origen de los comestibles?

Vamos a darle una ojeada a la interesante historia de la comida. Se sabe que la comida de las Américas tiene muchas influencias indígenas y españolas. Y no se puede olvidar que en la comida española hay influencia del Medio Oriente porque España estuvo bajo el dominio de los árabes por unos ocho siglos. Los nombres mismos de varios comestibles como la berenjena y la alcachofa son de origen árabe. Más adelante leeremos de la aceptación de estas legumbres en la cocina de las Américas, pero antes vamos a considerar la importancia de la historia de unas comidas muy sencillas.

Un taco de carne Vamos a observar las interesantes influencias en un simple taco. El taco de carne es una combinación de tortilla de maíz y carne de res con tomate y lechuga. Y es también una combinación de dos civilizaciones y culturas.

La tortilla de maíz es de las Américas. Hacía siglos que los indígenas de México—los mayas y aztecas—estaban comiendo tortillas de maíz antes de que llegaran los españoles. La tortilla era de maíz porque no había trigo. Los que introdujeron el trigo a las Américas fueron los españoles. También trajeron ganado. Antes de la llegada de los españoles no había vacas, ovejas y caballos en las Américas.

✓ Reading Check
¿Cómo es que el taco de carne es una combinación de dos civilizaciones?

▲ Tacos suaves de carne

Los tomates Es verdad que los españoles trajeron muchos productos, pero también encontraron muchos productos nuevos en América. Los españoles no conocían el maíz, ni la papa, ni el tomate. Eran los indígenas americanos los que cultivaban el tomate. Luego los españoles lo introdujeron en Europa donde lo cultivaban pero solo como decoración. ¿Te parecería posible que ellos tuvieran miedo a los tomates? Pues, así era. Ellos creían que eran venenosos y que si los comieran, morirían. En Inglaterra y Norteamérica no se comían tomates hasta el siglo diecinueve.

Las especias El mismo descubrimiento de las Américas por parte de los europeos se debe a la comida. Cristóbal Colón salió de España en busca de una nueva ruta a Asia porque en Asia había especias. En aquel entonces[1] las especias eran necesarias para conservar la comida. Muchas personas en Europa se estaban muriendo de hambre porque no tenían especias. Eran muy caras porque venían de Asia por tierra—en caravanas—y los viajes de Asia a Europa duraban años. Colón creía que por mar podría llegar al Oriente en menos tiempo. Quería ir a la India porque sabía que allí estaban las especias que buscaba pero sabemos que Colón nunca llegó a la India. Llegó a las Indias—en las Américas.

—«Favor de pasar la sal». —¡Qué cosa más sencilla! La sal. Pero había una vez que la gente se estaba luchando por sal. Pagaban a los soldados romanos con sal y de allí viene la palabra «salario». Y, ¿cuál es la palabra en inglés?

[1]En aquel entonces *At that time*

✓ **Reading Check**
¿Para qué usaban los europeos el tomate?

▲ Tumbet—un plato mallorquín tradicional

✓ **Reading Check**
En sus viajes, ¿qué buscaba Colón? ¿Por qué?

CULTURA
Un gran surtido de especias incluyendo el azafrán en un mercado en Granada, España

La influencia árabe Ahora vamos a volver a la influencia árabe en la cocina latina. La berenjena y la alcachofa son dos hortalizas que fueron introducidas en España por los moros (árabes). La berenjena, igual que en España, es muy apreciada en todo Latinoamérica. Se puede cortarla simplemente en rodajas y freírla o rebozarla en huevo batido y harina o pan rallado antes de echarla a la sartén. También se puede rellenarla de queso o de picadillo—carne picada de cerdo o vaca. Las recetas son muy parecidas en casi todos los países. En Chile la berenjena rellena con picadillo es muy popular. En Venezuela se comen berenjenas con vainitas. El plato se sirve ligeramente fría o a la temperatura ambiente². En la República Dominicana está riquísimo el caviar de berenjena. Es una mezcla de trozos de berenjena pelada con cebolla, pimiento dulce, tomates, cilantro y vinagre todo bien mezclado. Se sirve con hojas de lechuga o galletas saladas.

Las alcachofas no son tan apreciadas en Latinoamérica. Sin embargo la autora de un libro interesantísimo sobre la cocina latinoamericana encontró una receta chilena para preparar alcachofas con una salsa besamel³ y queso parmesano rallado. ¡Qué coincidencia que ella la encontrara en Chile! El poema que vamos a leer, *Oda a la alcachofa,* fue escrita por el famoso poeta chileno Pablo Neruda.

²temperatura ambiente
  room temperature

³besamel *bechamel*
  (una salsa de crema)

> ### ✓ Reading Check
> ¿Cómo es que hay influencia árabe en la comida latina?

▲ Artefacto mochica de un señor comiendo maíz, Perú

▲ Un plato de alcachofas rellenas de queso de parmesana

¿Comprendes?

VIDEO To learn about Latino food in the United States, watch **Cultura en vivo.**

A **Comparando y contrastando** Discute las diferentes influencias en la cocina española y la cocina latinoamericana. ¿Cómo es que existían estas influencias? ¿Cuáles eran las razones históricas?

B **Analizando** Completa el siguiente diagrama con información sobre un sencillo taco de carne.

ingredientes americanos	ingredientes europeos

C **Categorizando** Completa la siguiente tabla.

productos de origen indígena	productos de origen europeo

D **Recordando hechos** Contesta.
1. ¿Qué creían los europeos de los tomates?
2. ¿Cuáles son dos legumbres que los moros introdujeron en España?
3. ¿Cuáles son varias maneras en que se preparan las berenjenas?
4. ¿Cuál de estas dos legumbres es más apreciada en Latinoamérica—la berenjena o la alcachofa?
5. ¿En qué país encontró la autora de un libro sobre la cocina latinoamericana una receta para preparar alcachofas?

E **Analizando** Contesta.
1. ¿Cómo es que el mismo descubrimiento por parte de los españoles o europeos tenía que ver con la comida?
2. ¿Cuál es la derivación de la palabra *salary*?

F **Personalizando** ¿Qué hechos aprendiste en esta lectura que te sorprendieron?

Oda a la alcachofa
de Pablo Neruda

▲ Una escultura de Pablo Neruda en una playa de Isla Negra, Chile

INTRODUCCIÓN

Pablo Neruda nació en Chile en 1904. Además de ser maestro Neruda sirvió como cónsul chileno en varias ciudades españolas e hispanoamericanas.

Neruda se considera uno de los mejores poetas de todos los tiempos. Muchas de sus poesías surrealistas no son de fácil comprensión. Pero también hay en la obra de Neruda «el poeta realista, fotógrafo del cielo» como él mismo se llamó.

En la oda que sigue, *Oda a la alcachofa* tomada de sus *Odas elementales,* observarás un estilo sencillo y conciso de pocas palabras. El poeta se inspira en temas concretos y humildes y los poemas de esta fase de su creación van dirigidos a la persona sencilla.

Oda a la alcachofa 🎧

La alcachofa
de tierno corazón
se vistió de guerrero[1],
erecta, construyó
5 una pequeña cúpula,
se mantuvo
impermeable
bajo
sus escamas[2],
10 a su lado
los vegetales locos
se encresparon[3],
se hicieron
zarcillos[4], espadañas[5],
15 bulbos conmovedores[6],
en el subsuelo
durmió la zanahoria
de bigotes[7] rojos,
la viña
20 resecó[8] los sarmientos[9]

por donde sube el vino,
la col
se dedicó
a probarse faldas,
25 el orégano
a perfumar el mundo,
y la dulce
alcachofa
allí en el huerto,
30 vestida de guerrero,
bruñida[10]
como una granada,
orgullosa,
y un día
35 una con otra
en grandes cestos
de mimbre[11], caminó
por el mercado
a realizar su sueño[12]:
40 la milicia.

[1]guerrero *warrior*
[2]escamas *scales*
[3]se encresparon *curled up*
[4]zarcillos *tendrils*
[5]espadañas *bullrushes*
[6]conmovedores *moving, touching*

[7]bigotes *moustaches*
[8]resecó *dried out*
[9]sarmientos *vine shoots*
[10]bruñida *polished*
[11]mimbre *wicker*
[12]sueño *dream*

Estrategia

Visualizando Al leer, visualiza lo que está describiendo el poeta. Trata de hacer un cuadro mental de los distintos lugares por los cuales pasa la alcachofa.

Antes de leer

Antes de leer esta oda piensa en una alcachofa. Tanto mejor si has comido una. Si no, mira las fotografías que acompañan la oda para enterarte de la apariencia y composición de esta hortaliza.

Literatura

◀ Una alcachofa

Una granada ▼

Durante la lectura

Fíjate en la descripción que nos da el poeta de una alcachofa. ¿Habla el poeta de la alcachofa como si fuera una persona? Además, determina en cuántos lugares tiene lugar la acción.

Después de leer

¿Cómo explicas el uso del verbo «se vistió» a principios de la oda y «desvestimos» al final de la oda?

En hileras[13]
nunca fue tan
   marcial
como en la feria,
los hombres
45 entre las legumbres
con sus camisas
   blancas
eran
mariscales
de las alcachofas,
50 las filas apretadas[14],
las voces de
   comando,
y la detonación
de una caja que cae,
pero
55 entonces
viene
María
con su cesto,
escoge
60 una alcachofa,
no le teme,
la examina, la
   observa
contra la luz como si
   fuera un huevo,

la compra,
65 la confunde
en su bolsa
con un par de
   zapatos,
con un repollo y una
botella
70 de vinagre
hasta
que entrando a la
   cocina
la sumerge en la
   olla.

Así termina
75 en paz
esta carrera
del vegetal armado
que se llama
   alcachofa,
luego
80 escama por escama
desvestimos
la delicia
y comemos
la pacífica pasta
85 de su corazón verde.

[13] En hileras *In military file*
[14] apretadas *squashed, tightly packed*

¿Comprendes?

A **Analizando** Indica.

1. los atributos marciales o militares de la alcachofa
2. lo que tiene la alcachofa que la hace bien armada
3. legumbres a las que compara Neruda la alcachofa
4. tres lugares en que tiene lugar el poema
5. el sueño de la alcachofa

B **Analizando e interpretando** Escoge.

1. ¿Por qué diría el poeta que la col se dedicó a probarse faldas?
   a. Porque la col se compone de muchas hojas.
   b. Porque la col tiene la forma de una falda.
2. ¿Por qué diría el poeta que el orégano se dedicó a perfumar el mundo?
   a. El orégano es un perfume.
   b. El orégano tiene un olor fuerte y distintivo.
3. ¿Quiénes serán los marciales en el mercado?
   a. las alcachofas mismas
   b. los que trabajaban en el mercado
4. La palabra «detonación» añade al ambiente militar. ¿A qué se refiere la detonación?
   a. al ruido que hizo una caja que cayó
   b. a las voces de comando

C **Interpretando** ¿Cuál es el elemento de paz que introduce el poeta a la escena?

D **Describiendo** Contesta.

1. ¿Qué hace María con la alcachofa? ¿Cómo la trata? ¿Dónde la pone? ¿Qué más tiene en su bolsa?
2. ¿Qué hace María con la alcachofa en la cocina?
3. ¿Qué hacemos antes de comer una alcachofa? ¿Qué parte de la alcachofa comemos? ¿Cómo es?

E **Interpretando**

1. Un crítico ha dicho que Neruda es un gran virtuoso de las imágenes. El poeta representa las cosas en toda su humanidad. ¿Crees que Neruda humaniza a la alcachofa? Si contestas que sí, ¿cuáles son los elementos o rasgos humanos que encuentras en la alcachofa?
2. ¿Cuáles son los sentimientos que tienes hacia la alcachofa? ¿Por qué?

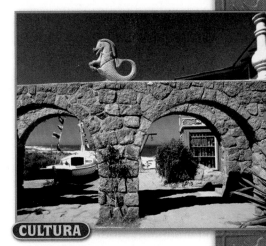

CULTURA

La entrada a la casa de Pablo Neruda en Isla Negra

Vocabulario

1 Identifica.

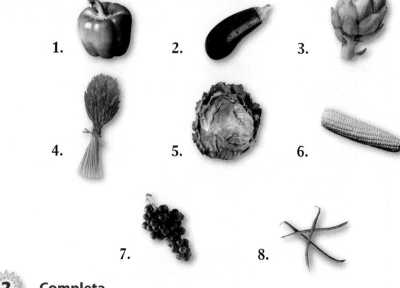

1.   2.   3.

4.   5.   6.

7.   8.

To review **Vocabulario,** turn to pages 272–273.

2 Completa.

9. El orégano es _____.

10. Se cultivan legumbres y frutas en _____.

11. Otra palabra que significa «col» es «_____».

12. Hay vides en _____.

13–14. Cortas la berenjena en _____ y las _____ en huevo batido y pan rallado.

15. La carne de una vaca es _____.

16. Cuando uno hace algo bueno debe estar _____.

17. Son los _____ los que se sientan a una mesa para comer juntos.

To review **la voz pasiva,** turn to page 276.

Gramática

3 Completa.

18. _____ abr_____ la tienda a las nueve de la mañana.

19. Las puertas _____ cierr_____ a las ocho de la noche.

20. _____ habl_____ español en México y Panamá.

21. España _____ invadida _____ los árabes en el siglo ocho.

22. Los países del continente sudamericano _____ colonizados _____ los españoles y los portugueses.

4 Completa con el pronombre relativo.

23. _____ habla ahora es el dueño del restaurante.

24–25. _____ preparan la comida son las cocineras y _____ se sientan juntos para comer la comida son los comensales.

26. _____ llegaron primero fueron mis primos.

27. Mis tíos fueron _____ llegaron tarde.

28. No hago siempre _____ debo hacer.

29. No nos importa _____ dice él.

30. Es mi amigo _____ hermana acaba de ganar el gran premio.

To review **los pronombres relativos,** turn to page 278.

5 Contesta.

31. ¿Hace cuánto tiempo que vives en la misma casa?

32. ¿Hace cuánto tiempo que estudias español?

33. ¿Hace mucho tiempo que se conocen tú y tu mejor amigo(a)?

To review **hace** and **hacía,** turn to page 280.

6 Completa.

34. _____ ocho siglos que los árabes estuvieron en España cuando los españoles los expulsaron.

35. _____ solamente un mes que su padre estaba enfermo cuando se murió.

Cultura

To review this cultural information, turn to pages 284–286.

7 Identifica.

36. dos productos de origen europeo

37. dos productos de origen americano

8 Contesta.

38. ¿Por qué no comían tomates los europeos?

39. ¿Cómo refleja el sencillo taco de carne la historia de la comida?

40. ¿Cómo es que hay influencias del Medio Oriente en la cocina española?

1 **Comunidades**

✔ *Talk about food in the United States*

Imagínate que estás viajando por un país latinoamericano y alguien te pregunta lo que se come aquí en Estados Unidos—lo que consideras una típica comida norteamericana. Se dice que no es muy fácil contestar esta pregunta. ¿Cómo la contestarías?

2 **La comida étnica**

✔ *Describe some ethnic meals from your family background*

Trabajen en grupos pequeños. Comparen y contrasten algunas comidas que comen en casa que tienen influencia de sus orígenes étnicos. ¿Hay muchas diferencias entre lo que comen ustedes? ¿Hay algunos platos que les interesan a todos?

3 **Hace mucho tiempo que lo hago.**

✔ *Talk about some things you have been doing for a long time*

Trabaja con un(a) compañero(a) de clase. Describan algunas cosas que ustedes hacen desde ya hace mucho tiempo—desde su niñez. Decidan lo que tienen en común.

CULTURA

Este joven cubano tiene una rebanada de pizza en cada mano.

4 **Yo en la cocina**

✔ *Discuss your talent or lack of talent in the kitchen*

¿Eres un(a) buen(a) cocinero(a) o no? Si por una razón u otra tuvieras que preparar una comida, ¿qué prepararías? Y, ¿cómo la prepararías? Da la receta.

5 **No me tomes el pelo.**

✔ *Talk about pulling someone's leg*

Piensa en algunas cosas que les dices a tus amigos o parientes cuando quieres tomarles el pelo. Dile a un(a) compañero(a) de clase lo que les dices. ¿Tienes el talento de convencerles que les estás hablando en serio o saben tus amigos enseguida lo que estás haciendo?

Tarea

To celebrate the cultural exchange between Spain and the Americas, a popular Hispanic food magazine is going to publish the best article on any Latin American or Spanish dish that combines ingredients from both worlds. Based on your own research and on information presented in the textbook, write a short essay about a dish that mixes Old World and New World elements.

Writing Strategy

Thesis statement One thing all essays have in common is a thesis statement in which you present the main theme, explain the purpose of your essay, and tie everything together. In a sense, the thesis statement is like a road map that guides the reader by telling him or her what to expect. As with an outline, it is a good idea to compose your thesis statement before writing your essay to help organize your ideas and ensure that you do not stray off topic.

❶ Prewrite

- Conduct preliminary research to choose a dish that blends ingredients from the Americas with those introduced by Spanish colonizers. Use the following list to help you find the dish that will be the focus of your essay.

PRODUCTOS DE LAS AMÉRICAS	PRODUCTOS TRAÍDOS POR LOS ESPAÑOLES
el aguacate	el ajo
el cacahuate (maní)	la almendra
el cacao	el arroz
el calabacín	el azúcar
la calabaza	la cabra
el camote (batata, papa dulce)	la cebolla

el chile (ají)	el cerdo
el frijol	la gallina
el girasol	la harina de trigo
el maíz	la lechuga
el pavo (guajalote)	el limón
la papa	la manzana
la papaya	la naranja
el pimiento	la oliva (aceituna)
la piña	la oveja
la quinoa	el queso
el tomate	la uva
la vainilla	la vaca
la yuca (casava)	la zanahoria

- Once you have chosen your dish, you will need to research the history and background of the dish, as well as of the ingredients.

- Make an outline of the different parts of your essay and write your thesis statement.

❷ Write

- Be careful not to plagiarize and remember to cite your sources.

- Do not attempt to translate from English to Spanish. Whenever possible, stick to vocabulary and grammar that you already know.

- Use the following grammar points learned in this chapter: both forms of the passive voice, two different relative pronouns, and at least one expression of time with **hace** or **hacía.**

Evaluate

Your teacher will evaluate you on proper use of vocabulary, correct spelling and grammar, logical structure, clarity of expression, and overall content and style.

Repaso del Capítulo 9

Gramática

- ### La voz pasiva *(page 276)*

  In Spanish, the passive voice is most frequently expressed by using the pronoun **se**. This **se** construction is also used when the subject is indefinite and the agent is not mentioned.

  Se venden legumbres en la verdulería.
  Se habla español en muchos países.

  The true passive is not frequently used in Spanish. The active voice is preferred.

  ACTIVE **Los moros conquistaron España en el siglo ocho.**
  PASSIVE **España fue conquistada por los moros en el siglo ocho.**

- ### Los pronombres relativos *(page 278)*

  The pronouns **el que, la que, los que,** and **las que** can be used as a subject or object and they can replace either a person or a thing.

  De todos mis hermanos es José el que tiene más talento.
  Of all my brothers Joe is the one who has the most talent.

  Note the sequence of tenses in the following sentences.

  El que habla ahora es mi hermano. *(present / present)*
  La que hablará mañana es mi hermana. *(future / present)*
  Los que hablaron ayer fueron mis primos. *(preterite / preterite)*

CULTURA

Un azulejo con la figura de un señor musulmán en la fachada de una casa en Ronda, España

  Lo que is a neuter relative pronoun.

  Lo que le hace falta a este plato es más sal.
  What this dish needs is more salt.

  Cuyo is an adjective equivalent to the English *whose* and agrees with the noun it modifies.

  Es la señora cuyos hijos son los dueños del restaurante.
  El cocinero cuyas recetas prefiero trabaja en este restaurante.

- ### Expresiones de tiempo con hace y hacía *(page 280)*

  The present tense is used with **hace** to express an action that began in the past and continues into the present. English uses the present perfect.

  Hace dos años que estoy aquí.   *I have been here for two years.*

  The imperfect tense is used with **hacía** to express what had been going on before something else happened.

  Hacía mucho tiempo que él lo sabía.   *He had known it for a long time.*

There are a number of cognates in this list. See how many you and a partner can find. Who can find the most? Compare your list with those of your classmates.

Vocabulario

Identifying more foods

las legumbres, las hortalizas	el pimiento	la carne	unas especias
la zanahoria	la alcachofa	la carne de res	el orégano
la col, el repollo	una mazorca de maíz	el cordero	el cilantro
las vainitas, las judías verdes	las hojas de lechuga, la hoja	el cerdo	el trigo
la berenjena		el picadillo, la carne picada	la harina
			las uvas

Talking about food preparation

el/la cocinero(a)	el pan rallado	la olla	rellenar
la rodaja	el aceite de oliva	cocinar	hervir
el huevo batido	el/la sartén	freír	rebozar

Other useful words and expressions

la viña	la huerta	cultivar
la vid	los comensales	
el huerto	orgulloso(a)	

Repaso cumulativo

Repasa lo que ya has aprendido

These activities will help you review and remember what you have learned so far in Spanish.

 1 Escucha las frases. Indica en una tabla como la de abajo si la frase se refiere al arte o a la literatura.

arte	literatura

 2 Haz una lista de los ingredientes que pondrías en una buena ensalada.

 3 Personaliza. Da respuestas personales.

1. ¿Cuáles son los comestibles que te gustan?
2. ¿Cuáles son algunos comestibles que no te gustan?
3. ¿Cómo te gusta la carne de res? ¿Casi cruda, a término medio o bien hecha?
4. ¿Te gustan más los mariscos o el pescado?
5. ¿Te gusta el postre?
6. ¿Cuáles son tus postres favoritos?
7. ¿Qué comes para el desayuno?
8. ¿Qué comes para el almuerzo?
9. ¿A qué hora desayunas?
10. ¿A qué hora almuerzas?

 4 Usa cada palabra en una frase original.

el primer plato   el postre   la sobremesa

el segundo plato   el cuchillo   el tenedor

el servicio   el menú   la cuenta

la cuchara

5 **Completa en el presente y el pretérito.**

1. Los meseros _____ la comida. (servir)
2. Yo _____ un biftec a término medio. (pedir)
3. El mesero me lo _____ como yo lo _____. (servir, pedir)
4. Tú _____ el pescado pero nosotros no lo _____. (freír, freír)
5. Él _____ todo y yo no _____ nada. (repetir, repetir)

6 **Crea una historia sobre la familia Suárez según los dibujos. Luego preséntala a la clase.**

Carreras

Aquí y Allí

Vamos a comparar Vamos a observar el impacto y la importancia de la globalización en Estados Unidos igual que en el mundo hispanohablante. Vamos a explorar también las oportunidades profesionales disponibles para el que tenga un conocimiento del español.

Objetivos

You will:

- talk about professions and occupations
- have a job interview
- discuss the importance of learning a second language
- read a short story by the famous Colombian writer Gabriel García Márquez

You will use:

- **por** and **para**
- the subjunctive in relative clauses

◄ El personal de esta empresa española en el Parque Tecnológico de San Sebastián es de muchas nacionalidades. Como muchas empresas multinacionales tienen que reclutar personal que hable una variedad de idiomas.

QuickPass

Go to glencoe.com
For: **Online book**
Web code: **ASD7844c10**

Introducción al tema
Carreras

El tema de este capítulo son carreras y oficios—el trabajo que se puede hacer con y sin preparación universitaria. Explorará también unas profesiones y oficios en los cuales el conocimiento del español te beneficiará.

▲ **California** Antonio Villaraigosa, alcalde de Los Ángeles

◄ **México** Una sucursal de un banco estadounidense en la Ciudad de México

Argentina Ejecutivos de una empresa multinacional en Buenos Aires participan en una teleconferencia con sus colegas en su oficina en Nueva York. El señor en la pantalla está usando su español en su oficina en Estados Unidos. ▼

▲ **España** Los abogados tienen clientes anglohablantes en su bufete en Madrid. Aunque ellos hablan inglés, ¿lo dominan bien?

▲ **Miami Beach** Estos dos policías están usando su español mientras ayudan a un joven latino.

Dental
Assistant
Needed
—
Spanish
Speaking
—
No Experience
Necessary

▲ **San Antonio** Están buscando un asistente dental que hable español. Y no es necesario que tenga experiencia.

▲ **Miami** Un congreso (una convención) donde están reclutando candidatos que hablen español para una variedad de empleos

Nueva York Esta guía en las Naciones Unidas habla con turistas y visitantes de todas partes del mundo. ▶

303

Profesiones

¿Cuál de las siguientes profesiones o carreras te interesaría?

la abogada

el ingeniero

la política (la alcaldesa de una ciudad, la senadora)

Oficios

el plomero, el fontanero

la albañil

¿Cuál de los siguientes oficios te interesaría?

Nota

Los nombres de muchas profesiones y oficios son palabras afines: asistente, ejecutivo, arquitecto, dentista, farmacéutico, programador de computadoras (informática); electricista, carpintero, mecánico(a), plomero (fontanero).

Los comerciantes trabajan para una
compañía (empresa, sociedad).
Los comerciantes se llaman también
hombres o mujeres de negocios.
Los comerciantes pueden ser también
dueños de una tienda.

Los contables preparan
estados financieros.

No puedo trabajar a tiempo completo.
Quiero un trabajo a tiempo parcial.

un anuncio
(clasificado)

Elena es una estudiante universitaria.
Lee los anuncios clasificados.
No puede ni quiere trabajar cuarenta
horas por semana.

Los funcionarios trabajan en
una oficina gubernamental
(de gobierno).

SOLICITUD DE EMPLEO

una solicitud
(aplicación) de
empleo

El señor está en la oficina del departamento de personal.
Se dice también «el servicio de recursos humanos».
El señor ha llenado una solicitud de empleo.
El candidato (aspirante) está teniendo una entrevista.
Está buscando un puesto que le pague bien.

Nota

En español, la palabra
general **oficina** cambia
según la profesión.
- el bufete del abogado
- el consultorio (la consulta)
  del médico
- el gabinete del dentista

trescientos cinco **305**

QuickPass

Go to glencoe.com
For: **Vocabulary practice**
Web code: **ASD7844c10**

ESCUCHAR

 1 Escucha y escoge de la lista la profesión que se describe.

los médicos	los contables
los arquitectos	los funcionarios
los comerciantes	los farmacéuticos
los carpinteros	los alcaldes
los ejecutivos	los dentistas

HABLAR

 2 Contesta. ¿A quién necesitas si…

1. tienes que reparar tu carro?
2. tienes un problema legal?
3. no te sientes bien, estás enfermo(a)?
4. el agua está goteando (saliendo) de la lavadora?
5. te duele una muela?
6. tienes una receta del médico?

HABLAR • ESCRIBIR

 3 Aquí tienes una lista de otras profesiones u oficios que conoces. Con un(a) compañero(a), describe el trabajo que hace cada uno(a).

1. el/la empleado(a) en una tienda
2. el/la mesero(a)
3. el/la agricultor(a)
4. el/la profesor(a)
5. el/la recepcionista
6. el/la asistente(a) de vuelo
7. el/la cocinero(a)
8. el/la pintor(a)
9. el/la mecánico(a)
10. el/la enfermero(a)

 4 **uego** Piensa en un oficio o profesión. Tu compañero(a) te puede hacer hasta tres preguntas para ayudarle a adivinar o acertar el oficio o la profesión en que estás pensando. Túrnense.

CULTURA

El pintor está pintando un cuadro del paisaje de la Costa Brava en España.

CULTURA

¿Qué expresión tiene en la cara este niño en el gabinete del dentista?

5 Contesta sobre una visita a un departamento de recursos humanos.

1. Anita está en una oficina del departamento de recursos humanos. ¿Estará buscando ella un puesto con la compañía?
2. ¿Es posible que ella esté un poco nerviosa?
3. ¿Quiere ella un trabajo que sea interesante y que le pague bien?
4. ¿Va a tener ella una entrevista?
5. ¿Debe Anita tener una carta de recomendación?
6. ¿Tendrá ella que llenar una solicitud de trabajo?

6 Parea.

1. el departamento
2. recursos humanos
3. un puesto
4. el candidato
5. anuncios

a. un trabajo, un empleo
b. el aspirante
c. el servicio
d. clasificados
e. personal

ESCUCHAR • HABLAR

7 Contesta según se indica.

1. ¿Juan busca trabajo? (sí)
2. ¿Qué ha leído? (un anuncio en el periódico)
3. ¿Qué compañía está reclutando (buscando) empleados? (Bancomar)
4. ¿Adónde va Juan? (al departamento de recursos humanos de Bancomar)
5. ¿Qué tiene que llenar? (una solicitud de empleo)
6. ¿A quién le da la solicitud? (a la recepcionista)
7. ¿Qué va a tener? (una entrevista)

EXPANSIÓN

Ahora, sin mirar las preguntas, cuenta la información en tus propias palabras. Si no recuerdas algo, un(a) compañero(a) te puede ayudar.

LEER • ESCRIBIR

8 Completa con una palabra apropiada.

1. Juan está buscando trabajo pero no quiere trabajar cuarenta horas por semana. Está buscando trabajo ____.
2. El que trabaja cuarenta horas por semana trabaja ____.
3. Su padre le dice que lea los ____ en el periódico.

FOLDABLES
Study Organizer

ENVELOPE FOLD
See page SH28 for help with making this foldable. Use this study organizer to talk about professions and occupations with a partner. On each tab, describe the work that is done at a particular job. Then pass the foldable to your partner who will use the clues to identify the professions or occupations. When you're finished, switch roles.

HABLAR

9 Personaliza. Da respuestas personales.

1. ¿Trabajas o has trabajado alguna vez?
2. ¿Dónde?
3. ¿Por qué trabajas o no trabajas?
4. ¿Recibes un sueldo (salario)?
5. ¿Qué haces con el dinero que ganas?
6. Si no trabajas y no recibes un sueldo, ¿de dónde recibes dinero? ¿Te dan tus padres una semana o una mesada?
7. Si recibes dinero cada mes (mensualmente), ¿recibes una semana o una mesada?

InfoGap For more practice using your new vocabulary, do Activity 10 on page SR11 at the end of this book.

EXPANSIÓN

Ahora, sin mirar las preguntas, cuenta la información en tus propias palabras. Si no recuerdas algo, un(a) compañero(a) te puede ayudar.

Comunicación

10 Trabaja con un(a) compañero(a). Vas a tener una entrevista para un trabajo a tiempo parcial. Uno(a) será el/la candidato(a) y el/la otro(a) será el/la empleado(a) en el departamento de personal. Pueden dar la entrevista dos veces cambiando de rol.

CULTURA

La empleada vende libros y materiales escolares en esta librería en Guadalajara, México.

Estudio de palabras

comerciar negociar comprando y vendiendo

el comercio el acto de vender y comprar; una tienda o almacén

el/la comerciante persona que se dedica a la compra y venta de mercancías; individuo que es propietario de un comercio

comercial relativo al comercio o a los comerciantes

vender traspasarle (darle) algo a alguien por un precio convenido

el/la vendedor(a) persona que vende algo; dependiente o empleado en una tienda

la venta acción y efecto de vender

1 Da lo contario.

1. comprar
2. la compra
3. el/la comprador(a)

2 Completa.

1. Una tienda de departamentos es una empresa _____.

2. El _____ puede ser un almacén o tienda y el propietario de tal empresa es _____.

3. Los joyeros _____ joyas: pulseras o brazaletes de oro y plata, anillos de diamantes y esmeraldas, etc. Son _____ que se dedican a la compra y _____ de joyas.

4. Mi prima trabaja en una agencia de automóviles. Ella es _____ de carros pero yo no sé la marca que _____ aunque sé que es una marca japonesa.

5. Ellos van a mudarse (cambiar de casa) y tienen su casa en _____.

CULTURA

La comerciante tiene un comercio o negocio exitoso vendiendo rosas en un puesto durante una fiesta en Barcelona.

 **QuickPass**

Go to glencoe.com
For: **Grammar practice**
Web code: ASD7844c10

Por y para

1. The prepositions **por** and **para** have very specific uses in Spanish. They are not interchangeable. These two prepositions are often translated into English as *for*. Such a translation is quite restrictive because these two words express many ideas in addition to *for*.

2. The preposition **para** is used to indicate destination or purpose.

> **El avión salió para Bogotá.**
> *The plane left for Bogota.*

> **Este regalo es para María.**
> *This gift is for Mary.*

> **Ella estudia para abogada.**
> *She is studying to be a lawyer.*

3. The preposition **por,** in contrast to **para,** is more circuitous. Rather than expressing a specific destination, **por** conveys the meanings *through, by,* and *along.*

> **Ellos viajaron por la América del Sur.**
> *They traveled through South America.*

> **Su barco pasó por las costas de las islas Galápagos.**
> *Their boat passed by the shores of the Galápagos Islands.*

> **El ladrón entró en la casa por la ventana.**
> *The thief entered the house through the window.*

4. **Por** also has the meanings *on behalf of, in favor of,* and *instead of.* Observe and analyze the difference in meaning in the following sentences.

> **Le compré el regalo para mi madre.**
> *I bought the gift for my mother. (I'm going to give the gift to my mother.)*

> **Compré el regalo por mi madre.**
> *I bought the gift for my mother. (The gift is for another person, but my mother could not go out to buy it so I went for her.)*

5. The preposition **por** is used after the verbs **ir, mandar, volver,** and **venir** in order to show the reason for the errand.

> **El joven fue a la tienda por pan.**
> *The young man went to the store for bread.*

> **Ellos mandaron por el médico.**
> *They sent for the doctor.*

CULTURA

Los hermanos fueron de compras en la Ciudad de México. Querían comprar un regalo para su mamá y se lo van a dar mañana.

Práctica

HABLAR

1 Contesta.

1. ¿Va a salir para Quito Josefa?
2. ¿Va a viajar por Ecuador?
3. ¿Va a andar por el casco antiguo Josefa?
4. ¿Va a comprar regalos para sus parientes?
5. Algunos amigos quieren que ella les compre unas cerámicas ecuatorianas y le han dado el dinero para comprarlas. ¿Va Josefa a comprar las cerámicas por ellos?

EXPANSIÓN

Ahora, sin mirar las preguntas, cuenta la información en tus propias palabras. Si no recuerdas algo, un(a) compañero(a) te puede ayudar.

CULTURA

La gente andaba por la Plaza de Armas en Quito, Ecuador.

LEER • ESCRIBIR

2 Completa sobre un día en Buenos Aires.

1. Hoy yo salí _____ el mercado a las ocho de la mañana.
2. Julia no pudo ir así que yo fui _____ ella.
3. Cuando salí del mercado, di un paseo _____ el centro de la ciudad.
4. Pasé _____ las tiendas de la calle Florida.
5. Entré en una de las tiendas y le compré un regalo _____ mi madre. Se lo voy a dar a ella mañana.
6. Cuando volví a casa, el hijo de Julia vino _____ las cosas que yo le había comprado en el mercado.

EXPANSIÓN

Ahora, sin mirar las frases, cuenta la información en tus propias palabras. Si no recuerdas algo, un(a) compañero(a) te puede ayudar.

CULTURA

La joven «comerciante» te venderá una bolsa para las compras en la calle Florida en Buenos Aires.

Por y para con expresiones de tiempo

1. The preposition **para** is used to indicate a deadline.

> **Ellos tienen que terminar el trabajo para el día ocho.**
> *They have to finish the work by the eighth.*

2. Por, in contrast to **para,** is used to define a period of time.

> **Los directores van a estar aquí por una semana.**
> *The directors are going to be here for a week.*

3. Por is also used to express an indefinite time.

> **Creo que ellos van a volver por diciembre.**
> *I think they are going to return around December.*

Práctica

HABLAR

3 Contesta.

1. ¿Pueden ustedes llegar para las ocho?
2. ¿Será posible tener los resultados para mañana?
3. ¿Por cuánto tiempo podrán ustedes quedarse aquí?
4. La última vez que ustedes vinieron, estuvieron por dos semanas, ¿no?
5. ¿Piensan ustedes volver otra vez por Pascuas?

LEER • ESCRIBIR

4 Completa.

Los árabes salieron del Norte de África __1__ España en el siglo ocho. Invadieron España en el año 711, y estuvieron en el país __2__ unos ocho siglos. Viajaron __3__ toda la península ibérica. Por eso, si uno hace un viaje __4__ España verá la influencia de los árabes en casi todas partes del país. Pero si uno viaja __5__ Andalucía en el sur del país, visitará sin duda la famosa Alhambra de Granada, el Alcázar de Sevilla y la Mezquita de Córdoba, tres monumentos famosos de los árabes. __6__ mañana yo tengo que preparar un informe sobre la influencia musulmana en España __7__ mi clase de español. Así que yo fui hoy a la biblioteca __8__ los libros que me hacían falta.

CULTURA

La gran Mezquita de Córdoba es una joya arquitectónica de los moros que estuvieron en España por ocho siglos.

Por y para con el infinitivo

1. When followed by an infinitive, **para** expresses purpose and means *in order to.*

> **Tengo que ir a la biblioteca para hacer investigaciones.**
> *I have to go to the library (in order) to do research.*

2. When **por** is followed by an infinitive, it expresses what remains to be done.

> **Me queda mucho por hacer.**
> *I still have a lot to do.*

3. The expression **estar para** means *to be about to* or *to be ready to.*

> **Ellos están para salir pero no sé lo que van a hacer porque está para llover.**
> *They are about (ready) to leave, but I don't know what they are going to do because it's about to rain.*

4. The expression **estar por** means *to be inclined to.* It does not mean that the action will definitely take place.

> **Estoy por salir porque hace buen tiempo.**
> *I'm in the mood to go out because the weather is nice.*

Práctica

HABLAR

5 Contesta.

1. ¿Vas a ir a tu cuarto para escribir tu currículum vitae?
2. ¿Lo has terminado o te queda mucho por hacer?
3. ¿A qué hora estarás listo(a) para salir?
4. ¿Estás por ir de compras o por ver un filme?
5. ¿Estás listo(a) para empezar a trabajar?

CULTURA

Estos jóvenes se preparan para muchas carreras diferentes en la biblioteca de la Universidad de Málaga en España.

CULTURA

Para comprar localidades (entradas) para el teatro tienes que hacer cola delante de la taquilla como hacen estos madrileños.

LEER • ESCRIBIR

6 Completa con **por** o **para**.

1. Ya me bañé y me vestí y ahora estoy _____ salir. Además quiero salir. Estoy _____ salir.
2. ¡Ay, pero mira! Está _____ llover.
3. Tendré que subir _____ mi paraguas.
4. Quiero ir al cine y _____ ir al cine tendré que tomar un taxi porque no hay bus que pase _____ el cine.
5. Me pregunto si tendré que hacer cola _____ comprar las entradas.
6. Estoy _____ divertirme. Al salir del cine voy a visitar uno de los mesones en Cuchilleros.
7. Trabajé todo el día y todavía me queda mucho _____ hacer.

Otros usos de por y para

1. **Para** is used to express a comparison.

> **Para cubano él habla muy bien el inglés.**
> *For a Cuban, he speaks English very well.*

> **Para norteamericano Roberto habla muy bien el español.**
> *For an American, Robert speaks Spanish very well.*

2. **Por** is used to express means, manner, or motive.

> **La carta llegó por correo.**
> *The letter arrived by mail.*

> **Los soldados lucharon por la libertad de su país.**
> *The soldiers fought for the freedom of their country.*

3. **Por** is used to express *in exchange for.*

> **Él me pagó cien dólares por el trabajo que hice.**
> *He paid me a hundred dollars for the work I did.*

> **Él cambió euros por dólares.**
> *He exchanged euros for dollars.*

4. **Por** is also used to express an opinion or estimation.

> **Yo lo tomé por francés, pero es español.**
> *I took him for French, but he is Spanish.*

5. **Por** is used to indicate measure or number.

> **Las papas se venden por kilo.**
> *Potatoes are sold by the kilo.*

> **Este avión vuela a 1.000 kilómetros por hora.**
> *This plane flies 1,000 kilometers per hour.*

CULTURA

En el famoso mercado La Boquería en Barcelona las patatas se venden por kilo.

Práctica

LEER • ESCRIBIR

7 Completa con **por** o **para**.

1. _____ español, el señor Lugones habla muy bien el francés.
2. _____ argentina, la señora Caravallo sabe mucho de Estados Unidos.
3. Ella vino a Miami en avión. Dijo que el avión volaba a más de mil kilómetros _____ hora.
4. Ella cambió sus pesos _____ dólares antes de salir de Argentina.
5. La primera vez que yo conocí a la señora Caravallo, yo la tomé _____ italiana. La verdad es que ella es de ascendencia italiana pero hace años que su familia vive en Argentina.
6. La señora Caravallo sabe que a mí me gustan mucho los zapatos argentinos. Ella me trajo dos pares. No quería que yo le pagara pero yo le di el dinero _____ los zapatos.

EXPANSIÓN

Ahora, sin mirar las frases, cuenta la información en tus propias palabras. Si no recuerdas algo, un(a) compañero(a) te puede ayudar.

ESCUCHAR • HABLAR

8 Contesta usando una expresión con **por** o **para**.

1. ¿Cuál es el destino del tren? ¿Córdoba?
2. ¿A quién vas a darle los regalos? ¿A tu prima?
3. Cuando vendiste tu bicicleta, ¿te dieron cien dólares?
4. Es mexicano pero habla muy bien el inglés, ¿verdad?
5. ¿Cuándo piensas venir? ¿En junio?
6. ¿Te queda mucho o poco trabajo?
7. ¿Cuándo lo terminarás? ¿La semana que viene?
8. Ellos pasaron mucho tiempo en España, ¿verdad?

CULTURA

Para una estación vieja, está en muy buenas condiciones, ¿no?

LEER • ESCRIBIR

9 Cambia cada frase usando **por** o **para**.

1. Hay un montón de trabajo *que tengo que* terminar.
2. Los chicos van ahora *en la dirección de* la ciudad.
3. Nos gusta viajar *en* Colombia.
4. Subimos al tren *con destino a* Granada.
5. Voy al mercado *en busca de* carne.
6. Tengo que estar allí *no más tarde de* las tres.
7. Estaremos en Cali *durante* siete días.
8. Andan *en* el parque.
9. Mis padres lo pagaron *en vez de* mí.
10. Papá no podía asistir, así que yo fui *en lugar de* él.
11. *A pesar de que es* rico, no es generoso.

El subjuntivo en cláusulas relativas

1. A relative clause describes or modifies a noun. If the noun refers to a definite person or thing, the indicative is used in the relative clause. If the noun refers to an indefinite person or thing, the subjunctive is used in the relative clause.

   Están buscando un asistente que hable español.
   Yo conozco a un asistente ejecutivo que habla español.

   Note that the **a personal** is omitted before an indefinite person.

2. The subjunctive can also be used in a relative clause that modifies a superlative or negative antecedent when the speaker or writer wishes to imply exaggeration.

   No hay persona que pinte como ella.
   Es el mejor libro que se haya escrito.

Nota

The **a personal** is never used after the verb **tener.**
   Tengo un amigo que habla español y francés.

CULTURA

Para el padre, no hay nadie que trabaje mejor que su hijo.

Práctica

VIDEO Want more help with the subjunctive? Watch **Gramática en vivo.**

Más práctica

■ Workbook, p. 10.8
◉ StudentWorks™ Plus

ESCUCHAR • HABLAR

10 Contesta.

1. ¿Quieres un puesto que te pague bien?
2. ¿Quieres un puesto que te permita viajar?
3. ¿Quieres trabajar en una oficina que esté cerca de tu casa?
4. ¿Tienes un puesto que te paga bien?
5. ¿Tienes un puesto que te permite viajar?
6. ¿Trabajas en una oficina que está cerca de tu casa?

ESCUCHAR • HABLAR • ESCRIBIR

11 Sigue el modelo.

MODELO   ser de aquí →
    —Buscamos un abogado que sea de aquí.
    —¿Ah, sí? Conozco a un abogado que es de aquí.

1. conocer las leyes del estado
2. poseer una licencia profesional
3. ser honesto
4. poder trabajar los fines de semana
5. tener mucha experiencia
6. hablar español

Refrán

Can you guess what the following proverb means?

Por el pan baila el perro, que no por el dueño.

Quiero un puesto que me permita viajar por el mundo hispanohablante.

¡Bravo!

You have now learned all the new vocabulary and grammar in this chapter. Continue to use and practice all that you know while learning more cultural information. ¡Vamos!

QuickPass

Go to glencoe.com
For: **Conversation practice**
Web code: **ASD7844c10**

SOLICITANDO UN PUESTO

ESTOY BUSCANDO UN PUESTO QUE ME INTERESE Y QUE ME PAGUE BASTANTE PARA PODER TENER UN POCO DE PLATA EXTRA.

¿QUIERES TRABAJAR A TIEMPO COMPLETO?

¿ME HABLAS EN SERIO?

PUES, EN EL PERIÓDICO SIEMPRE HAY UNOS ANUNCIOS PARA TRABAJO A TIEMPO PARCIAL.

¿SEGURO? NO LOS HE VISTO YO.

PUES, LEÍ UNO EL OTRO DÍA PARA VENDEDOR O VENDEDORA EN UNA TIENDA DE DEPARTAMENTOS.

PUES, ES POSIBLE QUE ME INTERESE.

PERO HAY QUE SABER HABLAR INGLÉS.

NO HAY PROBLEMA. YA HACE TRES AÑOS QUE ESTUDIO INGLÉS.

¿LO HABLAS BIEN?

SÍ, BASTANTE. TODOS ME DICEN QUE PARA MEXICANA HABLO MUY BIEN EL INGLÉS.

¡QUÉ VA!

LO IMPORTANTE ES QUE LO HABLAS.

MIL GRACIAS POR LA INFORMACIÓN. VOY A LLAMAR POR UNA ENTREVISTA.

¿Comprendes?

VIDEO To discuss career paths, watch **Diálogo en vivo.**

A Contesta según la información en la conversación.

1. ¿Qué tipo de trabajo está buscando Patricia?
2. ¿Quiere trabajar a tiempo completo?
3. ¿Qué ha visto Jaime?
4. ¿Puede aceptar Patricia un puesto que requiera un conocimiento del inglés? ¿Por qué?
5. ¿Qué opinión tienen sus amigos anglohablantes de su inglés?

B **Resumiendo** Cuéntale a un(a) compañero(a) toda la información sobre Patricia.

C **Analizando** Contesta.

1. Usa la imaginación. Decide por qué sería imposible que Patricia trabajara a tiempo completo.
2. ¿Qué hace Jaime para ayudar a Patricia a buscar trabajo?

CULTURA

La joven está buscando un puesto y está leyendo los anuncios clasificados en un periódico en Lima, Perú.

Una lengua importante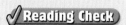

Antes de leer

¿Conoces a alguien que usa el español en su trabajo? ¿Qué hace esta persona?

No hay duda que el conocimiento de otro idioma te puede beneficiar en muchas carreras. En el mundo de globalización en que vivimos el comercio internacional tiene más y más importancia. En tal mundo, no es suficiente solo exportar nuestros productos al extranjero. Las grandes empresas de todas partes del mundo han llegado a ser multinacionales. Quiere decir que tienen instalaciones o sucursales[1] y filiales[2] en muchos países del mundo. Es posible que algún día trabajes con una compañía estadounidense y que tu oficina esté en Caracas, Panamá o Madrid. O es posible que trabajes con una compañía española o latinoamericana y que tu oficina esté en Miami, Los Ángeles o Chicago.

✓ Reading Check

Hoy en día, ¿qué está teniendo más y más importancia?

Es posible que el español en sí no sea una carrera. Pero el español con otra especialización te dará una ventaja tremenda. Si te especializas en la contabilidad, el marketing o la informática y conoces bien el español, podrás trabajar con una de las muchas empresas multinacionales. El español y tu otra especialización te ayudarán a encontrar un trabajo que te pague bien y que te dé la oportunidad de viajar y ver el mundo.

En esta época de globalización es posible que te sea necesario saber otro idioma—un tercer idioma. Una vez más el haber estudiado español te ayudará porque una vez que dominas un idioma es mucho más fácil adquirir otro. No te olvides: sigue con tus estudios del español porque te abrirá puertas interesantes y es posible que te dé oportunidades inesperadas.

✓ Reading Check

¿Qué es una empresa multinacional?

[1]sucursales *branches*
[2]filiales *affiliates*

Una compañía estadounidense entrega carga a todas partes del mundo.

¿Comprendes?

Más práctica

Workbook, pp. 10.9–10.10

StudentWorks™ Plus

VIDEO To learn about careers in the Spanish-speaking world, watch **Cultura en vivo.**

A Explicando Explica.

1. lo que es el comercio internacional
2. lo que es la globalización
3. como es posible que quizás trabajes para una empresa española y tu oficina esté en Estados Unidos
4. la importancia del español aunque no sea una carrera en sí
5. por qué el español te podrá ayudar a aprender un tercer idioma

CULTURA

Edificios modernos de empresas internacionales en una zona comercial de Madrid—Campo de las Naciones

B Personalizando Da respuestas personales.

1. ¿Has observado unas influencias de la globalización en tu propia vida? ¿Cuáles?
2. ¿Piensas seguir con tus estudios del español?
3. ¿Te gustaría tener un trabajo que te pagara bien y que te permitiera viajar y ver el mundo? ¿Por qué?

C Pronosticando consecuencias o resultados Contesta.

¿Tienes una idea de lo que quisieras ser de adulto? ¿Hay una profesión u oficio que te interese? ¿Es posible que el español te ayude en tu carrera?

Un día de éstos

de Gabriel García Márquez

▲ Una vista del pintoresco distrito colonial de la ciudad de Cartagena en la costa caribeña de Colombia

GeoVistas

To learn more about Colombia, take a tour on pages SH48–SH49.

Vocabulario

el/la madrugador(a) el que se levanta temprano por la mañana

la muñeca la parte del cuerpo donde se articula la mano con el brazo

una lágrima una gotita de agua que sale de los ojos cuando uno llora

enjuto(a) flaco

sordo(a) que no puede oír, que ha perdido el sentido del oído

hinchado(a) extendido, inflado

apresurarse tener prisa; ir rápido

amanecer empezar a aparecer la luz del día

Práctica

Completa con una palabra apropiada.

1. Él se cayó y se le torció el tobillo. Tiene el tobillo muy _____.
2. Ella no se levanta hasta las diez de la mañana. No es _____.
3. Tienes que hablarle en voz más alta porque es bastante _____.
4. Don Quijote es _____, no Sancho Panza.
5. Tienen que estar en el gabinete del dentista en cinco minutos. Tienen que _____ para no llegar tarde.
6. Ella patinaba y se cayó. Cree que tiene la _____ torcida.
7. Está llorando tanto que se le están saliendo _____.
8. Un madrugador ya está despierto cuando _____.

INTRODUCCIÓN

Gabriel García Márquez es uno de los escritores más importantes de las letras hispanas. Es el más brillante exponente de la tendencia literaria contemporánea denominada «realismo mágico».

García Márquez nació en Arataca, Colombia, en 1928. En la universidad estudió periodismo y leyes. Ha sido periodista en Barranquilla, Bogotá y Cartagena. Él escribió cuentos cortos para los periódicos donde trabajaba. Ahora escribe novelas y ya ha escrito muchas. Entre sus muchas novelas dos que son popularísimas son *Cien años de soledad* y *El amor en los tiempos del cólera.*

En 1982, García Márquez recibió el premio Nobel de Literatura.

El cuento que sigue «Un día de éstos» es de su obra *Los funerales de la Mamá Grande.* Los dos protagonistas ejercen profesiones muy distintas. Uno es dentista y el otro es político. ¡A ver como se comportan!

CULTURA

El famoso autor colombiano recibe el premio Nobel de Literatura en Estocolmo, Suecia.

FONDO HISTÓRICO

Antes de leer este cuento hay que conocer el fondo histórico. En 1948 el candidato liberal y laborista para presidente de Colombia fue asesinado. Este suceso produjo un clima de terror por todo el país. La lucha entre liberales y conservadores fue acompañada de mucha violencia. En una sola década, han perdido la vida más de 300.000 personas.

Monitoreando tu comprensión Monitoreando tu comprensión significa que siempre estás verificando si comprendes lo que estás leyendo. Si de vez en cuando no crees que estés entendiendo, hazte preguntas sobre las ideas principales, los personajes y eventos. Si no puedes contestar tu pregunta, repasa el texto. Lee con más cuidado y si es necesario pídele ayuda a alguien.

CULTURA

Se levanta el sol cuando amanece y se pone el sol cuando atardece. Aquí vemos una bonita puesta del sol sobre el mar Mediterráneo.

vidriera *drawer*
dentadura postiza *set of false teeth*
yeso *plaster*

cargadores *suspenders*

fresa *drill*
pulir *polish*

gallinazos *buzzards*
caballete *chimney cowl*

Durante la lectura

Fíjate en las emociones fuertes que tiene el dentista. ¿Por qué las tiene?

Un día de éstos 🎧

El lunes amaneció tibio y sin lluvia. Don Aurelio Escovar, dentista sin título y buen madrugador, abrió su gabinete a las seis. Sacó de la vidriera° una dentadura postiza° montada aún en el molde de yeso° y puso sobre la mesa un puñado de instrumentos que ordenó de mayor a menor, como en una exposición. Llevaba una camisa a rayas, sin cuello, cerrada arriba con un botón dorado, y los pantalones sostenidos con cargadores° elásticos. Era rígido, enjuto con una mirada que raras veces correspondía a la situación, como la mirada de los sordos.

Cuando tuvo las cosas dispuestas sobre la mesa rodó la fresa° hacia el sillón de resortes y se sentó a pulir° la dentadura postiza. Parecía no pensar en lo que hacía, pero trabajaba con obstinación, pedaleando en la fresa incluso cuando no se servía de ella.

Después de las ocho hizo una pausa para mirar el cielo por la ventana y vio dos gallinazos° pensativos que se secaban al sol en el caballete° de la casa vecina. Siguió trabajando con la idea de que antes del almuerzo volvería a llover. La voz destemplada de su hijo de once años lo sacó de su abstracción.

—Papá.

—¿Qué?

—Dice el alcalde que si le sacas una muela.

—Dile que no estoy aquí.

Estaba puliendo un diente de oro. Lo retiró a la distancia del brazo y lo examinó con los ojos a medio cerrar. En la salita de espera volvió a gritar su hijo.

—Dice que sí estás porque te está oyendo.

El dentista siguió examinando el diente. Sólo cuando lo puso en la mesa con los trabajos terminados, dijo:

—Mejor.

Volvió a operar la fresa. De una cajita de cartón donde guardaba las cosas por hacer, sacó un puente° de varias piezas y empezó a pulir el oro.

—Papá.

—¿Qué?

Aún no había cambiado de expresión.

—Dice que si no le sacas la muela te pega un tiro°.

Sin apresurarse, con un movimiento extremadamente tranquilo, dejó de pedalear en la fresa, la retiró del sillón y abrió por completo la gaveta° inferior de la mesa. Allí estaba el revólver.

—Bueno—dijo. —Dile que venga a pegármelo.

Hizo girar el sillón hasta quedar de frente a la puerta, la mano apoyada en el borde de la gaveta. El alcalde apareció en el umbral°. Se había afeitado la mejilla izquierda, pero en la otra, hinchada y dolorida, tenía una barba de cinco días. El dentista vio en sus ojos marchitos muchas noches de desesperación. Cerró la gaveta con la punta de los dedos y dijo suavemente:

—Siéntese.

—Buenos días—dijo el alcalde.

—Buenos—dijo el dentista.

Mientras hervían los instrumentos, el alcalde apoyó el cráneo en el cabezal de la silla y se sintió mejor. Respiraba un olor glacial. Era un gabinete pobre: una vieja silla de madera, la fresa de pedal y una vidriera con pomos de loza°.

puente dental bridge

te pega un tiro he'll shoot you

gaveta drawer

umbral doorway

pomos de loza small porcelain bottles

CULTURA

Una callecita de Cartagena, Colombia, que termina, o muere, en las orillas del mar Caribe

cancel de tela *cloth screen*	
cautelosa *cautious, careful*	
escupidera *spittoon, cuspidor*	
aguamanil *washstand*	
cordal inferior *bottom wisdom tooth*	
gatillo *forceps*	
se aferró *clung to, grasped*	
riñones *kidneys*	
muertos *deaths (you have caused)*	
crujido *crackle, creak*	
sudoroso *sweaty*	
jadeante *panting*	
guerrera *military jacket*	
a tientas *groping*	
trapo *rag*	
cielo raso desfondado *chipped ceiling*	
telaraña *spider web*	
araña *spider*	
haga buches *rinse*	
red *screen*	
misma vaina *same difference*	

Frente a la silla, una ventana con un cancel de tela° hasta la altura de un hombre. Cuando sintió que el dentista se acercaba el alcalde afirmó los talones y abrió la boca.

Don Aurelio Escovar le movió la cara hacia la luz. Después de observar la muela dañada, ajustó la mandíbula con una cautelosa° presión de los dedos.

—Tiene que ser sin anestesia—dijo.

—¿Por qué?

—Porque tiene un absceso.

El alcalde lo miró a los ojos. —Está bien—dijo, y trató de sonreír. El dentista no lo correspondió. Llevó a la mesa de trabajo la cacerola con los instrumentos hervidos y los sacó del agua con unas pinzas frías, todavía sin apresurarse. Después rodó la escupidera° con la punta del zapato y fue a lavarse las manos en el aguamanil°. Hizo todo sin mirar al alcalde. Pero el alcalde no lo perdió de vista.

Era un cordal inferior°. El dentista abrió las piernas y apretó la muela con el gatillo° caliente. El alcalde se aferró° a las barras de la silla, descargó toda su fuerza en los pies y sintió un vacío helado en los riñones°, pero no soltó un suspiro. El dentista sólo movió la muñeca. Sin rencor, más bien con una amarga ternura, dijo:

—Aquí nos paga veinte muertos°, teniente.

El alcalde sintió un crujido° de huesos en la mandíbula y sus ojos se llenaron de lágrimas. Pero no suspiró hasta que no sintió salir la muela. Entonces la vio a través de las lágrimas. Le pareció tan extraña a su dolor, que no pudo entender la tortura de sus cinco noches anteriores.

Inclinado sobre la escupidera, sudoroso°, jadeante°, se desabotonó la guerrera° y buscó a tientas° el pañuelo en el bolsillo del pantalón. El dentista le dio un trapo° limpio.

—Séquese las lágrimas—dijo.

El alcalde lo hizo. Estaba temblando. Mientras el dentista se lavaba las manos, vio el cielo raso desfondado° y una telaraña° polvorienta con huevos de araña° e insectos muertos. El dentista regresó secándose las manos.

—Acuéstese—dijo—y haga buches° de agua de sal.

El alcalde se puso de pie, se despidió con un displicente saludo militar, y se dirigió a la puerta estirando las piernas, sin abotonarse la guerrera.

—Me pasa la cuenta—dijo.

—¿A usted o al municipio?

El alcalde no lo miró. Cerró la puerta, y dijo, a través de la red° metálica:

—Es la misma vaina°.

¿Comprendes?

A **Recordando hechos** Contesta.
1. ¿Quién quiere que el dentista le saque una muela?
2. ¿Quién se lo dice al dentista?
3. ¿Cómo reacciona el dentista?
4. ¿Qué hará el alcalde si el dentista no le saca la muela?
5. ¿Qué saca el dentista de una gaveta antes de que entre en el gabinete el alcalde?
6. Según el dentista, ¿por qué era necesario sacarle la muela sin anestesia?

B **Describiendo** Describe.
1. al dentista
2. el gabinete del dentista
3. al alcalde mientras el dentista le sacaba la muela

C **Interpretando** Interpreta el significado de la conversación entre el dentista y el alcalde sobre el pago de la cuenta.

D **Analizando** Contesta sobre el estilo del autor.

¿Qué acciones introduce el autor en el cuento para hacerles sentir a sus lectores la tensión fuerte que existe entre el alcalde y el dentista?

Después de leer

¿Cuáles son tus reacciones ante la actitud y comportamiento del dentista?

Carreras

Si te interesa la odontología (ser dentista), prepara una lista de todos los términos relacionados con este campo que se encuentran en el cuento.

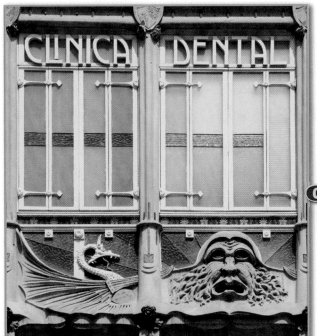

CULTURA

Una clínica dental en Palma de Mallorca

Vocabulario

1 **Completa.**

1–2. Otras palabras que se refieren a una oficina son _____ y _____.

3–4. Una _____ diseña un puente y un _____ lo construye.

5. Los _____ trabajan para el gobierno.

6. Para ser _____ hay que poder diseñar programas para la computadora.

7. El jefe de la administración de una ciudad se llama «el _____».

8. _____ va a preparar los medicamentos para la receta que le da Anita.

9. Su padre es representante de ventas y se dedica a la _____ de varias mercancías mexicanas.

10. Otra palabra que significa «empresa» es _____.

11. _____ hace cosas de madera.

12. Hay un problema con las luces en mi casa. Tengo que llamar a un _____.

13. Se puede decir el departamento de personal o de _____.

14–15. Antes de que una empresa te ofrezca un puesto es necesario tener una _____ y llenar una _____.

16. El entrevistador le ha dicho al _____ que es necesario hablar inglés y español.

17. En los periódicos hay _____ para los que buscan trabajo.

18. Trabajar cuarenta horas por semana es trabajar _____.

Gramática

2 **Completa con por o para.**

19. El tren sale _____ Barcelona.

20. Tenemos que estar allí _____ el día diez.

21. Vamos a estar _____ unos ocho días.

22. Después de terminar nuestro trabajo vamos a viajar _____ el país.

23–24. _____ norteamericano habla muy bien el español pero nadie lo toma _____ hispanohablante.

25–26. Yo compré el regalo _____ mi madre que quiere dárselo a mi hermana. El regalo es _____ mi hermana.

▲ El candidato tiene una entrevista en el departamento de recursos humanos de la empresa.

To review **Vocabulario,** turn to pages 304–305.

To review **por** and **para,** turn to pages 310, 312, 314.

Completa con por o para.

27. El cielo está muy nublado. Está _____ llover.

28. Estoy _____ divertirme. ¿Qué podemos hacer?

29. Ellos han llamado _____ ayuda.

30. Siempre está trabajando y le queda mucho _____ hacer.

31. Los huevos se venden _____ docena.

32. Él quiere darme dólares _____ euros.

To review **por** and **para**, turn to pages 310, 312, 314.

4 **Completa.**

33. Están buscando asistentes que _____ español. (hablar)

34. ¿Por qué? Ya tienen muchos asistentes que _____ español. (hablar)

35. Su padre trabaja con una compañía que _____ sucursales en otros países. (tener)

36. ¿Conoces una compañía que _____ oficinas en México? (tener)

To review **el subjuntivo en cláusulas relativas,** turn to page 316.

Cultura

5 **Contesta.**

37. ¿Qué es una compañía multinacional?

38. ¿Qué significa el mundo de globalización?

39–40. ¿Cuáles son dos maneras en que el español te podrá beneficiar en tu vida profesional?

To review this cultural information, turn to page 320.

CULTURA

Empleadas de una empresa
estadounidense en Lima, Perú

1 **Profesiones de interés**

✔ *Talk about professions and occupations*

Trabaja con un(a) compañero(a). Hablen de las profesiones u oficios en que tendrían interés. Expliquen por qué les interesaría cierta profesión.

2 **Una entrevista**

✔ *Interview a job candidate*

Eres un(a) empleado(a) en una agencia de empleos. Un(a) compañero(a) es un(a) candidato(a) para un puesto. Tú vas a darle una entrevista. Pregúntale sobre sus estudios, experiencia, aptitudes personales, talentos artísticos, etc. Luego cambien de rol.

CULTURA

¿Te interesaría pintar como esta artista en la Plaza Mayor en Cuenca, España?

3 **Un nuevo alumno hispano**

✔ *Talk about career possibilities*

El/La consejero(a) de orientación *(guidance counselor)* de tu escuela te ha pedido ayudar a un(a) estudiante hispanohablante que acaba de llegar de un país latinoamericano. Quiere que le hagas preguntas para determinar una carrera que le interese. Luego quiere que le expliques todo lo que tiene que hacer para prepararse para esa carrera.

4 **Un trabajo ideal**

✔ *Describe an ideal job*

Piensa en lo que tú considerarías un trabajo ideal o algo que a ti te gustaría hacer. Describe tu trabajo ideal a un(a) compañero(a). Luego cambien de rol.

5 **¡Seguir con el español! ¿Por qué?**

✔ *Discuss the importance of studying Spanish*

Tú y un(a) compañero(a) van a hablarles a los alumnos en una clase del primer año de español. Les van a decir por qué deben continuar con sus estudios del español. Les van a explicar por qué es muy importante el estudio del español. Traten de ser creativos y usen su sentido de humor.

Tarea

Imagine yourself in ten years applying for your "dream job." By then, you will have received further education in some area of specialization and will probably have acquired related work experience. Now that the job for which you have been preparing has become available, you must create a résumé **(currículum vitae)** that will show why you are a strong candidate for the position.

Writing Strategy

Persuasiveness When creating a résumé, your primary focus should be on how the job for which you are applying matches up with your background and your career goals. Since applying for a job is a formal process, it is always important to keep your audience in mind and to adhere to certain conventions or rules of professional communication. In order to convince the employer that you are indeed a highly qualified candidate, your writing—both in content and in form— should be persuasive.

1 Prewrite

- Begin by reflecting on what life will be like for you in ten years. Decide on a career that will suit your interests and that will draw upon your education and your work experience.

- Create a timeline or basic chronology of the jobs you will have worked and the training you will have received by then, making sure they relate in some way to the career you have chosen.

- You may also wish to make a list of additional information to be included in your résumé, such as a statement of your objectives, evidence of community service, and other personal achievements that will make your résumé stand out.

2 Write

- Although there are many different styles, most effective résumés contain information that is categorized under various headings. Within each category, the information is listed in reverse chronological order (starting with the most recent).

- The following headings may serve as a guideline: **Datos personales, Formación académica, Experiencia profesional, Idiomas, Informática, Otros datos (Servicio comunitario, Cualidades, Otras habilidades, Actividades, Intereses).**

- Be sure to narrow things down so that all information can fit on a single page. When describing your accomplishments, avoid unnecessary repetition and use strong or active verbs that will grab the reader's attention.

- When generating facts about your future self, feel free to be creative but also remember to take this assignment seriously and to view it as an opportunity to gain further practice for upcoming "real-world" situations.

Evaluate

Your teacher will evaluate you on proper use of vocabulary, correct spelling and grammar, completeness of information, and quality of content and style.

Gramática

- **Por y para** *(pages 310, 312, and 314)*
  The prepositions **por** and **para** have very specific uses.
  Para is used to represent a destination, purpose or reason, or readiness.
  It can also express a comparison or a deadline.

  > **Salen para Madrid.**
  > **El paquete es para María.**
  > **Estudia para ingeniero.**
  > **Están para salir.**
  > **Para cubano, habla bien el inglés.**
  > **Tiene que terminar para el día ocho.**

  Por, on the other hand, is more circuitous. It expresses *through, by, on behalf of, instead of,* and *in exchange for.* It expresses the reason for an errand, a period of time, indefinite time, means, manner, an opinion, or estimation. **Por** is also used to indicate a measure or number.

  > **Viajaron por España.**
  > **Entró por la ventana.**
  > **Compré el regalo por María.**
  > **Voy por agua.**
  > **Estuvieron por dos semanas.**
  > **Estarán por Navidad.**
  > **Lo toman por cubano, pero no lo es.**
  > **Estamos por** *(in the mood)* **salir.**
  > **Me dio pesos por dólares.**
  > **Se venden por kilo.**
  > **Ya tengo mucho por hacer.**

- **Subjuntivo en cláusulas relativas**
  (page 316)
  When a relative clause modifies an indefinite antecedent, the subjunctive is used in the clause. If the antecedent is definite the indicative is used.

  > **Estamos buscando alguien que tenga experiencia en ventas.**
  > **Conozco a alguien que tiene experiencia en ventas.**

CULTURA

El barco pasa por la costa de las islas Galápagos en Ecuador.

Vocabulario

Talking about offices and office personnel

la oficina
el bufete del
  abogado
el consultorio (la
  consulta) del

médico
el gabinete del
  dentista
el/la contable
el/la asistente(a)

ejecutivo(a)
el/la ejecutivo(a)
el/la programador(a)
  de computadoras
  (informática)

la empresa, la
  sociedad, la
  compañía
el estado financiero

Identifying some government workers

el gobierno
el/la político(a)

el/la senador(a)
el/la alcalde(sa)

el/la funcionario(a)
  gubernamental
  (de gobierno)

Talking about businesspeople

el/la comerciante

el hombre (la mujer)
  de negocios

el/la dueño(a)

el/la vendedor(a)

Identifying some professions

la carrera
la profesión

el/la arquitecto(a)
el/la ingeniero(a)

el/la abogado(a)
el/la dentista

el/la farmacéutico(a)

Identifying some trades

el oficio
el/la electricista

el/la plomero(a),
  el/la fontanero(a)

el/la carpintero(a)
el/la albañil

Talking about job opportunities

un puesto
el anuncio
  (clasificado)
el departamento
  de personal,

el servicio de
  recursos humanos
el/la candidato(a),
  el/la aspirante
la entrevista

el/la estudiante
  universitario(a)
la solicitud
  (aplicación) de
  empleo

el currículum vitae,
  el currículo
un trabajo
  a tiempo completo
  a tiempo parcial

Other useful words and expressions

llenar

 The words listed below come from this chapter's literary selection, *Un día de éstos*. They were selected to become part of your active vocabulary because of their relatively high frequency.

el/la madrugador(a)
la muñeca
una lágrima

enjuto(a)
sordo(a)
hinchado(a)

apresurarse
amanecer

Repaso cumulativo

Repasa lo que ya has aprendido

These activities will help you review and remember
what you have learned so far in Spanish.

 Escucha las frases. Indica en una tabla como la de abajo si la acción toma lugar en el pasado, el presente o el futuro.

en el pasado	en el presente	en el futuro

 Completa con el verbo hablar. Fíjate en las expresiones adverbiales para determinar el tiempo del verbo que necesitas.

1. Hace tres años que yo _____ español.
2. Pero yo no _____ español cuando era niño(a).
3. Yo le _____ a él ayer y _____ con él esta mañana.
4. No, no le _____ mañana.
5. Yo le _____ si pudiera pero nunca contesta su móvil ni sus correos electrónicos.
6. Yo le _____ antes de que llegue.
7. Yo le _____ antes de que llegara.

▲ El joven hace sus tareas en la biblioteca después de las clases.

 Personaliza. Da respuestas personales.

1. ¿Quién eres?
2. ¿Cuántos años tienes?
3. ¿A qué hora sales para la escuela?
4. ¿Conoces a mucha gente?
5. ¿Sabes mucho?
6. ¿Haces mucho trabajo?
7. ¿Conduces un carro?
8. ¿Siempre dices la verdad?
9. ¿Cómo vas a la escuela?
10. ¿Dónde estás ahora?

Completa con el pretérito o imperfecto.

1. Él lo hace ahora y lo _____ ayer.

2. Ellos lo dicen y siempre lo _____.

3. Yo voy con frecuencia pero no _____ mucho cuando era joven.

4. Abuelita me habla ahora y me _____ ayer también.

5. ¿Él da muchas fiestas? Sí, y como sabes, siempre _____ fiestas.

Completa para formar frases.

1. Quiero que tú _____.

2. Es necesario que ellos _____.

3. Prefiero que ustedes _____.

4. Te aconsejamos que _____.

5. Es importante que ella _____.

6. Yo le hablaré cuando _____.

7. Tú lo verás antes de que _____.

8. Esperaremos aquí hasta que ellos _____.

Completa para formar frases.

1. Quería que tú _____.

2. Fue necesario que ellos _____.

3. Preferiría que ustedes _____.

4. Te aconsejaríamos que _____.

5. Fue importante que ella _____.

6. Yo le hablé cuando _____.

7. Tú lo viste antes de que _____.

8. Esperaríamos hasta que ellos _____.

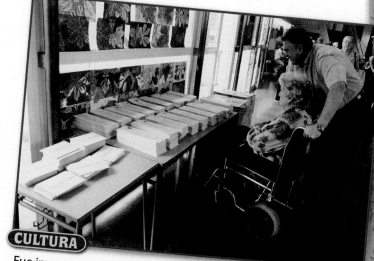

CULTURA

Fue importante que la señora supiera para quien votaba durante las elecciones para el Parlamento de Cataluña.

Student Resources

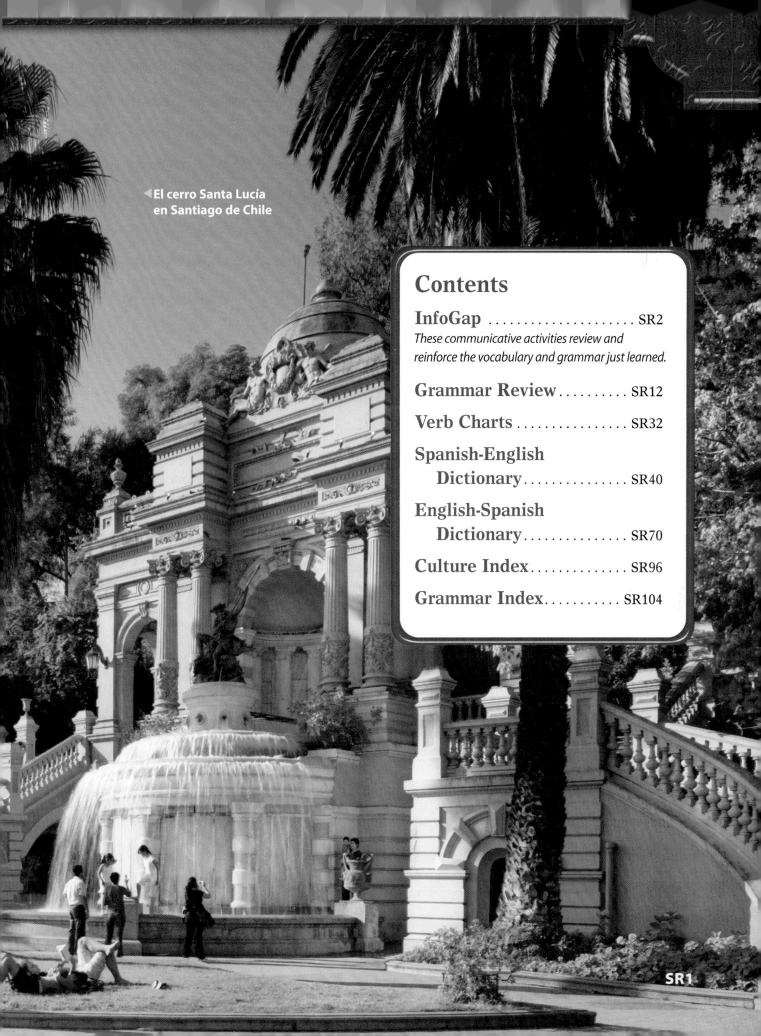

El cerro Santa Lucía
en Santiago de Chile

Contents

InfoGap

Activity 1

Alumno A Ask your partner the following questions. Correct answers are in parentheses.

1. ¿Qué quiere Marisa que su primo haga?
(*Marisa quiere que su primo se acueste.*)

2. ¿Qué quieren sus amigos que Marta haga?
(*Sus amigos quieren que Marta salga este fin de semana.*)

3. ¿Qué quieres que hagamos esta noche?
(*Quiero que miremos la tele esta noche.*)

4. ¿Qué quiere la madre de Diego que él haga? (*La madre de Diego quiere que él limpie la casa.*)

Alumno A Answer your partner's questions based on the cues below.

1. jugar tenis

2. preparar la comida

3. conducir con cuidado

4. decir la verdad

Alumno B Answer your partner's questions based on the cues below.

1. acostarse

2. salir este fin de semana

3. mirar la tele

4. limpiar la casa

Alumno B Ask your partner the following questions. Correct answers are in parentheses.

1. ¿Qué quieren los padres que sus hijos hagan?
(*Los padres quieren que sus hijos jueguen tenis.*)

2. ¿Qué quieres que yo haga?
(*Quiero que tú prepares la comida.*)

3. ¿Qué quiere Olivia que su hermana haga?
(*Olivia quiere que su hermana conduzca con cuidado.*)

4. ¿Qué quiere el profesor que sus alumnos hagan?
(*El profesor quiere que sus alumnos digan la verdad.*)

Activity 2

Alumno A Ask your partner the following questions. Correct answers are in parentheses.

1. ¿Qué se ha cortado la joven?
   (La joven se ha cortado el dedo.)

2. ¿Ella está en la ambulancia?
   (No, ella no está en la ambulancia.)

3. ¿Ella se ha hecho mucho daño?
   (No, ella no se ha hecho mucho daño.)

4. ¿Qué le pone la enfermera?
   (La enfermera le pone una venda.)

Alumno A Answer your partner's questions based on the photo below.

Alumno B Answer your partner's questions based on the photos below.

Alumno B Ask your partner the following questions. Correct answers are in parentheses.

1. ¿Qué se ha torcido el joven?
   (El joven se ha torcido el tobillo.)

2. ¿Habla el joven con los socorristas?
   (No, el joven no habla con los socorristas.)

3. ¿Con quién habla el joven?
   (El joven habla con la médica.)

4. ¿Está en una silla de ruedas?
   (Sí, está en una silla de ruedas.)

InfoGap

Alumno A Ask your partner the following questions. Correct answers are in parentheses.

1. ¿Qué quieres?
(Quiero que [tú] vayas conmigo a la fiesta de cumpleaños de mi prima.)

2. ¿Qué mandan tus padres?
(Mis padres mandan que yo asista al bautizo de mi sobrino.)

3. ¿Qué siente tu madre?
(Mi madre siente que mis abuelos no puedan asistir a su fiesta de cumpleaños.)

4. ¿Qué te sorprende?
(Me sorprende que mi hermana se case pronto.)

Alumno A Answer your partner's questions based on the cues below.

1. a la escuela

2. caminar

3. casarse

4. solo(a)

Alumno B Answer your partner's questions based on the cues below.

1. tú / ir conmigo a la fiesta de cumpleaños de mi prima

2. yo / asistir al bautizo de mi sobrino

3. mis abuelos / no poder asistir a su fiesta de cumpleaños

4. mi hermana / casarse pronto

Alumno B Ask your partner the following questions. Correct answers are in parentheses.

1. ¿Insisten tus padres en que vayas al cine?
(No, mis padres insisten en que yo vaya a la escuela.)

2. ¿Prefieres que tus amigas tomen el bus?
(No, prefiero que mis amigas caminen.)

3. ¿Estás contento(a) que tu hermano se gradúe?
(No, estoy contento[a] que mi hermano se case.)

4. ¿Desean tus padres que estudies con tus amigos? (No, mis padres desean que estudie solo[a].)

Alumno A Answer your partner's questions based on the pictures below.

Alumno A Ask your partner the following questions. Correct answers are in parentheses.

1. ¿Dónde está César?
   (César está en la lavandería.)

2. ¿Pone su ropa sucia en la lavadora o saca su ropa?
   (Pone su ropa sucia en la lavadora.)

3. ¿Dónde está Anita?
   (Anita está en el correo.)

4. ¿Qué hace allí?
   (Echa su tarjeta en el buzón.)

Alumno B Answer your partner's questions based on the pictures below.

1–2.

3–4.

Alumno B Ask your partner the following questions. Correct answers are in parentheses.

1. ¿Dónde trabaja Alonso?
   (Alonso trabaja en una peluquería.)

2. ¿Con qué paga el cliente, con dinero en efectivo o con cheque?
   (El cliente paga con dinero en efectivo.)

3. ¿Dónde está Gloria?
   (Gloria está enfrente del cajero automático.)

4. ¿Dónde está Susana, en el banco o en el correo?
   (Susana está en el banco.)

InfoGap

Activity 5

Alumno A Ask your partner the following questions. Correct answers are in parentheses.

1. ¿Qué era necesario?
   (Era necesario que todos se pusieran de pie.)

2. ¿Qué quería la profesora?
   (La profesora quería que los alumnos sacaran notas buenas.)

3. ¿Qué te sorprendió?
   (Me sorprendió que Juan no llegara a tiempo.)

4. ¿Qué es una lástima?
   (Es una lástima que nosotros perdamos la película.)

Alumno A Answer your partner's questions based on the cues below.

1. yo / levantarme temprano

2. la cocinera / freír el pescado

3. ellos / estudiar toda la noche

4. yo / pagar la cuenta

Alumno B Answer your partner's questions based on the cues below.

1. todos / ponerse de pie

2. los alumnos / sacar notas buenas

3. Juan / no llegar a tiempo

4. nosotros / perder la película

Alumno B Ask your partner the following questions. Correct answers are in parentheses.

1. ¿Qué quería tu madre?
   (Mi madre quería que yo me levantara temprano.)

2. ¿En qué insistió el cliente?
   (El cliente insistió en que la cocinera friera el pescado.)

3. ¿Qué será necesario?
   (Será necesario que ellos estudien toda la noche.)

4. ¿Qué dudó tu hermana?
   (Mi hermana dudó que yo pagara la cuenta.)

Alumno A Ask your partner the following questions. Correct answers are in parentheses.

1. ¿Cuándo podrás reclamar tu equipaje?
   (*Podré reclamar mi equipaje cuando llegue a mi destino.*)

2. ¿Cuándo hablarás con Marta?
   (*Hablaré con Marta antes de que cambie de tren.*)

3. ¿Cuándo saldrás?
   (*Saldré tan pronto como pueda.*)

4. ¿Cuándo alquilaste el carro?
   (*Alquilé el carro en cuanto llegué al aeropuerto.*)

Alumno A Answer your partner's questions based on the cues below.

1. antes de que / salir de la agencia

2. cuando / tener bastante dinero

3. después de que / encontrar la información

4. en cuanto / sentirme mejor

Alumno B Answer your partner's questions based on the cues below.

1. cuando / llegar a mi destino

2. antes de que / cambiar de tren

3. tan pronto como / poder

4. en cuanto / llegar al aeropuerto

Alumno B Ask your partner the following questions. Correct answers are in parentheses.

1. ¿Cuándo inspeccionarás el jeep?
   (*Inspeccionaré el jeep antes de que salga de la agencia.*)

2. ¿Cuándo viajarás?
   (*Viajaré cuando tenga bastante dinero.*)

3. ¿Cuándo devolviste el libro?
   (*Devolví el libro después de que encontré la información.*)

4. ¿Cuándo practicarás el esquí acuático?
   (*Practicaré el esquí acuático en cuanto me sienta mejor.*)

Activity 7

Alumno A Ask your partner the following questions. Correct answers are in parentheses.

1. Si tienes bastante tiempo, ¿qué harás?
(Si tengo bastante tiempo, escribiré una novela.)

2. Si ellos te hubieran preguntado, ¿qué habrías hecho?
(Si ellos me hubieran preguntado, les habría dicho la verdad.)

3. Si viajaras a Costa Rica, ¿qué harías?
(Si viajara a Costa Rica, iría a la playa.)

4. Si tienes bastante dinero, ¿qué harás? *(Si tengo bastante dinero, compraré un cuadro famoso.)*

Alumno A Use the cues below to answer your partner's questions.

1. eliminar la pobreza

2. ver más exposiciones

3. ir a la estación de esquí

4. celebrar

Alumno B Use the cues below to answer your partner's questions.

1. escribir una novela

2. decirles la verdad

3. ir a la playa

4. comprar un cuadro famoso

Alumno B Ask your partner the following questions. Correct answers are in parentheses.

1. Si fueras presidente(a), ¿qué harías?
(Si fuera presidente[a], eliminaría la pobreza.)

2. Si hubieras tenido más tiempo, ¿qué habrías hecho?
(Si hubiera tenido más tiempo, habría visto más exposiciones.)

3. Si nieva, ¿qué harás?
(Si nieva, iré a la estación de esquí.)

4. Si hubieras ganado el partido, ¿qué habrías hecho?
(Si hubiera ganado el partido, habría celebrado.)

Alumno A Ask your partner the following questions. Correct answers are in parentheses.

1. ¿Vas a salir?
(*Sí, voy a salir aunque es tarde.*)

2. ¿Vas a esquiar?
(*Sí, voy a esquiar aunque no haya nieve.*)

3. ¿Vas a decirle la verdad?
(*Sí, voy a decirle la verdad aunque es difícil.*)

4. ¿Vas a ir a la fiesta?
(*Sí, voy a ir a la fiesta aunque vaya solo[a].*)

Alumno A Answer your partner's questions with **sí** and the conjunction **aunque** based on the information provided.

1. No sabes si tienes el libro.

2. Es temprano.

3. No sabes si tienes que ir a pie.

4. Ya sabes que es caro.

Alumno B Answer your partner's questions with **sí** and the conjunction **aunque** based on the information provided.

1. Es tarde.

2. No sabes si habrá nieve.

3. Ya sabes que va a ser difícil.

4. No sabes si vas a ir solo(a).

Alumno B Ask your partner the following questions. Correct answers are in parentheses.

1. ¿Vas a estudiar?
(*Sí, voy a estudiar aunque no tenga el libro.*)

2. ¿Vas a despertarte?
(*Sí, voy a despertarme aunque es temprano.*)

3. ¿Vas a ir a la escuela?
(*Sí, voy a ir a la escuela aunque tenga que ir a pie.*)

4. ¿Vas a comprar el billete?
(*Sí, voy a comprar el billete aunque es caro.*)

InfoGap

Activity 9

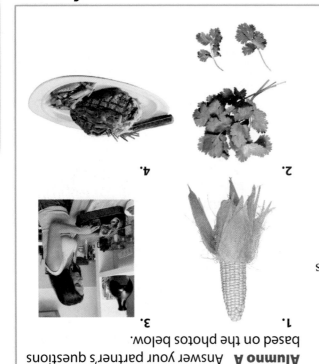

Alumno A Answer your partner's questions based on the photos below.

Alumno A Ask your partner the following questions. Correct answers are in parentheses.

1. ¿Qué quisieras comer?
   (*Quisiera comer una alcachofa.*)

2. ¿Qué hace la cocinera, reboza las rodajas o hierve el arroz?
   (*La cocinera hierve el arroz.*)

3. ¿Qué especia se cultiva en este huerto?
   (*Se cultiva el orégano en este huerto.*)

4. ¿Quiénes son ellos, los comensales o los cocineros?
   (*Son los comensales.*)

Alumno B Answer your partner's questions based on the photos below.

Alumno B Ask your partner the following questions. Correct answers are in parentheses.

1.  3.

2.  4.

1. ¿Qué necesitas, una zanahoria o una mazorca de maíz?
   (*Necesito una mazorca de maíz.*)

2. ¿Cuál es la especia que se usa?
   (*Se usa el cilantro.*)

3. ¿Prepara la cocinera la carne picada o el arroz?
   (*Prepara la carne picada.*)

4. ¿Qué pediste?
   (*Pedí la carne de res.*)

Alumno A Ask your partner the following questions. Correct answers are in parentheses.

1. ¿Raúl es ingeniero o político?
   (Raúl es ingeniero.)

2. ¿Está llenando una solicitud de empleo Elena o está leyendo los anuncios clasificados?
   (Elena está leyendo los anuncios clasificados.)

3. ¿Para qué profesión estudió Leonora?
   (Leonora estudió para ser abogada.)

4. ¿Felipe es funcionario o plomero?
   (Felipe es plomero.)

Alumno A Answer your partner's questions based on the pictures below.

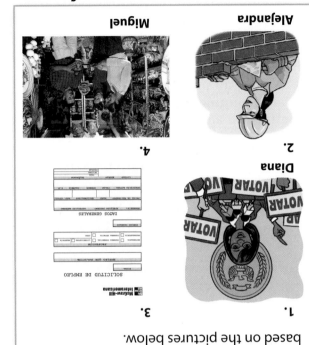

Alejandra

Miguel

Diana

1.

2.

3.

4.

Alumno B Answer your partner's questions based on the pictures below.

1.

Raúl

2.

Elena

3.

Lenora

4.

Felipe

Alumno B Ask your partner the following questions. Correct answers are in parentheses.

1. ¿Diana es contable o política?
   (Diana es política.)

2. ¿Alejandra es albañil o comerciante?
   (Alejandra es albañil.)

3. ¿Es una solicitud de empleo o un anuncio clasificado?
   (Es una solicitud de empleo.)

4. ¿Miguel es funcionario o comerciante?
   (Miguel es comerciante.)

Grammar Review

Nouns and articles

Nouns and definite articles

A noun is the name of a person, place, or thing. Unlike English, all nouns in Spanish have a gender—either masculine or feminine. Almost all nouns that end in **-o** are masculine and almost all nouns that end in **-a** are feminine. Note that the definite article **el** is used with masculine nouns. The definite article **la** is used with feminine nouns.

MASCULINE	FEMININE
el muchacho	**la muchacha**
el libro	**la escuela**
el curso	**la sala**

Nouns that end in **-e** can either be masculine or feminine. It is necessary for you to learn the gender.

MASCULINE	FEMININE
el padre	**la madre**
el restaurante	**la carne**
el nombre	**la leche**
el norte	**la gente**
el billete	**la nube**

Many nouns that end in **-e** and refer to a person can be either masculine or feminine.

el paciente	**la paciente**

It is also necessary to learn the gender of nouns that end in a consonant.

el comedor	**la flor**
el animal	**la capital**
el jamón	**la mujer**

Note, however, that nouns that end in **-ción, -dad, -tad** are always feminine.

la habitación	**la universidad**	**la dificultad**

Irregular nouns

There are not very many irregular nouns in Spanish. The ones you have learned so far are:

la mano   **el problema**   **la foto** (*from* **la fotografía**)

The following nouns end in **-a** but they are masculine.

el clima	el planeta
el día	el poema
el drama	el programa
el mapa	el telegrama

The following nouns that begin with **-a** or **-ha** are feminine. However because of the difficulty pronouncing the two **a** sounds together, they take the articles **el** and **un** in the singular. All other articles and adjectives are feminine.

el águila	las águilas
el agua	las aguas
el arma	las armas
el hacha	las hachas
el hambre	

Plural of nouns

To form the plural of nouns you add **-s** to nouns that end in a vowel. You add **-es** to nouns that end in a consonant. Note, too, that the definite articles **el** and **la** become **los** and **las** in the plural.

MASCULINE PLURAL	FEMININE PLURAL
los libros	las novelas
los cuartos	las casas
los coches	las carnes
los comedores	las flores

Nouns that end in **-z** change the **-z** to **-c** and add **-es.**

el lápiz	los lápices

Nouns that end in **-ción** drop the accent in the plural.

la estación	las estaciones
la conversación	las conversaciones

For special uses of the definite article, see page 245 in Chapter 8 of *¡Así se dice!* Level 3.

Indefinite articles

The indefinite articles are *a, an,* and *some* in English. They are **un, una, unos,** and **unas** in Spanish. Note that the indefinite article, like the definite article, must agree with the noun it modifies in both gender (masculine or feminine) and number (singular or plural).

	SINGULAR		PLURAL	
	un alumno	una alumna	unos alumnos	unas alumnas
	un café	una clase	unos cafés	unas clases
	un árbol	una flor	unos árboles	unas flores

For special uses of the indefinite article, see page 247 in Chapter 8 of *¡Así se dice!* Level 3.

Contractions

The prepositions **a** *(to, at)* and **de** *(of, from)* contract (combine) with the definite article **el** to form one word, **al** or **del.** There is no contraction with **la, los,** or **las.**

> **Voy al mercado; no vuelvo del mercado.**
> **Es el dinero del empleado, no del cliente.**

A personal

Remember that whenever a person is the direct object of the verb, it must be preceded by **a.** This **a personal** also contracts with **el.**

> **Conozco a Juan.**
> **Pero no conozco al hermano de Juan.**

Nouns and adjectives

Agreement of nouns and adjectives

An adjective is a word that describes a noun. An adjective must agree in gender (masculine or feminine) and number (singular or plural) with the noun it describes or modifies.

Adjectives that end in **-o** have four forms, the same as nouns that end in **-o.**

	SINGULAR	PLURAL
MASCULINE	el muchacho simpático	los muchachos simpáticos
FEMININE	la muchacha simpática	las muchachas simpáticas

Adjectives that end in **-e** have only two forms—singular and plural.

	SINGULAR	PLURAL
MASCULINE	el alumno inteligente	los alumnos inteligentes
FEMININE	la alumna inteligente	las alumnas inteligentes

Adjectives that end in a consonant have only two forms—singular and plural. Note that the plural ends in **-es.**

	SINGULAR	PLURAL
MASCULINE	**un curso fácil**	**dos cursos fáciles**
FEMININE	**una tarea fácil**	**dos tareas fáciles**

Adjectives of nationality

Adjectives of nationality that end in a consonant have four forms. Observe the following.

un joven francés	**unos jóvenes franceses**
una joven francesa	**unas jóvenes francesas**

Note that adjectives of nationality that end in **-s** or **-n (inglés, japonés, tailandés, alemán, catalán)** drop the written accent in all forms except the masculine singular.

Possessive adjectives

A possessive adjective tells who owns or possesses something—*my* book and *your* pencil. Like other adjectives in Spanish, possessive adjectives agree with the noun they modify. Note that only **nuestro** and *vuestro* have four forms.

MASCULINE SINGULAR	FEMININE SINGULAR	MASCULINE PLURAL	FEMININE PLURAL
mi tío	**mi tía**	**mis tíos**	**mis tías**
tu tío	**tu tía**	**tus tíos**	**tus tías**
su tío	**su tía**	**sus tíos**	**sus tías**
nuestro tío	**nuestra tía**	**nuestros tíos**	**nuestras tías**
vuestro tío	*vuestra tía*	*vuestros tíos*	*vuestras tías*

Since **su** can refer to many different people, it is often accompanied by a phrase that gives clarification.

su familia

la familia de Juan	**la familia de él**
la familia de María	**la familia de ella**
la familia de Juan y María	**la familia de ellos**

la familia de usted

la familia de ustedes

Demonstrative adjectives

Until recently the demonstrative pronoun (*this one, that one, these, those*) had to carry a written accent to differentiate it from a demonstrative adjective. That is no longer the case and the pronouns are the same as the adjectives.

In Spanish there are three demonstrative adjectives (pronouns): **este** (*this*), **ese** (*that*), and **aquel** (*that, farther away*). Each of the demonstratives has four forms and must agree in gender and number with the nouns it modifies or replaces.

MASCULINE SINGULAR	FEMININE SINGULAR	MASCULINE PLURAL	FEMININE PLURAL
este libro	esta chaqueta	estos libros	estas chaquetas
ese libro	esa chaqueta	esos libros	esas chaquetas
aquel libro	aquella chaqueta	aquellos libros	aquellas chaquetas

Suffixes

The suffixes **-ito, -ico,** and **-illo** can be added to nouns to convey the meaning *small*. They sometimes add an element of endearment.

> **Mamá y su hijito**
> **Quiere mucho a su abuelita.**
> **Es un chiquito (chiquillo).**

When a noun ends in **-e** or a consonant **-cito** is added.

> **mi cochecito**
> **un ratoncito**

-ísimo

The suffix **-ísimo** adds a superlative element to an adjective.

> **¡Buenísimo!**
> **Fue una experiencia fabulosísima.**

Comparative and superlative

Regular forms

You use the comparative (*more, -er*) and the superlative (*most, -est*) to compare people or things.

To form the comparative in Spanish you use **más** (or **menos**) before the adjective, adverb, or noun. The comparative is followed by **que: más... que.**

> **Él es más inteligente que los otros.**
> **Ella es más ambiciosa que los otros.**

Note that the comparative is followed by the subject pronoun or a negative word.

> más alto que yo (tú, él, nosotros)
> más alto que nadie

To form the superlative you use the definite article with **más.** Note that **de** follows the superlative: **el (la) más... de.**

> **Él es el más ambicioso de todos.**
> **Ella es la alumna más inteligente de todos.**

Irregular forms

The adjectives **bueno** and **malo** as well as the adverbs **bien** and **mal** have irregular comparative and superlative forms.

	COMPARATIVE	SUPERLATIVE
bueno	mejor	el/la mejor
malo	peor	el/la peor
bien	mejor	el/la mejor
mal	peor	el/la peor

> **Él es mejor jugador que su hermano.**
> **Pero su hermana Teresa es la mejor jugadora de los tres.**
> **La verdad es que ella juega mejor que nadie.**
> **Ella juega mejor que yo.**

(El) mayor and **(el) menor** are also comparative and superlative forms. They most often refer to age and sometimes size.

> **Mi hermano menor tiene trece años.**
> **Y mi hermana mayor tiene diecisiete.**
> **La Ciudad de México tiene el mayor número de habitantes.**

Comparison of equality

To compare things that have equal qualities (*as . . . as*) you use **tan... como** in Spanish. Note that **tan** can precede an adjective or an adverb.

> **Ella es tan inteligente como sus hermanos.**
> **Sus hermanos son tan inteligentes como ella.**
> **Ella habla tan rápido como los otros.**

To compare equal quantities (*as much . . . as, as many . . . as*) you use **tanto... como.** Since **tanto** is an adjective it must agree with the noun it modifies.

> **Él tiene tanta paciencia como su hermana.**
> **Susana no tiene tantos primos como yo.**

Note that the subject pronouns follow **como.**

Formation of adverbs

An adverb is formed by adding **-mente** to the feminine form of the adjective.

maravillosa	maravillosamente
clara	claramente
enorme	enormemente
fácil	fácilmente

If more than one adverb is used only the last one in the series has **-mente**.

Él habló clara y cómicamente.

Pronouns

A pronoun is a word that replaces a noun. Review the forms of the pronouns that you have learned so far.

SUBJECT PRONOUNS	DIRECT OBJECT PRONOUNS	INDIRECT OBJECT PRONOUNS	REFLEXIVE PRONOUNS	PREPOSITIONAL PRONOUNS
yo	me	me	me	mí
tú	te	te	te	ti
Ud., él, ella	lo, la	le	se	Ud., él, ella
nosotros(as)	nos	nos	nos	nosotros(as)
vosotros(as)	*os*	*os*	*os*	*vosotros(as)*
Uds., ellos, ellas	los, las	les	se	Uds., ellos, ellas

Remember that an object pronoun comes right before the conjugated form of the verb.

Ella me ve. **Ella nos habla.** **Ella lo ha escrito.**

The direct object pronoun is the direct receiver of the action of the verb. The indirect object is the indirect receiver of the action of the verb.

The direct object pronouns **lo, la, los, las** can refer to a person or a thing.

Ellos tiraron la pelota. **Ellos la tiraron.**

Ellos vieron a sus amigos. **Ellos los vieron.**

The indirect object pronouns **le, les** refer most frequently to people. They are often accompanied by a prepositional phrase for clarification.

Ella le habló { a él. / a ella. / a usted. } **Yo les hablé** { a ellos. / a ellas. / a ustedes. }

Note that the prepositional pronouns **mí** and **ti** form one word with **con**.

Yo voy contigo y tú vas conmigo.

Grammar Review

Double object pronouns

When there are two object pronouns in the same sentence, the indirect object pronoun always precedes the direct object pronoun.

Él me lo dijo.

Nuestros padres nos los dan.

¿Quién te lo dio?

The indirect object pronouns **le** and **les** change to **se** when used with a direct object pronoun (**lo, la, los, las**).

El profesor se lo explica muy bien.

¿Quién se las compró?

Se is often accompanied by a prepositional phrase to clarify its meaning.

Yo se lo di
$\begin{cases} \text{a usted.} \\ \text{a él.} \\ \text{a ella.} \\ \text{a ustedes.} \\ \text{a ellos.} \\ \text{a ellas.} \end{cases}$

Position of object pronouns

The object pronouns always precede the conjugated form of the verb.

José me vio.

El profesor se lo explicó a ustedes.

Ellos no lo han hecho.

With the progressive tenses or the infinitive the pronouns can either come before the helping verb or can be added to the present participle or the infinitive.

Ellos nos están ayudando.   **Ella te lo va a explicar.**

Ellos están ayudándonos.   **Ella va a explicártelo.**

Ella se la está vendiendo a ellos.   **Ellos nos quieren ayudar.**

Ella está vendiéndosela a ellos.   **Ellos quieren ayudarnos.**

Note that in order to maintain the same stress you add a written accent mark to the present participle with either one or two pronouns. You add an accent to the infinitive with two pronouns only.

The object pronouns are added to an affirmative command. They precede the negative command.

AFFIRMATIVE	NEGATIVE
Háblame.	**No me hables.**
Dáselo.	**No se lo des.**
Invítelos usted.	**No los invite.**
Díganmelo.	**No me lo digan.**

Note that in order to maintain the same stress, you add a written accent to the command with a pronoun.

Possessive pronouns

The possessive pronoun is used to replace a noun that is modified by a possessive adjective. The possessive pronoun must agree in number and gender with the noun it replaces. In almost all cases the possessive pronoun is accompanied by the appropriate definite article.

el mío	la mía	los míos	las mías
el tuyo	la tuya	los tuyos	las tuyas
el suyo	la suya	los suyos	las suyas
el nuestro	la nuestra	los nuestros	las nuestras
el vuestro	*la vuestra*	*los vuestros*	*las vuestras*

Since the pronoun **el suyo** can refer to so many things it is often clarified by a prepositional phrase:

el suyo	la suya	los suyos	las suyas
de usted	de usted	de usted	de usted
de ustedes	de ustedes	de ustedes	de ustedes
el de él	la de él	los de él	las de él
de ellos	de ellos	de ellos	de ellos
de ella	de ella	de ella	de ella
de ellas	de ellas	de ellas	de ellas

Yo tengo mi boleto, no el tuyo.

¿Dónde están tus maletas? No veo las tuyas; veo solo las de José.

Su carro está en el garaje y el nuestro está en la calle.

You will note that after the verb **ser**, the definite article is often omitted.

Aquella casa es nuestra.

¿Es suya esta cámara?

The definite article can be used, however, to give emphasis.

¿Aquel paquete? Es el mío. No es el tuyo.

Relative pronouns

The pronoun **que** introduces a clause that modifies a noun. **Que** can be used to replace a person or thing and can be either the subject or object of the clause.

> **El señor que habla es de aquí.**
>
> **El libro que está en la mesa es mío.**
>
> **El señor que vimos anoche es de aquí.**
>
> **El libro que escribió el señor es interesante.**

Que can also be used after a preposition but only when it refers to a thing.

> **Leí el libro de que hablas.**

A quien(es) can replace **que** only when it refers to a person and is the direct object of the clause.

> **El señor que (a quien) conocimos es de aquí.**

The pronoun **quien** must be used after a preposition when it refers to a person.

> **La persona (a quien, de quien, con quien) habla él es mi prima.**

The longer pronouns **el que, la que, los que,** and **las que** may be used as a subject or object of a clause and can refer to a person or a thing. They often convey the meaning *the one (ones) that* or *the one (ones) who.*

> **El que llega es mi hermano.**
>
> **(De todos los libros) el que lees es mi favorito.**
>
> **Las que están hablando ahora son mis primas.**

Lo que is a neuter pronoun which replaces a general or abstract idea rather than a specific antecedent.

> **Lo que necesito es más dinero.**
>
> **No sé lo que está diciendo.**

Cuyo is equivalent to the English *whose*. It is an adjective and agrees with the noun it modifies.

> **El señor cuya hija habla ahora es el director de la compañía.**
>
> **La señora cuyos documentos tienes va a viajar a Chile.**

Negative expressions

To make a sentence negative, you merely put **no** before the verb or before the object pronoun that precedes the verb.

> **El gato no está en el jardín.**
>
> **No lo veo.**

Review the following affirmative and negative expressions.

AFFIRMATIVE	NEGATIVE
algo	**nada**
alguien	**nadie**
siempre	**nunca**

> **Nadie está aquí.**

Note that in Spanish, unlike in English, more than one negative word can be used in the same sentence.

> **No ves a nadie.**
>
> **Ellos nunca hablan a nadie de nada.**

The negative of **también** is **tampoco**.

> **A Juan le gusta. A mí también.**
>
> **A Juan no le gusta. Ni a mí tampoco.**

Verbs such as interesar, aburrir, gustar

Note the construction with verbs such as **interesar** and **aburrir**.

> **La historia me interesa.**
> **Me interesa la historia.** } *History interests me.*

> **Los deportes no les aburren.**
> **No les aburren los deportes.** } *Sports don't bore them.*

Gustar functions the same as **interesar** and **aburrir**. It conveys the meaning *to like,* but it literally means *to please.*

Me			**Me**	
Te			**Te**	
Le	} **gusta el helado.**		**Le**	} **gustan los vegetales.**
Nos			**Nos**	
Les			**Les**	

Expressions with the infinitive

The infinitive is the form of the verb that ends in **-ar, -er,** or **-ir.** The infinitive often follows another verb.

> **Ellos quieren salir.**
> **Yo debo estudiar más.**
> **Me gusta leer.**

Three very common expressions that are followed by the infinitive are **tener que** *(to have to)*, **ir a** *(to be going to)*, and **acabar de** *(to have just)*.

> **Tengo que trabajar y estudiar más.**
> **Y voy a trabajar y estudiar más.**
> **Acabo de recibir una nota mala.**

You can use the expression **favor de** followed by an infinitive to ask someone in a polite way to do something.

> **Favor de escribir tu nombre.**
> **Favor de ayudarme.**

Note that the object pronoun is added to the infinitive.

Ser and estar

Spanish has two verbs that mean *to be.* They are **ser** and **estar** and each one has distinct uses.

Ser

You use **ser** to express a characteristic, where someone or something is from, or what something is made of.

> **Él es guapo. Es inteligente también.**
> **Ellos son de Nuevo México.**
> **Su casa es de adobe.**

Estar

You use **estar** to express a condition or location.

> **Él está muy cansado y está triste también.**
> **Madrid está en España.**
> **Sus amigos están en Madrid.**

Saber and conocer

Both **saber** and **conocer** mean *to know.*

Saber means to know a fact or to have information about something. With an infinitive it expresses to know how to do something.

> **Yo sé su número de teléfono.**
> **Sabemos que ella va a viajar.**
> **Todos saben usar el Internet.**

Conocer means *to know* in the sense of *to be familiar with.* It is used with people or complex, abstract concepts.

> **Yo conozco a su amigo Tadeo.**
> **Ellos conocen bien la historia de España.**

Reflexive verbs

When the subject is both the doer and receiver of the action of the verb, you have to use a reflexive pronoun with the verb. Study the following examples of the reflexive construction.

REFLEXIVE	NONREFLEXIVE
Ella se levanta.	**Ella levanta al niño.**
Él se divierte.	**Él divierte a sus amigos.**
Me cepillo.	**Cepillo a mi perro.**

When the reflexive is followed by an article of clothing or a part of the body, you use a definite article in Spanish. (In English the possessive adjective is used.)

> **Me lavo la cara y las manos.**
> **Ella tiene frío y se pone el suéter.**

Verb tenses

See the charts on page SR32 for the verb forms you have learned.

Verb tense usage

Present

You use the present tense to state what is taking place now or what always takes place.

> **Hablamos español.**
> **Juegan fútbol en el otoño.**
> **Siempre hacen la misma cosa.**

You can also use the present tense to express a future action.

> **Salen mañana.**
> **Vamos a México en julio.**

Preterite

You use the preterite to express an action that began and ended at a specific time in the past.

> **Ellos salieron la semana pasada.**
>
> **Nosotros llegamos ayer.**
>
> **Los árabes invadieron España en 711.**

Imperfect

You use the imperfect to describe a continuous, habitual action in the past. The time at which the action began or ended is not important.

> **Ellos siempre hacían la misma cosa.**
>
> **Yo los veía de vez en cuando.**
>
> **Ellos iban a España con frecuencia porque tenían una casa allí.**

You use the imperfect to describe things in the past.

> **Él era joven.**
>
> **Tenía solo dos años.**
>
> **Hacía buen tiempo.**
>
> **Su hermana era muy simpática.**

You use the imperfect to reminisce about past events.

> **Cuando yo era niño vivíamos en Puerto Rico y siempre celebrábamos el Día de los Reyes. Yo recuerdo bien que recibíamos nuestros regalos el seis de enero.**

You use the imperfect with verbs to express mental activities or emotions in the past.

> **Él lo creía.**
>
> **Querían hacerlo.**
>
> **Estaban contentos.**

Time expressions with hace, hacía

Hace is used with the present tense to express an action that began in the past and continues into the present.

> **¿Cuánto tiempo hace que estás en México?**
>
> **Hace dos años que asistimos a la misma escuela.**

Hacía is used with the imperfect tense to express an action that had been going on until something else occurred.

> **Hacía cinco años que ellos trabajaban en Puerto Rico cuando fueron a España.**
>
> **Hacía mucho tiempo que lo sabíamos.**

Future

The true future *will* is used less frequently in Spanish than in English.

> **Le hablaré a él mañana.**
>
> **Volverán la semana que viene.**

The present tense and the **ir a** + *infinitive* construction are often used to convey the future.

> **Le hablo a él mañana.**   **Le voy a hablar mañana.**
>
> **Vuelven la semana que viene.**   **Van a volver la semana que viene.**

Conditional

You use the conditional in Spanish the same as in English. It tells what would or could happen.

> **¿Iría él?**   **Sí, él iría.**
>
> **¿Lo sabrían ellos?**   **Sí, ellos lo sabrían.**
>
> **¿Estarías contento?**   **Sí, yo estaría contento.**

Present perfect

The present perfect is used to describe an action without reference to a specific past time. It is accompanied by time expressions such as **ya, todavía no, jamás, nunca.**

> **Nunca hemos hecho tal cosa.**
>
> **En mi vida he tenido dos accidentes.**
>
> **Todavía no han llegado.**

Pluperfect tense

The pluperfect tense is used to describe a past action that had actually taken place prior to another past action.

> **Ellos ya habían salido cuando nosotros llegamos.**
>
> **Lo había aprendido muchos años antes de empezar la secundaria.**

Future perfect

The future perfect is very seldom used. It conveys an action in the future that was completed prior to another future action.

> **Ellos lo habrán discutido antes de hablar con nosotros.**

Conditional perfect

The conditional perfect is used the same in Spanish as in English to explain what would have happened had something else not made it impossible.

> **Habríamos ido pero no pudimos porque no tuvimos bastante dinero.**
>
> **Él lo habría sabido pero nadie se lo dijo.**

Progressive tense

The progressive tense is formed by using the verb **estar** (or **ir, seguir**) and the present participle. You use the progressive to indicate that the action is actually taking place.

> **Estamos pasando tiempo en la playa.**
> **Estoy mirando a los niños.**
> **Están nadando en el mar.**

Subjunctive

You use the subjunctive in a dependent clause. As the word *subjunctive* implies, it is used to express a subjective action that is not necessarily a fact. It may or may not take place. So far you have learned the following uses of the subjunctive.

You use the subjunctive in a clause introduced by an expression of desire.

> **Quiero que ellos salgan ahora.**
> **Ellos quieren que estudiemos y que tengamos éxito.**
> **¿Prefieres que yo espere aquí?**
> **Él insiste en que tú lo sepas.**

You use the subjunctive following many impersonal expressions.

> **Es importante que lleguemos a tiempo.**
> **Es necesario que ellos lo sepan.**
> **Es mejor que tú lo hagas.**

The subjunctive follows the expressions **ojalá, quizás,** and **tal vez.**

> **¡Ojalá vengan a la fiesta!**
> **¡Quizá(s) vayan!**
> **¡Tal vez lo sepan!**

You use the subjunctive after an expression of doubt. The indicative is used with certainty.

CERTAINTY	DOUBT
Creo que les va a gustar.	**No creo que les guste.**
No dudo que vendrán.	**Dudo que vengan.**
Es cierto que lo saben.	**No es cierto que lo sepan.**

You use the subjunctive after expressions of emotion.

> **Estoy contento que ellos asistan.**
> **¡Qué pena que su padre esté enfermo!**
> **Siento que ellos no lo sepan.**

You use the subjunctive after expressions of advice, request, etc. Note that such expressions are used with an indirect object.

> *Te* **pido que lo hagas.**
> *Les* **aconsejamos** *a ustedes* **que presten atención.**

You use the subjunctive with any word that has **-quiera.**

> **quienquiera que seas y adondequiera que vayas y cuandoquiera que llegues**

You use the subjunctive in adverbial expressions introduced by **de manera que,**
para que.

> **Los padres trabajan duro para que sus hijos tengan una buena vida.**
>
> **El profesor habla claramente de manera que entendamos.**

The subjunctive is used after **aunque** (*even though*) when it is not known if the
information that follows will take place. The indicative is used when the action is real
or definite.

> **Saldremos aunque llueva.** (*even though it may rain*)
>
> **Saldremos aunque está lloviendo.** (*even though it is raining*)

The subjunctive is used in a relative clause that modifies an indefinite antecedent. The
indicative is used if the antecedent is definite. Note that the **a personal** is omitted
with an indefinite noun.

> **Buscamos un contable que tenga experiencia.**
>
> **Conocemos a un contable que tiene experiencia.**

Sequence of tenses with the subjunctive

The present subjunctive is used in any clause that requires the subjunctive when the
verb in the main clause is in the present or future tense. The imperfect subjunctive is
used when the verb in the main clause is in the preterite, imperfect, or conditional.

MAIN CLAUSE	DEPENDENT CLAUSE
present future → **que** (present subjunctive)	preterite imperfect → **que** (imperfect subjunctive) conditional
Quiero que él venga. **Querrán que él venga.**	**No quiso que él viniera.** **Quería que él viniera.** **Querría que él viniera.**
Es importante que ellos lo sepan. **Será importante que ellos lo sepan.**	**Fue importante que ellos lo supieran.** **Era importante que ellos lo supieran.** **Sería importante que ellos lo supieran.**
Te pido que lo hagas. **Te pediré que lo hagas.**	**Te pidió que lo hicieras.** **Te pedía que lo hicieras.** **Te pediría que lo hicieras.**
Busco una secretaria que hable español. **Buscaré una secretaria que hable español.**	**Busqué una secretaria que hablara español.** **Buscaba una secretaria que hablara español.** **Buscaría una secretaria que hablara español.**

Subjunctive with adverbial expressions of time

The subjunctive is used with an adverbial conjunction of time when it is not known if the action will really take place. If the action in the adverbial clause of time actually took place the indicative is used.

> **Voy a esperar hasta que lleguen ellos.**
>
> **Espera aquí hasta que lleguen.**   **Esperé hasta que llegaron.**
>
> **Esperaría hasta que llegaran.**

Note, however, that the conjunction **antes de que** is always followed by the subjunctive. If the verb in the main clause is in the past, the imperfect subjunctive is used.

> **Ellos llegarán antes de que nosotros salgamos.**
>
> **Ellos llegaron antes de que nosotros saliéramos.**

Present perfect subjunctive

You use the present perfect subjunctive in a clause that requires the subjunctive when the action would be prior to the action of the main verb.

> **Espero que hayan llegado.**
>
> **Dudamos que él lo haya hecho.**
>
> **Estamos contentos que todo haya salido bien.**

Pluperfect subjunctive

You use the pluperfect subjunctive in any clause introduced by a verb in the past when the action in the dependent clause would have taken place prior to the action in the main clause.

> **Yo dudaba mucho que él lo hubiera sabido.**
>
> **Estaría contento que hubieras tenido más éxito.**
>
> **Habríamos salido aunque hubiera llovido.**

Si clauses

Si clauses are referred to as contrary-to-fact clauses. The most common sequence of tenses for **si** clauses follows:

MAIN CLAUSE	SI CLAUSE
future	present indicative
conditional	imperfect subjunctive
conditional perfect	pluperfect subjunctive

Yo iré si tengo bastante dinero.

Yo iría si tuviera bastante dinero.

Yo habría ido si hubiera tenido bastante dinero.

Passive voice with se

The pronoun **se** is used to express something being done without saying by whom.

Se habla español en México. {
Spanish is spoken in Mexico.
One speaks Spanish in Mexico.
They speak Spanish in Mexico.

¿A qué hora se abre el restaurante?
Se sirven comidas mexicanas y peruanas.

Passive voice with ser

The true passive voice is used less frequently in Spanish than in English.

La ciudad fue invadida por el ejército.
El edificio fue destruido por un incendio.

Active voice is more commonly used than passive voice.

El ejército invadió la ciudad.
El incendio destruyó el edificio.

Imperative (commands)

You use the subjunctive form of the verb for all formal (**usted, ustedes**) commands and the negative familiar (**tú**) command.

Hable Ud.	**No hable Ud.**	**Hablen Uds.**	**No hablen Uds.**	**No hables.**
Coma Ud.	**No coma Ud.**	**Coman Uds.**	**No coman Uds.**	**No comas.**

You use the **usted** form of the present indicative for the familiar (**tú**) command.

Habla.
Come.

Note that you add the object pronouns to affirmative commands. The pronouns come before the negative command.

AFFIRMATIVE	NEGATIVE
Prepárelo.	**No lo prepare.**
Escríbanlo Uds.	**No lo escriban Uds.**
Háblame.	**No me hables.**

There are no irregular formal commands. You will find any irregular familiar (**tú**) commands in the verb charts that follow this Grammar Review.

Por and para

The prepositions **por** and **para** have very specific uses.

Para is used to represent a destination, purpose, reason, or readiness. It can also express a comparison or a deadline.

> **Salen para Madrid.**
> **El paquete es para María.**
> **Estudia para ingeniero.**
> **Están para salir.**
> **Para cubano, habla bien el inglés.**
> **Tiene que terminar para el día ocho.**

Por, on the other hand, is more circuitous. It expresses *through, by, on behalf of, instead of,* and *in exchange for.* It expresses the reason for an errand, a period of time or indefinite time, means, manner, as well as an opinion or estimation. **Por** is also used to indicate a measure or number.

> **Viajaron por España.**
> **Entró por la ventana.**
> **Compré el regalo por María.**
> **Voy por agua.**
> **Estuvieron por dos semanas.**
> **Estarán por Navidad.**
> **Lo toman por cubano, pero no lo es.**
> **Estamos por** *(in the mood)* **salir.**
> **Me dio pesos por dólares.**
> **Se venden por kilos.**
> **Ya tengo mucho por hacer.**

Verb Charts

REGULAR VERBS		
INFINITIVO	**hablar** *to speak*	**comer** *to eat*	**vivir** *to live*
PARTICIPIO PRESENTE	hablando	comiendo	viviendo
PARTICIPIO PASADO	hablado	comido	vivido

Simple Tenses		
INDICATIVO			
PRESENTE	hablo hablas habla hablamos *habláis* hablan	como comes come comemos *coméis* comen	vivo vives vive vivimos *vivís* viven
IMPERFECTO	hablaba hablabas hablaba hablábamos *hablabais* hablaban	comía comías comía comíamos *comíais* comían	vivía vivías vivía vivíamos *vivíais* vivían
PRETÉRITO	hablé hablaste habló hablamos *hablasteis* hablaron	comí comiste comió comimos *comisteis* comieron	viví viviste vivió vivimos *vivisteis* vivieron
FUTURO	hablaré hablarás hablará hablaremos *hablaréis* hablarán	comeré comerás comerá comeremos *comeréis* comerán	viviré vivirás vivirá viviremos *viviréis* vivirán
CONDICIONAL	hablaría hablarías hablaría hablaríamos *hablaríais* hablarían	comería comerías comería comeríamos *comeríais* comerían	viviría vivirías viviría viviríamos *viviríais* vivirían

Verb Charts

REGULAR VERBS *(continued)*

SUBJUNTIVO	hablar *to speak*	comer *to eat*	vivir *to live*
PRESENTE	hable hables hable hablemos *habléis* hablen	coma comas coma comamos *comáis* coman	viva vivas viva vivamos *viváis* vivan
IMPERFECTO	hablara hablaras hablara habláramos *hablarais* hablaran	comiera comieras comiera comiéramos *comierais* comieran	viviera vivieras viviera viviéramos *vivierais* vivieran

Compound Tenses

INDICATIVO			
PRESENTE PERFECTO	he hablado has hablado ha hablado hemos hablado *habéis hablado* han hablado	he comido has comido ha comido hemos comido *habéis comido* han comido	he vivido has vivido ha vivido hemos vivido *habéis vivido* han vivido
PLUSCUAM- PERFECTO	había hablado habías hablado había hablado habíamos hablado *habíais hablado* habían hablado	había comido habías comido había comido habíamos comido *habíais comido* habían comido	había vivido habías vivido había vivido habíamos vivido *habíais vivido* habían vivido
FUTURO PERFECTO	habré hablado habrás hablado habrá hablado habremos hablado *habréis hablado* habrán hablado	habré comido habrás comido habrá comido habremos comido *habréis comido* habrán comido	habré vivido habrás vivido habrá vivido habremos vivido *habréis vivido* habrán vivido
CONDICIONAL PERFECTO	habría hablado habrías hablado habría hablado habríamos hablado *habríais hablado* habrían hablado	habría comido habrías comido habría comido habríamos comido *habríais comido* habrían comido	habría vivido habrías vivido habría vivido habríamos vivido *habríais vivido* habrían vivido

REGULAR VERBS *(continued)*

SUBJUNTIVO

PRESENTE PERFECTO		
haya hablado	haya comido	haya vivido
hayas hablado	hayas comido	hayas vivido
haya hablado	haya comido	haya vivido
hayamos hablado	hayamos comido	hayamos vivido
hayáis hablado	*hayáis comido*	*hayáis vivido*
hayan hablado	hayan comido	hayan vivido

PLUSCUAM-PERFECTO		
hubiera hablado	hubiera comido	hubiera vivido
hubieras hablado	hubieras comido	hubieras vivido
hubiera hablado	hubiera comido	hubiera vivido
hubiéramos hablado	hubiéramos comido	hubiéramos vivido
hubierais hablado	*hubierais comido*	*hubierais vivido*
hubieran hablado	hubieran comido	hubieran vivido

Stem-changing verbs (-ar and -er verbs)

INFINITIVO	empezar (e→ie) *to begin*	perder (e→ie) *to lose*	recordar (o→ue) *to remember*	volver (o→ue) *to return*
INDICATIVO				
PRESENTE	empiezo	pierdo	recuerdo	vuelvo
	empiezas	pierdes	recuerdas	vuelves
	empieza	pierde	recuerda	vuelve
	empezamos	perdemos	recordamos	volvemos
	empezáis	*perdéis*	*recordáis*	*volvéis*
	empiezan	pierden	recuerdan	vuelven
SUBJUNTIVO				
PRESENTE	empiece	pierda	recuerde	vuelva
	empieces	pierdas	recuerdes	vuelvas
	empiece	pierda	recuerde	vuelva
	empecemos	perdamos	recordemos	volvamos
	empecéis	*perdáis*	*recordéis*	*volváis*
	empiecen	pierdan	recuerden	vuelvan

e→ie
Other verbs conjugated like **empezar** and **perder** are: **cerrar, comenzar, sentar(se), despertar(se), recomendar, pensar, defender, entender, querer, encender.**

o→ue
Other verbs conjugated like **recordar** and **volver** are: **acordar, almorzar, contar, costar, probar, encontrar, mostrar, soñar, acostar(se), devolver, mover, poder, jugar (u→ue).**

Stem-changing verbs (-ir verbs)

INFINITIVO	preferir (e→ie, i) *to prefer*	dormir (o→ue, u) *to sleep*	pedir (e→i, i) *to ask for*
PARTICIPIO PRESENTE	prefiriendo	durmiendo	pidiendo
INDICATIVO			
PRESENTE	prefiero prefieres prefiere preferimos *preferís* prefieren	duermo duermes duerme dormimos *dormís* duermen	pido pides pide pedimos *pedís* piden
PRETÉRITO	preferí preferiste prefirió preferimos *preferisteis* prefirieron	dormí dormiste durmió dormimos *dormisteis* durmieron	pedí pediste pidió pedimos *pedisteis* pidieron
SUBJUNTIVO			
PRESENTE	prefiera prefieras prefiera prefiramos *prefiráis* prefieran	duerma duermas duerma durmamos *durmáis* duerman	pida pidas pida pidamos *pidáis* pidan

e→ie, i

Other verbs conjugated like **preferir** are: **sentir(se), sugerir, mentir, divertir(se), advertir, invertir.**

o→ue

Another verb conjugated like **dormir** is **morir.**

e→i, i

Other verbs conjugated like **pedir** are: **repetir, servir, seguir, vestirse, freír, reír, sonreír, despedir(se).**

IRREGULAR VERBS

	abrir *to open*					
PARTICIPIO PASADO	abierto					

	andar *to walk*					
PRETÉRITO	anduve	anduviste	anduvo	anduvimos	*anduvisteis*	anduvieron

	conocer *to know, to be familiar with*					
PRESENTE	conozco	conoces	conoce	conocemos	*conocéis*	conocen

	cubrir *to cover*					
PARTICIPIO PASADO	cubierto					

	dar *to give*					
PRESENTE	doy	das	da	damos	*dais*	dan
PRETÉRITO	di	diste	dio	dimos	*disteis*	dieron
SUBJUNTIVO: PRESENTE	dé	des	dé	demos	*deis*	den

	decir *to say*					
PARTICIPIO PRESENTE	diciendo					
PARTICIPIO PASADO	dicho					
PRESENTE	digo	dices	dice	decimos	*decís*	dicen
PRETÉRITO	dije	dijiste	dijo	dijimos	*dijisteis*	dijeron
FUTURO	diré	dirás	dirá	diremos	*diréis*	dirán
CONDICIONAL	diría	dirías	diría	diríamos	*diríais*	dirían
IMPERATIVO FAMILIAR	di					

	devolver *to return (bring back)*					
PARTICIPIO PASADO	devuelto					

	escribir *to write*					
PARTICIPIO PASADO	escrito					

	estar *to be*					
PRESENTE	estoy	estás	está	estamos	*estáis*	están
PRETÉRITO	estuve	estuviste	estuvo	estuvimos	*estuvisteis*	estuvieron
SUBJUNTIVO: PRESENTE	esté	estés	esté	estemos	*estéis*	estén

	freír *to fry*					
PARTICIPIO PASADO	frito					

IRREGULAR VERBS *(continued)*

haber *to have (in compound tenses)*

PRESENTE	he	has	ha	hemos	*habéis*	han
PRETÉRITO	hube	hubiste	hubo	hubimos	*hubisteis*	hubieron
IMPERFECTO	había	habías	había	habíamos	*habíais*	habían
FUTURO	habré	habrás	habrá	habremos	*habréis*	habrán
CONDICIONAL	habría	habrías	habría	habríamos	*habríais*	habrían
SUBJUNTIVO: PRESENTE	haya	hayas	haya	hayamos	*hayáis*	hayan

hacer *to do, to make*

PARTICIPIO PASADO	hecho					
PRESENTE	hago	haces	hace	hacemos	*hacéis*	hacen
PRETÉRITO	hice	hiciste	hizo	hicimos	*hicisteis*	hicieron
FUTURO	haré	harás	hará	haremos	*haréis*	harán
CONDICIONAL	haría	harías	haría	haríamos	*haríais*	harían
IMPERATIVO FAMILIAR	haz					

ir *to go*

PARTICIPIO PRESENTE	yendo					
PRESENTE	voy	vas	va	vamos	*vais*	van
PRETÉRITO	fui	fuiste	fue	fuimos	*fuisteis*	fueron
IMPERFECTO	iba	ibas	iba	íbamos	*ibais*	iban
SUBJUNTIVO: PRESENTE	vaya	vayas	vaya	vayamos	*vayáis*	vayan
IMPERATIVO FAMILIAR	ve					

morir *to die*

PARTICIPIO PASADO	muerto

oír *to hear*

PRESENTE	oigo	oyes	oye	oímos	*oís*	oyen

poder *to be able to*

PARTICIPIO PRESENTE	pudiendo					
PRETÉRITO	pude	pudiste	pudo	pudimos	*pudisteis*	pudieron
FUTURO	podré	podrás	podrá	podremos	*podréis*	podrán
CONDICIONAL	podría	podrías	podría	podríamos	*podríais*	podrían

poner *to put*

PARTICIPIO PASADO	puesto					
PRESENTE	pongo	pones	pone	ponemos	*ponéis*	ponen
PRETÉRITO	puse	pusiste	puso	pusimos	*pusisteis*	pusieron
FUTURO	pondré	pondrás	pondrá	pondremos	*pondréis*	pondrán

IRREGULAR VERBS (continued)

querer *to want*

PRETÉRITO	quise	quisiste	quiso	quisimos	*quisisteis*	quisieron
FUTURO	querré	querrás	querrá	querremos	*querréis*	querrán
CONDICIONAL	querría	querrías	querría	querríamos	*querríais*	querrían

romper *to break*

PARTICIPIO PASADO	roto

saber *to know (how)*

PRESENTE	sé	sabes	sabe	sabemos	*sabéis*	saben
PRETÉRITO	supe	supiste	supo	supimos	*supisteis*	supieron
FUTURO	sabré	sabrás	sabrá	sabremos	*sabréis*	sabrán
CONDICIONAL	sabría	sabrías	sabría	sabríamos	*sabríais*	sabrían
SUBJUNTIVO: PRESENTE	sepa	sepas	sepa	sepamos	*sepáis*	sepan

ser *to be*

PRESENTE	soy	eres	es	somos	*sois*	son
PRETÉRITO	fui	fuiste	fue	fuimos	*fuisteis*	fueron
IMPERFECTO	era	eras	era	éramos	*erais*	eran
SUBJUNTIVO: PRESENTE	sea	seas	sea	seamos	*seáis*	sean
IMPERATIVO FAMILIAR	sé					

tener *to have*

PRESENTE	tengo	tienes	tiene	tenemos	*tenéis*	tienen
PRETÉRITO	tuve	tuviste	tuvo	tuvimos	*tuvisteis*	tuvieron
FUTURO	tendré	tendrás	tendrá	tendremos	*tendréis*	tendrán
CONDICIONAL	tendría	tendrías	tendría	tendríamos	*tendríais*	tendrían
IMPERATIVO FAMILIAR	ten					

traer *to bring*

PRESENTE	traigo	traes	trae	traemos	*traéis*	traen
PRETÉRITO	traje	trajiste	trajo	trajimos	*trajisteis*	trajeron

venir *to come*

PARTICIPIO PRESENTE	viniendo					
PRETÉRITO	vine	viniste	vino	vinimos	*vinisteis*	vinieron
FUTURO	vendré	vendrás	vendrá	vendremos	*vendréis*	vendrán
CONDICIONAL	vendría	vendrías	vendría	vendríamos	*vendríais*	vendrían
IMPERATIVO FAMILIAR	ven					

ver *to see*

PARTICIPIO PASADO	visto					
PRESENTE	veo	ves	ve	vemos	*veis*	ven
PRETÉRITO	vi	viste	vio	vimos	*visteis*	vieron
IMPERFECTO	veía	veías	veía	veíamos	*veíais*	veían

volver *to return*

PARTICIPIO PASADO	vuelto

Verb Charts

Spanish-English Dictionary

The Spanish-English Dictionary contains all productive and receptive vocabulary from **¡Así se dice!** Levels 1, 2, and 3. The locator numbers following each productive entry indicate the chapter and vocabulary section in which the word is introduced (e.g., 3.2 means Chapter 3, Vocabulary 2). Level 1 chapter/section numbers are light print (3.2); Level 2 numbers are *italic (3.2)*; Level 3 chapter/section numbers are **bold (3.2)**. LP refers to the Level 1 **Lecciones preliminares.** If no locator follows an entry, the word or expression is receptive.

a at; to
  a eso de las tres (cuatro, diez, etc.) at around three (four, ten, etc.) o'clock
  a fines de at the end of
  a la una (a las dos, a las tres…) at one o'clock (two o'clock, three o'clock), LP
  a lo lejos in the distance
  a lo menos at least
  a menos que unless
  a menudo often
  a pesar de in spite of
  a pie on foot, 3.2
  ¡A propósito! By the way!, 8.2
  ¿a qué hora? at what time?, LP
  a solas alone
  a tiempo on time, 10.2; *1.2*
  a veces at times, sometimes, 6.1; *1.2*
  a ver let's see
abajo down; below
  de abajo below
  (ir) para abajo (to go) down
abandonar el cuarto to check out *(hotel)*, 7
el **abismo** abyss
el/la **abogado(a)** lawyer, **10**
la **abolladura** dent, **6.2**
el **abono** fertilizer
  abordar to board, 10.2; *1.2*
  abordo aboard, on board, 10.2; *1.2*
  abotonarse to button
  abrazar(se) to hug (each other), **5**
el **abrazo** hug, **5**
  abreviado(a) abbreviated, shortened
  abrigado(a) wrapped up

el **abrigo** coat
  abril April, LP
  abrir to open, 4.2
  abrochado(a) fastened, 10.2; *1.2*
el/la **abuelo(a)** grandfather (grandmother) 2.1
los **abuelos** grandparents, 2.1
  abundoso(a) abundant
  aburrido(a) boring, 1.2
  aburrir to bore
  acá here, 11.2; *2.2*
  acabar de to have just (done something), 4.2
la **academia** school
  acaso perhaps, **3 (Lit.)**
  por si acaso just in case
  acceder to access
el **accidente** accident, *11.2;* **2.2**
el **aceite** oil, *4*
  el aceite de oliva olive oil, *9*
la **aceituna** olive, 4.2
el **acento** accent
la **aceptación** acceptance, success
  aceptar to accept, **6.2**
la **acera** sidewalk, *8.1*
  acercarse (a) to approach
  acomodado(a) wealthy, well-off, **8**
  acomodar to set *(bone)*, 11.2; *2.2*
  aconsejar to advise
  acontecer to happen
  acordarse (ue) to remember
  ¿Te acuerdas? Do you remember?
  acostarse (ue) to go to bed, 11.1; *2.1*
  acostumbrarse to get used to
el **acotamiento** shoulder *(road),* 9.1
la **actividad** activity
  actual present-day, current
  actuar to act, to take action
la **acuarela** watercolor, **7.1**
  acudir to go to

  acuerdo: de acuerdo okay, agreed; **estar de acuerdo con** to agree with, to be in agreement
  adelantar(se) to pass *(car),* 9.1
  adelante ahead
  ir hacia adelante to move forward, ahead
  además furthermore, what's more; besides
  además de in addition to, besides
  ¡Adiós! Good-bye!, LP
  adivinar to guess
  adjunto: el documento adjunto attached file, *6.1*
  admitir to admit
  ¿adónde? (to) where?, 3.2
la **aduana** customs, **6.1**
la **advertencia** warning
  advertir (ie, i) to warn
  aérea: la línea aérea airline, 10.1; *1.1*
  aeróbico(a) aerobic
el **aerodeslizador** hovercraft, hydrofoil
el **aeropuerto** airport, 10.1; *1.1;* **6.1**
el **afán** strong wish, desire, **3 (Lit.)**
  afeitarse to shave
  afición: tener (mucha) afición a to be (very) fond of
  aficionado(a): ser aficionado(a) a to like, to be a fan of
el/la **aficionado(a)** fan, 5.1
el/la **afiliado(a)** member, affiliate
  afine: la palabra afine cognate
  afirmar to dig in
  afortunados: los menos afortunados the less fortunate, the needy
las **afueras** suburbs, 2.2; outskirts, **6.2**
  agarrar velocidad to pick up speed

la **agencia** agency
   la agencia de alquiler car rental agency, **6.2**

el/la **agente** agent, 10.1; *1.1*; **6.2**

la **aglomeración** big city

agosto August, LP

agradable pleasant, friendly, agreeable, 6.1

agrario(a) agrarian

agresivo(a) aggressive

agrícola agricultural

el **agua** *(f.)* water, 4.1
   el agua corriente running water
   el agua mineral (con gas) (sparkling) mineral water, 4.2

el **aguacate** avocado, 10; **1**

el **águila** *(f.)* eagle

el **aguinaldo** Christmas gift, 5.2

el/la **ahijado(a)** godchild

ahora now

el **aire** air
   al aire libre open-air, outdoor, 7.2

el **aire acondicionado** air conditioning, 7

aislado(a) isolated

el **ají** chili pepper

el **ajo** garlic, *10*; **1**

al to the, on the, in the
   al aire libre open-air, outdoor, 7.2
   al borde mismo de right on the edge of
   al contrario on the contrary
   al lado de beside, next to, 2.2

la **alacena** cupboard

el **albañil** mason, 10

la **alberca** swimming pool, 7.1

el **albergue juvenil** youth hostel, 7

la **albóndiga** meatball, 4.2

el **álbum** album

la **alcachofa** artichoke, **9**
   las alcachofas salteadas sautéed artichokes

el/la **alcalde(sa)** mayor, **3.1**

alcanzar to reach

la **alcoba** bedroom

la **aldea** small village

alegrarse to rejoice, **3.1**

alegre happy, 6.1; **3.1**

la **alegría** happiness, joy, **3.1**

alejarse de to go away from

alemán(ana) German

los **alemanes** Germans

la **alfombrilla** mouse pad, *6.1*

el **álgebra** *(f.)* algebra

algo something; anything, 8.2

¿Algo más? Anything else?, 9.2

alguien someone, somebody, 8.2

algunos(as) some

el **alimento** food

las **alitas** wings, *10*; **1**

allá over there, 9.1

allí there

el **alma** *(f.)* soul

las **almejas** clams, *4*

la **almohada** pillow, *7*

el **almuerzo** lunch, 4.1
   tomar el almuerzo to have lunch, 4.1

¡Aló! Hello! *(on the phone)*

alpino: el esquí alpino downhill skiing

alquilar to rent, 7.1; *3.2*; **6.2**

alrededor de around, 2.2

los **alrededores** outskirts, surroundings

altivo(a) arrogant

alto(a) tall, 1.1; high, 3.1; upper
   la clase alta upper class
   la nota alta high grade, 3.1

la **altura** altitude

el/la **alumno(a)** student, 1.2

alzarse to rise **8**

amanecer to dawn, *10* (Lit.)

amargo(a) bitter

amarillo(a) yellow, 5.1

la **ambición** ambition

ambicioso(a) hardworking, 1.2

el **ambiente** atmosphere, environment, **7.2**

la **ambulancia** ambulance, *11.2*; **2.2**

la **América del Sur** South America

americano(a) American

el/la **amigo(a)** friend, 1.1

la **amistad** friendship

el **amo(a)** owner, **8**

el **amor** love, **5**

amurallado(a) walled

anaranjado(a) orange *(color)*, 5.1

ancho(a) wide, broad, *8.1*

el **ancla** anchor *(television)*, **8**

andar to go, to walk; to ride, *3.2*
   andar a caballo to ride a horse, *3.2*
   andar en bicicleta to ride a bike, *11.1*; **2.1**

el **andén** *(railway)* platform, *3.1*

andino(a) Andean, of the Andes

angosto(a) narrow, *8.1*

la **angustia** distress, anguish

el **anillo de boda** wedding ring, *3.1*

animado(a) lively

el **animal** animal

animar to cheer (somebody, something) on; to liven up

ánimo: estado de ánimo frame of mind

anoche last night, 7.1

anónimo(a) anonymous

el **anorak** anorak, ski jacket, 7.2

anotar to note

ansioso(a) anxious, worried

los **anteojos de sol** sunglasses, 7.1

el/la **antepasado(a)** ancestor

el **antepecho** parapet

anterior previous, *6.1*

antes de before, 3.2

antes de que before (doing something)

los **antibióticos** antibiotics

antiguo(a) ancient, old, *8.1*; former
   el casco (barrio) antiguo the old city, *8.1*

antipático(a) unpleasant, not nice 1.1

los **antojitos** snacks, nibbles, 4.2

anular to cancel

anunciar to announce

el **anuncio** announcement, **10**
   el anuncio clasificado classified ad, **10**

añadir to add, *10*; **1**

el **año** year, LP
   el Año Nuevo New Year
   el año pasado last year, 7.1
   ¿Cuántos años tiene? How old is he (she)?, 2.1
   cumplir... años to be (turn) . . . years old; **3.2**

apagado(a) put out, extinguished

apagar to turn off, 6.1

el **aparato** device

aparcar to park, *8.1*

aparentado(a) related

la **apariencia** appearance, looks
   ¿Qué apariencia tiene? What does he (she) look like?

el **apartamento** apartment, 2.2
   la casa de apartamentos apartment house

el **apartamiento** apartment, 2.2

aparte apart, on the side

apenas scarcely, hardly

apetecer to feel like, to crave

apetito: ¡Buen apetito! Bon appétit! Enjoy your meal!

Spanish-English Dictionary

aplaudir to applaud, to clap, 5.1

el **aplauso** applause, 5.1

recibir aplausos to be applauded, 5.1

la **aplicación de empleo** job application, **10**

aplicar to apply

apoderarse de to take by force, **4** (*Lit.*)

el **apodo** nickname, **5** (*Lit.*)

apoyar to lean, to support

apreciado(a) appreciated, liked

aprender to learn, 4.2

apresurado(a) hurried, **4**

apresurarse to be in a hurry, **10** (*Lit.*)

apretar to clench

el **apretón de manos** handshake

apropiado(a) appropriate

aproximadamente approximately

aquel(la) that, 9.1

aquí here, 9.1

Aquí lo (las, etc.) tienes. Here it (they) is (are).

árabe Arabic

aragonés(esa) from Aragon (*Spain*)

el **árbol** tree, 2.2

el **árbol de Navidad** Christmas tree, 5.2

el **arcén** shoulder (*road*), 9.1

el **archivo** file, 6.1

el **área** (*f.*) area

la **arena** sand, 7.1

argentino(a) Argentine

el **argumento** plot, 7.2

árido(a) dry, arid

la **aritmética** arithmetic

el **arma** (*f.*) weapon

armar to put up (*tent*), 11.2; 2.2

el **armario** closet, 7

la **arqueología** archaeology

el/la **arquitecto(a)** architect, **10**

arrendamiento: la agencia de arrendamiento car rental agency

arrendar (ie) to rent, **6.2**

la **arroba** the @ sign, 6.1

el **arroyo** brook

el **arroz** rice, 4.1

arrugado(a) wrinkled, **4**

el **arte** art, 1.2; **7.1**

arterial: la tensión arterial blood pressure, 6.2

la **artesanía** crafts, 9.2

el **artículo** article, **8**

el/la **artista** artist, **7.1**

asar to grill, to roast, 10; **1**

la **ascendencia** heritage, background

el **ascensor** elevator, 7

asegurar to assure

asegurarse to make sure

así thus, so, in this way

el **asiento** seat, 10.1; *1.1*; **6.1**

el **número del asiento** seat number, 10.1; *1.1*

asignar to assign, 6.2

la **asistencia médica** medical care

el/la **asistente(a) ejecutivo(a)** executive assistant, **10**

el/la **asistente(a) de vuelo** flight attendant, 10.2; *1.2*

asistir a to attend, 8.1

el **asno** donkey

el **aspa** (*f.*) sail (*windmill*)

el/la **aspirante** (job) candidate, **10**

astuto(a) astute, smart

el **asunto** business, affair

atacar to attack

atado(a) tied

el **ataúd** coffin, 3.2

la **atención** attention

¡Atención! Careful!

prestar atención to pay attention, 3.1

el **aterrizaje** landing, 10.2; *1.2*

aterrizar to land, 10.2; *1.2*

el/la **atleta** athlete

las **atracciones** rides (*amusement park*), 8.1

el **parque de atracciones** amusement park, 8.1

atraer to attract

atrapar to catch, 5.2

atrás: hacia atrás backwards

el **atributo** attribute, positive feature

el **atún** tuna, 9.2

aumentar to grow, to increase, to enlarge

aun even

aún still

aunque although, even though

el **auricular** (phone) receiver, *6.2*

ausente absent

el/la **ausente** absent, missing person

auténtico(a) authentic, real

el **autobús** bus, 8.1; *8.1*

perder el autobús to miss the bus, 8.1

automático(a) automatic, 10.1; *1.1*

el **distribuidor automático** boarding pass kiosk, 10.1; *1.1*; automatic dispenser, *3.1*

la **autopista** highway, 9.1

el/la **autor(a)** author

el **autoservicio** self-service (*restaurant, gas station*)

la **autovía** highway, 9.1

avanzado(a) difficult, 7.2; advanced

avaro(a) stingy

la **avenida** avenue, 8.1

la **aventura** adventure

la **avería** breakdown

averiado(a) broken-down

el **avión** airplane, 10.1; *1.1*

la **avioneta** small airplane

avisar to advise, **6** (*Lit.*)

avisar de to notify, to announce

ayer yesterday, 7.1

ayer por la tarde yesterday afternoon, 7.1

la **ayuda** help, assistance

ayudar to help, 10.1; *1.1*

el **ayuntamiento** city hall, **3.1**

el **azafrán** saffron

el **azúcar** sugar

azul blue, 2.1

el **azulejo** glazed tile, floor tile

B

el **bache** pothole

el **bacón** bacon, 4.1; **7**

el/la **bailador(a)** dancer

bailar to dance, 5.2

bajar to go down, 7.2; to download, 6.2

bajar(se) to get off (*train*), 3.2

la **bajeza** baseness

bajo(a) short, 1.1; low, 3.1; poor, lower-class

la nota baja low grade, 3.1

el **balcón** balcony

el **balneario** seaside resort, beach resort, 7.1

el **balón** ball, 5.1

el **baloncesto** basketball, 5.2

el **banco** bank, **4**

la **banda** band, 8.1; *5.2;* lane (*highway*)

la **banda municipal** municipal band, *5.2*

la **bandeja de entradas** inbox (*e-mail*), *6.1*

la **bandeja de enviados** sent mailbox (*e-mail*), *6.1*

la **bandera** flag

el **banquete** banquet, **3.1**

el **bañador** swimsuit, *7.1*

bañarse to take a bath, to bathe oneself

la **bañera** bathtub, *7*

el **baño** bath; bathroom

el **cuarto de baño** bathroom, *2.2; 7*

el **bar (bas/bat) mitzvah** bar (bas/bat) mitzvah

barato(a) inexpensive, cheap, *9.1*

Todo te sale más barato. It's all a lot cheaper (less expensive)., *9.1*

la **barba** beard

la **barbacoa** barbecue

barbaridad: ¡Qué barbaridad! That's awful!

¡Bárbaro! Great!, Awesome!, *5.2*

el **barbero** barber

el **barco** boat

el **barquito** small boat, *7.1*

la **barra** bar (*soap*), *11.2; 2.2;* counter, bar (*restaurant*)

la **barra de jabón** bar of soap, *11.2; 2.2*

la **barra de herramientas** toolbar, *6.1*

el **barrio** neighborhood, area, quarter, district, *8.1*

basado(a) en based on

base: a base de composed of

la **base** base, *5.2*

el **básquetbol** basketball, *5.2*

la **cancha de básquetbol** basketball court, *5.2*

¡Basta! That's enough!

bastante rather, quite, *1.2;* enough

el **bastón** ski pole, *7.2*

la **batalla** battle, **8**

el **bate** bat, *5.2*

el/la **bateador(a)** batter, *5.2*

batear to hit, to bat, *5.2*

batear un jonrón to hit a home run, *5.2*

el **batido** shake, smoothie, *4.2*

el **huevo batido** scrambled egg, *9*

el **baúl** trunk (*car*), *10.1; 1.1*

bautizar to baptize, *3.2*

el **bautizo** baptism, *3.2*

el **bebé** baby

beber to drink, *4.1*

la **bebida** beverage, drink, *4.1*

el **béisbol** baseball, *5.2*

el/la **beisbolista** baseball player, *5.2*

el **campo de béisbol** baseball field, *5.2*

el/la **jugador(a) de béisbol** baseball player, *5.2*

la **belleza** beauty

bello(a) beautiful

bendecir to bless

la **benzina** gas(oline)

la **berenjena** eggplant, **9**

besar to kiss, **5**

el **besito** little kiss (usually on the cheek), **5**

el **beso** kiss

la **bestia** beast, animal

los **biafranos** people from Biafra

la **biblioteca** library

la **bicicleta** bicycle, *2.2*

andar en bicicleta to ride a bike, *11.1; 2.1*

bien well, fine, LP

bien educado(a) polite, well-mannered, *6.1*

bien hecho(a) well-done (*meat*), *4*

estar bien to be (feel) well, fine, *6.2*

Muy bien. Very well., LP

el **bienestar** well-being

la **bienvenida: dar la bienvenida** to greet, to welcome

bienvenido(a) welcome

el **bife** beef

el **biftec** steak, *4*

el **billete** ticket, *10.1; 1.1;* bill, **4**

el **billete de ida y vuelta** round-trip ticket, *3.1*

el **billete electrónico** e-ticket, *10.1; 1.1*

el **billete sencillo** one-way ticket, *3.1*

la **biología** biology

el/la **biólogo(a)** biologist

el **bizcocho** cake, *5.1; 3.2*

blanco(a) white, *5.1*

la **blancura** whiteness

blando(a) soft

bloquear to block, *5.1*

el **blue jean** jeans, *9.1*

la **blusa** blouse, *3.1*

la **boca** mouth, *6.2*

la **boca del metro** subway entrance, *8.1*

la **bocacalle** intersection, *9.1*

el **bocadillo** sandwich, *4.1*

los **bocaditos** snacks

la **boda** wedding, *3.1*

la **bodega** grocery store

la **boletería** ticket window, *7.2; 3.1*

el **boleto** ticket, *7.2; 3.1*

el **boleto de ida y regreso** round-trip ticket, *3.1*

el **boleto electrónico** e-ticket, *10.1; 1.1*

el **boleto sencillo** one-way ticket, *3.1*

el **bolígrafo** pen, *3.1*

el **bolívar** bolivar (*currency of Venezuela*)

la **bolsa de dormir** sleeping bag, *11.2; 2.2*

bolsillo: el libro de bolsillo paperback, *3.1; 8*

la **bombilla** (*drinking*) container

los **bombones** candy

bonito(a) pretty, *1.1*

el **borde** side (*of a street, sidewalk*); edge

al borde mismo de right on the edge of

borrador: el botón borrador delete key, *6.1*

borrar to delete, *6.1*

el **bosque** woods

la **bota** boot, *7.2*

botar to throw out

botar la casa por la ventana to splurge

el **bote** can, *9.2*

la **botella** bottle, *9.2*

el **botón** button, key (*computer*), *6.1*

el **botón borrador** delete key, *6.1*

el **botón regresar (retroceder)** back button, *6.1*

Brasil Brazil

brasileño(a) Brazilian

bravo(a) rough, stormy

el **brazo** arm, *11.1; 2.1*

brillar to shine

bronce: de bronce bronze (*adj.*), *8.2; 7.1*

bronceador(a): la loción bronceadora suntan lotion, *7.1*

bucear to go snorkeling, *7.1;* to scuba dive

el **buceo** snorkeling, *7.1;* scuba diving

buen good, LP

estar de buen humor to be in a good mood, *6.1*

Hace buen tiempo. The weather is nice., LP

tener un buen sentido de humor to have a good sense of humor, *6.1*

Spanish-English Dictionary

bueno(a) good, 1.1; Hello!
(on the phone)

Buenas noches. Good
evening., LP

Buenas tardes. Good
afternoon., LP

Buenos días. Good
morning., Hello., LP

sacar notas buenas to get
good grades, 3.1

el **bufé** buffet, **3.1**

el **bufete del abogado** lawyer's
office, **10**

la **bufetería** dining car, *3.2*

el **burrito** burrito

el **bus** bus

el bus escolar school bus,
3.2

perder el autobús to miss
the bus, *8.1*

tomar el autobús to take
the bus

busca: en busca de seeking,
in search of

buscar to look for, to seek,
3.2

el **buzo** sweat suit, warm-ups,
11.1; **2.1**

el **buzón** mailbox, **4**

el **caballero** gentleman

el caballero andante knight
errant

el **caballete** easel, **7.1**

el **caballo** horse, *3.2*

andar a caballo to ride a
horse, *3.2*

montar a caballo to go
horseback riding, *8.2*

caber to fit

la **cabeza** head, *6.2;* **2.1**

tener dolor de cabeza to
have a headache, *6.2*

el **cabezal** headrest

la **cabina de mando** cockpit
(airplane)

la **cabina de peaje** tollbooth, *9.1*

el **cacahuate** peanut, *8.1*

el **cacahuete** peanut

la **cacerola** saucepan, *10;* **1**

el **cacique** leader, chief

cada each, every, *2.2*

caer to fall

caerse to fall, *11.2;* **2.2**

el **café** café, *4.2;* coffee, *4.1; 7*

la **cafetería** cafeteria, *4.1*

el coche cafetería dining
car, *3.2*

la **caída** drop

la llamada caída dropped
call *(cell phone)*, *6.2*

la **caja** cash register, *3.2;* box

el/la **cajero(a)** cashier, teller

el **cajero automático** ATM, **4**

el **cajón** box

la **calavera** skull, *5.1;* sweet cake
made for the Day of the
Dead

los **calcetines** socks, *5.1*

la **calculadora** calculator, *3.1*

el **caldo** broth

caliente hot, *4.1*

el chocolate caliente hot
chocolate, *4.1*

la **calle** street, *8.1*

la calle de sentido único
one-way street, *9.1*

calmo(a) calm, *6.1*

el **calor** heat

Hace calor. It's hot., LP

tener calor to be hot, *11.1;*
2.1

calzar to wear, to take *(shoe
size)*, *9.1*

¿Qué número calzas?
What size shoe do you
wear (take)?, *9.1*

la **cama** bed, *2.2; 7*

guardar cama to stay in
bed *(illness)*, *6.2*

hacer la cama to make the
bed, *7*

quedarse en la cama to
stay in bed, *11.1;* **2.1**

la **cámara digital** digital
camera, *7.1; 6.2*

el/la **camarero(a)** server, waiter
(waitress), *4; (hotel)*
housekeeper, *7*

los **camarones** shrimp, *4.2*

cambiar to change, *3.2;* **6.2**

cambio: en cambio on the
other hand

el **camello** camel, *5.2*

la **camilla** stretcher, *11.2;* **2.2**

caminar to walk, *5.1*

caminata: dar una caminata
to take a hike, *11.2; 2.2*

el **camino** road

ponerse en camino to set
off

tomar el camino to set out
for

el **camión** bus *(Mexico)*, *8.1;*
truck, *9.2*

la **camisa** shirt, *3.1*

**la camisa de manga corta
(larga)** short- (long-)
sleeved shirt, *9.1*

la **camiseta** T-shirt, *5.1*

el **campamento** camp

la **campana** bell tower

la **campanada** peal of the bell

el/la **campeón(ona)** champion

el/la **campesino(a)** farmer,
peasant, *8.2*

el **camping** camping, *11.2; 2.2;*
campsite

ir de camping to go
camping, *11.2; 2.2*

el **campo** field, *5.1; 8.2;* country,
countryside, *8.2*

el campo de béisbol
baseball field, *5.2*

el campo de fútbol soccer
field, *5.1*

la carrera a campo traviesa
cross-country race, *11.1;*
2.1

la casa de campo country
house, *8.2*

el **camposanto** cemetery, *5.1;* **3.2**

canadiense Canadian

el **canal** lane *(highway)*

la **canasta** basket, *5.2*

la **cancha** court, *5.2*

**la cancha de básquetbol
(tenis)** basketball (tennis)
court, *5.2*

la cancha de voleibol
volleyball court, *7.1*

la **candela** candle

el **cangrejo de río** crayfish

cansado(a) tired, *6.1*

el/la **cantante** singer, *8.1*

cantar to sing, *8.1*

la **cantidad** quantity, amount,
number of

la **cantina** cafeteria

el **cañón** canyon, *3.2*

la **capital** capital

el **capítulo** chapter, *7.2*

el **capó** hood *(car)*, *9.2*

la **cara** face, *6.1*

la **característica** feature, trait

¡Caramba! Good heavens!

el **carbón** coal

el/la **candidato(a)** candidate, **10**

el **cardo** thistle

cargado(a) thrown (over one's
shoulders); loaded

el **Caribe** Caribbean

el mar Caribe Caribbean
Sea

el **cariño** affection

cariñoso(a) adorable, affectionate, 2.1

caritativo(a) charitable

la **carne** meat, 4.1; *4;* **9**

    la carne de res beef, *4;* **9**

    la carne picada ground meat, **9**

el **carnet** driver's license, 9.2

el **carnet de identidad** ID card, 10.2; *1.2*

la **carnicería** butcher shop

caro(a) expensive, 9.1

la **carpa** tent, 11.2; *2.2*

    armar (montar) una carpa to put up a tent, 11.2; *2.2*

la **carpeta** folder, 3.2; *6.1*

la **carrera** race, *11.1;* **2.1**; career, **10**

    la carrera a campo traviesa cross-country race, *11.1;* **2.1**

    la carrera de larga distancia long-distance race, *11.1;* **2.1**

    la carrera de relevos relay race, *11.1;* **2.1**

la **carretera** highway, *9.1*

el **carril** lane *(highway),* 9.1

el **carrito** shopping cart, 9.2

el **carro** car, 2.2; *9.2*

    en carro by car

la **carta** letter, 4

la **casa** house, 2.2

    la casa de apartamentos apartment building, 2.2

    la casa de campo country house, 8.2

    en casa at home

    regresar a casa to go home, 3.2

el **casamiento** marriage, **3.1**

casarse to get married, **3.1**

el **casco** helmet, 7.2; *11.1;* **2.1**

el **casco antiguo** the old city, *8.1*

casi almost, practically, 8.2; *4*

    casi crudo rare *(meat),* 4

el **caso** case

    hacer caso to pay attention

castaño(a) brown, chestnut *(eyes, hair),* 2.1

castigar to punish, **5**

el **castillo** castle

la **casucha** shack

catarro: tener catarro to have a cold, 6.2

el/la **cátcher** catcher, 5.2

la **catedral** cathedral

la **categoría** category

catorce fourteen, LP

el **caucho** tire

causa: a causa de because of, on account of

cautivar to captivate, to charm

la **cazuela** saucepan, pot, *10;* **1**

el **CD** CD

la **cebolla** onion, 9.2; *10;* **1**

ceder to cede, to hand over

celebrar to celebrate, *5.2;* **3.2**

el **celular** cell phone, 6.1

el **cementerio** cemetery, *5.1;* **3.2**

la **cena** dinner, 4.1; **3.1**

cenar to have dinner, 4.1

el **cenote** natural water well

el **centro** downtown, 8.1; center

el **centro comercial** shopping center, mall, 9.1

cepillarse to brush, 11.1; *2.1*

    cepillarse los dientes to brush one's teeth, 11.1; *2.1*

el **cepillo** brush, 11.2; *2.2*

    el cepillo de dientes toothbrush, 11.2; *2.2*

las **cerámicas** ceramics, 9.2

cerca (de) near, 3.2

cercanías: el tren de cercanías suburban train, 6.2

cercano(a) near, nearby, close, 6.2

el **cerdo** pig, *8.2;* pork, **9**

    la chuleta de cerdo pork chop, *4;* **1**

el **cereal** cereal, 4.1

la **ceremonia** ceremony, **3.1**

    la ceremonia civil civil ceremony *(wedding),* **3.1**

cero zero, LP

cerrar (ie) to close, 11.2; *2.2*

la **cesta** basket

el **cesto** basket, 5.2

la **chacra** farm, 8.2

el **champán** champagne

el **champú** shampoo, 11.2; *2.2*

¡Chao! Good-bye!, Bye!, LP

la **chaqueta** jacket, 9.1

    la chaqueta de esquí ski jacket, anorak, 7.2

las **chauchas** green beans

chico(a) little

    A chico pajarillo, chico nidillo. Little bird, little nest.

el/la **chico(a)** boy, girl 5

chileno(a) Chilean

la **chimenea** fireplace, 5.2

el **chipotle** smoked jalapeño pepper

el **chiringuito** refreshment stand

el **chisme** rumor, gossip

el **choclo** corn

el **chocolate** chocolate, 4.1

    el chocolate caliente hot chocolate, 4.1

el **chorizo** Spanish sausage

la **choza** shack, 4 (Lit.)

la **chuleta de cerdo** pork chop, *4;* **1**

el **churro** (type of) doughnut

ciego(a) blind

el/la **ciego(a)** blind man (woman)

el **cielo** sky, 5.2

cien(to) one hundred, LP

la **ciencia** science, 1.2

cierto(a) true, certain, 6.1

la **cifra** number, 8

el **cilantro** cilantro, **9**

el **cincel** chisel, 7.1

cinco five, LP

cincuenta fifty, LP

el **cine** movie theater, movies, 8.2

    ir al cine to go to the movies, 8.2

el **cinturón de seguridad** seat belt, 10.2; *1.2*

la **circunstancia** circumstance

el/la **cirujano(a) ortopédico(a)** orthopedic surgeon, 11.2; **2.2**

la **ciudad** city, 2.2; *8.1*

civil: por (el, lo) civil civil, **3.1**

la **civilización** civilization

claro(a) clear

claro que of course

la **clase** class *(school),* 1.2; class *(ticket),* 3.1

    en primera (segunda) clase first-class (second-class), *3.1*

    la sala de clase classroom, 3.1

clavar con una multa to give (someone) a ticket, 9.1

la **clave de área** area code, 6.2

clic: hacer clic to click *(computer),* 6.1

el/la **cliente(a)** customer, 4.2; *7*

el **clima** climate

la **clínica** clinic

cobrar to cash, 4

la **cocción** cooking

cocer (ue) to cook, *10;* **1**

el **coche** car, 9.2; train car, 3.1

    el coche deportivo sports car, 9.2

    el coche comedor (cafetería) dining car, 3.2

el **cochinillo asado** roast suckling pig

la **cocina** kitchen, 2.2; *10;* **1**; stove, *10;* **1**; cooking, cuisine

cocinar to cook, *10;* **1**

el/la **cocinero(a)** cook, *10;* **1**

el **cocodrilo** crocodile

Spanish-English Dictionary

el **código** code

el **codo** elbow, 11.1; *2.1*

cogido(a) picked up, taken

la **col** cabbage, **9**

la **cola** cola (soda), 4.1; line (*of people*), 10.2; *1.2*

    hacer cola to wait in line, 10.2; *1.2*

el **colegio** secondary school, high school

el **colgador** hanger, *7*

colgar (ue) to hang up

la **colina** hill

la **colocación** placement

colocar to place, to put

colombiano(a) Colombian, 1.2

la **colonia** colony, **8**

colonial colonial, **8**

el **colonizador** colonizer, **8**

colonizar to colonize, **8**

el **color** color, 5.1

    de color marrón brown, 5.1

    ¿De qué color es? What color is it?

el **comando** command

combinado: el plato combinado combination plate

el **comedor** dining room, 2.2

    el coche comedor dining car, *3.2*

el/la **comensal** diner, **9**

comenzar (ie) to begin

comer to eat, 4.1

    dar de comer a to feed

el/la **comerciante** businessperson, **10**

los **comestibles** food, *4*

cometer to make (mistake); to commit

cómico(a) funny, comical, 1.1

la **comida** meal, 4.1; food

como like, as; since

¿cómo? how?; what?, 1.1

    ¿Cómo es él? What's he like? What does he look like?, 1.1

    ¿Cómo está...? How is...?

    ¡Cómo no! Sure! Of course!

cómodo(a) comfortable

comoquiera however

el/la **compañero(a)** companion

la **compañía** company, **8**

comparar to compare

el **compartimiento superior** overhead bin, 10.2; *1.2*

compartir to share

completar to complete, to fill in

completo(a) full, *3.2*; **6.1**

componer to compose, to make up

el **comportamiento** behavior, conduct, 6.1; **5**

comportarse to behave, **5**

la **composición** composition

la **compra** purchase, 9.2

el/la **comprador(a)** shopper, customer

comprar to buy, 3.2

compras: ir de compras to shop, to go shopping, 9.1

comprender to understand, 4.2; to include

la **comprensión** understanding

la **computadora** computer, 3.2; *6.1*

comunicarse to communicate with each other

la **comunión** communion

con with

    con frecuencia often

    con retraso (una demora) late, delayed, 10.2; *1.2*

el **concierto** concert, 8.1

el **conde** count

el **condimento** condiment, *10*; **1**

el **condominio** condominium

conducir to drive, 9.2; to lead

la **conducta** conduct, behavior, 6.1

    tener buena conducta to be well-behaved, 6.1

el/la **conductor(a)** driver, 9.2

conectado(a) on-line, connected

conectar to connect

la **conexión** connection

confeccionar to make, to prepare, *5.1*

la **conferencia** lecture

confesar to confess, to tell the truth

confiabilidad reliability

confiable reliable, trustworthy

confiar to entrust

la **confirmación** confirmation

confirmar to confirm (seat on a flight), **6.1**

conforme: estar conforme to agree, to be in agreement

confortar to soothe

confundir to mix up, to confuse

congelado(a) frozen, 9.2

los **productos congelados** frozen food, 9.2

el **congelador** freezer, *10*; **1**

el **conjunto** band, musical group, 8.1

conmovedor(a) moving

conocer to know, to be familiar with, 9.1; to meet

conocido(a) known

el/la **conocido(a)** acquaintance, **5**

el **conocimiento** knowledge

el **conquistador** conqueror

conquistar to conquer, **8**

consecuencia: por consecuencia as a result, consequently

el/la **consejero(a)** counselor

el **consejo** advice

considerar to consider

consiguiente: por consiguiente consequently

el **consomé** bouillon, consommé

la **consonante** consonant

constar (de) to consist of, to be made up of

la **consulta del médico** doctor's office, 6.2; **10**

consultar to consult

el **consultorio** doctor's office, 6.2; **10**

el/la **consumidor(a)** consumer

el/la **contable** accountant, **10**

contagioso(a) contagious

la **contaminación del aire** air pollution

contaminar to pollute

contar (ue) to tell, to count

contemporáneo(a) contemporary

el **contenido** contents

contento(a) happy, 6.1

contestar to answer, 3.1

continental: el desayuno continental Continental breakfast, *7*

el **continente** continent

continua: la línea continua solid line (*road*), *9.1*

continuar to continue

contra against

contraer matrimonio to get married

contrario(a) opposite; opposing

    al contrario on the contrary

    el equipo contrario opposing team, 7.1

contrastar to contrast
el **contrato** contract, **6.2**
contribuir to contribute
el **control de pasaportes** passport inspection, **6.1**
el **control de seguridad** security (checkpoint), 10.2; *1.2*
   pasar por el control de seguridad to go through security, 10.2; *1.2*
convencer to convince
convenir (ie) (en) to agree
la **conversación** conversation
conversar to converse
el **convertible** convertible, *9.2*
convertir (ie, i) to convert, to transform
copa: la Copa Mundial World Cup
la **copia** copy, *6.1*
   la copia dura hard copy, *6.1*
el **corazón** heart, **8**
la **corbata** tie, *9.1*
el **cordero** lamb, *4;* **9**
la **cordillera** mountain chain, range
la **corona** wreath, *5.1*
el **corral** corral, *8.2*
la **correa** conveyor belt, **6.1**
el/la **corredor(a)** runner *11.1;* **2.1**
el **correo** mail, **4**
el **correo electrónico** e-mail, *3.2;* **6.1**
correr to run, *5.2*
corresponder to correspond; to respond
corrido(a) unbolted, opened
cortar to cut off, *6.2;* to cut, to chop, *10;* **1**
   cortar en pedacitos to cut in small pieces, to dice, *10;* **1**
   cortar en rebanadas to slice, *10;* **1**
   Estás cortando. You're breaking up. *(telephone),* *6.2*
   Se nos cortó la línea. We've been cut off. *(telephone),* *6.2*
cortarse to cut oneself, *11.2;* **2.2**
el **corte de pelo** haircut, **4**
el **cortejo fúnebre** funeral procession, *3.2*
cortés polite, **5**
cortesano(a) of the court, courtly
la **cortesía** courtesy, LP
corto(a) short, *9.1;* **4**
   de manga corta short-sleeved, *9.1*

el pantalón corto shorts, *5.1*
la **corvina** corbina, drumfish
la **cosa** thing, *3.1*
la **cosecha** harvest, *8.2*
cosechar to harvest, *8.2*
cosmopolita cosmopolitan
la **costa** coast
costar (ue) to cost, *9.1*
   ¿Cuánto cuesta? How much does it cost?, *3.2*
costarricense Costa Rican
la **costumbre** custom
el **cráneo** skull, *5.1*
crear to create
crecer to grow
creer to believe, to think
   Creo que sí (que no). I (don't) think so.
la **crema dental** toothpaste, *11.2;* **2.2**
la **crema solar** suntan lotion, *7.1*
el/la **criado(a)** housekeeper; maid, **3 (Lit.)**
cristiano(a) Christian
criticar to criticize
el **cruce** crosswalk, pedestrian crossing, *8.1;* intersection, *9.1*
crudo(a) raw, *8.1*
   casi crudo rare *(meat),* **4**
   los vegetales crudos raw vegetables, crudités, *8.1*
cruzar to cross; to intersect, *9.1*
el **cuaderno** notebook, *3.1*
la **cuadra** *(city)* block, *9.1*
el **cuadro** painting, *8.2;* **7.1**
¿cuál? which? what?, LP
   ¿Cuál es la fecha de hoy? What is today's date?, LP
¿cuáles? which ones? what?
cualquier(a) any
cualquier otro(a) any other
cualquiera whichever, whatever
cuando when, *3.1*
¿cuándo? when?, *3.2*
cuanto: en cuanto as soon as; **en cuanto a** in terms of, as far as . . . is concerned
¿cuánto? how much?
   ¿A cuánto está(n)… ? How much is (are) . . . ?, *9.2*
   ¿Cuánto es? How much is it (does it cost)?, LP
¿cuántos(as)? how many?, *2.1*
   ¿Cuántos años tiene? How old is he (she)?, *2.1*
cuarenta forty, LP
el **cuarto** room, *2.2;* **7;** quarter

el cuarto de baño bathroom, *2.2;* **7**
el cuarto de dormir bedroom, *2.2*
el cuarto sencillo (doble) single (double) room, **7**
y cuarto quarter past (the hour), LP
cuatro four, LP
cuatrocientos(as) four hundred
el/la **cubano(a)** Cuban
el/la **cubanoamericano(a)** Cuban American
cubierto(a) covered; indoor
cubrir to cover
la **cuchara** tablespoon, **4**
la **cucharada** tablespoonful
la **cucharadita** teaspoonful
la **cucharita** teaspoon, **4**
el **cuchillo** knife, **4**
el **cuello** neck, *11.1;* **2.1;** collar
la **cuenca** basin *(river)*
la **cuenta** check *(restaurant),* *4.2;* **4;** account
   la cuenta corriente checking account, **4**
   darse cuenta de to realize, **8**
   por su cuenta on its own
   tomar en cuenta to take into account, **8**
el **cuento** story, *7.2*
la **cuerda** string
el **cuerpo** body, *11.1;* **2.1**
la **cueva** cave
¡Cuidado! Look out! Watch out!, **5**
   con (mucho) cuidado (very) carefully
   tener cuidado to be careful, *9.1*
cuidadoso(a) careful
cuidar to take care of, to care for
   ¡Cuídate! Take care of yourself!
la **culpa** blame, guilt
cultivar to work *(land);* to grow, *8.2;* **9**
culto(a) cultured
la **cultura** culture
el **cumpleaños** birthday, *8.1;* **3.2**
cumplir… años to be (turn) . . . years old
cumplir un sueño to fulfill a wish, to make a wish come true
la **cuota** toll
la **cúpula** dome
el **cura** priest, *3.1*
curarse to get better, to recover

Spanish-English Dictionary

Spanish-English Dictionary

el **currículo** curriculum vitae

el **currículum vitae** résumé, curriculum vitae, **10**

el **curso** class, course, 1.2

cuyo(a) whose

D

la **dama de honor** maid of honor, **3.1**

el **daño** harm

hacerse daño to harm oneself, to get hurt, *11.2;* **2.2**

dar to give, 3.1

dar de comer a to feed

dar la vuelta to turn around, *9.1*

dar un examen (una prueba) to give a test, 3.1

dar una caminata to take a hike, 11.2; *2.2*

dar una fiesta to throw a party, 8.1

darse cuenta de to realize

darse la mano to shake hands, **5**

datar to date *(time)*

los **datos** data, facts

de of, from, LP

¿de dónde? from where?, 1.1

de manera que so that, in such a way that

de modo que so that, in such a way that

De nada. You're welcome., LP

¿De parte de quién, por favor? Who's calling, please?, *6.2*

¿de qué nacionalidad? what nationality?, 1.1

de vez en cuando from time to time, 10.2; *1.2*

No hay de qué. You're welcome., LP

debajo de below, underneath, 10.2; *1.2*

deber should, 4.2; to owe

el **deber** duty

debido a owing to, **6.1**

la **debilidad** weakness

decidir to decide

decir to say, to tell

la **decisión** decision

tomar una decisión to make a decision

declinar to decline, **6.2**

decorar to decorate, 5.2

dedicado(a) devoted

el **dedo** finger, 11.1; *2.1*

el **dedo del pie** toe, *11.1;* **2.1**

deducirse to deduct

el **defecto** defect

defender (ie) to defend

definido(a) definite

dejar to leave (something), *4;* to let, to allow

dejar con to put an end to

dejar de to stop, to give up

dejar un mensaje to leave a message, *6.2*

dejar una propina to leave a tip, *4*

del of the, from the

delante de in front of, 2.2

delantero(a) front *(adj.)*, *8.1*

delgado(a) thin

demás: lo(s) demás the rest

los demás other people, **5 (Lit.)**

demasiado too *(adv.)*, too much

la **demora** delay, 10.2; *1.2;* **6.1**

con una demora late, 10.2; *1.2*

denominado(a) named, designated

la **densidad** density

dental: el tubo de crema dental tube of toothpaste, 11.2; *2.2*

dentífrica: la pasta dentífrica toothpaste

dentro de within

dentro de poco soon, shortly thereafter, 10.2; *1.2*

el **departamento** apartment, 2.2

el departamento de orientación guidance office

el departamento de personal human resources (personnel) department, **10**

el departamento de recursos humanos human resources department, **10**

el/la **dependiente(a)** salesperson, employee

el **deporte** sport, 5.1

el deporte de equipo team sport

el deporte individual individual sport

deportivo(a) *(related to)* sports

el coche deportivo sports car, *9.2*

depositar to deposit, **4**

deprimido(a) sad, depressed, 6.1

derecho straight (ahead), *9.1*

derecho(a) right, 11.1; *2.1*

a la derecha on the right, *9.1*

derrocar to bring down

la **derrota** defeat

derrotar to defeat

desafortunadamente unfortunately

desagradable unpleasant, not nice

desaparecer to disappear

desarrollarse to develop, **7.2**

el **desastre** disaster

desastroso(a) disastrous, catastrophic

el **desayuno** breakfast, 4.1; *7*

el desayuno americano American breakfast, *7*

el desayuno continental Continental breakfast, *7*

tomar el desayuno to have breakfast, 4.1

desbocado(a) runaway

descansar to rest, *11.1;* **2.1**

el **descapotable** convertible, *9.2*

descargar to download, *6.2;* to unload

descargado(a) carrying no load

descolgar (ue) (el auricular) to unhook (the telephone receiver), *6.2*

desconocido(a) unknown

desconsolado(a) very sad

descortés discourteous, rude

describir to describe

la **descripción** description

el **descubrimiento** discovery

el **descuento** discount

desde since; from

desear to want, to wish, 4.2

¿Qué desean tomar? What would you like *(to eat, drink)?*, 4.2

desembarcar to deplane, disembark, 10.2; *1.2*

desembocar to lead, to go (from one street into another), to come out onto

el **deseo** wish, desire

desesperado(a) desperate

desfilar to walk (in a parade or procession), *5.1*

el **desfile** parade, *5.2*

desgraciadamente unfortunately

deshuesado(a) deboned

el **desierto** desert

desinflada: la llanta desinflada flat tire, *9.2*

desnudar to strip, to lay bare

desnudo(a) naked

el **despacho** office, *4 (Lit.)*

despacio slow, slowly, *9.1*

despedirse (i, i) to say good-bye to, to take leave, *5*

despegar to take off *(plane)*, *10.2; 1.2*

el **despegue** takeoff *(plane)*, *10.2; 1.2*

despertarse (ie) to wake up, *11.1; 2.1*

después (de) after, *3.1;* later

después de que after (doing something)

destemplado(a) sharp, unpleasant

el/la **destinatario(a)** addressee, recipient, *6.1*

el **destino** destination, *3.1; 6.1*

con destino a (going) to; for, *10.2; 1.2*

las **desventajas** disadvantages

desvestir (i, i) to undress

el **detalle** detail

detenidamente thoroughly

el **detergente** detergent, *4*

detrás de in back of, behind, *2.2*

devolver (ue) to return *(something)*, *5.2*

el **día** day

Buenos días. Good morning., *LP*

el Día de los Muertos Day of the Dead, *5.1*

el Día de los Reyes Epiphany (January 6), *5.1*

hoy en día nowadays

¿Qué día es hoy? What day is it today?, *LP*

el **diablo** devil

el **diagnóstico** diagnosis

el **diálogo** dialogue

diario(a) daily

a diario on a daily basis

la rutina diaria daily routine, *11.1; 2.1*

el **diario** daily newspaper

el **dibujo** drawing, illustration

diciembre December, *LP*

el **dictado** dictation

dictar to dictate

diecinueve nineteen, *LP*

dieciocho eighteen, *LP*

dieciséis sixteen, *LP*

diecisiete seventeen, *LP*

el **diente** clove (of garlic)

los **dientes** teeth, *11.1; 2.1*

cepillarse (lavarse) los dientes to brush one's teeth, *11.1; 2.1*

la **dieta** diet

diez ten, *LP*

de diez en diez by tens

la **diferencia** difference

diferente different, *9.2*

difícil difficult, *1.2*

la **dificultad** difficulty

sin dificultad easily

difunto(a) dead, deceased, *5.1*

el/la **difunto(a)** deceased, dead person, *5.1*

¡Diga! Hello! *(on the phone)*

¡Dígame! Hello! *(on the phone)*

dinámico(a) dynamic, *6.1*

el **dinero** money, *3.2*

el dinero en efectivo cash, *4*

dirán: el «qué dirán» what people might say

la **dirección** address, *6.1;* direction

la dirección de correo electrónico (e-mail) e-mail address, *6.1*

las **direccionales** turn signals, *9.2*

dirigirse to head toward

el **disco** record

discreto(a) discrete

diseñar to design

el **disfraz** disguise, costume, *5.1*

disfrutar (de) to enjoy

displicente indifferent

disponerse to prepare (to do something)

disponible available, *6.1*

dispuesto(a) disposed, laid out

distancia: de larga distancia long-distance *(race)*, *11.1; 2.1*

distinguir to distinguish

distinto(a) different

distraer to distract

el **distribuidor automático** boarding pass kiosk, *10.1; 1.1;* ticket dispenser, *3.1*

el **distrito** district, area, section

divertido(a) fun, funny, amusing

divertir (ie, i) to amuse, *11.2; 2.2*

divertirse (ie, i) to have a good time, to have fun, *11.2; 2.2*

dividirse to divide, to separate, *7.2*

divino(a) divine, heavenly

doblar to turn, *9.1*

doble: el cuarto doble double *(hotel room)*, *7*

dobles doubles *(tennis)*, *5.2*

doce twelve, *LP*

la **docena** dozen

el **documento adjunto** attached file, *6.1*

el **dólar** dollar

doler (ue) to ache, to hurt, *6.2; 11.2; 2.2*

Le (Me, etc.) duele mucho. It hurts him (me, etc.) a lot., *11.2; 2.2*

Me duele(n)… My . . . ache(s)., *6.2*

el **dolor** pain, ache, *6.2*

tener dolor de cabeza to have a headache, *6.2*

tener dolor de estómago to have a stomachache, *6.2*

tener dolor de garganta to have a sore throat, *6.2*

el **domenical** Sunday newspaper

domesticado(a) domesticated

dominar to speak very well

el **domingo** Sunday, *LP*

dominicano(a) Dominican

la República Dominicana Dominican Republic

el **dominio** rule

el **dominó** dominos

donde where

¿dónde? where?, *1.1*

¿de dónde? from where?, *1.1*

dondequiera wherever

dorado(a) golden, (made of) gold

dormir (ue, u) to sleep

la bolsa de dormir sleeping bag, *11.2; 2.2*

el cuarto de dormir bedroom, *2.2*

el saco de dormir sleeping bag, *11.2; 2.2*

dormirse (ue, u) to fall asleep, *11.1; 2.1*

el **dormitorio** bedroom, *2.2*

dos two

doscientos(as) two hundred

el **drama** drama

driblar to dribble, *5.2*

la **ducha** shower, *11.1; 2.1*

Spanish-English Dictionary

tomar una ducha to take a
  shower, 11.1; *2.1*
la **duda** doubt
  sin duda without a doubt,
    doubtless
  duele(n): Me duele(n)...
    My . . . hurts (aches)., 6.2
    Me duele que... It hurts me
    that . . .
el **duelo** duel
el/la **dueño(a)** owner, **10**
  dulce sweet, *5.1*
    el pan dulce pastry, *7*
el **dulce** sweet
  durante during, 3.2
  durar to last
  duro(a) hard, difficult, 1.2
    la copia dura hard copy,
    6.1
el **DVD** DVD, 3.2

la **ebullición** boiling
  echar to throw, to expel
    echar a to start to (do
      something), **6 (Lit.)**
    echar una carta to mail a
      letter, **4**
  económico(a) inexpensive
  ecuatoriano(a) Ecuadoran,
    1.1
la **edad** age
  la Edad Media Middle
    Ages
el **edificio** building, 2.2
la **educación** education
  la educación física physical
    education, 1.2
  educado(a) mannered
    estar bien (mal)
      educado(a) to be polite
      (rude), 6.1
  efectuarse to take place
  egoísta selfish, egotistical
el/la **ejecutivo(a)** executive, **10**
el **ejemplo** example
  por ejemplo for example
los **ejercicios** exercises, 11.1; *2.1*
  ejercicios de respiración
    breathing exercises, *11.1;*
    2.1
  hacer ejercicios to exercise,
    11.1; **2.1**
el **ejército** army, **4 (Lit.)**
los **ejotes** green beans
  el the (*m. sing.*), 1.1

él he, 1.1
elaborar to make, to produce,
  5.1
electrónico(a) electronic,
  10.1; *1.1*
  el boleto (billete)
    electrónico e-ticket, 10.1;
    1.1
  el correo electrónico
    e-mail, 3.2; *6.1*
el **elefante** elephant
elegante elegant, fancy
elegir (i, i) to elect, to pick
elemental elementary
ella she, 1.1
ellos(as) they, 1.2
el **elote** corn
el **e-mail** e-mail, *6.1*
embarcar to board, 10.2; *1.2*
embargo: sin embargo
  however, nevertheless
el **embarque** boarding, 10.1; *1.1*
el **embotellamiento** traffic jam
emergencia: la sala de
  emergencia emergency
  room, *11.2;* **2.2**
la **emisión televisiva** television
  program, **8**
la **emisora de televisión**
  television station, **8**
emitir to broadcast, **8**
emocionante moving;
  exciting
emotivo(a) emotional,
  sensitive
la **empanada** meat pie, 4.2
empeorar to make worse, to
  worsen
empezar (ie) to begin, 5.1
el/la **empleado(a)** salesperson,
  employee, 3.2
la **empresa** company, **8**
empujar to push
en in; on; at
  en casa at home
enamorado(a) in love
el/la **enamorado(a)** sweetheart
enamorado(a) de in love with
enamorarse to fall in love, **5**
encaminarse to head toward
encantar to love, to adore, *6.2*
el **encanto** enchantment
encargar to put in charge,
  4 (Lit.)
encargarse to take it upon
  oneself
encender (ie) to light, *5.2*
encerrar (ie) to enclose; to
  lock up

encestar to make a basket
  (*basketball*), 5.2
la **enchilada** enchilada
encima: por encima
  de above, over, 5.2
encontrar (ue) to find, to
  encounter
encontrarse (ue) to be found;
  to meet
el **encuentro** encounter, meeting
la **encuesta** survey
endosar to endorse, **4**
el/la **enemigo(a)** enemy
energético(a) energetic, 6.1
la **energía** energy, 6.1
enero January, LP
enfadado(a) angry, mad, 6.1
enfadar to make angry, 6.1
enfadarse to get angry, **5**
la **enfermedad** illness
el/la **enfermero(a)** nurse, 6.2; *11.2;*
  2.2
enfermo(a) ill, sick, 6.2
el/la **enfermo(a)** sick person,
  patient
enfrente de in front of
¡Enhorabuena!
  Congratulations!, **3.1**
enjuto(a) thin, skinny,
  10 (Lit.)
enlatado(a) canned
enlazar to connect, *6.2*
enojado(a) angry, mad,
  annoyed, 6.1
enojar to make angry, to
  annoy, 6.1
enorme enormous
la **ensalada** salad, 4.1
enseguida right away, 4.2
enseñar to teach, 3.1; to show
entender (ie) to understand,
  8.2
entero(a) entire, whole
enterrado(a) buried, *5.1*
enterrar (ie) to bury
el **entierro** burial, *3.2*
entonces then
  en aquel entonces at that
    time
la **entrada** ticket, 8.1; entrée
  (*meal*); entrance
entradas: la bandeja de
  entradas e-mail inbox, *6.1*
entrar to enter, to go into, 5.1
  entrar en línea to go
    online, *6.1*
entre between, among
entregar to hand over, to
  deliver, **6 (Lit.)**

el/la **entrenador(a)** coach, manager

entretanto meanwhile

la **entrevista** interview, **10**

el/la **entrevistador(a)** interviewer

entusiasmado(a) enthusiastic

el **entusiasmo** enthusiasm, 6.1

enviados: la bandeja de enviados sent mailbox, *6.1*

enviar to send, 3.2

el **episodio** episode

la **época** times, period

el **equilibrio** balance

el **equipaje** luggage, baggage, 10.1; *1.1;* **6.1**

el equipaje de mano hand luggage, carry-on bags, 10.2; *1.2*

el **equipo** team, 5.1; equipment

el deporte de equipo team sport

la **equitación** horseback riding, *8.2*

equivocado(a) mistaken, wrong

escala: hacer escala to stop over, to make a stop, **6.1**

la **escalera** stairs, staircase, *8.1*

la escalera mecánica escalator, *8.1*

el **escalope de ternera** veal cutlet, *10;* **1**

el **escaparate** store window, 9.1

la **escena** scene

escoger to choose

escolar *(adj.)* school

el bus escolar school bus, 3.2

los materiales escolares school supplies, 3.1

la tarifa escolar student fare

escribir to write, 4.2

el **escrito** document, paper

escrito(a) written

el/la **escritor(a)** writer

escritorio: la pantalla de escritorio *(computer)* screen, *6.1*

escuchar to listen (to), 3.2

¿Me escuchas? Can you hear me? *(telephone), 6.2*

el **escudero** squire

la **escuela** school, 1.2

la escuela primaria elementary school

la escuela secundaria secondary school, high school, 1.2

el/la **escultor(a)** sculptor, 8.2; **7.1**

la **escultura** sculpture, **7.1**

ese(a) that, that one

eso: a eso de at about *(time)*

por eso for this reason, that is why

esos(as) those

la **espalda** back, 11.1; *2.1*

espantable horrendous

España Spain

español(a) Spanish *(adj.)*

el/la **español(a)** Spaniard

el **español** Spanish *(language); 1.2*

la **especia** spice, 9

la **especialidad** specialty

especialmente especially

específico(a) specific

espectacular spectacular

el **espectáculo** show, spectacle

el/la **espectador(a)** spectator

el **espejo** mirror, 11.1; *2.1*

espera: la sala de espera waiting room, *3.1*

esperar to wait (for), 10.2; *1.2;* to hope; to expect, **3.1**

el **espíritu** mind, spirit, *11.1;* **2.1**

la **esplendidez** splendor

espontáneo(a) spontaneous

la **esposa** wife, 2.1

el **esposo** husband, 2.1

la **esquela** obituary, *3.2*

el **esqueleto** skeleton, *5.1*

el **esquí** ski; skiing, 7.2

el esquí acuático (náutico) waterskiing, 7.1

el esquí alpino downhill skiing

el esquí nórdico cross-country skiing

el/la **esquiador(a)** skier, 7.2

esquiar to ski, 7.2

esquiar en el agua to water-ski, 7.1

la **esquina** corner, *8.1*

¿Está… , por favor? Is . . . there, please?, *6.2*

establecer(se) to establish; to settle, **8**

el **establecimiento** establishment, settling

el **establo** stable, *8.2;* manger

la **estación** season, LP; resort, 7.1; station, *3.1*

la estación de esquí ski resort, 7.2

la estación de ferrocarril (tren) railroad (train) station, *3.1;* **6.2**

la estación de metro subway (metro) station, *8.1*

la estación de servicio gas station, 9.2

¿Qué estación es? What season is it?, LP

estacionar to park

la **estadía** stay

el **estadio** stadium

el **estado financiero** financial statement, **10**

Estados Unidos United States

estadounidense from the United States

estallar to break out, to explode

la **estampilla** stamp, **4**

la **estancia** ranch, *8.2*

estar to be, 3.1

¿Está… ? Is . . . there?, 6.2

estar bien to feel fine, 6.2

estar cansado(a) to be tired, 6.1

estar contento(a) (triste, nervioso[a], etc.) to be happy (sad, nervous, etc.), 6.1

estar de buen (mal) humor to be in a good (bad) mood, 6.1

estar enfermo(a) to be sick, 6.2

estar para (+ infinitivo) to be about to (do something)

la **estatua** statue, *8.2;* **7.1**

la **estatura** stature, height

este(a) this, this one, 9.1

el **este** east

estereofónico(a) stereo

el **estilo** style

estimado(a) esteemed

estirarse to stretch, 11.1; *2.1;* **2.1**

el **estómago** stomach, 6.2

el dolor de estómago stomachache, 6.2

estos(as) these

la **estrategia** strategy

estrechamente closely

estrecho(a) narrow, *8.1*

la **estrella** star

estremecerse to shake

el **estrés** stress, 6.2

la **estrofa** stanza, 7.2

la **estructura** structure

el/la **estudiante** student

el/la estudiante universitario(a) university student, **10**

estudiantil: la tarifa estudiantil student fare

estudiar to study, 3.1

el **estudio** study

los estudios sociales social studies, 1.2

Spanish-English Dictionary

la **estufa** stove, *10;* **1**
estupendo(a) terrific, stupendous
la **etiqueta** luggage identification tag, **6.1**
la **etnia** ethnicity, ethnic group
étnico(a) ethnic
el **euro** euro *(currency of most of the countries of the European Union)*
Europa Europe
el **evento** event
evitar to avoid
el **examen** test, exam, 3.1
  el examen físico physical, 6.2
  examinar to examine, 6.2
  exceder to go over *(speed limit)*
  excelente excellent
la **excepción** exception
la **excursión** excursion, outing
el/la **excursionista** hiker
exigente demanding
exigir to demand, to require
existir exist
el **éxito** success, 6.1
  tener éxito to succeed, to be successful, 6.1
exótico(a) exotic
experimentar to try, to try out; to experience
el/la **experto(a)** expert, 7.2
explicar to explain
el/la **explorador(a)** explorer
la **exposición de arte** art show, exhibition, 8.2
la **expresión** expression
extenderse (ie) to extend
extranjero(a) foreign
  al extranjero abroad
extraño(a) strange
extraordinario(a) extraordinary

la **fábrica** factory
fabuloso(a) fabulous
fácil easy, 1.2
la **factura** bill
facturar el equipaje to check luggage, 10.1; *1.1*
la **falda** skirt, 3.1
el **fallecimiento** death, demise
falso(a) false
la **falta** lack
faltar to lack, not to have, 6.1

Le falta paciencia. He (She) has no patience., 6.1
la **familia** family, 2.1
familiar *(related to)* family
los **familiares** family members
famoso(a) famous
la **fantasía** fantasy
fantástico(a) fantastic
el/la **farmacéutico(a)** druggist, pharmacist
la **farmacia** pharmacy, drugstore, 6.2
el **favor** favor
  Favor de (+ infinitivo). Please (do something)., 11.2; *2.2*
  por favor please, LP
favorito(a) favorite
febrero February, LP
la **fecha** date, LP
  ¿Cuál es la fecha de hoy? What is today's date?, LP
fecundo(a) prolific
la **felicidad** happiness
feliz happy, 5.2
  ¡Felices Pascuas! Happy Easter!
  ¡Feliz Hanuka! Happy Hanukkah!, 5.2
  ¡Feliz Navidad! Merry Christmas!, 5.2
feo(a) unattractive, ugly, 1.1
la **feria** festival, fair, *5.1;* fairground
ferrocarril: la estación de ferrocarril train station, railroad station, *3.1,* **6.2**
festivo: el día festivo holiday
la **fiebre** fever, 6.2
  tener fiebre to have a fever, 6.2
fiel loyal, faithful
la **fiesta** party, 8.1; holiday, *5.1*
  dar una fiesta to throw a party, 8.1
  la fiesta de las luces festival of lights (Hanukkah), 5.2
fijarse to pay attention to, to concentrate on
fijo(a) fixed, unchanging
la **fila** line *(of people);* row *(of seats),* **6.1**
  estar en fila to wait in line
el **film** film, movie
el **filme** film, movie, 8.2
el **fin** end; death
  en fin in short
  el fin de semana weekend, 7.1

por fin finally
final: al final de at the end of
la **finca** farm, 8.2
fines: a fines de at the end of
fingir to pretend
firmar to sign, 3.1
físico(a) physical
  la apariencia física physical appearance, looks
  la educación física physical education, 1.2
flaco(a) thin
el **flan** flan, custard, 4.1
la **flauta** flute
la **flecha** arrow
flexible open-minded, flexible, 6.1
la **flor** flower, 2.2
el **foco** center, focal point
la **fogata** bonfire, campfire
el **fondo** background, **7.1**
  al fondo to (at) the bottom
los **fondos** funds, money, **4**
el/la **fontanero(a)** plumber, **10**
la **forma** form, piece, 10.2; *1.2;* shape
  la forma de identidad piece of ID, 10.2; *1.2*
formal formal, **5**
formar to form, to make up; to put together
el **formulario** form
forzado(a) forced
la **foto(grafía)** photo, 7.1
la **fractura** fracture
el **francés** French, 1.2
el **franciscano** Franciscan
franco(a) frank, sincere, candid
el **frasco** jar, 9.2
la **frase** sentence
la **frazada** blanket, **7**
frecuencia: con frecuencia often, frequently
frecuentemente frequently
freír (i, i) to fry, *4;* **1**
los **frenos** brakes, 9.2
la **frente** forehead, *11.1;* **2.1**
frente a in front of
fresco(a) cool, LP; fresh
  Hace fresco. It's cool *(weather).,* LP
los **frijoles** beans, 4.1
frío(a) cold, 4.2
  Hace frío. It's cold *(weather).,* LP
  tener frío to be cold, 11.1; *2.1*
el **frío** cold

frito(a) fried
las patatas (papas) fritas french fries, 4.1
frontal: la página frontal home page, *6.1*
la **frontera** border
la **fruta** fruit, 9.2
el puesto de frutas fruit stand, 9.2
la **frutería** fruit stand, 9.2
el **fuego** flame, heat, *10*; **1**
a fuego lento on low heat, *10*; **1**
los **fuegos artificiales** fireworks, *5.2*
la **fuente** fountain
fuera de outside
fuerte strong; substantial
las **fuerzas** (armed) forces
fumar: la señal de no fumar no-smoking sign, 10.2; *1.2*
el/la **funcionario(a) gubernamental (de gobierno)** government official, **10**
fundar to found
el **fútbol** soccer, 5.1
el campo de fútbol soccer field, 5.1
el fútbol americano football
el/la **futbolista** soccer player
el **futuro** future

G

el **gabinete del dentista** dentist's office, **9**
las **gafas para el sol** sunglasses, 7.1
el **galán** elegant man, heartthrob
gallardo(a) brave, dashing
las **galletas** crackers, 8.1
la **gallina** hen, *8.2*
galope: a galope galloping
la **gamba** shrimp, prawn
el **ganado** cattle, livestock, *8.2*
ganar to win, 5.1; to earn
ganas: tener ganas de to feel like
el **garaje** garage, 2.2
la **garganta** throat, 6.2
el dolor de garganta sore throat, 6.2
la **garita de peaje** tollbooth, *9.1*
gas: el agua mineral con gas carbonated (sparkling) mineral water, 4.2
la **gaseosa** soda, carbonated drink, 4.1

la **gasolina** gas
la **gasolinera** gas station, *9.2*
gastar to spend; to waste
el **gasto** expense
el/la **gato(a)** cat, 2.1; jack *(car)*, *9.2*
la **gaveta** drawer
el/la **gemelo(a)** twin, 2.1
general general
en general in general
por lo general usually, as a rule
generalmente usually, generally
el **género** genre, *7.2*
generoso(a) generous
la **gente** people, 9.1
la **geografía** geography
la **geometría** geometry
la **gesticulación** gesture
el **gigante** giant
el **gimnasio** gym(nasium), *11.1*; **2.1**
girar to turn, to swivel
la **gitanilla** little gypsy
el **globo** balloon
el/la **gobernador(a)** governor
el **gobierno** government, **10**
el **gol** goal, 5.1
meter un gol to score a goal, 5.1
el **golpe** blow; pat (on the back)
golpear to hit *(ball)*, 5.2
la **goma** tire, *9.2*
gordo(a) fat
el **gorro** ski hat, 7.2
gozar de to enjoy
grabar to record
Gracias. Thank you., LP
dar gracias a to thank
Mil gracias. Thanks a million.
gracioso(a) funny, 1.1
la **gramática** grammar
gran, grande big, large, 1.2
la **grandeza** greatness, grandeur
el **granero** barn, *8.2*
la **granja** farm, *8.2*
gratis for free
gratuito(a) free
grave serious
gris gray, 5.1
gritar to yell, to shout
el **grupo** group, 8.1
la **guagua** bus *(Puerto Rico, Cuba)*, 8.1
el **guante** glove, 5.2
la **guantera** glove compartment, *9.2*
guapo(a) attractive, good-looking, 1.1
guardar to guard, 5.1; to save, to keep, *6.1*

guardar cama to stay in bed *(illness)*, 6.2
la **guardería** shelter
guatemalteco(a) Guatemalan, 1.1
la **guerra** war, **8**
el **guerrero** warrior
la **guía** guidebook
la guía telefónica phone book, *6.2*
guiar to guide
el **guisante** pea, 9.2
la **guitarra** guitar
gustar to like, to be pleasing to, 5.1
el **gusto** pleasure; like; taste
Mucho gusto. Nice *(It's a pleasure)* to meet you, 1.2

H

haber to have *(in compound tenses)*
haber de (+ infinitivo) to have to (do something)
las **habichuelas** beans
las habichuelas tiernas green beans, string beans
la **habitación** bedroom; hotel room, 7
el/la **habitante** inhabitant
el/la **hablante** speaker
hablar to speak, to talk, 3.1
hablar en el móvil to talk on the cell phone
hablar por teléfono to talk on the phone
¿Hablas en serio? Are you serious?
Habría de (+ infinitivo). I (He, She) was supposed to (do something)., **4**
hace: Hace... años . . . years ago
Hace buen tiempo. The weather is nice., LP
¿Hace cuánto tiempo... ? How long . . . ?
Hace fresco. It's cool *(weather)*., LP
Hace frío. It's cold *(weather)*., LP
Hace mal tiempo. The weather is bad., LP
Hace (mucho) calor. It's (very) hot *(weather)*., LP
Hace sol. It's sunny., LP
Hace viento. It's windy., LP
hacer to do, to make, 10.2; *1.2*
hacer clic to click *(computer)*, 6.1

Spanish-English Dictionary

hacer cola to stand (wait) in line, 10.2; *1.2*

hacer ejercicios to exercise, *11.1*; **2.1**

hacer jogging to go jogging, *11.1*; **2.1**

hacer la cama to make the bed, 7

hacer la maleta to pack, 10.1; *1.1*

hacer planchas to do push-ups, *11.1*; **2.1**

hacer un viaje to take a trip, 10.1; *1.1*

hacerle caso to pay attention, 5 (Lit.)

hacerse daño to hurt oneself, *11.2*; **2.2**

el hacha (f.) ax

hacia toward

hacia atrás backwards

la hacienda ranch, 8.2

el hall concourse (train station), 3.1

hallar to find

el hambre (f.) hunger

    Me muero de hambre. I'm starving., 4

    tener hambre to be hungry, 4.1

la hamburguesa hamburger, 4.1

el Hanuka Hanukkah, 5.2

    ¡Feliz Hanuka! Happy Hanukkah!, 5.2

la harina flour, 9

hasta until; up to; as far as; even

    ¡Hasta luego! See you later!, LP

    ¡Hasta mañana! See you tomorrow!, LP

    ¡Hasta pronto! See you soon!, LP

hasta que until

hay there is, there are, 2.2

    hay que it's necessary to (do something), one must, 10.2; *1.2*

    Hay sol. It's sunny., LP

    No hay de qué. You're welcome., LP

    ¿Qué hay? What's new (up)?

la hazaña achievement

hebreo(a) Jewish, Hebrew, 5.2

el hecho fact

hecho(a): bien hecho(a) well-done (meat), 4

el helado ice cream, 4.1

el heno hay, 8.2

la herida wound, injury, *11.2*; **2.2**

el/la herido(a) injured person

el/la hermanastro(a) stepbrother (stepsister) 2.1

el/la hermano(a) brother (sister) 2.1

hermoso(a) beautiful

el héroe hero

la heroína heroine

herramientas: la barra de herramientas toolbar, 6.1

hervir (ie, i) to boil, 10; 1

el hielo ice, 7.2

    el patinaje sobre el hielo ice-skating, 7.2

la hierba grass, 8.2

las hierbas herbs

el hígado liver

higiénico: el rollo de papel higiénico roll of toilet paper, 11.2; **2.2**

el/la hijo(a) son (daughter), child, 2.1

    el/la hijo(a) único(a) only child, 2.1

los hijos children, 2.1

hinchado(a) swollen, *11.2*; **2.2**

hincharse to get swollen, to swell

hispano(a) Hispanic

hispanohablante Spanish-speaking

el/la hispanohablante Spanish speaker

la historia history, 1.2

el/la historiador(a) historian

la hoja sheet (of paper), 3.1; leaf (of lettuce), **9**

hojear to skim, to scan

¡Hola! Hello!, LP

el hombre man

el hombro shoulder, *11.1*; **2.1**

honesto(a) honest

honor: en honor de in honor of, **3.1**

honrado honest, upright

honroso(a) honorable

la hora hour; time, 10.1; *1.1*

    ¿a qué hora? at what time?, LP

    la hora de embarque boarding time, 10.1; *1.1*

    la hora de salida departure time, 10.1; *1.1*

    ¿Qué hora es? What time is it?, LP

el horario (train) schedule, timetable, 3.1

el horizonte horizon

el horno oven, 10; **1**

el horno de microondas microwave oven, 10; **1**

la hortaliza vegetable, 9

hospedarse to stay (in a hotel), 7

el hospital hospital

el hostal hostel, small (inexpensive) hotel, 7

el hotel hotel, 7

hoy today, LP

    ¿Cuál es la fecha de hoy? What's today's date?, LP

    hoy en día nowadays

    ¿Qué día es hoy? What day is it today?, LP

la huerta orchard, 8.2; **9**

el huerto vegetable garden, **9**

el hueso bone, 5.1; **2.2**

el/la huésped(a) guest, 7

el huevo egg, 4.1; 7

    el huevo batido scrambled egg, **9**

    los huevos pasados por agua soft-boiled eggs

    los huevos revueltos scrambled eggs, 7

huir to flee, 4 (Lit.)

humanitario(a) humanitarian

humano(a) human, 11.1; *2.1*

    el ser humano human being

humilde humble

el humor mood; humor

    estar de buen (mal) humor to be in a good (bad) mood, 6.1

    tener un buen sentido de humor to have a good sense of humor, 6.1

el huso horario time zone

el icono icon, *6.1*

ida y vuelta (regreso): un boleto (billete) de ida y vuelta (regreso) round-trip ticket, *3.1*

la idea idea

la identidad identification, 10.2; *1.2*

el carnet de identidad
ID card, 10.2; *1.2*
identificar to identify
el **idioma** language
la **iglesia** church, **3.1**
igual que as well as; like;
just as
iluminar to light up, to
illuminate, *5.2*
ilustre illustrious,
distinguished, **8**
la **imagen** picture, image
impaciente impatient, 6.1
impar odd *(numeric)*
impermeable waterproof
el **impermeable** raincoat
imponer to impose
importa: No importa. It
doesn't matter.
la **importancia** importance
importante important
imposible impossible
la **impresora** printer, 6.1
imprimir to print, 6.1
el **impuesto** tax
incluir to include, 6.2
¿Está incluido el servicio?
Is the tip included?, 4.2
incluso even
incomodar to inconvenience
increíble incredible
indicar to indicate
indígena native, indigenous,
9.2
el/la **indígena** indigenous
person
**individual: el deporte
individual** individual sport
individuales singles *(tennis)*,
5.2
índole character, nature
industrializado(a)
industrialized
inesperado(a) unexpected
la **inestabilidad** instability
infantil childlike
inferior bottom
el **infierno** hell
la **infinidad** infinity
la **influencia** influence
la **información** information, 3.2
la **informática** information
technology
el **informe** report
el/la **ingeniero(a)** engineer, **10**
el **inglés** English, 1.2
la **Inglaterra** England
el **ingrediente** ingredient
inhóspito(a) inhospitable,
desolate
inicial: la página inicial
home page, *6.1*

inicio: la página de inicio
home page, *6.1*
inmenso(a) immense
la **inmigración** immigration,
6.1
el **inodoro** toilet, *7*
inolvidable unforgettable
la **inquietud** restlessness,
agitation
insertar to insert, *3.1*
inspeccionar to inspect
inteligente intelligent, 1.2
intercambiar to exchange, *3.1*
el **interés** interest
interesante interesting, 1.2
interesar to interest, 5.1
las **intermitentes** turn signals,
9.2
el **Internet** Internet, 3.2; *6.1*
navegar el Internet to surf
the Net, 3.2; *6.1*
interurbano(a) city-to-city
intervenir (ie) to intervene
íntimo(a) close
la **introducción** introduction
introducir to insert, *6.2*
invertir (ie, i) to invest, **8**
el **invierno** winter, LP
la **invitación** invitation
el/la **invitado(a)** guest, **5**
invitar to invite
ir to go, 3.2
ir a (+ infinitivo) to be
going to (do something),
4.1
ir a casa to go home, 3.2
ir a pie to go on foot, 3.2
ir al cine to go to the
movies, 8.2
ir de camping to go
camping, 11.2; *2.2*
ir de compras to go
shopping, 9.1
irlandés(esa) Irish
la **isla** island
el **istmo** isthmus
italiano(a) Italian
izquierdo(a) left, 11.1; *2.1*
a la izquierda to the left,
9.1

el **jabón** soap, 11.2; *2.2*
**la barra (pastilla) de
jabón** bar of soap,
11.2; *2.2*
el jabón en polvo
powdered detergent, **4**
jamás never
el **jamón** ham, 4.1

el **sándwich de jamón
y queso** ham and
cheese sandwich, 4.1
el **jardín** garden, 2.2
el/la **jardinero(a)** outfielder, 5.2
jogging: hacer jogging to go
jogging, *11.1*; **2.1**
el **jonrón** home run
batear un jonrón to hit a
home run
joven young
el/la **joven** young person, 1.1
la **joya** jewel, piece of jewelry
judío(a) Jewish, *5.2*
las **judías verdes** green beans,
9.2; **9**
el **juego** game, 5.1
el **jueves** Thursday, LP
el/la **jugador(a)** player, 5.1
jugar (ue) to play, 5.1
**jugar (al) fútbol (béisbol,
básquetbol)** to play
soccer (baseball,
basketball), 5.1
el **jugo** juice, 4.1
el jugo de naranja orange
juice, 4.1; *7*
el **juguete** toy
juicio: a tu juicio in your
opinion
julio July, LP
junio June, LP
junto a next to
juntos(as) together

el **kilo** kilo(gram) (2.2 lbs.), 9.2
el **kilometraje** mileage, **6.2**
el **kilómetro** kilometer

la the *(f. sing.)*, 1.1; it, her
(pron.)
el **labio** lip
**laborable: el día
laborable** working day
el **laboratorio** laboratory
laborioso(a) hardworking
el/la **labrador(a)** farm worker
labrar to work *(land)*, 8.2
el **lacón** bacon, *7*
**lácteo(a): productos
lácteos** dairy products
el **lado** side
al lado de beside, next to,
2.2
ladrar to bark
el **lago** lake

Spanish-English Dictionary

la **lágrima** tear, **10 (Lit.)**

la **lámpara** lamp, 2.2

la **langosta** lobster, *4*

la **lanza** lance

el/la **lanzador(a)** pitcher, 5.2

lanzar to kick, to throw, 5.1

el **lapicero** ballpoint pen

el **lápiz** pencil, 3.1

largo(a) long, 5.1

a lo largo de along

el tren de largo recorrido long-distance train, **6.2**

las the (*f. pl.*); them (*pron.*)

lástima: ser una lástima to be a shame

lastimarse to harm oneself, to get hurt

la **lata** can, 9.2

latino(a) Latino

Latinoamérica Latin America

el/la **latinoamericano(a)** Latin American

el **lavabo** washbasin, sink, *7*

el **lavado** laundry, *4*

la **lavadora** washing machine, *4*

la **lavandería** laundromat, *4*

el **lavaplatos** dishwasher, **10; 1**

lavar to wash, 11.2; **2.2; 4**

lavarse to wash oneself, 11.1; *2.1*

lavarse el pelo (la cara, las manos) to wash one's hair (face, hands), 11.1; *2.1*

lavarse los dientes to clean (*brush*) one's teeth, 11.1; *2.1*

le to him, to her; to you (*formal*) (*pron.*)

la **lección** lesson

la **leche** milk, 4.1

el café con leche coffee with milk, café au lait

el **lechón asado** roast suckling pig

la **lechuga** lettuce, 4.1

la hoja de lechuga leaf of lettuce, *9*

la **lectura** reading

leer to read, 4.2

la **legumbre** vegetable, 4.1; **9**

lejano(a) distant; far-off

lejos (de) far (from), 3.2

a lo lejos in the distance

la **lengua** language

lentamente slowly

lento(a) slow, *11.1*; **2.1;** low (*heat*), **10; 1**

a fuego lento on low heat, *10;* **1**

el **león** lion

les to them; to you (*formal*) (*pron.*)

la **letra** letter (*of alphabet*)

las **letras** literature

levantar to raise, 3.1; to clear, *4;* to lift, *11.1;* **2.1**

levantar la mano to raise one's hand, 3.1

levantar la mesa to clear the table, *4*

levantar pesas to lift weights, *11.1;* **2.1**

levantarse to get up, 11.1; *2.1*

la **ley** law

la **leyenda** legend

liberar to free, to rid, *11.1;* **2.1**

la **libertad** freedom

la **libra** pound (*weight*)

libre free, unoccupied, 4.2; *3.2*

al aire libre outdoor, open-air

el tiempo libre spare time, 8.1

la **librería** bookstore

la **libreta de direcciones** (e-mail) address book, *6.1*

el **libro** book, 3.1

el libro de bolsillo paperback, *3.1;* **8**

la **licencia** driver's license, *9.2*

el **líder** leader

el **lienzo** canvas, *7.1*

la **liga** league

las Grandes Ligas Major Leagues

ligeramente lightly

ligero(a) light

el **límite de velocidad** speed limit

el **limón** lemon

la **limonada** lemonade

los **limpiaparabrisas** windshield wipers, *6.2*

limpiar to clean, *7*

limpio(a) clean, *7*

lindo(a) beautiful

la **línea** (*telephone*) line, 6.2; (*road*) line, 9.1

la línea continua solid line, *9.1*

Se nos cortó la línea. We've been cut off. (*phone*), 6.2

línea: en línea online, *6.1*

entrar en línea to go online, *6.1*

la **línea aérea** airline, 10.1; *1.1*

lío: ¡Qué lío! What a mess!, **6.1**

la **liquidación** sale, 9.1

listo(a) ready

la **litera** bunk

la **literatura** literature, **7.2**

la **llama** llama

la **llamada** (*telephone*) call, 6.2

la llamada perdida (caída) dropped call (*cell phone*), *6.2*

llamar to call, 11.2; *2.2*

llamarse to call oneself, to be called, named, 11.1; *2.1*

Me llamo… My name is . . . , 11.1; *2.1*

el **llano** plains

la **llanta** tire, 9.2

la llanta de repuesto (recambio) spare tire, 9.2

la **llave** key, *7*

la llave magnética magnetic key, *7*

la **llegada** arrival, 3.1

llegar to arrive, 4.1

llenar to fill, *9.2;* **10**

lleno(a) de full of, 6.1

llevar to carry; to wear, 3.1; to take; to bear; to have

llorar to cry

llover (ue) to rain

Llueve. It's raining., LP

lluvioso(a) rainy

lo it, him, you (*formal*) (*pron.*)

lo que what, that which

la **loción bronceadora** suntan lotion, sunblock, *7.1*

loco(a) crazy

el **lodo** mud

lógico(a) logical

lograr to achieve, to get, **8**

la **loncha** slice (*ham*)

la **lonja** slice (*ham*)

el **loro** parrot

los them (*m. pl.*) (*pron.*)

el **lote** lot, site

las **luces** lights, 5.2; headlights, *9.2*

la fiesta de las luces festival of lights (*Hanukkah*), 5.2

la **lucha** battle, fight, **8**

luchar to fight, **8**

luego later, LP; then, 3.2

¡Hasta luego! See you later!, LP

el **lugar** place; setting, *7.2*

en lugar de instead of
tener lugar to take place,
3.1
lujoso(a) luxurious
el **lunes** Monday, LP
la **luz** light, *5.2*
la luz roja red light, *9.1*

la **madera** wood
de madera wooden, **7.1**
la **madrastra** stepmother, *2.1*
la **madre** mother, *2.1*
los **madrileños** citizens of
Madrid
la **madrina** godmother, **3.2**
el/la **madrugador(a)** early riser,
11.1; *2.1*; **10 (Lit.)**
los **maduros** fried sweet bananas
el/la **maestro(a)** teacher; master
magnético(a) magnetic, *7*
magnífico(a) magnificent,
splendid
Magos: los Reyes Magos the
Three Wise Men, *5.2*
el **maíz** corn, *9.2*
la mazorca de maíz ear of
corn, **9**
mal bad
estar de mal humor to be
in a bad mood, *6.1*
Hace mal tiempo. The
weather is bad., LP
mal educado(a) ill-
mannered, rude, *6.1*
el **malecón** boardwalk
(seafront)
malentender (ie) to
misunderstand, **5**
el **malentendido**
misunderstanding, **5**
los **males** the evil (things), the
ills
la **maleta** suitcase, *10.1*; *1.1*; **6.1**
hacer la maleta to pack,
10.1; *1.1*
la **maletera** trunk *(of a car)*,
10.1; *1.1*
malicioso(a) malicious
malo(a) bad, *1.2*
sacar notas malas to get
bad grades, *3.1*
malquerer (ie) to dislike
mamá mom, mommy
mandar to send
el **mandato** command
la **mandíbula** jaw
el **mando** command, charge
la cabina de mando
cockpit

---

la **manejar** to drive
la **manera** manner, way
de ninguna manera in no
way, by no means
**manga: de manga corta
(larga)** short- (long-)
sleeved, *9.1*
el **maní** peanut, *8.1*
la **manía** habit, obsession,
6 (Lit.)
la **mano** hand, *3.1*
el equipaje de mano carry-
on luggage, *10.2*; *1.2*
levantar la mano to raise
one's hand, *3.1*
manso(a) gentle
la **manta** blanket, *7*
el **mantel** tablecloth, *4*
mantener (ie) to maintain
mantenerse en forma
to stay in shape
la **mantequilla** butter, *4.1*; *7*
la **manzana** apple, *9.2*; (city)
block, *9.1*
mañana tomorrow, LP
¡Hasta mañana!
See you tomorrow!, LP
la **mañana** morning
de la mañana A.M.
por la mañana in the
morning
el **mapa** map, **6.2**
la **máquina** machine
la **maquinaria** machinery,
equipment
el **mar** sea, ocean, *7.1*
el mar Caribe Caribbean
Sea
el **maratón** marathon, *11.1*; **2.1**
marcar to score, *5.1*; to dial,
6.2
marcar el número to dial
the number, *6.2*
marcar un tanto to score a
point, *5.1*
la **marcha** march
en marcha working
marchar to march
marchito(a) withered,
shriveled
el **marido** husband, *2.1*
el **marinero** sailor
el **mariscal** marshal
los **mariscos** shellfish, seafood, *4*
marrón: de color marrón
brown, *5.1*
el **martes** Tuesday, LP
marzo March, LP
mas but
más more, *9.1*
¡Qué… más… !
What a . . . !

---

la **máscara** mask, *5.1*
la máscara de oxígeno
oxygen mask, *10.2*; *1.2*
la **mascota** pet, *2.1*
matar to kill
las **matemáticas** mathematics,
math, *1.2*
los **materiales escolares** school
supplies, *3.1*
la **matrícula universitaria**
tuition, fees, **4**
el **matrimonio** marriage, **3.1**
el **mausoleo** mausoleum, *5.1*
máximo(a) highest, top
la velocidad máxima speed
limit, top speed
mayo May, LP
la **mayonesa** mayonnaise, *9.2*
mayor older, *2.1*
hacerse mayor to grow
older
el/la **mayor** the oldest, *2.1*; the
greatest
la **mayoría** majority
mayoritario(a) *(related to)*
majority
mazorca: la mazorca de maíz
ear of corn, **9**
me me *(pron.)*
mediano(a) medium,
medium-size
la **medianoche** midnight
el **medicamento** medicine, *6.2*
la **medicina** medicine, *6.2*
el/la **médico(a)** doctor, *6.2*
la **medida** measurement
las **medidas** measures
medio(a) half; middle
a término medio medium
(meat), *4*
la clase media middle class
y media half past (the
hour), LP
el **medio** means; ways; middle
el medio de transporte
means of transport, *8.1*
el **mediodía** noon
el **Medio Oriente** Middle East
**medios: los medios de
comunicación** media, **8**
la **mejilla** cheek, **5**
los **mejillones** mussels, *4*
mejor better
el/la **mejor** the best
mejorar to make better,
5 (Lit.)
menor younger, *2.1*; lesser
el/la **menor** the youngest, *2.1*; the
least
la **menora** menorah, *5.2*
menos less, *9.1*
a lo menos at least

Spanish-English Dictionary

menos cuarto a quarter to (the hour)

el **mensaje** message, *6.2*

   el mensaje de texto text message

   el mensaje instantáneo instant message

el/la **mensajero(a)** messenger

   mentir (ie, i) to lie, **8**

la **mentira** deceit, lie

el **menú** menu, *4.2; 4*

   menudo: a menudo often

el **mercado** market, *9.2*

la **mercancía** merchandise

la **merienda** snack, *4.2*

la **mermelada** jam, marmalade, *7*

el **mes** month, *LP*

la **mesa** table, *2.2; 4*

   levantar la mesa to clear the table, *4*

   poner la mesa to set the table, *4*

   quitar la mesa to clear the table, *4*

la **mesada** monthly allowance

el/la **mesero(a)** waiter (waitress), server, *4.2; 4*

la **meseta** meseta, plateau

la **mesita** table, *2.2; 4*

el **mesón** old-style bar, tavern

   meter to put, to place

   meter un gol to score a goal, *5.1*

el **metro** subway, metro, *8.1;* meter

   la boca del metro subway station entrance, *8.1*

   la estación de metro subway station, *8.1*

el **metrópoli** metropolis, big city

   mexicano(a) Mexican, *1.2*

la **mezcla** mixture

   mi(s) my

   mí me

el **miedo** fear

   tener miedo to be afraid, *7.2*

la **miel** honey, *3 (Lit.)*

el **miembro** member, *2.1*

   mientras while, *5.2*

el **miércoles** Wednesday, *LP*

la **migración** migration

   mil (one) thousand

el **millón** million

el/la **millonario(a)** millionaire

   mimado(a) spoiled *(person)*

el **mimo** mime, *8.1*

la **mina** mine

el **minuto** minute

   ¡Mira! Look!, *3.1*

la **mirada** gaze, look

   tener la mirada fijada to keep one's eyes fixed on

   mirar to look at, *3.2*

   mirarse to look at oneself, *11.1; 2.1*

la **misa** mass

la **miseria** poverty

la **misión** mission

   mismo(a) same, *1.2;* own; very

   misterioso(a) mysterious

   mixto(a) co-ed

la **mochila** backpack, knapsack, *3.1*

el/la **mochilero(a)** backpacker, hiker, *11.2; 2.2*

   viajar de mochilero to go backpacking, hiking

la **moda** fashion

los **modales** manners, *6.1; 5*

   tener buenos (malos) modales to have good (bad) manners, to be well-behaved (rude), *6.1*

   moderno(a) modern

   modesto(a) inexpensive

el/la **modista** fashion designer

el **modo** way

   molestar to bother, to annoy, *6.1*

la **molestia** nuisance, trouble, bother

el **molino de viento** windmill

el **monasterio** monastery

la **moneda** coin, *9.1; 4*

el **mono** monkey

el **monopatín** skateboard, *11.1; 2.1*

el **monstruo** monster

la **montaña** mountain, *7.2*

   la montaña rusa roller coaster, *8.1*

   montañoso(a) mountainous

   montar to put up *(tent)*, *11.2; 2.2;* to ride, *8.2*

   montar a caballo to go horseback riding, *8.2*

el **montón** bunch, heap

el **monumento** monument

la **moraleja** moral

   mórbido(a) morbid

   morder (ue) to bite

   moreno(a) dark-haired, brunette, *1.1*

   morir (ue, u) to die, *4*

el **morrón** sweet red pepper

el **mostrador** (ticket) counter, *10.1; 1.1*

   mostrar (ue) to show, *10.2; 1.2*

el **motivo** theme; reason, motive

el **móvil** cell phone, *3.2; 6.1*

el **movimiento** movement, *11.1; 2.1*

el **mozo** bellhop, *7;* young boy, lad, *5 (Lit.)*

el **MP3** MP3 player, *3.2; 6.2*

la **muchacha** girl, *1.1*

el **muchacho** boy, *1.1*

   mucho a lot, many, much, *2.2;* very, *LP*

   Hace mucho calor (frío). It's very hot (cold)., *LP*

   Mucho gusto. Nice to meet you., *1.2*

   ¡Mucho ojo! Careful!, *5*

   mudarse to move

los **muebles** furniture, *2.2*

la **muela** molar

la **muerte** death

   muerto(a) dead

el/la **muerto(a)** dead person, deceased, *5.1*

   el Día de los Muertos the Day of the Dead, *5.1*

la **mujer** wife, *2.1*

la **mula** mule

las **muletas** crutches, *11.2; 2.2*

   andar con muletas to walk on crutches, *11.2; 2.2*

la **multa** fine, *9.1*

   mundial: la Copa Mundial World Cup

el **mundo** world

   todo el mundo everyone

la **muñeca** wrist, *11.1; 2.1*

el **mural** mural

el/la **muralista** muralist

el **muro** wall

el **museo** museum, *8.2*

la **música** music, *1.2*

el/la **músico(a)** musician, *8.1*

   musitar to murmur, whisper, *3 (Lit.)*

el **muslo** thigh, *10; 1*

   muy very, *LP*

   muy bien very well, *LP*

N

   nacer to be born, **3.2**

el **nacimiento** birth

nacional national

la nacionalidad nationality, 1.1

¿de qué nacionalidad? what nationality?, 1.1

nada nothing, not anything, 8.2

De nada. You're welcome., LP

Nada más. Nothing else., 9.2

Por nada. You're welcome., LP; for no reason

nadar to swim, 7.1

nadie nobody, not anybody, 8.2

la nafta gasoline

la naranja orange (fruit), 4.1

la narrativa narrative, 7.2

natal pertaining to where someone was born

la naturaleza nature

la naturaleza muerta still life, 7.1

navegar la red (el Internet) to surf the Web (the Internet), 3.2; 6.1

la Navidad Christmas, 5.2

el árbol de Navidad Christmas tree, 5.2

¡Feliz Navidad! Merry Christmas!

necesario: Es necesario. It's necessary., 11.2; 2.2

necesitar to need, 3.2

negar (ie) to deny

negativo(a) negative

el negocio store, business

el hombre (la mujer) de negocios businessman (woman), 10

negro(a) black, 2.1

negroide negroid

nervioso(a) nervous, 6.1

el neumático tire, 9.2; 6.2

nevado(a) snowy, snow-covered

nevar (ie) to snow, 7.2

Nieva. It's snowing., LP

la nevera refrigerator, 10; 1

ni neither, nor

Ni idea. No idea.

nicaragüense Nicaraguan

el/la nieto(a) grandson (granddaughter), grandchild, 2.1

la nieve snow, 7.2

ninguno(a) none, not any

de ninguna manera in no way, by no means

la niñez childhood

el/la niño(a) boy, girl, child, 6.2

el nivel level.

no no

No hay de qué. You're welcome., LP

no obstante nevertheless

la noche night, evening

Buenas noches. Good evening., LP

esta noche tonight, 4.1

por la noche in the evening

la Nochebuena Christmas Eve, 5.2

la Nochevieja New Year's Eve

nombrar to name

el nombre name, 2.1

la noria Ferris wheel, 8.1

la norma norm, standard

normal normal, 6.2

el norte north

norteamericano(a) American, North American, 1.1

nos us

nosotros(as) we

la nota grade, mark, 3.1

sacar notas buenas (malas) to get good (bad) grades, 3.1

las noticias news, piece of news, 8

el noticiero news report, program

el/la noticiero(a) newscaster, 8

novecientos(as) nine hundred

la novela novel

el/la novelista novelist

noventa ninety, LP

la novia bride, 3.1; girlfriend 6 (Lit.)

noviembre November, LP

el novio groom, 3.1; boyfriend, 6 (Lit.)

los novios sweethearts

la nube cloud, 7.1

nublado(a) cloudy, 7.1

nuestro(a)(os)(as) our

nueve nine, LP

nuevo(a) new, 1.1

de nuevo again

el número shoe size, 9.1; number, 10.1; 1.1

el número del asiento seat number, 10.1; 1.1

el número de teléfono telephone number, 6.2

el número del vuelo flight number, 10.1; 1.1

¿Qué número calzas? What size shoe do you wear (take)?, 9.1

nunca never, not ever, 8.2

nupcial nuptial, wedding, 3.1

O

el obituario obituary, 3.2

el objetivo objective

obligatorio(a) required, obligatory

la obra work; work of art

la obra abstracta abstract work (of art), 7.1

la obra figurativa figurative work (of art), 7.1

observar to observe, to notice

el obstáculo obstacle

obstinado(a) obstinate, stubborn, 6.1

occidental western

el océano ocean

ochenta eighty, LP

ocho eight, LP

ochocientos(as) eight hundred

octubre October, LP

ocupado(a) occupied, 4.2; 3.2

ocurrir to happen

la oda ode

el odio hatred

el oeste west

la oficina office, 8.1; 9

ofrecer to offer

la ofrenda offering, 5.1

el oído ear, 6 (Lit.)

oír to hear, 8.1

Ojalá que… Would that . . . , I hope . . . , 11.2; 2.2

la ojeada glance, 8

dar una ojeada to take a look at

¡Ojo! Watch out! Be careful!

¡Mucho ojo! Careful!, 5

el ojo eye, 2.1

tener mucho ojo to be very careful

tener ojos azules (castaños, verdes) to have blue (brown, green) eyes, 2.1

la ola wave, 7.1

el óleo oil paint, 7.1

olfatear to sniff, to smell, 8

oliva: el aceite de oliva olive oil, 9

la olla pot, 10; 1

olvidar to forget, 5 (Lit.)

once eleven, LP

la onza ounce

opinar to think, to have an opinion

la opinión opinion

oponerse to be opposed

Spanish-English Dictionary

la **oportunidad** opportunity

el/la **opresor(a)** oppressor

oprimir to press, to push (*button, key*), **6.1**

opuesto(a) opposite

la **oración** sentence

el **orden** order

la **orden** order (*restaurant*), **4.2**

el **ordenador** computer, **3.2**; **6.1**

ordenar to order; to arrange

el **orégano** oregano, **9**

la **orfebrería** craftsmanship in precious metals

organizar to organize, to set up

el **órgano** organ

orgulloso(a) proud, **9**

oriental eastern

el **origen** origin, background

originarse to come from

las **orillas** banks, shores

a orillas de on the shores of

el **oro** gold

la **orquesta** orchestra, band

la **orquídea** orchid

ortopédico(a): el/la cirujano(a) ortopédico(a) orthopedic surgeon, **11.2**; **2.2**

oscuro(a) dark

el **otoño** autumn, fall, LP

otorgar to give, to grant, **8**

otro(a) other, another

otros(as) others

el **oxígeno** oxygen

la máscara de oxígeno oxygen mask, **10.2**; **1.2**

¡Oye! Listen!, **1.2**

P

---

paceño(a) of, from La Paz

pacer to graze, **8.2**

la **paciencia** patience, **6.1**

paciente patient (*adj.*), **6.1**

el/la **paciente** patient, **6.2**

el **padrastro** stepfather, **2.1**

el **padre** father, **2.1**

los **padres** parents, **2.1**

el **padrino** best man, **3.1**; godfather, **3.2**

pagar to pay, **3.2**

la **página** page

la página de inicio (inicial, frontal) home page, **6.1**

el **pago** pay, wages

el **país** country

el **paisaje** landscape

la **paja** straw, **5.2**

el **pájaro** bird

el **paje** page, **3.1**

la **palabra** word

la palabra afine cognate

el **palacio** palace

la **palma** palm tree

la **paloma** pigeon

la **palta** avocado

el **pan** bread

el pan dulce pastry, **7**

el pan rallado bread crumbs, **9**

el pan tostado toast, **4.1**; **7**

la **panadería** bakery

el **panecillo** roll, **4.1**; **7**

el **panqueque** pancake

la **pantalla** screen, **6.1**

la pantalla de escritorio (computer) screen, monitor, **6.1**

el **pantalón** pants, **3.1**

el pantalón corto shorts, **5.1**

el pantalón largo long pants, **9.1**

la **panza** belly

el **pañuelo** handkerchief

la **papa** potato, **4.1**

las papas fritas french fries, **4.1**

el **papel** paper, **3.1**; role

la hoja de papel sheet of paper, **3.1**

el rollo de papel higiénico roll of toilet paper, **11.2**; **2.2**

el **paquete** package, **9.2**

par even (*numeric*)

el **par** pair, **9.1**

el par de zapatos pair of shoes, **9.1**

para for; in order to

el **parabrisas** windshield, **9.1**

la **parada** stop, station, **3.2**

la parada de autobús bus stop, **8.1**

el **parador** inn

el **paraguas** umbrella

el **paraíso** paradise

parar(se) to stop, **9.1**

parear to match

parecer to seem, to look like

a mi (tu, su) parecer in my (your, his) opinion

¿Qué te parece? What do you think?

parecido(a) similar

la **pareja** couple, **3.1**

parentesco(a): una relación parentesca a relationship of kinship

el/la **pariente** relative, **2.1**

el **parking** parking lot, **8.1**

el **parque** park, **11.2**; **2.2**

el parque de atracciones amusement park, **8.1**

parquear to park

el **parqueo** parking lot, **8.1**

el **parquímetro** parking meter, **9.1**

el **párrafo** paragraph

la **parrilla** grill, *10*; **1**

la **parte** part; place

¿De parte de quién, por favor? Who's calling, please?, **6.2**

en muchas partes in many places

la mayor parte the greatest part, the most

participar to participate, to take part in

el **partido** game, **5.1**

el **pasabordo** boarding pass

pasado(a) last, **7.1**

el año pasado last year, **7.1**

la semana pasada last week, **7.1**

el **pasaje de la vida** life passage, **3**

el/la **pasajero(a)** passenger, **10.1**; **1.1**

el **pasaporte** passport, **10.2**; **1.2**

pasar to pass, to go, **5.2**; to spend (*time*), **7.1**; to pass (*car*), **9.1**

pasar un rato to spend some time

pasarlo bien to have a good time, to have fun, **11.2**; **2.2**

pasar por el control de seguridad to go through security, **10.2**; **1.2**

¿Qué pasa? What's going on? What's happening?

¿Qué te pasa? What's the matter (with you)?

la **Pascua (Florida)** Easter

pascual (*related to*) Easter

el **paseo** avenue, walk, **8.1**

dar un paseo to take a walk

dar un paseo en bicicleta to take a (bike) ride

el **pasillo** aisle, 10.2; *1.2;* **6.1**
la **pasta dentífrica** toothpaste
el **pastel** cake, 8.1; **3.2**
la **pastilla** bar *(soap)*
los **patacones** slices of fried plantain
patada: dar una patada to stamp
la **patata** potato, 4.1
    las patatas fritas french fries, 4.1
el **patín** ice skate, 7.2
el/la **patinador(a)** ice-skater, 7.2
el **patinaje** skating, 7.2; *11.1;* **2.1**
    el patinaje en línea in-line skating, *11.1;* **2.1**
    el patinaje sobre hielo ice-skating, 7.2
    patinar to skate, to go skating, 7.2; *11.1;* **2.1**
    patinar en línea to go in-line skating, *11.1;* **2.1**
    patinar sobre el hielo to ice-skate, 7.2
la **patria** country, fatherland
el/la **patrón(ona)** patron, 5.1
    el/la santo(a) patrón(ona) patron saint, 5.1
    patronal pertaining to a patron saint, 5.1
pausado(a) slow, deliberate
pavimentado(a) paved
el **pavimento** pavement
el **peaje** toll, *9.1*
    la cabina (garita) de peaje tollbooth, *9.1*
el/la **peatón(ona)** pedestrian, *8.1*
peatonal related to pedestrians, *8.1*
el **pecho** chest, *11.1;* **2.1**
la **pechuga (de pollo)** (chicken) breast, 10; **1**
el **pedacito** little piece, 10; **1**
pedalear to pedal
el **pedazo** piece
pedir (i, i) to ask for, to request, 4
peinarse to comb one's hair, *11.1;* **2.1**
el **peine** comb, 11.2; *2.2*
pelar to peel, 10; **1**
la **película** movie, film, 8.2
el **peligro** danger
peligroso(a) dangerous
pelirrojo(a) redheaded, 1.1
el **pelo** hair, 2.1
    tener el pelo rubio (castaño, negro) to have blond (brown, black) hair, 2.1
la **pelota** ball *(baseball, tennis),* 5.2
    la pelota vasca jai alai

la **peluquería** hair salon, 4
el/la **peluquero(a)** hair stylist, 4
la **pena** pain, sorrow; pity
    ¡Qué pena! What a shame!, 5.1
pendiente steep
la **pendiente** incline
el **pensamiento** thought
pensar (ie) to think, 5.1
    pensar en to think about
    ¿Qué piensas? What do you think?, 5.1
el **peón** peasant, farm laborer, *8.2*
peor worse
el/la **peor** worst
el **pepino** cucumber, 10; **1**
pequeño(a) small, little, 1.2
la **percha** hanger, *7*
percibir to perceive
perder (ie) to lose, 5.1; to miss, 8.1
    perder el vuelo to miss the flight, **6.1**
perdida: la llamada perdida dropped call *(cell phone),* **6.2**
la **pérdida** loss
perdón pardon me, excuse me
perdurar to last, to endure
la **peregrinación** pilgrimage
perezoso(a) lazy, 1.2
el **periódico** newspaper, *3.1;* 8
el/la **periodista** journalist, 8
permanecer to remain
permiso: Con permiso. Excuse me., 10.1; *1.1*
el **permiso de conducir** driver's license, *9.2*
permitir to permit
pero but
el/la **perro(a)** dog, 2.1
la **persona** person
el **personaje** character *(in a novel, play),* **7.2**
la **personalidad** personality, 6.1
la **perspectiva** perspective, 7.1
pertenecer to belong
peruano(a) Peruvian
la **pesa** weight, *11.1;* **2.1**
    levantar pesas to lift weights, *11.1;* **2.1**
pesar to weigh, 6.1
    a pesar de in spite of
la **pescadería** fish market
el **pescado** fish, 4.1
pescar to fish
el **peso** peso *(monetary unit of several Latin American countries);* weight, **6.1**

picada: la carne picada ground meat, 9
el **picadillo** ground meat, 9
picar to nibble on; to chop; to mince, 10; **1**
picaresco(a) picaresque
el/la **pícher** pitcher, 5.2
el **pico** mountain top, peak, 7.2
el **pie** foot, 5.1; *2.1*
    a pie on foot, 3.2
    de pie standing
piedad: sin piedad mercilessly
la **piedra** stone
la **pierna** leg, 11.1; *2.1*
la **pieza** bedroom; piece; part
la **pila** swimming pool; baptismal font, **3.2**
el **pimentón** pepper *(vegetable)*
la **pimienta** pepper *(spice),* 4
el **pimiento** bell pepper, 9.2; *10;* **1**
el **pin** PIN
el **pincel** paintbrush, **3** (Lit.)
el **pinchazo** flat tire, *9.2*
los **pinchitos** kebabs, 4.2
pintado(a) painted
pintar to paint, 7.1
el/la **pintor(a)** painter, artist, 8.2; **7.1**
pintoresco(a) picturesque, **7.1**
la **pintura** paint, painting, 7.1
las **pinzas** tongs
la **piña** pineapple, 9.2
la **piscina** swimming pool, 7.1
el **piso** floor, 2.2; apartment *(Spain)*
la **pista** ski slope, 7.2; runway, 10.2; *1.2;* lane *(highway)*
    la pista de patinaje ice-skating rink, 7.2
la **pizca** pinch
la **pizza** pizza, 4.1
placentero(a) pleasant
el **plan** structure, layout
la **plancha de vela** windsurfing; sailboard, 7.1
    practicar la plancha de vela to windsurf, to go windsurfing, 7.1
planchar to iron, 4
planchas: hacer planchas to do push-ups, *11.1;* **2.1**
planear to plan
el **planeta** planet
plano: el primer plano foreground, 7.1
plano(a) flat, **7.1**
el **plano** map, *9.1*
la **planta** plant, 2.2
la **plata** silver

Spanish-English Dictionary

el **plátano** banana, 9.2
el **platillo** home plate, 5.2; saucer, 4
el **plato** dish (food); plate, 4; course (meal)
la **playa** beach, 7.1
la **plaza** square, plaza, 8.1; seat (train, plane), 3.2; 6.1
el/la **plomero(a)** plumber, 10
la **pluma** (fountain) pen
la **población** population
pobre poor
el/la **pobre** poor boy (girl)
poco(a) a little; few, 2.2
  dentro de poco soon; shortly thereafter
  un poco más a little more
poder (ue) to be able, 5.1
el **poema** poem, 7.2
la **poesía** poetry, poem, 7.2
el/la **poeta** poet, 7.2
el/la **policía** police officer
policíacas: novelas policíacas mysteries, detective fiction
el/la **político(a)** politician, 10
la **póliza** policy, 6.2
el **pollo** chicken, 4.1; 10; 1
polvoriento(a) dusty
poner to put, to place, to set, 10.2; 1.2; to make (someone something)
  poner al fuego to heat, 10; 1
  poner la mesa to set the table, 4
  poner unos puntos (unas suturas) to give (someone) stitches, 11.2; 2.2
ponerse to put on (clothes), 11.1; 2.1; to become, to turn
  ponerse de pie to stand up, 5
  ponerse en marcha to start moving
popular popular
por for, by
  por ejemplo for example
  por encima de over, 5.2
  por eso that's why, for this reason
  por favor please, LP
  por fin finally
  por hora per hour
  por la mañana in the morning
  por la noche at night, in the evening
  por la tarde in the afternoon

por lo general in general
Por nada. You're welcome., LP; for no reason
¿por qué? why?, 3.2
¡Por supuesto! Of course!
los **porotos** green beans (Chile)
porque because, 3.2
el/la **porrista** cheerleader
portátil: la computadora portátil laptop computer
el/la **porteño(a)** person from Buenos Aires
la **portería** goal (box), 5.1
el/la **portero(a)** goalie, 5.1
portugués(esa) Portuguese
poseer to possess
posible possible
positivo(a) positive
el **postre** dessert, 4.1
practicar to practice (sport)
  practicar la plancha de vela (la tabla hawaiana) to go windsurfing (surfing), 7.1
  practicar yoga to do yoga, 11.1; 2.1
el **precio** price, 9.1
precolombino(a) pre-Columbian
la **preferencia** preference
preferir (ie, i) to prefer
el **prefijo del país** country code, 6.2
la **pregunta** question, 3.1
preguntar to ask (a question)
el **premio** prize, award
prender to turn on, 6.1
la **prensa** press, 8
preparar to prepare; to get ready
la **prepa(ratoria)** high school
presenciar to witness, to attend
presentar to introduce
los **presentes** those present, the attendees
el **préstamo** loan, 4
  el préstamo a corto (largo) plazo short- (long-) term loan, 4
prestar: prestar atención to pay attention, 3.1
presumir to presume
el **pretendiente** suitor
primario(a): la escuela primaria elementary school
la **primavera** spring, LP
primero(a) first, LP

el **primer plano** foreground, 7.1
el **primero de enero (febrero, etc.)** January (February, etc.) 1, LP
en primera clase first class, 3.2
el/la **primo(a)** cousin, 2.1
la **princesa** princess
principal main
el/la **principiante** beginner, 7.2
prisa: de prisa fast, hurriedly
  a toda prisa with full speed
privado(a) private, 2.2
probable probable, likely
probarse (ue) to try on
el **problema** problem
  No hay problema. No problem.
procedente de coming, arriving from, 10.2; 1.2
el **procedimiento** step (recipe)
la **procesión** procession, parade, 5.1
producir to produce
el **producto** product; food, 9.2
  los productos congelados frozen food, 9.2
la **profesión** profession, occupation, 10
profesional professional
el/la **profesor(a)** teacher, 1.2
profundo(a) deep
el **programa de televisión** television program, 8
el/la **programador(a) de computadoras** computer programmer, 10
prohibido(a) forbidden, 9.1
prometer to promise
la **promoción** (sales) promotion, 8
el **pronombre** pronoun
pronto: ¡Hasta pronto! See you soon!, LP
la **propaganda** advertising, 8
propenso(a) prone to
la **propina** tip (restaurant), 4
propio(a) own, 5.1
propósito: ¡A propósito! By the way! 8.2
  el propósito benévolo charitable purpose
la **prosa** prose, 7.2
el/la **protagonista** protagonist, 7.2
protectora: la loción protectora sunblock
el **provecho** benefit, 5 (Lit.)
próximo(a) next, 3.2

la **prueba** test, exam, 3.1
publicar to publish
la **publicidad** advertising, **8**
el **público** audience
el **pueblo** town
el **puente** bridge
la **puerta** gate *(airport),* 10.2; *1.2;* door, *9.2*
    la puerta de salida gate *(airport),* 10.2; *1.2;* **6.1**
    la puerta delantera (trasera) front (back) door *(bus)*
el **puerto** port
puertorriqueño(a) Puerto Rican, 1.1
pues well
el **puesto** market stall, 9.2; position *(job),* **10**
puesto que since
los **pulmones** lungs
pulsar to press *(button, key),* 6.1
la **pulsera** bracelet
pulso: tomar el pulso to take someone's pulse, 6.2
la **punta de los dedos** fingertips
el **punto** point; dot *(Internet),* 6.1; stitch, *11.2;* **2.2**
    poner puntos (a alguien) to give (somebody) stitches, *11.2;* **2.2**
puntual punctual
el **puñado** handful, **4 (Lit.)**
el **pupitre** desk, 3.1

Q

que that; who
¿qué? what? how?, LP
    ¿a qué hora? at what time?, LP
    ¿de qué nacionalidad? what nationality?
    No hay de qué. You're welcome., LP
    ¿Qué desean tomar? What would you like (to eat)?, 4.2
    ¿Qué día es hoy? What day is it today?, LP
    ¿Qué hay? What's new (up)?
    ¿Qué hora es? What time is it?, LP
    ¡Qué lío! What a mess!, **6.1**
    ¡Qué… más… ! What a . . . !
    ¿Qué pasa? What's going on? What's happening?, 3.1
    ¡Qué pena! What a shame!, 5.1

¿Qué tal? How are things? How are you?, LP
¿Qué tal le gustó? How did you like it? *(formal)*
¿Qué tiempo hace? What's the weather like?, LP
quebrarse (ie) to break, *11.2;* **2.2**
quedar (bien) to fit, to look good on, 9.1
    Esta chaqueta no te queda bien. This jacket doesn't fit you., 9.1
quedar(se) to remain, to stay, *11.1;* **2.1**
quemarse to burn, *10;* **1**
querer (ie) to want, to wish, 5.1; to love
querido(a) dear, beloved
el **queso** cheese, 4.1
    el sándwich de jamón y queso ham and cheese sandwich, 4.1
el **quetzal** quetzal *(currency of Guatemala)*
¿quién? who?, 1.1
    ¿De parte de quién, por favor? Who's calling, please?, 6.2
¿quiénes? who? *(pl.),* 1.2
quince fifteen, LP
la **quinceañera** fifteen-year-old girl
quinientos(as) five hundred
el **quiosco** kiosk, newsstand, 3.1
quisiera I'd like
quitar la mesa to clear the table, 4
quitarse to take off *(clothes),* 11.1; *2.1*
quizá(s) maybe, perhaps, 7.2

R

el **racimo** bunch *(grapes)*
el/la **radio** radio
la **radiografía** X ray, *11.2;* **2.2**
    Le toman (hacen) una radiografía. They're taking an X ray of him (her)., *11.2;* **2.2**
la **raja** slice *(melon)*
la **rama** branch
el **rancho** ranch, 8.2
la **ranura** slot, 6.2
rápidamente quickly
rápido(a) fast
la **raqueta** *(tennis)* racket, 5.2
raro(a) rare
el **rascacielos** skyscraper, *8.1*
el **rato** time, while

pasar un rato to spend some time
el **ratón** mouse, 6.1
rayas: a rayas striped
el **rayón** scratch, **6.2**
la **raza** breed
la **razón** reason
    tener razón to be right
el/la **realista** realist
realista royalist
realizarse to happen, to come to pass
rebajar to lower *(prices),* 9.1
la **rebanada** slice *(bread),* 10; **1**
    cortar en rebanadas to slice, *10;* **1**
rebasar to pass *(car),* 9.1
rebozar to coat *(with batter),* 9
la **recámara** bedroom, 2.2
recambio: la rueda (llanta) de recambio spare tire, 9.2
la **recepción** front desk *(hotel),* 7; reception, *3.1*
el/la **recepcionista** hotel clerk, 7
el/la **receptor(a)** catcher, 5.2
la **receta** prescription, 6.2; recipe, *10;* **1**
recetar to prescribe, 6.2
recibir to receive, 4.1; to catch
    recibir aplausos to be applauded, 5.1
recién recently, newly
    los recién casados newlyweds, 3.1
    el/la recién llegado(a) person who has just arrived, **5**
    el/la recién nacido(a) newborn, 3.2
reciente recent
reclamar to claim, 6.1
el **reclamo de equipaje** baggage claim, 6.1
recoger to collect, to gather, to pick up 6.1
recomendar (ie) to recommend
reconocer to recognize
recordar (ue) to remember
el **recorrido** trip, route
    el tren de largo recorrido long-distance train, 6.2
el **recorte** trim *(hair),* **4**
los **recuerdos** memories
recuperar to claim, to get back
la **red** the Web, 3.2; *6.1;* net, 5.2
    navegar la red to surf the Web, 3.2; *6.1*
    pasar por encima de la red to go over the net, 5.2
reducido(a) reduced

Spanish-English Dictionary

reducir to reduce; to set *(bone)*, *11.2;* **2.2**

  reducir la velocidad to reduce speed, *9.1*

reemplazar to replace

refacción: la rueda (llanta) de refacción spare tire

reflejar to reflect

reflexionar to think about, to reflect on

el **refresco** soft drink, *4.2*

el **refrigerador** refrigerator, *10;* **1**

refrito(a) refried

el **refugio** refuge

el **regalo** gift, present, *8.1;* **3.1**

regatear to bargain, *9.2*

el **régimen** diet

la **región** region

el **registro de matrimonio** wedding register, **3.1**

la **regla** rule

regresar to go back, to return, *3.2*

  el botón regresar back button, back key, *6.1*

  regresar a casa to go home, *3.2*

regreso: el boleto de ida y regreso round-trip ticket, *3.1*

regular regular, average

la **reina** queen

reinar to rule, to reign; to prevail

reír (i, i) to laugh

relacionado(a) related

relacionar to relate, to connect

relacionarse to mix with, to have contact with

relevos: la carrera de relevos relay race, *11.1;* **2.1**

religioso(a) religious

rellenar to fill, to put filling in, *9*

el **reloj** watch, *6 (Lit.)*

el **rencor** resentment

rendir (i, i) honor to honor

renombrado(a) famous

rentar to rent, *7.1; 3.2;* **6.2**

repartido(a) distributed, split up among

repasar to review

el **repaso** review

repente: de repente suddenly, all of a sudden

repetir (i, i) to repeat, *4;* to have seconds *(meal), 4*

el **repollo** cabbage, *9*

el **reportaje** report, *8*

la **república** republic

  la República Dominicana Dominican Republic

repuesto: la rueda (llanta) de repuesto spare tire, *9.2*

requerir (ie, i) to require

la **reserva** reservation

la **reservación** reservation, *7*

reservar to reserve, *7*

resfriado(a) stuffed up *(cold), 6.2*

el **resorte** spring (mechanical)

respetado(a) respected

respetar to respect

respetuoso(a) respectful

la **respiración** breathing, *11.1;* **2.1**

respirar to breathe

responsable responsible

la **respuesta** answer

el **restaurante** restaurant, *4*

resuelto(a) resolute, determined

resultar to turn out to be

resumirse to be summed up

retirar to withdraw, *4*

el **retraso** delay, *10.2; 1.2*

  con retraso late, *10.2; 1.2*

el **retrato** portrait

retroceder: el botón retroceder back button, back key, *6.1*

el **retrovisor** rearview mirror, **6.2**

la **reunión** meeting, get-together

reunirse to meet, to get together

revisar to check *(ticket), 3.2*

el/la **revisor(a)** conductor, *3.2*

la **revista** magazine, *3.1;* **8**

revolver (ue) to stir, *10;* **1**

revueltos: los huevos revueltos scrambled eggs, *7*

el **rey** king

  el Día de los Reyes Epiphany (January 6), *5.2*

  los Reyes Magos the Three Wise Men, *5.2*

rico(a) rich; delicious

  ¡Qué rico! How delicious!

rígido(a) stiff

la **rima** rhyme, **7.2**

el **rincón** corner

los **riñones** kidneys

el **río** river

el **risco** cliff, *3.2*

el **ritmo** rhythm

el **rito** rite

robar to steal

la **roca** rock, stone

el **rocín** donkey; nag

la **rodaja** slice *(lemon, cucumber);* **9**

rodar (ue) to roll

rodeado(a) surrounded

rodear con los brazos to put one's arms around

la **rodilla** knee, *11.1;* **2.1**

la **rodillera** kneepad, *11.1;* **2.1**

rogar (ue) to beg

rojo(a) red, *5.1*

  la luz roja red light, *9.1*

el **rol** role

el **rollo de papel higiénico** roll of toilet paper, *11.2;* **2.2**

el **rompecabezas** puzzle

romperse to break, *11.2;* **2.2**

  Se rompió la pierna. He (She) broke his (her) leg., *11.2;* **2.2**

la **ropa** clothing, *9.1*

  la ropa para lavar dirty clothes, *4*

  la ropa sucia dirty clothes, **4**

la **ropaje** wardrobe

la **rosa** rose

rosado(a) pink, *5.1*

roto(a) broken

el **rótulo** sign, *9.1*

rubio(a) blonde, *1.1*

la **rueda** tire, *9.2*

  la rueda de repuesto (recambio) spare tire, *9.2*

  la silla de ruedas wheelchair, *11.2;* **2.2**

el **ruido** noise

las **ruinas** ruins

la **ruta** route

la **rutina diaria** daily routine, *11.1;* **2.1**

el **sábado** Saturday, LP

la **sábana** sheet, *7*

saber to know, *9.1*

sabio(a) wise, *5 (Lit.)*

el **sabor** flavor, *10;* **1;** taste

sacar to get, *3.1;* to take, *7.1*

  sacar fotos to take pictures, *7.1*

sacar notas buenas (malas) to get good (bad) grades, 3.1

el **sacerdote** priest, 8

el **saco de dormir** sleeping bag, 11.2; *2.2*

el **sacrificio** sacrifice

la **sal** salt, *4*

la **sala** living room, 2.2
   la sala de clase classroom, 3.1
   la sala de emergencia emergency room, 11.2; **2.2**
   la sala de espera waiting room, 3.1

salado(a) salty

el **saldo** sale, 9.1; *(bank)* balance, *4*

la **salida** departure, 10.1; *1.1;* exit, *9.1*
   la hora de salida time of departure, 10.1; *1.1*
   la puerta de salida gate *(airport),* 10.2; *1.2*

salir to leave; to go out, 8.1; to turn out, to result
   Todo te sale más barato. Everything costs a lot less.; It's all a lot less expensive., 9.1

el **salón** room *(museum),* 8.2

la **salsa** sauce, gravy, *10; 1;* dressing

saltar to jump (over)

salteado(a) sautéed

la **salud** health, 6.1

saludar to greet, **5**

el **saludo** greeting, LP

salvar to save

la **sandalia** sandal, 9.2

el **sándwich** sandwich, 4.1
   el sándwich de jamón y queso ham and cheese sandwich, 4.1

la **sangre** blood

sano(a) healthy

el/la **santo(a)** saint
   el/la santo(a) patrón(ona) patron saint, *5.1*

el **sarape** blanket

el/la **sartén** skillet, frying pan, *10; 1*

satisfacer to satisfy

el **sato** a type of dog from Puerto Rico

sea: o sea or, in other words

la **secadora** dryer, *4*

secarse to dry oneself

seco(a) dry

secundario(a): la escuela secundaria high school, 1.2

la **sed** thirst, 4.1
   tener sed to be thirsty, 4.1

el **sedán** sedan, *9.2*

seguir (i, i) to follow, *4;* to continue, *9.1*

según according to

segundo(a) second
   el segundo tiempo second half *(soccer),* 5.1
   en segunda clase second-class *(ticket),* 3.1

seguramente surely, certainly

seguridad: el control de seguridad security *(airport),* 10.2; *1.2*
   el cinturón de seguridad seat belt, 10.2; *1.2*

seguro que certainly

seguro(a) sure; safe

los **seguros contra todo riesgo** comprehensive insurance, **6.2**

seis six, LP

seiscientos(as) six hundred

seleccionar to choose, *3.1*

el **sello** stamp, *4*

la **selva** jungle, forest

el **semáforo** traffic light, *8.1*

la **semana** week, LP; weekly allowance
   el fin de semana weekend, 7.1
   la semana pasada last week, 7.1

sembrar (ie) to plant, to sow, *8.2*

el **seminómada** seminomad

el/la **senador(a)** senator, **10**

sencillo(a) one-way, *3.1;* single *(hotel room), 7;* simple
   el billete (boleto) sencillo one-way ticket, *3.1*
   el cuarto sencillo single room, *7*

la **senda** path, *3.2*

sentado(a) seated

sentarse (ie) to sit down, 11.1; *2.1*

el **sentido** direction, *9.1;* sense, 6.1
   la calle de sentido único one-way street, *9.1*

sentir (ie, i) to be sorry; to feel
   Lo siento mucho. I'm very sorry.

sentirse (ie, i) to feel

la **señal** sign, 10.2; *1.2*
   la señal de no fumar no-smoking sign, 10.2; *1.2*

señalar to point out

el **señor** sir, Mr., gentleman, LP

la **señora** Ms., Mrs., madam, LP

los **señores** Mr. and Mrs.

la **señorita** Miss, Ms., LP

el **sepelio** burial, **3.2**

septiembre September, LP

ser to be

el **ser** being
   los seres humanos human beings
   los seres vivientes living beings

serio(a) serious, 1.1
   ¿Hablas en serio? Are you serious?

el **servicio** tip, 4.2; restroom, 10.2; *1.2;* service, *9.2*
   ¿Está incluido el servicio? Is the tip included?, 4.2
   la estación de servicio gas station, service station, *9.2*

la **servilleta** napkin, *4*

servir (i, i) to serve, *4*
   servir de to serve as

servirse (i, i) de to use

sesenta sixty, LP

setecientos(as) seven hundred

setenta seventy, LP

severo(a) harsh, strict

si if

sí yes, LP

siempre always, 8.2

siento: Lo siento mucho. I'm very sorry., 5.1

la **sierra** mountain range

el/la **siervo(a)** slave, serf

la **siesta** nap

siete seven, LP

el **siglo** century

el **significado** meaning

significar to mean

siguiente following

la **silla** chair, 2.2
   la silla de ruedas wheelchair, *11.2;* **2.2**

el **sillón** armchair

similar similar

simpático(a) nice, 1.1

simpatizar con to sympathize with

sin without

sincero(a) sincere

sino but rather

el **síntoma** symptom

el **sistema** system

el **sitio** space *(parking)*

el **sitio Web** Web site, *6.1*

el/la **snowboarder** snowboarder, 7.2

las **sobras** leftovers

sobre on, on top of; about
   sobre todo above all, especially

el **sobre** envelope, *4*

Spanish-English Dictionary

Spanish-English Dictionary

la **sobremesa** dessert; after-dinner conversation

sobrepasar to surpass, **8**

la **sobrepoblación** overpopulation

sobrevivir to survive

sobrevolar (ue) to fly over

el/la **sobrino(a)** nephew (niece), 2.1

social social

los estudios sociales social studies, 1.2

la **sociedad** society; company, corporation, **10**

el/la **socio(a)** member, partner

socorrer to help

el/la **socorrista** paramedic, 11.2; **2.2**

el **sofá** sofa, 2.2

el **sol** sun, 7.1

Hace (Hay) sol. It's sunny., LP

tomar el sol to sunbathe, 7.1

solamente only

solar: la crema solar suntan lotion, 7.1

solas: a solas alone

el **soldado** soldier, **8**

soler (ue) to be used to, to do something usually

solicitar to apply for

la **solicitud de empleo** job application, **10**

solo only

solo(a) single; alone; lonely

soltar (ue) to release

el/la **soltero(a)** single, unmarried person

el **sombrero** hat

el **son** sound

sonar (ue) to ring, 6.1

soñar (ue) to dream

el **sonido** sound

la **sonrisa** smile, 6.1

la **sopa** soup

soplar to blow (wind)

sordo(a) deaf, **10 (Lit.)**

sorprender to surprise, **3.1**

la **sorpresa** surprise, 4.1

sospechas: tener sospechas to be suspicious

sostener (ie) to support; to hold up

su(s) his, her, their, your (formal)

suavemente softly

subir to go up, 7.2; to get on (train, etc.), 3.1

el **subsuelo** subsoil

subterráneo(a) underground

los **suburbios** suburbs, 2.2; **6.2**

suceder to happen, **5 (Lit.)**

el **suceso** event

sucio(a) dirty, 7

Sudamérica South America

sudamericano(a) South American

el/la **suegro(a)** father- (mother-) in-law

suele(n): see **soler**

el **suelo** ground, floor

el **suelto** change (money), **4**

el **sueño** dream

tener sueño to be sleepy

la **suerte** luck

¡Buena suerte! Good luck!

¡Qué suerte tengo! How lucky I am!, 9.1

el **suéter** sweater, 11.1; **2.1**

sufrir to suffer

sugerir (ie, i) to suggest

sujetar to subject, to subdue, **4 (Lit.)**

sumergir to submerge, to immerse

sumiso(a) submissive, docile

la **superficie** surface, **7.1**

superior upper, top

el compartimiento superior overhead bin (airplane), 10.2; 1.2

el **supermercado** supermarket, 9.2

el **sur** south

la América del Sur South America

el **surfing** surfing, 7.1

surgir to come up with, to arise

el **surtido** assortment

sus his, her, their, your (formal)

el **suspiro** breath

sustituir to substitute (for)

el **susto** fear

la **sutura** stitch, 11.2; **2.2**

suturar to give (someone) stitches

el **SUV** SUV, 9.2

T

el **tabaquero** cigar maker

la **tabla** chart, table

la **tabla hawaiana** surfboard, 7.1

practicar la tabla hawaiana to surf, to go surfing, 7.1

tacaño(a) stingy, cheap, 9.1

el **taco** taco

la **tajada** slice (ham, meat), 9.2

tal such

¿Qué tal? How are things? How are you?, LP

¿Qué tal tu clase de español? How's your Spanish class?

tal como such as

tal vez maybe, perhaps, 7.2

el **talento** talent, **7.2**

la **talla** size, 9.1

¿Qué talla usas? What size do you take?, 9.1

tallar to carve, **7.1**

el **taller** workshop, **7.1**

el **talón** heel (of a shoe); luggage claim ticket, **6.1**

el **tamaño** size

también also, too, 1.2

el **tambor** drum

el **tamborín** small drum

tampoco not . . . either, neither

tan so

tan… como as . . . as

tan pronto como as soon as

el **tanque** gas tank, 9.2; **6.2**

el **tanto** score, point, 5.1

marcar un tanto to score a point, 5.1

tanto(a) so much

tanto(a)… como as much . . . as

tantos(as)… como as many . . . as

la **tapa** lid, 10; **1**

tapar to cover (pot)

las **tapas** snacks, nibbles, 4.2

el **tapón** traffic jam

la **taquilla** box office, ticket window, 8.2

tardar: no tardar en not to take long (to do something)

tarde late, 10.2; **1.2**

la **tarde** afternoon

ayer por la tarde yesterday afternoon, 7.1

Buenas tardes. Good afternoon., LP

la **tarea** homework; task

la **tarifa** fare, 3.1; price, **6.2**

la **tarjeta** card; pass

la tarjeta de abordar boarding pass

la tarjeta de crédito credit card, 3.1

la tarjeta de embarque boarding pass, 10.1; 1.1

---

la **tarjeta postal** postcard, *4*
la **tarjeta telefónica**
telephone card, *6.2*
la **tarta** cake, 8.1; **3.2**
la **tasa de interés** interest rate, **4**
el **taxi** taxi, 10.1; *1.1*
el/la **taxista** taxi driver, 10.1; *1.1*
la **taza** cup, 4.1; *4*
te you *(fam. pron.)*
el **té** tea
el **teclado** keyboard, *6.1*
el/la **técnico(a)** technician
la **tecnología** technology
tejano(a) Texan
los **tejidos** fabrics, 9.2
la **tele** TV
telefónico(a) *(related to)*
phone, *6.2*
la **guía telefónica** phone
book, *6.2*
la **tarjeta telefónica** phone
card, *6.2*
el **teléfono** telephone
hablar por teléfono to
speak on the phone
el **número de teléfono**
phone number, *6.2*
el **teléfono celular** cell
phone, *6.1*
el **teléfono público** pay
phone, *6.2*
la **telenovela** serial, soap opera
el **telesilla** chairlift, ski lift, 7.2
el **telesquí** ski lift, 7.2
la **televisión** television
el **tema** theme
temblar (ie) to tremble, to
shake
tembloroso(a) trembling
la **temperatura** temperature,
7.2
temprano(a) early, 11.1; *1.2*
el **tenderete** market stall, 9.2
el **tenedor** fork, *4*
tener (ie) to have, 2.1
tener... años to be . . . years
old, 2.1
tener calor (frío) to be hot
(cold), 11.1; *2.1*
tener catarro to have a
cold, 6.2
tener cuidado to be careful,
9.1
tener dolor de... to have
a(n) . . . -ache, 6.2
**tener el pelo rubio (castaño,
negro)** to have blond
(brown, black) hair, 2.1
tener éxito to be successful,
6.1
tener fiebre to have a fever,
6.2
tener ganas de to feel like

tener hambre to be hungry,
4.1
tener lugar to take place
tener miedo to be afraid,
7.2
**tener ojos azules (castaños,
verdes)** to have blue
(brown, green) eyes, 2.1
tener que to have to (do
something), 4.1
tener sed to be thirsty, 4.1
el/la **teniente** deputy mayor
el **tenis** tennis, 5.2
la **cancha de tenis**
tennis court, 5.2
jugar (al) tenis to play
tennis, 5.2
los **tenis** sneakers, tennis shoes,
9.1
el/la **tenista** tennis player
la **tensión** tension, stress,
11.1; **2.1**
la **tensión arterial** blood
pressure, *6.2*
tercer(o)(a) third
terco(a) stubborn, 6.1
terminar to end, to finish
término: a término medio
medium *(meat)*, *4*
el **término** term
la **ternera** veal, *10*; *1*
el **escalope de ternera** veal
cutlet, *10*; *1*
la **ternura** tenderness
el/la **terrateniente** landowner
la **terraza** terrace, balcony
el **terremoto** earthquake
el **tesoro** treasure
ti you
tibio(a) lukewarm
el **ticket** ticket, 7.2
el **tiempo** weather, LP; half
(soccer), 5.1
a tiempo on time, 10.2; *1.2*
a tiempo completo full-
time, **10**
a tiempo parcial part-time,
10
**Hace buen (mal)
tiempo.** The weather is
nice (bad)., LP
¿Qué tiempo hace? What's
the weather like?, LP
el **segundo tiempo** second
half *(soccer)*, 5.1
la **tienda** store, 3.2
la **tienda de ropa** clothing
store, 9.1
la **tienda de campaña** tent, 11.2;
2.2
tierno(a) tender; affectionate
la **tierra** land, 8.2
el **tigre** tiger

los **timbales** small drums,
kettledrums
el **timbre (sonoro)** ringtone, *6.2*
tímido(a) shy
el/la **tío(a)** uncle (aunt), 2.1
los **tíos** aunt and uncle, 2.1
el **tiovivo** merry-go-round, *8.1*
típico(a) typical
el **tipo** type, 6.1
el **tiquete** ticket, *9.1*
tirar to throw, 5.2
el **titular** headline, **8**
el **título** title; degree
la **toalla** towel, 7.1; *7*
el **tobillo** ankle, *11.1*; **2.1**
el **tocadiscos** record player
tocar to touch, 5.1; to play
(musical instrument), 8.1; *5.2*
¡Te toca a ti! It's your turn!
el **tocino** bacon, 4.1; *7*
todavía still; yet
todo(a) everything; all
sobre todo above all,
especially
todo el mundo everyone,
5.2
todos(as) everyone, 8.1;
everything; all
en todas partes everywhere
tomar to take, 3.1; to have
(meal), 4.1
**tomar el almuerzo (el
desayuno)** to have lunch
(breakfast), 4.1
tomar el bus to take the
bus
tomar el pulso a alguien to
take someone's pulse, 6.2
tomar el sol to sunbathe,
7.1
tomar en cuenta to take
into account, **8**
tomar fotos to take
pictures, 7.1
**tomar la tensión arterial a
alguien** to take someone's
blood pressure, 6.2
tomar un examen to take a
test, 3.1
tomar una ducha to take a
shower, 11.1; *2.1*
tomar una radiografía to
take an X ray of someone,
11.2; **2.2**
el **tomate** tomato, 4.1
la **tonelada** ton
el **tono** dial tone, *6.2*
tontería: ¡Qué tontería!
How silly! What nonsense!
las **tonterías** foolish things
tonto(a) foolish, crazy
torcerse (ue) to sprain, to
twist, *11.2*; **2.2**

Spanish-English Dictionary

Se torció el tobillo.
He (She) sprained his (her) ankle., *11.2*; **2.2**

torcido(a) sprained, twisted

la **torre** tower

la **torta** cake, *4.1*; **3.2**; sandwich

la **tortilla** tortilla

la **tos** cough, *6.2*

tener tos to have a cough, *6.2*

toser to cough, *6.2*

la **tostada** tostada

las **tostadas** toast, *4.1*

tostado(a) toasted

el pan tostado toast, *4.1*; *7*

los **tostones** slices of fried plantain, *4.2*

trabajar to work, *3.2*; *8.2*

el **trabajo** work, **10**

tradicional traditional

traer to carry, to bring, to take, *10.1*; *1.1*

el **tráfico** traffic, *8.1*

el **traje** suit

el **traje de baño** swimsuit, *7.1*

el **traje de novia** wedding dress, **3.1**

tranquilo(a) calm, *6.1*

transbordar to transfer (trains), *3.2*; **6.2**

el **tránsito** traffic

la **transmisión manual** manual transmission, *6.2*

transporte: los medios de transporte means of transportation, *8.2*

tras behind

trasero(a) back, *7.1*

trasladar to move (something); to transfer

el **tratamiento** treatment

tratar to treat

tratar de to try to (do something)

tratar de desviar to try to dissuade

través: a través de through; over

la **travesía** crossing

traviesa: a campo traviesa cross-country (race), *11.1*; **2.1**

el **trayecto** stretch (of road)

trece thirteen, LP

el **trecho** stretch (distance)

treinta thirty, LP

treinta y uno thirty-one, LP

el **tren** train, *3.1*; **6.2**

el tren de cercanías suburban train, **6.2**

el tren de largo recorrido long-distance train, **6.2**

tres three, LP

trescientos(as) three hundred

el **trigo** wheat, *8.2*; **9**

triste sad, *6.1*

la **tristeza** sadness, sorrow

el **trocito** little piece

la **trompeta** trumpet

las **tropas** troops

tropical tropical

el **trotamundos** globe-trotter

el **trozo** piece

la **trucha** trout

el **T-shirt** T-shirt

tu(s) your (*fam.*)

tú you (*sing. fam.*)

el **tubo de crema dental** tube of toothpaste, *11.2*; **2.2**

la **tumba** grave, tomb, *5.1*

turbarse to be disturbed; to be altered

el **turismo** tourism

el/la **turista** tourist

tutear to use «**tú**» when addressing someone

U

u or (used instead of **o** before words beginning with **o** or **ho**)

Ud., usted you (*sing.*) (*formal*)

Uds., ustedes you (*pl.*) (*formal*)

último(a) last; final

un(a) a, an, *1.1*

la **una** one o'clock, LP

único(a) only, *2.1*; one-way, *9.1*

la calle de sentido único one-way street, *9.1*

el/la hijo(a) único(a) only child, *2.1*

la **unidad** unit

el **uniforme** uniform, *3.1*

la **universidad** university

universitario(a) (related to) university, college

el/la **universitario(a)** college student

uno(a) one, LP

unos(as) some

urbano(a) urban, *8.1*

usar to use, *3.2*; to wear (size), *9.1*

¿Qué talla usas? What size do you wear (take)?, *9.1*

el **uso** use

el/la **usuario(a)** user

la **uva** grape, *9.2*; **9**

V

la **vaca** cow, *8.2*

las **vacaciones** vacation, *7.1*

estar de vacaciones to be on vacation

vacante vacant

vacilar to hesitate

el **vacío** void, empty space

vacío(a) empty, *9.2*; *3* (Lit.)

vagar to wander, to roam

el **vagón** train car, *3.1*

la **vainilla** vanilla

las **vainitas** green beans, **9**

Vale. Okay.; It's a good idea.

más vale que... it is better that . . .

No vale. It's not worth it., *7.1*

valeroso(a) brave

valiente brave, courageous, valiant

el **valle** valley

el **valor** bravery, valor

¡Vamos! Let's go!

varios(as) several

el **varón** man, boy

vasco(a) Basque

la pelota vasca jai-alai

el **vaso** glass, *4.1*

el **váter** toilet, *7*

veces: a veces at times, sometimes, *6.1*

el/la **vecino(a)** neighbor

el **vegetal** vegetable, *4.1*

los vegetales crudos raw vegetables, crudités, *8.1*

vegetariano(a) vegetarian, *4.1*

veinte twenty, LP

veinticinco twenty-five, LP

veinticuatro twenty-four, LP

veintidós twenty-two, LP

veintinueve twenty-nine, LP

veintiocho twenty-eight, LP

veintiséis twenty-six, LP

veintisiete twenty-seven, LP

veintitrés twenty-three, LP

veintiuno twenty-one, LP

la **vela** candle, *8.1*; *5.2*; **3.2**

vela: **la plancha de vela**
windsurfing; sailboard, 7.1

velar to keep watch

el **velo** veil, **3.1**

la **velocidad** speed, *9.1*

la velocidad máxima speed
limit, *9.1*

el **velorio** wake, **3.2**

la **venda** bandage, *11.2;* **2.2**

el/la **vendedor(a)** merchant, 9.2;
10

vender to sell, 6.2

venenoso(a) poisonous

venezolano(a) Venezuelan

venir (ie) to come, 10.2; *1.2*

**el verano (año, mes) que
viene** next summer (year,
month), *8.2*

la **venta** small hotel

las **ventajas** advantages

la **ventanilla** ticket window, 7.2,
3.1; window *(plane),* 10.2;
1.2; **6.1**

ventoso(a) windy

ver to see, 4.2

no tener nada que ver con
not to have anything to do
with

el **verano** summer, LP

el **verbo** verb

la **verdad** truth

Es verdad. That's true
(right)., 9.1

¿Verdad? Right?

verdadero(a) real, true

verde green, 2.1

las judías verdes green
beans, 9.2; **9**

la **verdulería** greengrocer
(vegetable) store, 9.2

la **verdura** vegetable, 4.1

verificar to check, **6.2**

verosímil true-to-life

el **verso** verse, **7.2**

el **vestido** dress, 9.1

el vestido de novia
wedding dress

vestirse (i, i) to get dressed,
to dress, **4**

la **vez** time

a veces at times,
sometimes, 6.1; *1.2*

cada vez each time, every
time

de vez en cuando from
time to time, occasionally,
10.2; *1.2*

en vez de instead of

una vez más (once) again,
one more time

la **vía** track, *3.1;* lane *(highway)*

viajar to travel

viajar en avión (tren) to
travel by plane (train)

el **viaje** trip, voyage 10.1; *1.1*

hacer un viaje to take a
trip, 10.1; *1.1*

la **víctima** victim

la **vid** grapevine, **9**

la **vida** life

el **video** video

viejo(a) old, 2.2

el **viento** wind, LP

Hace viento. It's windy.,
LP

el **viernes** Friday, LP

la **villa** small town, **5** (Lit.)

el **vinagre** vinegar, *4*

el **vino** wine

la **viña** vineyard, **9**

el **violín** violin

la **virtud** virtue

visitar to visit, 8.2

la **víspera de Año Nuevo**
New Year's Eve

la **vista** view; sight

perder la vista to lose sight
of

la **viuda (del difunto)** widow,
3.2

vivir to live, 4.1

vivo(a) lively

los **vivos** the living

la **vocal** vowel

el **volante** steering wheel,
9.2

volar (ue) to fly

el **volcán** volcano

volcar to flip over

el **voleibol** volleyball, 7.1

la cancha de voleibol
volleyball court, 7.1

volver (ue) to return, 5.1

volver a casa to go back
(return) home, 8.1

volver a (+ infinitivo) to do
(something) again

volverse to turn around

vosotros(as) you *(pl.)*

la **voz** voice

en voz alta aloud

el **vuelo** flight, 10.1; *1.1;* **6.1**

el número del vuelo flight
number, 10.1; *1.1*

el vuelo directo direct
flight, **6.1**

el vuelo sin escala non-
stop flight, **6.1**

**vuelta: un boleto (billete)
de ida y vuelta** round-trip
ticket, *3.1*

la **vuelta** lap, *11.1;* **2.1**

Vuestra Merced Your
Highness

Y

y and, LP

y cuarto a quarter past
(the hour), LP

y media half past
(the hour), LP

ya already

¡Ya voy! I'm coming!,
11.2; *2.2*

el **yeso** cast *(medical),* 11.2;
2.2; plaster, **7.1**

yo I; me

el **yoga** yoga, *11.1;* **2.1**

Z

la **zanahoria** carrot, 9.2; *10;* **1**

las **zapatillas** (sports) shoes,
sneakers, 5.1

los **zapatos** shoes, 9.1

la **zona** area, zone

el **zoológico** zoo, *8.1*

el **zumo** juice *(Spain)*

English-Spanish Dictionary

The English-Spanish Dictionary contains all productive and receptive vocabulary from ¡Así se dice! Levels 1, 2, and 3. The locator numbers following each productive entry indicate the chapter and vocabulary section in which the word is introduced (e.g., 3.2 means Chapter 3, Vocabulary 2). Level 1 chapter/section numbers are light print (3.2); Level 2 numbers are *italic (3.2)*; Level 3 chapter/section numbers are **bold (3.2)**. LP refers to the Level 1 **Lecciones preliminares.** If no locator follows an entry, the word or expression is receptive.

A

@ la arroba, *6.1*

a, an un(a), 1.1

able: to be able poder (ue), 5.1

aboard abordo (de), 10.2; *1.2*

about sobre; *(time)* a eso de

above por encima de, 5.2

  above all sobre todo

abroad al extranjero

abstract work (of art) la obra abstracta, **7.1**

to **accept** aceptar, **6.2**

accident el accidente, *11.2;* **2.2**

accompanied by acompañado(a) de, *3.2*

according to según

accountant el/la contable, **10**

ache el dolor, **6.2**

to **ache** doler (ue), **6.2**; *11.2;* **2.2**

  My . . . ache(s). Me duele(n)... , **6.2**

to **achieve** lograr, **8**

acquaintance el/la conocido(a), **5**

activity la actividad

to **add** añadir, **10**; **1**

addition: in addition to además de

address la dirección, *6.1*

  address book la libreta de direcciones, *6.1*

  e-mail address la dirección de correo electrónico (e-mail), *6.1*

addressee el/la destinatario(a), *6.1*

adorable cariñoso(a), 2.1; adorable

advanced avanzado(a), **7.2**

advantage la ventaja

advertising la propaganda, la publicidad, **8**

to **advise** aconsejar; avisar, **6 (Lit.)**

afraid: to be afraid tener miedo, 7.2

after después (de), 3.1; *(time)* y; después de que

  It's ten after one. Es la una y diez., LP

afternoon la tarde

  Good afternoon. Buenas tardes., LP

  this afternoon esta tarde, 7.1

  yesterday afternoon ayer por la tarde, 7.1

again de nuevo

against contra

age la edad

agency la agencia

agent el/la agente, 10.1; *1.1;* **6.2**

ago: . . . years (months, etc.) ago hace... años (meses, etc.)

agricultural agrícola

air el aire

  open-air (outdoor) café (market) el café (mercado) al aire libre

  air conditioning el aire acondicionado, *7*

airline la línea aérea, 10.1; *1.1*

airplane el avión, 10.1; *1.1*

airport el aeropuerto, 10.1; *1.1;* **6.1**

aisle el pasillo, 10.2; *1.2;* **6.1**

album el álbum

algebra el álgebra

all todo(a), 6.2; todos(as), 8.1

  above all sobre todo

to **allow** dejar

almost casi, 8.2; *4*

alone solo(a); a solas

already ya

also también, 1.2

although aunque

always siempre, 8.2

A.M. de la mañana

ambulance la ambulancia, *11.2;* **2.2**

American americano(a)

among entre

to **amuse** divertir (ie, i), 10.2; *1.2*

amusement park el parque de atracciones, *8.1*

  amusement park ride la atracción, *8.1*

amusing divertido(a)

anchor *(television)* el ancla, **8**

ancient antiguo(a), *8.1*

and y, LP

Andean andino(a)

angry enfadado(a), enojado(a), *6.1*

  to get angry enfadarse, **5**

  to make angry enfadar, *6.1*

animal el animal

ankle el tobillo, *11.1;* **2.1**

announcement el anuncio, **10**

to **annoy** molestar, enojar, *6.1*

another otro(a)

answer la respuesta

to **answer** contestar, 3.1

any cualquier

  any other cualquier otro(a)

anybody alguien, 8.2

anything algo, 8.2

  Anything else? ¿Algo más?, 9.2

apartment el apartamento, el apartamiento, el departamento, 2.2; el piso

  apartment building la casa de apartamentos, 2.2

appearance la apariencia

to **applaud** aplaudir, 5.1

  to be applauded recibir aplausos, 5.1

applause el aplauso, 5.1

apple la manzana, 9.2

appreciated apreciado(a)

to **approach** acercarse a

April abril, LP

archaeology la arqueología

architect el/la arquitecto(a),
10.1

area la zona; el área *(f.)*

area code la clave de área, *6.2*

Argentine argentino(a)

arithmetic la aritmética

arm el brazo, 11.1; *2.1*

army el ejército, **4 (Lit.)**

around alrededor de, 2.2;
(time) a eso de

arrival la llegada, *3.1*

to arrive llegar, 4.1

arriving from procedente de,
10.2; *1.2*

art el arte, 1.2; **7.1**

  art show (exhibition)
la exposición de arte, 8.2

artichoke la alcachofa, **9**

  artichoke (sautéed) la
alcachofa salteada

article el artículo, **8**

artist el/la artista;
el/la pintor(a), 8.2; **7.1**

as como

  as . . . as tan… como

  as many . . . as tantos(as)…
como

  as much . . . as tanto(a)…
como

  as soon . . . as en cuanto,
tan pronto como

to ask (a question) preguntar

to ask for pedir (i, i), *4*

assign asignar, *6.2*

assistance la ayuda

assistant: executive assistant
el/la asistente(a) ejecutivo(a),
10

at a, en

  at (@) sign la arroba, *6.1*

  at around *(time)* a eso de

  at home en casa, 2.2

  at night por la noche; de
noche

  at one o'clock (two o'clock,
three o'clock . . .) a la una
(a las dos, a las tres...), LP

  at times a veces, 6.1; *1.2*

  at what time? ¿a qué hora?,
LP

athlete el/la atleta

ATM el cajero automático, **4**

atmosphere el ambiente, *7.2*

attached file el documento
adjunto, *6.1*

to attend asistir (a), 8.1

attention: to pay attention
prestar atención, 3.1

attractive guapo(a), 1.1

August agosto, LP

aunt la tía, 2.1

aunt and uncle los tíos, 2.1

author el/la autor(a)

automatic automático(a),
10.1; *1.1*

  automatic dispenser el
distribuidor automático, *3.1*

autumn el otoño, LP

available disponible, **6.1**

avenue la avenida, *8.1*

avocado el aguacate, *10; 1;*
la palta

Awesome! ¡Bárbaro!, 5.2

ax el hacha *(f.)*

B

back la espalda, 11.1; *2.1*

back *(adj.)* trasero(a), **7.1**

  back button *(key)* el botón
regresar (retroceder), *6.1*

  back door la puerta trasera,
8.1

back: in back of detrás de, 2.2

background la ascendencia;
el fondo, **7.1**

backpack la mochila, 3.1

backpacker el/la mochilero(a),
11.2; *2.2*

backwards hacia atrás

bacon el tocino, el bacón, 4.1;
7; el lacón, *7*

bad malo(a), 1.2; mal, LP

  The weather is bad. Hace
mal tiempo., LP

  to be in a bad mood estar
de mal humor, 6.1

  to get bad grades sacar
notas malas, 3.1

baggage el equipaje, 10.1; *1.1*

  baggage claim el reclamo
de equipaje, **6.1**

  baggage claim ticket
el talón, **6.1**

  carry-on baggage el equipaje
de mano, 10.1; *1.1*

bakery la panadería

balance *(bank)* el saldo, **4**

balcony el balcón

ball *(soccer, basketball)*
el balón, 5.1; *(volleyball)*
el balón, 7.1; *(baseball,
tennis)* la pelota, 5.2

  to hit the ball batear, 5.2;
golpear, 5.2

  to kick (throw) the ball
lanzar el balón, 5.1

balloon el globo

ballpoint pen el bolígrafo,
3.1; el lapicero, la pluma

banana el plátano, 9.2

  fried sweet bananas los
maduros

band *(music)* la banda, 8.1;
5.2; el conjunto, 8.1

  city band la banda
municipal, *5.2*

bandage la venda, *11.2;* **2.2**

bank el banco, **4**

banquet el banquete, **3.1**

baptism el bautizo, **3.2**

baptismal font la pila, **3.2**

to baptize bautizar, **3.2**

bar: bar of soap la barra
de jabón, 11.2; *2.2;*
la pastilla de jabón

to bargain regatear, 9.2

barn el granero, *8.2*

base *(baseball)* la base, 5.2

baseball el béisbol, 5.2

  baseball field el campo de
béisbol, 5.2

  baseball game el juego
(partido) de béisbol, 5.2

  baseball player el/la
jugador(a) de béisbol,
el/la beisbolista, 5.2

basket *(basketball)* el cesto,
la canasta, 5.2

  to make a basket encestar,
meter el balón en la cesta,
5.2

basketball el básquetbol, el
baloncesto, 5.2

  basketball court la cancha
de básquetbol, 5.2

bat el bate, 5.2

to bat batear, 5.2

bath el baño, 2.2; *7*

bathing suit el bañador,
el traje de baño, 7.1

bathroom el cuarto de baño,
2.2; *7*

bathtub la bañera, *7*

batter el/la bateador(a), 5.2

battle la lucha, la batalla, **8**

to be ser, 1.1; estar, 3.1

  to be able (to) poder (ue),
5.1

  to be about to (do
something) estar para (+
infinitivo)

  to be afraid tener miedo,
7.2

  to be applauded recibir
aplausos, 8.1

  to be born nacer, **3.2**

  to be called (named)
llamarse, 11.1; *2.1*

  to be careful tener cuidado,
9.1

English-Spanish Dictionary

to be cold (hot) tener frío (calor), 11.1; *2.1*

to be cut off cortar la línea (a alguien), *6.2*

to be familiar with conocer, 9.1

to be fine (well) estar bien, 6.2

to be going to (do something) ir a (+ infinitivo), 4.1

to be happy estar contento(a), alegre, 6.1

to be hungry tener hambre, 4.1

to be in a good (bad) mood estar de buen (mal) humor, 6.1

to be in a hurry apresurarse, **10 (Lit.)**

to be in the mood for estar por

to be pleasing (to someone) gustar, 5.1

to be ready to (do something) estar para (+ infinitivo)

to be sad estar triste, deprimido(a), 6.1

to be sick estar enfermo(a), 6.2

to be sorry sentir (ie, i)

to be successful tener éxito, 6.1

to be thirsty tener sed, 4.1

to be tired estar cansado(a), 6.1

to be (turn) . . . years old cumplir... años, **3.2**

to be . . . years old tener... años, 2.1

beach la playa, 7.1

beach resort el balneario, 7.1

beans los frijoles, 4.1

   green beans (string beans) las judías verdes, 9.2; **9;** las vainitas, **9**

beautiful bello(a), hermoso(a)

because porque, 3.2

bed la cama, 2.2; *7*

   to go to bed acostarse (ue), 11.1; *2.1*

   to make the bed hacer la cama, *7*

   to stay in bed guardar cama, 6.2; quedarse en la cama, 11.1; *2.1*

bedroom el cuarto de dormir, la recámara, 2.2; la habitación, *7*; el dormitorio, la alcoba, la pieza

beef la carne de res, *4*; **9;** el bife

before antes de, 3.2

beforehand antes, 10.1; *1.1*

to **beg** rogar (ue)

to **begin** empezar (ie), 5.1; comenzar (ie)

beginner el/la principiante, 7.2

to **behave** comportarse, **5**

behaved: to be well-behaved tener buena conducta, 6.1

behavior la conducta, el comportamiento, 6.1; **5**

behind detrás de, 2.2

to **believe** creer

bell pepper el pimiento, 9.2; *10;* **1**

bell tower la campana

bellhop el mozo, *7*

to **belong** pertenecer

below debajo de, 10.2; *1.2*

benefit el provecho, **5 (Lit.)**

beside al lado de, 2.2

besides además

best el/la mejor

best man el padrino, **3.1**

better mejor

between entre

beverage la bebida, el refresco, 4.1

bicycle la bicicleta, 2.2

   to ride a bicycle andar en bicicleta, 11.1; **2.1**

big gran, grande, 1.2

bike ride: to go for a bike ride dar un paseo en bicicleta

bike riding: to go bike riding andar en bicicleta, 11.1; **2.1**

bill la factura; el billete, **4**

biologist el/la biólogo(a)

biology la biología

bird el pájaro

birthday el cumpleaños, 8.1; **3.2**

black negro(a), 2.1

blanket la manta, la frazada, *7*

block (city) la cuadra, la manzana, 9.1

to **block** bloquear, 5.1

blond(e) rubio(a), 1.1

   to have blond hair tener el pelo rubio, 2.1

blood pressure la tensión arterial, 6.2

blouse la blusa, 3.1

to **blow (wind)** soplar

blue azul, 2.1

blue jeans el blue jean, 9.1

board: on board abordo (de), 10.2; *1.2*

to **board** embarcar, abordar, 10.2; *1.2*

boarding el embarque, 10.1; *1.1*

   boarding pass la tarjeta de embarque, 10.1; *1.1;* el pasabordo, la tarjeta de abordar

   boarding pass kiosk el distribuidor automático, 10.1; *1.1*

   boarding time la hora de embarque, 10.1; *1.1*

boat (small) el barquito, 7.1

body (human) el cuerpo (humano), 11.1; *2.1*

to **boil** hervir (ie, i), *10;* **1**

boiling la ebullición

bone el hueso, *5.1;* **2.2**

   to set the bone reducir, acomodar el hueso, *11.2;* **2.2**

book el libro, 3.1

boot la bota, 7.2

border la frontera

to **bore** aburrir

boring aburrido(a), 1.2

born: to be born nacer, 3.2

to **bother** molestar, enfadar, enojar, 6.1

bottle la botella, 9.2

box office la taquilla, 8.2

boy el muchacho, 1.1; el niño, 6.2; el chico, **5;** el mozo, **5 (Lit.)**

boyfriend el novio, **6 (Lit.)**

brakes los frenos, 9.2

   to put on (apply) the brakes poner los frenos

brave valeroso(a)

Brazilian brasileño(a)

bread el pan

   bread crumbs el pan rallado, **9**

to **break** romper; romperse, quebrarse (ie), *11.2;* **2.2**

   He (She) broke his (her) leg. Se rompió (Se quebró) la pierna., *11.2;* **2.2**

breakdown la avería

breakfast el desayuno, 4.1; *7*

  Continental breakfast el desayuno continental, *7*

  to have breakfast tomar el desayuno, 4.1; desayunarse

breaking: You're breaking up. (telephone) Estás cortando., *6.2*

breast (chicken) la pechuga, *10;* **1**

breathing la respiración, *11.1;* **2.1**

  breathing exercises los ejercicios de respiración, *11.1;* **2.1**

breed la raza

bride la novia, **3.1**

to **bring** traer, 10.1; *1.1*

to **bring down** derrocar

broad ancho(a), *8.1*

to **broadcast** emitir, **8**

broken roto(a); quebrado(a)

bronze (adj.) de bronce, 8.2; **7.1**

brother el hermano, 2.1

brown castaño(a), 2.1; de color marrón, 5.1

  to have brown eyes tener ojos castaños, 2.1

  to have brown hair tener el pelo castaño, 2.1

brunette moreno(a), 1.1

brush el cepillo, 11.2; *2.2*

  toothbrush el cepillo de dientes, 11.2; *2.2*

to **brush** cepillar, 11.1; *2.1*

  to brush one's hair cepillarse, 11.1; *2.1*

  to brush one's teeth cepillarse (lavarse) los dientes, 11.1; *2.1*

buffet el bufé, **3.1**

building el edificio, 2.2

bunk la litera

burial el entierro, el sepelio **3.2**

buried enterrado(a), *5.1*

to **burn** quemarse, *10;* **1**

burrito el burrito

to **bury** enterrar (ie)

bus el autobús, el camión, la guagua, *8.1;* el bus

  bus stop la parada de autobús (de camiones, de guaguas), 8.1

  school bus el bus escolar, 3.2

  to miss the bus perder el autobús, 8.1

businessman el hombre de negocios, **10**

businessperson el/la comerciante, **10**

businesswoman la mujer de negocios, **10**

but pero

butcher shop la carnicería

butter la mantequilla, 4.1; *7*

button el botón, *6.1*

  back button el botón regresar (retroceder), *6.1*

  delete button el botón borrador, *6.1*

to **buy** comprar, 3.2

by por; en

  by plane (car, bus) en avión (carro, autobús)

  by tens de diez en diez

  By the way! ¡A propósito!, 8.2

Bye! ¡Chao!, LP

cabbage el repollo, la col, **9**

café el café, 4.2

  outdoor café el café al aire libre

cafeteria la cafetería, 4.1

cake la torta, 4.1; **3.2;** el bizcocho, *5.1;* **3.2;** el pastel, la tarta, 8.1; **3.2**

calculator la calculadora, 3.1

call (phone) la llamada, *6.2*

  dropped call la llamada perdida (caída), *6.2*

to **call** llamar, 11.2; *2.2*

  Who's calling, please? ¿De parte de quién, por favor?, *6.2*

calm calmo(a), tranquilo(a), 6.1

camel el camello, *5.2*

camera la cámara, 7.1; *6.2*

  digital camera la cámara digital, 7.1; *6.2*

camping el camping, 11.2; *2.2*

  to go camping ir de camping, 11.2; *2.2*

can el bote, la lata, 9.2

Canadian canadiense

candidate el/la aspirante, el/la candidato(a), **10**

candle la vela, 8.1; *5.2;* **3.2**

canned enlatado(a)

canvas el lienzo, **7.1**

canyon el cañón, *3.2*

cap el gorro, 7.2

capital la capital

car el carro, 2.2; *9.2;* el coche, *9.2; (train)* el coche, el vagón, *3.1*

  dining car el coche comedor (cafetería), la bufetería, *3.1*

  sports car el coche deportivo, *9.2*

car rental agency la agencia de alquiler, *6.2*

carbonated drink la gaseosa, 4.1

card la tarjeta, 3.1; *6.2;* el carnet, 10.2; *1.2*

  credit card la tarjeta de crédito, 3.1

  ID card el carnet de identidad, 10.2; *1.2*

  phone card la tarjeta telefónica, *6.2*

career la carrera, **10**

careful: to be careful tener cuidado, *9.1*

  Careful! ¡Cuidado!, ¡Mucho ojo!, **5**

carefully con cuidado

Caribbean Sea el mar Caribe

carrot la zanahoria, 9.2; *10;* **1**

to **carry** llevar, 3.1; traer, 10.1; *1.1*

  carry-on luggage el equipaje de mano, 10.2; *1.2*

cart el carrito, 9.2; *3.1*

to **carve** tallar, **7.1**

case: in case en caso de; por si acaso

cash register la caja, 3.2

cash el dinero en efectivo, **4**

to **cash** cobrar, **4**

cashier el/la cajero(a)

cast (medical) el yeso, 11.2; *2.2*

castle el castillo

cat el/la gato(a), 2.1

to **catch** atrapar, *5.2*

  catcher el/la cátcher, el/la receptor(a), *5.2*

Catholic católico(a)

cattle el ganado, *8.2*

to **cause** causar

to **celebrate** celebrar, *5.2;* **3.2**

celebration la celebración

cell phone el móvil, 3.2, *6.1;* el celular, *6.1*

cemetery el cementerio, el camposanto, *5.1;* **3.2**

century el siglo

ceramics las cerámicas, 9.2

cereal el cereal, 4.1

ceremony la ceremonia, **3.1**

  civil ceremony (wedding) la ceremonia civil, **3.1**

English-Spanish Dictionary

certain cierto(a), *6.1*

chair la silla, 2.2

chairlift el telesilla, el telesquí, 7.2

change *(monetary)* suelto, **4**

to **change** cambiar, *3.2;* **6.2**

    to change trains (transfer) transbordar, *3.2*

chapter el capítulo, **7.2**

character el personaje, **7.2**

charitable purpose el propósito benévolo

cheap barato(a), 9.1

    It's all a lot cheaper. Todo te sale más barato., 9.1

check *(restaurant)* la cuenta, *4.2;* **4**

to **check** *(ticket)* revisar, *3.2;* *(facts)* verificar, **6.2**

to **check luggage** facturar el equipaje, 10.1; *1.1*

to **check out** *(hotel room)* abandonar el cuarto, *7*

checking account la cuenta corriente, **4**

cheek la mejilla, **5**

cheese el queso, 4.1

    ham and cheese sandwich el sándwich de jamón y queso, 4.1

chemistry la química

chest el pecho, *11.1;* **2.1**

chicken el pollo, 4.1; *10;* **1**

    chicken breast la pechuga de pollo, *10;* **1**

    chicken thigh el muslo de pollo, *10;* **1**

    chicken wings las alitas de pollo, *10;* **1**

child el/la niño(a), 6.2

children los hijos, 2.1

Chilean chileno(a)

chili pepper el ají

chisel el cincel, *7.1*

chocolate el chocolate, 4.1

    hot chocolate el chocolate caliente, 4.1

to **choose** escoger; seleccionar, *3.1*

chop: pork chop la chuleta de cerdo, *10;* **1**

to **chop** picar, *10;* **1**

Christian cristiano(a)

Christmas la Navidad, las Navidades, *5.2*

    Christmas Eve la Nochebuena, *5.2*

Christmas gift el aguinaldo, *5.2*

Christmas tree el árbol de Navidad, *5.2*

Merry Christmas! ¡Feliz Navidad!

church la iglesia, *3.1*

cilantro el cilantro, **9**

city la ciudad, 2.2; *8.1*

city hall el ayuntamiento, *3.1*

civil civil

    civil ceremony *(wedding)* la ceremonia civil, *3.1*

    por (el, lo) civil civil, *3.1*

civilization la civilización

to **claim** reclamar, **6.1**

clams las almejas, *4*

to **clap** aplaudir, 5.1

clarinet el clarinete

class *(school)* la clase; el curso, 1.2; *(ticket)* la clase, *3.1*

    first– (second–) class en primera (segunda) clase, *3.1*

classified ad anuncio clasificado, **10**

classroom la sala de clase, 3.1

clean limpio(a), *7*

to **clean** limpiar, *7*

to **clear the table** levantar (quitar) la mesa, *4*

clerk el/la empleado(a), 3.1; el/la dependiente(a)

to **click** *(computer)* hacer clic, *6.1*

cliff el risco, *3.2*

climate el clima

close (to) cerca (de)

to **close** cerrar (ie), *11.2;* **2.2**

closet el armario, *7*

clothes la ropa, 9.1

    dirty clothes la ropa para lavar, la ropa sucia *4*

clothes hanger la percha, el colgador, *7*

clothing la ropa, 9.1

    clothing store la tienda de ropa, 9.1

cloud la nube, *7.1*

cloudy nublado(a), *7.1*

clove (of garlic) el diente

coach el/la entrenador(a)

coast la costa

to **coat (with batter)** rebozar, **9**

code: area code la clave de área, *6.2*

    country code el prefijo del país, *6.2*

co-ed mixto(a)

coffee el café, 4.1; *7*

coffin el ataúd, *3.2*

cognate la palabra afine

coin la moneda, *9.1;* **4**

cola la cola, 4.1

cold el frío; frío(a), 4.2; *(illness)* el catarro, 6.2

    It's cold *(weather).* Hace frío., LP

    to be cold tener frío, 11.1; *2.1*

    to have a cold tener catarro, 6.2

to **collect** recoger, **6.1**

college la universidad

Colombian colombiano(a), 1.2

colonial colonial, **8**

to **colonize** colonizar, **8**

colonizer el colonizador, **8**

colony la colonia, **8**

color el color, 5.1

comb el peine, *11.2;* **2.2**

to **comb one's hair** peinarse, 11.1; *2.1*

to **come** venir (ie)

    I'm coming! ¡Ya voy!, *11.2;* **2.2**

to **come out onto** desembocar

comical cómico(a), gracioso(a), 1.1

coming from procedente de, *10.2;* **1.2**

companion el/la compañero(a)

company la compañía, la empresa, la sociedad, **8**

to **complete** completar

completely totalmente

composition la composición

computer la computadora, el ordenador, *3.2;* **6.1**

    computer programmer el/la programador(a) de computadoras, **10**

concert el concierto, 8.1

concourse *(train station)* el hall, *3.1*

condiment el condimento, *10;* **1**

condo(minium) el condominio

conduct la conducta, el comportamiento, 6.1

conductor *(train)* el revisor, *3.2*

to **confirm (seat on a flight)** confirmar, **6.1**

Congratulations!
¡Enhorabuena!, **3.1**

to **connect** enlazar, **6.2**

connected conectado(a)

connection la conexión

to **conquer** conquistar, **8**

consonant la consonante

to **consult** consultar

to **contain** contener (ie)

contemporary
contemporáneo(a)

continent el continente

Continental breakfast
el desayuno continental, *7*

to **continue** continuar;
seguir (i, i), *9.1*

contract el contrato, **6.2**

contrary: on the contrary
al contrario

conversation la conversación

convertible el descapotable, el
convertible, *9.2*

conveyor belt la correa, **6.1**

to **convince** convencer

cook el/la cocinero(a), *10;* **1**

to **cook** cocinar, cocer (ue), *10;* **1**

cooking la cocción

cool fresco(a), LP

It's cool *(weather).* Hace
fresco., LP

copy la copia, *6.1*

hard copy la copia dura, *6.1*

corn el maíz, *9.2;* el elote,
el choclo

ear of corn la mazorca de
maíz, *9*

corner la esquina, *8.1*

corporation la sociedad, **10**

corral el corral, *8.2*

to **cost** costar (ue), *9.1*

How much does it cost?
¿Cuánto cuesta?, *3.2*

Costa Rican costarricense

costume el disfraz, *5.1*

cough la tos, *6.2*

to have a cough tener tos, *6.2*

to **cough** toser, *6.2*

counter *(airline)* el mostrador,
10.1; 1.1

country el país; el campo, *8.2*

country code el prefijo
del país, *6.2*

country house la casa
de campo, *8.2*

Spanish-speaking countries
los países hispanohablantes

countryside el campo, *8.2*

couple la pareja, *3.1*

course el curso, *1.2*

court la cancha, *5.2*

basketball (tennis) court
la cancha de básquetbol
(tenis), *5.2*

volleyball court la cancha
de voleibol, *7.1*

courtesy la cortesía, LP

cousin el/la primo(a), *2.1*

to **cover** cubrir, tapar

cow la vaca, *8.2*

crackers las galletas, *8.1*

crafts la artesanía, *9.2*

crazy loco(a)

credit card la tarjeta
de crédito, *3.1*

to **cross** cruzar, *9.1*

cross-country *(skiing)*
el esquí nórdico, *7.2; (race)*
la carrera a campo traviesa,
11.1; **2.1**

crosswalk el cruce, *8.1*

crutches las muletas, *11.2;* **2.2**

to walk on crutches andar
con muletas, *11.2;* **2.2**

Cuban cubano(a)

Cuban American
cubanoamericano(a)

cucumber el pepino, *10;* **1**

cuisine la cocina

culture la cultura

cup la taza, *4.1; 4*

curriculum vitae
el currículum vitae, **10**

custard el flan, *4.1*

custom la costumbre

customer el/la cliente(a), *4.2; 7*

customs la aduana, *6.1*

to **cut** cortar, *10;* **1**

to cut (up) in small pieces
cortar en pedacitos, *10;* **1**

cut off: We've been cut off.
(telephone) Se nos cortó la
línea., *6.2*

to **cut oneself** cortarse, *11.2;* **2.2**

cutlet: veal cutlet el escalope
de ternera, *10;* **1**

daily diario(a)

daily routine la rutina
diaria, *11.1;* **2.1**

dairy products los productos
lácteos

to **dance** bailar, *5.2*

danger el peligro

dangerous peligroso(a)

dark-haired moreno(a), *1.1*

data los datos

date la fecha, LP

What's today's date?
¿Cuál es la fecha
de hoy?, LP

daughter la hija, *2.1*

to **dawn** amanecer, **10 (Lit.)**

day el día, LP; la fiesta, *5.1*

the Day of the Dead el Día
de los Muertos, *5.1*

patron saint's day la fiesta
patronal, *5.1*

What day is it (today)?
¿Qué día es hoy?, LP

dead muerto(a), difunto(a), *5.1*

**dead person, deceased
person** el/la muerto(a),
el/la difunto(a), *5.1*

deaf sordo(a), **10 (Lit.)**

dear querido(a)

death la muerte

deboned deshuesado(a)

December diciembre, LP

to **decide** decidir

to **decline** declinar, **6.2**

to **decorate** decorar, *5.2*

deep profundo(a)

definition la definición

delay el retraso, la demora,
10.2; 1.2; **6.1**

to **delete** borrar, *6.1*

delete key *(computer)*
el botón borrador, *6.1*

delicious delicioso(a); rico(a)

to **deliver** entregar, **6 (Lit.)**

to **demand** exigir

dent la abolladura, **6.2**

dentist's office el gabinete
del dentista, *9*

departure la salida, *10.1; 1.1*

departure gate la puerta
de salida, *10.2; 1.2;* **6.1**

departure time la hora
de salida, *10.1; 1.1*

to **depend** depender (ie) (de)

to **deplane** desembarcar

to **deposit** depositar, **4**

to **describe** describir

description la descripción

desert el desierto

desk el pupitre, *3.1*

desolate inhóspito(a)

dessert el postre, *4.1*

destination el destino, *3.1;* **6.1**

detergent el detergente, **4**

powdered detergent
el jabón en polvo, **4**

to **develop** desarrollarse, *7.2*

device el aparato

English-Spanish Dictionary

diagnosis el diagnóstico

to **dial** marcar el número, *6.2*

dial tone el tono, *6.2*

to **dice** cortar en pedacitos, *10;* **1**

dictation el dictado

to **die** morir (ue, u), *4*

diet la dieta

difference la diferencia

different diferente, *9.2*

difficult difícil; duro(a), *1.2;* avanzado(a), *7.2*

difficulty la dificultad

digital camera la cámara digital, *7.1; 6.2*

diner el/la comensal, **9**

dining car el coche comedor (cafetería), la bufetería, *3.2*

dining room el comedor, *2.2*

dinner la cena, *4.1;* **3.1**

  to have dinner cenar, *4.1*

direction (road) sentido, *9.1*

  in each direction en cada sentido, *9.1*

directions las direcciones

dirty sucio(a), *7*

disadvantage la desventaja

disagreeable desagradable

to **disappear** desaparecer

to **discover** descubrir

to **disembark** desembarcar, *1.2*

disguise el disfraz, *5.1*

dish el plato, *4*

dishwasher el lavaplatos, *10;* **1**

dispenser: automatic boarding pass dispenser el distribuidor automático, *10.1;* **1.1**

distance: long distance de larga distancia, *11.1;* **2.1**

distinguished ilustre, **8**

district el casco, el barrio, *8.1*

to **dive** bucear, *7.1*

to **divide** dividirse, **7.2**

divine divino(a)

to **do** hacer, *10.2; 1.2*

  to do homework hacer las tareas

  to do push-ups hacer planchas, *11.1;* **2.1**

  to do yoga practicar yoga, *11.1;* **2.1**

doctor el/la médico(a), *6.2*

  doctor's office el consultorio, la consulta, *6.2;* **10**

document el documento

  attached document el documento adjunto, *6.1*

dog el/la perro(a), *2.1*

dollar el dólar

Dominican dominicano(a)

  Dominican Republic la República Dominicana

door la puerta, *9.2*

  front (back) door la puerta delantera (trasera)

dot (Internet) el punto, *6.1*

double (room) el cuarto doble, *7*

doubles (tennis) dobles, *5.2*

doubt la duda

to **doubt** dudar

doughnut (type of) el churro

down: to go down bajar, *7.2*

downhill skiing el esquí alpino, *7.2*

to **download** bajar, descargar, *6.2*

downtown el centro, *8.1*

dozen la docena

drama el drama

drawing el dibujo

dream el sueño

dress el vestido, *9.1*

to **dress** vestirse (i, i), *4*

to **dribble** driblar (con el balón), *5.2*

drink (beverage) la bebida, *4.1;* el refresco, *4.2*

to **drink** beber, *4.1*

to **drive** conducir, manejar, *9.2*

driver el/la conductor(a), *9.2*

driver's license el permiso de conducir, la licencia, el carnet, *9.2*

dropped call la llamada caída (perdida), *6.2*

drugstore la farmacia, *6.2*

dry seco(a)

dryer la secadora, *4*

during durante, *3.2*

DVD el DVD, *3.2*

dynamic dinámico(a), *6.1*

e-mail el correo electrónico, *3.2; 6.1;* el e-mail

  e-mail address la dirección de correo electrónico (e-mail), *6.1*

e-mail inbox la bandeja de entradas, *6.1*

e-ticket el boleto (billete) electrónico, *10.1; 1.1*

each cada, *2.2*

eagle el águila *(f.)*

ear el oído, **6 (Lit.)**

early temprano, *11.1; 2.1*

early riser el/la madrugador(a), *11.1; 2.1;* **10 (Lit.)**

to **earn** ganar

easel el caballete, **7.1**

easily sin dificultad, *7.2*

east el este

easy fácil, *1.2*

to **eat** comer, *4.1*

  to eat breakfast (lunch) tomar el desayuno (el almuerzo), *4.1*

  to eat dinner cenar, *4.1*

Ecuadoran ecuatoriano(a), *1.1*

education la educación

  physical education la educación física, *1.2*

egg el huevo, *4.1; 7*

  scrambled eggs los huevos revueltos, *7;* los huevos batidos, **9**

eggplant la berenjena, **9**

eight ocho, LP

eight hundred ochocientos(as)

eighteen dieciocho, LP

eighty ochenta, LP

either tampoco *(afer negation)*

elbow el codo, *11.1; 2.1*

electronic electrónico(a), *10.1; 1.1*

elementary school la escuela primaria

elevator el ascensor, *7*

eleven once, LP

else: Anything else? ¿Algo más?, *9.2;* **Nothing else.** Nada más., *9.2*

emergency room la sala de emergencia, *11.2; 2.2*

employee el/la empleado(a), *3.2;* el/la dependiente(a)

empty vacío(a), *9.2;* **3 (Lit.)**

enchilada la enchilada

end el fin

  at the end (of) al final (de); a fines de

to **end** terminar

to **endorse** endosar, *4*

energetic energético(a), *6.1*

English-Spanish Dictionary

energy la energía, 6.1
engine el motor
engineer el/la ingeniero(a), **10**
English *(language)* el inglés, 1.2
to enjoy disfrutar; gozar
to enjoy oneself divertirse (ie, i), 11.2; *2.2*
enormous enorme
enough bastante; suficiente
to enter entrar, 5.1
enthusiasm el entusiasmo, 6.1
enthusiastic lleno(a) de entusiasmo, 6.1; entusiasmado(a)
entire entero(a)
entrance la entrada; *(subway)* la boca del metro, *8.1*
envelope el sobre, **4**
environment el ambiente, **7.2**
Epiphany el Día de los Reyes, *5.2*
equal igual
escalator la escalera mecánica, *8.1*
especially especialmente; sobre todo
to establish estalecer(se), **8**
ethnic étnico(a)
euro el euro
European europeo(a)
even aun; hasta
even *(numeric)* par
evening la noche
Good evening. Buenas noches., LP
in the evening por la noche
yesterday evening anoche, *7.1*
every cada, 2.2; todos(as)
every day (year) todos los días (años)
everybody todo el mundo *5.1;* todos(as), 8.1
everyone todo el mundo *5.1;* todos(as), 8.1
everything todo, 6.2
everywhere en todas partes
exactly exactamente
exam el examen, la prueba, 3.1
physical exam el examen físico, 6.2
to take an exam tomar un examen, 3.1
to examine examinar, 6.2
example: for example por ejemplo
to exceed exceder
excellent excelente

exception la excepción
to exchange intercambiar, **3.1**
Excuse me. Con permiso., 10.1; *1.1*
executive el/la ejecutivo(a), **10**
executive assistant el/la asistente(a) ejecutivo(a), **10**
exercise los ejercicios, *11.1; 2.1*
to exercise hacer ejercicios, *11.1; 2.1*
exhibition la exposición (de arte), 8.2
to exist existir
exit la salida, *9.1*
exotic exótico(a)
to expect esperar, **3.1**
expensive caro(a), 9.1
less expensive más barato, 9.1
expert el/la experto(a), 7.2
to explain explicar
expressway la autopista, la autovía, *9.1*
extraordinary extraordinario(a)
eye el ojo, 2.1
to have blue (green, brown) eyes tener ojos azules (verdes, castaños) 2.1

fabrics los tejidos, 9.2
fabulous fabuloso(a)
face la cara, 6.1
fact el hecho
fair la feria, 5.1
fall el otoño, LP
to fall caerse, *11.2;* **2.2**
to fall asleep dormirse (ue, u), *11.1; 2.1*
to fall in love enamorarse, **5**
false falso(a)
family la familia, 2.1
family *(adj.)* familiar
famous famoso(a)
fan el/la aficionado(a), 5.1
fantastic fantástico(a)
far lejos (de), 3.2
fare la tarifa, *3.1*
farm la finca, la granja, la chacra, *8.2*
farmer el/la campesino(a), el peón, *8.2*
farmhand el peón, *8.2*
to fascinate fascinar

fast rápido(a)
fastened abrochado(a), 10.2; *1.2*
fat gordo(a)
father el padre, 2.1
favor el favor
favorite favorito(a)
fear el miedo
feature la característica
February febrero, LP
to feel sentirse (ie, i)
to feel like (doing something) tener ganas de (+ infinitivo)
Ferris wheel la noria, *8.1*
fertilizer el abono
festival la feria, *5.1*
festival of lights (Hanukkah) la fiesta de las luces, *5.2*
fever la fiebre, 6.2
to have a fever tener fiebre, 6.2
few poco(a), pocos(as), 2.2
a few unos(as)
fewer menos
field el campo, 5.1; *8.2*
baseball field el campo de béisbol, 5.2
soccer field el campo de fútbol, 5.1
fifteen quince, LP
fifteen-year-old girl la quinceañera
fifty cincuenta, LP
to fight luchar, **8**
figurative work (of art) la obra figurativa, **7.1**
file el archivo, *6.1;* el documento
attached file el documento adjunto, *6.1*
to fill llenar, *9.2;* **10;** *(put filling in)* rellenar, **9**
to fill up *(gas tank)* llenar el tanque, *9.2;* **6.2**
film el filme, la película, 8.2; el film
finally por fin
financial statement el estado financiero, **10**
to find encontrar (ue)
fine la multa, *9.1*
fine *(adj.)* bien, LP
to be fine estar bien, 6.2
finger el dedo, *11.1; 2.1*
to finish terminar
fire el fuego, *10;* **1**
fireplace la chimenea, 5.2
fireworks los fuegos artificiales, 5.2

English-Spanish Dictionary

first primero(a), LP

   first-class primera clase, *3.1*

   first of January el primero de enero, LP

fish el pescado, *4.1*

fish market la pescadería

to **fit** quedar, *9.1*

   This jacket doesn't fit you. Esta chaqueta no te queda bien., *9.1*

five cinco, LP

five hundred quinientos(as)

flame el fuego, *10; 1*

   on a low flame (heat) a fuego lento, *10; 1*

flan el flan, *4.1*

flat plano(a), **7.1**; (*tire*) el pinchazo, *9.2*

flavor el sabor, *10; 1*

to **flee** huir, *4* (Lit.)

flight el vuelo, *10.1; 1.1;* **6.1**

   direct flight el vuelo directo, **6.1**

   flight attendant el/la asistente(a) de vuelo, *10.2; 1.2*

   flight number el número del vuelo, *10.1; 1.1*

   non-stop flight el vuelo sin escala, **6.1**

to **flip over** volcar

floor el piso, *2.2*

flower la flor, *2.2*

flute la flauta

to **fly** volar (ue)

folder la carpeta, *3.2;* **6.1**

to **follow** seguir (i, i), *4*

following siguiente

food la comida, *4.1;* los comestibles, *4;* el alimento

   frozen food los productos congelados, *9.2*

foot el pie, *5.1; 2.1*

   on foot a pie, *3.2*

football el fútbol americano

for por, para; con destino a, *10.2; 1.2*

   for example por ejemplo

forbidden prohibido(a), *9.1*

foreground el primer plano, **7.1**

forehead la frente, *11.1;* **2.1**

foreign extranjero(a)

to **forget** olvidar, *5* (Lit.)

fork el tenedor, *4*

form la forma, *10.2; 1.2*

formal formal, **5**

former antiguo(a)

forty cuarenta, LP

fountain pen la pluma, *5.1*

four cuatro, LP

four hundred cuatrocientos(as)

fourteen catorce, LP

fracture la fractura

free libre, *4.2; 3.2*

to **free** liberar, *11.1;* **2.1**

freezer el congelador, *10; 1*

French el francés, *1.2;* (*adj.*) francés(esa), *4*

french fries las papas (patatas) fritas, *4.1*

frequently con frecuencia, frecuentemente

fresh fresco(a)

Friday el viernes, LP

fried frito(a)

friend el/la amigo(a), *1.1;* el/la compañero(a)

friendly agradable, *6.1*

from de, LP; desde

   from time to time de vez en cuando

   from where? ¿de dónde?, *1.1*

front (*adj.*) delantero(a), *8.1*

   in front of delante de, *2.2*

   front desk (*hotel*) la recepción, *7*

   front door (*car, bus*) la puerta delantera, *8.1*

frozen congelado(a), *9.2*

   frozen food los productos congelados, *9.2*

fruit la fruta, *9.2*

   fruit stand la frutería, el puesto de frutas, *9.2*

to **fry** freír (i, i), *4; 1*

frying pan el/la sartén, *10; 1*

full completo(a), *3.2;* **6.1**

full of lleno(a) de, *6.1*

full-time a tiempo completo, **10**

fun: to have fun divertirse (ie, i), pasarlo bien, *11.2; 2.2*

funds los fondos, *4*

funeral procession el cortejo fúnebre, *3.2*

funny cómico(a); gracioso(a), *1.1;* divertido(a)

furious furioso(a)

furniture los muebles, *2.2*

future el futuro

G

game el juego; (*match*) el partido, *5.1*

garage el garaje, *2.2*

garden el jardín, *2.2*

garlic el ajo, *10; 1*

gasoline la gasolina, la nafta, la benzina

gas station la estación de servicio, la gasolinera, *9.2*

gas tank el tanque, *9.2*

gate (*airport*) la puerta de salida, *10.2; 1.2;* **6.1**

to **gather** recoger, **6.1**

general general

   generally, in general en general, por lo general

generous generoso(a)

genre el género, **7.2**

gentle manso(a)

gentleman el señor, LP

geography la geografía

geometry la geometría

German alemán(ana)

to **get** sacar, *3.1;* lograr, **8**

   to get angry enfadarse, **5**

   to get good (bad) grades sacar notas buenas (malas), *3.1*

to **get dressed** ponerse la ropa, *11.1; 2.1;* vestirse (i, i), *4*

to **get off** (*train, bus*) bajar(se), *3.2*

to **get on** (*train, bus*) subir, *3.1;* (*plane*) abordar, *10.2; 1.2*

to **get together** reunirse

to **get up** levantarse, *11.1; 2.1*

gift el regalo, *8.1;* **3.1;**

   Christmas gift el aguinaldo, *5.2*

girl la muchacha, *1.1;* la niña, *6.2;* la chica, **5**

   fifteen-year-old girl la quinceañera

girlfriend la novia, *6* (Lit.)

to **give** dar, *3.1;* otorgar, **8**

   to give an exam dar un examen (una prueba), *3.1*

   to give back devolver (ue)

   to give (someone) stitches poner unos puntos (unas suturas) (a alguien)

   to give (throw) a party dar una fiesta, *8.1*

   to give up renunciar

glance la ojeada, **8**

glass (drinking) el vaso, 4.1; *4*

glove el guante, 5.2

glove compartment
la guantera, *9.2*

to **go** ir, 3.2; pasar, 5.2; andar, *3.2*

Let's go! ¡Vamos!

**to be going
(to do something)**
ir a (+ infinitivo), 4.2

to go back regresar, 3.2;
volver (ue), 5.1

to go bike riding andar
en bicicleta, *11.1;* **2.1**

to go camping
ir de camping, 11.2; *2.2*

to go down bajar, 7.2

to go for a hike dar una
caminata, 11.2; *2.2*

to go home regresar a casa,
ir a casa, 3.2; volver (ue)
a casa, 8.1

to go horseback riding
andar a caballo, *3.2;*
montar a caballo, 8.2

to go ice-skating patinar
sobre el hielo, 7.2

to go in-line skating
patinar en línea, *11.1;* **2.1**

to go jogging hacer
jogging, *11.1;* **2.1**

to go on a trip hacer un
viaje

to go online entrar en
línea, *6.1*

to go out salir, 8.1

to go over the net pasar
por encima de la red, 5.2

**to go rollerblading (inline
skating)** patinar en línea,
11.1; **2.1**

to go scuba diving bucear

to go shopping
ir de compras, 9.1

to go skiing esquiar, 7.2

to go snorkeling bucear,
7.1

to go surfing practicar
la tabla hawaiana, 7.1

to go swimming nadar, 7.1

to go through pasar por,
10.2; *1.2*

to go to bed acostarse (ue),
11.1; **2.1**

to go to the movies
ir al cine, 8.2

to go up subir, 7.2

to go waterskiing esquiar
en el agua, 7.1

to go windsurfing practicar
la plancha de vela, 7.1

goal el gol, 5.1

to score a goal meter un gol,
5.1

goal (box) la portería, 5.1

goalie el/la portero(a), 5.1

godchild el/la ahijado(a)

godfather el padrino, **3.2**

godmother la madrina, **3.2**

going to con destino a, 10.2; *1.2*

gold el oro

good buen, LP; bueno(a), 1.1

to be in a good mood
estar de buen humor, 6.1

to get good grades
sacar notas buenas, 3.1

Good afternoon. Buenas
tardes., LP

Good evening. Buenas
noches., LP

Good morning. Buenos
días., LP

Good-bye. ¡Adiós!; ¡Chao!, LP

to say good-bye despedirse
(i, i), **5**

good-looking guapo(a),
bonito(a), 1.1

government el gobierno, **10**

government official
el/la funcionario(a)
gubernamental
(de gobierno), **10**

grade la nota, 3.1

high grade la nota alta, 3.1

low grade la nota baja, 3.1

to get good (bad) grades
sacar notas buenas
(malas), 3.1

grandchildren los nietos, 2.1

granddaughter la nieta, 2.1

grandfather el abuelo, 2.1

grandmother la abuela, 2.1

grandparents los abuelos, 2.1

grandson el nieto, 2.1

to **grant** otorgar, **8**

grape la uva, 9.2; **9**

grapevine la vid, **9**

grass la hierba, *8.2*

grave la tumba, *5.1*

gravy la salsa, *10;* **1**

gray gris, 5.1

to **graze** pacer, *8.2*

great gran, grande

Great! ¡Bárbaro!, 5.2

greater (greatest) part
(la) mayor parte

green verde, 2.1

green beans las judías verdes,
9.2; **9;** las vainitas, **9**

green pepper el pimiento, 9.2;
10; **1**

**greengrocer
(vegetable) store**
la verdulería, 9.2

to **greet** saludar, **5**

greeting el saludo, LP

grill la parrilla, *10;* **1**

to **grill** asar, *10;* **1**

groom el novio, **3.1**

ground el suelo

group (musical) el grupo,
el conjunto, 8.1

to **grow (agriculture)** cultivar,
8.2; **9**

to **guard** guardar, 5.1

Guatemalan guatemalteco(a),
1.1

to **guess** adivinar

guest el/la invitado(a); *(hotel)*
el/la cliente(a), el/la
huésped(a), *7*

guitar la guitarra, 8.1

guy el tipo, 6.1

gymnasium el gimnasio,
11.1; **2.1**

habit la manía, **6 (Lit.)**

hair el pelo, 2.1

to brush one's hair
cepillarse, *11.1;* **2.1**

to comb one's hair
peinarse, *11.1;* **2.1**

**to have blond (brown, black)
hair** tener el pelo rubio
(castaño, negro), 2.1

haircut el corte de pelo, **4**

hair salon la peluquería, **4**

hair stylist el/la peluquero(a),
4

half (soccer) el tiempo, 5.1

second half (soccer)
el segundo tiempo, 5.1

half past (hour) y media, LP

ham el jamón, 4.1

ham and cheese sandwich
el sándwich de jamón
y queso, 4.1

hamburger la hamburguesa,
4.1

hand la mano, 3.1

to raise one's hand levantar
la mano, 3.1

handful el puñado, **4 (Lit.)**

to **hand over** entregar, **6 (Lit.)**

handsome guapo(a), 1.1

hanger la percha, el colgador,
7

Hanukkah el Hanuka, *5.2*

English-Spanish Dictionary

to **happen** pasar; ocurrir; suceder, **5 (Lit.)**

    What's happening?
    ¿Qué pasa?

happiness la alegría, **3.1**; la felicidad

happy alegre, 6.1; **3.1**; contento(a), 6.1; feliz, *5.2*

    Happy Hanukkah!
    ¡Feliz Hanuka!, *5.2*

hard difícil, duro(a), 1.2

hard copy la copia dura, *6.1*

hardworking ambicioso(a), 1.2

harvest la cosecha, *8.2*

to **harvest** cosechar, *8.2*

hat el sombrero; *(ski)* el gorro, *7.2*

to **have** tener (ie), 2.1; haber *(in compound tenses)*

    to have a cold tener catarro, *6.2*

    to have a cough tener tos, *6.2*

    to have a fever tener fiebre, *6.2*

    to have a good time pasarlo bien, divertirse (ie, i), 11.2; *2.2*

    to have a headache tener dolor de cabeza, *6.2*

    to have a party dar una fiesta, *8.1*

    to have a snack tomar una merienda, *4.2*

    to have a sore throat tener dolor de garganta, *6.2*

    to have a stomachache tener dolor de estómago, *6.2*

    to have blond (brown, black) hair tener el pelo rubio (castaño, negro), *2.1*

    to have blue (brown, green) eyes tener ojos azules (castaños, verdes), *2.1*

    to have breakfast (lunch) tomar el desayuno (el almuerzo); *4.1*

    to have dinner cenar, *4.1*

    to have fun pasarlo bien, divertirse (ie, i), 11.2; *2.2*

    to have just (done something) acabar de (+ infinitivo), *4.2*

    to have to (do something) tener que, *4.1*

hay el heno, *8.2*

he él, 1.1

head la cabeza, 6.2; *2.1*

headache: to have a headache tener dolor de cabeza, *6.2*

headlights las luces, *9.2*

headline el titular, **8**

health la salud, *6.1*

to **hear** oír, 8.1

    ¿Can you hear me? (telephone)
    ¿Me escuchas?, *6.2*

heart el corazón, **8**

heat el calor; el fuego, *10*; **1**

    on low heat a fuego lento, *10*; **1**

to **heat** poner en el fuego, *10*; **1**

heavy pesado(a)

heel *(of a shoe)* el talón

height la altura

Hello! ¡Hola!, LP; *6.2*; *(on the phone)* ¡Diga!, ¡Dígame!, ¡Aló!, ¡Bueno!

helmet el casco, 7.2; *11.1*; **2.1**

help la ayuda

to **help** ayudar, 10.1; *1.1*

hen la gallina, *8.2*

her *(pron.)* la

    to her *(pron.)* le

her su(s)

here aquí, 9.1; acá, 11.2; *2.2*

    Here it (they) is (are).
    Aquí lo (la, los, etc.) tienes.

hero el héroe

heroine la heroína

Hi! ¡Hola!, LP

high alto(a), 3.1

high school la escuela secundaria, 1.2; el colegio

highway la autopista, la autovía, la carretera, *9.1*

hike: to take (go for) a hike dar una caminata, 11.2; *2.2*

hiker el/la mochilero(a), 11.2; *2.2*

him *(pron.)* lo

    to him *(pron.)* le

his su(s)

Hispanic hispano(a)

history la historia, 1.2

to **hit** *(baseball)* batear; *(tennis, volleyball)* golpear, *5.2*

    to hit a home run batear un jonrón, *5.2*

holiday la fiesta, *5.1*

home la casa, 2.2; a casa; *3.2*

    at home en casa

    to go home regresar a casa, *3.2*; volver (ue) a casa, 8.1

home page la página de inicio (inicial, frontal), *6.1*

home plate el platillo, *5.2*

home run el jonrón, *5.2*

    to hit a home run batear un jonrón, *5.2*

homework las tareas

honest honesto(a)

honor: in honor of en honor de, *3.1*

hood *(car)* el capó, *9.2*

to **hope** esperar, *3.1*

    I hope . . . Ojalá... , *11.2*; **2.2**

horse el caballo, *3.2*

horseback riding la equitación, *8.2*

    to go horseback riding andar a caballo, *3.2*; montar a caballo, *8.2*

hospital el hospital

hostel: youth hostel el albergue juvenil, el hostal, *7*

hot: to be hot tener (ie) calor, *11.1*; **2.1**

    It's (very) hot (weather). Hace (mucho) calor., LP

hot caliente, 4.1

hotel el hotel, *7*

    small (inexpensive) hotel el hostal, *7*

hotel clerk el/la recepcionista, *7*

hour la hora

house la casa, 2.2

    apartment house la casa de apartamentos, 2.2

    private house la casa privada, 2.2

housekeeper la camarera, *7*; el/la criado(a), **3 (Lit.)**

how? ¿cómo?, 1.1; ¿qué?, LP

    How are things going? ¿Qué tal?, LP

    How are you? ¿Qué tal?, LP; ¿Cómo estás?

    How much does it cost? ¿Cuánto cuesta?, *3.2*

    How much is (are) . . . ? ¿A cuánto está(n)… ?, *9.2*

    How much is it? ¿Cuánto es?, LP

    How old is he (she)? ¿Cuántos años tiene?, *2.1*

how long . . . ? ¿Hace cuánto tiempo... ?

how many? ¿cuántos(as)?, *2.1*

how much? ¿cuánto?, *3.1*

however comoquiera
hug el abrazo, **5**
to **hug (each other)** abrazar(se), **5**
human humano(a), 11.1; *2.1*
human being el ser humano
human resources department
el departamento de personal
(de recursos humanos), **10**
humble humilde
**humor: to have a good sense
of humor** tener un buen
sentido de humor, 6.1
hundred cien(to), LP
hunger el hambre *(f.)*
hungry: to be hungry tener
hambre, 4.1
hurried apresurado(a), **4**
hurry: to be in a hurry
apresurarse, **10 (Lit.)**
to **hurt** doler (ue), 6.2; *11.2; **2.2***
It hurts him (me, etc.) a lot.
Le (Me, etc.) duele mucho.,
*11.2; **2.2***
**My head (stomach, etc.)
hurts.** Me duele la cabeza
(el estómago, etc.), *11.2; **2.2***
to **hurt (oneself)** hacerse daño,
*11.2; **2.2***
husband el esposo, el marido,
2.1

I yo, 1.1
ice el hielo, 7.2
ice cream el helado, 4.1
ice skate el patín, 7.2
to **ice-skate** patinar sobre
el hielo, 7.2
ice-skater el/la patinador(a), 7.2
ice-skating el patinaje sobre
(el) hielo, 7.2
ice-skating rink la pista
de patinaje, 7.2
icon el icono, *6.1*
ID card el carnet
de identidad, 10.2; *1.2*
idea la idea
idealist el/la idealista
identification la identidad,
10.2; *1.2*
piece of identification
la forma de identidad,
10.2; *1.2*
to **identify** identificar
if si
ill enfermo(a), 6.2
ill-mannered mal educado(a),
6.1
illness la enfermedad

illustrious ilustre, **8**
to **imagine** imaginar
immediately enseguida, 4.2;
inmediatamente
immense inmenso
immigration la inmigración,
6.1
impatient impaciente, 6.1
important importante
impossible imposible
in en
in back of detrás de, 2.2
in front of delante de, 2.2
in general por lo general
inbox *(e-mail)* la bandeja
de entradas, *6.1*
incline la pendiente
to **include** incluir, *6.2*
Is the tip included? ¿Está
incluido el servicio?, 4.2
to **increase** aumentar
incredible increíble
to **indicate** indicar
indigenous indígena, 9.2
individual: individual sport
el deporte individual
inexpensive barato(a), 9.1
influence la influencia
to **inform** informar
information la información,
3.2
ingredient el ingrediente
inhabitant el/la habitante
inhospitable inhóspito(a)
injured herido(a)
injury la herida, *11.2; **2.2***
in-line skating el patinaje
en línea, *11.1; **2.1***
to go in-line skating
patinar en línea, *11.1; **2.1***
inn el parador
to **insert** insertar, *3.1;* introducir,
6.2
instead of en vez de
instrument el instrumento
**insurance: comprehensive
insurance** los seguros
contra todo riesgo, **6.2**
intelligent inteligente, 1.2
interest el interés
to **interest** interesar, 5.1
interesting interesante, 1.2
international internacional,
10.1; *1.1*
interest rate la tasa de interés,
4
Internet el Internet, 3.2; *6.1*
to surf the Net navegar
el Internet, 3.2; *6.1*
to **interrupt** interrumpir

to **intersect** cruzarse
intersection la bocacalle,
el cruce, *9.1*
interview la entrevista, **10**
to **interview** entrevistar
interviewer
el/la entrevistador(a)
to **invest** invertir (ie, i), **8**
to **invite** invitar
Irish irlandés(esa)
to **iron** planchar, **4**
Is . . . there, please? ¿Está… ,
por favor?, *6.2*
island la isla
it lo, la
Italian italiano(a)

jack *(car)* el/la gato(a), *9.2*
jacket la chaqueta, 9.1
ski jacket la chaqueta
de esquí, el anorak, 7.2
jam la mermelada, **7**
January enero, LP
Japanese japonés(esa)
jar el frasco, 9.2
jeans el blue jean, 9.1
Jewish judío(a), hebreo(a), *5.2*
job application la aplicación
(la solicitud) de empleo, **10**
jogging: to go jogging
hacer jogging, *11.1; **2.1***
journalist el/la periodista, **8**
juice el jugo, el zumo, 4.1
orange juice el jugo
de naranja, 4.1; **7**
July julio, LP
June junio, LP
**just: to have just
(done something)**
acabar de (+ infinitivo), 4.2
just as (like) igual que

kebabs los pinchitos, 4.2
to **keep** guardar, *6.1*
key la llave, **7;** *(computer)*
el botón, *6.1*
back key el botón regresar
(retroceder), *6.1*
delete key el botón
borrador, *6.1*
magnetic key la llave
magnética, **7**
keyboard el teclado, *6.1*

English-Spanish Dictionary

to **kick** lanzar, 5.1
kilogram el kilo, 9.2
kilometer el kilómetro
kind la clase
king el rey
 the Three Kings (Wise Men)
 los Reyes Magos, 5.2
kiosk *(newsstand)* el quiosco,
 3.1; *(ticket dispenser)*
 el distribuidor automático, 3.1
kiss el beso; *(little, often on
 cheek)* el besito, 5
to **kiss** besar, 5
kitchen la cocina, 2.2; *10;* **1**
knapsack la mochila, 3.1
knee la rodilla, 11.1; *2.1*
kneepad la rodillera, *11.1;* **2.1**
knife el cuchillo, *4*
to **know** saber; conocer, 9.1
 **to know how (to do
 something)** saber, 9.1

to **lack** faltar, 6.1
 He/She lacks . . . Le falta... ,
 6.1
lamb el cordero, *4;* **9**
lamp la lámpara, 2.2
land la tierra, *8.2*
to **land** aterrizar, 10.2; *1.2*
landing el aterrizaje, 10.2; *1.2*
landowner el/la terrateniente
landscape el paisaje
lane *(highway)* el carril, *9.1;*
 la pista, la vía, la banda,
 el canal
language la lengua
lap *(track)* la vuelta, *11.1;* **2.1**
laptop computer
 la computadora portátil
large gran, grande, 1.2
last pasado(a) *7.1;* último(a)
 last night anoche, 7.1
 last week la semana pasada,
 7.1
 last year el año pasado, 7.1
to **last** durar
late tarde; con retraso (una
 demora), 10.2; *1.2*
later luego, LP; más tarde;
 después
 See you later! ¡Hasta
 luego!, LP
Latin America Latinoamérica

Latin American
 latinoamericano(a)
Latino latino(a)
to **laugh** reír
laundromat la lavandería, *4*
laundry el lavado, *4*
lawyer's office el bufete
 del abogado, **10**
lazy perezoso(a), 1.2
to **lead** *(from one street into
 another)* desembocar
leaf (of lettuce) la hoja
 de lechuga, **9**
league la liga
to **learn** aprender, 4.2
least: at least a lo menos
to **leave** salir, 8.1
to **leave** *(something)* dejar, *4*
 to leave a message dejar
 un mensaje, *6.2*
 to leave a tip dejar una
 propina, *4*
left izquierdo(a), 11.1; *2.1*
 to the left a la izquierda, *9.1*
leftovers las sobras
leg la pierna, 11.1; *2.1*
lemon el limón
lemonade la limonada
less menos, 9.1
lesson la lección
to **let** dejar; permitir
letter la carta, *4*
letter *(of alphabet)* la letra
lettuce la lechuga, 4.1
 leaf of lettuce la hoja
 de lechuga, **9**
lid la tapa, *10;* **1**
to **lie** mentir (ie, i), **8**
life la vida
 life passage el pasaje de la
 vida, *3*
to **lift** levantar, *11.1;* **2.1**
 to lift weights levantar
 pesas, *11.1;* **2.1**
light la luz, 5.2
 red light la luz roja, *9.1*
 traffic light el semáforo, *8.1*
to **light** encender (ie), 5.2
to **light up** iluminar, 5.2
lightly ligeramente
lights las luces, *5.2;*
 (headlights) las luces, 9.2
 festival of lights (Hanukkah)
 la fiesta de las luces, *5.2*
like como

to **like** gustar, 5.1; encantar, *6.2*
 **What would you like
 (to eat)? ¿Qué desean
 tomar?, 4.2
line *(of people)* la cola, 10.2;
 1.2; la fila
 to wait in line hacer cola,
 10.2; *1.2;* estar en fila
line la línea, *6.2*
 solid line *(road)* la línea
 continua, *9.1*
to **line up** hacer cola, 10.2; *1.2*
lion el león
lip el labio
to **listen to** escuchar, 3.2
 Listen! ¡Oye!, 1.2
literary literario(a)
literature la literatura, *7.2;*
 las letras
little pequeño(a), 1.2
 a little poco(a), 2.2
to **live** vivir, 4.1
livestock el ganado, *8.2*
living room la sala, 2.2
loan el préstamo, *4*
 short- (long-) term loan
 el préstamo a corto (largo)
 plazo, *4*
lobster la langosta, *4*
logical lógico(a)
long largo(a), 5.1
long-distance *(race)* de larga
 distancia, *11.1;* **2.1**
long-sleeved de manga larga,
 9.1
Look! ¡Mira!, 3.1
to **look at** mirar, 3.2
to **look at oneself** mirarse, 11.1;
 2.1
to **look for** buscar, 3.2
 Look out! ¡Cuidado!, **5**
to **lose** perder (ie), 5.1
lot: a lot mucho(a), LP;
 muchos(as), 2.1
lotion: suntan lotion
 la crema solar, la loción
 bronceadora, 7.1
love el amor, **5**
 in love with
 enamorado(a) de
 loved one el/la amado(a)
to **love** encantar, *6.2;* querer (ie)
 She loves the music. Le
 encanta la música.
low bajo(a), 3.1
 low (heat), a fuego lento,
 10; **1**
to **lower** *(price)* rebajar, 9.1

luck: How lucky I am!
¡Qué suerte tengo!, 9.1

luggage el equipaje, 10.1; *1.1;*
6.1

  carry-on luggage el equipaje
de mano, 10.1; *1.1*

  luggage cart el carrito, *3.1*

  luggage claim ticket,
el talón, **6.1**

  luggage identification tag
la etiqueta, **6.1**

  to check luggage facturar
el equipaje, 10.1; *1.1*

lunch el almuerzo, 4.1

  to have lunch tomar el
almuerzo, 4.1

luxurious lujoso(a)

mad enojado(a), enfadado(a),
6.1

madam (la) señora, LP

made hecho(a)

magazine la revista, *3.1;* **8**

magnetic magnético(a), *7*

magnificent magnífico(a)

maid la camarera, *7;* el/la
criado(a), **3 (Lit.)**

  maid of honor la dama
de honor, **3.1**

mail el correo, **4**

  e-mail el correo
electrónico, *6.1*

to **mail a letter** echar una carta, **4**

mailbox el buzón, **4**

main principal

majority la mayoría; *(adj.)*
mayoritario(a)

to **make** hacer, 10.2; *1.2;*
confeccionar, elaborar, *5.1*

  to make a basket
(basketball) encestar, 5.2

  to make a stopover hacer
escala, **6.1**

  to make better mejorar,
5 (Lit.)

  to make the bed hacer
la cama, *7*

mall el centro comercial, 9.1

man el hombre

manners los modales, 6.1; **5**

  to have good (bad)
manners tener buenos
(malos) modales, 6.1

manual transmission
la transmisión manual, **6.2**

many muchos(as), 2.2

  as many . . . as tantos(as)…
como

how many? ¿cuántos(as)?,
2.1

map el plano, *9.1;* el mapa, **6.2**

marathon el maratón, *11.1;* **2.1**

March marzo, LP

mark la nota, 3.1

  bad (low) mark la nota
mala (baja), 3.1

  good (high) mark la nota
buena (alta), 3.1

  to get good (bad) marks
sacar notas buenas
(malas), 3.1

market el mercado, 9.2

  native market el mercado
indígena, 9.2

market stall el puesto,
el tenderete, 9.2

marmalade la mermelada, *7*

marriage el matrimonio,
el casamiento, **3.1**

married: to get married
casarse, **3.1**

mask la máscara, *5.1*

mason el albañil, **10**

to **match** parear

mathematics las matemáticas,
1.2

mausoleum el mausoleo, *5.1*

maximum máximo(a)

May mayo, LP

maybe quizá, quizás, tal vez,
7.2

mayonnaise la mayonesa, 9.2

mayor el/la alcalde(sa), **3.1**

me *(pron.)* me

  to (for) me a (para) mí

meal la comida, 4.1

to **mean** significar

means of transport el medio
de transporte, *8.1*

meat la carne, 4.1; *4;* **9**

  ground meat la carne
picada, el picadillo, **9**

meatball la albóndiga, 4.2

meat pie la empanada, 4.2

media los medios
de comunicación, **8**

medicine el medicamento,
la medicina, 6.2

medium *(meat)* a término
medio, *4*

medium-sized mediano(a)

to **meet** encontrarse (ue);
conocer

member el miembro, 2.1;
el/la socio(a)

menorah la menora, *5.2*

menu el menú, 4.2; *4*

merchant el/la
vendedor(a), 9.2; **10**

Merry Christmas!
¡Feliz Navidad!

merry-go-round el tiovivo,
8.1

mess: What a mess! ¡Qué lío!,
6.1

message el mensaje, *6.2*

meter el metro

Mexican mexicano(a)

Mexican American
mexicanoamericano(a), 1.2

microwave oven el horno de
microondas, *10;* **1**

Middle Ages la Edad Media

midnight la medianoche

mile la milla

mileage el kilometraje, **6.2**

milk la leche, 4.1

million el millón

  a million dollars un millón
de dólares

mime el mimo, *8.1*

to **mince** picar, *10;* **1**

mind el espíritu, *11.1;* **2.1**

mineral water el agua
mineral, 4.2

mirror el espejo, 11.1; *2.1*

Miss (la) señorita, LP

to **miss (the bus, the flight)**
perder (ie) (el autobús,
el vuelo), 8.1; **6.1**

to **misunderstand** malentender
(ie), **5**

misunderstanding
el malentendido, **5**

mobile phone el móvil, 3.2,
6.1; el celular, *6.1*

modern moderno(a)

mom mamá

moment el momento

monastery el monasterio

Monday el lunes, LP

money el dinero, 3.2

monitor *(computer)*
la pantalla de escritorio, *6.1*

month el mes, LP

monument el monumento

mood el humor, 6.1

  to be in a good (bad) mood
estar de buen (mal)
humor, 6.1

moon la luna

more más, 9.1

morning la mañana

  Good morning. Buenos
días., LP

  in the morning por la
mañana; de la mañana

English-Spanish Dictionary

mother la madre, 2.1
motive el motivo
mountain la montaña, 7.2
mountaintop el pico, 7.2
mouse el ratón, *6.1*
mousepad la alfombrilla, *6.1*
mouth la boca, 6.2
to **move** mover (ue)
movement el movimiento, *11.1;* **2.1**
movie la película, el filme, 8.2; el film
movie theater el cine, 8.2
movies: to go to the movies ir al cine, 8.2
MP3 player el MP3, 3.2; *6.2*
Mr. (el) señor, LP
Mr. and Mrs. (los) señores
Mrs. (la) señora, LP
Ms. (la) señorita, (la) señora, LP
much mucho(a), LP
  as much . . . as tan… como, *11.2;* **2.2**
  How much is it (does it cost)? ¿Cuánto es?, LP; ¿Cuánto cuesta?, 3.2
mud el lodo
to **murmur** musitar, **3 (Lit.)**
museum el museo, 8.2
music la música, 1.2
musician el/la músico(a), 8.1
mussels los mejillones, *4*
must deber
my mi(s)
mysterious misterioso(a)

name el nombre, 2.1
  My name is . . . Me llamo… , 11.1; *2.1*
  What is your name? ¿Cómo te llamas?, 11.1; *2.1;* ¿Cuál es su nombre?
napkin la servilleta, *4*
narrative la narrativa, **7.2**
narrow angosto(a), estrecho(a), *8.1*
national nacional
nationality la nacionalidad, 1.1
  what nationality? ¿de qué nacionalidad?, 1.1
native indígena, 9.2
native person el/la indígena
nature la naturaleza

near cerca de, 3.2; cercano(a), **6.2**
necessary necesario(a)
  It's necessary. Es necesario., *11.2;* **2.2**
  it's necesssary to (do something) hay que, 10.2; *1.2*
neck el cuello, *11.1;* **2.1**
necktie la corbata, 9.1
to **need** necesitar, 3.2
negative negativo(a)
neighbor el/la vecino(a)
neighborhood el casco, el barrio, *8.1*
neither tampoco
nephew el sobrino, 2.1
nervous nervioso(a), 6.1
net *(World Wide Web)* la red, 3.2; *6.1; (tennis),* 5.2
  to surf the Net navegar el Internet, 3.2; *6.1*
never nunca, 8.2; jamás
new nuevo(a), 1.1
  New Year el Año Nuevo
  New Year's Eve la Nochevieja, la víspera del Año Nuevo
newborn el/la recién nacido(a), **3.2**
newlyweds los recién casados, **3.1**
news la(s) noticia(s), **8**
newscaster el/la noticiero(a), **8**
newspaper el periódico, *3.1;* **8**
newsstand el quiosco, *3.1*
next próximo(a), *3.2;* que viene, 8.2
  next stop la próxima parada, *3.2*
  next summer (year, etc.) el verano (año, etc.) que viene, 8.2
next to al lado de, 2.2
Nicaraguan nicaragüense
nice simpático(a), 1.1; *(weather)* buen (tiempo)
  Nice to meet you. Mucho gusto., 1.2
  The weather is nice. Hace buen tiempo., LP
nickname el apodo, **5 (Lit.)**
niece la sobrina, 2.1
night la noche
  at night por la noche
  Good night. Buenas noches., LP

last night anoche, 7.1
nine nueve, LP
nine hundred novecientos(as)
nineteen diecinueve, LP
ninety noventa, LP
no no, LP; ninguno(a)
  by no means de ninguna manera
nobody nadie, 8.2
none ninguno(a)
noon el mediodía
no one nadie, 8.2
normal normal, 6.2
north el norte
North American norteamericano(a), 1.1
no-smoking sign la señal de no fumar, 10.2; *1.2*
not no, 1.2
notebook el cuaderno, 3.1
nothing nada, 8.2
  Nothing else. Nada más., 9.2
novel la novela
novelist el/la novelista
November noviembre, LP
now ahora
nowadays hoy en día
number el número, 10.1; *1.1;* la cifra, **8**
  flight number el número del vuelo, 10.1; *1.1*
  seat number el número del asiento, 10.1; *1.1*
  telephone number el número de teléfono, 6.2
nuptial nupcial, **3.1**
nurse el/la enfermero(a), 6.2; *11.2;* **2.2**

obituary la esquela, el obituario, **3.2**
object el objeto
objective el objetivo
obligatory obligatorio(a)
to **observe** observar
obsession la manía, **6 (Lit.)**
obstinate obstinado(a), 6.1
occasionally de vez en cuando
occupation la profesión, **10**
occupied ocupado(a), 4.2; *3.2*
ocean el océano
o'clock: It's two o'clock. Son las dos., LP

October octubre, LP
odd *(numeric)* impar
of de, LP
    Of course! ¡Cómo no!;
      ¡Claro!
    of the del, de la
to **offer** ofrecer
offering la ofrenda, *5.1*
office la oficina, *8.1;* **9;**
    el despacho, **4 (Lit.)**
    doctor's office la consulta
      del médico, *6.2;* **10**
official: government official
    el/la funcionario(a)
    gubernamental
    (de gobierno), **10**
often con frecuencia, a menudo
oil el aceite, *4*
    olive oil el aceite de oliva, **9**
oil paint el óleo, *7.1*
okay de acuerdo
old viejo(a), *2.2;* antiguo(a), *8.1*
    How old is he (she)?
      ¿Cuántos años tiene?, *2.1*
    old city el casco (barrio)
      antiguo, *8.1*
older mayor, *2.1*
oldest el/la mayor, *2.1*
olive la aceituna, *4.2*
on sobre; en
    on board abordo, *10.2; 1.2*
    on foot a pie, *3.2*
    on the edge of al borde
      mismo de
    on time a tiempo, *10.2; 1.2*
    on top of sobre
one uno; un(a), LP
one hundred cien(to), LP
one thousand mil
one-way (ticket) el boleto
    (billete) sencillo, *3.1;* **(street)**
    la calle de sentido único, *9.1*
onion la cebolla, *9.2;* **10; 1**
online: to go online
    entrar en línea, *6.1*
only único(a), *2.1;* solo;
    solamente
to **open** abrir, *4.2*
open-air al aire libre, *7.2*
open-minded flexible, *6.1*
opinion la opinión
opponents el equipo
    contrario, *7.1*
opposite el contrario
or o, u *(used instead of o in
    front of words beginning
    with o or ho)*
orange *(color)* anaranjado(a),
    5.1

orange *(fruit)* la naranja, *4.1*
    orange juice el jugo (zumo)
      de naranja, *4.1; 7*
orchard la huerta, *8.2;* **9**
to **order** *(restaurant)* la orden, *4.2*
to **order** *(restaurant)* pedir (i, i)
oregano el orégano, **9**
to **organize** organizar
origin el origen
orthopedic surgeon
    el/la cirujano(a)
    ortopédico(a), *11.2;* **2.2**
other otro(a)
    any other cualquier otro(a)
    other people los demás,
      5 (Lit.)
our nuestro(a), nuestros(as)
outdoor al aire libre, *7.2*
outfielder el/la jardinero(a),
    5.2
outskirts los alrededores,
    las afueras, *6.2*
oven el horno, *10;* **1**
over por encima de, *5.2*
overhead bin el
    compartimiento superior,
    10.2; 1.2
overpopulation
    la sobrepoblación
owing to debido a, **6.1**
own propio(a), *5.1*
owner el amo, **8 (Lit.);**
    el/la dueño(a), **10**
oxygen mask la máscara de
    oxígeno, *10.2; 1.2*

P

to **pack** hacer la maleta, *10.1; 1.1*
package el paquete, *9.2*
page la página; el paje, **3.1**
    home page la página
      de inicio (inicial, frontal),
      6.1
pain el dolor, *6.2*
paint la pintura, **7.1**
to **paint** pintar, **7.1**
paintbrush el pincel, **3 (Lit.);**
    7.1
painter el/la pintor(a), *8.2;*
    7.1
painting el cuadro, *8.2;* **7.1;**
    la pintura
pair el par, *9.1*
    pair of shoes el par
      de zapatos, *9.1*
pants el pantalón, *3.1*
    long pants el pantalón
      largo, *9.1*

paper el papel, *3.1*
    sheet of paper la hoja
      de papel, *3.1*
    toilet paper el papel
      higiénico, *11.2; 2.2*
paperback (book) el libro
    de bolsillo, *3.1;* **8**
parade el desfile, *5.2*
    to walk in a parade
      desfilar, *5.1*
paramedic el/la socorrista,
    11.2; **2.2**
parents los padres, *2.1*
park el parque, *11.2; 2.2*
to **park** aparcar, *8.1;* estacionar,
    parquear
parka el anorak, *7.2*
parking lot el parking,
    el parqueo, *8.1*
parking meter
    el parquímetro, *9.1*
part la parte
    **the greatest part, the
      majority** la mayor parte
part-time a tiempo parcial,
    10
party la fiesta, *8.1*
    to (have) throw a party
      dar una fiesta, *8.1*
to **pass** pasar, *5.2;* *(car)*
    adelantar(se), rebasar, pasar,
    9.1
passenger el/la pasajero(a),
    10.1; 1.1
passport el pasaporte, *10.2; 1.2*
    passport inspection
      el control de pasaportes,
      6.1
past el pasado
pastry el pan dulce, *7*
path la senda, *3.2*
patience la paciencia, *6.1*
patient el/la paciente, *6.2*
patient *(adj.)* paciente, *6.1*
patron saint el/la santo(a)
    patrón(ona), *5.1*
    patron saint's day la fiesta
      patronal, *5.1*
pavement el pavimento
to **pay** pagar, *3.2*
    to pay attention prestar
      atención, *3.1;* hacerle caso,
      5 (Lit.)
pay phone el teléfono público,
    6.2
pea el guisante, *9.2*
peaceful tranquilo(a), *6.1*
peak el pico, *7.2*
peanut el cacahuate, el maní,
    8.1; el cacahuete

English-Spanish Dictionary

peasant el campesino, el peón, *8.2*

pedestrian el/la peatón(ona), *8.1*

  pedestrian crossing el cruce peatonal, *8.1*

to **peel** pelar, *10; 1*

pen el bolígrafo, *3.1*; el lapicero, la pluma

pencil el lápiz, *3.1*

people la gente, *9.1*

  other people los demás, **5 (Lit.)**

pepper *(spice)* la pimienta, *4;* *(bell pepper)* el pimiento, *9.2; 10; 1*; el pimentón; el ají; el chipotle; el morrón

perhaps quizá, quizás, tal vez, *7.2;* acaso, **3 (Lit.)**

to **permit** permitir

person la persona

  person who just arrived el/la recién llegado(a), **5**

personality la personalidad, *6.1*

perspective la perspectiva, **7.1**

Peruvian el/la peruano(a)

peso el peso

pet la mascota, *2.1*

pharmacist el/la farmacéutico(a)

pharmacy la farmacia, *6.2*

phone el teléfono

  cell phone el móvil, *3.2, 6.1*; el (teléfono) celular, *6.1*

  pay phone el teléfono público, *6.2*

  phone book la guía telefónica, *6.2*

  phone call la llamada telefónica, *6.2*

  phone card la tarjeta telefónica, *6.2*

  phone number el número de teléfono, *6.2*

  phone receiver el auricular, *6.2*

  public phone el teléfono público, *6.2*

  to pick up the phone descolgar (ue) el auricular, *6.2*

  to speak on the phone hablar por teléfono

photo(graph) la foto(grafía), *7.1*

  to take photos sacar (tomar) fotos, *7.1*

physical *(exam)* el examen físico, *6.2*

  physical education la educación física, *1.2*

physics la física

piano el piano

to **pick up** recoger, *6.1*

to **pick up** *(phone)* descolgar (ue) el auricular, *6.2*

to **pick up** *(speed)* agarrar velocidad

picture la foto(grafía); la imagen

  to take pictures sacar (tomar) fotos, *7.1*

picturesque pintoresco(a); **7.1**

piece el pedazo, el trozo (trocito)

  little piece el pedacito, *10; 1*

pig el cerdo, *8.2*; el cochinillo, el lechón, el chancho

pillow la almohada, *7*

pinch la pizca

pineapple la piña, *9.2*

pink rosado(a), *5.1*

pitcher *(baseball)* el/la pícher, el/la lanzador(a), *5.2*

pizza la pizza, *4.1*

place el lugar, **7.2**; el sitio

to **plan** planear

plane el avión, *10.1; 1.1*

planet el planeta

plant la planta, *2.2*

to **plant** sembrar (ie), *8.2*

plantain: slices of fried plantain los tostones, *4.2*; los patacones

plaster el yeso, **7.1**

plate el plato, *4*

platform *(railway)* el andén, *3.1*

to **play** *(sport)* jugar (ue), *5.1*; *(musical instrument)* tocar, *8.1; 5.2*

  to play soccer (baseball, etc.) jugar (al) fútbol (béisbol, etc.), *5.1*

player el/la jugador(a), *5.1*

  baseball player el/la jugador(a) de béisbol, el/la beisbolista, *5.2*

plaza la plaza, *8.1*

pleasant agradable, *6.1*; placentero(a)

please por favor, *LP*; favor de (+ infinitivo), *11.2; 2.2*

pleasure: It's a pleasure to meet you. Mucho gusto.

plot el argumento, *7.2*

plumber el/la fontanero(a), el/la plomero(a), **10**

P.M. de la tarde, de la noche

poem el poema, *7.2*

poet el/la poeta, *7.2*

poetry la poesía, *7.2*

point el tanto, *5.1*; el punto

  to score a point marcar un tanto, *5.1*

to **point out** señalar

policy la póliza, *6.2*

polite bien educado(a), *6.1*; cortés, **5**

politician el/la político(a), **10**

polluted contaminado(a)

pollution la contaminación

pool la piscina, la alberca, *7.1*; la pila

poor pobre

popular popular

population la población

pork el cerdo, **9**

pork chop la chuleta de cerdo, *4; 1*

portrait el retrato

Portuguese portugués(esa)

position el puesto, **10**

to **possess** poseer

possibility la posibilidad

possible posible

postcard la tarjeta postal, *4*

pot la olla, la cacerola, la cazuela *10; 1*

potato la papa, la patata, *4.1*

  french fried potatoes las papas (patatas) fritas, *4.1*

pothole el bache

practically casi, *8.2*

to **practice** practicar

to **prefer** preferir (ie, i), *5.2; 4*

to **prepare** preparar; confeccionar, *5.1*

to **prescribe** recetar, *6.2*

prescription la receta, *6.2*

present el regalo, *8.1*

  Christmas present el aguinaldo, *5.2*

to **present** presentar

president el/la presidente(a)

press la prensa, **8**

to **press** *(button)* oprimir, pulsar, *6.1*

pretty bonito(a), 1.1; hermoso(a)

previous anterior, *6.1*

price el precio, 9.1; la tarifa, **6.2**

priest el cura, **3.1**; el sacerdote, **8**

primary primario(a)

to **print** imprimir, *6.1*

printer la impresora, *6.1*

private privado(a), 2.2

probable probable

problem el problema

procession la procesión, *5.1*

product el producto, 9.2

profession la profesión, **10**

promotion (sales) la promoción, **8**

prose la prosa, **7.2**

protagonist la protagonista, **7.2**

proud orgulloso(a), **9**

public público(a)

Puerto Rican puertorriqueño(a), 1.1

pulse el pulso, 6.2

to **punish** castigar, **5**

purchase la compra, 9.2

to **push (button)** oprimir, pulsar, *6.1*

push-ups: to do push-ups hacer planchas, *11.1;* **2.1**

to **put** poner, 10.2; *1.2;* meter, 5.2

to **put in charge** encargar, **4 (Lit.)**

to **put on (clothes)** ponerse, 11.1; *2.1; (brakes)* poner los frenos

to **put up (tent)** armar, montar, 11.2; *2.2*

puzzle el rompecabezas

quarter (city) el casco, el barrio, *8.1; (time)* el cuarto, LP

a quarter past (the hour) y cuarto, LP

question la pregunta, 3.1

to ask a question preguntar, 3.1

quickly rápidamente

quiet tranquilo(a), calmo(a), 6.1

quite bastante, 1.2

race la carrera, *11.1;* **2.1**

cross-country race la carrera a campo traviesa, *11.1;* **2.1**

long-distance race la carrera de larga distancia, *11.1;* **2.1**

relay race la carrera de relevos, *11.1;* **2.1**

racket la raqueta, 5.2

railroad el ferrocarril, *3.1*

railroad platform el andén, *3.1*

railroad station la estación de ferrocarril, *3.1;* **6.2**

to **rain** llover (ue)

It's raining. Llueve., LP

raincoat el impermeable

to **raise** levantar, 3.1

to raise one's hand levantar la mano, 3.1

ranch la hacienda, la estancia, el rancho, 8.2

rare (meat) casi crudo, *4*

rate la tarifa; la tasa

rather bastante, 1.2

raw crudo(a), 8.1

raw vegetables los vegetales crudos, 8.1

reaction la reacción

to **read** leer, 4.2

reading la lectura

ready listo(a)

to **realize** darse cuenta de, **8**

really realmente

rearview mirror el retrovisor, **6.2**

reason la razón, el motivo

to **receive** recibir, 4.1

receiver (telephone) el auricular, 6.2

reception la recepción, **3.1**

recipe la receta, 10; **1**

recipient el/la destinatario(a), *6.1*

to **recognize** reconocer

to **recommend** recomendar (ie)

record el disco

red rojo(a), 5.1

red light la luz roja, 9.1

redheaded pelirrojo(a), 1.1

to **reduce (price)** rebajar, 9.1

to **reduce (speed)** reducir la velocidad, 9.1

reduced reducido(a)

refrigerator el refrigerador, la nevera, *10;* **1**

region la región

to **rejoice** alegrarse, **3.1**

relative el/la pariente, 2.1

relay: relay race la carrera de relevos, *11.1;* **2.1**

reliability la confiabilidad

religious religioso(a)

to **remain** quedarse, 11.1; *2.1*

to **remember** recordar (ue)

to **rent** alquilar, rentar, 7.1; *3.2;* **6.2;** arrendar (ie), **6.2**

to **repeat (take second helping)** repetir (i, i), *4*

report el reportaje, **8**

to **represent** representar

republic la república

Dominican Republic la República Dominicana

to **request** pedir (i, i), *4*

to **require** exigir

required obligatorio(a)

reservation la reservación, *7;* la reserva

to **reserve** reservar, *7*

resort: seaside resort el balneario, 7.1

ski resort la estación de esquí, 7.2

rest: the rest lo(s) demás

to **rest** descansar, *11.1;* **2.1**

restaurant el restaurante, *4*

restroom el servicio, 10.2; *1.2*

result el resultado

résumé el currículum vitae, **10**

to **return** regresar, 3.2; volver (ue), 5.1; **to return (something)** devolver (ue), 5.2

review el repaso

to **review** repasar

rhyme la rima, **7.2**

rice el arroz, 4.1

rich rico(a)

to **rid** liberar, *11.1;* **2.1**

ride: to go for a (bike) ride dar un paseo en bicicleta

to **ride (horse)** andar a caballo, *3.2;* montar a caballo, 8.2; *(bicycle)* andar en bicicleta, *11.1;* **2.1**

English-Spanish Dictionary

rides *(amusement park)* las atracciones, *8.1*

right derecho(a), 11.1; *2.1*

  right on the edge of al borde mismo de

  to the right a la derecha, *9.1*

  right: That's right! ¡Verdad!

right away enseguida, 4.2

to **ring** sonar (ue), *6.1*

  ringtone el timbre (sonoro), *6.2*

  rink *(ice-skating)* la pista de patinaje, 7.2

to **rise** alzarse, *8*

  rite el rito

  river el río

roast asado(a)

  roast suckling pig el cochinillo asado, el lechón asado, el chancho asado

to **roast** asar, *10;* **1**

roll *(bread)* el panecillo, 4.1; *7*

roll of toilet paper el rollo de papel higiénico, 11.2; *2.2*

rollerblading el patinaje en línea, *11.1;* **2.1**

rollerblading: to go rollerblading patinar en línea, *11.1;* **2.1**

roller coaster la montaña rusa, *8.1*

romantic romántico(a)

room el cuarto, 2.2; *7;* *(museum)* el salón, 8.2

  bathroom el cuarto de baño, 2.2; *7*

  bedroom el cuarto de dormir, la recámara, 2.2; el dormitorio, la habitación, la alcoba, la pieza

  classroom la sala de clase, 3.1

  dining room el comedor, 2.2

  emergency room la sala de emergencia, 11.2; **2.2**

  living room la sala, 2.2

  restroom el servicio, 10.2; *1.2*

  single (double) room el cuarto sencillo (doble), *7*

  waiting room la sala de espera, *3.1*

round-trip *(ticket)* el boleto (billete) de ida y vuelta (regreso), *3.1*

routine la rutina, 11.1; *2.1*

  daily routine la rutina diaria, 11.1; *2.1*

row *(of seats)* la fila, **6.1**

rude mal educado(a), 6.1

ruins las ruinas

rule la regla

to **run** correr, 5.2

runner el/la corredor(a), *11.1;* **2.1**

running water el agua corriente

runway la pista, 10.2; *1.2*

rural rural

S

sad triste, deprimido(a), 6.1

saffron el azafrán

sailboard la plancha de vela, 7.1

saint el/la santo(a), *5.1*

  patron saint el/la santo(a) patrón(ona), *5.1*

salad la ensalada, 4.1

sale el saldo, la liquidación, 9.1

salesperson el/la empleado(a), 3.2; el/la dependiente(a)

salt la sal, *4*

salty salado(a)

same mismo(a), 1.2

sand la arena, 7.1

sandal la sandalia, 9.2

sandwich el sándwich, el bocadillo, 4.1; la torta

  ham and cheese sandwich el sándwich de jamón y queso, 4.1

satisfied satisfecho(a)

to **satisfy** satisfacer

Saturday el sábado, LP

sauce la salsa, *10;* **1**

saucepan la cacerola, la cazuela, la olla, *10;* **1**

saucer el platillo, *4*

sausage el chorizo

to **save** guardar, *6.1*

saxophone el saxófono

to **say** decir, *3.2*

  to say good-bye despedirse (i, i), *5*

scenery el paisaje

schedule *(train)* el horario, *3.1*

school la escuela, 1.2; el colegio; la academia

  elementary school la escuela primaria

  high school la escuela secundaria, 1.2; el colegio

school *(adj.)* escolar

  school bus el bus escolar, 3.2

  school supplies los materiales escolares, 3.1

science la ciencia, 1.2

score el tanto, 5.1

  to score a goal meter un gol, 5.1

  to score a point marcar un tanto, 5.1

scrambled: scrambled eggs los huevos revueltos, *7;* los huevos batidos, **9**

scratch el rayón, **6.2**

screen *(computer)* la pantalla de escritorio, *6.1;* la pantalla, **6.1**

scuba diving el buceo

  to go scuba diving bucear

sculptor el/la escultor(a), 8.2; **7.1**

sculpture la escultura, 8.2; **7.1**

sea el mar, 7.1

  Caribbean Sea el mar Caribe

seafood los mariscos, *4*

search: in search of en busca de

to **search** buscar, 3.2

seaside resort el balneario, 7.1

season la estación, LP

  What season is it? ¿Qué estación es?, LP

seat el asiento, 10.1; *1.1;* **6.1**; la plaza, 3.2; **6.1**

  seat number el número del asiento, 10.1; *1.1*

seat belt el cinturón de seguridad, 10.2; *1.2*

second segundo(a), 5.1

   second-class segunda clase, *3.1*

   second half *(soccer)* el segundo tiempo, 5.1

secondary secundario(a), 1.2

security *(checkpoint)* el control de seguridad, 10.2; *1.2*

   to go through security pasar por el control de seguridad, 10.2; *1.2*

sedan el sedán, 9.2

   four-door sedan el sedán a cuatro puertas, *9.2*

to **see** ver, 4.2

   let's see a ver

   See you later! ¡Hasta luego!, LP

   See you soon! ¡Hasta pronto!, LP

   See you tomorrow! ¡Hasta mañana!, LP

to **seem** parecer

   It seems to me . . . Me parece…

to **select** seleccionar, *3.1*

   self-service *(restaurant, gas station)* el autoservicio

to **sell** vender, 6.2

senator el/la senador(a), **10**

to **send** enviar, 3.2; mandar

sense: sense of humor el sentido de humor, 6.1

   to have a good sense of humor tener un buen sentido de humor, 6.1

sent mailbox la bandeja de enviados, *6.1*

sentence la frase, la oración

September septiembre, LP

serious serio(a), 1.1

to **serve** servir (i, i), *4*

   to serve as servir (i, i) de

server el/la mesero(a), 4.2, *4*; el/la camarero(a), *4*

service el servicio, 9.2

to **set** *(table)* poner la mesa, *4*; *(bone)* reducir, acomodar el hueso, *11.2*; **2.2**

setting el lugar, *7.2*

to **settle** establecer(se), **8**

seven siete, LP

seven hundred setecientos(as)

seventeen diecisiete, LP

seventy setenta, LP

several varios(as)

shack la choza, *4* **(Lit.)**; la casucha

to **shake** *(drink)* el batido, 4.2

to **shake hands** dar(se) la mano, **5**

shame: What a shame! ¡Qué pena!, 5.1

   to be a shame ser una lástima

shampoo el champú, 11.2; *2.2*

shape la forma

she ella, 1.1

sheet la sábana, *7*

sheet of paper la hoja de papel, 3.1

shellfish los mariscos, *4*

shirt la camisa, 3.1

   short- (long-) sleeved shirt la camisa de manga corta (larga), 9.1

shoe size el número, 9.1

   What size shoe do you wear (take)? ¿Qué número calzas?, 9.1

shoes las zapatillas, 5.1; los zapatos, 9.1

to **shop** ir de compras, 9.1

shopping cart el carrito, 9.2

shopping center el centro comercial, 9.1

short *(person)* bajo(a), 1.1; *(length)* corto(a), 9.1; *4*

short-sleeved de manga corta, 9.1

shorts el pantalón corto, 5.1

should deber, 4.2

shoulder *(road)* el acotamiento, el arcén, 9.1; *(body)* el hombro, *11.1*; **2.1**

to **show** mostrar (ue), 10.2; *1.2*; enseñar

shower la ducha, 11.1; *2.1*

   to take a shower tomar una ducha, 11.1; *2.1*

shrimp los camarones, 4.2

shy tímido(a)

sick enfermo(a), 6.2

sick person el/la enfermo(a)

side el lado

sidewalk la acera, 8.1

sign la señal, 10.2; *1.2*; *(road)* el rótulo, *9.1*

   no-smoking sign la señal de no fumar, 10.2; *1.2*

to **sign** firmar, **3.1**

similar similar

since desde; como

sincere sincero(a); franco(a)

to **sing** cantar, 8.1

singer el/la cantante, 8.1

single solo(a); **(room)** un cuarto sencillo, *7*

singles *(tennis)* individuales, 5.2

sink el lavabo, *7*

sir (el) señor, LP

sister la hermana, 2.1

to **sit down** sentarse (ie), 11.1; *2.1*

site (Web site) el sitio, *6.1*

six seis, LP

six hundred seiscientos(as)

sixteen dieciséis, LP

sixty sesenta, LP

size *(clothing)* la talla; *(shoes)* el número, 9.1

   What size (clothing) do you wear (take)? ¿Qué talla usas?, 9.1

   What size (shoe) do you wear (take)? ¿Qué número calzas?, 9.1

to **skate** patinar, 7.2; *11.1*; **2.1**

   to ice-skate patinar sobre el hielo, 7.2

   to in-line skate (rollerblade) patinar en línea, *11.1*; **2.1**

skateboard el monopatín, *11.1*; **2.1**

skating el patinaje, 7.2; *11.1*; **2.1**

skeleton el esqueleto, *5.1*

ski el esquí, 7.2

   ski hat el gorro, 7.2

   ski jacket la chaqueta de esquí, el anorak, 7.2

   ski lift el telesilla, el telesquí, 7.2

   ski pole el bastón, 7.2

   ski resort la estación de esquí, 7.2

   ski slope la pista, 7.2

to **ski** esquiar, 7.2

   to water-ski esquiar en el agua, 7.1

skier el/la esquiador(a), 7.2

skiing el esquí, 7.2

   cross-country skiing el esquí nórdico

   downhill skiing el esquí alpino, 7.2

   waterskiing el esquí acuático (náutico), 7.1

skillet el/la sartén, *10*; **1**

skinny enjuto(a), **10 (Lit.)**

skirt la falda, 3.1

skull el cráneo, la calavera, *5.1*

sky el cielo, 5.2

skyscraper el rascacielos, 8.1

to **sleep** dormir (ue, u)

sleeping bag el saco (la bolsa) de dormir, 11.2; *2.2*

English-Spanish Dictionary

sleeved: short- (long-) sleeved de manga corta (larga), *9.1*

slice la tajada, *9.2;* la rebanada, *10;* **1;** *(ham)* la lonja, la loncha; *(lemon, cucumber)* la rodaja, **9;** *(melon)* la raja

to **slice** cortar en rebanadas, *10;* **1**

slope la pista, *7.2*

slot la ranura, *6.2*

slow lento(a), *11.1;* **2.1**

slowly despacio, *9.1*

small pequeño(a), *1.2*

to **smell** olfatear, **8**

smile la sonrisa, *6.1*

smoking: no-smoking sign la señal de no fumar, *10.2;* *1.2*

smoothie el batido, *4.2*

snack la merienda; las tapas, los antojitos, *4.2;* los bocaditos

sneakers las zapatillas, *5.1;* los tenis, *5.2*

to **sniff** olfatear, **8**

to **snorkel** bucear, *7.1*

snorkeling el buceo, *7.1*

snow la nieve, *7.2*

to **snow** nevar (ie), *7.2*

It's snowing. Nieva., LP

snowboarder el/la snowboarder, *7.2*

so tan; *(thus)* así

so that para que, de modo que, de manera que

soap el jabón, *11.2;* **2.2**

bar of soap la barra de jabón, *11.2;* **2.2;** la pastilla de jabón

soap opera la telenovela

soccer el fútbol, *5.1*

soccer field el campo de fútbol, *5.1*

social studies los estudios sociales, *1.2*

socks los calcetines, *5.1*

soda la cola, la gaseosa, *4.1*

sofa el sofá, *2.2*

soft blando(a)

soft drink el refresco, *4.2*

soldier el soldado, **8**

solid line (road) la línea continua, *9.1*

some algunos(as); unos(as)

someone alguien, *8.2*

something algo, *8.2*

sometimes a veces, *6.1;* *1.2;* de vez en cuando

son el hijo, *2.1*

soon pronto, LP; dentro de poco, *10.2;* *1.2*

as soon as en cuanto

See you soon! ¡Hasta pronto!, LP

sore throat: to have a sore throat tener dolor de garganta, *6.2*

sorry: to be sorry sentir (ie, i)

I'm very sorry. Lo siento mucho., *5.1*

soul el alma *(f.)*

soup la sopa

south el sur

South America la América del Sur, la Sudamérica

to **sow** sembrar (ie), *8.2*

space el espacio; *(parking)* el sitio (para estacionar)

Spain España

Spanish (language) el español, *1.2;* *(person)* el/la español(a)

Spanish (adj.) español(a)

Spanish speaker el/la hispanohablante

Spanish-speaking hispanohablante

spare time el tiempo libre, *8.1*

spare tire la rueda (llanta) de repuesto (recambio), *9.2*

to **speak** hablar, *3.1*

to speak on the phone hablar por teléfono

special especial

specialty la especialidad

spectator el/la espectador(a)

speed la velocidad, *9.1*

speed limit la velocidad máxima, *9.1;* el límite de velocidad

to **spend (time)** pasar, *7.1;* *(money)* gastar

spice la especia; **9**

spirit el espíritu, *11.1;* **2.1**

to **splurge** botar la casa por la ventana

spoon (tablespoon) la cuchara, *4;* *(teaspoon)* la cucharita, *4*

sport el deporte, *5.1*

individual sport el deporte individual

team sport el deporte de equipo

sports (related to) deportivo(a)

sports car el coche deportivo, *9.2*

to **sprain** torcerse (ue), *11.2;* **2.2**

He (She) sprained his (her) ankle. Se torció el tobillo., *11.2;* **2.2**

spring la primavera, LP

square (town) la plaza, *8.1*

stable el establo, *8.2*

stadium el estadio

stairs la escalera, *8.1*

stall (market) el puesto, el tenderete, *9.2*

stamp la estampilla, el sello, *4*

to **stand in line** hacer cola, *10.2;* *1.2;* estar en fila

to **stand up** ponerse de pie, **5**

standing de pie

stanza la estrofa, *7.2*

star la estrella

to **start to (do something)** echar a, **6** **(Lit.)**

starving: I'm starving. Me muero de hambre., *4*

state el estado

station (train) la estación de ferrocarril (tren), *3.1;* **6.2;** *(subway)* la estación de metro, *8.1;* *(gas)* la estación de servicio, la gasolinera, *9.2*

statue la estatua, *8.2;* **7.1**

stay la estadía

to **stay** quedarse, *11.1;* **2.1**

to stay in bed (illness) guardar cama, *6.2;* **to stay in bed (idleness)** quedarse en la cama, *11.1;* **2.1**

to **stay** *(in a hotel)* hospedarse, 7

steak el biftec, 4

steep pendiente

steering wheel el volante, 9.2

stepbrother el hermanastro, 2.1

stepfather el padrastro, 2.1

stepmother la madrastra, 2.1

stepsister la hermanastra, 2.1

still todavía

still life la naturaleza muerta, **7.1**

stingy tacaño(a), 9.1

to **stir** revolver (ue), 10; **1**

stitch el punto, la sutura, 11.2; **2.2**

    to give (someone) stitches poner unos puntos (unas suturas) (a alguien), 11.2; **2.2**

stomach el estómago, 6.2

    to have a stomachache tener dolor de estómago, 6.2

stone la piedra

stop la parada, 3.2

    next stop la próxima parada, 3.1

    to make a stopover hacer escala, **6.1**

to **stop** parar(se), 9.1

store la tienda, 3.2

story el cuento, **7.2;** la historia

stove la cocina, la estufa, 10; **1**

straight (ahead) derecho, 9.1

    to go straight (ahead) seguir (i, i) derecho, 9.1

straw la paja, 5.2

street la calle, 8.1

    one-way street la calle de sentido único, 9.1

stress el estrés, 6.2; las tensiones, 11.1; **2.1**

stretch *(distance)* el trecho

to **stretch** estirarse, 11.1; **2.1; 2.1**

stretcher la camilla, 11.2; **2.2**

string beans las judías verdes, 9.2

strong fuerte

stubborn obstinado(a), terco(a), 6.1

student el/la alumno(a), 1.2; el/la estudiante; *(adj.)* estudiantil, escolar, 3.1

    university student el/la estudiante universitario(a), **10.2**

study el estudio

    social studies los estudios sociales, 1.2

to **study** estudiar, 3.1

stuffed up *(head cold)* resfriado(a), 6.2

stupendous estupendo(a)

style el estilo

to **subject** sujetar, **4 (Lit.)**

suburbs las afueras, los suburbios, 2.2; **6.2**

subway el metro, 8.1

    subway entrance la boca del metro, 8.1

    subway station la estación de metro, 8.1

to **succeed** tener éxito, 6.1

success el éxito, 6.1

successful: to be successful tener éxito, 6.1

such tal

suddenly de repente

to **suffer** sufrir

sugar el azúcar

to **suggest** sugerir (ie, i)

suitcase la maleta, 10.1; *1.1;* **6.1**

    to pack one's suitcase hacer la maleta, 10.1; *1.1*

summer el verano, LP

sun el sol

to **sunbathe** tomar el sol, 7.1

Sunday el domingo, LP

sunglasses los anteojos de sol, las gafas para el sol, 7.1

sunny: It's sunny. Hace (Hay) sol., LP

suntan lotion la crema solar, la loción bronceadora, 7.1

supermarket el supermercado, 9.2

supplies: school supplies los materiales escolares, 3.1

supposed to: I (He, She) was supposed to (do something). Habría de (+ infinitivo)., **4**

sure seguro(a)

to **surf** practicar la tabla hawaiana, 7.1

to **surf the Web (the Net)** navegar la red (el Internet), 3.2; **6.1**

surface la superficie, **7.1**

surfboard la tabla hawaiana, 7.1

surfing la tabla hawaiana, el surfing, 7.1

    to go surfing practicar la tabla hawaiana, el surfing, 7.1

surgeon:

    orthopedic surgeon el/la cirujano(a) ortopédico(a), 11.2; **2.2**

to **surpass** sobrepasar, **8**

surprise la sorpresa, 4.1

to **surprise** sorprender, **3.1**

survey la encuesta

SUV el SUV, 9.2

sweat suit el buzo, 11.1; **2.1**

sweater el suéter, 11.1; **2.1**

sweet dulce, 5.1

to **swim** nadar, 7.1

swimming pool la piscina, la alberca, 7.1; la pila

swimsuit el bañador, el traje de baño, 7.1

swollen hinchado(a), 11.2; **2.2**

symptom el síntoma

system el sistema

T-shirt la camiseta, 5.1; el T-shirt

table la mesa, la mesita, 2.2; *4*

    to clear the table levantar (quitar) la mesa, *4*

    to set the table poner la mesa, *4*

tablecloth el mantel, *4*

tablespoon la cuchara, *4; (in recipe)* la cucharada

to **take** tomar, 3.1; traer, 10.1; *1.1;* sacar, 7.1

    to take (by force) apoderarse de, **4 (Lit.)**

    to take *(size)* usar, calzar, 9.1

    to take a bath bañarse

    to take a flight tomar un vuelo

    to take a hike dar una caminata, 11.2; *2.2*

    to take a shower tomar una ducha, 11.1; *2.1*

    to take a test tomar un examen, 3.1

    to take a trip hacer un viaje, 10.1; *1.1*

    to take an X ray of someone tomar una radiografía, 11.2; *2.2*

    to take into account tomar en cuenta, **8**

    to take pictures (photos) sacar (tomar) fotos, 7.1

English-Spanish Dictionary

to take place tener lugar, **3.1**

to take someone's blood pressure tomar la tensión arterial, 6.2

to take someone's pulse tomar el pulso, 6.2

to take the (school) bus tomar el bus (escolar), 3.2

to **take off** *(airplane)* despegar, 10.2; *1.2; (clothes)* quitarse, 11.1; *2.1*

to **take out** sacar

taken ocupado(a), 4.2; *3.2*

takeoff el despegue, 10.2; *1.2*

talent el talento, **7.2**

to **talk** hablar, 3.1

to talk on a cell phone hablar en el móvil

to talk on the phone hablar por teléfono

tall alto(a), 1.1

tank *(car)* el tanque, 9.2

taste el gusto

tax el impuesto

taxi el taxi, 10.1; *1.1*

taxi driver el/la taxista, 10.1; *1.1*

tea el té

to **teach** enseñar, 3.1

teacher el/la profesor(a), 1.2

team el equipo, 5.1

team sport el deporte de equipo

tear la lágrima, **10 (Lit.)**

teaspoon la cucharita, *4; (in recipe)* la cucharadita

teeth los dientes, 11.1; *2.1*

to brush one's teeth cepillarse (lavarse) los dientes, 11.1; *2.1*

telegram el telegrama

telephone el teléfono

pay telephone el teléfono público, *6.2*

(related to) **telephone** telefónico(a), *6.2*

telephone book la guía telefónica, *6.2*

telephone call la llamada telefónica, *6.2*

telephone card la tarjeta telefónica, *6.2*

telephone line la línea, *6.2*

telephone number el número de teléfono, *6.2*

telephone receiver el auricular, *6.2*

to pick up the telephone descolgar (ue) el auricular, *6.2*

to speak on the telephone hablar por teléfono

television la televisión, la tele

television program la emisión televisiva, el programa de televisión, **8**

television station la emisora de televisión, **8**

temperature la temperatura, 7.2

ten diez, LP

tennis el tenis, 5.2

tennis court la cancha de tenis, 5.2

tennis player el/la tenista, 5

tennis racket la raqueta, 5.2

tennis shoes los tenis, 9.1

to play tennis jugar (ue) (al) tenis, 5.2

tension la tensión, *11.1;* **2.1**

tent la carpa, la tienda de campaña, 11.2; *2.2*

to put up a tent armar, montar una carpa (una tienda de campaña), 11.2; *2.2*

terrace la terraza

terrible terrible

test el examen, la prueba, 3.1

to give a test dar un examen (una prueba), 3.1

to take a test tomar un examen, 3.1

Texan tejano(a)

text message el mensaje de texto

Thank you. Gracias., LP

that aquel, aquella, 9.1; ese(a)

that *(one)* eso

the el, la, los, las, 1.1

their su(s)

them las, los, les

to them *(pron.)* les

theme el tema

then luego, 3.2

there allí, allá, 9.1

Is . . . there? ¿Está… ?, *6.2*

there is, there are hay, 2.2

therefore por eso

these estos(as)

they ellos(as), 1.2

thigh el muslo, *10;* **1**

thin flaco(a); delgado(a); enjuto(a), **10 (Lit.)**

thing la cosa, 3.1

to **think** pensar (ie), 5.1

What do you think? ¿Qué piensas?, 5.1

thirsty: to be thirsty tener sed, 4.1

thirteen trece, LP

thirty treinta, LP

thirty-one treinta y uno, LP

this este(a), 9.1

those aquellos(as), esos(as)

thousand mil

three tres, LP

the Three Wise Men los Reyes Magos, 5.2

three hundred trescientos(as)

throat la garganta, 6.2

to have a sore throat tener dolor de garganta, 6.2

to **throw** lanzar, tirar, 5.2

to throw (give) a party dar una fiesta, 8.1

Thursday el jueves, LP

thus así

ticket el boleto, el ticket, 7.2; *3.1;* la entrada, 8.1; el billete, 10.1; *1.1;* el tiquet(e); *(car)* la multa, 9.1

e-ticket el boleto (billete) electrónico, 10.1; *1.1*

one-way ticket el boleto (billete) sencillo, *3.1*

round-trip ticket el boleto (billete) de ida y vuelta (regreso), *3.1*

to give (someone) a ticket clavar con una multa, 9.1

ticket counter *(airport)* el mostrador, 10.1; *1.1*

ticket dispenser el distribuidor automático, *3.1*

ticket window la ventanilla, la boletería, 7.2, *3.1;* la taquilla, 8.2

tie la corbata, 9.1

tiger el tigre

time la hora, LP; 10.1; *1.1;*
el tiempo, 8.1; la vez

at times (sometimes)
a veces, 6.1; *1.2*

at what time? ¿a qué hora?,
LP

boarding time la hora
de embarque, 10.1; *1.1*

departure time la hora
de salida, 10.1; *1.1*

from time to time de vez
en cuando, 10.2, *1.2*

full-time a tiempo completo

on time a tiempo, 10.2; *1.2*

part-time a tiempo parcial

spare time el tiempo libre,
8.1

What time is it? ¿Qué hora
es?, LP

timetable el horario, *3.1*

timid tímido(a)

tip el servicio, 4.2; la propina, *4*

Is the tip included? ¿Está
incluido el servicio?, 4.2

tire la llanta, la goma,
el neumático, la rueda, *9.2;*
6.2; el caucho

flat tire el pinchazo, *9.2*

spare tire la rueda (llanta)
de repuesto (recambio), *9.2*

tired cansado(a), 6.1

to a

toast las tostadas, el pan
tostado, 4.1; *7*

today hoy, LP

What day is it today?
¿Qué día es hoy?, LP

What is today's date?
¿Cuál es la fecha de hoy?,
LP

toe el dedo del pie, *11.1;* **2.1**

together juntos(as)

toilet el inodoro, el váter, *7*

toilet paper el papel
higiénico, *11.2;* **2.2**

roll of toilet paper el rollo
de papel higiénico, *11.2;*
2.2

toll el peaje, *9.1;* la cuota

tollbooth la cabina (garita)
de peaje, *9.1*

tomato el tomate, 4.1

tomb la tumba, *5.1*

tomorrow mañana, LP

See you tomorrow!
¡Hasta mañana!, LP

tonight esta noche, 4.1

too también, 1.2

toolbar la barra de
herramientas, *6.1*

toothbrush el cepillo
de dientes, *11.2;* **2.2**

toothpaste la crema dental,
11.2; **2.2;** la pasta dentífrica

tube of toothpaste el tubo
de crema dental, *11.2;* **2.2**

to **touch** tocar, 5.1

tourist el/la turista

toward hacia

towel la toalla, *7.1;* *7*

town el pueblo; la villa,
5 (Lit.)

town square la plaza, 8.1

toy el juguete

track *(train)* la vía, *3.1*

traffic el tráfico, 8.1;
el tránsito

traffic jam el tapón

traffic light el semáforo, *8.1;*
la luz roja, *9.1*

trail el camino; la senda, *3.2*

train el tren, *3.1;* **6.2**

long-distance train el tren
de largo recorrido, **6.2**

suburban train el tren
de cercanías, **6.2**

train car el coche, el vagón, *3.1*

train conductor el/la
revisor(a), *3.2*

train station la estación
de ferrocarril (tren), *3.1*

to **transfer** *(train)* transbordar,
3.2; **6.2**

**transmission: manual
transmission**
la transmisión manual, **6.2**

**transportation: means of
transportation** los medios
de transporte, *8.2*

to **travel** viajar

tree el árbol, 2.2

trim *(hair)* el recorte, *4*

trip el viaje, 10.1; *1.1*

to take a trip hacer un
viaje, 10.1; *1.1*

trombone el trombono

truck el camión, *9.2*

true *(adj.)* verdadero(a);
cierto(a), *6.1*

That's true. Es verdad., *9.1*

trunk *(car)* el baúl,
la maletera, 10.1; *1.1*

truth la verdad

to **try** tratar de

tube el tubo, *11.2;* **2.2**

Tuesday el martes, LP

tuna el atún, *9.2*

to **turn** doblar, *9.1*

to **turn around** dar la vuelta,
9.1

to **turn off** apagar, *6.1*

to **turn on** prender, *6.1*

to **turn ... years old**
cumplir... años, **3.2**

turn signals las direccionales,
9.2

TV la tele

twelve doce, LP

twenty veinte, LP

twenty-eight veintiocho, LP

twenty-five veinticinco, LP

twenty-four veinticuatro, LP

twenty-nine veintinueve, LP

twenty-one veintiuno, LP

twenty-seven veintisiete, LP

twenty-six veintiséis, LP

twenty-three veintitrés, LP

twenty-two veintidós, LP

twin el/la gemelo(a), 2.1

to **twist** torcerse, *11.2;* **2.2**

two dos, LP

two hundred doscientos(as)

type el tipo, 6.1

typical típico(a)

U

ugly feo(a), 1.1

unattractive feo(a), 1.1

uncle el tío, 2.1

under debajo de, 10.2; *1.2*

underneath debajo de, 10.2;
1.2

to **understand** comprender, 4.2;
entender (ie), 8.2

unfortunately
desgraciadamente

to **unhook** *(telephone receiver)*
descolgar (ue) el auricular, *6.2*

uniform el uniforme, 3.1

United States Estados Unidos

from the United States
estadounidense

university la universidad

university tuition, fee
la matrícula universitaria, *4*

unless a menos que

unoccupied libre, 4.2; *3.2*

unpleasant antipático(a), 1.1;
desagradable

until hasta, LP; hasta que

English-Spanish Dictionary

up: to go up subir, 7.2
upper superior
urban urbano(a), *8.1*
us (*pl. pron.*) nos
to **use** usar, 3.2

V

vacation las vacaciones, 7.1
vanilla (*adj.*) de vainilla
various varios(as)
veal la ternera, *10; 1*
veal cutlet el escalope
de ternera, *10; 1*
vegetable la legumbre,
la verdura, el vegetal, 4.1; *9*;
la hortaliza, *9*
vegetable garden el huerto, *9*
vegetable store (greengrocer)
la verdulería, 9.2
vegetarian vegetariano(a), 4.1
veil el velo, **3.1**
Venezuelan venezolano(a)
verse el verso, **7.2**
very muy, LP; mucho, LP
It's very hot (cold). Hace
mucho calor (frío)., LP
Very well. Muy bien, LP
view la vista
vinegar el vinagre, *4*
vineyard la viña, *9*
violin el violín
to **visit** visitar, 8.2
volcano el volcán
volleyball el voleibol, 7.1
volleyball court la cancha
de voleibol, 7.1
vowel la vocal

W

to **wait (for)** esperar, 10.2; *1.2*
to wait in line hacer cola,
10.2; *1.2*; estar en fila
waiter (waitress)
el/la mesero(a), 4.2, *4;*
el/la camarero(a), *4*
waiting room la sala
de espera, *3.1*
wake el velorio, **3.2**

to **wake up** despertarse (ie),
11.1; *2.1*
to **walk** caminar, 5.1; andar
to walk in a procession
desfilar, *5.1*
to **want** querer (ie), 5.1; desear,
4.2
war la guerra, **8**
warm-ups (*clothing*) el buzo,
11.1; **2.1**
to **warn** advertir (ie, i)
warning la advertencia
to **wash** lavar, 11.2; *2.2;* **4**
to **wash oneself** lavarse, 11.1; *2.1*
**to wash one's hair (face,
hands)** lavarse el pelo
(la cara, las manos), 11.1;
2.1
washbasin el lavabo, *7*
washing machine la lavadora, **4**
watch el reloj, *6* (Lit.)
to **watch** mirar, 3.2; ver, 4.2
Watch out! ¡Cuidado!, **5**
water el agua (*f.*), 4.1
running water el agua
corriente
(sparkling) mineral water
el agua mineral (con gas),
4.2
watercolor la acuarela, **7.1**
waterskiing el esquí acuático
(náutico), 7.1
to water-ski esquiar
en el agua, 7.1
wave la ola, 7.1
way la manera
to lose one's way perder (ie)
el camino
we nosotros(as)
wealthy acomodado(a), **8**
weapon el arma (*f.*)
to **wear** llevar, 3.1; (*shoe size*)
calzar, 9.1; (*clothing size*)
usar, 9.1
weather el tiempo, LP
It's cold (weather).
Hace frío., LP
It's cool (weather).
Hace fresco., LP
The weather is bad.
Hace mal tiempo., LP
The weather is nice.
Hace buen tiempo., LP
What's the weather like?
¿Qué tiempo hace?, LP

Web la red, 3.2; *6.1*
to surf the Web navegar
la red, 3.2; *6.1*
Web site el sitio Web, *6.1*
wedding la boda, **3.1**
wedding dress el traje
de novia, **3.1**
wedding register el registro
de matrimonio, **3.1**
wedding ring el anillo
de boda, **3.1**
Wednesday el miércoles, LP
week la semana, LP
last week la semana pasada,
7.1
weekend el fin de semana, 7.1
to **weigh** pesar, *6.1*
weight la pesa, *11.1;* **2.1;**
(*of something*) el peso, **6.1**
weights: to lift weights
levantar pesas, *11.1;* **2.1**
welcome: You're welcome.
De nada., Por nada., No hay
de qué., LP
well bien, LP; pues
Very well. Muy bien., LP
well-done (*meat*) bien
hecho(a), *4*
well-known renombrado(a)
well-mannered bien
educado(a), *6.1*
west el oeste
what ¿qué?, ¿cuál?, ¿cuáles?,
LP; ¿cómo?, 1.1
at what time? ¿a qué hora?,
LP
What a mess! ¡Qué lío!, **6.1**
What a shame! ¡Qué pena!,
5.1
What day is it (today)?
¿Qué día es hoy?, LP
**What does he (she, it) look
like?** ¿Cómo es?, 1.1
**What's happening?
What's going on?** ¿Qué
pasa?, 3.1
What is he (she, it) like?
¿Cómo es?, 1.1
What is today's date?
¿Cuál es la fecha de hoy?,
LP
what nationality? ¿de qué
nacionalidad?, 1.1
What's new (up)?
¿Qué hay?

What size (clothing) do you wear (take)? ¿Qué talla usas?, 9.1

What size shoe do you wear (take)? ¿Qué número calzas?, 9.1

What would you like (to eat)? ¿Qué desean tomar?, 4.2

What time is it? ¿Qué hora es?, LP

whatever cualquier(a)

wheat el trigo, *8.2;* **9**

wheelchair la silla de ruedas, *11.2;* **2.2**

when cuando, 3.1

when? ¿cuándo?, 3.2

whenever cuandoquiera

where donde

where? ¿dónde?, 1.1; **(to) where?** ¿adónde?, 3.2

from where? ¿de dónde?, 1.1

wherever dondequiera

which? ¿cuál?, LP; ¿cuáles?

whichever cualquier(a)

while mientras, *5.2*

to **whisper** musitar, **3 (Lit.)**

white blanco(a), 5.1

who? ¿quién?, 1.1; ¿quiénes?, 1.2

Who's calling, please? ¿De parte de quién, por favor?, 6.2

whoever quienquiera

whole entero(a)

whose cuyo(a)(os)(as)

why? ¿por qué?, 3.2

wide ancho(a), *8.1*

widow la viuda, **3.2**

wife la esposa, la mujer, 2.1

to **win** ganar, 5.1

wind el viento, LP

window (store) el escaparate, 9.1; **(plane)** la ventanilla, 10.2; *1.2;* **6.1**

windshield el parabrisas, 9.1

windshield wipers los limpiaparabrisas, **6.2**

windsurfing la plancha de vela, 7.1

to go windsurfing practicar la plancha de vela, 7.1

windy: It's windy. Hace viento., LP

wings las alitas, *10;* **1**

winter el invierno, LP

wise sabio(a), **5 (Lit.)**

the Three Wise Men los Reyes Magos, *5.2*

wish el afán, **3 (Lit.)**

to **wish** desear, 4.2

with con

to **withdraw** retirar, **4**

within dentro de

without sin, 7.2

woman la dama

wooden de madera, **7.1**

word la palabra

work el trabajo, **10;** *(art)* la obra

abstract work (of art) la obra abstracta, **7.1**

figurative work (of art) la obra figurativa, **7.1**

to **work** trabajar, 3.2; *(land)* cultivar, labrar, *8.2*

workshop el taller, **7.1**

world el mundo

World Cup la Copa Mundial

worldwide mundial

worse peor

worst el/la peor

worth: It's not worth it. No vale., 7.1

Would that . . . Ojalá que… , *11.2;* **2.2**

wound la herida, *11.2;* **2.2**

wreath la corona, *5.1*

wrinkled arrugado(a), **4**

wrist la muñeca, *11.1;* **2.1**

to **write** escribir, 4.2

written escrito(a)

wrong erróneo(a)

X ray la radiografía, *11.2;* **2.2**

They're taking an X ray (of him or her). Le toman (hacen) una radiografía., *11.2;* **2.2**

Y

year el año, LP

last year el año pasado, 7.1

to be turning . . . years old cumplir… años

to be . . . years old tener… años, 2.1

yellow amarillo(a), 5.1

yes sí, LP

yesterday ayer, 7.1

yesterday afternoon ayer por la tarde, 7.1

yesterday evening anoche, 7.1

yet aún; todavía

yoga el yoga, *11.1;* **2.1**

to do yoga practicar yoga, *11.1;* **2.1**

you tú; *(sing. form.)* usted; *(pl. form.)* ustedes; *(pl. fam.)* vosotros(as); *(fam. pron.)* ti; te; *(form. pron.)* le

You're welcome. De (Por) nada.; No hay de qué., LP

young person el/la joven, 1.1

younger menor, 2.1

youngest el/la menor, 2.1

your *(fam.)* tu(s); *(form.)* su(s)

It's your turn! ¡Te toca a ti!

youth hostel el albergue juvenil, el hostal, 7

Z

zero cero, LP

zone la zona

zoo el zoológico, *8.1*

English-Spanish Dictionary

Culture Index

Numbers in light print indicate that the cultural reference was introduced in a prior level.
Numbers in bold print indicate that the cultural reference is introduced in Level 3.

A

A Julia de Burgos **256–258**

amigos R1, R7, **R18,** R34, **R38, R60,** 20, 21, 23, 26, 30, **32,** 42, 42, 52, **68,** 71, 73, 73, **75, 76,** 90, **92,** 103, 112, 111, 112, 130, 132, **132–133,** 133, **134, 148, 149, 150,** 153, **157,** 170, 196, 230, 239, 266, 275, 326, 370

Andes 22, 58, 59, **78,** 88–89, 252, 265, 282, 350, 386, 387

Andorra 236

Año Nuevo 137, 143

Argentina en general, **R45, R55, R57, 30, 283,** 326; Aconcagua, 58, 386; La Angostura, **R26;** la bandera, 165; Bariloche, R52, 11, **132–133,** 252, 253, 339; La Boca (barrio de Buenos Aires), **214;** Buenos Aires, **R9, R31, R43, R46,** 3, **3,** 17, 19, 33, 37, **48,** 56, **59, 77, 99,** 100, 105, 113, **117,** 119, **120,** 122, **123,** 127, 132, **135,** 160, **160,** 161, **167,** 171, 191, 202, 213, 231, 234, 240, 244, 264, 264, **275,** 281, 286, 289, 296, 299, **302,** 310, **311,** 331, 344, 345, 347, 355, 361, 365; La Casa Rosada (Buenos Aires), 17, 345; las cataratas del Iguazú, 229; el Catedral Cerro, 252; el cementerio de la Recoleta (Buenos Aires), **63;** Cerro Bayo, **R30;** El Cruce, **R32;** el lago Nahuel Huapi, **R28,** 253; el Parque Nacional Los Glaciares, 37, 365; el Parque Nacional Nahuel Huapi, 252; la Patagonia, 250; Puerto Madryn, 238; Rawson, 166; Salta, 231; San Telmo (barrio de Buenos Aires), **R46; La tecnología de**

hoy y ayer, 190; **Tráfico y más tráfico, 286;** Trelew, **42,** 338

arte en general, **R54, 204, 205, 330; Las artes, 220–222;** las Bellas Artes, **207;** Botero, Fernando (escultor y pintor colombiano), **202;** la cerámica, **259,** 321; *Los cubos de la memoria* de Agustín Ibarrola, **231;** Dalí, Salvador (artista surrealista español), **203; Un día de cultura latina,** 282; *Hispanic Institute* (Nueva York, Estados Unidos), 272, 287; **Un hostal y un parador** (una estadía en un albergue juvenil en Argentina), 216; Ibarrola, Agustín (escultor y pintor español), **231;** Kahlo, Frida (pintora mexicana), **202, 236,** 264; *La liberación del peón* de Diego Rivera, **221;** Miró, Joan (artista español), **203;** un mural cubano, **200–201;** un mural en un edificio de la Universidad Autónoma de México, **227;** mural de Julia de Burgos, **257;** Museo del Barrio (Nueva York, Estados Unidos), 272; Olmedo Patino, Dolores (artista mexicana), 137; Orozco, José Clemente (muralista mexicano), 282; Rivera, Diego (pintor mexicano), **220, 221,** 264; Velázquez, Diego (pintor español), **204;** *Zapatistas* de José Clemente Orozco, 283

artesanía en general, 209, 227; canastas, 90; tejidos, 71, 82

aztecas 284, 403, 405

B

baile 137, 264, 265, 405; Ballet

Folklórico de México, 284

banderas 165, 185, 206, **224, 234–235**

bienestar 28–29, 30, 31, 35, 39, **43, 45,** 48, **54,** 131, 192–194, 203, 324–325, 326, 327, 332, 335, 338, 339, 344, 376; las farmacias en los países hispanos, 195, 201, 202; el hospital, **31, 38, 47,** 327, 334, 343; **Médicos Sin Fronteras, 50, 51,** 346, 347; **Vida activa y buena salud, 48–49,** 344–345

Bolívar, Simón 145

Bolivia ¡A Bolivia ya!, 184; Laguna Verde, **193;** Llapallapani, 265; La Paz, **R48–R49,** 21, 180, **184;** el lago Titicaca, **177, 184, 185;** el volcán Licancabur, **193**

Botero, Fernando 202

Burgos, Julia de 256–257

C

Cabeza de Vaca, Álvaro Núñez 252

cafés y restaurantes R13, R17, **R46, R58–R59, R60,** R65, R66, R67, 2, **3,** 12, **22, 76,** 102–103, 104–105, 108, 109, 110, 111, 112, 113, 115, 119, 120–122, 123, 124, 125, 126, 127, 129, 132, 133, 135, 138, 140, 148, 149, 152, 154, **160, 161,** 210, 244, 253, **255, 275, 281,** 285, 298, 299, 306, 318, 340; **Restaurantes de España y Latinoamérica, 120–122; Sé lo que pedí,** 124

California 236; Baja, 170; East Los Angeles, **237;** Los Ángeles,

Culture Index

Culture Index

Culture Index

Culture Index

Culture Index

N

O

Culture Index

Culture Index

Culture Index

Grammar Index

Grammar Index

pluperfect tense 108 (4); subjunctive mood, 212 (7)

poder present indicative, R17; preterite tense, R31; **pudiera,** 140 (5)

poner present indicative, R7; preterite tense, R31

por to convey meanings *through, by, along, on behalf of, in favor of,* and *instead of,* and after **ir, mandar, venir,** and **volver,** 310 (10); to define a period of time or to express an indefinite time, 312 (10); after infinitive to express what remains to be done, 313 (10); **estar por,** 313 (10); to express means, manner, or motive, 314 (10); to express *in exchange for,* 314 (10); to express an opinion or estimation, 314 (10); to indicate measure or number, 314 (10); (*See also* **para**)

possessive adjectives 76 (3)

possessive pronouns 76 (3)

preferir present indicative, R17; present subjunctive, 43 (2)

present perfect tense R66; subjunctive mood, 212 (7)

present tense of regular and irregular verbs, R7; of **ir, dar,** and **estar,** R7; of verbs with irregular **yo** form, R7; of **ser,** R7; subjunctive mood, 8–9 (1); (*See also* irregular verbs; stem-changing verbs; subjunctive mood)

preterite tense of regular verbs, R29; verbs with a spelling change in the preterite (**buscar, caer, empezar, jugar, leer**), R29; of **dar,** R29; of irregular verbs, R31; uses of the preterite and the imperfect, R54

producir present indicative, R7

pronouns reflexive pronouns, R19; indirect object pronouns, R46; direct object pronouns, R53; double object pronouns, R64; object pronouns with commands, 11, 13 (1); possessive pronouns, 76 (3); relative pronouns, 278 (9)

querer present indicative, R17; preterite tense, R31; **quisiera,** 140 (5)

reflexive pronouns R19

reflexive verbs R19

relative clauses 316 (10)

relative pronouns 278 (9)

saber present indicative, R7; preterite tense, R31; present subjunctive, 9 (1)

salir present indicative, R7

ser present indicative, R7; preterite tense, R31; imperfect tense, R43; present subjunctive, 9 (1)

si clauses *if* clauses and sequence of tenses, 214 (7)

stem-changing verbs present indicative, R17; present subjunctive, 43 (2)

subjunctive mood present subjunctive: regular forms, 8 (1); irregular forms, 9 (1); subjunctive form used as formal (**usted, ustedes**) command, 11 (1); used as negative familiar (**tú**) command, 13 (1); subjunctive with impersonal expressions, 40 (2); after **¡Ojalá!, ¡Quizás!,** and **¡Tal vez!,** 42 (2); stem-changing verbs, 43 (2); subjunctive to express wishes, 72 (3); subjunctive to express emotion, 74 (3); subjunctive to express doubt, 104 (4); subjunctive in adverbial clauses, 106 (4); imperfect subjunctive: formation and use, 140 (5); sequence of tenses for using present and imperfect subjunctive, 140 (5); subjunctive vs. infinitive, 143 (5); subjunctive with adverbial conjunctions of time, 176 (6); sequence of tenses with adverbial conjunctions of time, 176 (6); subjunctive to express implied commands, suggestions, and advice, 178 (6); present perfect subjunctive, 212 (7); pluperfect subjunctive, 212 (7); subjunctive with **aunque,** 242 (8); subjunctive with **-quiera,** 244 (8); subjunctive in relative clauses, 316 (10)

suffixes diminutives **-ito, -illo (-ico),** 144 (5); absolute superlative **-ísimo,** 144 (5)

tener preterite tense, R31

traer present indicative, R7; preterite tense, R31

tuteo 149 (5)

venir preterite tense, R31

ver imperfect tense, R43

volver present indicative, R17

voseo 149 (5)

Credits

Photo Credits

Credits